English Prose and Criticism, 1900-1950

AMERICAN LITERATURE, ENGLISH LITERATURE, AND WORLD LITERATURES IN ENGLISH: AN INFORMATION GUIDE SERIES

Series Editor: Theodore Grieder, Curator, Division of Special Collections, Fales Library, New York University

Associate Editor: Duane DeVries, Associate Professor, Polytechnic Institute of New York, Brooklyn

Other books on English literature in this series:

ENGLISH DRAMA TO 1660 (EXCLUDING SHAKESPEARE)—*Edited by Frieda Elaine Penninger*

ENGLISH DRAMA, 1660-1800—*Edited by Frederick M. Link*

ENGLISH DRAMA AND THEATRE, 1800-1900—*Edited by L.W. Conolly and J.P. Wearing*

ENGLISH DRAMA, 1900-1950—*Edited by E.H. Mikhail*

MODERN DRAMA IN AMERICA AND ENGLAND, 1950-1970—*Edited by Richard H. Harris*

ENGLISH FICTION, 1660-1800—*Edited by Jerry C. Beasley*

ENGLISH FICTION, 1900-1950 (volume 1)—*Edited by Thomas Jackson Rice*

ENGLISH FICTION, 1900-1950 (volume 2)—*Edited by Thomas Jackson Rice*

CONTEMPORARY FICTION IN AMERICA AND ENGLAND, 1950-1970—*Edited by Alfred F. Rosa and Paul A. Echholz*

OLD AND MIDDLE ENGLISH POETRY TO 1500—*Edited by Walter H. Beale*

ENGLISH POETRY, 1660-1800—*Edited by Donald C. Mell*

ENGLISH ROMANTIC POETRY, 1800-1835—*Edited by Donald H. Reiman*

ENGLISH POETRY, 1900-1950—*Edited by Emily Ann Anderson*

CONTEMPORARY POETRY IN AMERICA AND ENGLAND, 1950-1970—*Edited by Martin E. Gingerich*

ENGLISH PROSE, PROSE FICTION, AND CRITICISM TO 1660—*Edited by S.K. Heninger, Jr.*

ENGLISH PROSE AND CRITICISM IN THE NINETEENTH CENTURY—*Edited by Harris W. Wilson and Diane Long Hoeveler*

The above series is part of the
GALE INFORMATION GUIDE LIBRARY

The Library consists of a number of separate series of guides covering major areas in the social sciences, humanities, and current affairs.

General Editor: Paul Wasserman, Professor and former Dean, School of Library and Information Services, University of Maryland

Managing Editor: Denise Allard Adzigian, Gale Research Company

English Prose and Criticism, 1900-1950

A GUIDE TO INFORMATION SOURCES

Volume 42 in the American Literature, English Literature, and World Literatures in English Information Guide Series

Christopher C. Brown

*Assistant Professor of English
University of South Carolina
Columbia*

William B. Thesing

*Assistant Professor of English
University of South Carolina
Columbia*

Gale Research Company
Book Tower, Detroit, Michigan 48226

Library of Congress Cataloging in Publication Data

Brown, Christopher C.
   English prose and criticism, 1900-1950.

   (American literature, English literature, and
world literatures in English information guide
series ; v. 42)
      Bibliography: p.
      Includes indexes.
      1. English prose literature—20th century—
Bibliography.   2. English prose literature—20th
century—History and criticism—Bibliography.
I. Thesing, William B. II. Title. III. Series:
Gale information guide library. American literature,
English literature, and world literatures in English
information guide series ; v. 42.
Z2014.P795B76   1983   [PR801]   016.828'91208'09   83-11581
ISBN 0-8103-1236-0

Copyright © 1983 by
Christopher C. Brown and William B. Thesing

No part of this book may be reproduced in any form without permission in writing from the publisher, except by a reviewer who wishes to quote brief passages or entries in connection with a review written for inclusion in a magazine or newspaper. Manufactured in the United States of America.

To
Joyce and Jane

VITAE

Christopher C. Brown received his B.A. from the University of Rochester in 1971, his M.A. from Duke University in 1972, and his Ph.D. from Duke in 1977. He is currently assistant professor of English at the University of South Carolina, Columbia. His concentration is modern British literature, and he has published on Hudson, Ford, Eliot, and Lawrence.

William B. Thesing is assistant professor of English at the University of South Carolina, Columbia, whose faculty he joined in 1977. He holds the M.A. and Ph.D. degrees from Indiana University. His publications include THE LONDON MUSE: VICTORIAN POETIC RESPONSES TO THE CITY, winner of the 1980 SAMLA Studies Award, as well as articles on Victorian figures and the teaching of composition.

CONTENTS

Journal Abbreviations ix
Acknowledgments xvii
Introduction xix

Generic and Period Studies
    Bibliographies 3
    Literary Histories 6
    Studies of Biography and Autobiography................ 10
    Studies of the Essay and Prose Style 13
    Studies of Literary Criticism........................ 16
    Studies of Travel Writing 22

Individual Authors
    W.H. Auden (1907-73) 27
    Max Beerbohm (1872-1956)............................ 37
    Hilaire Belloc (1870-1953).......................... 48
    Christopher Caudwell [Christopher St. John Sprigg] (1907-37).... 69
    G.K. Chesterton (1874-1936) 74
    Cyril Connolly (1903-74) 98
    Joseph Conrad (1857-1924) 102
    Norman Douglas (1868-1952) 110
    T.S. Eliot (1888-1965).............................. 117
    William Empson (1906-) 153
    Ford Madox Ford (1873-1939) 161
    E.M. Forster (1879-1970)............................ 170
    Edmund Gosse (1849-1928) 179
    R.B. Cunninghame Graham (1852-1936) 199
    Robert Graves (1895-) 208
    Philip Guedalla (1889-1944)......................... 219
    W.H. Hudson (1841-1922) 224
    T.E. Hulme (1883-1917) 231
    Aldous Huxley (1894-1963) 238
    D.H. Lawrence (1885-1930) 251
    T.E. Lawrence (1888-1935) 271

Contents

F.R. Leavis (1895-1978) 279
C.S. Lewis (1898-1963) 300
Wyndham Lewis (1882-1957) 314
John Middleton Murry (1889-1957) 332
George Orwell [Eric Blair] (1903-50) 342
Herbert Read (1893-1968) 357
I.A. Richards (1893-1979) 368
George Saintsbury (1845-1933) 387
Siegfried Sassoon (1886-1967) 398
George Bernard Shaw (1856-1950) 403
Osbert Sitwell (1892-1969) 425
Lytton Strachey (1880-1932) 432
H.M. Tomlinson (1873-1958) 445
H.G. Wells (1866-1946) 450
Virginia Woolf (1882-1941) 470
W.B. Yeats (1865-1939) 488

Indexes
    Author Index 509
    Title Index 529

JOURNAL ABBREVIATIONS

The following abbreviations of journal titles follow the MLA INTERNATIONAL BIBLIOGRAPHY Master List and Table of Abbreviations.

ABR	AMERICAN BENEDICTINE REVIEW
ADAM	ADAM INTERNATIONAL REVIEW
AEB	ANALYTICAL AND ENUMERATIVE BIBLIOGRAPHY
AL	AMERICAN LITERATURE: A JOURNAL OF LITERARY HISTORY, CRITICISM, AND BIBLIOGRAPHY
ALITASH	ACTA LITTERARIA ACADEMIAE SCIENTIARUM HUNGARICAE
AN&Q	AMERICAN NOTES AND QUERIES
AQ	AMERICAN QUARTERLY
AR	ANTIOCH REVIEW
ARIELE	ARIEL: A REVIEW OF INTERNATIONAL ENGLISH LITERATURE
ARQ	ARIZONA QUARTERLY
ASCH	AMERICAN SCHOLAR
BB	BULLETIN OF BIBLIOGRAPHY
BFORUM	BOOK FORUM: AN INTERNATIONAL TRANSDISCIPLINARY QUARTERLY
BJA	BRITISH JOURNAL OF AESTHETICS
BMMLA	BULLETIN OF THE MIDWEST MODERN LANGUAGE ASSOCIATION
BNYPL	BULLETIN OF THE NEW YORK PUBLIC LIBRARY
BSUF	BALL STATE UNIVERSITY FORUM
CALR	CALCUTTA REVIEW
CATHW	CATHOLIC WORLD
CCC	COLLEGE COMPOSITION AND COMMUNICATION
CE	COLLEGE ENGLISH
CENTR	CENTENNIAL REVIEW
CHIR	CHICAGO REVIEW

Journal Abbreviations

CJ	CLASSICAL JOURNAL
CL	COMPARATIVE LITERATURE
CLC	COLUMBIA LIBRARY COLUMNS
CLQ	COLBY LIBRARY QUARTERLY
CLS	COMPARATIVE LITERATURE STUDIES
CONL	CONTEMPORARY LITERATURE
CONNR	CONNECTICUT REVIEW
CONTEMPR	CONTEMPORARY REVIEW (London, England)
CQ	CAMBRIDGE QUARTERLY
CREV	CHESTERTON REVIEW: THE JOURNAL OF THE CHESTERTON SOCIETY
CRITI	CRITICAL INQUIRY
CRITQ	CRITICAL QUARTERLY
DELTAES	DELTA: REVUE DE CENTRE D'ETUDES ET RECHERCHE SUR LES ECRIVAINS DU SUD AUX ETATS-UNIS
DHLR	D. H. LAWRENCE REVIEW
DOWNR	DOWNSIDE REVIEW
DQR	DUTCH QUARTERLY REVIEW OF ANGLO-AMERICAN LETTERS
DR	DALHOUSIE REVIEW
DSA	DICKENS STUDIES ANNUAL
DSN	DICKENS STUDIES NEWSLETTER
EA	ETUDES ANGLAISES: GRAND-BRETAGNE, ETATS-UNIS
E&S	ESSAYS AND STUDIES (London, England)
EDH	ESSAYS BY DIVERS HANDS
EFT	ENGLISH FICTION IN TRANSITION (later ELT)
EIC	ESSAYS IN CRITICISM: A QUARTERLY JOURNAL OF LITERARY CRITICISM
EIE	ENGLISH INSTITUTE ESSAYS
EIGOS	EIGO SEINEN (Tokyo)
EIRE	EIRE-IRELAND: A JOURNAL OF IRISH STUDIES
EJ	ENGLISH JOURNAL
ELH	ELH (formerly JOURNAL OF ENGLISH LITERARY HISTORY)
ELLS	ENGLISH LITERATURE AND LANGUAGE (Tokyo, Japan)
ELN	ENGLISH LANGUAGE NOTES
ELT	ENGLISH LITERATURE IN TRANSITION (formerly EFT)

Journal Abbreviations

EM	ENGLISH MISCELLANY: A SYMPOSIUM OF HISTORY, LITERATURE AND THE ARTS
ENGR	ENGLISH RECORD
ES	ENGLISH STUDIES: A JOURNAL OF ENGLISH LANGUAGE AND LITERATURE
ESA	ENGLISH STUDIES IN AFRICA: A JOURNAL OF THE HUMANITIES
EXPLOR	EXPLORATION (Normal, Ill.)
FORUMH	FORUM (Houston, Texas)
FRG	FOCUS ON ROBERT GRAVES
FWF	FAR-WESTERN FORUM: A REVIEW OF ANCIENT AND MODERN LETTERS
GAR	GEORGIA REVIEW
HLQ	HUNTINGTON LIBRARY QUARTERLY: A JOURNAL FOR THE HISTORY AND INTERPRETATION OF ENGLISH AND AMERICAN CIVILIZATION
HTR	HARVARD THEOLOGICAL REVIEW
HUDR	HUDSON REVIEW
IOWAR	IOWA REVIEW
JAAC	JOURNAL OF AESTHETICS AND ART CRITICISM
JAF	JOURNAL OF AMERICAN FOLKLORE
JEGP	JOURNAL OF ENGLISH AND GERMANIC PHILOLOGY
JES	JOURNAL OF EUROPEAN STUDIES
JHI	JOURNAL OF THE HISTORY OF IDEAS
JJQ	JAMES JOYCE QUARTERLY
JML	JOURNAL OF MODERN LITERATURE
JNT	JOURNAL OF NARRATIVE TECHNIQUE
JP	JOURNAL OF PHILOSOPHY
JPC	JOURNAL OF POPULAR CULTURE
JRUL	JOURNAL OF THE RUTGERS UNIV. LIBRARIES
KR	KENYON REVIEW
KSJ	KEATS-SHELLEY JOURNAL: KEATS, SHELLEY, BYRON, HUNT, AND THEIR CIRCLES
L&P	LITERATURE AND PSYCHOLOGY
LCRIT	LITERARY CRITERION (Mysore, India)
LHY	LITERARY HALF-YEARLY

Journal Abbreviations

MBL	MODERN BRITISH LITERATURE
MCNR	MCNEESE REVIEW
MD	MODERN DRAMA
MFS	MODERN FICTION STUDIES
MHREV	MALAHAT REVIEW: AN INTERNATIONAL QUARTERLY OF LIFE AND LETTERS
MILTONS	MILTON STUDIES
MINNR	MINNESOTA REVIEW
MLN	MLN (formerly MODERN LANGUAGE NOTES)
MLQ	MODERN LANGUAGE QUARTERLY
MLR	MODERN LANGUAGE REVIEW
MLS	MODERN LANGUAGE STUDIES
MODA	MODERN AGE: A QUARTERLY REVIEW
MP	MODERN PHILOLOGY: A JOURNAL DEVOTED TO RESEARCH IN MEDIEVAL AND MODERN LITERATURE
MQ	MIDWEST QUARTERLY: A JOURNAL OF CONTEMPORARY THOUGHT
MR	MASSACHUSETTS REVIEW: A QUARTERLY OF LITERATURE, THE ARTS AND PUBLIC AFFAIRS
NC	NUOVA CORRENTE: REVISTA DI LETTERATURA
NCF	NINETEENTH-CENTURY FICTION
NEQ	NEW ENGLAND QUARTERLY: A HISTORICAL REVIEW OF NEW ENGLAND LIFE AND LETTERS
NGC	NEW GERMAN CRITIQUE: AN INTERDISCIPLINARY JOURNAL OF GERMAN STUDIES
NHJ	NATHANIEL HAWTHORNE JOURNAL
NLH	NEW LITERARY HISTORY: A JOURNAL OF THEORY AND INTERPRETATION
NR	NASSAU REVIEW
NYRB	NEW YORK REVIEW OF BOOKS
NYTBR	NEW YORK TIMES BOOK REVIEW
OL	ORBIS LITTERARUM: INTERNATIONAL REVIEW OF LITERARY STUDIES
PAPS	PROCEEDINGS OF THE AMERICAN PHILOSOPHICAL SOCIETY
PBA	PROCEEDINGS OF THE BRITISH ACADEMY
PBSA	PBSA: PAPERS OF THE BIBLIOGRAPHICAL SOCIETY OF AMERICA

PHR	PHILOSOPHICAL REVIEW
PHS	PHILOSOPHICAL STUDIES: AN INTERNATIONAL JOURNAL FOR PHILOSOPHY IN THE ANALYTIC TRADITION
PLL	PAPERS ON LANGUAGE AND LITERATURE
PMLA	PUBLICATIONS OF THE MODERN LANGUAGE ASSOCIATION
PNR	PN REVIEW
POETRYR	POETRY REVIEW
PPR	PHILOSOPHY AND PHENOMENOLOGICAL RESEARCH
PQ	PHILOLOGICAL QUARTERLY (Iowa City, Ia.)
PR	PARTISAN REVIEW
PRS	PRAIRIE SCHOONER
QJS	QUARTERLY JOURNAL OF SPEECH
QQ	QUEEN'S QUARTERLY
QR	QUARTERLY REVIEW
REL	REVIEW OF ENGLISH LITERATURE (now ARIEL)
RES	REVIEW OF ENGLISH STUDIES
RLV	REVUE DES LANGUES VIVANTES
RMS	RENAISSANCE AND MODERN STUDIES
ROMN	ROMANCE NOTES
RQ	RIVERSIDE QUARTERLY
RS	RESEARCH STUDIES
SAB	SOUTH ATLANTIC BULLETIN
SAF	STUDIES IN AMERICAN FICTION
SAQ	SOUTH ATLANTIC QUARTERLY
SATR	SATURDAY REVIEW
SDR	SOUTH DAKOTA REVIEW
SEER	SLAVONIC AND EAST EUROPEAN REVIEW
SFQ	SOUTHERN FOLKLORE QUARTERLY
SFS	SCIENCE-FICTION STUDIES
SHAWR	SHAW REVIEW (formerly SHAW BULLETIN)
SHR	SOUTHERN HUMANITIES REVIEW
SHS	SHAKESPEARE SURVEY: AN ANNUAL SURVEY OF SHAKE-SPEARIAN STUDY AND PRODUCTION
SLITI	STUDIES IN THE LITERARY IMAGINATION
SNNTS	STUDIES IN THE NOVEL

Journal Abbreviations

SOQ	SOUTHERN QUARTERLY
SOR	SOUTHERN REVIEW (Baton Rouge, La.)
SORA	SOUTHERN REVIEW: LITERARY AND INTERDISCIPLINARY ESSAYS (Adelaide, Australia)
SP	STUDIES IN PHILOLOGY
SR	SEWANEE REVIEW
SRC	STUDIES IN RELIGION/SCIENCES RELIGIEUSES: REVUE CANADIENNE/A CANADIAN JOURNAL
SSL	STUDIES IN SCOTTISH LITERATURE
STC	STUDIES IN THE TWENTIETH CENTURY
SWR	SOUTHWEST REVIEW
TAMR	TAMARACK REVIEW
TCL	TWENTIETH CENTURY LITERATURE: A SCHOLARLY AND CRITICAL JOURNAL
TLS	TIMES LITERARY SUPPLEMENT
TQ	TEXAS QUARTERLY
TSB	THOREAU SOCIETY BULLETIN
TSE	TULANE STUDIES IN ENGLISH
TSL	TENNESSEE STUDIES IN LITERATURE
TSLL	TEXAS STUDIES IN LITERATURE AND LANGUAGE
UCQ	UNIVERSITY COLLEGE QUARTERLY
UKCR	UNIVERSITY OF KANSAS CITY REVIEW
ULR	UNIVERSITY OF LEEDS REVIEW
UNS	UNIVERSITY OF NEBRASKA STUDIES
UTQ	UNIVERSITY OF TORONTO QUARTERLY
UWR	UNIVERSITY OF WINDSOR REVIEW
VN	VICTORIAN NEWSLETTER
VP	VICTORIAN POETRY
VQR	VIRGINIA QUARTERLY REVIEW
VS	VICTORIAN STUDIES
VWQ	VIRGINIA WOOLF QUARTERLY
WHR	WESTERN HUMANITIES REVIEW
WN	A WAKE NEWSLETTER: STUDIES IN JAMES JOYCE'S FINNEGAN'S WAKE
WR	WESTERN REVIEW

Journal Abbreviations

WWR	WALT WHITMAN REVIEW
YER	YEATS ELIOT REVIEW
YES	YEARBOOK OF ENGLISH STUDIES
YR	YALE REVIEW
YSE	YALE STUDIES IN ENGLISH

ACKNOWLEDGMENTS

We wish to thank Theodore Grieder, Duane DeVries, Thomas J. Rice, Joel A. Myerson, Patrick G. Scott, Matthew J. Bruccoli, and J. Albert Robbins for their suggestions and encouragement during the preparation of this guide. We also express our gratitude to our past chairman, William H. Nolte, and our present chairman, George L. Geckle, for providing us with summer grants and research release time. We also thank the University of South Carolina Research and Productive Scholarship Committee for providing us with a grant during 1979. Because of the support of that funding and further departmental support, we were able to make use of the superb talents of the following research assistants, to whom we owe a special debt of gratitude: Steve Garrison, Jenny MacDougall, Tyler Smith, Dave Kellish, and Kathy Pavlakovich. We are also most grateful to Harriet Oglesbee and Lori Finger, interlibrary loan librarians, and to Jane Thesing, Beth Woodard, Jean Rhyne, Paula Swope, and Michael Freeman, reference librarians at the Thomas Cooper Library, University of South Carolina, for the cheerful and efficient help that they provided us. Further, staff members at the libraries of the University of North Carolina, Duke University, University of Pennsylvania, Indiana University, Washington University, and Northwestern University offered invaluable assistance during our several research trips. Elizabeth Thomas cheerfully and carefully typed the entire manuscript.

Finally, we owe the greatest debt to our wives, Joyce Brown and Jane Thesing, for the patient support and loving inspiration they have shown during the many months of work on this project.

INTRODUCTION

This guide is a primary and secondary bibliography of nonfictional prose in modern British literature. It is alphabetically ordered, letter by letter, and annotated throughout, except in the rare cases of self-explanatory titles. The annotations are descriptive, but a majority also include evaluation. Brief quotations from a book or article are given when deemed useful. Some of the authors listed in this book are little known or studied; the nonfictional prose of others, such as Ford or D.H. Lawrence, has been slighted in favor of their more famous fictional works. Since many of the primary titles are works not widely familiar, our annotations of them represent a special contribution of our volume, and we hope that they will address a substantial educational need. Our annotations of the criticism on these works also aim at offering new insights into the relatively unstudied area of modern British nonfictional prose. We hope that readers will use our volume as a starting point for their own research.

Organized in two parts, the book first lists general studies germane to the subject and then the nonfictional prose of thirty-seven authors and the criticism treating each. We have selected our writers solely from the modern British <u>literary</u> world. The thirty-seven have been chosen for the high quality of their nonfictional prose (Sassoon, for instance), for their representativeness of the period's trends in various forms (Empson, for instance), or for both (Eliot, for instance).

The first part, "Generic and Period Studies," is in six sections:

1. <u>Bibliographies.</u> A selected list of bibliographies treating various genres of nonfictional prose and of bibliographies with a period focus.

2. <u>Literary Histories.</u> A selected list of histories of modern British literature with substantial treatment of the nonfiction.

3. <u>Studies of Biography and Autobiography.</u> A selected list of theoretical works and of histories of the forms in modern British literature.

4. <u>Studies of the Essay and Prose Style.</u> A selected list of theoretical works and of histories of the form and the subject in modern British literature.

Introduction

5. Studies of Literary Criticism. A selected list of theoretical works and of histories of the form in modern British literature.
6. Studies of Travel Writing. A selected list of theoretical works and of histories of the form in modern British literature.

The second part, "Individual Authors," examines thirty-seven writers in alphabetical order. The name of each is abbreviated to initials in the annotations of his or her section; when it appears elsewhere in the volume it is given fully. Collected editions of an author's works, where they exist, are described in a headnote. Each writer is dealt with in five categories:

1. Nonfictional Prose. A list of the author's books and pamphlets of nonfictional prose of fifty or more pages. Shorter pieces of extraordinary importance are also listed. The editions recorded are first British; first American editions are also noted when they exist.
2. Works Edited by Others. A selected list of the author's works compiled by others. Almost all of these are posthumous. Most are essay collections.
3. Bibliography. A selected list of primary and secondary bibliographies.
4. Biography. A selective list of biographies with significant information on the writing history of the nonfiction, the critical reception of it, and so forth.
5. Criticism. A list of critical books, chapters in critical books, and critical articles with substantial treatment of the author's nonfictional prose. Dissertations and criticism in foreign languages are not included, nor book reviews unless of special interest. For the reader's convenience, essays by the author mentioned in the annotations of this section are followed by the short titles of the collection containing them, if they are collected. For example, in the following sample entry--a listing and annotation of a critical article by John M. Lothian in which he discusses Huxley's essay "Wordsworth in the Tropics"--DO WHAT YOU WILL is the title of the essay collection containing Huxley's essay and AH stands for Aldous Huxley:

> Lothian, John M. "Wordsworth North of Forty-Nine." ABERDEEN UNIVERSITY REVIEW, 33 (1950), 245-51.
>
> > Argues that in "Wordsworth in the Tropics" (DO WHAT YOU WILL) AH shows that it is he (not Wordsworth) who wants nature easy and pretty.

The terminal date for this present information guide is in general January 1, 1981. However, some important material--especially critical books and primary essay collections--published after that date up to June 1, 1982, has been included.

In dividing our work on this project, Christopher C. Brown assumed principal responsibility for: Connolly, Conrad, Douglas, Ford, Forster, Graham, Hudson, Hulme, Huxley, D.H. Lawrence, T.E. Lawrence, C.S. Lewis, Murry, Read, Saintsbury, Shaw, Tomlinson, Wells, and Woolf; William B. Thesing assumed

Introduction

principal responsibility for: Auden, Beerbohm, Belloc, Caudwell, Chesterton, Eliot, Empson, Gosse, Graves, Guedalla, Leavis, Wyndham Lewis, Orwell, Richards, Sassoon, Sitwell, Strachey, and Yeats. Each of us has checked the other's work. All decisions about the editorial plan or annotations have been joint ones. The final volume is the responsibility of both editors.

GENERIC AND PERIOD STUDIES

BIBLIOGRAPHIES

ANNUAL REVIEW NUMBER. JML, 1 (1971--).

A yearly volume with reviews, some lengthy and signed, of critical books arranged under the names of the numerous modern authors included. Articles are also listed, and there is a section annotating literary histories.

Bailey, Richard W., and Dolores M. Burton, eds. ENGLISH STYLISTICS: A BIBLIOGRAPHY. Cambridge, Mass.: M.I.T. Press, 1968.

An excellent bibliography, most of which treats "English Stylistics in the Twentieth Century." Under such topic headings as "Diction," "Tropes," and "Statistical Approaches," the works are listed alphabetically by author with sizable annotations for the more important.

Bailey, Richard W., Dolores M. Burton et al., eds. "1966 Annual Bibliography on Style." STYLE, 1 (1967), 257-81. Continued in subsequent volumes.

A comprehensive, well-annotated listing of works on style, including prose style. Appearing in every volume except 5 and 9, the bibliography since the fourth volume is arranged alphabetically by author under such headings as "Theoretical Orientations," "Syntax," and "Imagery, Diction, and Figures of Speech."

"Bibliography, News, and Notes." EFT [later ELT], 1 (1957), 6-43, and continuing through 18 (1975), 47-75.

Heavy annotation of critical books and articles grouped under the authors treated such as Gosse, Strachey, Graham, and Hudson.

Carlock, Mary Sue, ed. "Writings about the Autobiography: A Selective Bibliography." BB, 26 (1969), 1-2.

A selective list of twentieth-century books and articles in English about autobiography as practiced in several historical periods. Useful listing with no annotations.

Bibliographies

"Current Literature: II." ENGLISH STUDIES, 27 (1946), 44-58. Continued in subsequent volumes.

> Includes handy reviews of the year's work in and about such nonfiction as criticism and biography.

Lauterbach, Edward S., and W. Eugene Davis, eds. THE TRANSITIONAL AGE IN BRITISH LITERATURE, 1880-1920. Troy, N.Y.: Whitston, 1973.

> Part 2 is a handy research guide with selected primary and secondary bibliographies for 177 writers of the specified period. It includes many of the figures treated in this study.

Matthews, William, ed. BRITISH AUTOBIOGRAPHIES: AN ANNOTATED BIBLIOGRAPHY OF BRITISH AUTOBIOGRAPHIES PUBLISHED OR WRITTEN BEFORE 1951. Berkeley and Los Angeles: Univ. of California Press, 1955.

> Arranged alphabetically by author; includes brief annotations of titles.

Mellown, Elgin W., ed. A DESCRIPTIVE CATALOGUE OF THE BIBLIOGRAPHIES OF 20TH CENTURY BRITISH POETS, NOVELISTS, AND DRAMATISTS. Troy, N.Y.: Whitston, 1978.

> An annotated listing of primary and secondary bibliographies of modern British authors.

Milic, Louis, ed. STYLE AND STYLISTICS: AN ANALYTICAL BIBLIOGRAPHY. New York: Free Press, 1967.

> Lists over eight hundred items in five categories: theoretical studies of style, studies of analytical methodology, studies of specific styles, bibliographies on style, and miscellaneous studies. Milic annotates by a systematized topic notation.

Riches, Phyllis M., ed. AN ANALYTICAL BIBLIOGRAPHY OF UNIVERSAL COLLECTED BIOGRAPHY: COMPRISING BOOKS PUBLISHED IN THE ENGLISH TONGUE IN GREAT BRITAIN AND IRELAND, AMERICA AND THE BRITISH DOMINIONS. Detroit: Gale Research Co., 1980.

> An index to biographies on figures from various historical periods.

Temple, Ruth Z., and Martin Tucker, eds. A LIBRARY OF LITERARY CRITICISM: MODERN BRITISH LITERATURE. 4 vols. New York: Ungar, 1966-75.

> Includes primary bibliographies and brief selections of critical responses to over four hundred twentieth-century British writers. Volume 4 updates the selections and adds over fifty more authors; bibliographical entries are also brought up to date for all figures.

_____. TWENTIETH CENTURY BRITISH LITERATURE: A REFERENCE GUIDE AND BIBLIOGRAPHY. New York: Ungar, 1968.

Bibliographies

   An extremely useful book for the student of modern literature.
   Part 1 lists and briefly annotates literary histories, collections
   of critical essays, special studies of genres and theory; part 2
   lists and briefly identifies works by individual authors.

Willison, I.R., ed. THE NEW CAMBRIDGE BIBLIOGRAPHY OF ENGLISH
LITERATURE: VOLUME 4: 1900-1950. Cambridge: The Univ. Press, 1972.

   The major bibliography of the period, indispensable for its unannotated, chronologically arranged, primary and secondary
   listings on everybody who is anybody in poetry, fiction, drama,
   and nonfictional prose.

Winslow, Donald J., ed. "Current Bibliography on Life-Writing." BIOGRAPHY,
2 (1979), 342-47.

   A useful annotated bibliography which includes books and articles
   about biography and autobiography published during 1978-79. The
   survey is to be an annual feature of the journal.

THE YEAR'S WORK IN ENGLISH STUDIES. London: English Association,
1921. Continued in subsequent volumes.

   Although less useful than other annual reviews--partly because
   less finely organized--this does contain some discussion of criticism
   of nonfiction writers in its twentieth-century section.

LITERARY HISTORIES

Batho, E.C., and Bonamy Dobrée. THE VICTORIANS AND AFTER (1830-1914). London: Cresset, 1950.

> The section on "Criticism and Essays" offers very brief, introductory assessments of works by Saintsbury, Gosse, Hudson, Cunninghame Graham, Beerbohm, Belloc, and Chesterton.

Bergonzi, Bernard. HEROES' TWILIGHT: A STUDY OF THE LITERATURE OF THE GREAT WAR. Atlantic Highlands, N.J.: Humanities, 1980.

> Chapter 8 offers insightful critical treatment of war-related autobiographies by Sassoon, Graves, Wyndham Lewis, and T.E. Lawrence.

Chapple, J.A.V. DOCUMENTARY AND IMAGINATIVE LITERATURE, 1880-1920. New York: Barnes and Noble, 1970.

> Connects history with the literature of the period through thematic organization. It includes brief discussion of prose by Chesterton, Eliot, Graham, Graves, Hudson, D.H. Lawrence, Sassoon, Shaw, Strachey, Wells, and Yeats.

Chew, Samuel E., and Richard D. Altick. "Anthropology; Travel; History; Criticism." In A LITERARY HISTORY OF ENGLAND. Ed. Albert C. Baugh et al. Englewood Cliffs, N.J.: Prentice-Hall, 1967. Pp. 1589-1605.

> A standard survey of literary history, now somewhat out-of-date. The section treats T.E. Lawrence, Cunninghame Graham, Hudson, Belloc, Chesterton, Strachey, Guedalla, Saintsbury, Gosse, and others.

Cunliffe, J.W. ENGLISH LITERATURE IN THE TWENTIETH CENTURY. Folcroft, Pa.: Folcroft, 1973.

> Discusses religious, social, and political developments of the period. It includes separate chapters on Shaw, Yeats, Conrad, Wells, Strachey, and on "Essays, Journalism and Travel" (covers

Hudson, Gosse, Chesterton, and T. E. Lawrence). Cunliffe tends
to value nonfiction prose over prose fiction.

Daiches, David. THE PRESENT AGE IN BRITISH LITERATURE. Bloomington:
Indiana Univ. Press, 1958.

> Includes a useful chapter on "Critical and General Prose."
> Daiches demonstrates how modern criticism has become less
> impressionistic and less academic. He treats such important
> figures as Hulme, Eliot, Richards, Leavis, and Read.

Evans, B. Ifor. ENGLISH LITERATURE BETWEEN THE WARS. London:
Methuen, 1948.

> Includes background chapters and individual chapters on Forster,
> Joyce, D. H. Lawrence, Aldous Huxley, Woolf, Yeats, and
> Eliot. The two chapters "The New Biography" and "War and
> the Writer" offer pertinent discussions of works by Strachey,
> Guedalla, Belloc, Chesterton, Sassoon, and T. E. Lawrence.

Ford, Boris, ed. THE MODERN AGE. Baltimore: Penguin, 1973.

> Outlines main developments in literary criticism and devotes
> more detailed discussion to prose works by Wyndham Lewis and
> T. S. Eliot.

Fraser, G. S. THE MODERN WRITER AND HIS WORLD. New York: Criterion
Books, 1955.

> Chapter 5, "The Trends of Criticism," offers some useful analysis
> of ideas and style in works by Saintsbury, Chesterton, Belloc,
> Hulme, Eliot, Wyndham Lewis, D. H. Lawrence, Murry, Woolf,
> Forster, Strachey, Orwell, Leavis, Richards, and Empson.

Gillie, Christopher. MOVEMENTS IN ENGLISH LITERATURE, 1900-1940.
Cambridge: The Univ. Press, 1975.

> Includes individual chapters on D. H. Lawrence, Yeats, and
> Eliot as well as a chapter on "The Critical Decade, 1930-1940,"
> which focuses on works by Orwell, Auden, Richards, and Leavis.

Hynes, Samuel. EDWARDIAN OCCASIONS: ESSAYS ON ENGLISH WRITING
IN THE EARLY TWENTIETH CENTURY. London: Routledge, 1972.

> Keen assessments of such prose writers and critics as Wells, Shaw,
> Woolf, Conrad, Ford, Chesterton, Belloc, Forster, and Hulme.
> The sense of "radical social and literary change" is an important
> unifying dimension in the Edwardian period.

Lehmann, John, ed. THE CRAFT OF LETTERS IN ENGLAND: A SYMPOSIUM.
Westport, Conn.: Greenwood, 1974.

Literary Histories

The following essays are relevant and valuable introductory surveys: "Biography," "The New Criticism," "The Bloomsbury Tradition in English Literary Criticism," "Historical Writing," and "The Literature of Ideas."

Lester, John A., Jr. JOURNEY THROUGH DESPAIR, 1880-1914: TRANS-FORMATIONS IN BRITISH LITERARY CULTURE. Princeton, N.J.: Princeton Univ. Press, 1968.

> Analyzes differing responses of writers who seek to establish bases for "significant imaginative life" in an era of crisis. Works by Chesterton, Conrad, Eliot, Forster, Hudson, D.H. Lawrence, Shaw, and Yeats are discussed.

Robson, W.W. MODERN ENGLISH LITERATURE. London: Oxford Univ. Press, 1970.

> Offers concise, often keen critical interpretations of major developments. It includes brief discussions of such nonfictional writers as Shaw, Wells, Chesterton, Belloc, D.H. Lawrence, Auden, Empson, Graves, and Orwell, and is especially good on criticism in the thirties.

Routh, Harold V. ENGLISH LITERATURE AND IDEAS IN THE TWENTIETH CENTURY. New York: Russell, 1970.

> Focuses on prose styles and ideologies of such writers as Beerbohm, Chesterton, Belloc, Gosse, Hudson, Graham, Wells, Shaw, Eliot, Richards, Sassoon, and Strachey. Routh assesses each writer's contribution to literary progress and innovation.

Sampson, George, and R.C. Churchill. THE CONCISE CAMBRIDGE HISTORY OF ENGLISH LITERATURE. Cambridge: The Univ. Press, 1970.

> Chapters 14 and 16 offer rich introductory surveys of the early twentieth-century writers' achievements in biography, critical and miscellaneous prose, travel writing, and so forth. The section on "Criticism and Culture" is especially good in its treatments of Eliot, Murry, and Leavis.

Scott-James, Rolfe A. FIFTY YEARS OF ENGLISH LITERATURE, 1900-1950. London: Longmans, 1951.

> Chapter 6 offers a helpful discussion of such essayists as Chesterton, Belloc, and Beerbohm; chapter 15 analyzes prose writings by T.E. Lawrence, Strachey, and other minor figures.

Swinnerton, Frank. THE GEORGIAN LITERARY SCENE, 1910-1935: A PANORAMA. London: Hutchinson, 1950.

> Useful book which examines Shaw and Wells as "Teachers"; Belloc

and Chesterton as Catholic liberals; Graham, Hudson, Conrad, Tomlinson, Douglas as travel writers; Beerbohm, Ford, and Murry as "Literary Men"; Graves, Sassoon, and Osbert Sitwell as wartime writers; Strachey and Woolf as leaders of the Bloomsbury group; Huxley and Lewis as exponents of pessimism; Eliot as leader of "the new Academicism."

Tindall, William York. FORCES IN MODERN BRITISH LITERATURE, 1885-1956. New York: Vintage, 1956.

> An indispensable guide through the period. Discussion is arranged chronologically within several categories which treat aspects of the period's history, meanings, and values. Tindall treats prose and criticism of Auden, Caudwell, Eliot, Empson, Graves, Hudson, Richards, and a few others. He is especially good on leftist writers of the 1930s.

Ward, Alfred C. TWENTIETH-CENTURY ENGLISH LITERATURE, 1901-1960. London: Methuen, 1964.

> Offers brief but useful outlines of forms and writers. Chapter 5 treats such essayists and critics as Beerbohm, Chesterton, Richards, Eliot, and Leavis; chapter 6 discusses travel writers Hudson and Graham as well as such biographers as Belloc, Strachey, and Gosse.

STUDIES OF BIOGRAPHY AND AUTOBIOGRAPHY

Altick, Richard. LIVES AND LETTERS: A HISTORY OF LITERARY BIOGRAPHY IN ENGLAND AND AMERICA. Westport, Conn.: Greenwood, 1979.

> A section on "The Modern Age" provides an insightful analysis of the effects of the "Stracheyan Revolution." Gosse's works are also discussed, to a lesser degree.

Bates, E. Stuart. INSIDE OUT: AN INTRODUCTION TO AUTOBIOGRAPHY. Oxford: Blackwell, 1936.

> Good basic introduction to the nature and variety of autobiographical material, which includes brief treatments of Hudson and Yeats.

Bruss, Elizabeth W. AUTOBIOGRAPHICAL ACTS: THE CHANGING SITUATION OF A LITERARY GENRE. Baltimore: Johns Hopkins Univ. Press, 1976.

> Useful theoretical consideration of the audience's and autobiographer's roles in, features and forms of, and rules and sanctions for autobiographical writing. Bruss treats both theoretical and practical definitions of the genre, with an emphasis on linguistic matters.

Clifford, James L. FROM PUZZLES TO PORTRAITS: PROBLEMS OF A LITERARY BIOGRAPHER. Chapel Hill: Univ. of North Carolina Press, 1970.

> Concise discussion of the problems of handling evidence and the art of writing biography. Clifford emphasizes practical rather than theoretical concerns and includes discussion of Strachey, Woolf, and Beerbohm.

_____, ed. BIOGRAPHY AS AN ART: SELECTED CRITICISM, 1560-1960. New York: Oxford Univ. Press, 1962.

> A worthwhile collection of essays on the nature and function of biography, which includes items by Gosse, Saintsbury, Strachey, and Woolf. Clifford's introduction offers superb insights on the art versus craft debate.

Studies of Biography and Autobiography

Edel, Leon. LITERARY BIOGRAPHY. London: Rupert Hart-Davis, 1957.

    Treats the theoretical concepts of subject, quest, criticism, psychoanalysis, and time in writing literary biography. He discusses Strachey, Woolf, and Yeats.

Ellmann, Richard. GOLDEN CODGERS: BIOGRAPHICAL SPECULATIONS. New York: Oxford Univ. Press, 1973.

    Good consideration of the present difficulties of literary biography. Ellmann discusses such figures as Conrad, Eliot, Forster, Gosse, Joyce, Lawrence, Strachey, and Yeats.

_____. LITERARY BIOGRAPHY. Oxford, Engl.: Clarendon Press, 1971.

    Brief, but stimulating essay. Despite new psychological approaches which make biographers seem relentlessly "intrusive," Ellmann warns that the intricacies of great minds can never be fully understood.

Garraty, John. THE NATURE OF BIOGRAPHY. New York: Knopf, 1957.

    A historical survey of biographical methods from Plutarch to Gosse, Guedalla, and Strachey. Garraty stresses the rule of "honesty" and assesses the present state of the biographical art.

Johnson, Edgar. ONE MIGHTY TORRENT: THE DRAMA OF BIOGRAPHY. New York: Macmillan, 1955.

    Impressive study of the arts of biography and autobiography from the sixteenth through the twentieth centuries. Johnson praises Strachey, condemns Guedalla, and offers brief commentaries on Gosse and D.H. Lawrence.

Kendall, Paul. THE ART OF BIOGRAPHY. New York: Norton, 1965.

    Chapter 5, "Contemporary Biography," offers a worthwhile overview of practices that have developed since World War I. Kendall examines the style, technique, and influence of Gosse, Sitwell, and especially Strachey.

Longaker, Mark. CONTEMPORARY BIOGRAPHY. Philadelphia: Univ. of Pennsylvania Press, 1934.

    Includes a valuable first chapter which surveys both traditional and experimental trends in "the modern vogue of biography." There are also significant chapters on Strachey, Guedalla, and Belloc.

Nicolson, Harold. THE DEVELOPMENT OF ENGLISH BIOGRAPHY. London: Hogarth, 1928.

Studies of Biography and Autobiography

Chapter 6, "The Present Age," treats works by Gosse and Strachey and predicts the end of "pure" biography as the genre combines with elements of psychology.

Olney, James. METAPHORS OF SELF: THE MEANING OF AUTOBIOGRAPHY. Princeton, N.Y.: Princeton Univ. Press, 1972.

A major theoretic statement of the "presentness" of the form: "a metaphor of the self at the summary moment of composition." Olney discusses works by Montaigne, Jung, Fox, Darwin, Newman, Mill, and T.S. Eliot.

_____, ed. AUTOBIOGRAPHY: ESSAYS THEORETICAL AND CRITICAL. Princeton, N.J.: Princeton Univ. Press, 1980.

An important collection of theoretic essays.

Shapiro, Stephen. "The Dark Continent of Literature: Autobiography." CLS, 5 (1968), 421-54.

Argues that autobiography is an important form of imaginative literature that is too often ignored by modern critics. Shapiro examines rhetorical strategies in works by Yeats, Osbert Sitwell, and a range of foreign writers.

Shelston, Alan. BIOGRAPHY. New York: Harper and Row, 1977.

A brief but enlightening discussion of some problems of the form and the balance between author and subject, fact and fiction. Shelston devotes some attention to Gosse, D.H. Lawrence, Strachey, and Woolf.

Shumaker, Wayne. ENGLISH AUTOBIOGRAPHY: ITS EMERGENCE, MATERIALS, AND FORM. Berkeley and Los Angeles: Univ. of California Press, 1954.

Discusses the history and modes of autobiography and devotes some attention to Chesterton, Gosse, and Yeats.

STUDIES OF THE ESSAY AND PROSE STYLE

Baum, Paull. THE OTHER HARMONY OF PROSE: AN ESSAY IN ENGLISH PROSE RHYTHM. Durham, N.C.: Duke Univ. Press, 1952.

> A learned and witty treatment of the subject which opts for a loose "stress" conception of English prose rhythm.

Brown, Huntington. PROSE STYLES: FIVE PRIMARY TYPES. Minneapolis: Univ. of Minnesota Press, 1966.

> Perceives five basic types, each with distinguishing formal features: hortatory, expository, the aphoristic "prophetic," legalese, and "colloquial, rough-and-ready story telling."

Burton, S.H. THE CRITICISM OF PROSE. London: Longman, 1973.

> Good basic introduction to such technical features of both historical and modern prose style as tone, diction, structure, rhythms, and imagery. Reference is made to selections from Orwell, D.H. Lawrence, and others.

De la Mare, Walter. POETRY IN PROSE. New York: Oxford Univ. Press, 1937.

> Shows that good prose is poetic and contains many of the techniques of poetry.

Dobrée, Bonamy. ENGLISH ESSAYISTS. Folcroft, Pa.: Folcroft, 1973.

> A brief impressionistic history that selects Beerbohm, Chesterton, Woolf, Eliot, and Read for treatment as modernist essayists.

_____. MODERN PROSE STYLE. Westport, Conn.: Greenwood, 1978.

> Cites numerous modern British prose writers in defining style as personal voice and adducing examples in "descriptive prose," "explanatory prose," and "emotive prose." Dobrée feels British prose is becoming more colloquial.

Studies of the Essay and Prose Style

Eleanore, Sister Mary. THE LITERARY ESSAY IN ENGLISH. Boston: Ginn, 1923.

> A college text, this entails an interesting attempt to break the essay into several types, with brief evaluations of the major practitioners of each.

Freeman, Donald, ed. LINGUISTICS AND LITERARY STYLE. New York: Holt, Rinehart and Winston, 1970.

> An important collection of essays on applying linguistic techniques to the analysis of style, including prose style and prose rhythm.

Graves, Robert. THE READER OVER YOUR SHOULDER: A HANDBOOK FOR WRITERS OF ENGLISH PROSE. With Alan Hodge. New York: Random House, 1979.

> An informative discussion of "the principles of clear statement" as well as the history and types of English prose styles.

Hough, Graham. STYLE AND STYLISTICS. London: Routledge and Kegan Paul, 1969.

> An intelligent compact survey of approaches to style. After a historical overview, Graham has chapters on linguistic and literary contributions and on eight major theorists.

Lucas, F.L. STYLE. London: Cassell, 1955.

> Although Lucas has chapters on metaphors and prose harmony, most of the work concerns his thesis that the best style exhibits a pleasing personality, showing such features as good humor and vitality. Several modern British writers of nonfictional prose are cited disapprovingly, especially Saintsbury.

Miles, Josephine. STYLE AND PROPORTION: THE LANGUAGE OF PROSE AND POETRY. Boston: Little, Brown, 1967.

> Includes an interesting attempt to evaluate the historical development of British prose style through close analysis of passages, some by Connolly, Orwell, Read, Lawrence, and Shaw. Modern British prose is seen as a compromise between the old "sinewy" style (emphasizing verbs) and the "Mandarin" adjectival.

Murry, John Middleton. THE PROBLEM OF STYLE. London: Oxford Univ. Press, 1960.

> One of Murry's most important works, consisting of six lectures delivered at Oxford in 1921. Rejecting a rhetorical conception of style, he defines it as "universal significance" communicated largely by way of metaphor.

Studies of the Essay and Prose Style

Read, Herbert. ENGLISH PROSE STYLE. London: Bell, 1928.

> A guide to prose style, with examples drawn from great stylists, of whom Swift is the most consistently fine according to Read. The first section discusses such topics as onomatopoeia and metaphor; the second includes a survey of various kinds of prose.

Rucker, Mary E. "The Literary Essay and the Modern Temper." PLL, 11 (1975), 317-35.

> A useful review of changing attitudes toward the familiar essay in the twentieth century as industrialism and deterministic science caused it to be replaced by the more "functional" and polemic article.

Saintsbury, George. A HISTORY OF ENGLISH PROSE RHYTHM. Westport, Conn.: Greenwood, 1978.

> A survey from the Old English period to the later nineteenth century that applies Saintsbury's foot system to prose and stresses the importance of variety in prose rhythm.

Scholes, Robert, and Carl H. Klaus. ELEMENTS OF THE ESSAY. New York: Oxford Univ. Press, 1969.

> A critical study of the essay emphasizing its five "basic forms": the essay as essay, as story, as play, as poem, as dramatic monologue. The authors include detailed commentaries on essays by D.H. Lawrence, Orwell, and Forster.

Sutherland, James. "The Nineteenth Century and After." In his ON ENGLISH PROSE. Toronto: Univ. of Toronto Press, 1957. Pp. 82-110.

> Briefly cites the nonfiction of Saintsbury, Woolf, and D.H. Lawrence as exemplifying the modern trend toward colloquial prose.

Thomson, J.A.K. CLASSICAL INFLUENCES ON ENGLISH PROSE. London: Allen and Unwin, 1956.

> On classical models of such forms as biography and travel literature.

Ullman, Stephen. LANGUAGE AND STYLE. New York: Barnes and Noble, 1964.

> This contains a highly useful summary of the approaches of semantics to stylistic analysis; almost all the passages discussed are from French literature.

STUDIES OF LITERARY CRITICISM

Adams, Hazard. THE INTERESTS OF CRITICISM: AN INTRODUCTION TO LITERARY THEORY. New York: Harcourt, Brace and World, 1969.

> An excellent presentation of ancient and modern ideas on critical issues such as the imitative or creative nature of literature, the didactic purpose of literature, and the like. Adams concludes with chapters on the warfare over New Criticism, and on "violent" critics like Pound and Lawrence.

Bloomfield, Paul. "The Bloomsbury Tradition and English Literary Criticism." In THE CRAFT OF LETTERS IN ENGLAND: A SYMPOSIUM. Ed. John Lehmann. Westport, Conn.: Greenwood, 1974. Pp. 160-82.

> Examines the intellectual climate that influenced literary criticism by Strachey and Woolf.

Casey, John. THE LANGUAGE OF CRITICISM. London: Methuen, 1966.

> A discussion of the ways in which criticism is capable of a philosophic, rational (rather than emotive) response to literature, with sections on Eliot, Murry, and Leavis.

Crane, R.S. CRITICAL AND HISTORICAL PRINCIPLES OF LITERARY HISTORY. Chicago: Univ. of Chicago Press, 1971.

> A worthwhile inquiry into the principles that have directed the writing of literary history from ancient Greece to the present day.

_____. THE LANGUAGES OF CRITICISM AND THE STRUCTURE OF POETRY. Toronto: Univ. of Toronto Press, 1953.

> On how critical assumptions determine the findings of Aristotelian, New Critical, and Jungian-Freudian approaches to poetic structure.

Daiches, David. CRITICAL APPROACHES TO LITERATURE. New York: Longman, 1979.

Studies of Literary Criticism

Part 1 lays out in chronological order the major critical conceptions of literature; part 2 discusses various methods of "practical" criticism; part 3 discusses the relation of criticism to such disciplines as history and psychology. There are sections on Richards, Eliot, and Empson.

Demetz, Peter. MARX, ENGELS, AND THE POETS: ORIGINS OF MARXIST LITERARY CRITICISM. Chicago: Univ. of Chicago Press, 1967.

A useful introduction to past and present developments (1850-1950) in Marxist criticism. Criticism by Engels, Marx, Lukács, and others is examined and analyzed.

Eliot, T.S. SELECTED ESSAYS. New York: Harcourt, 1950.

In the important essays "Tradition and the Individual Talent" and "The Function of Criticism," Eliot proclaims his critical principles; in other essays he draws new attention to classicism and the metaphysicals.

Frye, Northrop. ANATOMY OF CRITICISM. Princeton, N.J.: Princeton Univ. Press, 1957.

The major work of archetypal criticism, discussing the archetypal symbols and patterns in literary genres.

Gross, John. THE RISE AND FALL OF THE MAN OF LETTERS: A STUDY OF THE IDIOSYNCRATIC AND THE HUMANE IN MODERN LITERATURE. New York: Macmillan, 1969.

An excellent, informed history of the breed in the nineteenth and twentieth centuries with discussions of Saintsbury, Gosse, Chesterton, Eliot, Murry, Orwell, Leavis, and many others.

Handy, William J., ed. A SYMPOSIUM ON FORMALIST CRITICISM. Austin: Univ. of Texas, 1965.

Significant collection of four theoretical essays exhibiting various approaches to formalist criticism by four distinguished scholars-- John Crowe Ransom, Elder Olson, Eliseo Vivas, and Kenneth Burke.

Hirsch, E.D., Jr. VALIDITY IN INTERPRETATION. New Haven, Conn.: Yale Univ. Press, 1967.

The major theoretical assertion that literature is open to correct and agreed-upon interpretation.

Hobsbaum, Philip. THEORY OF CRITICISM. Bloomington: Indiana Univ. Press, 1970.

Studies of Literary Criticism

    A brilliant discussion of how great literary works engender critical agreement and of the ways lesser works do not.

Hoffman, Frederick J. "The Scholar-Critic: Trends in Contemporary British and American Literary Study." MLQ, 26 (1965), 1-15.

    A provocative article which examines uses and abuses in both modern criticism and scholarship.

Hough, Graham. "English Criticism." In THE TWENTIETH-CENTURY MIND: HISTORY, IDEAS, AND LITERATURE IN BRITAIN. Ed. C. B. Cox and A. E. Dyson. London: Oxford Univ. Press, 1972. Vol. 1, pp. 475-84.

    Brief but useful survey of main critical trends from 1900 to 1918. Hough is especially good on Yeats and academic critics such as Saintsbury.

Hyman, Stanley Edgar. THE ARMED VISION: A STUDY IN THE METHODS OF MODERN LITERARY CRITICISM. Westport, Conn.: Greenwood, 1978.

    A controversial, readable study of the nature and ancestry of the modern critical method. Hyman argues for an integrated and practical methodology. In ten chapters, he explains the contributions of such critics as Eliot, Empson, and Richards.

Jones, A. R. "Literary Criticism." In THE TWENTIETH-CENTURY MIND: HISTORY, IDEAS, AND LITERATURE IN BRITAIN. Ed. C. B. Cox and A. E. Dyson. London: Oxford Univ. Press, 1972. Vol. 2, pp. 457-73.

    Brief but helpful survey of main critical trends from 1918 to 1945. Jones offers insightful commentary on Eliot, Richards, Empson, and Leavis.

Kaplan, Morton, and Robert Kloss. "Psychoanalysis and Literary Criticism." In their THE UNSPOKEN MOTIVE: A GUIDE TO PSYCHOANALYTIC LITERARY CRITICISM. New York: Free Press, 1973. Pp. 3-43.

    A lucid and balanced introduction to the concerns of psychoanalytic critical theory.

Krieger, Murray. THE NEW APOLOGISTS FOR POETRY. Westport, Conn.: Greenwood, 1977.

    A philosophical discussion of how such modern critical issues as the creative process, the aesthetic object, and the function of poetry relate to science, language, cognition, and the imagination. Krieger offers worthwhile insights on Hulme, Eliot, and Richards.

_____. THEORY OF CRITICISM: A TRADITION AND ITS SYSTEM. Baltimore: Johns Hopkins Univ. Press, 1976.

A complex discussion emphasizing the poet as form-maker rather than as imitator; it discusses Eliot and Richards.

Lemon, Lee T. THE PARTIAL CRITICS. New York: Oxford Univ. Press, 1965.

Regrets the extreme specialization of critical approaches to poetry. Lemon inquires into the theoretical and practical consistencies of positions held to rigidly by critics at first and then later abandoned. Lemon scrutinizes approaches of Eliot, Empson, Hulme, Leavis, Richards, and others.

Lodge, David. "Crosscurrents in Modern English Criticism." In his THE NOVELIST AT THE CROSSROADS AND OTHER ESSAYS ON FICTION AND CRITICISM. Ithaca, N.Y.: Cornell Univ. Press, 1971. Pp. 247-86.

An exceedingly handy survey, especially good on the academic critics.

McDowell, Frederick P.W., ed. THE POET AS CRITIC. Evanston, Ill.: Northwestern Univ. Press, 1967.

An interesting collection of six essays on the subject of the relationship between a poet's creative and critical functions and psychology.

Madden, William A. "The Divided Tradition of English Criticism." PMLA, 73 (1958), 69-80.

The divided tradition which "underlies modern English criticism" can be traced back to Arnold's "Christian and non-Christian, romantic and nonromantic notions." Madden treats the reactions in Eliot, Hulme, Richards, Read, and Yeats.

Morrison, Claudia C. FREUD AND THE CRITIC. Chapel Hill: Univ. of North Carolina Press, 1968.

Although the study emphasizes primarily American critics who were attracted early on to Freudian criticism, reference is made to Herbert Read and other British practitioners.

O'Connor, William Van. AN AGE OF CRITICISM, 1900-1950. Chicago: Regnery, 1952.

Describes the general character of various critical movements in America. Includes extended commentary on Empson and Richards.

Pulos, C.E. "The New Critics and the Language of Poetry." UNS, No. 19 (1958), 1-93.

Studies of Literary Criticism

    A useful monograph which is a historical study of the new critic's concern with language. The study argues that the two schools of criticism linked to the imagists and I.A. Richards are "different phases of the same basic movement." Seven critics are treated, including Ford, Hulme, Eliot, Richards, and Empson.

Richards, I.A. PRINCIPLES OF LITERARY CRITICISM. London: Kegan Paul, 1924.

    An important work applying linguistics and psychology to the study of poetic meaning.

Righter, William. LOGIC AND CRITICISM. New York: Chilmark Press, 1963.

    An examination of the possibilities of critical value judgments and of the precision of critical language, with sections on Richards and Empson.

Ruthven, R.K. CRITICAL ASSUMPTIONS. Cambridge: The Univ. Press, 1979.

    An excellent comprehensive survey of differing critical assumptions on such issues as whether literature should be complex or simple, whether it should be imitative or original, whether it is the product of inspiration or contrivance, and the like.

Vivas, Eliseo. CREATION AND DISCOVERY. South Bend, Ind.: Regnery-Gateway, 1966.

    A collection of Vivas' essays on aesthetics. Two pieces find Eliot's objective correlative and Richards' psychological theory confused.

Watson, George. THE LITERARY CRITICS: A STUDY OF ENGLISH DESCRIPTIVE CRITICISM. Totowa, N.J.: Biblio, 1973.

    A basic history of English criticism, which includes commentary on Eliot, Richards, Empson, Leavis, Orwell, and others.

Wellek, René. CONCEPTS OF CRITICISM. New Haven, Conn.: Yale Univ. Press, 1963.

    Thirteen essays seeking to define the roles of literary history, criticism, and theory and such concepts as realism and romanticism. The final essay outlines "The Main Trends of Twentieth-Century Criticism."

West, Alick. CRISIS AND CRITICISM AND LITERARY WRITINGS. New York: Beekman, 1975.

    A Marxist embrace of Romanticism's social consciousness that attacks the individualistic, expressive idea of literary creation, with chapters analyzing the perceptions and errors of Eliot, Read, and Richards on the subject.

Wimsatt, William, and Cleanth Brooks. LITERARY CRITICISM: A SHORT HISTORY. Chicago: University of Chicago Press, 1978.

A classic literary history that offers readable and unified discussions. The esteemed scholars offer useful commentary on Richards, Eliot, Yeats, Empson, and other modern critics.

STUDIES OF TRAVEL WRITING

Butor, Michel. "Travel and Writing." MOSAIC 8, No. 1 (1974), 1-16.

    A difficult treatise on the psychological analogies and influences between travelling and reading and writing.

Day, Martin S. "Travel Literature and the Journey Theme." FORUMH, 12, No. 2 (1975), 37-47.

    An authoritative survey of travel writing which argues it is not a genre but an expression of the archetypal journey of life.

Fedden, Robin. ENGLISH TRAVELLERS IN THE NEAR EAST. London and New York: Longmans, Green, 1958.

    A forty-page history of British travel writing on Arabia, with a brief chapter on T. E. Lawrence.

Fussell, Paul. ABROAD: BRITISH LITERARY TRAVELING BETWEEN THE WARS. New York: Oxford Univ. Press, 1980.

    An excellent, well-informed survey of modern British travelling and travel writing. There are chapters on individual authors, including Norman Douglas and D. H. Lawrence, and thematic chapters treating various aspects of travel as social history.

Hunt, Bishop C., Jr. "Travel Metaphors and the Problem of Knowledge." MLS, 6, No. 1 (1976), 44-47.

    On the historical evolution of travelling as a metaphor for learning in literature.

Keith, W. J. THE RURAL TRADITION: A STUDY OF THE NON-FICTION PROSE WRITERS OF THE ENGLISH COUNTRYSIDE. Toronto: Univ. of Toronto Press, 1974.

    A useful survey of the principal writers of nonfiction on rural themes in British literary history. It includes chapters on Hudson, Edward Thomas, Henry Williamson, and H.J. Massingham.

Peyre, Henri. "Reflections on the Literature of Travel." In TRAVEL, QUEST, AND PILGRIMAGE AS A LITERARY THEME: STUDIES IN HONOR OF REINO VIRTANEN. Ed. Frans C. Amelinckx and Joyce N. Megay. Lincoln, Nebr.: Society of Spanish and Spanish-American Studies, 1978. Pp. 7-23.

> Contains a brief historical review of western travel writing, but primarily focuses on French practitioners.

Spengemann, William C. "Eternal Maps and Temporal Voyages." EXPLOR, 2 (1974), 1-7.

> Associates travel writing from the Renaissance on with the modern conception of reality as temporal experience rather than as timeless ideal.

INDIVIDUAL AUTHORS

W.H. AUDEN (1907-73)

NONFICTIONAL PROSE

A CERTAIN WORLD: A COMMONPLACE BOOK. New York: Viking, 1970.

> A selection of quotations from many sources on topics ranging from aging to writing. WHA intersperses some reflections of his own and says that he considers the compilation to be "a sort of autobiography."

THE DYER'S HAND AND OTHER ESSAYS. New York: Random House, 1962. London: Faber, 1963.

> A collection of thirty-four essays, including "Reading," "Writing," "Making, Knowing and Judging," "The Poet and The City," "American Poetry," "Postscript: Christianity and Art," and "Music in Shakespeare."

EDUCATION TODAY--AND TOMORROW. With J.C. Worsley. London: Hogarth, 1939.

> Education's place in the English social system, from grammar school to university.

THE ENCHAFED FLOOD: OR THE ROMANTIC ICONOGRAPHY OF THE SEA. New York: Random House, 1950. London: Faber, 1951.

> In three essays, WHA formulates a theory of romanticism from a limited number of works by such writers as Wordsworth, Lewis Carroll, Melville, Ibsen, Baudelaire, and Valéry.

JOURNEY TO A WAR. With Christopher Isherwood. London: Faber; New York: Random House, 1939.

> A prose and verse record of experiences in China. At the war front, WHA witnesses the war and speculates that Europeans may be joining the action soon. Some meditations concerning the metaphysical reasons for war are also provided.

W.H. Auden

LETTERS FROM ICELAND. With Louis MacNeice. London: Faber; New York: Random House, 1937.

> A travel book in verse and prose about Iceland. The authors convey their impressions of the land and its people, including farmers, fishermen, busmen, children, and so forth.

MAKING, KNOWING, AND JUDGING. Oxford, Engl.: Clarendon Press, 1956. New York: Oxford Univ. Press, 1957.

> WHA's inaugural lecture as Professor of Poetry delivered before the University of Oxford, June 11, 1956; WHA presents his views on the nature and function of poetry. Reprinted in DYER'S HAND.

THE ORATORS: AN ENGLISH STUDY. London: Faber, 1932.

> An experimental treatment, mostly in prose, of war, mobilization, and an airman's experiences.

SECONDARY WORLDS. London: Faber, 1968. New York: Random House, 1969.

> A collection of four essays that were given by WHA at the University of Kent as the inaugural T.S. Eliot Memorial Lectures. The first lecture deals with the martyr as dramatic hero; the second with the Icelandic Sagas; the third with opera; the fourth with the problems of a Christian writer. The unifying theme is that "the relation between those secondary worlds which we call works of art and the primary world of our everyday social experience is a problem which concerns every artist."

SELECTED ESSAYS. London: Faber, 1962.

> A collection of ten essays, all of which appear in DYER'S HAND.

WORKS EDITED BY OTHERS

THE ENGLISH AUDEN: POEMS, ESSAYS AND DRAMATIC WRITINGS, 1927-1939. Ed. Edward Mendelson. London: Faber, 1977.

> Reprints ORATORS as well as twenty-seven essays and reviews. Mendelson states that he chose "those essays and reviews that best serve as a commentary on the poems and on Auden's changing ideas of poetry's social role."

FOREWORDS AND AFTERWORDS. Ed. Edward Mendelson. New York: Random House, 1973.

> A selection of forty-six essays reprinted from books for which

WHA wrote introductions or reviews. The book serves as a
valuable index to WHA's literary opinions over three decades
(1943 to 1973), and a complete listing of the original
appearances is given at the end of the book.

BIBLIOGRAPHY

Beach, Joseph Warren. THE MAKING OF THE AUDEN CANON. Minneapolis: Univ. of Minnesota Press, 1957.

> Treats textual alterations made in WHA's poems and some prose passages; includes a chapter on ORATORS and LETTERS FROM ICELAND as well as a brief bibliography.

Bloomfield, B.C., and Edward Mendelson, eds. W.H. AUDEN, A BIBLIOGRAPHY, 1924-1969. 2nd ed. Charlottesville: Univ. Press of Virginia, 1972.

> Revised and expanded edition of Bloomfield's initial effort. The definitive bibliography.

Callan, Edward, ed. AN ANNOTATED CHECKLIST OF THE WORKS OF W. H. AUDEN (1924-1957). Denver: Swallow, 1958.

> A primary bibliography which includes brief descriptive annotations of WHA's critical and expository prose. In a prefatory note, Callan points out that "Although W.H. Auden is primarily known as a poet, nearly four-fifths of the more than three hundred items in this checklist refer to critical and expository prose." Useful as a complete list of WHA's essays and reviews.

——. "An Annotated Checklist of the Works of W.H. Auden (1924-1957)." TCL, 4 (1958), 30-50.

> The article edition which is more widely available than the Swallow limited edition.

——. "W.H. Auden: Annotated Checklist II (1958-1969)." TCL, 16 (1970), 27-56.

> Continues the format of the earlier edition and extends the number of entries to 501.

Clancy, Joseph, comp. "A W.H. Auden Bibliography 1924-1955." THOUGHT, 30 (1955), 260-70.

> Includes books by WHA as well as over one hundred uncollected materials such as essays, reviews, and introductions to books. There is also a list of one hundred critical books and articles about WHA, some of which are negative.

W.H. Auden

Gingerich, Martin E., ed. W.H. AUDEN: A REFERENCE GUIDE. Boston: Hall, 1977.

> A comprehensive listing of writings about WHA, 1931-1976, with a helpful index. Concise and competent annotations for almost all items.

Todd, Ruthven, comp. "Writings by W.H. Auden (1929-1937)." NEW VERSE, Nos. 26-7 (1937), 32-46.

> Lists WHA's published volumes, ten articles in books, and ten miscellaneous prose pieces into 1937. Todd says: "This checklist is for readers, not for bibliographers or collectors."

BIOGRAPHY

Carpenter, Humphrey. W.H. AUDEN: A BIOGRAPHY. Boston: Houghton Mifflin, 1981.

> A candid and scholarly biography which explores in great detail the influences on WHA's life and work. Carpenter provides well-focused insights into the circumstances surrounding the composition of WHA's various works and describes their styles, themes, and ideas.

Mendelson, Edward. EARLY AUDEN. New York: Viking Press, 1981.

> An important and valuable study which analyzes WHA's writings against their biographical and historical background. The study focuses on his career between 1927 and 1939. Mendelson includes excellent analyses of WHA's social, moral, and aesthetic ideas and comments on his developing style.

NEW VERSE, Nos. 26-27 (1937). Auden Double Number.

> A special issue which treats various aspects of WHA's life, work, and politics. Contributors include Isherwood, MacNeice, Spender, Grigson, Day Lewis, Rickword, and others.

Osborne, Charles. W.H. AUDEN: THE LIFE OF A POET. New York: Harcourt, 1979.

> A readable, well-researched biography which delightfully interweaves some personal anecdotes. Osborne quotes from, but rarely analyzes, WHA's works.

SHENANDOAH, 18 (1967). Special Auden Issue.

> Contains fourteen biographical and tribute essays by such writers as E.R. Dodds, Bonamy Dobrée, Julian Symons, and Robert Lowell.

Spender, Stephen, ed. W. H. AUDEN: A TRIBUTE. New York: Macmillan, 1975.

> A collection of thirty-six new essays, many by WHA's friends, and "covering as much as possible of different periods of his life." More valuable as reminiscence than as critical study.

CRITICISM

Bahlke, George W. THE LATER AUDEN: FROM "NEW YEAR LETTER" TO ABOUT THE HOUSE. Rutgers, N.J.: Rutgers Univ. Press, 1970.

> Contains a very useful chapter on "Auden's Literary Criticism," which discusses in detail ENCHAFED FLOOD and DYER'S HAND.

Blair, John G. THE POETIC ART OF W.H. AUDEN. Princeton, N.J.: Princeton Univ. Press, 1965.

> Sees WHA as an anti-Romantic and a moralist. Blair discusses mainly the poetry, but he also provides some biographical information and refers to a number of WHA's critical essays.

Bogan, Louise. "W.H. Auden." In her A POET'S ALPHABET. New York: McGraw-Hill, 1970. Pp. 32-35.

> Brief discussion of the travel book LETTERS. Bogan argues that the two authors had the same attitude toward the strange Icelandic landscape--that of a detached amateur. However, the "two noticed different things."

Bone, Christopher. "W.H. Auden in the 1930's: The Problem of Individual Commitment to Political Action." ALBION, 4, No. 1 (1972), 3-11.

> Bone argues that in JOURNEY, WHA directly confronts the problem of individual commitment to collective political action. WHA considers the present wartime situation and metaphysical reasons behind all wars.

Brooks, Cleanth. "W.H. Auden as a Critic." KR, 26 (1964), 173-89.

> Discusses several of WHA's critical essays, including "Balaam and the Ass" (DYER'S HAND) and "Squares and Oblongs" (SELECTED ESSAYS). Brooks concludes that "his possession of a coherent and responsible theory accounts for Auden's having become one of the soundest as well as one of the most exciting critics of our day."

Buell, Frederick. W.H. AUDEN AS A SOCIAL POET. Ithaca, N.Y.: Cornell Univ. Press, 1973.

Though primarily a study of the relationship between WHA's poetry and politics, Buell discusses JOURNEY, LETTERS and ORATORS in some detail.

Burgum, Edwin Berry. "Three English Radical Poets." NEW MASSES, 12 (1934), 33-36.

> Discusses ORATORS and compares WHA with Spender and Day Lewis. Burgum feels that they "have turned to Communism as a way out."

Callan, Edward. "Auden on Christianity and Criticism." THE CHRISTIAN SCHOLAR, 46 (1963), 168-73.

> Callan argues that the essays in DYER'S HAND reveal an indebtedness to Kierkegaard's aesthetic works, although "Auden displays some skepticism towards Kierkegaard's theological speculations." WHA's literary criticism also displays a profound knowledge of "the techniques of his craft."

―――. "Auden's Ironic Masquerade: Criticism as Morality Play." UTQ, 35 (1966), 133-43.

> Callan demonstrates how WHA's THE SEA AND THE MIRROR epitomizes the critical theory underlying his essays in DYER'S HAND. The intellectual scheme underlying both is "Kierkegaard's triad of aesthetic, ethical, and religious spheres."

―――. "The Development of W.H. Auden's Poetic Theory since 1940." TCL, 4 (1958), 79-91.

> WHA's critical writings are valuable sources of information because they often illuminate themes in his poetry. The criticism also records "the view of life and the theory of art from which his poetry stems."

Cox, R.G. "Auden as Critic and Poet." SCRUTINY, 18 (1951), 158-61.

> A negative report. Cox feels that ENCHAFED FLOOD lacks discipline and a controlling focus.

Daiches, David. "Poetry in the 1930's--II: W.H. Auden and Stephen Spender." In his POETRY AND THE MODERN WORLD. Chicago: Univ. of Chicago Press, 1940. Pp. 219-29.

> Close analysis of all parts of ORATORS, which Daiches calls WHA's "most obscure work" because of the shifting point of view, ambiguous symbols, hero-villain figure, and abrupt transitions.

Davison, Trevor. "The Method of Auden's 'The Orators.'" DUJ, N.S. 32 (1971), 167-78.

> Intelligent and informal discussion of ORATORS. Davison argues that paradox is "inherent in its method" since the work was not written to illustrate a preconceived thesis but "it actually originated as an attempt to substantiate didacticism, to inject it with new effectiveness on the surrealist model."

Duchene, Francois. THE CASE OF THE HELMETED AIRMAN: A STUDY OF W.H. AUDEN'S POETRY. London: Chatto and Windus, 1972.

> Argues that WHA maintained a detached perspective like that of "the hawk or the helmeted airman." Duchene discusses mainly the poetry but there are numerous references to the essays in DYER'S HAND and ENCHAFED FLOOD.

Everett, Barbara. AUDEN. Edinburgh: Oliver and Boyd, 1964.

> Everett employs WHA's prose writings, including JOURNEY TO A WAR and LETTERS FROM ICELAND, to elucidate the poems.

Faulkner, Peter. "Auden as Scrutineer." DUJ, N.S. 32 (1970), 56-60.

> WHA published a number of reviews in the early numbers of SCRUTINY. Faulkner discusses the content and thought in these reviews, and shows how they reveal the doubts of WHA in his early career.

Fletcher, John Gould. "Poet of Courage." POETRY, 42 (1933), 110-13.

> Fletcher objects to the obscurity of ORATORS "which may be read as a satire on the English public-school system" or "as a piece of buffoonery" or "as a fragmentary autobiography" or "as a sort of manifesto for an unwritten poem."

Forster, E.M. "THE ENCHAFED FLOOD." In his TWO CHEERS FOR DEMOCRACY. New York: Harcourt, 1951. Pp. 265-68.

> Impressionistic reaction to ENCHAFED FLOOD. Forster analyzes briefly the book's three sections and finds himself left with the admonition that "we must either build the city or die."

Fraser, G.S. "The Young Prophet." NEW STATESMAN AND NATION, 51 (1956), 102-03.

> Compares ORATORS to Carlyle's PAST AND PRESENT. Fraser concludes that WHA was a courageous prophet; he was right "to harangue and clamour" and to suggest social remedies.

Greenburg, Herbert. QUEST FOR THE NECESSARY: W.H. AUDEN AND THE DILEMMA OF DIVIDED CONSCIOUSNESS. Cambridge, Mass.: Harvard Univ. Press, 1968. Pp. 51-57.

>   Psychological analysis of "Journal of an Airman" section of ORATORS.

Greenburg, Martin. "Auden as Critic." NATION, 170 (1950), 407-08.

>   Negative reaction to ENCHAFED FLOOD. Greenburg feels the book lacks a strong critical faculty, is "oddly schematic," and has a "surface manner" of approach to the subject of Romanticism.

Hoggart, Richard. AUDEN: AN INTRODUCTORY ESSAY. New Haven, Conn.: Yale Univ. Press, 1951.

>   The first full-length study of WHA's work. Hoggart includes brief discussions of the themes and techniques of JOURNEY TO A WAR, LETTERS FROM ICELAND, and ORATORS.

Hoskins, Katherine Bail. TODAY THE STRUGGLE. Austin: Univ. of Texas Press, 1969.

>   Presents WHA's political outlook "On the Left" in the 1930's and discusses in more detail WHA's purposes in JOURNEY and LETTERS.

Johnson, Richard A. MAN'S PLACE: AN ESSAY ON AUDEN. Ithaca, N.Y.: Cornell Univ. Press, 1973.

>   A philosophical approach to WHA. Johnson includes some references to several essays in DYER'S HAND and to ENCHAFED FLOOD to make his points.

Magnusson, Sigurdur A. "Auden in Iceland." ICELAND REVIEW, 2, No. 3 (1964), 30.

>   Discusses the visit to Iceland in 1936 of WHA and Louis MacNeice. Magnusson maintains that their account in LETTERS FROM ICELAND is "candid and unsentimental" as well as accurate.

Mendelson, Edward. "The Coherence of Auden's THE ORATORS." ELH, 35 (1968), 114-33.

>   The themes of human failure and divine success contribute to the "coherent structure" of ORATORS. The bulk of ORATORS details the search for a secular leader but it ends with an absurd affirmation whereby "the individual self is divinely inspired."

W.H. Auden

Ohmann, Richard M. "Auden's Sacred Awe." COMMONWEAL, 78 (1963), 279-81.

> Ohmann praises DYER'S HAND for three reasons: the essays represent "fifteen years' worth of major comments on literature"; they serve as a gloss on WHA's poetry; they scrutinize carefully moral and emotional experience, thus preserving the author from "the charge of ideological fickleness."

Paulin, Tom. "LETTERS FROM ICELAND: Going North." In THE 1930S: A CHALLENGE TO ORTHODOXY. Ed. John Lucas. New York: Barnes and Noble, 1978. Pp. 59-77.

> A valuable appreciation of LETTERS FROM ICELAND in which Paulin argues that the work "offers a response to history, politics and society which is not only still valid, but which has still to be followed." The book should be seen not as a travel book but as significant social, political, and cultural commentary.

Porter, Peter. "The Achievement of Auden." SSENG, 4 (1978-79), 73-113.

> Balanced and comprehensive assessment of WHA's reputation and his achievements in both poetry and criticism. Porter briefly treats LETTERS FROM ICELAND, JOURNEY TO A WAR, and the several essay collections; he concludes that WHA's criticism tends to be discursive and "full of quirks," but free of academic orthodoxies. The "true landmarks" are in the poetry.

Powell, Dilys. "Advance Guard." In her DESCENT FROM PARNASSUS. London: Cresset Press, 1934. Pp. 173-94.

> Argues that ORATORS is filled with obscure allusions and in it "prophecy is still stronger than precept." The Airman is a confused figure who struggles against "both personal weakness and national peril."

Sellers, W.H. "New Light on Auden's THE ORATORS." PMLA, 82 (1967), 455-64.

> Seeks to clarify the thematic coherence of ORATORS, WHA's "most puzzling work." Sellers argues that "Auden set about in THE ORATORS to diagnose the contemporary human condition in a series of discontinuous but not disconnected parables."

Spears, Monroe K. "The Nature of Modernism: The City." In his DIONYSUS AND THE CITY. New York: Oxford Univ. Press, 1970. Pp. 82-90.

> Brief discussion of ENCHAFED FLOOD and DYER'S HAND. Spears points out that in his critical prose, WHA has "extensively discussed the City and related symbols."

W.H. Auden

──────. THE POETRY OF W.H. AUDEN: THE DISENCHANTED ISLAND. New York: Oxford Univ. Press, 1963.

> The most comprehensive study to date. Spears includes information on WHA's life and work not found elsewhere; for some facts, Spears consulted WHA himself. The concluding chapter presents some perceptive analysis of WHA's criticism.

Spender, Stephen. "Airmen, Politics and Psychoanalysis." In his THE DESTRUCTIVE ELEMENT: A STUDY OF MODERN WRITERS AND BELIEF. London: Cape, 1935. Pp. 251-77.

> Discusses "Journal of an Airman," Book II of ORATORS. Spender shows that because the airman is alone he is bound to fail: "There is never any really revolutionary issue . . . because the airman has no friends." Further, he is like "the contemporary writer who hates the social system under which he exists."

Warren, Robert Penn. "Twelve Poets." AMERICAN REVIEW, 3 (1934), 221-27.

> Although Warren admits that the system of reference and symbol in ORATORS is "a personal, if not arbitrary matter," he ultimately concludes that it derives from "an actual subtlety of thought and effect."

Woodcock, George. "Auden--Critic and Criticized." SR, 82 (1975), 685-97.

> Discussion of some essays in FOREWORDS AND AFTERWORDS. Woodcock comes to the general conclusion that the essays reveal "the scope of Auden's culture and knowledge" but furnish personal, autobiographical details in a highly selective manner.

Wright, George T. W.H. AUDEN. New York: Twayne, 1969.

> A basic critical-analytical interpretation of WHA's works, including DYER'S HAND, ENCHAFED FLOOD, and ORATORS.

Young, Dudley. "Still Life Inside the Whale." PNR, 18 (1980), 39-49.

> A provocative discussion which examines the grounds for WHA's rise to prominence in the thirties.

MAX BEERBOHM (1872-1956)

THE WORKS OF MAX BEERBOHM, 10 volumes (London: Heinemann, 1922-28), collects most of the nonfictional prose.

NONFICTIONAL PROSE

AND EVEN NOW. London: Heinemann, 1920. New York: Dutton, 1921.

> Probably the finest collection of MB's essays. Of the twenty essays, the more important are: "Hosts and Guests," "Servants," "In Homes Unblest," "Something Defensible," and "The Crime."

AROUND THEATRES. 2 vols. London: Heinemann, 1924. New York: Knopf, 1930.

> Reprints 153 critical essays written by MB for the SATURDAY REVIEW between 1898 and 1910. The contributions are arranged in chronological order and deal mainly with the London theatre.

A CHRISTMAS GARLAND. London: Heinemann; New York: Dutton, 1912.

> Collection of eighteen literary parodies of contemporary English writers, including Bennett, Chesterton, Conrad, Galsworthy, and Wells. A work of the highest quality.

A DEFENCE OF COSMETICS. New York: Dodd, Mead, 1922.

> Separate reprint of the essay originally entitled "The Pervasion of Rouge" (WORKS, 1896). In a tongue-in-cheek manner, MB pays homage to the young, delicate beauty of the music-hall artist, Cissy Loftus.

LYTTON STRACHEY. The Rede Lecture. London: Macmillan; New York: Knopf, 1943.

> Personal reminiscences of Strachey. MB strongly objects to the

application of the term "a debunker" to Strachey's efforts and
he includes a brief discussion of VICTORIANS and ELIZABETH.

MAINLY ON THE AIR. London: Heinemann, 1946. New York: Knopf, 1947.

Collects six BBC broadcasts, including "London Revisited," "Speed," "Music Halls of My Youth," and "Advertisements," and adds six essays, including "A Note on the Einstein Theory," "From Bloomsbury to Bayswater," and "The Top Hat."

MORE. London and New York: Lane, 1899.

Collects twenty of MB's early essays, including "Actors," "Madame Tussaud's," "Sign-Boards," "The Blight on the Music Halls," "Fashion and Her Bicycle," "At Covent Garden," and "Ouida" (her books are "amazing in their sustained vitality").

A SELECTION FROM AROUND THEATRES. New York: Knopf, 1930.

An abridged edition of the original AROUND THEATRES.

SEVEN MEN. London: Heinemann, 1919. New York: Knopf, 1920.

Satiric sketches of six men (semifictional and semiautobiographical). MB functions as a character in each tale and as the seventh man.

SEVEN MEN AND TWO OTHERS. London: Heinemann, 1950.

Reprints SEVEN MEN (1919) and adds the story of "Felix Argallo and Walter Ledgett," which was previously included as "Not That I Would Boast" in VARIETY OF THINGS.

A VARIETY OF THINGS. London: Heinemann; New York: Knopf, 1928.

Contains two stories, one play, and nine essays, including "Not That I Would Boast," "A Social Success," "The Guerdon" (a parody of Henry James's style), "A Note on the Einstein Theory," and "The Spirit of Caricature." The American edition includes a vituperative "Note" in which MB condemns pirated publications of his work.

WORKS AND MORE. London: Lane, 1930.

Collects WORKS (1896) and MORE (1899).

THE WORKS OF MAX BEERBOHM. New York: Scribner's, 1896. As THE WORKS OF MAX BEERBOHM WITH A BIBLIOGRAPHY BY JOHN LANE. London: Lane, 1896.

Despite the tongue-in-cheek title, the book collects only seven of MB's early essays, including "Dandies and Dandies," "The Pervasion of Rouge," and "King George the Fourth" (a defense and answer to Thackeray's denunciation). The American edition omits the Lane bibliography.

YET AGAIN. London: Chapman and Hall, 1909. New York: Lane, 1910.

A collection of twenty-two essays and nine word pictures. Some essays included are: "Seeing People Off," "A Memory of a Midnight Express" (terror and sorrow), "A Club in Ruins," "Whistler's Writing," "A Morris for May-Day" (on Morris-dancers), "The Naming of Streets," and "The Humor of the Public." In a "Words for Pictures" edition, MB transforms paintings (such as "Macbeth and the Witches" by Corot) into verbal sketches.

WORKS EDITED BY OTHERS

THE BODLEY HEAD MAX BEERBOHM. Ed. David Cecil. London: Bodley Head, 1970.

A valuable anthology which includes four sketches, thirteen general essays, six parodies, and six essays of dramatic criticism.

THE INCOMPARABLE MAX: A COLLECTION OF WRITINGS OF SIR MAX BEERBOHM. Ed. S.C. Roberts. London: Heinemann, 1962.

A fairly representative selection which includes thirty-three essays, sketches, parodies, criticisms, and broadcasts.

LAST THEATRES, 1904-1910. Ed. Rupert Hart-Davis. London: Rupert Hart-Davis, 1970.

Collects all of MB's dramatic criticism written between 1904 and 1910 which did not appear in AROUND THEATRES.

MAX BEERBOHM: SELECTED ESSAYS. Ed. N.L. Clay. London: Heinemann, 1958.

Collects twenty of MB's essays, including "Madame Tussaud's," "Laughter," "London Revisited," "Speed," "Music Halls of My Youth," and "Advertisements." Brief but helpful notes are provided for most of the essays.

MORE THEATRES 1898-1903. Ed. Rupert Hart-Davis. New York: Taplinger, 1969.

Collects all of MB's dramatic criticism written between 1898 and 1903 which did not appear in AROUND THEATRES.

A PEEP INTO THE PAST AND OTHER PROSE PIECES. Ed. Rupert Hart-Davis. London: Heinemann, 1972.

    Selects twenty-eight essays written by MB over a period of fifty years. The items (arranged chronologically) are drawn from a variety of sources and include the title essay (a satire on Wilde), "My Ambitions," "Miss Dustworth and Miss Libman" (two retired, impoverished actresses), and "Remembered Meals" (on French cuisine).

A SELECTION FROM AROUND THEATRES. Garden City, N.Y.: Doubleday, 1960.

BIBLIOGRAPHY

Gallatin, A. E., comp. SIR MAX BEERBOHM: BIBLIOGRAPHICAL NOTES. Cambridge, Mass.: Harvard Univ. Press, 1944.

    Lists MB's collected and separately printed works, some of his uncollected and unpublished writings, introductions written for various books, and selected works about MB.

Gallatin, A. E., and L. M. Oliver, eds. A BIBLIOGRAPHY OF THE WORKS OF MAX BEERBOHM. Soho Bibliographies. Cambridge, Mass.: Harvard Univ. Press, 1952.

    Reprinted, with revisions and additions, from the HARVARD LIBRARY BULLETIN (1951). Lists and describes MB's collected and separately published works, with an appendix listing Harvard's holdings of MB's manuscripts, typescripts, letters, and memorabilia.

Riewald, Jacobus Gerhardus, ed. "A Bibliography." In his SIR MAX BEERBOHM, MAN AND WRITER. The Hague: Nijhoff, 1953. Pp. 213-343.

    Excellent primary and secondary bibliography. Riewald provides detailed information on the printing and revision history of MB's essays. Some of the items in his secondary checklist are of minor importance.

BIOGRAPHY

Behrman, S. N. PORTRAIT OF MAX: AN INTIMATE MEMOIR OF SIR MAX BEERBOHM. New York: Random House, 1960.

    Behrman recalls and records conversations with MB, often on literary topics. Informal but informative. Summarizes, with little analysis, some of the following works: AND EVEN NOW, AROUND THEATRES, A CHRISTMAS GARLAND, MAINLY ON THE AIR, and VARIETY OF THINGS. Includes forty illustrations.

Cecil, David. MAX, A BIOGRAPHY. London: Constable, 1964.

> The authorized biography, begun several months after MB's death and supervised by his widow. Like many standard biographies, Cecil quotes generously from MB's works and letters but avoids critical analysis. Includes slight documentation and thirty illustrations.

Wilson, Edmund. "A Miscellany of Max Beerbohm." In his THE BIT BETWEEN MY TEETH: A LITERARY CHRONICLE OF 1950-1965. New York: Farrar, 1965. Pp. 41-62.

> From remembered conversations (1954), Wilson presents the spectrum of MB's literary opinions--for example, his preference for James and his hostility toward Shaw.

CRITICISM

Acton, Harold. "Max Beerbohm: A Dandy among English Classics." EDH, 38 (1975), 1-14.

> A favorable but general discussion based on the premise that MB was "a fine writer within a narrow range."

Auden, W.H. "One of the Family." In his FOREWORDS AND AFTERWORDS. New York: Random House, 1973. Pp. 367-83.

> General and sometimes humorous discussion of MB's personality and writings. Auden speaks of MB's "table-talk criticism" which was wisely confined to "the few writers he knew well."

Boas, Guy. "The Magic of Max." BLACKWOOD'S MAGAZINE, 260 (1946), 341-50.

> High praise for MB's essays, which mix laughter and philosophy. Boas treasures the "elfin" quality of MB's art: in MB's essays and portraits, "there must be some essence of the artist himself interpenetrated, however subtly, with that of the subject."

Braybrooke, Patrick. "Max Beerbohm, Swinburne, and Other Things." In his PEEPS AT THE MIGHTY. Philadelphia: Lippincott, 1927. Pp. 43-58.

> Praises MB's essays for being entertaining and untaxing reading material.

Bross, Addison C. "Beerbohm's 'The Feast' and Conrad's Early Fiction." NCF, 26 (1971), 329-36.

> Explains how MB's parody in A CHRISTMAS GARLAND exploits several features of Conrad's early style.

Max Beerbohm

Cecil, David. "Introduction." In his THE BODLEY HEAD MAX BEERBOHM. London: Bodley Head, 1970. Pp. 7-18.

> Cecil argues that all of MB's work is homogeneous: "an expression of the same personality and the same attitude towards his art"--that of the entertainer with a comic genius. However, Cecil stresses that MB tempered his work with intelligence and good sense.

Clay, N. L. "Introduction." In his MAX BEERBOHM: SELECTED ESSAYS. London: Heinemann, 1958. Pp. vii-xviii.

> Includes a brief biographical sketch and a discussion of MB's career as a writer. Although Clay insists that his humor is "to be enjoyed, not analyzed or dissected," he offers some insights into MB's prose style.

Cross, Wilbur J. "The Humor of Max Beerbohm." YR, 13 (1924), 209-27.

> Theoretical and critical study of the characteristics of MB's humor by a distinguished scholar. AND EVEN NOW and A CHRISTMAS GARLAND are singled out for special praise.

Felstiner, John. THE LIES OF ART: MAX BEERBOHM'S PARODY AND CARICATURE. New York: Knopf, 1972.

> Intelligent critical study of MB's aesthetics. The book traces MB's emerging views of the artist's function and stresses the nineties' idea of the literary artist's "masked" detachment.

_____. "Max Beerbohm and the Wings of Henry James." KR, 29 (1967), 449-71.

> A highly intelligent discussion of MB's "masked" point of view as a parodist, with particular reference to MB's critique of James. Felstiner values "The Guerdon" over "The Mote in the Middle Distance" (two of MB's parodies of James from VARIETY OF THINGS).

Gorman, Herbert S. "'The Incomparable Max.'" In his PROCESSION OF MASKS. Boston: Brimmer, 1923. Pp. 57-71.

> Detailed critical analysis of MB's prose. Gorman stresses that MB uses complex strategies of irony and is not a mere humorist.

Grushow, Ira. "The Chastened Dandy: Beerbohm's 'Hilary Maltby and Stephen Braxton.'" PLL, 8, supplement (1972), 149-64.

> A well-documented attempt to unravel the autobiographical elements of two of the figures in SEVEN MEN, a work which assumes "almost Chaucerian dimensions" in its ironic reverberations.

Max Beerbohm

Hillebrand, Harold N. "Max Beerbohm." JEGP, 19 (1920), 254-69.

> Useful survey of MB's early prose, including his critical essays and parodies. Includes some discussion of MB's philosophy of art and calls MB "the most artistic of all the English literati."

Huss, Roy. "The Aesthete as Realist." In THE SURPRISE OF EXCELLENCE. Ed. J. G. Riewald. Hamden, Conn.: Archon, 1974. Pp. 113-22.

> Explains how MB's dramatic criticism relies on the principles of realism.

――――. "Max the 'Incomparable' on GBS the 'Irrepressible.'" SHAWR, 5 (1962), 10-20.

> Surveys in some detail MB's critical reactions to G. B. Shaw. Although MB at first expressed an "ambivalent feeling" about Shaw's ability as a playwright, he found in MAN AND SUPERMAN a "compensating freshness and skill."

Kronenberger, Louis. "Max Beerbohm." In his THE REPUBLIC OF LETTERS. New York: Knopf, 1955. Pp. 224-35.

> Discusses several essays by MB. Kronenberger sees the personality of "the perfect trifler" in MB's works but he feels that careful study of the writings will guarantee their classic status.

Langbaum, Robert. "Max and Dandyism." VP, 4 (1966), 121-26.

> Argues that dandyism was MB's "armor" to protect himself against ironical scrutiny and comments briefly on how he won his reputation "from the very world he satirized."

Ledger, Marshall. "Ring around A CHRISTMAS GARLAND." In AEOLIAN HARPS: ESSAYS IN LITERATURE IN HONOR OF MAURICE BROWNING CRAMER. Ed. Donna G. and Douglas C. Fricke. Bowling Green, Ohio: Bowling Green Univ. Press, 1976. Pp. 227-46.

> Intelligent discussion of the serious achievement of MB's parodies in A CHRISTMAS GARLAND. Ledger makes a convincing case that "Beerbohm works himself up from the subservient position of parodist into the position of master over the original, overtaking the artist on his own grounds and, . . . [thus] laying claim to the title of artist." The best examples of this principle of artistic mastery are the parodies of James, Conrad, Kipling, and Shaw.

Littell, Philip. "An Immortal Writer." In his BOOKS AND THINGS. New York: Harcourt, 1919. Pp. 201-07.

> Praises MB's prose style in a superficial, impressionistic manner.

Lynch, J. G. Bohun. MAX BEERBOHM IN PERSPECTIVE. New York: Knopf, 1922.

> Earliest book-length study and appreciative survey of MB's work. Lynch seeks to integrate the study of the artistic impulse behind MB's caricatures and writings. The commentary on the prose style of MB's essays and parodies is particularly useful. Includes sixteen illustrations.

Lynd, Robert. "Mr. Max Beerbohm." In his BOOKS AND AUTHORS. London: Cobden-Sanderson, 1922. Pp. 153-67.

> Discusses MB's early works and concludes that MB is most successful as a writer of parodies and sketches.

McElderry, Bruce R., Jr. MAX BEERBOHM. New York: Twayne, 1972.

> Good introductory study of MB's life and works set against the cultural background of the nineties and early decades of this century. Summaries and brief critiques of most of MB's works are provided. Includes a useful chapter (3) on MB's dramatic criticism, a general evaluation chapter (7), an index which lists individual essays discussed, and a brief bibliography.

_____. "Max Beerbohm: Essayist, Caricaturist, Novelist." In ON STAGE AND OFF: EIGHT ESSAYS IN ENGLISH LITERATURE. Ed. John W. Ehrstine et al. Pullman: Washington State Univ. Press, 1968. Pp. 76-86.

> Brief but praiseworthy discussion of some of MB's essays, especially the dramatic criticism.

Mix, Katherine L. MAX AND THE AMERICANS. Brattleboro, Vt.: Greene, 1974.

> Cut-and-paste catalog of MB's ambivalent reactions to American politics and culture.

_____. "Max on Shaw." SHAWR, 6 (1963), 100-104.

> Plodding survey of MB's positive and negative opinions of G. B. Shaw. Over many years, a "paradoxical pattern" emerges: "praise mingled with censure, or disapproval veiled in commendation."

Moers, Ellen. "Epilogue: Sir Max Beerbohm." In her THE DANDY: BRUMMELL TO BEERBOHM. New York: Viking, 1960. Pp. 315-30.

> A critical study of dandyism, the last chapter of which is devoted to MB and his early essays on dandyism. Moers comments on MB's distanced perspective and concludes that his dandyism was "one from which all heroic qualities had been stripped away: arrogance, class superiority, exclusivism."

Max Beerbohm

Riewald, J.G. SIR MAX BEERBOHM, MAN AND WRITER: A CRITICAL ANALYSIS WITH A BRIEF LIFE AND A BIBLIOGRAPHY. The Hague: Nijhoff, 1953.

> Brief biography with extensive critical discussion of MB's essays, parodies, and criticism. Although the schema of dividing and subdividing MB's works and techniques is awesome, the discussion of the form and content of MB's prose is extensive and illuminating. Riewald analyzes such technical features as MB's syntax and vocabulary. The primary and secondary bibliography is invaluable.

_____, ed. THE SURPRISE OF EXCELLENCE: MODERN ESSAYS ON MAX BEERBOHM. Hamden, Conn.: Archon, 1974.

> Collects twenty essays (all but two previously published) on MB's life and works written by important friends and distinguished critics between 1943 and 1970. (Relevant contributions are listed separately.)

Roberts, S.C. "Introduction." In his THE INCOMPARABLE MAX. New York: Dodd, Mead, 1962. Pp. xi-xviii.

> Enumerates MB's achievements as a writer of essays and parodies. Roberts views MB's dramatic criticism as "a duty"; praises A CHRISTMAS GARLAND as "a supreme example of the critical value inherent in parody"; and detects MB's highest powers as an essayist in SEVEN MEN and AND EVEN NOW.

_____. "Max Beerbohm." In his DR. JOHNSON AND OTHERS. Cambridge: The Univ. Press, 1958. Pp. 156-76.

> Brief and somewhat perceptive discussion of MB's criticism, essays, and parodies.

Shand, John. "Max." In NINETEENTH CENTURY AND AFTER, 132 (1942), 84-87.

> Brief discussion of MB's dramatic criticism, which emphasizes its balanced quality. Shand provides examples of MB's fresh enthusiasm, even temper, and patience in reviewing plays.

Smith, Logan Pearsall. "Sir Max Beerbohm." ATLANTIC MONTHLY, 170 (November 1942), 88-90.

> Brief but lively essay in which Smith pays tribute to MB, "his old friend and fellow perfectionist."

Stanford, Derek. "Sir Max Beerbohm." CONTEMPR, 190 (1956), 11-14.

> Appreciative tribute which stresses the development of MB's art over many decades. Stanford praises MB's "tough yet subtle

and ironic common-sense" and sees in his dramatic criticism "the clear victory of the urban spirit."

────── . "The Writings of Sir Max Beerbohm." MONTH, 13 (1955), 352-65.

Discusses some of the topics and strategies in MB's essays and parodies. Stanford makes the interesting observation that MB sometimes serves as "a judge and scrutinist of his own process of composition."

Stein, Joseph. "The New Woman and the Decadent Dandy." DR, 55 (1975), 54-62.

Stein examines WORKS and MORE and YET AGAIN and comes to the conclusion that although MB had "a great respect for the feminine intellect," he viewed the emergence of women "as a direct assault on the supremacy of the male and the reign of the dandy."

Stevenson, David. "Irony and Deception." In THE SURPRISE OF EXCELLENCE. Ed. J. G. Riewald. Hamden, Conn.: Archon, 1974. Pp. 65-76.

Some valuable analysis of the strategies implicit in MB's prose style, with particular attention to his "ironic type of candor." In the essays, irony is a critical device which "demands cooperation on the part of the reader."

Tuell, Anne K. "The Prose of Mr. Beerbohm." SAQ, 30 (1931), 190-99.

A highly impressionistic discussion of MB's prose which often obscures the points of analysis. Tuell concludes that as a prose writer, MB is "a connoisseur of manner, dandy of the phrase, but he has always found fact more alluring than form."

Wells, Stanley. "Shakespeare in Max Beerbohm's Theatre Criticism." SHS, 29 (1976), 133-44.

Argues that the proportion of Shakespearian comment in MB's dramatic criticism is serious but "relatively small" because MB was more interested in contemporary plays and was "temperamentally unresponsive to much in Shakespeare." In fact, MB often argued that Shakespeare's plays should be performed less frequently.

Wilson, Edmund. "In Analysis of Max Beerbohm." In his CLASSICS AND COMMERCIALS: A LITERARY CHRONICLE OF THE FORTIES. New York: Farrar, 1950. Pp. 431-41.

Praises MB's distinguished criticism and analyzes the intricate nature of MB's point of view in several of his works.

Woolf, Virginia. "The Modern Essay." In her THE COMMON READER. FIRST SERIES. London: Hogarth, 1925. Pp. 274-76.

    Praises MB as a young, modern essayist who "brought personality into literature" again and as a perfectionist in matters of style.

HILAIRE BELLOC (1870-1953)

NONFICTIONAL PROSE

THE AFTERMATH, OR GLEANINGS FROM A BUSY LIFE CALLED UPON THE OUTER COVER FOR PURPOSES OF SALE "CALIBAN'S GUIDE TO LETTERS." London: Duckworth, 1903.

    A guide to modern journalism in which HB provides advice on reviewing, political appeals, interviewing, editing, style, and other matters.

AVRIL: BEING ESSAYS ON THE POETRY OF THE FRENCH RENAISSANCE. London: Duckworth, 1904.

    Critical essays which stress the sixteenth-century French tradition of mingling civilizations of the south and the north. The six poets treated are: Charles of Orleans, Villon, Marot, Ronsard, DuBellay, and Malherbe.

THE BATTLE GROUND. London: Cassell; Philadelphia: Lippincott, 1936.

    A history of lands in the Middle East to 1187 A.D. with the chapter on "The Christian Victory" serving as the book's climax. Specific details of military battles are emphasized.

THE BOOK OF THE BAYEUX TAPESTRY. London: Chatto and Windus, 1914. New York: Putnam's, 1916.

    HB provides the introduction and historical narrative to accompany the color facsimiles of the art treasures of Normandy's small village.

THE CAMPAIGN OF 1812, AND THE RETREAT FROM MOSCOW. London: Nelson, 1924. As NAPOLEON'S CAMPAIGN OF 1812 AND THE RETREAT FROM MOSCOW. New York and London: Harper, 1926.

    Close analysis of the military adventure which ruined Napoleon.

HB draws insightful conclusions concerning military strategy from diagrams and reports; his analysis of the centralized Russian monarchy, however, is dated.

THE CATHOLIC CHURCH AND HISTORY. London: Burns, Oates and Washbourne, 1926.

A succinct presentation of "the arguments drawn from History" which oppose the Catholic Church's claim to speak with divine and infallible authority.

CHARACTERS OF THE REFORMATION. London: Sheed and Ward, 1936. New York: Image Books, 1958.

Twenty-three profiles of key men and women who fought for or against the Reformation plus an essay on the "Nature of the Reformation." Some historical figures treated include: Henry VIII, Thomas More, Richelieu, Cromwell, and Descartes.

CHARLES THE FIRST, KING OF ENGLAND. London: Cassell; Philadelphia: Lippincott, 1933.

Traces the background and circumstances of the rebellion in which "the wealthier classes . . . gradually ousted the Crown and took over its power." Against the background of these historical circumstances, HB examines the character and reactions of Charles Stuart.

A COMPANION TO MR. WELLS'S <u>OUTLINE OF HISTORY</u>. London: Sheed and Ward, 1926.

A trenchant, thorough refutation of H. G. Wells's treatment of Christianity by a Catholic. HB accuses Wells of "satisfied ignorance" and a rabid hatred of tradition. The book engendered Wells's MR. BELLOC OBJECTS.

THE CONTRAST. London: Arrowsmith, 1923.

Perceptive essay which compares Europe and America. Many transformations are noted as HB elucidates the physical, social, political, military, religious, literary, linguistic, and diplomatic contrasts. The chapter on "The Jewish Problem" is controversial.

A CONVERSATION WITH A CAT, AND OTHERS. London: Cassell; New York: Harper, 1931.

Thirty-nine essays on such topics as architecture, autobiography, fashion, royalty, Jonathan Swift, and poetic reputation.

A CONVERSATION WITH AN ANGEL AND OTHER ESSAYS. London: Cape, 1928. New York: Harper, 1929.

Thirty-four essays on such phenomena as poverty, epigrams, laughter, speeches, diaries, and advertising, and on such figures as Dickens, George II, Gibbon, and Macaulay.

THE COUNTY OF SUSSEX. London: Cassell, 1936.

HB presents the physical nature, historical development, and individual character of his favorite county, Sussex. A revised and expanded version of SUSSEX. With a sense of urgency, HB records his memories of an area he believes is "in peril of dissolution."

CRANMER, ARCHBISHOP OF CANTERBURY, 1533-1556. London: Cassell; Philadelphia: Lippincott, 1931.

HB states his purpose: "This is not a life of [Thomas] Cranmer; it is a study of his character and motives, with exposition of, and emphasis upon, his literary genius and its legacy to the Church of England."

THE CRISIS OF OUR CIVILIZATION. London: Cassell; New York: Fordham Univ. Press, 1937.

HB's thesis is that Christian civilization of Western Europe "has arrived at a crisis where it is in peril of death." HB traces the origins of that civilization, the main lines of its development, and the institutions it produced. The enfeebling consequences of the "disaster" called "The Reformation" are analyzed and lamented. He recommends restricting modern monopolies, curbing the money power, widening the distribution of private property, and reconversion to Catholicism.

CROMWELL. London: Cassell, 1934.

A biographical study of Oliver Cromwell which examines the "real" nature of his motives. HB debunks myths surrounding Cromwell, myths generated by past military, religious, and patriotic quarrels. Heavy attention is paid to Cromwell as a military man and as the embodiment of "the new wealth and the new religion."

THE CRUISE OF THE NONA. London: Constable, 1925.

Travel adventures at sea blended with meditations of a middle-aged man; HB provides philosophy and tempered joy. One of HB's most significant books.

THE CRUSADES: THE WORLD'S DEBATE. Science and Culture. London: Cassell; Milwaukee: Bruce, 1937.

Outlines the religious issues and recreates the drama of medieval warfare associated with the Crusades. HB regards the movement as a conflict between Christendom and the "Anti-Christ"; he also sees it as a "subject for romance" and analyzes in detail the errors of the military campaign.

DANTON: A STUDY. London: Nisbet, 1899. New York: Scribner's, 1902.

An unbiased biographical study which strives to connect Danton's motives with "the creed of the time." HB shows how Danton's "spirit," "energy," and "practical grasp of things" formed the strength of France in the two years of his prominence, 1792-93. A revised edition was published in 1928.

DO WE AGREE? A DEBATE BETWEEN G.K. CHESTERTON AND BERNARD SHAW, WITH HILAIRE BELLOC IN THE CHAIR. Hartford, Conn.: Mitchell, 1928.

HB's contributions are slight, but he does conclude that industrial civilization's "monstrous wickedness, folly, ineptitude" will probably soon lead to catastrophe, a desert, or mass slavery.

ECONOMICS FOR HELEN. London: Arrowsmith, 1924.

A basic discussion of the fundamental principles of economics -- land, labor, capital, production, money--and of some basic political applications--property rights, capitalism, socialism.

ELIZABETHAN COMMENTARY. London: Cassell, 1942. As ELIZABETH: CREATURE OF CIRCUMSTANCE. New York: Harper, 1942.

A biography which treats the physical, mental, and spiritual condition of Elizabeth Tudor against the historical background of her age.

AN ESSAY ON THE NATURE OF CONTEMPORARY ENGLAND. London: Constable, 1937.

A brief sociological essay which identifies and describes the three main characteristics of modern England--"Aristocratic, Protestant, and Commercial."

AN ESSAY ON THE RESTORATION OF PROPERTY. London: The Distributist League, 1936.

A supplement to SERVILE STATE (see p. 58). This brief treatise advocates a plan of action--the ownership of property by private and free individuals.

Hilaire Belloc

ESSAYS OF A CATHOLIC LAYMAN IN ENGLAND. London: Sheed and Ward, 1931.

> Sixteen personal and controversial essays on different subjects related to religion. HB speculates on the relationship between church and state, the church and capitalism, the church and science, and the church and history. The essay "On Usury" is famous.

ESTO PERPETUA: ALGERIAN STUDIES AND IMPRESSIONS. London: Duckworth, 1906.

> One of HB's best travel books. HB explores the fascinating geographical and historical contrasts of northern Africa.

EUROPE AND THE FAITH. London: Constable; New York: Paulist Press, 1920.

> After a cornerstone essay on "The Catholic Conscience of History," HB traces the history of religious faith from the Roman Empire through the Middle Ages to the Reformation. Several chapters focus specifically on developments in Britain.

THE EYE-WITNESS: BEING A SERIES OF DESCRIPTIONS AND SKETCHES. London: Nash, 1908.

> Interesting collection of historical sketches in which HB uses historical figures to describe briefly and directly important incidents from B.C. 55 to A.D. 1906.

FIRST AND LAST. London: Methuen, 1911.

> Collects forty-one essays including "On Cheeses," "On Historical Evidence," "St. Patrick," "On the Reading of History," "Companions of Travel," and "'King Lear.'"

THE FOUR MEN, A FARRAGO. London and New York: Nelson, 1912.

> Conversations on a range of topics are exchanged among the author, a poet, a sailor, and Grizzlebeard (all sides of HB himself) while on a tour of the Sussex countryside.

THE FREE PRESS. London: Allen and Unwin, 1918.

> Sociological treatise on the powers and responsibilities of journalists in a capitalistic country. HB stresses that the free press must make truth known and expose corrupt politics.

THE FRENCH REVOLUTION. London: Williams and Norgate; New York: Holt, 1911.

Hilaire Belloc

In his history HB faults the monarchy's dullness. In helpful chapter divisions, he concentrates on the political, biographical, historical, military, and religious aspects of the political upheaval.

A GENERAL SKETCH OF THE EUROPEAN WAR: THE FIRST PHASE. Vol. 1. London: Nelson, 1915. As THE ELEMENTS OF THE GREAT WAR. New York: Hearst's, 1915-16.

HB outlines the historical causes which produced the conflict and compares the strengths and weaknesses of the opposing sides. Volume 1 covers the outbreak of hostilities and HB offers clear explanations and simplified diagrams for the reader.

A GENERAL SKETCH OF THE EUROPEAN WAR: THE SECOND PHASE. Vol. 2. London: Nelson, 1916.

Discusses the early battles of the war. Volume 2 explores the component details of the Battle of the Marne.

THE GREAT HERESIES. London: Sheed and Ward, 1938.

A theological survey in which HB defines and describes "the main attacks upon the Catholic Church which have marked her long history."

THE GREAT INQUIRY. London: Duckworth, 1903.

Witty, satirical investigation, mainly in dialog form, of a cabinet committee's dealings with England's fiscal and other problems. G.K. Chesterton supplied some humorous illustrations for the slim volume.

HILLS AND THE SEA. London: Methuen, 1906. New York: Dutton, 1929.

A collection of thirty-eight Anglo-European travel sketches which describe the people and the land. The essays entitled "The North Sea," "On Ely," "Carcassonne," "The Channel," and "The Arena" are representative.

THE HISTORIC THAMES. London: Dent; New York: Dutton, 1907.

HB describes the topography and history of the Thames valley which "has in the past supported the government and the wealth of England."

A HISTORY OF ENGLAND. Vol. 1: B.C. 55 TO A.D. 1066. London: Methuen, 1925; Vol. 2: A.D. 1066-1348 (1927); Vol. 3: A.D. 1348-1525 (1928); Vol. 4: A.D. 1525-1612 (1931).

Hilaire Belloc

A general survey of the historical development of Britain as its people embraced pagan, Catholic, and Protestant faiths. HB's general theses are that "religion is the determining force of society" and that the island's institutions are derived from Roman civilization rather than German ancestry.

THE HOUSE OF COMMONS AND MONARCHY. London: Allen and Unwin, 1920.

A political treatise which argues that although the House of Commons was once formed by an aristocratic state, England has lost its "aristocratic temper." Thus, the governing body is without function and it cannot be reformed.

HOW THE REFORMATION HAPPENED. London: Cape, 1928.

HB outlines the main causes and events of the Reformation which destroyed united Christendom. He laments the effects of the conflict: the end of Catholicism as "the culture of Europe" which has led to "its present peril of dissolution."

JAMES THE SECOND. Philadelphia: Lippincott, 1928. London: Faber, 1934.

A balanced character portrait which focuses on several key conflicts in the life of James the Second. His establishment of the British Navy is stressed in one chapter. His personal temperament, beliefs, accomplishments, and defeats are presented selectively.

THE JEWS. London: Constable, 1922.

As an "attempt at justice," HB expounds upon the "pressing problem" of the treatment of Jews in Europe. He outlines the general and special "causes of friction" in the past and present; he offers as the just solution "a full recognition of separate nationality."

JOAN OF ARC. London: Cassell, 1929.

An uncritical and undocumented popularized biography which celebrates the piety and condemns the execution of Joan of Arc.

THE LAST DAYS OF THE FRENCH MONARCHY. London: Chapman and Hall, 1916.

Belloc offers dramatic descriptions of the last years (1789-1793) of the doomed royal family during the French Revolution. He blames Marie-Antoinette and Lafayette for the turn of events. Also, he admires the calm courage of Louis XVI just before his execution. Includes fifty illustrations from the period.

THE LAST RALLY: A STORY OF CHARLES II. New York: Harper, 1939. London: Cassell, 1940.

> A sequel and companion to MONARCHY. HB deals with Charles II, who was Stuart King of England as well as contemporary and first cousin of King Louis XIV of France. The reasons for and the consequences of the monarch's failure to "tame" the money powers are discussed in great detail. The subsequent rise of London as well as the material triumphs of aristocratic commerce and wealth are prophesied.

MARIE ANTOINETTE. London: Methuen; New York: Doubleday, 1909.

> HB offers a tragic biography of the ill-fated Queen of France: "In person she was not considerable, in temperament not distinguished; but her fate was enormous."

MILTON. London: Cassell, 1935. Philadelphia: Lippincott, 1955.

> Milton is considered against the historical backdrop of "that complete transformation which turned the English from Catholic to Protestant . . . from a peasantry to a capitalist society." Special critical attention is devoted to Milton's poetry.

MINIATURES OF FRENCH HISTORY. London and New York: Nelson, 1925.

> Thirty-one short historical sketches of key moments in French history, from 599 B.C. to 1914 A.D. Some sketches include famous men such as William the Conqueror and King Louis IX; other moments are rendered from the perspective of unknown foot soldiers involved in crucial battles.

MONARCHY: A STUDY OF LOUIS XIV. London: Cassell, 1938. As LOUIS XIV. New York and London: Harper, 1938.

> A study of King Louis XIV of France organized around the central theme of "the eternal conflict between One Man Government and the Rich." HB admires the king's ability to successfully stand up to the money power.

MR. BELLOC STILL OBJECTS TO MR. WELL'S OUTLINE OF HISTORY. London: Sheed and Ward, 1926.

> Historical criticism in which HB offers a lively reply to H.G. Wells's MR. BELLOC OBJECTS TO THE OUTLINE OF HISTORY (1926).

MRS. MARKHAM'S NEW HISTORY OF ENGLAND: BEING AN INTRODUCTION FOR YOUNG PEOPLE TO THE CURRENT HISTORY & INSTITUTIONS OF OUR TIME. Kensington, Engl.: Cayme, 1926.

Hilaire Belloc

A satirical book designed to instruct adolescents "in the institutions and recent history of our beloved country." Topics covered include: industrial insurance, League of Nations, law courts, Parliament, and the police.

NAPOLEON. London: Cassell; Philadelphia: Lippincott, 1932.

A sympathetic biography of Napoleon up to his defeat at Waterloo. HB admires Napoleon's near success of uniting Europe and stabilizing its culture.

THE OLD ROAD (FROM CANTERBURY TO WINCHESTER). London: Constable, 1904.

HB discusses the origins of the road in antiquity and describes significant sites and interesting people between Winchester and Canterbury.

ON. London: Methuen, 1923.

Collects thirty essays on such diverse topics as educational reform, footnotes, bad verse, climate, sailing, and cathedrals.

ON ANYTHING. London: Constable, 1910.

Collects thirty-eight essays, mainly on travel sites and literary figures or products. The essays on Swinburne, Milton, and Hans Christian Andersen are significant.

ON EVERYTHING. London: Methuen, 1909.

Collects thirty-nine essays, including "On Song," "On the Rights of Property," "The Economist," "The Reasonable Press," "On London and the Houses in It," and "On Fantastic Books."

ON NOTHING AND KINDRED SUBJECTS. London: Methuen, 1908.

Thirty-one essays on such topics as ignorance, advertisements, tea, railways, national debts, fishermen, hermits, and death.

ON SOMETHING. London: Methuen, 1910.

Collects thirty essays, many dealing with HB's travels to real and imaginary lands.

ON THE PLACE OF GILBERT CHESTERTON IN ENGLISH LETTERS. London: Sheed and Ward, 1940.

A short, appreciative study of HB's intimate friend. HB discusses Chesterton's nationalism, precision of thought, use of parallelism, and his literary, humane, and religious interests.

PARIS. London: Arnold, 1900.

With affection and in detail, HB traces the history of Paris from its origins through the Middle Ages and the Renaissance. His commentary ends with the year 1789, though there are brief condemnatory references to landmarks destroyed by the Commune of 1871.

THE PARTY SYSTEM. With Cecil Chesterton. London: Swift, 1911.

A controversial discussion of political realities in England which calls for restoring power to the people.

THE PATH TO ROME. London: Allen; New York: Putnam's, 1902.

HB's best travel book is a delightful blend of wisdom and humor as the author leads the reader to appreciate the rich tradition of Europe and Catholicism.

PLACES. London: Cassell, 1942.

HB collects "many an impression of the travel of the sort which I fear can never be repeated in a ruined world." Highlights include descriptive essays on Scandinavia, Russia, France, Spain, Portugal, and the Near East.

THE PYRENEES. London: Methuen, 1909.

Original and useful travel information for those walking or driving through the Pyrenees. The roads, paths, geography, politics, and inns of the region are treated in minute detail. Includes sketches and maps drawn by HB.

THE QUESTION AND THE ANSWER. Science and Culture Series. New York: Bruce, 1932. London: Longmans, Green, 1938.

HB explains "to the rational skeptic how and why a Catholic believes what he does."

RETURN TO THE BALTIC. London: Constable, 1938.

After forty-three years HB returns to Scandinavia to explore the changes in the landscape and in himself. The last third of the book deals with Poland.

RICHELIEU, A STUDY. London: Benn; Philadelphia: Lippincott, 1929.

A biography which analyzes Richelieu's effect on the breaking of Christendom "into a mosaic of nationalities" and the splitting of "the Catholic and the Protestant culture." His genius and dedicated toil failed to secure religious and cultural unity in Europe.

THE RIVER OF LONDON. London: Foulis, 1912.

Historical topography of the Thames River.

THE ROAD. London: Hobson, 1923. New York: Harper, 1925.

As a nonexpert, HB offers a general sketch of the theory and history of highway transportation from the Middle Ages to the 1920's, with special attention to the British roads.

ROBESPIERRE: A STUDY. London: Nisbet, 1901. New York: Scribner's, 1902.

A well-researched biography which does an excellent job of balancing the drama and the facts of one of the key figures of France's Reign of Terror. Reissued with a new preface in 1927.

THE SERVILE STATE. London: Foulis, 1912. New York: Holt, 1946.

An important theoretical treatise pleading for the restoration of the institution of private property and looking to the Middle Ages as a model society. In this broad sociological survey, HB rejects both capitalism and socialism in favor of distributism-- individual ownership of property and land as the basis of society. The volume has become HB's most influential work.

A SHORTER HISTORY OF ENGLAND. London: Harrap, 1934.

An abridged version of the four-volume work designed for use in the schools.

SHORT TALKS WITH THE DEAD, AND OTHERS. Kensington, Engl.: Cayme, 1926.

Twenty-nine essays on good versus bad poetry, Byron, Wordsworth, opportunity, fools, advertising, and other topics.

THE SILENCE OF THE SEA, AND OTHER ESSAYS. London: Cassell, 1941.

Collects forty-eight essays including "On Skulls," "Bunyan," "Boswell," "Jane Austen," "On Euphemism," "On Hats," and "On Fame."

SIX BRITISH BATTLES. Bristol, Engl.: Arrowsmith, 1931.

Collects previously published monographs on the battles of Blenheim, Crecy, Malplaquet, Tourcoing, Poitiers, and Waterloo. In each case, HB explains the political circumstances which led to the battle and outlines the military action in detail.

THE STANE STREET: A MONOGRAPH. London: Constable, 1913.

After a general discussion of Roman roads in Britain, HB traces the history surrounding one such road from Chichester through Merton Abbey to London Bridge. Illustrations and maps are supplied.

SURVIVALS AND NEW ARRIVALS. London: Sheed and Ward, 1929.

In a series of essays, HB examines the forces of opposition--old and new--arrayed against the Catholic Church.

SUSSEX. London: Adam and Charles Black, 1906.

HB's first attempt to sketch the local history and situation of his beloved home county.

THE TACTICS AND STRATEGY OF THE GREAT DUKE OF MARLBOROUGH. London: Arrowsmith, 1933.

Military history which analyzes the superior character of Marlborough as a commander in six strategic operations.

THIS AND THAT, AND THE OTHER. London: Methuen; New York: Dodd, Mead, 1912.

Forty essays covering such concepts as atheism, fame, omens, jokes, and such people as pedants, servants, spies, and charlatans. The essay "The Higher Criticism" is famous for its attack on German scholars' studies of the Bible.

TOWNS OF DESTINY. New York: McBride, 1927. As MANY CITIES. London: Constable, 1928.

Important and enduring human settlements in Spain, Portugal, France, Germany, and the Mediterranean area are discussed.

THE TWO MAPS OF EUROPE, AND SOME OTHER ASPECTS OF THE GREAT WAR. London: Pearson, 1915.

A comparison between German and British ideas, written under the influence of wartime prejudices.

WARFARE IN ENGLAND. London: Williams and Norgate; New York: Holt, 1912.

After describing the strategical topography of England, HB describes the military strategy of the Roman conquest, the Norman conquest, medieval warfare, the Civil Wars, and the Scotch Wars.

WHY I AM A CATHOLIC. New York: Macmillan, 1932.

Written with four others. In an essay HB defends the faith in personal, historical, and theological terms.

WILLIAM THE CONQUEROR. London: Davies, 1933.

A short popular biography of the Norman invader which focuses on his accomplishments as military and political leader.

WOLSEY. London: Cassell; Philadelphia: Lippincott, 1930.

A biography in which HB presents a sometimes biased interpretation of the "character and motive in him [Cardinal Wolsey] and his contemporaries" during the controversial time of the Reformation.

WORKS EDITED BY OTHERS

ADVICE. Ed. Evelyn Waugh. London: Harvill Press, 1960.

HB's delightful wisdom concerning food, wine, and home economy is offered here from an unpublished manuscript written in 1935.

A PICKED COMPANY: BEING A SELECTION FROM THE WRITINGS OF H. BELLOC. Ed. E.V. Lucas. London: Methuen, 1915.

Selections drawn from seventeen books by HB. The volume includes seventeen essays as well as several entries from the historical studies and the travel sketches.

AT THE SIGN OF THE LION, AND OTHER ESSAYS FROM THE BOOKS OF HILAIRE BELLOC. Ed. T.B. Mosher. Portland, Me.: T.B. Mosher, 1916.

A selection of five essays which are written in an autumnal atmosphere and treat the finalities of rest, death, and sacramental states.

BELLOC: A BIOGRAPHICAL ANTHOLOGY. Ed. Herbert Van Thal. New York: Knopf, 1970.

An extensive anthology of extracts from HB's work (1891-1940) which represents his many-sided genius and the variety of his interests. Brief notes introduce the selections, which are arranged in chronological order.

Hilaire Belloc

BELLOC ESSAYS. Ed. Anthony Forster. London: Methuen, 1955.

> Reprints thirty-seven essays from eight of HB's volumes. Some helpful notes are provided at the end of the book.

HILAIRE BELLOC: AN ANTHOLOGY OF HIS PROSE AND VERSE. Ed. W. N. Roughead. Philadelphia: Lippincott, 1951.

> Includes "representative" selections of HB's prose, printed chronologically.

HILAIRE BELLOC'S PREFACES: WRITTEN FOR FELLOW AUTHORS. Ed. J. A. DeChantigny. Chicago: Loyola Univ. Press, 1971.

> Reproduces in facsimile thirty-seven prefaces by HB which were written between 1899 and 1938.

HILAIRE BELLOC'S STORIES, ESSAYS, AND POEMS. 2nd ed. Ed. J. B. Morton. London: Dent, 1957.

> Includes selections of HB's essays, literary criticism, travel sketches, biographies, and military history.

ONE THING AND ANOTHER. Ed. Patrick Cahill. London: Hollis and Carter, 1955.

> A miscellany of thirty-eight uncollected essays written by HB for various journals and books. Topics include: walking, cooking, selecting books, spelling, and military history. Brief notes are provided by the editor.

ON SAILING THE SEA: A COLLECTION OF THE SEAGOING WRITINGS OF HILAIRE BELLOC. Ed. W. N. Roughead. London: Methuen, 1939.

> Collects various essays by HB about the sea and sailing. First appearance in book form for the essays "Armada Weather," "Foreign Entry," "Channel Fog," and "Headlands."

SELECTED ESSAYS OF HILAIRE BELLOC. Ed. J. B. Morton. London: Methuen, 1948.

> Reprints fifty-four essays from seven previously published volumes. Topics range from cheese and irony to Milton and immortality.

BIBLIOGRAPHY

Cahill, Patrick, ed. THE ENGLISH FIRST EDITIONS OF HILAIRE BELLOC. London: [published by the author], 1953.

> A chronological list of 153 books and pamphlets written by HB. Includes detailed bibliographical notes.

Haynes, Renée, comp. "A Select Bibliography." HILAIRE BELLOC. London: Longmans, Green, 1958. Pp. 31-35.

> Chronological list of primary books and a brief list of selected secondary books.

BIOGRAPHY

Jebb, Eleanor, and Reginald Jebb. TESTIMONY TO HILAIRE BELLOC. London: Methuen, 1956.

> HB's daughter and her husband offer their characterizations of the man and his work. Highly appreciative and random impressions of HB's "many-sided genius" are rendered in a study that offers more biography and background than critical analysis.

Lowndes, Marie Belloc. THE YOUNG HILAIRE BELLOC. New York: Kenedy, 1956.

> A memoir written by HB's sister which focuses on his early years.

Morton, John Bingham. HILAIRE BELLOC: A MEMOIR. London: Hollis and Carter, 1955.

> A brief appreciative memoir by a friend who knew HB over the last thirty years of his life. The chapters dealing with HB at sea, in London, and on tour provide some significant background information concerning his prose works.

Pearson, Hesketh. "Hilaire Belloc." In his LIVES OF THE WITS. London: Heinemann, 1962. Pp. 269-85.

> A lively sketch of HB's career and personality. To Pearson, HB was restless and compulsive, a man whose "prejudices and preferences were strongly expressed."

Speaight, Robert. THE LIFE OF HILAIRE BELLOC. New York: Farrar, Straus, 1957.

> The authorized and most complete biography. Speaight had access to HB's private papers and correspondence and he is thoroughly familiar with HB's works and the reminiscences of those who knew him. An excellent and balanced biography with some critical analysis of the writings. Speaight offers superficial treatment of HB's historical and fiscal theories.

CRITICISM

Braybrooke, Patrick. SOME THOUGHTS ON HILAIRE BELLOC. Philadelphia: Lippincott, 1923.

As a journalist Braybrooke devotes extensive discussion to HB's attitude to the press. He also treats HB "as a politician, as a theologian, as an anti-Jew, as an historian of the French Revolution, as a writer of essays and as a lover of Sussex." An early, curious critical assessment.

Burdett, Osbert. "Hilaire Belloc." LONDON MERCURY, 30 (1934), 133-41.

Praises HB's prose as "authentic" and "oratorical." Burdett calls CRUISE OF THE NONA "the most companiable, possibly the most beautiful" and HOW THE REFORMATION HAPPENED the "most useful" of HB's works.

Coffey, Thomas P. "Belloc: Tiger on the Doorstep." CATHW, 189 (1959), 217-23.

Describes HB's prose style as "clear and nervous and effortless in appearance." Although his reputation is not yet fixed, he is to be admired as a controversial fighter and a humanist.

Corrin, Jay P. G.K. CHESTERTON AND HILAIRE BELLOC: THE BATTLE AGAINST MODERNITY. Athens: Ohio Univ. Press, 1981.

A detailed treatment of HB's and Chesterton's social and political opinions, with particular attention to the movement called Distributism. Corrin analyzes both the positive and negative consequences of of two men's influence and cooperation.

DeChantigny, J.A. "About Hilaire Belloc." In HILAIRE BELLOC'S PREFACES: WRITTEN FOR FELLOW AUTHORS. Ed. J.A. DeChantigny. Chicago: Loyola Univ. Press, 1971. Pp. 27-33.

Brief appreciative overview of HB's career and writings.

Gauss, Christian. "Introduction." In his THE SERVILE STATE. New York: Holt, 1946. Pp. ix-xvi.

Gauss recommends SERVILE STATE to the American reading public and demonstrates how the ideas in the study are relevant to America's situations and problems after World War II.

Hamilton, Robert. HILAIRE BELLOC: AN INTRODUCTION TO HIS SPIRIT AND WORK. London: Organ, 1945.

An appreciative introductory study. Hamilton believes that the "spirit of Catholic humanism" is "the key to the understanding and full appreciation of HB's work." Four broad divisions of HB's writings are treated: history, sociology, essays, and verse.

Haynes, Renée. HILAIRE BELLOC. British Council Pamphlet. London: Longmans, Green, 1953.

A useful introduction to HB's personality and literary career.

Although Haynes believes that HB's claim to immortality will rest on his poetry, she admits that some prose will also survive because it provides "enlarging joy to lovers of pre-industrial Europe and the sea." Includes a select bibliography.

Hollis, Christopher. "Foreword." In HILAIRE BELLOC'S PREFACES: WRITTEN FOR FELLOW AUTHORS. Ed. J.A. DeChantigny. Chicago: Loyola Univ. Press, 1971. Pp. 13-25.

> Revealing commentary on HB's prefaces, which Hollis argues also helps show the "versatility of [HB's] genius." Hollis concentrates on HB's religious and political persuasions.

Jago, David. "The Stoicism of Hilaire Belloc." RENASCENCE, 27 (1975), 89-100.

> An intelligent essay which considers the aesthetic implications of the positive and negative sides to HB's sensibility.

James, Stanley B. "Hilaire Belloc--the Good European." CATHW, 151 (1940), 288-93.

> Argues that there are limitations to HB's outlook and that clear distinctions between what is a good Catholic and a good European must be drawn.

Jebb, Reginald. "Introduction." In SONNETS AND VERSE. Ed. W.N. Roughead. London: Duckworth, 1978. Pp. xiii-xxiii.

> Provides a brief sketch of selected events and influences that shaped HB's poetry and prose.

Jerrold, Douglas. "On the Influence of Hilaire Belloc." In FOR HILAIRE BELLOC: ESSAYS IN HONOUR OF HIS 72ND BIRTHDAY. Ed. Douglas Woodruff. London: Sheed and Ward, 1942. Pp. 9-17.

> A general appraisal of HB's influence. Jerrold affirms the validity of HB's political and economic theories and calls THE SERVILE STATE "the most penetrating and prophetic piece of political pamphleteering of the century."

Kantra, Robert A. "Irony in Belloc." RENASCENCE, 17 (1965), 131-36.

> Uses Northrop Frye's literary theory to analyze and compare THE FOUR MEN and THE PATH TO ROME.

Keating, Karl. "The Servile State and Hilaire Belloc: Edwardian Radical." CREV, 6 (1979-80), 131-35.

> Brief but extremely lucid explanation of HB's economic and political theory in THE SERVILE STATE.

Kenny, Herbert A. "Hilaire Belloc: His Future." CATHW, 183 (1956), 452-55.

Weighs the advantages and disadvantages of HB's genius and predicts that "If civilization rallies, it will be around him."

Knox, Ronald. "Introduction." In BELLOC ESSAYS. Ed. Anthony Forster. London: Methuen, 1955. Pp. vii-ix.

Brief explanation of HB as "a bundle of contradictions." Knox believes that always the true cast of HB's mind "was one of profound melancholy"; this outlook made him a good satirist.

Las Vergnas, Raymond. "Hilaire Belloc." In his CHESTERTON, BELLOC, BARING. Trans. C.C. Martindale. London: Sheed and Ward, 1938. Pp. 50-87.

Praises HB's lucidity and guarded irony. Concludes HB is best as a European historian. Wide-ranging survey--with superficial analysis--of most of HB's writings.

Lynd, Robert. "Mr. G.K. Chesterton and Mr. Hilaire Belloc." In his OLD AND NEW MASTERS. London: Unwin, 1919. Pp. 25-41.

Brief comparison between the two literary men. Lynd calls HB's genius "schoolmasterish" and Chesteron's genius "uproarious." Discusses THE FOUR MEN.

MacCarthy, Desmond. "Borrow and Belloc." In his EXPERIENCE. London: Putnam, 1935. Pp. 272-74.

In spite of its "militant" Catholicism, THE PATH TO ROME is well-written and contains interesting descriptions as well as "energetic reflections."

McCarthy, John P. "The Edwardian Political Milieu of Chesterbelloc." CREV, 4 (1978), 219-31.

A careful examination of the late Victorian and Edwardian periods of English history prompts "a reevaluation of the importance and perceptiveness" of HB's and Chesterton's political and social works. Explains why he values HB's "prophetic" work, THE SERVILE STATE.

_____. HILAIRE BELLOC: EDWARDIAN RADICAL. Indianapolis: Liberty Press, 1978.

A valuable analysis of HB's social and political ideas with extended treatment of THE SERVILE STATE. McCarthy sees HB as a lone prophet who suggested "the close correlation between the growth in state power and the enhancement of certain private interests," especially state-capitalism. A well-documented study which defines HB's position within a larger political tradition.

Hilaire Belloc

MacCurtain, Austin. "The Redeemed Pagan." STUDIES, 46 (1957), 207-12.

> Discusses the difficulties of writing a biography of HB and concludes that events up to 1918 deserve the fullest attention. Praises Speaight's biography but argues that he errs in analyzing HB's Catholicism.

McMahon, Francis E. "Belloc and America." COMMONWEAL, 66 (1957), 343-46.

> Examines HB's social and political ideas as well as his influence on Americans. Good discussion of THE CONTRAST.

Madeleva, Sister M. "Belloc as Biographer: Three Splendors and a Saint." BOOKMAN, 72 (1931), 607-12.

> A Catholic nun ranks HB's "secular" biographies in order of relative merit: "RICHELIEU, good; MARIE ANTIONETTE, better; WOLSEY, best." She calls JOAN OF ARC "a brochure in devotional, unexpanded style."

Mandell, C.C., and E.B. Shanks. HILAIRE BELLOC: THE MAN AND HIS WORK. London: Methuen, 1916.

> The authors argue that the whole of HB's work is based "on tradition and authority." An early and often dogmatic critical assessment of HB's reputation. The chapters on HB as stylist, historian, and traveller are of interest.

Mason, Michael. "In Retrospect: Chesterbelloc." TWENTIETH CENTURY, 177-78, nos. 1039 and 1040 (1968-69), 84-87.

> A revaluation of Chesterton's and HB's reputations. Mason stresses that HB was more politically involved. Although HB's topical journalism and ignorance of science and technology are drawbacks, his historical and other serious writings will survive.

Morton, J.B. "Introduction." In his HILAIRE BELLOC'S STORIES, ESSAYS, AND POEMS. 2nd ed. London: Dent, 1957. Pp. v-viii.

> Maintains that HB wrote with clarity, energy, and excellence "on every subject which engaged his pen." Describes briefly HB's "unmistakable" style and unfailing sense of form.

_____. "Introduction." In his SELECTED ESSAYS OF HILAIRE BELLOC. London: Methuen, 1948. Pp. v-xii.

> Values the stamp of HB's many moods and militant Catholicism on the diverse range of essays. Morton also stresses two great traits of HB's prose style: "lucidity and vitality."

Nisbet, Robert. "Introduction." In his THE SERVILE STATE. Indianapolis: Liberty Classics, 1977. Pp. 13-26.

> Nisbet explains cogently the background and implications of HB's sociological and political ideas. He concludes that "just as Belloc predicted, we find the real liberties of individuals diminished and constricted by the Leviathan we have built in the name of equality."

Pearson, Hesketh. "G.K. Chesterton and Hilaire Belloc." LISTENER, 55 (1956), 886-87.

> Anecdotal sketch of the important literary relationship between the two men.

Poynter, J.W. HILAIRE BELLOC KEEPS THE BRIDGE: AN EXAMINATION OF HIS DEFENSE OF ROMAN CATHOLICISM. London: Watts, 1929.

> A brief and heated defense of the enduring greatness of the Roman Church against HB's constricting interpretations of its history and policies. Berates HB's "narrow" apologies for a church of "despotism and obscurantism." Discusses especially HB's CATHOLIC CHURCH AND HISTORY (1926).

Pryce-Jones, Alan. "A French Romantic in England." THE LISTENER, 57 (1957), 480-81.

> Provides memories and impressions of HB's "fascinating" character. Pryce-Jones maintains that HB failed to treat certain themes because he was "much more deeply engaged by his hates than by his affections."

Purcell, J.M. "The Road to the SERVILE STATE." CREV, 6 (1979-80), 136-43.

> Concise discussion of the intellectual sources of HB's SERVILE STATE. Purcell also briefly outlines the history of the book's reputation.

Shanks, Edward. "Mr. Belloc: Some Characteristics." In his FIRST ESSAYS ON LITERATURE. London: Collins, 1923. Pp. 125-47.

> A general discussion in which Shanks praises and explains four characteristics of HB's work: lucid, humorous, firm, and controversial.

Speaight, Robert. "Hilaire Belloc." THE MONTH, N.S. 10 (1953), 133-40.

> Tribute to HB's prolific career, his rational critique of modern civilization, and his "humanist way" of being a Catholic.

Thody, Philip. "The Cosmic Pessimism of Hilaire Belloc." ULR, 13 (1970), 73-88.

> Primarily a study of HB's poetry; however, Thody provides clear explanations of HB's social vision and its contradictions.

Wells, H. G. MR. BELLOC OBJECTS TO THE OUTLINE OF HISTORY. The Forum Series. London: Watts, 1926.

> A refutation of HB's COMPANION TO MR. WELLS'S OUTLINE OF HISTORY. Opening with the statement, "I am the least controversial of men," Wells closes by accusing HB of impudence, ignorance, and dishonesty.

Wilhelmsen, Frederick. HILAIRE BELLOC: NO ALIENATED MAN. A STUDY IN CHRISTIAN INTEGRATION. London: Sheed and Ward, 1954.

> Focuses on HB's Christian humanism and "the vision of integrated humanity concretized in his work." An interesting introduction to HB's ideas that sometimes becomes abstract or dogmatic in making critical assessments.

CHRISTOPHER CAUDWELL
[CHRISTOPHER ST. JOHN SPRIGG] (1907-37)

NONFICTIONAL PROSE

Except for the seven detective novels and five textbooks on aviation, all of CC's books are posthumously printed.

WORKS EDITED BY OTHERS

THE CONCEPT OF FREEDOM. Ed. George Thomson. London: Lawrence and Wishart, 1965.

    Reprints most of STUDIES and CRISIS.

THE CRISIS IN PHYSICS. Ed. Hyman Levy. London: Lane, 1939.

    The first five chapters of the book are complete but the rest consists of notes. The bourgeois view of economics and society as an eternal and immutable mode also colors bourgeois physical theory. CC suggests an alternative theory to Einstein's stable structure of the universe.

FURTHER STUDIES IN A DYING CULTURE. Ed. Edgell Rickword. London: Bodley Head, 1949.

    Five essays on such topics as bourgeois aesthetics and psychology. The essays on "Beauty" and "Consciousness" are the most significant.

ILLUSION AND REALITY: A STUDY OF THE SOURCES OF POETRY. London: Macmillan, 1937.

    CC's major work on aesthetics in which he spells out the implications for poetry of Marxist theory. The final chapter, "The Future of Poetry," is especially doctrinaire. The second half of the book discusses the relation of poetry to dream, fantasy, and illusion.

Christopher Caudwell

ROMANCE AND REALISM: A STUDY IN ENGLISH BOURGEOIS LITERATURE. Ed. Samuel Hynes. Princeton, N.J.: Princeton Univ. Press, 1970.

> Discusses English literature since Shakespeare in terms of its relationship to history, physics, and economics. CC described the purpose of the book as "the tracing of those chief social changes which produced change in the form and technique of the novel and poetry."

STUDIES AND FURTHER STUDIES IN A DYING CULTURE. New York: Dodd, 1949.

> Reprint of the two titles published separately in 1938 and 1949, respectively.

STUDIES IN A DYING CULTURE. Ed. John Strachey. London: Lane, 1938.

> Eight essays on literary, psychological, and philosophical subjects. Of particular interest are the essays, "G.B. Shaw," "D.H. Lawrence," "Love," and "Liberty."

BIBLIOGRAPHY

Munton, Alan, and Alan Young, comps. SEVEN WRITERS OF THE ENGLISH LEFT: A BIBLIOGRAPHY OF LITERATURE AND POLITICS, 1916-1980. New York: Garland, 1981.

> A useful bibliography which includes the most up-to-date and comprehensive listing of editions of CC's writings. Brief commentaries are interspersed.

BIOGRAPHY

Beard, Paul. "Biographical Note." In his POEMS. London: Lawrence and Wishart, 1965. Pp. 3-5.

> Succinct survey of CC's life written by his close friend. Beard maintains that CC's "earnestness made any intellectual pretence impossible to him."

Thomson, George. "Biographical Note." In his ILLUSION AND REALITY: A STUDY OF THE SOURCES OF POETRY. New York: International Publishers, 1937. Pp. 3-5.

> Brief sketch of CC's career. CC was a "quiet, well-spoken young man who wrote books for a living," but later he became a "man of action."

CRITICISM

Currie, Robert. "Christopher Caudwell: Marxist Illusion, Jungian Reality." BJA, 18 (1978), 291-99.

> With copious documentation, Currie demonstrates how the principal doctrines in ILLUSION AND REALITY are based on the psychological and anthropological theories of Jung. Thus, for a full understanding of the work, one must look beyond its surface Marxism.

Doyle, Brian. "The Necessity of Illusion: The Writings of Christopher Caudwell." L&H, 6 (1980), 235-48.

> Surveys recent assessments of CC's work and argues that he is unique among Marxist critics in his valuing of poetry. Doyle defends CC against a host of critics.

Draper, Michael. "Christopher Caudwell's Illusions." RMS, 21 (1977), 80-100.

> Brief summaries of most of CC's major works and ideas with even briefer critical comments on them. The discussion is loosely tied to the central idea that "to master reality, man creates and commits himself to illusions, which he then struggles to realize."

Frankel, Hyman. "Christopher Caudwell." WORLD NEWS AND VIEWS, 27, No. 7 (1947), 76-77.

> Concise discussion of CC's conversion to communism, and the works ILLUSION, STUDIES, and CRISIS.

Harap, Louis. "Caudwell, Critic." NEW MASSES, 57, No. 8 (1945), 22-23.

> Calls ILLUSION "the most profound historical materialist study on art in English." Harap admits, however, that the work has serious limitations: CC's method of generalizing and characterizing broad trends is "hazardous" and, at times, his style is unnecessarily abstract and involved.

_____. "Christopher Caudwell, Marxist Critic, Poet and Soldier." THE WORKER, 2, No. 47 (24 November 1946), 9.

> Praises CC as a great mind who integrated Marxist theory and practice in his writings. Harap surveys the range of CC's interests and briefly discusses the significance of his "brilliant essays."

Hawley, Andrew R. "Art for Man's Sake: Christopher Caudwell as Communist Aesthetician." CE, 30 (1968), 1-19.

Christopher Caudwell

By way of comprehensive survey of the literary critics of the 1930s, Hawley argues that of the British intellectuals on the left, CC alone made an "important contribution to the ethical and political theory of literature."

Hynes, Samuel. "Introduction." In his ROMANCE AND REALISM: A STUDY IN ENGLISH BOURGEOIS LITERATURE. Princeton, N.J.: Princeton Univ. Press, 1970. Pp. 3-28.

Hynes argues that the meaning and value of CC's works are as historical documents belonging to the 1930's, a time when communism served as a surrogate religion. Also, Hynes stresses CC's talent as a gifted synthesizer: his criticism "became more than partisan; it became profound."

Levy, Hyman. "Introduction." In his THE CRISIS IN PHYSICS. London: Lane, 1939. Pp. v-xiii.

Argues that CC said some extremely significant things about physics and the crisis of the scientist in a capitalist society.

Margolies, David N. THE FUNCTION OF LITERATURE: A STUDY OF CHRISTOPHER CAUDWELL'S AESTHETICS. New York: International Publishers, 1969.

Favorable, Marxist commentary that sees CC as "perhaps the first critic to take a fully social and fully Marxist view of art." In a clear and stimulating manner, Margolies demonstrates how CC's outstanding contribution to Marxist aesthetics is his theory of the immediate and future functions of literature.

Matthews, G.M., et al. "The Caudwell Discussion." MODERN QUARTERLY, 6, n.s. (1950-51), 16-33, 107-34, 259-75, 340-58.

The first extended commentary on CC with contributions from fourteen British Marxist critics. This lively series presents the pros and cons of the content and validity of CC's political and literary theories.

Ray, Paul C. "The Anti-Surrealism of Christopher Caudwell." CLS, 6 (1969), 61-67.

While granting that ILLUSION is the best Marxist analysis of literature by an Englishman, Ray points out that CC's rejection of the surrealist synthesis of Engels and Freud forces him into awkward self-contradictions and finally his position is close to the surrealists.

Rickword, Edgell. "Preface." In his FURTHER STUDIES IN A DYING CULTURE. London: Bodley Head, 1949. Pp. 7-11.

Views the central theme of the essays as "the unity of thinking and doing." Rickword praises CC's intellectual curiosity as well as his realistic understanding of economic conditions in the thirties.

Strachey, John. "Introduction." In his STUDIES IN A DYING CULTURE. London: Lane, 1938. Pp. v-xvi.

High praise for CC's last books which "show a sharp gain in precision, in capacity to focus." Strachey argues that STUDIES is unified by CC's concept of human liberty.

Thomson, George. "Introduction." In his THE CONCEPT OF FREEDOM. London: Lawrence and Wishart, 1965. Pp. 7-8.

Brief biographical and critical assessment. Thomson calls CC "one of those rare geniuses in whom the scientist and the artist are combined" and the first critic to make a "systematic attempt" to work out a Marxist theory of aesthetics.

Williams, Raymond. CULTURE AND SOCIETY, 1780-1950. New York: Harper, 1958.

A hostile estimate of CC, found on pages 275-80, as a literary critic because he "has little to say, of actual literature, that is even interesting" and "for the most part his discussion is not even specific enough to be wrong."

G.K. CHESTERTON (1874-1936)

THE MINERVA EDITION OF THE WORKS OF G.K. CHESTERTON, 9 volumes (Library Press, 1926), contains ALARMS AND DISCURSIONS, ALL THINGS CONSIDERED, CHARLES DICKENS, FANCIES VERSUS FADS, A MISCELLANY OF MEN, TREMENDOUS TRIFLES, and THE USES OF DIVERSITY.

NONFICTIONAL PROSE

ALARMS AND DISCURSIONS. London: Methuen, 1910. New York: Dodd, Mead, 1911.

> Thirty-nine essays, including "The Nightmare," "The Man and His Newspaper," "The Futurists," and several other essays which categorize types of men.

ALFRED TENNYSON. With Richard Garnett. The Bookman Biographies. London: Hodder and Stoughton, 1903. New York: Pott, 1904.

> Brief but vivid impression of the man with some critical discussion of his poetry.

ALL IS GRIST: A BOOK OF ESSAYS. London: Methuen, 1931. New York: Dodd, Mead, 1932.

> Thirty-eight essays, ranging from discussions of Dante to Mencken and Trollope to Shaw. Other provocative essays treat slang, nudists, quacks, and business education.

ALL I SURVEY: A BOOK OF ESSAYS. London: Methuen; New York: Dodd, Mead, 1933.

> Forty-four essays, covering such literary figures as Scott, Stevenson, and Swift, as well as such topics as taxes, war memorials, love, and bad poetry.

G.K. Chesterton

ALL THINGS CONSIDERED. London: Methuen; New York: Lane, 1908.

    Selects witty essays from GKC's weekly contributions to the ILLUSTRATED LONDON NEWS. Topics treated include: success, sport, women, spiritualism, humanitarianism, and fairy tales.

THE APPETITE OF TYRANNY. New York: Dodd, Mead, 1915.

    Includes "Letters to an Old Garibaldian" and "The Barbarism of Berlin."

APPRECIATIONS AND CRITICISMS OF THE WORKS OF CHARLES DICKENS. London: Dent; New York: Dutton, 1911.

    Collects twenty-three introductions written by GKC for the Everyman editions of Dickens' novels.

AS I WAS SAYING: A BOOK OF ESSAYS. London: Methuen; New York: Dodd, Mead, 1936.

    Thirty-six essays, including discussions of Coleridge, Meredith, Morris, and Voltaire, as well as GKC's ideas on poetry, blondes, and widows. One of the best volumes of GKC's essays.

AUTOBIOGRAPHY. London: Hutchinson, 1936. As THE AUTOBIOGRAPHY OF G.K. CHESTERTON. New York: Sheed and Ward, 1936.

    GKC provides important information on his life and works. The book is well-organized and provides many details concerning his youth, his beginnings in Fleet Street, his war against political corruption, his friendships, and his conversion.

AVOWALS AND DENIALS: A BOOK OF ESSAYS. London: Methuen, 1934. New York: Dodd, Mead, 1935.

    Thirty-six essays which treat such figures as Blake, Wordsworth, and Shaw, as well as such lively topics as enfranchised women, melodrama, and jazz.

THE BARBARISM OF BERLIN. London: Cassell, 1914.

    Wartime articles collected from the DAILY MAIL. GKC vents his wrath against Germany in this propagandistic pamphlet.

THE CATHOLIC CHURCH AND CONVERSION. London: Burns, Oates and Washbourne; New York: Macmillan, 1926.

    GKC defends and explains his Catholic faith and concludes that the Catholic Church's "very antiquity preserves an attitude of novelty."

G.K. Chesterton

CHARLES DICKENS. London: Methuen, 1906. As CHARLES DICKENS: A CRITICAL STUDY. New York: Dodd, Mead, 1906.

> Appreciative biographical and critical study of the great Victorian novelist.

CHAUCER. London: Faber; New York: Farrar and Rinehart, 1932.

> Critical discussion of Chaucer's works and times, with some attention to his religious ideas.

A CHESTERTON CALENDAR. London: Kegan Paul, 1911.

> A day-by-day compilation which includes selections from many of GKC's prose writings published before 1911.

CHRISTENDOM IN DUBLIN. London: Sheed and Ward, 1932. New York: Sheed and Ward, 1933.

> Brief account of GKC's visit to the Eucharistic Congress held in Dublin in 1932.

THE CRIMES OF ENGLAND. London: Palmer and Hayward, 1915. New York: Lane, 1916.

> GKC examines the past hundred years of England's diplomacy. The "crimes" were whenever England betrayed France and favored Prussia. He concludes that England should be more alert and assertive. In various sections, GKC argues that "Teutonism" is a fairy tale and he condemns "Kultur preached by Unkultur."

THE DEFENDANT. London: Johnson, 1901. New York: Dodd, Mead, 1902.

> Sixteen essays, including the essay "A Defence of Detective Stories," which calls for heroes and art in the city. Other topics defended include farce, penny dreadfuls, and slang.

ESSAYS OF TO-DAY AND YESTERDAY. London: Harrap, 1928.

> Collects seven essays (all previously published) including "A Defence of Nonsense," "Thomas Carlyle," and travel essays on America and Ireland.

EUGENICS AND OTHER EVILS. London: Cassell, 1922. New York: Dodd, Mead, 1927.

> Social criticism which expresses capitalism's collectivist tendencies. GKC launches a sustained attack against any agency's interference with families or reproductive methods.

G.K. Chesterton

THE EVERLASTING MAN. London: Hodder and Stoughton; New York: Dodd, Mead, 1925.

> An important extended reply to H. G. Wells's OUTLINE OF HISTORY.

FANCIES VERSUS FADS. London: Methuen; New York: Dodd, Mead, 1923.

> Thirty essays, on such literary figures as Shakespeare, Milton, and Bennett, and such topics as butterflies, toys, and divorce.

FIVE TYPES: A BOOK OF ESSAYS. London: A. L. Humphreys, 1910. New York: Holt, 1911.

> A slim collection of essays on Byron, Pope, Stevenson, Rostand, and Charles II.

G. F. WATTS. London: Duckworth; Chicago: Rand McNally, 1904.

> An important assessment of the nineteenth-century painter's work and intentions.

GENERALLY SPEAKING: A BOOK OF ESSAYS. London: Methuen, 1928. New York: Dodd, Mead, 1929.

> Forty-two articles, including essays on detective novels, Byron, and Hardy. Many essays deal with cultural phenomena--golf, movies, funeral customs, Christmas, and prohibition.

GEORGE BERNARD SHAW. London and New York: Lane, 1909.

> Some perceptive critical commentary on Shaw's art and ideas.

HERETICS. London and New York: Lane, 1905.

> Twenty essays on various writers of the nineties. The positions of several "false prophets" (Kipling, Shaw, and Wells) are questioned. Other essays on the family as well as on poverty and democracy are valuable as social history.

IRISH IMPRESSIONS. London: Collins, 1919. New York: Lane, 1920.

> Articles written for the NEW WITNESS when GKC visited Ireland.

LEO TOLSTOY. The Bookman Biographies. New York: Pott; London: Hodder and Stoughton, 1904.

> GKC's six-page contribution discusses Tolstoy's influence upon later political acts of heroic consistency.

G.K. Chesterton

A MISCELLANY OF MEN. London: Methuen; New York: Dodd, Mead, 1912.

> Thirty-seven essays on such figures as the poet, the gardener, the sentimental Scot, the sultan, and the contented man. The essays demonstrate GKC's blend of exaggeration and common sense.

THE NEW JERUSALEM. London: Hodder and Stoughton, 1920. New York: Doran, 1921.

> GKC records his impressions of his visit to Palestine. The last chapter on Zionism is highly controversial.

ORTHODOXY. London: Lane; New York: Dodd, Mead, 1908.

> The most important of GKC's writings on Christian apologetics. In a major work, GKC traces his experiences which led him to discover orthodox Christianity.

THE OUTLINE OF SANITY. London: Methuen, 1926. New York: Dodd, Mead, 1927.

> GKC outlines his political plan of Distributionism, which sought "the restoration of liberty through the distribution of property."

THE RESURRECTION OF ROME. London: Hodder and Stoughton; New York: Dodd, Mead, 1930.

> A travel book dealing with GKC's visit to Rome in 1929.

ROBERT BROWNING. English Men of Letters. London: Macmillan; New York: Grosset and Dunlap, 1903.

> A popular biographical and critical study of a major Victorian poet. Some quotations are rendered--unreliably--from memory.

ROBERT LOUIS STEVENSON. The Bookman Biographies. London: Hodder and Stoughton, 1927. New York: Dodd, Mead, 1928.

> Brief but instructive biography, with some critical discussion of the Victorian novelist's works.

ST. FRANCIS OF ASSISI. London: Hodder and Stoughton, 1923. Garden City, N.Y.: Doubleday, 1924.

> GKC's sketch of the saint who loved animals was an instant popular success.

ST. THOMAS OF AQUINAS. London: Hodder and Stoughton; New York: Sheed and Ward, 1933.

A serious introduction to Thomistic ideas which won the approval of Aquinas scholars.

A SHORT HISTORY OF ENGLAND. London: Chatto and Windus; New York: Lane, 1917.

A less than comprehensive survey of the high spots of England's past. GKC reveals his strong love for Catholic France and discusses England's relations with that land.

SIDELIGHTS ON NEW LONDON AND NEWER YORK, AND OTHER ESSAYS. London: Sheed and Ward; New York: Dodd, Mead, 1932.

Twenty-eight light essays, including treatments of such literary figures as Dickens, Shakespeare, and Shaw, and such controversial developments in America as prohibition and skyscrapers.

THE SUPERSTITION OF DIVORCE. London: Chatto and Windus; New York: Lane, 1920.

GKC bitterly condemns the growing number of divorces and blames the trend on a capitalist conspiracy. Without a reformed moral and economic system, social disaster looms as a possibility.

THE THING. London: Sheed and Ward, 1929. New York: Dodd, Mead, 1930.

Collects thirty-five essays on religious topics.

THOMAS CARLYLE. With J. E. Hodder Williams. The Bookman Biographies. London: Hodder and Stoughton; New York: Pott, 1903.

Brief but instructive impression of Carlyle's life and thoughts. GKC argues that Carlyle is a flawed historian because of his "impatience with other men's ideas."

TREMENDOUS TRIFLES. London: Methuen; New York: Dodd, Mead, 1909.

Thirty-nine sketches, which in GKC's words "amount to no more than a sort of sporadic diary." Some titles include: "A Piece of Chalk," "The Dickensian," and "The Toy Theatre."

TWELVE TYPES. London: Humphreys, 1902. As VARIED TYPES. New York: Dodd, Mead, 1903.

Twelve biographical and critical sketches of primarily Victorian figures: William Morris, Tolstoy, Carlyle, and C. Bronte. (The American edition includes eight additional essays.)

G.K. Chesterton

THE USES OF DIVERSITY. A BOOK OF ESSAYS. London: Methuen, 1920. New York: Dodd, Mead, 1921.

> Thirty-five articles covering detective and historical fiction as well as such figures as Dickens, Meredith, and Tennyson.

UTOPIA OF USERERS AND OTHER ESSAYS. New York: Boni and Liveright, 1917.

> Collects twenty-six essays that GKC contributed to the DAILY HERALD between 1913 and 1914. GKC attacks British society and warns against rule by captains of industry.

THE VICTORIAN AGE IN LITERATURE. London: Williams and Norgate; New York: Holt, 1913.

> A general, but still useful critical survey of GKC's impressions of the Victorian Age.

W.M. THACKERAY. With Lewis Melville. The Bookman Biographies. London: Hodder and Stoughton; New York: Pott, 1903.

> Popular literary biography and criticism.

THE WELL AND THE SHALLOWS. London and New York: Sheed and Ward, 1935.

> Thirty-nine controversial essays on religious and social issues. Some essays included are: "The Collapse of Materialism," "Three Foes of the Family," "Sex and Property," "Why Protestants Prohibit," and the most important--"Where is the Paradox?"

WHAT I SAW IN AMERICA. London: Hodder and Stoughton; New York: Dodd, Mead, 1922.

> GKC records his impressions of his first lecture tour around America, 1919-20.

WHAT'S WRONG WITH THE WORLD. London: Cassell; New York: Dodd, Mead, 1910.

> GKC offers his ideas about and conflicts with society. In this reactionary collection of essays, he calls for a return to the freedom of an age before modern capitalism.

WILLIAM BLAKE. London: Duckworth; New York: Dutton, 1910.

> Brief biographical and critical study of Blake's writings and philosophy.

WILLIAM COBBETT. London: Hodder and Stoughton, 1925; New York: Dodd, Mead, 1926.

> A useful introduction to Cobbett's life and significance.

WORKS EDITED BY OTHERS

THE APOSTLE AND THE WILD DUCKS, AND OTHER ESSAYS. Ed. Dorothy Collins. London: Elek, 1975.

> Previously uncollected essays, including some interesting discussions of literary figures such as Ruskin, Shelley, Austen, and Hardy.

A CHESTERTON CATHOLIC ANTHOLOGY. Ed. Patrick Braybrooke. New York: Kennedy, 1928.

> Selected religious writings with a foreword by Father O.F. Dudley.

CHESTERTON ESSAYS. Ed. K.E. Whitehorn. London: Methuen, 1953.

> A title in the Methuen's Modern Classics Series.

CHESTERTON ON SHAKESPEARE. Ed. Dorothy Collins. Chester Springs, Pa.: Dufour Editions, 1921.

> Reprints from various sources thirty-two of GKC's essays on Shakespeare's works and critical reputation.

THE COLOURED LANDS. Ed. Maisie Ward. London: Sheed and Ward, 1938.

> A delightful posthumous collection which includes some previously unpublished prose pieces, including "Dreams," "The Artistic Side," and "The Phantom Butler." Contains interesting illustrations done by GKC.

COME TO THINK OF IT . . . A BOOK OF ESSAYS. Ed. J.P. de Fonseka. London: Methuen, 1930.

> Collects forty-three essays, most previously published in ILLUSTRATED LONDON NEWS. Topics range from Keats to psychoanalysis and from preaching to prohibition.

THE COMMON MAN. London: Sheed and Ward, 1950.

> Forty-four previously uncollected essays and introductions, including discussions of James, Johnson, and Tolstoy.

THE END OF THE ARMISTICE. Ed. F.J. Sheed. London: Sheed and Ward, 1940.

G.K. Chesterton

> Selected essays in which GKC analyzes the problem in Germany's position and intentions in Europe. The sections on "Prussianism" and "Hitlerism" were especially controversial and prophetic.

ESSAYS AND POEMS. Ed. Wilfred Sheed. Harmondsworth, Engl.: Penguin, 1958.

> A handy collection.

ESSAYS BY G.K. CHESTERTON. Ed. John Guest. London: Collins, 1939.

> John Guest provides a brief appreciative preface to this selection of GKC's essays on various topics.

G.K. CHESTERON: AN ANTHOLOGY. Ed. D.B. Wyndham Lewis. London: Oxford Univ. Press, 1957.

> An interesting selection with an important introduction by Lewis.

G.K.C. AS M.C.: BEING A COLLECTION OF THIRTY-SEVEN INTRODUCTIONS BY G.K.C. Ed. J.P. de Fonseka. London: Methuen, 1929.

> Selected introductions that GKC contributed to various books between 1903 and 1909. Some titles include "Matthew Arnold," "Dr. Johnson," "Gilbert and Sullivan," and "Literary London."

G.K. CHESTERTON: A SELECTION FROM HIS NON-FICTIONAL PROSE. Ed. W.H. Auden. London: Faber, 1970.

> Thirty-six essays, two-thirds on literary topics (mainly Victorian writers), and one third on philosophic matters (e.g., "Darwinism and Morality," "Nature and Logic," and "Mythology and Philosophy").

THE GLASS WALKING-STICK, AND OTHER ESSAYS FROM THE ILLUSTRATED LONDON NEWS, 1905-1936. Ed. Dorothy Collins. London: Methuen, 1955.

> Forty essays (previously uncollected) on such miscellaneous topics as Shakespeare, Fielding, and the Victorians. There are also several important essays on literary genres: "Poetry in Action," "On the Essay," and "On the True Artists."

A GLEAMING COHORT. Ed. E.V. Lucas. London: Methuen, 1926.

> Selects thirty-seven essays, covering such figures as Milton, Tennyson, and Dickens, and such objects as cheese, lampposts, and toys.

A HANDFUL OF AUTHORS: ESSAYS ON BOOKS AND WRITERS. Ed. Dorothy Collins. London: Sheed and Ward, 1953.

G.K. Chesterton

> Thirty-seven of GKC's previously uncollected critical essays and articles on various books and authors.

LUNACY AND LETTERS. Ed. Dorothy Collins. London: Sheed and Ward, 1958.

> Thirty-eight previously uncollected essays (from the DAILY NEWS, 1901-11), including "The Poetry of Cities," "The Meaning of Dreams," "The Meaning of the Theatre," and "Good Stories Spoilt by Great Authors." The essays are light and nonpolitical in nature.

THE MAN WHO WAS CHESTERTON: THE BEST ESSAYS, STORIES, POEMS AND OTHER WRITINGS OF G.K. CHESTERTON. Ed. Raymond T. Bond. New York: Dodd, Mead, 1937.

> An impressive anthology which includes a collection of over a hundred essays and selections from GKC's books, including "On the Prison of Jazz," "Marriage and the Modern Mind," "On American Morals," and "The Real Journalist." A valuable book which does as well as any one volume can to convey the spectrum of GKC's varied achievements.

THE MAN WHO WAS ORTHODOX: A SELECTION FROM THE UNCOLLECTED WRITINGS OF G.K. CHESTERTON. Ed. A.L. Maycock. London: Dobson, 1963.

> An anthology which arranges extracts from ninety-eight previously uncollected articles (1891-1936) on religious themes.

ON RUNNING AFTER ONE'S HAT AND OTHER WHIMSIES. Ed. E.V. Knox. New York: McBride, 1933.

> An anthology of GKC's humorous writings.

SELECTED ESSAYS. Ed. Dorothy Collins. London: Methuen, 1949.

> Valuable representative selection of sixty-one essays, covering such figures as Voltaire, Dickens, Belloc, and Trollope, and such diverse experiences as cab rides, funerals, gardening, shopping, and writing.

A SHILLING FOR MY THOUGHTS. Ed. E.V. Lucas. London: Methuen, 1916.

> A selection of several of GKC's early essays, stories, and other writings.

THE SPICE OF LIFE, AND OTHER ESSAYS. Ed. Dorothy Collins. Beaconsfield, Engl.: Finlayson, 1964.

Previously uncollected essays on several literary genres, works, and writers, as well as on such topics as religion, philosophy, and travel at home and abroad.

STORIES, ESSAYS, AND POEMS. Ed. Ernest Rhys. London: Dent, 1935.

An anthology in the Everyman Series. GKC offered his assistance in choosing the selections.

BIBLIOGRAPHY

Sullivan, John, ed. "Chesterton Bibliography Continued." CREV, 2 (1975-76), 94-98. Continued in subsequent volumes.

Corrects and adds to Sullivan's book-length bibliographies.

_____. CHESTERTON CONTINUED: A BIBLIOGRAPHICAL SUPPLEMENT. London: Univ. of London Press, 1968.

Sullivan adds items published between 1956 and 1966 to his 1958 bibliography (below). Also reprints several uncollected essays.

_____. G.K. CHESTERTON: A BIBLIOGRAPHY. London: Univ. of London Press, 1958.

The best primary bibliography on GKC. Includes a descriptive listing of GKC's books and pamphlets, with checklists of GKC's contributions to books, articles, translations, and miscellaneous materials. Also includes a list in chronological order of 138 books and articles about GKC.

BIOGRAPHY

Barker, Dudley. G.K. CHESTERTON: A BIOGRAPHY. London: Constable, 1973.

Well-organized biography on GKC which offers commentary on most of his major works. A succinct and readable account of GKC's ideas and literary connections. Chapter 13 deals with his journalism; chapter 16 with his essays.

Titterton, W.R. G.K. CHESTERTON: A PORTRAIT. London: Ouseley, 1936.

A fellow journalist comments on some of GKC's essays.

Ward, Maisie. G.K. CHESTERTON. New York: Sheed and Ward, 1943.

The authorized and most useful biography of GKC. Ward draws a portrait of GKC's personality from memoir material obtained from friends, and also analyzes the growth of GKC's ideas in both published and unpublished works.

_____. RETURN TO CHESTERTON. New York: Sheed and Ward, 1952.

A supplement to the 1943 biography (above). Ward surveys some unpublished letters and memoirs to round out the portrait of GKC.

CRITICISM

Asquith, Michael. "GKC: Prophet and Jester." LISTENER, 47 (1952), 390-91.

Comments on GKC's serious method and humorous style.

Auden, W.H. "G.K. Chesterton's Non-Fictional Prose." PROSE, 1 (1970), 17-28.

Analyzes the strengths and weaknesses of GKC's journalism.

Baker, Richard, John J. Connolly, and Ronald Zudeck. "Notes on Chesterton's Notre Dame Lectures in Victorian Literature." CREV, 4 (1977-78), 115-44; 285-301.

A trio of scholars record their notes on what GKC had to say concerning such figures as Carlyle, Darwin, Newman, and Thackeray.

Belloc, Hilaire. "Gilbert Chesterton." In ONE THING AND ANOTHER. Ed. Patrick Cahill. London: Hollis and Carter, 1955. Pp. 171-76.

Brief, but interesting essay on the relationship between GKC's style and meaning; Belloc stresses his friend's logical and rational bent.

_____. ON THE PLACE OF GILBERT CHESTERTON IN ENGLISH LETTERS. New York: Sheed and Ward, 1940.

Important study of GKC's ideas and themes. Belloc stresses the "social philosophy" of nationalism and historical perspective as well as religious emphasis on faith and charity in GKC's work. Praises GKC's style for its "precision of thought," lucidity, and "capacity for parallelism." Selects THE THING as GKC's best work.

Bergonzi, Bernard. "Chesterton and/or Belloc." CRITQ, 1 (1959), 64-71.

Predicts that GKC's nonfictional prose on an array of topics constitutes his most important achievement. Although GKC is more genial than Belloc, he is also "too rationalistic."

Bogaerts, Anthony M.A. CHESTERTON AND THE VICTORIAN AGE. New York: Haskell House, 1966.

> A somewhat prosaic assessment of GKC's studies of the period (THE VICTORIAN AGE IN LITERATURE) and such writers as Dickens, Browning, and Stevenson. Chapter 6 treats GKC as a literary critic who prefers "healthy, optimistic and interesting literature."

Bradbrook, B.R. "The Literary Relationship between G.K. Chesterton and Karel Capek." SEER, 39 (1961), 327-38.

> Demonstrates the influences of GKC's use of paradoxes on Capek's works.

Braybrooke, Patrick. GILBERT KEITH CHESTERTON. Philadelphia: Lippincott, 1922.

> A friend's appreciative survey of GKC's works with some critical commentary. The chapter entitled "The Essayist" is of some value, as are chapters dealing with GKC's treatment of Dickens, Thackeray, Browning, and Shaw.

_____. THE WISDOM OF G.K. CHESTERTON. London: Palmer, 1929.

> A supplement to his earlier study (1922). Here Braybrooke offers more insightful, if selective, critical commentary in such chapters as "The Critic," "The Essayist," "The Historian," and "The Traveller."

Brown, Father (Monsignor John O'Connor). "GKC Recognita Decennalia." NINETEENTH CENTURY AND AFTER, 139-40 (1946), 301-07.

> Sees GKC's approach to life as a combination of a deep, constant intuition and a childlike attitude toward everything. Includes a brief discussion of GKC as humorist and journalist.

Cammaerts, Emile. THE LAUGHING PROPHET: THE SEVEN VIRTUES AND G.K. CHESTERTON. London: Methuen, 1937.

> Sentimental portrait of GKC, the good warrior who wages "an eternal fight against the vices of civilization." Stresses examples of Christian virtues in GKC's life and works.

Canovan, Margaret. "Chesterton's Attack on the Proto-Nazis: New Light on the Black Legend." CREV, 3 (1976-77), 246-59.

Defends GKC's attack on eugenics and stresses his "genuine kinship with ordinary men." GKC is a great polemical writer because of his talent for using "vivid concrete examples."

_____. G.K. CHESTERTON: RADICAL POPULIST. New York: Harcourt, 1977.

Well-organized discussion of GKC's social and political ideas concerning education, patriotism, property, socialism, women, and so forth. Canovan admires the variety of GKC's outlook, but concludes that "populism as an ideology is incoherent."

Chambers, Leland H. "Gide, Santayana, Chesterton, and Browning." CLS, 7 (1970), 216-28.

In a complex, but well-argued essay, Chambers demonstrates that GKC's study of Browning (1903) sparked Gide's enthusiasm for the poet.

THE CHESTERTON REVIEW (CREV), 1974-- . 2 times per year.

This is the journal of the G.K. Chesterton Society. Publishes critical articles on all aspects of GKC's life and work.

[Chesterton, Cecil]. G.K. CHESTERTON--A CRITICISM. London: Alston Rivers, 1908.

An early negative assessment of GKC as a propagandist, which was published anonymously by his brother. The individualistic features of GKC's ideas are analyzed in several chapters.

Chisholm, Sir Joseph. G.K. CHESTERTON AND HIS BIOGRAPHER. Webster Groves, Mo.: International Mark Twain Society, 1945.

Brief survey of GKC's life and works. Chisholm feels that the heart of his prose style is "lucidity."

Churchill, R.C. "Chesterton on Dickens: The Legend and the Reality." DSN, 5 (1974), 34-38.

High praise for GKC as the leading Dickens critic of his day.

Clarke, Margaret. "Chesterton the Classicist." DUBLIN REVIEW, 229 (1955), 51-67.

Discusses the influence of GKC's classical studies on his essays and his brand of Christian humanism.

Clipper, Lawrence J. G.K. CHESTERTON. Twayne's English Author Series. New York: Twayne, 1974.

G.K. Chesterton

> Competent general introduction to GKC's life and works. Clipper values GKC as "an audacious and prolific polymath in an age of narrow specialists" and places him in the tradition of Christian humanism. Superficial discussion of GKC's prose style.

Conlon, D.J., ed. G.K. CHESTERTON: THE CRITICAL JUDGMENTS, I: 1900-1937. Antwerp, Belgium: Antwerp Studies in English Literature, 1976.

> Reprints selected contemporary reviews of most of GKC's published books between 1900 and 1937. An introduction and brief annotations identifying the critics are provided.

Corrin, Jay P. G.K. CHESTERTON AND HILAIRE BELLOC: THE BATTLE AGAINST MODERNITY. Athens: Ohio Univ. Press, 1981.

> A detailed treatment of GKC's and Belloc's social and political opinions, with particular attention to the movement called Distributism. Corrin analyzes both the positive and negative consequences of the two men's influence and cooperation.

_____. "The Formation of the Distributist Circle." CREV, 1 (1975), 52-83.

> Discusses the establishment of the Distributist political movement and GKC's dealings with Belloc and others.

Cunningham, Lawrence S. "Chesterton as Mystic." ABR, 26 (1975), 16-24.

> Relates GKC's religious writings to the mystic tradition.

_____. "Chesterton Reconsidered." THOUGHT, 47 (1972), 271-79.

> Sees continuing significance in GKC's theological writings.

De Blácam, Aodh. "Defender of the Faith: Chesterton's First Conversion." IRISH MONTHLY, 73 (1945), 47-55.

> Analyzes GKC's early spiritual crises and his movement toward faith based on "mystical materialism."

Derus, David L. "Chesterton as Literary Critic." RENASCENCE, 25 (1972-73), 103-12.

> A thorough and balanced assessment of GKC's critical theory. Derus faults GKC as a critic because of his dogmatism and shifting points of view.

_____. "The Chesterton Style: Patterns and Paradox." CREV, 4 (1977-78), 45-49.

> A valuable study of GKC's prose style. Derus analyzes closely

and intelligently both the surface features and philosophical
implications of "the artist's" style.

Donaghy, Henry J. "Chesterton on Shaw's Views of Catholicism." SHAWR,
10 (1967), 108-16.

> Explains why GKC thought Shaw was mistaken about Catholicism:
> "the answer lies in what Chesterton thought was Shaw's inability
> to understand paradox."

Dooley, David J. "Chesterton as Satirist." CREV, 6 (1980), 233-53.

> Dooley distinguishes between GKC's use of humor and satire
> in his writings. Good analysis.

Eaker, J. Gordon. "G. K. Chesterton among the Moderns." GAR, 13 (1959),
152-60.

> GKC's faith in reason and common sense--based on Thomistic
> metaphysics--led him to attack the doctrines of modernism.

Edwards, Dorothy. "G. K. Chesterton." In SCRUTINIES: CRITICAL ESSAYS
BY VARIOUS WRITERS. Ed. Edgell Rickword. London: Wishart, 1928. Pp.
30-40.

> Harsh attack on GKC, a "cocksure" writer who "cannot distinguish
> between symbols and facts."

Engel, Elliot D. "The Wizard of Boz: G. K. Chesterton and Dickensian
Humour." CREV, 3 (1976-77), 211-29.

> Comprehensive discussion of GKC's writings about Dickens'
> comedy. Engel concludes that GKC "gave a much more exacting
> and critical commentary on Dickens's work than most recent
> scholars realize."

Evans, David. "The Making of G. K. Chesterton's HERETICS." YES, 5
(1975), 207-13.

> Traces the origin of several essays in HERETICS to essays GKC
> contributed to the DAILY NEWS (1901-04).

Evans, Maurice. G. K. CHESTERTON. Cambridge: The Univ. Press, 1939.

> Good basic discussion of GKC's philosophical and political beliefs.
> The brief chapters on "The Essays" and "Style and Argument" are
> particularly valuable. Concludes that GKC's "best essays were
> undoubtedly written before the war."

Feeney, Leonard. "The Metaphysics of Chesterton." THOUGHT, 17 (1942),
22-36.

Discusses GKC's fascinated interest in metaphysical statements.

Furlong, William B. GBS/GKC: SHAW AND CHESTERTON, THE META-
PHYSICAL JESTERS. University Park: Penn. State Univ. Press, 1970.

> A valuable and detailed study of the personal and literary
> relationship of Shaw and GKC between 1901 and 1936. Furlong
> provides background material and analysis of GKC's impressive
> critical study of Shaw.

Green, V.H.H. "Gilbert Keith Chesterton." THEOLOGY, 43 (1941), 93-101, 150-55.

> Interesting discussions of GKC's humor and Christian theology
> which focus on the concepts of his rebellion and Christian
> humanism.

Hamilton, Robert. "The Rationalist from Fairyland." QR, 305 (1967), 444-53.

> Praises GKC's sensibility and creative use of the faculty of
> reason.

Hart, Jeffrey. "In Praise of Chesterton." YR, 53 (1963), 49-60.

> A valuable retrospective essay which attacks some misunder-
> standings of GKC's social, religious, and political beliefs.
> Hart values GKC's concentrated prose style.

Hetzler, Leo A. "Chesterton and the Man in the Forest." CREV, 1 (1974-75), 11-18.

> Interesting discussion of GKC's treatment of the themes of
> "primal intuition and mystical insights" in several of his essays.

_____. "George McDonald and G.K. Chesterton." DUJ, 37 (1976), 176-82.

> Treats the various influences of McDonald's writings on GKC's
> religious outlook and on his personality.

Hollis, Christopher. G.K. CHESTERTON. Writers and Their Work Series.
London: Longmans, 1950.

> Brief but handy introduction to GKC's work and thought. Hollis
> primarily discusses GKC's religious writings as related to "the
> supreme Christian paradox."

_____. THE MIND OF CHESTERTON. London: Hollis and Carter, 1970.

> Focusing on GKC's nonfiction in some detail, Hollis demonstrates
> the relationship between GKC's religious, social, and political

ideas. Chapter 13, "The Secular Biographer," supplies useful
commentary on GKC's treatment of various historical and literary
figures. This staunchly Catholic interpretation is somewhat biased.

Hunt, Peter. "Chesterton on Education." FAITH & REASON, 4, No. 1
(1978), 48-59.

> Analyzes GKC's opinions on education and endorses "the sunlit
> sanity of his vision." Hunt admires GKC as "the greatest
> generalist" of his times; he refers to WHAT'S WRONG WITH
> THE WORLD and several relevant essays.

_____. "Colin Clark, Small Farming, the Guild System and Chesterton."
CREV, 4 (1978), 165-81.

> Appreciative discussion of the implications of GKC's historical
> and political writings. Hunt stresses the intimate relationship
> between GKC's Distributist social philosophy and the need to
> escape "gigantic units" in business, education, and government.

Hunter, Lynette. G.K. CHESTERTON: EXPLORATIONS IN ALLEGORY.
London: Macmillan, 1979.

> Traces the developments in GKC's religious and philosophical
> ideas. Brief discussion of twelve essays; full treatment of GKC's
> criticism.

John, V.V. "The Chestertonian Style." CATHW, 184 (1957), 369-74.

> Praises, but doesn't really analyze, GKC's prose style.

Jones, W.S. Handley. "G.K. Chesterton and the Discovery of Christianity."
In his THE PRIEST AND THE SIREN AND OTHER LITERARY STUDIES. London:
Epworth, 1953. Pp. 13-29.

> Argues that GKC's religious faith, the "vitalizing root" of his
> thinking, was strongly humanistic.

Kelly, Hugh. "G.K. Chesterton: His Philosophy of Life." STUDIES, 31
(1942), 83-97.

> Compares GKC's style and substance; Kelly concludes that con-
> servative checks are evident.

Kenner, Hugh. PARADOX IN CHESTERTON. New York: Sheed and Ward,
1947.

> Controversial and very important assessment of GKC's achievement.
> Kenner condemns GKC's artistic medium--"he merely did not
> polish what he made"--but praises his Thomist message. Kenner

illuminates GKC's metaphysical side and provides a close analysis of his style.

Las Vergnas, Raymond. CHESTERTON, BELLOC, BARING. Trans. C.C. Martindale. New York: Sheed and Ward, 1938.

> Includes a fifty-page general, appreciative summary of GKC's religion of "good news." Marred by an impressionistic style.

Lea, F.A. "G.K. Chesterton." In MODERN CHRISTIAN REVOLUTIONARIES: AN INTRODUCTION TO THE LIVES AND THOUGHT OF KIERKEGAARD, ERIC GILL, G.K. CHESTERTON, C.F. ANDREWS, AND BERDGAEU. Ed. Donald Attwater. New York: Devin-Adair, 1947. Pp. 89-160.

> Admiring and fairly comprehensive treatment of GKC's character and writings. To Lea, the "first essential fact" about GKC is that "he was one of the last important English men of letters to embrace orthodox Christianity in toto."

_____. THE WILD KNIGHT OF BATTERSEA: G.K. CHESTERTON. Modern Christian Revolutionaries Series. London: Clarke, 1945.

> Brief but intelligent treatment of GKC. Lea admires the fruitful marriage of intellect and imagination in GKC's works.

Leigh, David J. "Chesterton and Modern Drama." RENASCENCE, 28 (1975-76), 171-80.

> Finds the better side of GKC's critical method in his essays on Ibsen and Shaw. Leigh pieces together an appreciative "Chestertonian philosophy of the theater."

Lewis, D.B. Wyndham. "Introduction." In his G.K. CHESTERTON: AN ANTHOLOGY. London: Oxford Univ. Press, 1957. Pp. iii-xxi.

> A useful survey of GKC's career and works.

Lowther, F.H. "G.K. Chesterton: The Man and His Work." LONDON QUARTERLY REVIEW, 168 (1943), 335-41.

> Stresses the importance of religious emotion and the autobiographical strain in GKC's works.

Lunn, Arnold. "G.K. Chesterton." In his ROMAN CONVERTS. London: Chapman and Hall, 1924. Pp. 211-65.

> In HERETICS and ORTHODOXY, GKC proves himself to be a thoughtful critic of modern ideas and various religious creeds. However, Lunn concludes that GKC's argument for Catholic doctrine is not fully convincing.

McCarthy, John P. "The Edwardian Political Mileau of Chesterbelloc."
CREV, 4 (1978), 219-31.

> A valuable analysis of the social and political climate in which
> GKC formed his opinions.

Macdonald, Gregory. "The Other Face: Chesterton's Later Journalism."
CREV, 1 (1975), 84-99.

> Macdonald offers some controversial clarifications concerning
> GKC's work with G. K.'s WEEKLY.

McLuhan, Marshall. "G. K. Chesterton: A Practical Mystic." DR, 15
(1936), 455-64.

> Balanced appreciation of both GKC's religious ideas and his
> social outlook. Compares his democratic sympathies to those
> of Dickens.

Marie Virginia, Sister. G. K. CHESTERTON'S EVANGEL. New York:
Benziger, 1937.

> Extended, appreciative discussion of GKC's religious convictions,
> with superficial analysis of the works.

MARK TWAIN QUARTERLY, 1 (Spring 1937): Special GKC Memorial Issue.

> Sixteen friends and scholars render appreciative estimates of
> GKC's life and works. Contributors include Frank Swinnerton,
> Alfred Noyes, Patrick Braybrooke, and G. B. Shaw.

Martin, John. "Some Theological Implications of Chesterton's Style." CREV,
5 (1978-79), 121-37.

> Examines various passages from GKC's prose writings and con-
> cludes that just as he believed the Word of God was made
> Flesh, so he tried hard to ensure that the word of man took on
> flesh by becoming "concrete and effective."

Mason, Michael. THE CENTER OF HILARITY. London: Sheed and Ward,
1959.

> Original study which stresses GKC's joie de vivre and sees in
> his works a synthesis of the outlooks and styles of D. H. Lawrence
> and T. S. Eliot.

──────. "In Retrospect: Chesterbelloc." TWENTIETH CENTURY, 177-78,
nos. 1039 and 1040 (1968-69), 84-87.

> General discussion of the important relationship between GKC
> and Belloc.

Masterman, C. F. G.   "G. K. Chesterton: An Appreciation."   BOOKMAN, 16 (1903), 595-97.

    An early and half-appreciative account of GKC as master of paradox, and a true believer.   Concludes that it will be as a poet that GKC will contribute most to literature.

Maurois, Andre.   "G. K. Chesterton."   In his PROPHETS AND POETS. London: Cassell, 1936.   Pp. 141-74.

    Survey of GKC's life and works which stresses the elements of optimism, democracy, and reaction.

Monod, Sylvere.   "1900-1920:   The Age of Chesterton."   DICKENSIAN, 66, (1970), 101-20.

    Admires GKC's courage, determination, and optimism in defending Dickens' reputation during its "leaner years."   Monod demonstrates why GKC was the most important figure in Dickens studies between 1900 and 1920.

Murray, Henry.   "G. K. Chesterton."   BOOKMAN, 38 (1910), 63-69.

    Early critical discussion which offers some perceptive insights concerning GKC's work as an essayist and stylist.

Noyes, Alfred.   "The Centrality of Chesterton."   QR, 291 (1953), 43-50.

    GKC is unique among the moderns because of his romantic rediscovery of the "laws of God and nature."

Orage, Alfred R.   "Mr. G. K. Chesterton."   In his THE ART OF READING. New York: Farrar and Rinehart, 1930.   Pp. 242-45.

    Examines some of GKC's polemical essays and perceives a disparity between form and content: GKC's clever style is sometimes inappropriate to his topic.

Pearson, Hesketh.   "G. K. Chesterton and Hilaire Belloc."   Snapshots of My Senior Series.   LISTENER, 55 (1956), 886-87.

    Anecdotal sketch of the important literary relationship of the two men.

Petitpas, Harold M.   "Chesterton's Metapoetics."   RENASCENCE, 23 (1971), 137-44.

    An attempt to assess GKC's contribution to poetic theory which unfortunately leads the reader through a forest of jargon.

Pfleger, Karl. "Chesterton, The Adventurer of Orthodoxy." In his WRESTLERS WITH CHRIST. Trans. E. I. Watkin. New York: Sheed and Ward, 1936. Pp. 159-81.

>Dry sketch of GKC as prophet and defender of a personal form of orthodoxy.

Pritchett, V. S. "Secret Terrors." NEW STATESMAN, 87 (1974), 804-05.

>Admires GKC's DICKENS and other sensible and lively books written in the first decade of his writing career before an "excess of facility swept him out into the sea of print."

Purnell, George. "The Humour of Chesterton." CREV, 2 (1975-76), 1-21.

>A rather pedestrian attempt to classify GKC's humor into nine categories, such as witticisms, analogy, sugarcoating, nonsense, and satire.

Raymond, John. "Jee Kaycee." NEW STATESMAN AND NATION, 53 (1957), 384-85.

>A negative report. Raymond finds GKC's writings to be "homogeneous" and he questions the value of his social prophecy.

Reckitt, Maurice B. "Belloc and Chesterton: The Study of an Impact." In his THE WORLD AND THE FAITH: ESSAYS OF A CHRISTIAN SOCIOLOGIST. London: Faith Press, 1954.

>Compares the two men's personalities and analyzes mutual influences.

_____. "G. K. Chesterton: A Christian Prophet for England Today." In his THE WORLD AND THE FAITH: ESSAYS OF A CHRISTIAN SOCIOLOGIST. London: Faith Press, 1954.

>Thoughtful discussion of problems of the time and GKC's solutions for them.

Schmude, Karl G. THE MAN WHO WAS CHESTERTON: A CENTENARY ESSAY 1874-1974. Melbourne: CTS Publications, 1974.

>A fairly comprehensive survey of GKC's life and works, with some attention to the critical reception.

Scott, William T. "Chesterton as Writer and Critic; Chesterton as a Religious Writer." In his CHESTERTON AND OTHER ESSAYS. Cincinnati: Jennings and Graham, 1912. Pp. 11-39, 43-75.

>Early, appreciative commentary on GKC as Christian apologist with a pugnacious personality.

G.K. Chesterton

Sewell, Elizabeth. "G.K. Chesterton: The Giant Upside-Down." THOUGHT, 30 (1955), 555-76.

> Attempts to describe the "darker," decadent side of GKC.

Shaw, G.B. "The Case against Chesterton." NEW STATESMAN (13 May 1916), 133-36.

> A rather rambling essay in which Shaw uses various examples to show how GKC "compromises himself" both as an anti-Modernist and an anti-Socialist.

―――. PEN PORTRAITS AND REVIEWS. London: Constable, 1932.

> Collects four witty reviews and commentaries on GKC's studies of Shaw and Shavian issues.

Sheed, Wilfrid. "Introduction." In his GKC's ESSAYS AND POEMS. Baltimore: Penguin, 1958. Pp. 9-20.

> Praises GKC as a prose writer who has original ideas and a lively style.

Slosson, Edwin E. "G.K. Chesterton." In his SIX MAJOR PROPHETS. Boston: Little, Brown, 1917. Pp. 129-89.

> General and unsympathetic survey of GKC's philosophical views and defenses of orthodoxy.

Sprug, Joseph W., ed. AN INDEX TO G.K. CHESTERTON. Washington, D.C.: Catholic Univ. Press, 1966.

> A curious and comprehensive subject index of GKC's ideas as contained in almost one hundred books and other writings. Of value to concordance aficionados.

Sullivan, John, ed. G.K. CHESTERTON: A CENTENARY APPRAISAL. New York: Barnes and Noble, 1974.

> Excellent collection of fourteen essays by such distinguished scholars as Dudley Barker, Ian Boyd, Dorothy Collins, P.B. Furbank, and John Sullivan. The essays treat GKC's personality, writings, and critical reputation.

Versfeld, M. "Chesterton and St. Thomas." ESA, 4 (1961), 128-46.

> Superficial explanation of GKC's Thomistic "vision of reality" and the importance of the "image" as a cornerstone for the two men's philosophies.

Ward, Leo R. "The Innocence of G.K. Chesterton." MODA, 19 (1975), 146-56.

> Appreciative commentary upon GKC's orthodox writings.

Ward, Wilfrid P. "Mr. Chesterton among the Prophets." In his MEN AND MATTERS. London: Longmans, 1914. Pp. 105-44.

> Discusses ORTHODOXY in detail and ranks GKC's thinking with Burke's and Coleridge's. Concludes that GKC is a serious and important writer.

Waring, Hubert. "G.K. Chesterton: Prince of Essayists." FORTNIGHTLY REVIEW, N.S. 142 (1937), 588-95.

> General estimate of GKC's accomplishments as an essayist. GKC's propagandistic outlook mars his stories but enhances the value of his essays.

West, Julius. G.K. CHESTERTON: A CRITICAL STUDY. London: Secker, 1915.

> West appreciates the high quality of GKC's prose style, but condemns his political and religious views. A biased study to be used with appropriate care.

White, Albert C. [Alan Handsacre]. AUTHORDOXY: BEING A DISCURSIVE EXAMINATION OF MR. G.K. CHESTERTON'S ORTHODOXY. London: Lane, 1921.

> One of the unconverted responds point-by-point to GKC's arguments in ORTHODOXY. Fair, if argumentative.

Wills, Garry. CHESTERTON: MAN AND MASK. New York: Sheed and Ward, 1961.

> A dense and sometimes confusing study which focuses on the psychological conflict between realism and solipsism in GKC's outlook. The conclusion that GKC adopted various "masks" throughout his career is not convincing.

Wilson, Edmund. "Meetings with Max Beerbohm." ENCOUNTER, 21 (1963), 16-22.

> Calls GKC's prose style "mechanical and monotonous."

CYRIL CONNOLLY (1903-74)

NONFICTIONAL PROSE

THE CONDEMNED PLAYGROUND: ESSAYS 1927-1944. London: Routledge, 1945. New York: Macmillan, 1946.

> A collection of thirty-six pieces on literature and travel, most written during the thirties. It contains a series of parodies: "Ninety Years of Novel-Reviewing" satirizes the cliches of reviewers; "Told in Gath" lampoons Huxley.

ENEMIES OF PROMISE. London: Routledge, 1935. Boston: Little, Brown, 1939.

> CC's first nonfiction work, a fascinating conglomeration of literary criticism and autobiography of his years at Eton. Part 1 discusses "Mandarin" literary style (e.g., James) threatened by the "new vernacular" (e.g., Lawrence). Part 2 examines causes for the failure of modern authorial careers, such as the lures of journalism and politics. While retailing the usual public school horrors, part 3 attributes CC's sense of personal failure to the "romantic" attitudes engendered at Eton, unfitting him for practical success.

THE EVENING COLONNADE. London: Bruce and Watson, 1973. New York: Harcourt, 1975.

> CC's final collection, similar to PREVIOUS CONVICTIONS in scope and arrangement, consisting of essays from the sixties. There are numerous pieces on the moderns, including Genet, Mailer, Lowell, and Ian Fleming.

IDEAS AND PLACES. London: Weidenfeld and Nicolson; New York. Harper, 1953.

> Mostly a collection of numerous editorials from CC's journal HORIZON from D-Day to 1949. Many deal with the economic problems of authorship and the antihumanist environment of the cold war.

THE MODERN MOVEMENT: ONE HUNDRED KEY BOOKS FROM ENGLAND, FRANCE AND AMERICA, 1880-1950. London: Deutsch, 1965. New York: Atheneum, 1966.

> Conceiving of modernism as combining Enlightenment clarity and irony with Romantic sensibility, CC lists his one hundred most important books, with brief evaluative comments on each.

LES PAVILLONS: FRENCH PAVILIONS OF THE EIGHTEENTH CENTURY. London: Hamilton; New York: Macmillan, 1962.

> Treats thirty-nine "garden houses," with pictures by Jerome Zerbe. CC contributes a learned introduction and prefaces to each house.

PREVIOUS CONVICTIONS. London: Hamilton; New York: Harper, 1963.

> A collection of numerous brief essays, most from the SUNDAY TIMES after 1950. Part 1 consists of travel essays and essays on animals (a life-long love). Part 2 has essays on British eighteenth-century literature and French nineteenth-century literature. Part 3, treating modernist literature, includes two or more essays on Wilde, Lawrence, Joyce, Hemingway, and Fitzgerald. Part 4 consists of humorous satires, including send-ups of the beat generation and James Bond.

THE UNQUIET GRAVE: A WORD CYCLE. London: Curwen Press, 1944. New York: Harper, 1945.

> CC's best-known book, a collection of musings on life with appropriate quotations from classical authors (western and eastern) up to moderns such as Eliot and Hemingway. It addresses the modernist sense of angst and bemoans the eternal dualism of the human condition: man torn between passion and reason, the desires for individualism and community. It was issued under the pseudonym "Palinurus," Aeneas' unlucky helmsman, who, analyzed as possessing the "will-to-failure," constitutes CC's self-image.

BIOGRAPHY

ADAM INTERNATIONAL REVIEW, 39, Nos. 385-90 (1974-75).

> A memorial number on CC, collecting over twenty brief pieces on his life and writing. Those by A.E. Ellis, G.S. Fraser, T.S. Matthews, Alan Pryce-Jones, and Denys Sutton are listed separately.

Ellis, A.E. "Te Palinure Petens." ADAM, 39, Nos. 385-90 (1974-75), 40-49.

Cyril Connolly

    An acquaintance provides anecdotal vignettes about an "eighteenth century aphorist" in a pessimistic age.

Fraser, G. S. "On Not Knowing Cyril Connolly." ADAM, 39, Nos. 385-90 (1974-75), 68-73.

    Judges CC's true gift to be criticism.

Lambert, J. W. "To Hell with Masterpieces." ENCOUNTER, 44, No. 5 (1975), 82-89.

    A colleague's memories of CC as a reviewer for the SUNDAY TIMES.

Lehmann, John. "Friend of Promise." ENCOUNTER, 44, No. 5 (1975), 79-82.

    Reviews CC's career in light of the idea that he never found his proper literary form.

Matthews, T. S. "A Note on Cyril and Edmund." ADAM, 39, Nos. 385-90 (1974-75), 76-79.

    Compares CC's personality with Edmund Wilson's to the advantage of neither.

Pryce-Jones, Alan. "A Socratic Elder." ADAM, 39, Nos. 385-90 (1974-75), 23-26.

    Discusses CC as an upholder of the first-rate in life and letters.

Quennell, Peter. "Cyril Connolly." ENCOUNTER, 44, No. 5 (1975), 77-79.

    A balanced sketch of CC's personality, noting the tensions in it between romanticism and classicism, the fear of insecurity and the need to engender it.

Spender, Stephen. CYRIL CONNOLLY. Edinburgh: Tragara Press, 1978.

    A fifteen-page obituary, emphasizing CC's comic capacity.

Sutton, Denys. "The Discerning Judge of the Arts." ADAM, 39, Nos. 385-90 (1974-75), 49-51.

    Emphasizes CC's eighteenth-century personality in connection with LES PAVILLONS.

Wain, John. "Lost Horizons?" ENCOUNTER, 16, No. 1 (1961), 66-71.

    CC's persona is that of the failed writer. His "oversated" Etonian sensibility leads him to undervalue contemporary letters.

CRITICISM

Ewart, Gavin. "Cyril Connolly." LONDON MAGAZINE, 3, No. 9 (1963), 35-50.

> A useful, chronologically arranged survey of CC's works, emphasizing his wit and his Francophile tendency.

Lienhardt, R. G. "From Playground to Grave." SCRUTINY, 13 (1945), 224-29.

> An antagonistic review of UNQUIET GRAVE and CONDEMNED PLAYGROUND that finds CC's style too Paterian and his criticism uninformed by objective, defined values.

Wilson, Edmund. "A Cry from THE UNQUIET GRAVE." In his CLASSICS AND COMMERCIALS: A LITERARY CHRONICLE OF THE FORTIES. New York: Farrar, Straus, 1950. Pp. 280-85.

> Admiring reviews of THE UNQUIET GRAVE and CONDEMNED PLAYGROUND. CC's lack of engagement with his time is defended.

JOSEPH CONRAD (1857-1924)

The Heinemann edition (London: Heinemann, 1921-27), the "Uniform Edition" (London: Dent, 1923-28), the "Medallion Edition" (London: Gresham, 1925), and the "Memorial Edition" (Garden City, N.Y.: Doubleday, 1925) all contain PERSONAL RECORD, MIRROR OF THE SEA, and NOTES ON LIFE AND LETTERS.

NONFICTIONAL PROSE

THE MIRROR OF THE SEA: MEMOIRS AND IMPRESSIONS. London: Methuen; New York: Harper, 1906.

> A vivid memoir of JC's experiences at sea, addressing such topics as prevailing winds, the London docks, and types of commanders. The volume also depicts JC's introduction to the sinister quality of the ocean in a youthful rescue attempt and contains a long, exciting narrative about his gun-running activities for the Carlist cause.

NOTES ON LIFE AND LETTERS. London: Dent; Garden City, N.Y.: Doubleday, 1921.

> A collection of thirteen essays on "Letters" and thirteen on "Life," written throughout JC's career. Of special note are brief pieces on James and Crane and the long essay "Autocracy and War" (1905) which discusses with remarkable foresight the approaching conflagration in Russia specifically and Europe generally.

A PERSONAL RECORD. New York: Harper, 1912. As SOME REMINISCENCES. London: Nash, 1912.

> A series of vignettes from JC's past, based mainly on his Polish and maritime experiences, but also containing a few interesting passages on his early reading. The theme of the volume is fidelity: JC depicts his abandonment of Poland and his heroic ancestors for other loyalties to the sea and to fiction.

WORKS EDITED BY OTHERS

CONGO DIARY: AND OTHER UNCOLLECTED PIECES. Ed. Zdzislaw Najder. Garden City, N.Y.: Doubleday, 1978.

> Contains "all of Joseph Conrad's writings intended for publication" hitherto uncollected. This includes very minor pieces of nonfiction and the "Up-River Book," JC's technical notes on the navigation of the Congo River.

"Conrad's Diary." Ed. Richard Curle. YR, 15 (1926), 254-66.

> Prints JC's diary of his Congo experience in 1890. Some of the incidents JC records are used in HEART OF DARKNESS.

CONRAD'S MANIFESTO: PREFACE TO A CAREER. Ed. David R. Smith. Northampton, Mass.: Gehenna Press, 1966.

> A collection of manuscript facsimiles (and transcriptions) of the NIGGER preface in its several versions.

CONRAD'S PREFACES TO HIS WORKS. Ed. Edward Garnett. London: Dent, 1937.

> The most important of these is the preface to THE NIGGER OF THE NARCISSUS, wherein JC expresses his artistic credo.

JOSEPH CONRAD ON FICTION. Ed. Walter F. Wright. Regents Critics Series. Lincoln: Univ. of Nebraska Press, 1964.

> An extremely useful compilation of JC's letters, essays, and prefaces treating the subject.

LAST ESSAYS. Ed. Richard Curle. London: Dent; Garden City, N.Y.: Doubleday, 1926.

> A collection of nineteen pieces, mostly written in JC's last years. It includes a fond, thirty-eight page memoir of Crane, a brief essay on THE RED BADGE OF COURAGE, and "The Congo Diary."

BIBLIOGRAPHY

Beebe, Maurice, comp. "Criticism of Joseph Conrad: A Selected Checklist." MFS, 10 (1964), 81-106.

> Has sections on general studies and studies of individual works.

"Conrad Bibliography: A Continuing Checklist." CONRADIANA, 2 (1969), 135-46. Continued in subsequent volumes.

Arranged alphabetically by author, this is compiled by several hands.

Ehrsam, Theodore G., ed. A BIBLIOGRAPHY OF JOSEPH CONRAD. Metuchen, N.J.: Scarecrow, 1969.

An alphabetically arranged primary and secondary bibliography; the secondary section is not annotated.

Lohf, Kenneth A., and Eugene P. Sheehy, eds. JOSEPH CONRAD AT MID-CENTURY: EDITIONS AND STUDIES, 1895-1955. Minneapolis: Univ. of Minnesota Press, 1957.

Very useful, with both primary and secondary sections.

Teets, Bruce E., and Helmut E. Gerber, eds. JOSEPH CONRAD: AN ANNOTATED BIBLIOGRAPHY OF WRITINGS ABOUT HIM. DeKalb: Northern Illinois Univ. Press, 1971.

A superb secondary bibliography, organized by year rather than by topic.

Wise, Thomas J., ed. A CONRAD LIBRARY: A CATALOGUE OF PRINTED BOOKS, MANUSCRIPTS AND AUTOGRAPH LETTERS BY JOSEPH CONRAD, COLLECTED BY THOMAS JAMES WISE. London: Privately printed, 1928.

Probably the best primary bibliography, but difficult to obtain.

BIOGRAPHY

Baines, Jocelyn. JOSEPH CONRAD: A CRITICAL BIOGRAPHY. New York: McGraw-Hill, 1960.

A major critical biography which contains brief discussions of the nonfictional prose and demonstrates that JC's account in MIRROR of his smuggling operations is romanticized.

Karl, Frederick R. JOSEPH CONRAD: THE THREE LIVES. New York: Farrar, 1979.

A mammoth study of JC's "lives" as a Pole, a seaman, and a writer, which includes factual information on the writing of the nonfiction.

Morf, Gustav. THE POLISH HERITAGE OF JOSEPH CONRAD. New York: Smith, 1930.

A good treatment of JC's Polish experience; Morf cites the political essays on Poland collected in NOTES.

Sherry, Norman. CONRAD'S EASTERN WORLD. Cambridge: The Univ. Press, 1966.

> The most detailed treatment of JC's sea experience; Sherry occasionally cites MIRROR.

CRITICISM

The Preface to THE NIGGER OF THE NARCISSUS is referred to as the Preface in the annotations of this section.

Berthoud, Jacques. JOSEPH CONRAD: THE MAJOR PHASE. Cambridge: The Univ. Press, 1978.

> In chapter 1, Berthoud discusses the relationship between JC's lives as a sailor and author depicted in RECORD; RECORD suggests that the qualities of restraint, solidarity, and fidelity apply to both.

Fleishman, Avrom. CONRAD'S POLITICS: COMMUNITY AND ANARCHY IN THE FICTION OF JOSEPH CONRAD. Baltimore: Johns Hopkins Press, 1967.

> Discusses "Autocracy and War," "Poland Revisited" (NOTES), and other political essays in arguing that JC comes to embrace a social communalism.

Gedder, Gary. "Conrad and the Fine Art of Understanding." DR, 47 (1967-68), 492-503.

> An excellent discussion of JC's "sympathetic imagination" that cites a great deal of the nonfiction.

Goldknopf, David. "What's Wrong with Conrad: Conrad on Conrad." CRITICISM, 10 (1968), 54-64.

> Discerns vague rhetoric and sloppy thought in JC's prefaces.

Gray, Hugh. "Conrad's Political Prophecies." LIFE AND LETTERS TODAY, 24 (1940), 134-39.

> The accuracy of JC's "Autocracy and War" (NOTES) noted by an Englishman in 1940.

Hay, Eloise Knupp. "Conrad's Self-Portraiture." CONRADIANA, 8 (1976), 191-202.

> An examination of the artistry in JC's memoirs, noting, for example, the paralleling of JC with Ulysses in MIRROR and with Quixote in RECORD.

Joseph Conrad

———. "Impressionism Limited." In JOSEPH CONRAD: A COMMEMORATION. Ed. Norman Sherry. London: Macmillan, 1976. Pp. 54-64.

> The Preface indicates that JC rejected impressionism to the extent it dealt with surfaces rather than "the inner truth."

Hervouet, Yves. "Conrad and Anatole France." ARIELE, 1, No. 1 (1970), 84-99.

> Cites passages in NOTES, RECORD, and the preface to CHANCE in demonstrating France's influence on JC.

Higdon, David Leon. "The Text and Context of Conrad's First Critical Essay." In JOSEPH CONRAD: COMMEMORATIVE ESSAYS. Ed. Adam Gillon and Ludwik Krzyzanowski. New York: Astra Books, 1975. Pp. 97-105.

> On the history of the "Author's Note" for ALMAYER'S FOLLY.

Hodges, Robert R. THE DUAL HERITAGE OF JOSEPH CONRAD. The Hague: Mouton, 1967.

> Contains a discussion of "Poland Revisited," "A Note on the Polish Problem," and "The Crime of Partition" (NOTES) pointing out errors of fact and logic.

Joy, Neill R. "Conrad's 'Preface' to THE NIGGER OF THE 'NARCISSUS': The Lost Typescript Recovered." CONRADIANA, 9 (1977), 17-33.

> A detailed account of the Preface's textual evolution.

Karl, Frederick R. "Joseph Conrad's Literary Theory." CRITICISM, 2 (1960), 317-35.

> Cites the Preface, RECORD, and the essays on James and Maupassant (NOTES) in discussing JC's affinities with other literary theorists.

———. A READER'S GUIDE TO JOSEPH CONRAD. Rev. ed. New York: Farrar, 1969.

> Karl, in chapter 1, reviews the Preface, some of the literary essays, and the Author's Notes of the collected edition. Handy.

Kertzer, J.M. "Conrad's Personal Record." UTQ, 44 (1975), 290-303.

> A penetrating analysis of the fictional techniques JC employs in RECORD.

La Bossiere, Camille Rene. "The Eastern Logic of Conrad's ARS POETICA." CONRADIANA, 11 (1979), 267-80.

Employs the Preface and other nonfictional works in arguing JC rejects "western" logic for a subjective "eastern" alliance of contradictions.

Nettels, Elsa. "Conrad and Stephen Crane." CONRADIANA, 10 (1978), 267-83.

Reviews the three Crane essays (NOTES, LAST ESSAYS) in examining Crane's influence on JC.

_____. "James and Conrad on the Art of Fiction." TSLL, 14 (1972), 529-43.

An excellent comparison, which cites JC's nonfictional prose throughout.

Paterson, John. "Joseph Conrad: To Make You See." In his THE NOVEL AS FAITH: THE GOSPEL ACCORDING TO JAMES, HARDY, CONRAD, JOYCE, LAWRENCE AND VIRGINIA WOOLF. Boston: Gambit, 1973. Pp. 69-106.

Cites heavily the major works of nonfictional prose throughout in an excellent explication of JC's belief that the novelist should represent, not preach.

Rose, Alan M. "Conrad and the Sirens of the Decadence." TSLL, 11 (1969), 795-810.

Cites the Preface throughout in noting JC's several affinities (e.g., descriptive impressionism) with the Decadence.

Said, Edward W. JOSEPH CONRAD AND THE FICTION OF AUTOBIOGRAPHY. Cambridge, Mass.: Harvard Univ. Press, 1966.

Contains brief discussions of the autobiographies, and perceives Baudelaire's influence in MIRROR.

Smith, David R. "Conrad's Manifesto: Preface to a Career." In his CONRAD'S MANIFESTO: PREFACE TO A CAREER. Northampton, Mass.: Gehenna Press, 1966. Pp. 47-79.

A lengthy discussion of the writing history of the Preface.

Solomon, Eric. "Chapter VI." In his STEPHEN CRANE IN ENGLAND: A PORTRAIT OF THE ARTIST. Columbus: Ohio State Univ. Press, 1964. Pp. 91-118.

Cites the Crane essays in LAST ESSAYS in discussing the personal and professional relationships between the two authors.

Tarnawski, Wit. "Conrad's A PERSONAL RECORD." CONRADIANA, 1, No. 2 (1969), 55-58.

> A brief discussion of the excusatory manner in which JC describes his abandonment of Poland.

Thomas, Edward. "'Truer than History.'" ARIELE, 1, No. 1 (1970), 65-72.

> We should eschew applying Marxist and Freudian contexts to JC; his nonfictional prose itself is an adequate guide.

Thorburn, David. CONRAD'S ROMANTICISM. New Haven, Conn.: Yale Univ. Press, 1974.

> Thorburn's chapter 3 is a penetrating analysis of RECORD and MIRROR, centering on narrative technique and style. RECORD is less pretentiously romantic than MIRROR.

Watt, Ian. "Conrad's Preface to THE NIGGER OF THE 'NARCISSUS.'" NOVEL, 7 (1974), 101-15.

> A close explication which draws interesting parallels between the Preface and the thoughts of such writers as Wordsworth and Pater. Excellent.

_____. "Joseph Conrad: Alienation and Commitment." In THE ENGLISH MIND: STUDIES IN THE ENGLISH MORALISTS PRESENTED TO BASIL WILLEY. Ed. Hugh Sykes Davies and George Watson. Cambridge: The Univ. Press, 1964. Pp. 257-78.

> Quotes from the Preface and various essays in NOTES (e.g., "Henry James: An Appreciation") in emphasizing JC's "commitment" rather than his "alienation."

Weston, John Howard. "THE NIGGER OF THE 'NARCISSUS' and Its Preface." In THE NIGGER OF THE "NARCISSUS": AN AUTHORITATIVE TEXT, BACKGROUNDS AND SOURCES, REVIEWS AND CRITICISM. Ed. Robert Kimbrough. New York: Norton, 1979. Pp. 339-53.

> An excellent discussion of how the Preface's key conception of "solidarity" does and does not fit NIGGER OF THE "NARCISSUS" and the fiction in general.

Wolfe, Peter. "Conrad's THE MIRROR OF THE SEA: An Assessment." MCNR, 15 (1964), 36-45.

> Review of the basic themes and techniques in the volume.

Worth, George J. "Conrad's Debt to Maupassant in the Preface to THE NIGGER OF THE 'NARCISSUS.'" JEGP, 54 (1955), 700-704.

Similarities between the Preface and Maupassant's preface to PIERRE ET JEAN noted.

Wright, Walter F. "Introduction: Conrad's Critical Perspectives." In his JOSEPH CONRAD ON FICTION. Lincoln: Univ. of Nebraska Press, 1964. Pp. ix-xiv.

A brief overview of JC's prose.

_____. "'The Truth of My Own Sensations.'" MFS, 1, No. 1 (1955), 26-29.

Cites several of the prose works, including the Preface and MIRROR, in discussing JC's treatment of the problem of authorial subjectivity.

Zabel, Morton Dauwen. "Introduction." In his THE MIRROR OF THE SEA AND A PERSONAL RECORD. Garden City, N.Y.: Doubleday, 1960. Pp. ix-xlix.

A lengthy, important discussion of the psychology underlying JC's two autobiographies, of their factual background, and of their relationship with his fiction.

_____. "Introduction to UNDER WESTERN EYES." In CONRAD: A COLLECTION OF CRITICAL ESSAYS. Ed. Marvin Mudrick. Englewood Cliffs, N.J.: Prentice-Hall, 1966. Pp. 111-44.

Briefly summarizes the political essays in NOTES by way of introducing UNDER WESTERN EYES.

NORMAN DOUGLAS (1868-1952)

NONFICTIONAL PROSE

AN ALMANAC. London: Chatto and Windus, 1945.

> Privately printed in Lisbon in 1941, this is a collection of pithy sayings selected from ND's previous books.

ALONE. London: Chapman and Hall, 1921.

> ND's fourth travel book, which depicts a tour of Italy during WWI. Written in parts with almost Laurentian spleen ("Consider well your neighbor, what an imbecile he is"), ND contrasts wartime bureaucracy and militarism with Italian sanity.

BIRDS AND BEASTS OF THE GREEK ANTHOLOGY. London: Chapman and Hall, 1928. New York: Cape, 1929.

> A learned survey of the wild creatures in Greek poetry. First published privately in Florence in 1927.

CAPRI: MATERIALS FOR A DESCRIPTION OF THE ISLAND. Florence: Orioli, 1930.

> The collected edition of nine monographs and an index on Capri issued between 1904 and 1915. The pieces range from the forests of the island to the pirates associated with it.

D.H. LAWRENCE AND MAURICE MAGNUS: A PLEA FOR BETTER MANNERS. Florence: Privately printed, 1924.

> ND's response to D.H. Lawrence's "Introduction" to Maurice Magnus' posthumous MEMOIRS OF THE FOREIGN LEGION.
> In the very introduction to Magnus' book, Lawrence had attacked the American as a cad and had drawn an unfavorable portrait of ND. ND replies that both he and Magnus have been victims of the "novelist's touch," which distorts for the sake of effect.

EXPERIMENTS. London: Chapman and Hall; New York: McBride, 1925.

> A collection of previously published stories and critical articles, including a revised version of D.H. LAWRENCE AND MAURICE MAGNUS. Two of the more interesting praise Charles Doughty for the personality and intellectual curiosity evident in ARABIA DESERTA and Edgar Allan Poe for his analytical powers.

FOOTNOTE ON CAPRI. London: Sidgwick and Jackson, 1952.

> A posthumously published rehash of ND's writings on Capri, with photographs by Islay Lyons.

FOUNTAINS IN THE SAND: RAMBLES AMONG THE OASES OF TUNISIA. London: Secker, 1912.

> ND's second travel book, on the harsh land of Tunisia. The work is highly critical of the fatalistic Arab mentality: "Mahomet is the desert-maker."

HOW ABOUT EUROPE?: SOME FOOTNOTES ON EAST AND WEST. London: Chatto and Windus, 1930. As GOOD-BYE TO WESTERN CULTURE: SOME FOOTNOTES ON EAST AND WEST. New York: Harper, 1930.

> A cantankerous assault on the standardization of Western culture. Evoking the name of Nietzsche (the book is dedicated to Nietzsche's English translator), ND deplores the leveling effect of Christianity, government regulation, mass education, and the like. The volume was privately printed in Florence in 1929.

LATE HARVEST. London: Drummond, 1946.

> This odd volume consists of seventeen brief essays on the writing and publishing history of ND's works, five book reviews written by ND for the ENGLISH REVIEW, and SUMMER ISLANDS.

LONDON STREET GAMES. London: St. Catherine Press, 1916.

> A volume describing the many games of East End children, supposedly in their own words. The book celebrates the inventiveness and individualism of this game playing as opposed to the conforming effect of organized sports.

LOOKING BACK: AN AUTOBIOGRAPHICAL EXCURSION. London: Chatto and Windus; New York: Harcourt, 1933.

> ND's memoirs, supposedly recording the memories evoked from drawing old calling cards at random from a vase. ND speaks openly of his sexual adventures throughout. The sections on Hudson, Lawrence, and Rupert Brooke are of interest.

Norman Douglas

OLD CALABRIA. London: Secker, 1915. New York: Modern Library, 1927.

> ND's third and most diverting travel volume, on southern Italy. It ranges over topics from Milton to the Flying Monk. The presentation is less idealized than in SIREN LAND; nonetheless, the "harshly-vibrant surroundings" induce health.

ONE DAY. Florence: Privately printed, 1929.

> ND musing on THE POETS OF THE GREEK ANTHOLOGY and other matters while overlooking Athens one day.

PANEROS. Florence: Orioli, 1930. As PANEROS: SOME WORDS ON APHRODISIACS AND THE LIKE. London: Chatto and Windus, 1931. New York: McBride, 1932.

> A learned discussion of aphrodisiacs, suitably written in an archaic style. Tiger's testicles, truffles, and many others are examined in turn, but, ND concludes, variety is the finest of all.

SIREN LAND. London: Dent; New York: Dutton, 1911.

> ND's first travel book, inviting the northern reader to the psychological "purgation and readjustment" afforded by Capri and the Sorrentine Peninsula. The narrative ranges widely over the terrain and legends of the region, and includes a learned discussion of the sirens who have come to rest there. Two chapters contrast Tiberius, whose sanity typifies the area, and a masochistic nun of Capri, whose insanity does not.

SUMMER ISLANDS: ISCHIA AND PONZA. London: Desmond Harmsworth; New York: Colophon, 1931.

> This consists of two essays published years previously in the ENGLISH REVIEW. Treats the appearance and legendary history of two volcanic islands off Naples.

THREE OF THEM. London: Chatto and Windus, 1930.

> A collection of three previously published works representing ND's abilities as scientist, fiction writer, and travel writer: "On the Herpetology of the Grand Duchy of Baden" (from the journal ZOOLOGIST, 1894), "Nerinda" (from UNPROFESSIONAL TALES, 1901), and ONE DAY.

TOGETHER. London: Chapman and Hall; New York: McBride, 1923.

> ND's fifth travel book, on a tour of the Tyrol in 1919 where he had grown up. More smiling in tone than ALONE, the book presents a series of vivid portraits of his family and ancestors

and of his own youthful pranks. ND is accompanied by "Mr. R," whose difficulty in learning English is a running gag.

VENUS IN THE KITCHEN. London: Heinemann, 1952. New York: Viking, 1953.

A collection of aphrodisiacal recipes.

WORKS EDITED BY OTHERS

NORMAN DOUGLAS: A SELECTION FROM HIS WORKS. Ed. D.M. Low. London: Chatto and Windus, 1955.

Contains selections from the major travel books, and from LONDON STREET GAMES, EXPERIMENTS, BIRDS AND BEASTS, PANEROS, and LOOKING BACK.

BIBLIOGRAPHY

McDonald, Edward D., ed. A BIBLIOGRAPHY OF THE WRITINGS OF NORMAN DOUGLAS. Philadelphia: Centaur Book Shop, 1927.

Not seen.

Woolf, Cecil, ed. A BIBLIOGRAPHY OF NORMAN DOUGLAS. Soho Bibliographies. London: Rupert Hart-Davis, 1954.

The best primary bibliography, with detailed bibliographic annotations. Woolf has sections on ND's books and pamphlets, contributions to books and pamphlets, contributions to periodicals, and on translations of ND's works.

BIOGRAPHY

Cunard, Nancy. GRAND MAN: MEMORIES OF NORMAN DOUGLAS WITH EXTRACTS FROM HIS LETTERS, AND APPRECIATIONS BY KENNETH MACPHERSON, HAROLD ACTON, ARTHUR JOHNSON, CHARLES DUFF, AND VICTOR CUNARD AND A BIBLIOGRAPHICAL NOTE BY CECIL WOOLF. London: Secker and Warburg, 1954.

A breathless tribute to ND, whom Cunard knew in his later years. The first section is of some use as background to the writings; the last section consists of brief summaries of all the volumes.

FitzGibbon, Constantine. "Norman Douglas: Memoir of an Unwritten Biography." ENCOUNTER, 43, No. 3 (1974), 23-37.

An intimate and amusing piece on ND's life on Capri written by a distant relative and would-be biographer. An episode involving "Muriel Draper" in LOOKING BACK is elucidated.

Holloway, Mark. NORMAN DOUGLAS: A BIOGRAPHY. London: Secker and Warburg, 1976.

The best biography, with detailed information on the writing history and reception of the nonfiction, and some critical commentary as well.

CRITICISM

Aldington, Richard. "Norman Douglas and Calabria." ATLANTIC MONTHLY, 163 (1939), 757-60.

A casually-written tribute to OLD CALABRIA that includes a brief history of the region ND treats.

Davenport, John. "Norman Douglas." TWENTIETH CENTURY, 151 (1952), 359-67.

A pedestrian review of the career.

FitzGibbon, Constantine. NORMAN DOUGLAS: A PICTORIAL RECORD. New York: McBride, 1953.

This contains a straightforward review of the career which mentions all the books and also contains sixteen photographs of ND arranged chronologically.

Flint, R.W. "Norman Douglas." KR, 14 (1952), 660-68.

Judges OLD CALABRIA, LOOKING BACK, SIREN LAND, BIRDS AND BEASTS, ALONE, TOGETHER, FONTAINS IN THE SAND, and PANEROS to be the best efforts of an author whose "literary reputation must remain a small one."

Flory, Evelyn A. "Norman Douglas and the Scientific Spirit." ELT, 14 (1971), 167-77.

A handy review of ND's scientific and quasi-scientific writings. His scientific habits--close observation, for example--are reflected in the travel books.

Fraser, Keath. "Norman Douglas and D.H. Lawrence: A Sideshow in Modern Memoirs." DHLR, 9 (1976), 283-95.

A discussion of the bitter squabble between ND and D.H. Lawrence over their mutual parasite, Maurice Magnus. Lawrence drew an

unflattering portrait of Magnus in the "Introduction" to Magnus'
MEMOIRS OF THE FOREIGN LEGION; ND attacked the portrait
as inaccurate in D.H. LAWRENCE AND MAURICE MAGNUS:
A PLEA FOR BETTER MANNERS.

Greenlees, Ian. NORMAN DOUGLAS. Writers and Their Work. London:
Longmans, 1957.

> A glowing appreciation, written by a friend of ND, which
> judges ND to be "the greatest travel writer of his generation."
> Greenlees casually reviews the travel writing and picks OLD
> CALABRIA as the author's best book.

Karl, Frederick R. "Joseph Conrad, Norman Douglas, and the ENGLISH
REVIEW." JML, 2 (1972), 342-56.

> A detailed examination of Conrad's attempts to place ND's
> nonfiction in the ENGLISH REVIEW and elsewhere.

Leary, Lewis. NORMAN DOUGLAS. Columbia Essays on Modern Writers.
New York: Columbia Univ. Press, 1968.

> A brief, useful survey of the career by a scholar less than taken
> with ND.

Lindeman, Ralph D. NORMAN DOUGLAS. Twayne's English Author Series.
New York: Twayne, 1965.

> The best critical book. Chapter 2, on the ideas behind the
> literature, chapter 3, on the techniques of the travel books,
> and chapter 5, on ND's literary style are quite good.

Low, D.M. "Introduction." In his NORMAN DOUGLAS: A SELECTION
FROM HIS WORKS. London: Chatto and Windus, 1955. Pp. 9-24.

> A good, short introduction, especially interesting for its dis-
> cussion of Ouida's influence on ND.

Lynd, Robert. "Mr. Norman Douglas's Dislikes." In his BOOK AND
AUTHORS. London: Cobden-Sanderson, 1922. Pp. 256-62.

> Notes the lively but bitter hatred of people and places in
> ALONE.

McDonald, Edward D. "The Early Work of Norman Douglas." BOOKMAN,
66 (1927), 42-46.

> A useful review of the first unprofessional part of the career,
> including discussion of the zoological articles.

Swan, Michael. "The Living Dead--II: Norman Douglas and the Southern World." LONDON MAGAZINE, 3, No. 6 (1956), 49-55.

> An article discussing ND's rejection of aestheticism in favor of pure rationalism.

Tomlinson, H. M. NORMAN DOUGLAS. London: Chatto and Windus, 1931.

> An appreciation that stresses the travel writing; ND is much better at it than D. H. Lawrence, according to Tomlinson.

Webster, H. T. "Norman Douglas: A Reconsideration." SAQ, 49 (1950), 226-36.

> Protesting the popular view of ND as a novelist (because of SOUTH WIND), Webster praises the nonfiction, which is essentially autobiographical and owes much of its interest to the author's personality. "Norman Douglas may thus be seen as a sort of twentieth-century Samuel Johnson, who is also his own Boswell."

Wheatley, Elizabeth D. "Norman Douglas." SR, 40 (1932), 55-67.

> A balanced review of the career, which praises the mythopoeic style of the nonfiction.

Wilson, Edmund. "The Nietzschean Line." In his THE SHORES OF LIGHT. New York: Farrar, 1952. Pp. 485-91.

> An assault on ND's "diluted and inconsistent Nietzscheanism" (i.e., his antidemocratic attitudes) in HOW ABOUT EUROPE?

T.S. ELIOT (1888-1965)

NONFICTIONAL PROSE

AFTER STRANGE GODS: A PRIMER OF MODERN HERESY. London: Faber; New York: Harcourt, Brace, 1934.

>Essays given as lectures at the University of Virginia in 1933. Because of the controversial nature--including some anti-Semitic statements--TSE requested that this work not be reprinted.

DANTE. London: Faber, 1929.

>Expands a shorter essay of same title in SACRED WOOD. Dante is valued as a pure poet who created an objective world apart from his own personality.

ELIZABETHAN ESSAYS. London: Faber, 1934.

>Collects eleven critical essays on such Elizabethan dramatists as Marlowe, Shakespeare, and Heywood. With the exception of the essay on John Marston, all essays are reprinted from SELECTED ESSAYS (1932).

ESSAYS, ANCIENT AND MODERN. London: Faber; New York: Harcourt, Brace, 1936.

>Collects ten essays, including some previously published. The three essays "Religion and Literature," "Catholicism and International Order," and "Modern Education and the Classics" present TSE's opinions on cultural and religious matters.

EZRA POUND: HIS METRIC AND POETRY. New York: Knopf, 1917.

>An early and brief analysis of Pound's innovative art. Pound himself made corrections and changes on the manuscript.

FOR LANCELOT ANDREWES: ESSAYS ON STYLE AND ORDER. London: Faber and Gwyer, 1928. Garden City, N.Y.: Doubleday, Doran, 1929.

> A collection of eight critical essays, with a preface. The essays on Andrewes, F.H. Bradley, Baudelaire, and Irving Babbitt are important for understanding the development of TSE's own art and ideas.

THE FRONTIERS OF CRITICISM. Minneapolis: Univ. of Minnesota Press, 1956.

> TSE examines the sometimes hostile relationship between authors and critics. Reprinted in ON POETRY AND POETS (1957).

GEORGE HERBERT. Writers and Their Work. London: Longmans, Green, 1962.

> A sympathetic biography of the religious poet.

HOMAGE TO JOHN DRYDEN: THREE ESSAYS ON POETRY OF THE SEVENTEENTH CENTURY. London: Hogarth, 1924.

> Significant positive revaluations of the poetry of John Dryden, Andrew Marvell, and several metaphysical poets.

THE IDEA OF A CHRISTIAN SOCIETY. London: Faber, 1939. New York: Harcourt, Brace, 1940.

> TSE outlines his theory of the Christian community. "Guardians" are to lead other members of society to duties and epiphanies.

JOHN DRYDEN: THE POET, THE DRAMATIST, THE CRITIC. New York: Holliday, 1932.

> Three appreciative essays on Dryden's contributions to three genres. TSE values Dryden's poetry for its distinctively English voice, his drama for its techniques, and his criticism for its rational defense of "sanity" in literary works.

KNOWLEDGE AND EXPERIENCE IN THE PHILOSOPHY OF F.H. BRADLEY. London: Faber; New York: Farrar, Straus, 1964.

> TSE's doctoral dissertation for Harvard was completed in 1916 but was published for the first time just before his death. Includes two appendixes on Leibniz.

THE LITERATURE OF POLITICS. London: Conservative Political Centre, 1955.

> Text of a lecture delivered to a conservative political group on 19 April 1955. Reprinted in TO CRITICIZE THE CRITIC AND OTHER WRITINGS (1965).

T.S. Eliot

NOTES TOWARDS THE DEFINITION OF CULTURE. London: Faber, 1948. New York: Harcourt, Brace, 1949.

> Six chapters, with introductory and concluding material. TSE provides important definitions of culture, class, and education and explores the relationships between culture, religion, and politics in the Western world.

ON POETRY AND POETS. London: Faber; New York: Farrar, Straus and Cudahy, 1957.

> Important collection of sixteen critical essays on such figures as Virgil, Davies, Milton, Johnson, and Yeats. Other essays provide stimulating discussions of such topics as poetry's social function, minor poetry, a classic, and the like.

POETRY AND DRAMA. London: Faber; Cambridge, Mass.: Harvard Univ. Press, 1951.

> A brief discussion of the aims and purposes of poetic drama.

THE SACRED WOOD: ESSAYS ON POETRY AND CRITICISM. London: Methuen, 1920. New York: Knopf, 1921.

> TSE's first collection includes eighteen critical essays of original and important significance. Besides "Tradition and the Individual Talent," the essays on Swinburne, Marlowe, Hamlet, Blake, and Dante have become classics.

SELECTED ESSAYS, 1917-1932. London: Faber; New York: Harcourt, Brace, 1932.

> Selects TSE's choice prose up to 1932. The more important of the thirty-two critical essays included are: "Tradition and the Individual Talent," "The Function of Criticism," as well as original and sometimes controversial assessments of the works of Marlowe, Shakespeare, Swinburne, Arnold, Pater, and several Renaissance poets and dramatists. A subsequent edition with the addition of four essays was issued in 1950.

THOUGHTS AFTER LAMBETH. London: Faber, 1931.

> TSE explains the need for the Christian church to save the fallen world. Reprinted in SELECTED ESSAYS, 1932.

THE THREE VOICES OF POETRY. Cambridge: The Univ. Press, 1953. New York: Cambridge Univ. Press, 1954.

> Offers three classifications of poetry: 1) "the poet talking to himself or to nobody"; 2) "the poet addressing an audience"; 3) "the poet when he attempts to create a dramatic character speaking in verse."

T.S. Eliot

TO CRITICIZE THE CRITIC AND OTHER WRITINGS. London: Faber; New York: Farrar, Straus and Giroux, 1965.

> Reprints nine studies, all published between 1917 and 1961. Some topics discussed include: American literature and language, the aims of education, vers libre, and political thinking.

THE USE OF POETRY AND THE USE OF CRITICISM: STUDIES IN THE RELATION OF CRITICISM TO POETRY IN ENGLAND. London: Faber; Cambridge, Mass.: Harvard Univ. Press, 1933.

> Essays given as the Charles Eliot Norton Lectures at Harvard University, 1932-33. In addition to an introduction and conclusion, the book contains six important essays on the Countess of Pembroke, Dryden, Wordsworth and Coleridge, Shelley and Keats, Matthew Arnold, and the modern mind. TSE's central theme is that while the exact use and value of poetry cannot be determined, it cannot serve as a substitute for religion.

WHAT IS A CLASSIC? London: Faber, 1945.

> Defines a classic in terms of realizing fully a language's potentials despite its limitations. Virgil is a true classic. Reprinted in ON POETRY AND POETS (1957).

WORKS EDITED BY OTHERS

POINTS OF VIEW. Ed. John Hayward. London: Faber, 1941.

> Reprints selections--with TSE's approval--from his critical writings. The book serves as an introduction to TSE's work in prose and Hayward supplies titles, sources, and dates for the various selections.

SELECTED PROSE. Ed. John Hayward. London and Baltimore: Penguin, 1953.

> Hayward divides selected prose writings by TSE into two categories: literary and social criticism. The essays on vers libre, Virgil, Dante, and Yeats are published here for the first time in book form.

SELECTED PROSE OF T.S. ELIOT. Ed. Frank Kermode. New York: Harcourt, Farrar; London: Faber, 1975.

> Selects thirty-one of TSE's essays (some are extracts) and arranges them chronologically into three groups: "Essays of Generalization," "Appreciations of Individual Authors," and "Social and Religious Criticism."

BIBLIOGRAPHY

Canary, Robert H. T.S. ELIOT: THE POET AND HIS CRITICS. Chicago: American Library Association, 1982.

    Chapter 3, "The Social Critic," surveys critical commentary on TSE's social writings.

Eames, Elizabeth R., and Alan M. Cohn, comps. "Some Early Reviews by T.S. Eliot." PBSA, 70 (1976), 420-24.

    Addenda to Gallup.

Frank, Mechthild, Armin Paul Frank, and K.P.S. Jochum, comps. T.S. ELIOT CRITICISM IN ENGLISH, 1916-1965: A SUPPLEMENTARY BIBLIOGRAPHY. Edmonton, Canada: Yeats Eliot Review, 1978. (YER Monog. 1.)

    A supplement to Martin which adds 1,300 items in chronological order. Includes a range of items written in English on TSE's work and life--from anecdotes and parodies to books and articles. Items are annotated sporadically and many items listed are of extremely minor significance.

Fry, Varian, comp. "A Bibliography of the Writings of Thomas Stearns Eliot." THE HOUND AND HORN, 1 (1928), 214-18; 320-24.

    An early list.

Gallup, Donald, ed. T.S. ELIOT: A BIBLIOGRAPHY. Rev. ed. London: Faber, 1969.

    A complete listing of all editions of books and pamphlets by TSE as well as his contributions to periodicals and translations of his works into foreign languages. The authoritative primary bibliography.

Gunter, Bradley. THE MERRILL CHECKLIST OF T.S. ELIOT. Columbus, Ohio: Merrill, 1970.

    A handy selective guide for students which lists TSE's major book publications and important secondary works.

Ludwig, Richard M. "T.S. Eliot." In SIXTEEN MODERN AMERICAN AUTHORS. Ed. Jackson R. Bryer. New York: Norton, 1973.

    An excellent survey article which describes fairly and accurately the trends in TSE research and criticism from 1916 to 1972.

Martin, Mildred. A HALF-CENTURY OF ELIOT CRITICISM: AN ANNOTATED BIBLIOGRAPHY OF BOOKS AND ARTICLES IN ENGLISH, 1916-1965. Lewisburg, Pa.: Bucknell Univ. Press, 1972.

> Very useful for writings on TSE through 1965. Includes a full listing in chronological order of criticism in English, cogent annotations for almost all entries, and convenient cross-indexes by subject, author, and title.

Ricks, Beatrice, comp. T.S. ELIOT: A BIBLIOGRAPHY OF SECONDARY WORKS. Metuchen, N.J.: Scarecrow, 1980.

> Useful compilation which divides works about TSE into three divisions: drama, poetry, and criticism. There is also an extensive general criticism section. Annotations or brief quotations given only in the interest of title clarification. Includes convenient indexes of topics and critics.

Tate, Allen. "Thomas Stearns Eliot." In his SIXTY AMERICAN POETS, 1896-1944. Washington, D.C.: Library of Congress, 1954. Pp. 24-39, 153-54.

> Lists TSE's publications and selected books about him.

Unger, Leonard, ed. T.S. ELIOT: A SELECTED CRITIQUE. New York: Rinehart, 1948.

> Contains an excellent bibliography of writings about TSE's works to 1948.

BIOGRAPHY

Bergonzi, Bernard. T.S. ELIOT. Masters of World Literature. New York: Macmillan, 1972.

> A concise critical biography, which concentrates on the public details of TSE's literary career. Bergonzi does not discuss TSE's private life nor does he use the poetry "as material for a biography." Includes brief discussions of "Dante," FOR LANCELOT ANDREWES, HAMLET, HOMAGE TO JOHN DRYDEN, and IDEA OF A CHRISTIAN SOCIETY.

Gordon, Lyndall. ELIOT'S EARLY YEARS. New York: Oxford Univ. Press, 1977.

> This is the best look at TSE's early years (some biography, some criticism), but it dwells too much on the idea of a religious epiphany in his life and works.

Howarth, Herbert. NOTES ON SOME FIGURES BEHIND T.S. ELIOT. Boston: Houghton Mifflin, 1964.

> Critical biography which presents a mosaic of figures who influenced TSE's intellectual development and taste through World War II. Discusses IDEA OF CHRISTIAN SOCIETY.

Montgomery, Marion. "Eliot's Autobiography." ILLINOIS QUARTERLY, 37, No. 2 (1974), 57-64.

    Interesting discussion of the problems involved in viewing SELECTED ESSAYS and later criticism as TSE's autobiography.

Sencourt, Robert. T.S. ELIOT: A MEMOIR. Ed. Donald Adamson. New York: Dodd, Mead, 1971.

    TSE from the perspective of a fellow expatriate who influenced TSE's conversion to Anglicanism and his ideas on metaphysical literature. The recollections and impressions, though an interesting tribute, do not add up to a biography. Includes brief treatment of TSE as critic and reviewer.

Spender, Stephen. T.S. ELIOT. Modern Masters. London: Fontana, 1975.

    An insightful blend of biography and literary criticism by a man of letters who knew TSE. The chapters on "Poet-Critic, Critic-Poet," "Ideas of Poetry," and "Politics" are especially helpful for understanding TSE's literary and social criticism.

Tate, Allen, ed. T.S. ELIOT: THE MAN AND HIS WORK. London: Chatto and Windus, 1967.

    Includes many memoirs and reminiscences with some discussion of his work and critical reputation.

CRITICISM

Acton, H.B. "Discussion: Religion, Culture, and Class." ETHICS, 60 (1950), 120-30.

    Observes contradictions in TSE's social theories as outlined in NOTES TOWARDS THE DEFINITION OF CULTURE.

Aiken, Conrad. "Mr. Eliot in the Wilderness." NR, 88 (1936), 326-37.

    Harsh analysis of ESSAYS ANCIENT AND MODERN. Aiken objects to the melancholy and religious strains in the essays.

_____. "Retreat." DIAL, 86 (1929), 628-30.

    Harsh attack on TSE's ideas as expressed in FOR LANCELOT ANDREWES. Aiken maintains that TSE "seeks a refuge from humanity in Grace, from personality in dogma, and from the present in the past."

_____. "The Scientific Critic." FREEMAN, 2 (1921), 593-94.

    Questions the promises of SACRED WOOD; insightful in drawing the lines for later critical discussion of the collection of essays.

Aldington, Richard. "A Critic of Poetry." POETRY, 17 (1921), 345-48.

    High praise for SACRED WOOD, which shows TSE's classicism, intelligence, and realism at its best.

_____. "Mr. Eliot on Seneca." NATION AND ATHENAEUM, 42 (1927), 159.

    Aldington comments on TSE's critical approach and specifically examines his scholarship on the Elizabethan's use of Seneca.

Allan, Mowbray. T.S. ELIOT'S IMPERSONAL THEORY OF POETRY. Lewisburg, Pa.: Bucknell Univ. Press, 1974.

    Examines the influence on TSE's poetry of his critical ideas. Concludes that "much of Eliot's critical thought was derived from the idealist theory of knowledge," and his critical practice is "an effort to escape" from the Romantic tradition.

Antrim, Harry T. T.S. ELIOT'S CONCEPT OF LANGUAGE: A STUDY OF ITS DEVELOPMENT. Gainesville: Univ. of Florida Press, 1971.

    Traces the process of TSE's triumph over his Romantic inheritance in his essays, poetry, and drama. The major movement is "from irony to contemplation."

Austin, Allen. T.S. ELIOT: THE LITERARY AND SOCIAL CRITICISM. Bloomington: Indiana Univ. Press, 1971.

    Discusses HAMLET, IDEA OF A CHRISTIAN SOCIETY, KNOWLEDGE AND EXPERIENCE, NOTES TOWARD THE DEFINITION OF CULTURE, and SACRED WOOD.

_____. "T.S. Eliot's Objective Correlative." UKCR, 26 (1959), 133-40.

    Explains that the term must be related to a character's emotional motivations.

_____. "T.S. Eliot's Theory of Dissociation." CE, 23 (1962), 309-12.

    Intelligent discussion of TSE's critical term "dissociation of sensibility."

_____. "T.S. Eliot's Theory of Personal Expression." PMLA, 81 (1966), 303-07.

A brief essay on TSE's theories concerning the impersonality of the poet. Austin believes TSE's theory is "one of indirect personal expression" in a given poem.

Bantock, G.H. T.S. ELIOT AND EDUCATION. London: Faber, 1970.

An introduction to TSE's ideas on education, culture, and society that is intended "primarily for students." Extensive quotations from TSE's works in order to demonstrate clearly their "unconventionality."

_____. "T.S. Eliot's View of Society." CRITQ, 15 (1973), 37-46.

Relates TSE's social criticism to the themes of individual identity and social equality.

Barfoot, Gabriella. "Dante in T.S. Eliot's Criticism." EM, 23 (1972), 231-46.

Praises TSE's "insights" into Dante in SACRED WOOD.

Barrett, William. "Aristocracy and/or Christianity." KR, 11 (1949), 489-96.

Finds TSE's positions in NOTES TOWARDS THE DEFINITION OF CULTURE to be not very well thought out.

Bateson, F.W. "Criticism's Lost Leader." In THE LITERARY CRITICISM OF T.S. ELIOT: NEW ESSAYS. Ed. David Newton-De Molina. London: Athlone, 1977. Pp. 1-19.

Discusses the implications and reception of the shift from "diffused scepticism" in TSE's early criticism to the moral "humility" and "general social surrender" of his later criticism. Bateson compares TSE's development to Wordsworth's decline of powers.

Belgion, Montgomery. "In Memory of T.E. Hulme." SATR, 4 (1927), 154-55.

Brief but illuminating discussion which relates the philosophies of Hulme and TSE.

Blackmur, R.P. "The Dangers of Authorship." HOUND AND HORN, 7 (1934), 719-26.

Examines AFTER STRANGE GODS and deplores TSE's use of the litmus test of Christianity for judging literature.

_____. "In the Hope of Straightening Things Out." KR, 13 (1951), 303-14.

An interesting attempt to discover the coherence of TSE's criticism by relating it to his overall personality. Discussion focuses on TRADITION AND THE INDIVIDUAL TALENT.

———. "It Is Later Than He Thinks." In his THE EXPENSE OF GREATNESS. New York: Arrow, 1940. Pp. 239-44.

> Brief discussion of TSE's ideas in IDEA OF A CHRISTIAN SOCIETY.

———. "T.S. Eliot." HOUND AND HORN, 1 (1928), 291-319.

> Discusses TSE's work as a critic and stresses his intellectual as opposed to emotional interest in literature.

———. "T.S. Eliot in Prose." POETRY, 42 (1933), 44-49.

> Praises TSE's original and intelligent ideas in JOHN DRYDEN and SELECTED ESSAYS 1917-1932. Blackmur pleads for an objective judgment of the writings, devoid of TSE's religious convictions.

Blackmur, R.P., et al. "Mr. Eliot and Notions of Culture: A Discussion." PR, 11 (1944), 302-12.

> Four critics analyze and attack TSE's NOTES TOWARDS THE DEFINITION OF CULTURE from various perspectives.

Blissett, William. "Pater and Eliot." UTQ, 22 (1953), 261-68.

> Attempts to explain TSE's belittling of Pater in the essay "Arnold and Pater" (SELECTED ESSAYS) in terms of the maturation of TSE's tastes.

Bolgan, Anne C. "The Philosophy of F.H. Bradley and the Mind and Art of T.S. Eliot: An Introduction." In ENGLISH LITERATURE AND BRITISH PHILOSOPHY: A COLLECTION OF ESSAYS. Ed. S.P. Rosenbaum. Chicago: Univ. of Chicago Press, 1971. Pp. 251-77.

> A good introductory survey of TSE's accomplishments as philosopher and literary critic.

Bollier, Ernest Philip. "Mr. Eliot's 'Tradition and the Individual Talent' Reconsidered." UNIV. OF COLORADO STUDIES IN LANGUAGE AND LITERATURE, no. 6 (1957), 103-18.

> Reviews TSE's canon in light of the beliefs in his early essay. Interesting study of TSE's growth as a critic.

———. "T.S. Eliot and John Milton: A Problem in Criticism." TSE, 8 (1958), 165-92.

> An intelligent and comprehensive analysis of TSE's attitude toward Milton. Bollier contrasts TSE's treatment of Milton as a composing poet with his reception by the general reading public.

_____. "T.S. Eliot and THE SACRED WOOD." COLORADO QUARTERLY, 8 (1960), 308-17.

> Praises the book as an important classic which fostered new ideas "about the nature of poetry and criticism."

Boyd, John D. "T.S. Eliot as Critic and Rhetorician: The Essay on Jonson." CRITICISM, 11 (1969), 167-82.

> Close analysis of TSE's rhetorical strategies in the Jonson essay: Boyd finds imprecision and contradictions.

Bradbrook, M.C. "Eliot's Critical Method." In T.S. ELIOT, A STUDY OF HIS WRITINGS BY SEVERAL HANDS. Ed. B. Rajan. London: Dobson, 1947. Pp. 119-28.

> Balanced discussion of TSE's criticism and reception over a twenty-five year period.

_____. T.S. ELIOT. Rev. ed. London: Longmans, 1965.

> Includes a chapter on "The Critic and the Man of Letters."

Braybrooke, Neville, ed. T.S. ELIOT: A SYMPOSIUM FOR HIS SEVENTIETH BIRTHDAY. New York: Farrar, 1958.

> Fifty scholars and friends discuss TSE's personality and work from various perspectives. The cluster of essays on "T.S. Eliot as Classical Scholar; Political Writer; Moralist" are especially relevant.

Bredin, Hugh. "T.S. Eliot and Thomistic Scholasticism." JHI, 33 (1972), 299-306.

> Demonstrates how Aquinas influenced TSE as philosopher but not as poet.

Brombert, Victor H. THE CRITICISM OF T.S. ELIOT: PROBLEMS OF AN 'IMPERSONAL THEORY' OF POETRY. New Haven, Conn.: Yale Univ. Press, 1949.

> A forty-two page study which examines the problems of TSE's shifting view of the role of belief in evaluating poetry.

Brooks, Cleanth. "T.S. Eliot: Discourse to the Gentiles." In THE HIDDEN GOD: STUDIES IN HEMINGWAY, FAULKNER, YEATS, ELIOT, AND WARREN. New Haven, Conn.: Yale Univ. Press, 1963. Pp. 68-97.

> Discusses TSE's strategy for writing about Christianity in modern society.

Brown, Wallace Cable. "Mr. Eliot without the Nightingales." UKCR, 14 (1947), 31-38.

> An interesting revaluation of SACRED WOOD.

Buck, Philo M., Jr. "Faith of Our Fathers--T.S. Eliot." In his DIRECTIONS IN CONTEMPORARY LITERATURE. New York: Oxford Univ. Press, 1942. Pp. 261-90.

> Examines TSE's religious views in his essays and poems and compares him with Dante.

Buckley, Vincent. POETRY AND MORALITY: STUDIES ON THE CRITICISM OF MATTHEW ARNOLD, T.S. ELIOT AND F.R. LEAVIS. London: Chatto and Windus, 1959.

> Two chapters discuss the principles of TSE's literary social criticism in AFTER STRANGE GODS, SACRED WOOD, SELECTED ESSAYS, and USE OF POETRY. The two chapters emphasize concepts of order, impersonality, and tradition.

Burke, Kenneth. "The Allies of Humanism Abroad." In THE CRITIQUE OF HUMANISM. Ed. C. Hartley Grattan. New York: Brewer and Warren, 1930. Pp. 183-87.

> Argues that Eliot reconciles the theories of Maurras and Babbitt. Burke raises interesting questions about the functions of religion and humanism in society.

Bush, Douglas. "No Small Program." VQR, 25 (1949), 287-90.

> Offers some favorable commentary and analysis of TSE's ideas and proposals in NOTES TOWARDS THE DEFINITION OF CULTURE.

_____. PARADISE LOST IN OUR TIME: SOME COMMENTS. Ithaca, N.Y.: Cornell Univ. Press, 1945.

> A competent, point-by-point retort, found on pages 8-23, to TSE's criticisms of Milton's style and ideas.

Calverton, V.F. "T.S. Eliot: An Inverted Marxian." MODERN MONTHLY, 8 (1934), 372-73.

> Interesting reading of AFTER STRANGE GODS. Calverton posits that what Marxists call ideology, TSE calls tradition, so that his social theories are inverted accordingly.

Cameron, J.M. "T.S. Eliot as a Political Writer." In T.S. ELIOT: A SYMPOSIUM FOR HIS SEVENTIETH BIRTHDAY. Ed. Neville Braybooke. New York: Farrar, Straus and Cudahy, 1958. Pp. 138-51.

Examines the relationship between Anglicanism and TSE's idea of society.

Carne-Ross, D. S. "T. S. Eliot: Tropheid." ARION, 4 (1965), 5-20.

Good analysis of TSE's use of the classics in his critical and religious writings.

Cattani, Georges. T. S. ELIOT. Trans. Claire Pace and Jean Stewart. London: Merlin Press, 1966.

Chapter 6, "Aesthetics and Criticism, Culture and Christianity," treats TSE's literary and social criticism, but puts an exaggerated emphasis on "a moral preoccupation."

Chace, William M. "T. S. Eliot: The Plea against Consciousness." MOSAIC, 5, No. 1 (1971), 133-43.

Focusing on the central concept of "consciousness," Chace examines TSE's social and political theories in AFTER STRANGE GODS, IDEA OF A CHRISTIAN SOCIETY, and NOTES TOWARDS THE DEFINITION OF CULTURE.

Child, Ruth C. "The Early Critical Work of T. S. Eliot: An Assessment." CE, 12 (1951), 269-75.

Emphasizes TSE's positive and negative influence on the New Criticism as well as his contributions to literary reputations and critical vocabulary.

Collin, W. E. "T. S. Eliot the Critic." SR, 39 (1931), 419-24.

Collin was one of the first to value TSE's penchant for the critical method of rigorous analysis which eschewed impressionistic subjectivism.

Condon, James P. "Notes on T. S. Eliot's 'What Is a Classic?': The Classical Norm and Social Existence." CJ, 73 (1977-78), 176-78.

A brief but intelligent essay. In posing the question TSE aids classical studies; in answering it "he proceeds to offer criteria to the entire literary métier, and . . . to society at large."

Cormican, L. A. "Mr. Eliot and Social Biology." SCRUTINY, 17 (1950), 2-13.

One of the unconverted finds TSE's arguments in NOTES TOWARDS THE DEFINITION OF CULTURE unconvincing and vague.

Cowley, V. J. E. "A Source for T. S. Eliot's 'Objective Correlative.'" RES, 26 (1975), 320-21.

Suggests the source of the term is one of John Henry Newman's sermons (1839).

Crewe, J.V. "T.S. Eliot: A Metaphysical Problem." ESA, 15, No. 2 (1972), 105-14.

Discusses TSE's THE METAPHYSICAL POETS.

Czamanske, Palmer, and Karl Hertz. "The Beginning of T.S. Eliot's Theory of Culture." CRESSET, 15 (1952), 9-21.

An interesting study which demonstrates roots of NOTES TOWARDS THE DEFINITION OF CULTURE in TSE's early essays.

Daniells, J.R. "T.S. Eliot and His Relation to T.E. Hulme." UTQ, 2 (1933), 380-96.

Clear analysis of TSE's ideas in relation to Hulme's.

Davie, Donald. "Anglican Eliot." SORA, N.S. 9 (1973), 93-104.

Argues the significance of TSE's alliance with the nonintellectual "British Establishment." Refers to IDEA OF A CHRISTIAN SOCIETY.

Davis, Robert Gorham. "The New Criticism and the Democratic Tradition." ASCH, 19 (1949), 9-19.

Famous inflammatory essay which aligns TSE and the New Criticism against democracy.

Dawson, Christopher. "Mr. T.S. Eliot on the Meaning of Culture." MONTH, N.S. 1 (1949), 151-57.

Dawson agrees with TSE's perspective in NOTES TOWARDS THE DEFINITION OF CULTURE and provides some important comparisons between TSE's and Matthew Arnold's definitions of culture.

DeLaura, David J. "Pater and Eliot: The Origin of the Objective Correlative." MLQ, 26 (1965), 426-31.

Explains the critical terms and demonstrates how the two critics embody opposite approaches in the practice of literary criticism (Pater, subjective; TSE objective).

_____. "The Place of the Classics in T.S. Eliot's Christian Humanism." In HEREDITAS: SOME ESSAYS IN THE MODERN EXPERIENCE OF THE CLASSICAL. Ed. Frederick Will. Austin: Univ. of Texas Press, 1964. Pp. 153-97.

A valuable and broad-based study of TSE's views concerning

the place of the classics, religion, and humanism in modern civilization.

Dobrée, Bonamy. "The Present Century." In his ENGLISH ESSAYISTS. London: Collins, 1946. Pp. 44-46.

> Describes TSE's prose style as a conflation of Bacon's and Montaigne's.

Donoghue, Denis. "Eliot and the CRITERION." In THE LITERARY CRITICISM OF T.S. ELIOT. Ed. David Newton-De Molina. London: Athlone, 1977. Pp. 20-41.

> Argues that TSE's aim in the CRITERION was to stress European tradition and to attack "native provincialism." The article examines some of TSE's prose contributions and explains why the journal failed.

Duffy, John J. "T.S. Eliot's Objective Correlative: A New England Commonplace." NEQ, 42 (1969), 108-15.

> Examines the use of the term in nineteenth-century New England by Washington Allston, James Marshall, and others.

Duncan, Joseph Ellis. "Eliot and the Twentieth Century Revival." In his THE REVIVAL OF METAPHYSICAL POETRY. Minneapolis: Univ. of Minnesota Press, 1959. Pp. 143-64.

> A scholarly analysis of the relationship between TSE's criticism and the revaluation of metaphysical poetry. Points out that TSE's essays in THE METAPHYSICAL POETS were "often not clearly understood but seldom doubted" by his admirers.

Ellis, P.G. "The Development of T.S. Eliot's Historical Sense." RES, 23 (1972), 291-301.

> This revaluation focuses on TRADITION AND THE INDIVIDUAL TALENT.

Every, Brother George. "The Way of Rejections." In T.S. ELIOT: A SYMPOSIUM. Ed. Richard March and Thurairajah Tambimuttu. Freeport, N.Y.: Books for Libraries Press, 1968. Pp. 181-88.

> Examines TSE's political and religious beliefs.

Falck, Colin. "Hurry Up, Please! It's Time." REVIEW, 1 (1962), 59-64.

> Examines TSE's proposals in NOTES TOWARDS THE DEFINITION OF CULTURE and AFTER STRANGE GODS and finds them inadequate for remedying modern society's pressing problems.

Fekete, John. "T.S. Eliot." In his THE CRITICAL TWILIGHT: EXPLORATIONS IN THE IDEOLOGY OF ANGLO-AMERICAN LITERARY THEORY FROM ELIOT TO McLUHAN. London: Routledge and Kegan Paul, 1977. Pp. 21-25.

> A Marxist critique of TSE's critical theories about the impersonality of the artist.

Ferguson, Francis. "Golden Candlesticks." HOUND AND HORN, 2 (1929), 297-99.

> Sympathetic survey of the emergence of TSE's ideas from SACRED WOOD through FOR LANCELOT ANDREWES.

———. "Hamlet as an Artistic Failure." HUDR, 2 (1949), 166-70.

> Another critic disapproves of TSE's interpretation of HAMLET as "an artistic failure."

———. "T.S. Eliot and His Impersonal Theory of Art." In THE AMERICAN CARAVAN. Ed. Van Wyck Brooks et al. New York: Macaulay, 1927. Pp. 446-53.

> A provocative discussion of the tenuous balance between aesthetic and moral problems in TSE's writings.

Fernandez, Ramon. "The Classicism of T.S. Eliot." In his MESSAGE. Trans. Montgomery Belgion. New York: Harcourt, Brace, 1927. Pp. 295-304.

> Straightforward and concise explanations of TSE's classicism.

Frank, Armin P. "T.S. Eliot's Concept of Tradition and the American Background." JAHRBUCH FÜR AMERIKASTUDIEN, 16 (1971), 151-61.

> Interprets TSE's concepts of "tradition" and the "historical sense" in terms of a "predominantly American theological tradition, that of typological thought."

———. "T.S. Eliot's Objective Correlative and the Philosophy of F.H. Bradley." JAAC, 30 (1972), 311-17.

> Argues that Bradley's philosophizing is "self-defeating" and that because of such philosophical despair TSE soon abandoned the discipline for the realm of art. The basic idea of the objective correlative was derived from Bradley's writings on the problem of knowledge.

Freed, Lewis. "Eliot and Bradley: A Review." T.S. ELIOT REVIEW, 3, Nos. 1 and 2 (1976), 29-58.

> With profuse documentation, Freed demonstrates how and why Bradley was "a central influence on Eliot as critic."

_____. T. S. ELIOT, AESTHETICS AND HISTORY. LaSalle, Ill.: Open Court, 1962.

> Explores the influence of such figures as Aristotle, Kant, and F. H. Bradley on TSE's critical theories. Concludes that TSE's literary theory is based primarily on Bradley's philosophy.

_____. T. S. ELIOT: THE CRITIC AS PHILOSOPHER. West Lafayette, Ind.: Purdue Univ. Press, 1979.

> After studying TSE's Harvard dissertation on Bradley, Freed arrives at some new conclusions about influence and critical concepts. Thorough treatment of the "philosophic ingredient" in TSE's critical prose and his writing about education, culture, religion, and politics.

Gardner, Helen Louise. "Shakespeare in the Age of Eliot." TLS, No. 3243 (23 April 1964), 335.

> Brief but stimulating speculations on how TSE influenced Shakespearean criticism over several decades.

George, Arapura G. T. S. ELIOT: HIS MIND AND ART. New York: Asia Publishing House, 1969.

> A rather unbalanced existentialist interpretation of TSE's work. Various chapters treat F. H. Bradley, TSE's aesthetic principles, as well as his literary and social criticism.

Gillis, Everett A. "T. S. Eliot and the Classical Tradition." In CLASSICAL MYTHOLOGY IN TWENTIETH-CENTURY THOUGHT AND LITERATURE. Ed. Wendell M. Aycock and Theodore M. Klein. Lubbock: Texas Tech Press, 1980. Pp. 215-31.

> Examines the impact of the classics on TSE's "formulation of his special 'impersonal' theory of poetry" and his use of "allusory materials drawn from classical sources." Gillis provides a detailed discussion of the essay "Tradition and the Individual Talent," with its classical ideal of the artist's objective role.

Glicksberg, Charles I. "T. S. Eliot as Critic." ARQ, 4 (1948), 225-36.

> Blames TSE's conversion to Anglo-Catholicism for the decline of his literary criticism.

Gray, Piers. T. S. ELIOT'S INTELLECTUAL AND POETIC DEVELOPMENT, 1909-1922. Atlantic Highlands, N. J.: Humanities, 1982.

> A refreshing study of some literary and philosophical sources that influenced TSE's own ideas and writings.

Greenberg, Clement. "The Plight of Our Culture: Industrialism and Class Mobility." COMMENTARY, 15 (1953), 558-66.

> Interesting essay which argues that NOTES TOWARDS THE DEFINITION OF CULTURE is not really applicable to modern problems.

Gupta, N. Das. "T.S. Eliot." In his PLATO TO ELIOT: A LITERARY CRITICISM. London: Probsthain, 1965. Pp. 185-98.

> A pedestrian summary of some of TSE's critical ideas.

Guttman, Allen. "From Brownson to Eliot: The Conservative Theory of Church and State." AQ, 17 (1965), 483-500.

> Finds TSE to be unique in his advocacy of a fruitful union of church and state.

Harding, D.W. "Christian or Liberal?" SCRUTINY, 8 (1939), 309-13.

> Argues that IDEA OF A CHRISTIAN SOCIETY presents a blueprint for a sober and restrictive society where "we must now choose between working for a new Christian culture and accepting a pagan one, whether fascist or communist."

──────. "Mr. Eliot at Harvard." SCRUTINY, 2 (1933), 289-92.

> Discusses TSE's ideas on a poet's beliefs as he expresses them in THE USE OF POETRY.

Harrison, John R. THE REACTIONARIES: A STUDY OF THE ANTIDEMOCRATIC INTELLIGENTSIA. New York: Schocken Books, 1966.

> Discusses in general terms, on pages 145-62, AFTER STRANGE GODS and NOTES TOWARDS THE DEFINITION OF CULTURE. Relies heavily on Raymond Williams' previous analysis in CULTURE AND SOCIETY (1958).

Hayakawa, S. Ichiye. "Mr. Eliot's Auto da Fé." SR, 42 (1934), 365-71.

> Condemns the narrowness of TSE's concepts of race, morality, and tradition as outlined in AFTER STRANGE GODS.

Hayward, John. PROSE LITERATURE SINCE 1939. London: Longmans, Green, 1947.

> Reports on TSE's critical activities since 1939. Calls IDEA OF A CHRISTIAN SOCIETY important but intellectual.

Headings, Philip R. T.S. ELIOT. New York: Twayne, 1964.

> A good introductory study which devotes passing attention to a range of TSE's critical essays.

Higgins, Bertram. "The Critical Method of T.S. Eliot." In SCRUTINIES II. Ed. Edgell Rickword. London: Wishart, 1931. Pp. 54-71.

> Praises the clarity of TSE's "particular criticism" (essays in THE SACRED WOOD). However, Higgins objects to the "prudential" ethic in the essays.

Holder, Alan. "T.S. Eliot on Henry James." PMLA, 79 (1964), 490-97.

> Comprehensive survey of TSE's opinions on James. Holder concludes that TSE "rather cavalierly waves James's criticism aside as inconsequential," but admires his fiction.

Hough, Graham. "The Poet as Critic." In THE LITERARY CRITICISM OF T.S. ELIOT. Ed. David Newton-De Molina. London: Athlone, 1977. Pp. 42-63.

> An interesting essay which argues that one reason why TSE's early criticism held authority was because he was both a poet and a critic. In the twenties, Pound helped foster the status of such an identity. In later years, TSE admitted "some quite specific limitations of the poet-critic's range."

House, Humphrey. "Mr. Eliot as a Critic." NEW OXFORD OUTLOOK, 1 (1933), 95-105.

> A balanced and detailed commentary on TSE's attack on John Milton's poetry.

Howarth, Herbert. "Eliot and Milton: The American Aspect." UTQ, 30 (1961), 150-62.

> A provocative, Jungian interpretation of TSE's relationship to John Milton.

Hutchins, Robert Maynard. "T.S. Eliot on Education." MEASURE, 1 (1950), 1-8.

> Views NOTES TOWARDS THE DEFINITION OF CULTURE from yet another angle. TSE thought highly of this essay.

Hyman, Stanley Edgar. "Poetry and Criticism: T.S. Eliot." ASCH, 30 (1961), 43-55.

> Relates the use of various allusions in TSE's poem "Sweeney among the Nightingales" to the ideas in his essay "Tradition and the Individual Talent."

Hynes, Samuel. "The Trials of a Christian Critic." In THE LITERARY CRITI-
CISM OF T.S. ELIOT. Ed. David Newton-De Molina. London: Athlone,
1977. Pp. 64-88.

> Compares TSE's development as a social critic with that of
> Matthew Arnold: TSE realized fully the problems involved in
> reaching beyond literature to treat cultural issues. A provoca-
> tive discussion of the reasons for TSE's "failure" as a Christian
> critic in twentieth-century society.

Johnson, Lesley. "T.S. Eliot." In her THE CULTURAL CRITICS: FROM
MATTHEW ARNOLD TO RAYMOND WILLIAMS. London: Routledge and
Kegan Paul, 1979. Pp. 122-30.

> Brief but provocative discussion of TSE's concepts of community
> and culture in IDEA OF A CHRISTIAN SOCIETY and NOTES
> TOWARDS THE DEFINITION OF CULTURE.

Johnson, Maurice. "T.S. Eliot on Satire, Swift, and Disgust." PLL, 5
(1969), 310-15.

> A fresh treatment of TSE's critical views on satire.

Kenner, Hugh. THE INVISIBLE POET: T.S. ELIOT. New York: McDowell,
Obolensky, 1959.

> Insightful, intelligent, but advanced study of TSE's poems,
> plays, and criticism.

_____. "Mr. Eliot's New Book." HUDR, 2 (1949), 289-94.

> Sees NOTES TOWARDS THE DEFINITION OF CULTURE as a
> "meditation on order" and defends it as such.

_____, ed. T.S. ELIOT: A COLLECTION OF CRITICAL ESSAYS. Engle-
wood Cliffs, N.J.: Prentice-Hall, 1962.

> Reprints nineteen essays by eminent scholars with varied per-
> spectives. Only a few of the essays deal with TSE's prose
> writings.

Kermode, Frank. "The Classic." UNIV. OF DENVER QUARTERLY, 9 (1974),
1-33.

> A scholarly analysis of TSE's definition of the term "classic"
> that includes such Roman distinctions between "relative,"
> "absolute," and "imperialist" classics.

_____. "Dissociation of Sensibility." KR, 19 (1957), 169-94.

> Insightful analysis of the meaning and importance of the critical
> term.

_____. "Introduction." In his SELECTED PROSE OF T.S. ELIOT. New York: Harcourt, Farrar, 1975. Pp. 11-27.

>   Cogent and masterful survey of the development of TSE's critical ideas.

_____. ROMANTIC IMAGE. London: Routledge and Kegan Paul, 1957.

>   Important study which places TSE, critic, in the Romantic-Symbolist tradition.

Kingsmill, Hugh. "Goethe, Wordsworth, and Mr. Eliot." ENGR, 57 (1933), 667-70.

>   Attempts to refute TSE's disparaging remarks in THE USE OF POETRY concerning the limitations of Goethe and Wordsworth.

Kirk, Russell. ELIOT AND HIS AGE: T.S. ELIOT'S MORAL IMAGINATION IN THE TWENTIETH CENTURY. New York: Random House, 1971.

>   Provides summaries of and background material for IDEA OF A CHRISTIAN SOCIETY, NOTES TOWARDS THE DEFINITION OF CULTURE, and THE USE OF POETRY.

Knickerbocker, William S. "Bellwether: An Exercise in Dissimulatio." SR, 41 (1933), 64-79.

>   Compares the criticism and prose of Matthew Arnold and TSE. A valuable article.

Kojecký, Roger. T.S. ELIOT'S SOCIAL CRITICISM. London: Faber, 1971.

>   An excellent study of TSE's social and religious writing, which includes discussions of "Dante" and IDEA OF A CHRISTIAN SOCIETY.

Kramer, Jurgen. "T.S. Eliot's Concept of Tradition: A Revaluation." NGC, 6 (1975), 20-30.

>   Uses such Marxist critics as Walter Benjamin to examine the following concepts related to TSE's criticism: function of traditional literature, influence of past writers, the idea of revaluation, and "dissociation of sensibility." Well-documented and intelligent article.

Krieger, Murray. "The Critical Legacy of Matthew Arnold: Or, the Strange Brotherhood of T.S. Eliot, I.A. Richards, and Northrop Frye." SORA, N.S. 5 (1969), 457-74.

>   Provocative analysis of TSE's antagonistic attitude to Arnold;

he is especially "repelled" by the idea that poetry might become a substitute for religion. Also compares insightfully TSE to Richards' and Frye's positions.

Kumar, Jitendra. "Consciousness and Its Correlates: Eliot and Husserl." PPR, 28 (1968), 332-52.

Compares Husserl's IDEAS with TSE's KNOWLEDGE AND EXPERIENCE.

Kuna, F.M. "T.S. Eliot's Dissociation of Sensibility and the Critics of Metaphysical Poetry." EIC, 13 (1963), 241-52.

Kuna is wary of TSE's and other modern critics' interpretations of what seventeenth-century poets intended.

Leavis, F.R. "Approaches to T.S. Eliot." SCRUTINY, 15, No. 1 (1947), 56-67.

Discussion of SACRED WOOD and USE OF POETRY.

———. "Mr. Eliot, Mr. Wyndham Lewis and Lawrence." SCRUTINY, 3 (1934), 184-91.

Compares an earlier essay on Lawrence with AFTER STRANGE GODS and concludes that TSE's critical powers have indeed weakened to the point of heresy.

———. "Mr. Eliot and Education." SCRUTINY, 5, No. 1 (1936), 84-89.

Discusses TSE's ideas in ESSAYS ANCIENT AND MODERN.

———. "Mr. Eliot and Milton." SR, 57 (1949), 1-30.

Argues that TSE's revised comments on Milton demonstrate less critical acumen.

———. "T.S. Eliot's Stature as Critic: A Revaluation." COMMENTARY, 26 (1958), 399-410.

Despite his early literary prowess, TSE is essentially conventional in thought. Extended discussion of ON POETRY AND POETS.

LeBrun, Philip. "T.S. Eliot and Henry Bergson." RES, 18 (1967), 149-61, 274-86.

Argues that Bergson's ideas about time, change, and consciousness "greatly influenced" TSE's concepts of tradition, artistic sensibility, and the objective correlative.

Lee, Brian. THEORY AND PERSONALITY: THE SIGNIFICANCE OF T.S. ELIOT'S CRITICISM. London: Athlone, 1979.

> Informed by many references to the history and philosophy of science, Lee offers fresh interpretations of some of TSE's fundamental critical and social concepts. Includes a helpful bibliography of secondary sources.

Levy, William Turner. "The Idea of the Church in T.S. Eliot." CHRISTIAN SCHOLAR, 41 (1958), 587-600.

> Levy provides a lucid explanation of TSE's conception of the nature and function of the church in society as outlined in several of TSE's essays.

Lu, Fei-Pai. T.S. ELIOT: THE DIALECTICAL STRUCTURE OF HIS THEORY OF POETRY. Chicago: Univ. of Chicago Press, 1966.

> Important but difficult treatment of the major critics of TSE's prose. Includes a seventeen-page bibliography of works on TSE's criticism.

Lucy, Seán. T.S. ELIOT AND THE IDEA OF TRADITION. London: Cohen and West, 1960.

> Attempts to trace "fundamental themes and ideas" in each level of TSE's work. About half of the discussion focuses on TSE's critical studies. Heavy reliance on lengthy quotations.

Marcus, Philip L. "T.S. Eliot and Shakespeare." CRITICISM, 9 (1967), 63-79.

> Detailed analysis of TSE's evolving and often "idiosyncratic" responses to Shakespeare's work from 1919 to 1955.

Margolis, John D. T.S. ELIOT'S INTELLECTUAL DEVELOPMENT 1922-1939. Chicago: Univ. of Chicago Press, 1972.

> Includes discussions of AFTER STRANGE GODS, DANTE, FOR LANCELOT ANDREWES, HOMAGE TO JOHN DRYDEN, IDEA OF A CHRISTIAN SOCIETY, SACRED WOOD, and TRADITION AND THE INDIVIDUAL TALENT. Important and well-documented study.

Marks, Emerson R. "T.S. Eliot and the Ghost of S.T.C." SR, 72 (1964), 262-80.

> A comparison of TSE's political and social ideas in IDEA OF A CHRISTIAN SOCIETY and NOTES TOWARDS THE DEFINITION OF CULTURE with selected writings by Coleridge reveals some resemblances in outlook.

Martin, Graham. ELIOT IN PERSPECTIVE: A SYMPOSIUM. London: Macmillan, 1970.

> The second part of this collection includes seven important essays which relate TSE to such figures as F.H. Bradley, Matthew Arnold, and to various religious, social, literary, and cultural circles.

Matthiessen, F.O. THE ACHIEVEMENT OF T.S. ELIOT: AN ESSAY ON THE NATURE OF POETRY. 3rd ed., rev. and enl. New York: Oxford Univ. Press, 1959.

> Perhaps the best discussion of the critical basis for TSE's poetry. Includes excellent chapters on "Tradition and the Individual Talent," "The Problem for the Contemporary Artist," and "The 'Objective Correlative.'"

Maxwell, D.E.S. "Eliot, History, and Contemporary Culture." ESC, 6 (1980), 232-43.

> A wide-ranging discussion which attempts to examine how TSE's essays and poetry made use of historical and contemporary events.

Moloney, Michael F. "The Critical Faith of Mr. T.S. Eliot." THOUGHT, 22 (1947), 297-314.

> Summarizes TSE's critical theories and stresses their religious implications.

Montgomery, Marion. "Eliot, Wordworth, and the Problem of Personal Emotion in the Poet." SHR, 2, No. 2 (1968), 185-97.

> Draws on TSE's TRADITION AND THE INDIVIDUAL TALENT to compare him to the poet Wordsworth.

―――. "Through a Glass Darkly: Eliot and the Romantic Critics." SWR, 58 (1973), 327-35.

> Examines the influence of TSE's commitment to Christianity on his perception of several Romantic critics.

Morse, J.I. "T.S. Eliot in 1921: Toward the Dissociation of Sensibility." WHR, 30 (1976), 31-40.

> Interesting study of the way in which TSE's "selective unfairness" toward Matthew Arnold operates and what it reveals "about Eliot's own poetics."

Muir, Edwin. "Mr. Eliot's Criticism." CALENDAR OF MODERN LETTERS, 1 (1925), 242-44.

Praises Eliot's criticism as fundamentally "sound" and "comprehensive"; however, Muir regrets TSE's depreciation of the poets Milton and Wordworth.

Murry, Byron D. "Tradition and the Eliot Critical Talent." CONNR, 9, No. 2 (1976), 2-15.

Points out that James Russell Lowell's criticism paralleled TSE's "in many ways" and strongly suggests that Lowell influenced TSE's approach to criticism. Not entirely convincing.

Newton-De Molina, David, ed. THE LITERARY CRITICISM OF T.S. ELIOT: NEW ESSAYS. London: Athlone, 1977.

Collects nine new and important essays on various aspects of TSE's literary criticism. Contributors include F.W. Bateson, Denis Donoghue, and Graham Hough.

Noonan, James. "Poetry and Belief in the Criticism of T.S. Eliot." QQ, 79 (1972), 388-96.

Comprehensive analysis of TSE's developing ideas on the relation of poetry and belief in critical writings from 1927 to 1955.

Osterwalder, Hans. T. S. ELIOT: METAPHOR AND METONYMY, A STUDY OF HIS ESSAYS AND PLAYS IN TERMS OF ROMAN JAKOBSON'S TYPOLOGY. Zurich: Francke Verlag Bern, 1978.

Includes a labored analysis of the "poetic function" of language in some of TSE's essays. TSE moves from a bipolar phase through a leveling period to a final equilibrium.

Panichas, George A. "T. S. Eliot and the Critique of Liberalism." MODA, 18 (1974), 145-62.

A conservative critic argues that TSE's contribution to the critique of modern liberalism is "considerable." Panichas reviews the harsh reception of TSE's AFTER STRANGE GODS and other social criticism with the view of upgrading his reputation.

Parkinson, Thomas. "Intimate and Impersonal: An Aspect of Modern Poetics." JAAC, 16 (1958), 373-83.

Discusses the modernist theory of impersonality in art and concludes that some critics make stronger endorsements of it than TSE does.

Paul, Leslie. "A Conversation with T. S. Eliot." KR, 27 (1965), 11-21.

An important interview conducted in 1958 in which TSE gives his views on religion, politics, and the function of the poet in modern society.

Peacock, R. "Eliot's Contribution to Criticism of Drama." In THE LITERARY CRITICISM OF T.S. ELIOT. Ed. David Newton-De Molina. London: Athlone, 1977. Pp. 89-110.

> TSE's drama criticism has three main parts: the Elizabethan essays, assessments of contemporary theatre, and statements about an ideal of poetic drama. Peacock shows how the three divisions are all related by TSE's "two-dimensional interest" as both critic and practitioner.

Peterson, Sven. "Mr. Eliot in THE SACRED WOOD." GREY FRIAR, 8 (1965), 33-43.

> Expresses reservations about the validity of TSE's theory of impersonality when applied to various critical situations.

Pound, Ezra. "Mr. Eliot's Solid Merit." NEW ENGLISH WEEKLY, 5 (1934), 297-99.

> Important defense of TSE's criticism. Reprinted in POLITE ESSAYS (London: Faber and Faber, 1937), pages 98-105.

Powell, Dilys. "The Poetry of T.S. Eliot." LIFE AND LETTERS, 7 (1931), 386-419.

> Although this appreciative survey essay deals mainly with TSE's poetry, it makes succinct use of some of TSE's prose statements for illuminating the meaning of the poems.

Praz, Mario. "T.S. Eliot and Dante." SOR, 2 (1937), 525-48.

> The most intelligent discussion of the influence of Dante on TSE's poetic language and prose theories.

──────. "T.S. Eliot as a Critic." In T.S. ELIOT: THE MAN AND HIS WORK. Ed. Allen Tate. London: Chatto and Windus, 1967. Pp. 262-77.

> Argues that a survey of TSE's critical opinions reveals that he is "an empirical critic" whose "real guide is not logic but intuition." Shows how various critical ideas involve "a myth or an image."

Quennell, Peter. "T.S. Eliot the Critic." NEW STATESMAN AND NATION, N.S. 4 (1932), 377-78.

> Brief but valuable analysis of TSE's prose style in SELECTED ESSAYS 1917-1932.

Quiller-Couch, Arthur T. "Tradition and Orthodoxy." In his THE POET AS CITIZEN AND OTHER PAPERS. Cambridge: The Univ. Press, 1934. Pp. 44-61.

> Harsh commentary on AFTER STRANGE GODS. The author argues that liberalism is an important tradition and not a temporary blight on society and condemns TSE's dogmatic tendency to move toward totalitarianism.

Raina, M. L. "T. S. Eliot's Criticism of the Novel." RS, 40 (1972), 81-94.

> Raina is impressed by the range of interest and sympathy TSE showed for many novelists. A useful article which assembles scattered references.

Rajan, B. "Milton and Eliot: A Twentieth-Century Acknowledgment." MILTONS, 11 (1978), 115-29.

> Uses TSE's developing response to Milton as an example of how "studious circumvention may well be a natural mode of relationship with the past until the order-seeking consciousness has advanced to a point where a more direct confrontation is possible."

Rajnath. T. S. ELIOT'S THEORY OF POETRY: A STUDY OF THE CHANGING CRITICAL IDEAS IN THE DEVELOPMENT OF HIS PROSE AND POETRY. Atlantic Highlands, N. J.: Humanities Press, 1981.

> Rajnath provides a scholarly but diffuse study of TSE's developing critical theories concerning poetry.

Raleigh, John H. "The New Criticism as an Historical Phenomenon." CL, 11 (1959), 21-28.

> Examines TSE's place in the critical movement: in his organicism he is akin to Coleridge and opposed to the utilitarian and scientific outlook of Bentham and I. A. Richards.

_____. "Revolt and Revaluation in Criticism, 1900-1930." In THE DEVELOPMENT OF AMERICAN CRITICISM. Ed. Floyd Stovall. Chapel Hill: Univ. of North Carolina Press, 1955. Pp. 159-98.

> Examines TSE's influence on American criticism in the 1920's and stresses TSE's emphasis on European attitudes and past traditions.

Ransom, John Crowe. "T. S. Eliot: The Historical Critic." In his NEW CRITICISM. Norfolk, Conn.: New Directions, 1941. Pp. 135-208.

> A meaningful discussion of TSE's essays on Jonson and the metaphysical poets.

_____. "T. S. Eliot on Criticism." SATR, 10 (1934), 574.

    Valuable essay on TSE's reluctance to develop a critical scheme for discussing the literature he so loves.

Reed, Henry. "If and Perhaps and But." LISTENER, 49 (1953), 1017-18.

    Brief but useful analysis of TSE's prose style.

Rees, Thomas Richard. "T. S. Eliot, Rémy de Gourmont, and Dissociation of Sensibility." In STUDIES IN COMPARATIVE LITERATURE. Ed. Waldo F. McNeir. Louisiana Univ. Studies, Humanities Series, No. 11. Baton Rouge: Louisiana State Univ. Press, 1962. Pp. 186-98.

    Explains and approves TSE's use of the critical phrase "dissociation of sensibility."

Rice, Philip Blair. "The Critic as Prophet." POETRY, 50, No. 1 (1937), 51-54.

    Comments on TSE's strategy in ESSAYS ANCIENT AND MODERN.

Righter, William. "The Philosophical Critic." In THE LITERARY CRITICISM OF T. S. ELIOT. Ed. David Newton-De Molina. London: Athlone, 1977. Pp. 111-38.

    A dense and circuitous essay which examines, with the aid of much theoretical jargon, the ambiguities inherent in the notion of the "philosophical critic."

Robson, W. W. "Eliot's Later Criticism." REVIEW, 1 (1962), 52-58.

    A balanced but incomplete discussion of TSE's criticism, focusing on ON POETRY AND POETS.

_____. "A Poet's Notebook: THE USE OF POETRY AND THE USE OF CRITICISM." In THE LITERARY CRITICISM OF T. S. ELIOT. Ed. David Newton-De Molina. London: Athlone, 1977. Pp. 139-59.

    Robson admits the considerable biographical interest of THE USE OF POETRY and adds that it is the "beginning of Eliot's major concern with public questions." However, Robson values the book most for its important statements of critical principles concerning "the responsibility of the poet" and the functions of poetry.

Salmon, Christopher V. "Critics and Criticism." NC, 115 (1934), 359-69.

    Discusses THE USE OF POETRY in terms of the narrow focus of the critic's function in society.

Savage, Derek S. "The Orthodoxy of T.S. Eliot." In his THE PERSONAL PRINCIPLE. London: Routledge, 1944. Pp. 91-112.

>An antireligious discussion of TSE's essays and poems.

Scarfe, Francis. "Notes on the Individual Talent." STC, No. 3 (1969), 1-14.

>Analysis of TSE's TRADITION AND INDIVIDUAL TALENT.

──────. "Two Lectures: The Classics and the Man of Letters, and the Music of Poetry." POETRY (London), 10 (1944), 239-42.

>Intelligent analysis of two of TSE's lectures which were later printed as essays.

Schneider, Elisabeth. T.S. ELIOT: THE PATTERN IN THE CARPET. Berkeley and Los Angeles: Univ. of California Press, 1975.

>Perceptive references to ON POETRY AND POETS, SELECTED ESSAYS, TO CRITICIZE THE CRITIC, and USE OF POETRY are used to illuminate important developments in TSE's poetry.

Schuchard, Ronald. "Eliot and Hulme in 1916: Toward a Revaluation of Eliot's Critical and Spiritual Development." PMLA, 88 (1973), 1083-94.

>Argues that Hulme had a significant effect on TSE's religious position as early as 1916: Hulme's work influenced the "esthetic, authoritarian, and moral assumptions that underlie Eliot's classicism and Christian humanism."

──────. "'First Rate Blasphemy': Baudelaire and the Revised Christian Idiom of T.S. Eliot's Moral Criticism." ELH, 42 (1975), 276-95.

>Well-documented and detailed examination of TSE's use of Baudelaire "in developing his theory for the moral valuation of literature."

──────. "'Our mad poetics to confute': The Personal Voice in T.S. Eliot's Early Poetry and Criticism." OL, 31 (1976), 208-23.

>Interesting approach which sees TSE absorbed with the interior world of the poet in his early literary criticism. The critical prose shows a personal voice and defines "a method of re-personalization for the critical process."

──────. "T.S. Eliot as an Extension Lecturer, 1916-1919." RES, 25 (1974), 163-73, 292-304.

>Interesting and detailed presentation of TSE's syllabuses from this period in order to demonstrate the extent of his grounding in French and English literature, literary criticism, philosophy, and

so on, "as he began to formulate his own critical positions."

Schwartz, Delmore. "Literary Dictatorship of T. S. Eliot." PR, 16 (1949), 119-37.

    Offers a comprehensive schema of TSE's critical theories.

Shapiro, Karl. "T. S. Eliot: The Death of Literary Judgment." In his IN DEFENSE OF IGNORANCE. New York: Random House, 1960. Pp. 35-60.

    Harsh attack on TSE as "an institution unto himself." Charges that TSE's theories are borrowed wholesale from T. E. Hulme.

Sharrock, Roger. "The Critical Revolution of T. S. Eliot." ARIELE, 2 (1971), 26-42.

    Examines the tone in TSE's criticism and finds an authoritative personal tone with a calculated shock effect: a combination of "trenchant orthodoxy and striking unorthodoxy."

―――. "Eliot's 'Tone.'" In THE LITERARY CRITICISM OF T. S. ELIOT. Ed. David Newton-De Molina. London: Athlone, 1977. Pp. 160-83.

    Uses aesthetic theory of F. H. Bradley and others to explore "the elusive question of tone" in TSE's early critical writings. Sharrock describes the tone of the early essays in these terms: "urgency," a "dandy's assurance and poise," "scepticism," and "frequent deviousness and occasional mystery." Intelligent analysis of TSE's early prose style.

Simon, Brian. "The Defence of Culture." COMMUNIST REVIEW, 4 (1949), 763-68.

    With many rhetorical flourishes, Simon condemns TSE's intellectual elitism and "contempt and fear of the masses" in NOTES TOWARDS THE DEFINITION OF CULTURE.

Smith, Carol H. T. S. ELIOT'S DRAMATIC THEORY AND PRACTICE, FROM SWEENEY AGONISTES TO THE ELDER STATESMAN. Princeton, N. J.: Princeton Univ. Press, 1963.

    An excellent study which includes perceptive analysis of TSE's critical writings about the nature and function of drama.

Smith, James. "Notes on the Criticism of T. S. Eliot." EIC, 22 (1972), 333-61.

    A chatty survey which touches superficially on most of TSE's critical writings. Points out relationships to Thomas Hobbes.

Soldo, John J. "Knowledge and Experience in the Criticism of T. S. Eliot."
ELH, 35 (1968), 284-308.

> A scholarly essay which sees TSE as "solidly entrenched" in the tradition of British idealism and explains the "deep impact" of Bradley's system of absolute idealism on TSE's theoretical criticism.

Spender, Stephen. "How Shall We Be Saved?" HORIZON, 1 (1940), 51-56.

> On TSE's IDEA OF A CHRISTIAN SOCIETY.

──── . "T. S. Eliot in His Criticism." In his THE DESTRUCTIVE ELEMENT. London: Cape, 1935. Pp. 153-75.

> Partially disapproves of TSE's critical theories.

Srinath, C. N. "T. S. Eliot's Dramatic Theory and Practice." LCRIT, 12, No. 4 (1975), 64-79.

> An unfocused essay that relates TSE's dramatic theories to his own plays. Concludes that TSE's influence has not been so extensive in modern drama.

Stapleton, Laurence. THE ELECTED CIRCLE: STUDIES IN THE ART OF PROSE. Princeton, N.J.: Princeton Univ. Press, 1973.

> Chapter 8 treats TSE's early essays and reviews. In an original discussion, Stapleton links the clarity in TSE's early prose to the young writer's surrounding sociological milieu.

Stead, C. K. "Eliot, Arnold, and the English Poetic Tradition." In THE LITERARY CRITICISM OF T. S. ELIOT. Ed. David Newton-De Molina. London: Athlone, 1977. Pp. 184-206.

> An intelligent and valuable essay which raises many important and provocative questions "by re-reading Eliot's criticism against the background of Arnold's." Stead concludes that although TSE contributed much in his criticism on the Metaphysicals as well as the Jacobean dramatists, his criticism failed to look "squarely" at the tenets of Romanticism (as Arnold attempted to do).

Steadman, John M. "Eliot and Husserl: The Origin of the Objective Correlative." N & Q, 5 (1958), 261-62.

> TSE probably indebted to Husserl and "apparently the first to transfer this term from logical theory to literary criticism."

Stevenson, David L. "An Objective Correlative for T.S. Eliot's HAMLET." JAAC, 13 (1954), 69-79.

> TSE's claim that the play is "an artistic failure" forces the alert

reader to appreciate the successful "originality of the dramatic structure" devised by Shakespeare.

Stone, Geoffrey. "Morals and Poetry." AMERICAN REVIEW, 9 (1937), 58-63.

Compares the critical standards of TSE and I.A. Richards.

Takács, Ferenc. "Some Themes of Unification in T.S. Eliot's Criticism." ALITASH, 20 (1978), 164-72.

Outlines a "strategy of unities and disunities" in TSE's essays on the way language functions in prose and poetry and on the idea of a "popular" literature.

Takayanagi, Shunichi. "About the Center of the Silent Word--T.S. Eliot and Lancelot Andrewes." ELLS, 7 (1970), 37-81.

Extended discussion of essays in FOR LANCELOT ANDREWES.

Tanner, Stephen L. "T.S. Eliot and Paul Elmer More on Tradition." ELN, 8 (1971), 211-15.

Stresses the importance of critical term "historical sense" in "Tradition and the Individual Talent" (SACRED WOOD) and traces the influence of both that term and concept of tradition to More.

Thomas, R. Hinton. "Culture and T.S. Eliot." MODERN QUARTERLY (London), 6 (1951), 147-62.

Leftist assessment of TSE's social and political theories in NOTES TOWARDS THE DEFINITION OF CULTURE.

Thompson, Eric. T.S. ELIOT: THE METAPHYSICAL PERSPECTIVE. Crosscurrents: Modern Critiques. Carbondale: Southern Illinois Univ. Press, 1963.

A difficult and specialized study which examines the relationship of TSE's Harvard thesis on F.H. Bradley to his early critical writings. Includes discussion of HAMLET, THE METAPHYSICAL POETS, and essays written between 1917 and 1923.

Tillyard, E.M.W. "Milton's Visual Imagination." In his THE MILTONIC SETTING, PAST AND PRESENT. New York: Barres and Noble, 1966. Pp. 90-104.

Outlines TSE's early essays which found fault with Milton's style. Tillyard offers a balanced and informed reply to TSE's negative assessments.

Trilling, Lionel. "Elements That Are Wanted." PR, 7 (1940), 367-79.

Suggestive comments from a liberal on the value of TSE's view of a Christian society to any "rational and naturalistic philosophy."

Turnell, G. Martin. "Tradition and T. S. Eliot." COLOSEUM, 1 (1934), 44-54.

A well-reasoned analysis of AFTER STRANGE GODS in which the author refuses to follow TSE's leap of equating the Anglican and European traditions.

Unger, Leonard. T. S. ELIOT. Pamphlets on American Writers. Minneapolis: Univ. of Minnesota Press, 1961.

A brief but competent introduction to most of TSE's work.

―――――. T. S. ELIOT: MOMENTS AND PATTERNS. Minneapolis: Univ. of Minnesota Press, 1966.

Collects seven critical essays written by Unger over three decades. Many of TSE's essays, including "Dante" and "Hamlet" (SELECTED ESSAYS) are discussed.

―――――, ed. T. S. ELIOT: A SELECTED CRITIQUE. New York: Rinehart, 1948.

Thirty-one essays (most previously published) which provide a spectrum of critical response to TSE's works.

Van Doren, Mark. "Seventeenth-Century Poetry and Twentieth-Century Critics." In STUDIES IN METAPHYSICAL POETRY. Ed. Theodore Spencer and Mark Van Doren. New York: Columbia Univ. Press, 1939. Pp. 21-29.

Attaches high value to TSE's critical appreciations and analyses of metaphysical poetry in essays from METAPHYSICAL POETS.

Verma, Rajendra. ROYALIST IN POLITICS, T. S. ELIOT AND POLITICAL PHILOSOPHY. London: Asia Publishing House, 1968.

Includes discussions of TSE's concepts of culture, tradition, democracy, and religion. Special attention paid to a "literary appraisal" of NOTES TOWARDS THE DEFINITION OF CULTURE and IDEA OF A CHRISTIAN SOCIETY.

Vivas, Eliseo. "The Objective Correlative of T. S. Eliot." AMERICAN BOOKMAN, 1 (1944), 7-18.

Vivas concludes that the theory of expression posited by TSE's critical principle is not verifiable in either psychological or aesthetic terms.

Ward, David. "The Cult of Impersonality: Eliot, St. Augustine, and Flaubert." EIC, 17 (1967), 169-82.

> Discusses SELECTED ESSAYS and points out "the ingenious looseness of argument which underlies the persuasive surface of the criticism." The essays should be taken as "interim reports" and not as final, authoritative statements.

---------. "Eliot, Murray, Hoover, and the Idea of Tradition: 'So I Assumed in Double Part. . . .'" EIC, 18 (1968), 47-59.

> Relates TSE's ideas in SELECTED ESSAYS, AFTER STRANGE GODS, and NOTES TOWARDS A DEFINITION OF CULTURE to the work of anthropologists and other scholars--Frazer, Murray, Cornford, and Jane Harrison.

Warren, Austin. "Continuity in T.S. Eliot's Criticism." EAST WEST REVIEW, 1 (1964), 1-12.

> Argues the influence of Irving Babbitt on TSE's ideas in THE USE OF POETRY.

Wasson, Richard. "T.S. Eliot's Antihumanism and Antipragmatism." TSLL, 10 (1968), 445-55.

> Well-documented discussion of how TSE's critical and social thoughts reflect the continuing debate between pragmatists and idealists.

Watson, C.B. "T.S. Eliot and the Interpretation of Shakespearean Tragedy in Our Time." EA, 17 (1964), 502-21.

> TSE's analysis of Shakespeare's flawed philosophical stance has fostered too many religious interpretations of his plays by modern critics.

Webster, Grant T. "T.S. Eliot as Critic: The Man Behind the Masks." CRITICISM, 8 (1966), 336-48.

> Surveys TSE's criticism and various reactions to it; argues that "the man behind the masks" has a sense of humility and humor as well as an acute literary sensitivity.

Weinblatt, Alan. "T.S. Eliot and the Historical Sense." SAQ, 77 (1978), 282-95.

> Draws on THE USE OF POETRY, ON POETRY AND POETS, and SELECTED ESSAYS in order to relate the concept of "the historical sense" to such concerns of TSE's as the past, audience, style, and poetics.

Weisberg, Robert. "T.S. Eliot: The Totemic-Mosaic Dream." BMMLA, 8, No. 2 (1975), 24-44.

>Discusses AFTER STRANGE GODS as a utopian book that is illuminated by the anthropological concept of totemism.

Wellek, René. "Criticism of T.S. Eliot." SR, 64 (1956), 398-443.

>Detailed assessment of TSE's career as critic. Wellek concludes that TSE's early criticism is better than his later work.

Whiteside, George. "T.S. Eliot's Dissertation." ELH, 34 (1967), 400-424.

>Provides a close examination (chapter by chapter) of TSE's doctoral dissertation on F.H. Bradley's philosophy "for the benefit of anyone who wonders what is in it but has no time or inclination to read it."

Williams, Orlo. CONTEMPORARY CRITICISM OF LITERATURE. London: Parsons, 1924. Pp. 89-94, 143-54.

>Discusses essays in SACRED WOOD and concludes that although TSE is a serious critic, his outlook and opinions are too scientific and impersonal.

Williams, Raymond. "Second Thoughts: T.S. Eliot on Culture." EIC, 6 (1956), 302-18.

>A critical but fair discussion of NOTES TOWARDS THE DEFINITION OF CULTURE and IDEA OF A CHRISTIAN SOCIETY.

_____. "T.S. Eliot." In his CULTURE AND SOCIETY, 1780-1950. New York: Columbia Univ. Press, 1958. Pp. 227-43.

>Discusses IDEA OF A CHRISTIAN SOCIETY and NOTES TOWARDS THE DEFINITION OF CULTURE from a leftwing perspective.

Williamson, George. A READER'S GUIDE TO T.S. ELIOT: A POEM-BY-POEM ANALYSIS. 2nd ed. New York: Noonday, 1966.

>Chapter 2, "The Use of His Criticism," provides a basic introduction to TSE's literary essays.

_____. THE TALENT OF T.S. ELIOT. Seattle: Univ. of Washington Chapbooks, No. 32, 1929.

>Important early comments on the relation of TSE's ideas to his poetry and on his relation to Donne. Based on an earlier critical essay of the same title in SR, 35 (1927), 284-95.

Wilson, Edmund. "T.S. Eliot." In his AXEL'S CASTLE. New York: Scribner's, 1931. Pp. 93-131.

> A general but influential early evaluation which includes some discussion of the developments in TSE's prose writings.

Wimsatt, W.K. "Eliot's Weary Gestures of Dismissal." MR, 7, (1966), 584-90.

> A significant review essay by a noted literary critic. Wimsatt focuses on TSE's TO CRITICIZE THE CRITIC AND OTHER WRITINGS.

Winston, George P. "Washington Allston and the Objective Correlative." BUR, 11 (1962), 95-108.

> Suggests a possible nineteenth-century source for the critical phrase made famous by TSE.

Winters, Yvor. "T.S. Eliot, the Illusion of Reaction." KR, 3 (1941), 7-30, 221-39.

> Lively and unfavorable essay which suggests that TSE contradicts himself and is overly influenced by Pound.

Wiseman, James. "Of Loneliness and Communion." DRAMA CRITIQUE, 5, No. 1 (1962), 14-21.

> Discusses TSE's ideas in IDEA OF A CHRISTIAN SOCIETY.

Wollheim, Richard. "Eliot and F.H. Bradley: An Account." In ELIOT IN PERSPECTIVE. Ed. Graham Martin. New York: Humanities, 1970. Pp. 169-93.

> Helpful and extended discussion of TSE's KNOWLEDGE AND EXPERIENCE IN THE PHILOSOPHY OF F.H. BRADLEY.

Woodward, Daniel A. "John Quinn and T.S. Eliot's First Book of Criticism." PBSA, 56 (1962), 259-65.

> Discusses the circumstances which generated EZRA POUND: HIS METRIC AND POETRY. TSE states that "it was through Pound himself that I was commissioned to write the book."

Wright, Nathalia. "A Source for T.S. Eliot's 'Objective Correlative.'" AL, 41 (1970), 589-91.

> Points to Washington Allston's LECTURES ON ART, AND POEMS (1850) as possible source of TSE's term.

Zabel, M.D. "The Use of the Poet." POETRY, 44 (1934), 32-37.

> Sparkling analysis of TSE's THE USE OF POETRY.

WILLIAM EMPSON (1906-   )

NONFICTIONAL PROSE

MILTON'S GOD. London: Chatto and Windus, 1961. New York: New Directions, 1962.

> A controversial study because of its blatantly anti-Christian approach to Milton's PARADISE LOST. WE demonstrates how Milton makes God "noticeably less wicked than the traditional Christian one." WE added an appendix in 1965 which outlines Milton's alleged intrigues against King Charles.

SEVEN TYPES OF AMBIGUITY: A STUDY OF ITS EFFECTS ON ENGLISH VERSE. London: Chatto and Windus, 1930. New York: Harcourt, 1931.

> In WE's most important work of literary criticism he uses the technique of close verbal analysis to discuss the nuances evident in an impressive range of literary examples. WE's youthful prose style is sometimes uneven, tedious, and dogmatic. WE published several subsequent revised editions (in 1947 and 1953).

SOME VERSIONS OF PASTORAL. London: Chatto and Windus, 1935. As ENGLISH PASTORAL POETRY. New York: Norton, 1938.

> WE applies the method of close verbal analysis to longer passages and several complete works, from Renaissance poems to ALICE IN WONDERLAND. He defines pastoral as "the process of putting the complex into the simple." Sociological implications of pastoral theme are also treated.

THE STRUCTURE OF COMPLEX WORDS. London: Chatto and Windus; New York: New Directions, 1951.

> WE's most difficult and ambitious book consists of a theoretical analysis of key language patterns in works by Shakespeare, Pope, Milton, and others. In his discussions WE also draws from the fields of anthropology, philosophy, and psychology.

BIBLIOGRAPHY

Johnson, Michael L., comp. "William Empson: A Chronological Bibliography." BB, 29 (1972), 134-39.

    A nearly comprehensive chronological bibliography of WE's published work from 1927 to 1970. WE's early reviews in GRANTA (1926-1929) are not included. No items are annotated. Johnson expands and updates Lowbridge's citations.

Lowbridge, Peter, comp. "An Empson Bibliography." THE REVIEW, 6 and 7 (1963), 63-73.

    A helpful bibliography which covers material up to April 1963. Omits WE's early contributions to GRANTA. The entries are in chronological order, with the following divisions: poetry, criticism, reviews, selected correspondence, and miscellaneous.

Megaw, Moira, comp. "An Empson Bibliography." In WILLIAM EMPSON: THE MAN AND HIS WORK. Ed. Roma Gill. London and Boston: Routledge and Kegan Paul, 1974. Pp. 213-44.

    The most detailed and complete bibliography on WE's works from 1927 to 1973. Includes reviews and articles that WE contributed to Cambridge journals (especially GRANTA) as an undergraduate. Divisions include poetry, reviews, criticism, letters; no annotations are provided.

Willis, John H., comp. "Selected Bibliography." In his WILLIAM EMPSON. Columbia Essays on Modern Writers. New York: Columbia Univ. Press, 1969. Pp. 46-48.

    A handy listing of principal works by and critical works about WE.

CRITICISM

Adams, Robert Martin. "Empson and Bentley: Something about Milton Too." PR, 21 (1954), 178-89.

    Close examination of WE's analysis of Milton's works in SOME VERSIONS. Adams concludes: "To read Empson hard is always useful and pleasant because his mistakes are as much fun as his perceptions."

Alpers, Paul. "Empson on Pastoral." NLH, 10 (1978), 101-23.

    Thoughtful analysis of WE's seemingly "idiosyncratic" manner and outlook in SOME VERSIONS, with some references to SEVEN TYPES. Explains how WE's "idea of pastoral" is central to his sense of poetry and of life. Discusses WE's concepts of language, style, and social convention.

Bradbrook, M.C. "The Ambiguity of William Empson." In WILLIAM EMPSON: THE MAN AND HIS WORK. Ed. Roma Gill. London: Routledge and Kegan Paul, 1974. Pp. 2-12.

> An undergraduate contemporary of WE's admires his perceptions of Nature and the human situation in his poems as well as in SEVEN TYPES and SOME VERSIONS.

———. "The Criticism of William Empson." SCRUTINY, 2 (1933), 253-57.

> Admires the "intellectual closeness and keenness" of WE's SEVEN TYPES as well as its "educating function." However, Bradbrook wishes WE would also evaluate the works he analyzes.

Cox, R.G. "Ambiguity Revised." SCRUTINY, 15 (1948), 148-52.

> A negative assessment of SEVEN TYPES. Cox faults WE's tone of "undergraduate smartness," his "lack of control," and his misquotation of texts. He also condemns the "fantastic" extravagances of SOME VERSIONS.

Dodsworth, Martin. "Empson at Cambridge." THE REVIEW, 6 and 7 (1963), 3-13.

> A good account of WE's years at Cambridge. Claims early critics have overlooked the "underlying seriousness" and tragic force of WE's early writings.

Fraser, George [S.]. "The Man within the Name: William Empson as Poet, Critic, and Friend." In WILLIAM EMPSON: THE MAN AND HIS WORK. Ed. Roma Gill. London: Routledge and Kegan Paul, 1974. Pp. 52-75.

> Argues that a poet's imagination suffuses WE's criticism. There is a "wholeness" in WE's personality and writing: "It is this plain directness of manner that has helped to give him his wide influence."

Fuller, John. "Empson's Tone." THE REVIEW, 6 and 7 (1963), 21-25.

> Values WE's prose over his verse because his "mind at work" is easier to follow in the criticism. A blend of generalization and detailed analyses marks WE's "critical character."

Fuller, Roy. "Too High-Flown a Genius? William Empson's Poetry Prose." ENCOUNTER, 53 (1979), 41-48.

> High praise for WE's critical prose: "He changed the way we

read; he imported a new probing, ranging, informal style into criticism."

Gardner, Philip, and Averil Gardner. THE GOD APPROACHED: A COMMENTARY ON THE POEMS OF WILLIAM EMPSON. London: Chatto and Windus, 1978.

> Primarily provides analysis on a poem-by-poem basis; however, the introduction offers a survey of WE's career and in discussing the poetry, illuminations from WE's own prose are often called upon.

Gill, Roma, ed. WILLIAM EMPSON: THE MAN AND HIS WORK. London: Routledge and Kegan Paul, 1974.

> A collection of fifteen tributes to WE's life, interests, and work, plus a bibliography by Moira Megaw. The essay contributions by Bradbrook, Fraser, Hough, Miller, Richards, Stock, and Wain are annotated separately.

Glicksberg, Charles I. "William Empson: Genius of Ambiguity." DR, 29 (1950), 366-77.

> Admires the virtuosity and rationalism of WE's analyses of ambiguity and poetry; however, he is too often carried to extremes which are misleading and far-fetched. A provocative and largely negative discussion of WE's strategies in SEVEN TYPES and SOME VERSIONS.

Hobsbaum, Philip. "Empson as Critical Practitioner." THE REVIEW, 6 and 7 (1963), 14-20.

> Values both WE and F.R. Leavis as practical critics. Contrasts their different approaches to Keats's "Ode on a Grecian Urn." WE sees it as an aesthetic paradox; to Leavis the paradox is a moral one.

Hough, Graham. "An Eighth Type of Ambiguity." In WILLIAM EMPSON: THE MAN AND HIS WORK. Ed. Roma Gill. London: Routledge and Kegan Paul, 1974. Pp. 76-97.

> Uses the concept of multiple meaning in SEVEN TYPES as a departure point for a highly intelligent exploration of the question of literary intention. Concludes that the surface of the text and the author's inferred intention must serve as a complementary basis for interpretation.

Jensen, James. "The Construction of SEVEN TYPES OF AMBIGUITY." MLQ, 27 (1966), 243-59.

> Stresses the open-minded outlook to various critical approaches

by WE at the time he wrote SEVEN TYPES and reconstructs "as
far as possible" the origins and conditions of its composition. Explains why the work has a "structural ungainliness" and why it
fails to implement "a coherently workable critical theory."

_____. "Some Ambiguous Preliminaries: Empson in THE GRANTA." CRITI-
CISM, 8 (1966), 349-61.

Examines some of WE's early prose contributions to GRANTA in
an effort to trace the origins of SEVEN TYPES in the full context of the Cambridge experience. Shows how WE blends the
"subjectivist orientation" of Robert Graves and Laura Riding with
the "more objective or rationalistic auspices" of I. A. Richards.

Kenner, Hugh. "Alice in Empsonland." In his GNOMON: ESSAYS IN
CONTEMPORARY LITERATURE. New York: McDowell, Obolensky, 1958.
Pp. 249-62.

Argues that WE's analytic method for discussing poetry fails to
grapple with the complexities of longer poems. Kenner also
charges that the organization of COMPLEX WORDS "isn't particularly rigorous."

McLuhan, H. M. "Poetic vs. Rhetorical Exegesis: The Case for Leavis against
Richards and Empson." SR, 52 (1944), 266-76.

Stresses that I. A. Richards and WE in their devices for analyzing
poetry have neither aimed at nor succeeded in the "literary
evaluation" of poems. Concludes that these two critics "are
thus rhetoricians" and recommends the "superior relevance" of
Leavis' critical method.

Mason, H. A. "W. Empson's Criticism." SCRUTINY, 4 (1936), 431-34.

Regrets that SOME VERSIONS lacks the "vigour and exuberance"
of SEVEN TYPES. Further, the pastoral theme "imperfectly binds"
WE's second book which is full of digressions.

Miller, Karl. "Empson Agonistes." In WILLIAM EMPSON: THE MAN AND
HIS WORK. Ed. Roma Gill. London: Routledge and Kegan Paul, 1974.
Pp. 41-48.

An interesting and sympathetic discussion of WE's "recoil from
Christianity" in several controversial writings. Also includes a
good analysis of WE's politics and prose style.

Norris, Christopher. WILLIAM EMPSON AND THE PHILOSOPHY OF LITERARY
CRITICISM. London: Athlone, 1978.

An intelligent and valuable study of WE's literary criticism.
Norris attempts to explain why the books have "invited mis-

understanding." Emphasizing the philosophical approach, he explains the necessary interaction between WE's theoretical and practical criticism. Concludes that humanistic rationalism "forms a coherent and developing background to each of his books." WE's criticism encompasses his "complicated feelings and baffled rationality" better than the poetry can.

Olsen, Elder. "William Empson, Contemporary Criticism, and Poetic Diction." In CRITICS AND CRITICISM: ANCIENT AND MODERN. Ed. R.S. Crane. Chicago: Univ. of Chicago Press, 1952. Pp. 45-82.

> A rhetorician launches a harsh attack on WE's shifting definitions of "ambiguity" and his other critical terms. Olsen soon leaves WE's works to examine the many aspects of "new criticism." In general, the new critics rate diction "as entirely too important."

Ransom, John Crowe. "I.A. Richards: The Psychological Critic. And William Empson, His Pupil." In his THE NEW CRITICISM. Norfolk, Conn.: New Directions, 1941. Pp. 101-31.

> Offers a fair amount of praise for WE's SEVEN TYPES: "The thing that engages his close analysis is the cognitive content." Ransom exercises his own imagination on some of WE's already extensive analyses of poems.

――――. "Mr. Empson's Muddles." SOR, 4 (1938), 322-39.

> A valuable article by an important critic who discusses fully why he approaches WE's criticism "with admiration and also with caution." Explains the subtle relationship between the poet's original intention and WE's later interpretations of a given poem.

THE REVIEW: A MAGAZINE OF POETRY AND CRITICISM, 6 and 7 (1963). A special issue on WE.

> Includes contributions by Martin Dodsworth, Colin Falck, John Fuller, Philip Hobsbaum, Peter Lowbridge, Christopher Ricks, and Saul Tonster. Also includes a WE interview and bibliography.

Richards, I.A. "Semantic Frontiersman." In WILLIAM EMPSON: THE MAN AND HIS WORK. Ed. Roma Gill. London: Routledge and Kegan Paul, 1974. Pp. 98-108.

> WE's senior supervisor at Cambridge presents a significant appraisal of his pupil's valuable work in literary semantics: He "raised the standards of ambition and achievement in a difficult and very hazardous art." Richards explains WE's techniques in SEVEN TYPES and COMPLEX WORDS.

———. "William Empson." FURIOSO, 1, No. 3 (12 January 1940), Supplement page.

    WE's mentor provides an interesting account of the genesis of SEVEN TYPES. He stresses WE's independent thinking and predicts the book's "persistent" and "distinctive" influence.

Robson, W.W. "More Empson than Milton?" THE OXFORD REVIEW, 1 (1966), 19-28.

    Robson wishes to register an "honest difference of opinion" about WE's reading of Milton's works in MILTON'S GOD.

Sale, Roger. "The Achievement of William Empson." HUDR, 19 (1966), 369-90.

    Extensive examination of WE's four critical books and the receptions accorded to them. Sale selects SOME VERSIONS as WE's best book: "As a modern work of persuasion it is unrivaled."

———. "The Achievement of William Empson." In his MODERN HEROISM: ESSAYS ON D.H. LAWRENCE, WILLIAM EMPSON, AND J.R.R. TOLKIEN. Berkeley and Los Angeles: Univ. of California Press, 1973. Pp. 107-92.

    An expanded version of Sale's appreciative essay in HUDR. Sale provides extensive and insightful discussions of SEVEN TYPES and SOME VERSIONS; he provides much briefer analyses of MILTON'S GOD and COMPLEX WORDS.

Sleight, Richard. "Mr. Empson's Complex Words." EIC, 2 (1952), 325-37.

    Sleight proclaims: "Irritating, difficult and wrongheaded though it often is, THE STRUCTURE OF COMPLEX WORDS is unquestionably the most important contribution to critical theory since [T.S. Eliot's] THE SACRED WOOD." A balanced and thoughtful discussion of WE's method of verbal analysis in COMPLEX WORDS.

Smith, James. "Books of the Quarter." THE CRITERION, 10 (1931), 738-42.

    A famous attack on WE's critical method in SEVEN TYPES. Smith believes that the first business of a critic of poetry is to pass conclusive value judgments. Questions WE's "vagueness about the nature and scope of ambiguity."

Stock, A.G. "NEW SIGNATURES in Retrospect." In WILLIAM EMPSON: THE MAN AND HIS WORK. Ed. Roma Gill. London: Routledge and Kegan Paul, 1974. Pp. 126-44.

    A restrospective assessment of the hope of revolution among young Leftist intellectuals during the 1930's. Discusses WE's politics and friendships with some of these writers.

William Empson

Strickland, Geoffrey. "The Criticism of William Empson." MANDRAKE, 2 (1954-55), 320-31.

> Useful evaluative survey of WE's critical writings. Strickland praises the "vitality" of the early criticism, but is troubled by the "dubious brilliance" of the later work. Strickland defines WE's idea of criticism and measures its degrees of "flexibility" and "resistance."

Wain, John. "Reflections on Johnson's LIFE OF MILTON." In WILLIAM EMPSON: THE MAN AND HIS WORK. Ed. Roma Gill. London: Routledge and Kegan Paul, 1974. Pp. 117-25.

> Appreciative defense of WE's expression of his personal views on religion, politics, and society in MILTON'S GOD. Compares WE's and Samuel Johnson's approaches to writing about Milton.

Willis, John H. WILLIAM EMPSON. Columbia Essays on Modern Writers. New York: Columbia Univ. Press, 1969.

> A handy introductory survey of WE's life and principal works. Willis traces the influence of I.A. Richards on WE's critical ideas and discusses individual poems in detail. Includes a selected bibliography.

FORD MADOX FORD (1873-1939)

Volume 1 of THE BODLEY HEAD FORD MADOX FORD (London: Bodley Head, 1962) along with THE GOOD SOLDIER collects numerous brief pieces drawn from ANCIENT LIGHTS, HEART OF THE COUNTRY, PORTRAITS FROM LIFE, and RETURN TO YESTERDAY. Volume 5 is the same as YOUR MIRROR TO MY TIMES (p. 165).

NONFICTIONAL PROSE

ANCIENT LIGHTS AND CERTAIN NEW REFLECTIONS: BEING THE MEMORIES OF A YOUNG MAN. London: Chapman and Hall, 1911. As MEMORIES AND IMPRESSIONS: A STUDY IN ATMOSPHERES. New York: Harper, 1911.

> Treats the literary climate in the 80's and 90's. FMF includes portraits of his grandfather, Madox Brown, and of the principal authors of the late Victorian period, some of whom, like Rossetti, FMF knew in his youth. FMF regrets the tameness of the current literary period as compared to theirs.

BETWEEN ST. DENNIS AND ST. GEORGE: A SKETCH OF THREE CIVILIZATIONS. London and New York: Hodder and Stoughton, 1915.

> The companion volume to WHEN BLOOD IS THEIR ARGUMENT, written as a reply to pacifists like Shaw.

THE CINQUE PORTS: A HISTORICAL AND DESCRIPTIVE RECORD. London: Blackwood, 1900.

> A treatise on the history and present state of Hastings, Winchelsea, Rye, Hythe, and Romney, as well as Dover and Sandwich.

THE CRITICAL ATTITUDE. London: Duckworth, 1911.

> A collection of eight essays on various literary topics. The most important piece, "English Literature of Today--II," examines Edwardian novelists and praises James, Conrad, and Moore.

ENGLAND AND THE ENGLISH: AN INTERPRETATION. New York: McClure, Phillips, 1907.

> Collects THE SOUL OF LONDON, THE HEART OF THE COUNTRY, and THE SPIRIT OF THE PEOPLE.

THE ENGLISH NOVEL: FROM THE EARLIEST DAYS TO THE DEATH OF JOSEPH CONRAD. Philadelphia: Lippincott, 1929. London: Constable, 1930.

> A casual study which deplores the sentimentality of the nineteenth-century British "nuvvle" and praises the "aloofness" of Flaubert and his school.

FORD MADOX BROWN: A RECORD OF HIS LIFE AND WORK. London and New York: Longmans, 1896.

> A long, detailed biography of the painter, containing liberal quotations from letters and diaries. Brown, an associate of the Pre-Raphaelites, was FMF's grandfather.

GREAT TRADE ROUTE. London: Unwin; New York: Oxford Univ. Press, 1937.

> A long digressive volume supposedly on the trade route from China to the West but focusing on the northern and southern United States. The culture and moderation of the South are preferred to the industrialism and militarism of the North. Along with PROVENCE, this volume represents FMF at his colloquial best.

HANS HOLBEIN THE YOUNGER: A CRITICAL MONOGRAPH. London: Duckworth; New York: Dutton, 1905.

> An informed and admiring survey of Holbein's career. Holbein possessed, as FMF emphasizes throughout, "a gift of keenly observing his fellow-men, and of rendering them dispassionately."

THE HEART OF THE COUNTRY: A SURVEY OF A MODERN LAND. London: Alston Rivers, 1906.

> Evocative sketches of the country, both in its realistic aspects and as an image of Arcadia.

HENRY JAMES: A CRITICAL STUDY. London: Secker, 1913. New York: Boni, 1915.

> A casual treatment of James's themes, background, and techniques. FMF emphasizes that James is a realist, not a moralist.

IT WAS THE NIGHTINGALE. Philadelphia: Lippincott, 1933. London: Heinemann, 1934.

> FMF's autobiography of his post-war years, written with the technical artistry of a novel. The book is packed with anecdotes about everyone from E.V. Lucas to Gertrude Stein, and recounts the conception of the PARADE'S END tetralogy. The last section deals with FMF's experience editing the TRANSATLANTIC REVIEW.

JOSEPH CONRAD: A PERSONAL REMEMBRANCE. London: Duckworth; Boston: Little, Brown, 1924.

> Rehearses the history of FMF's and Conrad's collaborations and contains an important section on the tenets of Impressionism the two evolved. FMF also writes amusing vignettes of Conrad, who wished to be "an English country gentleman of the time of Lord Palmerston."

THE MARCH OF LITERATURE: FROM CONFUCIUS' DAY TO OUR OWN. New York: Dial, 1938. As THE MARCH OF LITERATURE: FROM CONFUCIUS TO MODERN TIMES. London: Unwin, 1939.

> A long survey of world literature intended to introduce students to FMF's favorite authors.

A MIRROR TO FRANCE. London: Duckworth; New York: Boni, 1926.

> A parallel volume to THE SPIRIT OF THE PEOPLE, with chapters on the Left Bank, French politics, French wives, and the like.

NEW YORK ESSAYS. New York: Rudge, 1927.

> A collection of thoroughly delightful essays about the American scene and authors, written and published in New York. The most important pieces are on Crane, James, and the American expatriates.

NEW YORK IS NOT AMERICA. London: Duckworth, 1927. As NEW YORK IS NOT AMERICA: BEING A MIRROR TO THE STATES. New York: Boni, 1927.

> Sees New York, "large, loose, easy and tolerant," as a sanctuary in vulgar America.

NO ENEMY: A TALE OF RECONSTRUCTION. New York: Macaulay, 1929.

> A memoir of WWI, written as an extended interview with the French poet "Gringore" (an invention of FMF).

PORTRAITS FROM LIFE. Boston: Houghton Mifflin, 1937. As MIGHTIER

Ford Madox Ford

THAN THE SWORD: MEMOIRS AND CRITICISMS. London: Unwin, 1938.

> A collection of impressionistic portraits of James, Crane, Hudson, Conrad, Lawrence, Hardy, Wells, Galsworthy, Turgenev, Dreiser, and Swinburne.

THE PRE-RAPHAELITE BROTHERHOOD: A CRITICAL MONOGRAPH. London: Duckworth; New York: Dutton, 1907.

> A frequently biting history of the Brotherhood, which FMF knew well. He is particularly acerbic in his treatment of Holman Hunt.

PROVENCE: FROM MINSTRELS TO THE MACHINE. Philadelphia: Lippincott, 1935. London: Unwin, 1938.

> A lovely impressionistic rendering of Provencal history and characteristics. Provence is both an "earthly paradise" and a "frame of mind" to FMF.

RETURN TO YESTERDAY. London: Gollancz, 1931. New York: Liveright, 1932.

> A long memoir centering on the personal relationships (not always smooth) of FMF with Crane, Conrad, and James. The book also contains sections on FMF's encounters with the political left, Fleet Street, and New York.

ROSSETTI: A CRITICAL ESSAY ON HIS ART. London: Duckworth; New York: Dutton, 1902.

> A study of Rossetti's career as a painter, written in a cool and balanced manner that is unusual for FMF. "Rossetti's real gift, his essential talent, was that of catching emotions. . . . "

THE SOUL OF LONDON: A SURVEY OF A MODERN CITY. London: Alston Rivers, 1905.

> Vivid sketches of upper and lower class existence in London. FMF emphasizes the multiplicity of the city.

THE SPIRIT OF THE PEOPLE: AN ANALYSIS OF THE ENGLISH MIND. London: Alston Rivers, 1907.

> The final volume in the series that includes THE SOUL OF LONDON and THE HEART OF THE COUNTRY. The best chapters deal with the Englishman's social and religious codes.

THUS TO REVISIT: SOME REMINISCENCES. London: Chapman and Hall; New York: Dutton, 1921.

> Divided into two main parts: "Prosateurs" and "The Battle of

the Poets." The first centers on the struggle for technical innovations by FMF, Conrad, and James, with fond (if inaccurate) portraits of Hudson and Crane; the second describes the more drastic innovations of the Pound group.

WHEN BLOOD IS THEIR ARGUMENT: AN ANALYSIS OF PRUSSIAN CULTURE. London and New York: Hodder and Stoughton, 1915.

> A volume of war propaganda, complete with a historical survey of Germany. FMF concludes, "Germany has produced no art of a really capital kind since 1870, and all German art and learning have been steadily on the downgrade since 1848."

WOMEN AND MEN. Paris: Three Mountain Press, 1923.

> A humorous examination of the war between the sexes: "Roughly speaking, in Germany the woman is better drilled than in England."

WORKS EDITED BY OTHERS

CRITICAL WRITINGS OF FORD MADOX FORD. Ed. Frank MacShane. Lincoln: Univ. of Nebraska Press, 1964.

> A collection of FMF's critical writings mostly treating the novel; some of these are essays originally published in periodicals.

YOUR MIRROR TO MY TIMES: THE SELECTED AUTOBIOGRAPHIES AND IMPRESSIONS OF FORD MADOX FORD. Ed. Michael Killigrew. New York: Holt, Rinehart and Winston, 1971.

> Selections from the nonfiction arranged chronologically to form the "novel" of FMF's life.

BIBLIOGRAPHY

Beebe, Maurice, and Robert G. Johnson, comps. "Criticism of Ford Madox Ford: A Selected Checklist." MFS, 9 (1963), 94-100.

> Very selected, with sections on the major novels.

Gerber, Helmut, et al., eds. "Ford Madox Ford: An Annotated Checklist of Writings about Him." EFT [now ELT], 1, No. 2 (1958), 2-19. Continued in subsequent volumes.

> Organized alphabetically by author.

Harvey, David Dow, ed. FORD MADOX FORD, 1873-1939: A BIBLIOG-

RAPHY OF WORKS AND CRITICISM. Princeton, N.J.: Princeton Univ. Press, 1962.

>An excellent primary bibliography with sections on FMF's books, contributions to books by others, manuscripts and letters, and contributions to periodicals. Harvey also includes secondary sections on books and articles about FMF.

BIOGRAPHY

MacShane, Frank. THE LIFE AND WORKS OF FORD MADOX FORD. New York: Horizon Press, 1965.

>The biography touches on most of the nonfictional prose and focuses especially on the ideas expressed in PROVENCE and GREAT TRADE ROUTE.

Mizener, Arthur. THE SADDEST STORY: A BIOGRAPHY OF FORD MADOX FORD. New York: World, 1971.

>Contains material on the writing history of all of the nonfiction volumes and analyzes the more important.

CRITICISM

Bornhauser, Fred. "Ford as Art Critic." SHENANDOAH, 4, No. 1 (1953), 51-59.

>Paraphrases ROSSETTI and HANS HOLBEIN.

Borowitz, Helen Osterman. "The Paint Beneath the Prose: Ford Madox Ford's Pre-Raphaelite Ancestry." MFS, 21 (1975-76), 483-98.

>Cites the art books in attempting to show the influence of the Pre-Raphaelites' painting styles on FMF's writing style.

Cassell, Richard A. FORD MADOX FORD: A STUDY OF HIS NOVELS. Baltimore: Johns Hopkins Press, 1961.

>Cites the nonfiction frequently in delineating FMF's Pre-Raphaelite background and his theories of fiction.

──────. "Images of Collapse and Reconstruction: Ford's Vision of Society." ELT, 19 (1976), 265-82.

>Briefly cites ENGLAND AND THE ENGLISH in discussing FMF's social views.

Conrad, Jessie. JOSEPH CONRAD AND HIS CIRCLE. London: Jarrolds, 1935.

> Contains enraged passages on the inaccuracies in JOSEPH CONRAD.

Cox, James Trammell. "Ford's 'Passion for Provence.'" ELH, 28 (1961), 383-98.

> Briefly cites NIGHTINGALE, RETURN TO YESTERDAY, and PROVENCE in noting courtly love conventions in THE GOOD SOLDIER.

Davis, Harold E. "Conrad's Revisions of THE SECRET AGENT: A Study in Literary Impressionism." MLQ, 19 (1958), 244-54.

> Cites RETURN TO YESTERDAY and other prose works in discussing FMF's influence on the revisions.

Gabbay, Lydia Rivlin. "The Four Square Coterie: A Comparison of Ford Madox Ford and Henry James." SNNTS, 6 (1974), 439-53.

> Notes some satirical passages aimed at James in HENRY JAMES.

Green, Robert. FORD MADOX FORD: PROSE AND POLITICS. Cambridge: The Univ. Press, 1981.

> This contains heavy reference to the nonfiction in establishing how FMF's political attitudes affect the major novels.

Herendon, Richard. "The Genesis of Conrad's 'Amy Foster.'" SP, 57 (1960), 549-66.

> Cites material in THE CINQUE PORTS as a source for Conrad's story.

Huntley, H. Robert. "Ford, Holbein and Dürer." SAB, 30, No. 3 (1965), 4-6.

> A study of character types in THE FIFTH QUEEN. Huntley discusses FMF's theory of historical evolution of psychological types set forth in ENGLAND AND THE ENGLISH and suggested earlier in HANS HOLBEIN by the differences between Holbein's and Dürer's portraits.

Hynes, Samuel. "Ford and the Spirit of Romance." MFS, 9 (1963), 17-24.

> Notes the "romancing" tendency in the nonfiction.

Karl, Frederick R. "Joseph Conrad's Literary Theory." CRITICISM, 2 (1960), 317-35.

>Discusses FMF's doctrines for novelistic technique set forth in JOSEPH CONRAD.

Leer, Norman. THE LIMITED HERO IN THE NOVELS OF FORD MADOX FORD. East Lansing: Michigan State Univ. Press, 1966.

> A direct treatment (ch. 5) of FMF's nonfiction of the thirties, which, according to Leer, is better than the fiction. Frightened by the political climate, FMF becomes a prophet preaching an agrarian ideal in such works as PROVENCE and GREAT TRADE ROUTE. He places "increasing emphasis on the moral relevance of art, as opposed to its more dispassionate rendering of reality. . . ."

MacShane, Frank. "Ford Madox Ford and His Contemporaries: The Techniques of the Novel." EFT [now ELT], 4, No. 1 (1961), 2-11.

> Quotes from THE CRITICAL ATTITUDE and other works in discussing FMF's ideas about the novel.

_____, ed. FORD MADOX FORD: THE CRITICAL HERITAGE. Boston: Routledge and Kegan Paul, 1972.

> Contains contemporary reviews of most of the nonfictional books.

Meixner, John A. FORD MADOX FORD'S NOVELS: A CRITICAL STUDY. Minneapolis: Univ. of Minnesota Press, 1962.

> Cites FMF's prose treating fictional technique (e.g., JOSEPH CONRAD) in the introductory chapter.

Moser, Thomas C. THE LIFE IN THE FICTION OF FORD MADOX FORD. Princeton, N.J.: Princeton Univ. Press, 1980.

> Involves considerable discussion of the nonfiction (chs. 5 and 8) in laying out the biographical and psychological influences in FMF's career.

Pulos, C.E. "The New Critics and the Language of Poetry." UNS, 19 (1958), 8-14.

> Cites several of the prose works in noting that FMF "urged poets to choose subject matter possessing significance for their own age, to express themselves in an efficient language, and to project or render rather than to report effects."

Seiden, Melvin. "The Living Dead--VI: Ford Madox Ford and His Tetralogy." LONDON MAGAZINE, 6, No. 8 (1959), 45-55.

> Quotes from "The Women of the Novelists" [THE CRITICAL ATTITUDE] in discussing Christopher Tietjen's attitudes toward women in PARADE'S END.

Smith, Grover. FORD MADOX FORD. Columbia Essays on Modern Writers. New York: Columbia Univ. Press, 1972.

> A penetrating summary of the career, this mostly deals with the fiction but does contain some mention of the nonfictional works, judging those of the 1930's superior to the novels.

Stang, Sondra J. FORD MADOX FORD. Modern Literature Monographs. New York: Ungar, 1977.

> Contains brief, useful discussions of "The Autobiographical Writing" and "The Books on Culture."

Vidan, Ivo. "Ford's Interpretation of Conrad's Technique." In JOSEPH CONRAD: A COMMEMORATION. Ed. Norman Sherry. London: Macmillan, 1976. Pp. 183-93.

> An excellent critique of FMF's ideas about the novel in JOSEPH CONRAD, itself a novel in fact.

Wagner, Geoffrey. "Ford Madox Ford: The Honest Edwardian." EIC, 17 (1967), 75-87.

> Briefly cites ENGLAND AND THE ENGLISH in noting FMF's criticism of the upper class.

Wiley, Paul L. NOVELIST OF THREE WORLDS: FORD MADOX FORD. Syracuse, N.Y.: Syracuse Univ. Press, 1962.

> Places the utopian tendencies in PROVENCE and GREAT TRADE ROUTE in the tradition of other modern writers like Yeats and Lawrence.

E.M. FORSTER (1879-1970)

The "Abinger Edition" (London: Arnold, 1972--) includes TWO CHEERS (vol. 11) and GOLDSWORTHY LOWES DICKINSON (vol. 13).

NONFICTIONAL PROSE

ABINGER HARVEST. London: Arnold; New York: Harcourt, 1936.

Primarily a collection of previously published essays, arranged under these headings: "The Present," "Books," "The Past," and "The East." Among the more important works are "Notes on the English Character" (which is emotionally undeveloped), "Liberty in England" (a political credo), "T. S. Eliot" (guilty of willful obscurity), "Joseph Conrad: A Note" (he has no philosophy, only opinions), and an admiring piece on "The Early Novels of Virginia Woolf." The volume concludes with "The Abinger Pageant," written by EMF on behalf of a country church in the parish of Abinger.

ALEXANDRIA: A HISTORY AND A GUIDE. Alexandria, Egypt: Whitehead Morris, 1922.

Less amusing than PHAROS AND PHARILLON, ALEXANDRIA is a straightforward account of the city's political and cultural history (first section) and of its present attractions (second section). EMF was a Red Cross volunteer in Alexandria during WWI.

ASPECTS OF THE NOVEL. London: Arnold; New York: Harcourt, 1927.

An influential and famous work, written originally as the Clark lectures. EMF prefers character to plot and damns writers he dislikes--Scott, Meredith, James--with the faint praise of being good plotters. Despite its quirkiness, the study makes important observations on the distinction between flat and round character, the use of rhythm (motif) in the novel, and the ability of the realistic genre to manifest "fantasy" and "prophecy."

GOLDSWORTHY LOWES DICKINSON. London: Arnold; New York: Harcourt, 1934.

>EMF's tribute to "Goldie" Dickinson, a Cambridge don, based both on Dickinson's own autobiographical writings and EMF's long friendship with him. Unlike EMF in his strenuous political activities (he was a founder of the League of Nations), Dickinson clearly influenced EMF's humanistic values. The book is also a glowing portrait of Cambridge life in general.

THE HILL OF DEVI. London: Arnold; New York: Harcourt, 1953.

>A volume of EMF's letters written home during two visits to India in 1912 and 1921, together with some historical sketches. During the latter stay, he was private secretary to the Maharajah of Dewas Senior, the principal figure of the book. Many of the experiences EMF records were used in A PASSAGE TO INDIA, such as the religious festival in the novel's third part.

MARIANNE THORNTON: A DOMESTIC BIOGRAPHY. London: Arnold; New York: Harcourt, 1956.

>A "domestic biography" of EMF's great aunt, whose bequest enabled him to attend Cambridge. The pious Thorntons and their house, Battersea Rise, represent virtues EMF sorely misses.

PHAROS AND PHARILLON. Richmond, Engl.: Hogarth; New York: Knopf, 1923.

>A collection of humorous sketches depicting Alexandria's legendary past and more mundane present; Pharos was the huge lighthouse of the city and Pharillon its diminutive successor.

TWO CHEERS FOR DEMOCRACY. London: Arnold; New York: Harcourt, 1951.

>An extensive collection of essays (most written after 1936) on politics and art. Two of the more significant political essays are "The Challenge of Our Time" (to combine economic socialism and personal independence) and "What I Believe" (he believes in personal relationships and democracy). The more important pieces on art include "Art for Art's Sake," "The Raison d'Etre of Criticism," "Virginia Woolf," and "English Prose between 1918 and 1939."

WORKS EDITED BY OTHERS

ALBERGO EMPEDOCLE AND OTHER EARLY WRITINGS. Ed. George H. Thomson. New York: Liveright, 1971.

A collection of minor essays written between 1900 and 1915. The previously uncollected works are arranged under these headings: "Cambridge Humor," "Bourgeois Values versus Inspiration," "For the Working Men's College," "India," and "The Arts and War."

E.M. FORSTER: A TRIBUTE. Ed. K. Natwar-Singh. New York: Harcourt, 1964.

The second edition of this book collects passages dealing with India from several of EMF's nonfictional prose works.

E.M. FORSTER: SELECTED WRITINGS. Ed. G.B. Parker. London: Heinemann, 1968.

The first section of this book consists of essays drawn from ABINGER, TWO CHEERS, ASPECTS, and THE HILL OF DEVI.

BIBLIOGRAPHY

Beebe, Maurice, and Joseph Brogunier, comps. "Criticism of E.M. Forster: A Selected Checklist." MFS, 7 (1961), 284-92.

Alphabetically arranged, with general sections and sections on individual works. Not annotated.

Borrello, Alfred, ed. E.M. FORSTER: AN ANNOTATED BIBLIOGRAPHY OF SECONDARY MATERIALS. Scarecrow Author Bibliographies. Metuchen, N.J.: Scarecrow, 1973.

An annotated secondary bibliography, chronologically arranged. Borrello indexes EMF's books only if they appear in secondary titles, not secondary contents.

Gerber, Helmut, Frederick P.W. McDowell et al., eds. "E.M. Forster: An Annotated Checklist of Writings about Him." EFT [now ELT], 2, No. 1 (1959), 4-27. Continued in subsequent volumes.

Alphabetically arranged; annotated.

Kirkpatrick, Brownlee Jean, ed. A BIBLIOGRAPHY OF E.M. FORSTER. [1965]. Rev. ed. London: Rupert Hart-Davis, 1968.

The best primary bibliography, with sections on books, contributions to books, contributions to periodicals, translations (of EMF's works), and miscellanea such as recordings.

McDowell, Frederick P.W., ed. E.M. FORSTER: AN ANNOTATED BIBLIOGRAPHY OF WRITINGS ABOUT HIM. DeKalb: Northern Illinois Univ. Press, 1976.

Compiles over 1900 well-annotated pieces on EMF's work; chronologically organized with good indexes. The best secondary bibliography.

BIOGRAPHY

Furbank, P.N. E.M. FORSTER: A LIFE. 2 vols. London: Secker, 1977-78.

The best biography, useful for background information on the nonfiction.

CRITICISM

Baker, James R. "Forster's Voyage of Discovery." TQ, 18, No. 2 (1975), 99-118.

A survey of EMF's career, showing the contemporary relevance of his views on the splintered western mentality and culture. Baker touches on most of the nonfiction prose volumes. For instance, both ALEXANDRIA and PHAROS depict the collapse of Alexander's dream of unity.

Booth, Wayne C. "E.M. Forster as Essayist." In A RHETORIC OF IRONY. Chicago: Univ. of Chicago Press, 1974. Pp. 185-90.

A sensitive, if brief, explication of EMF's social essay "Me, Them and You" (ABINGER) demonstrating when the essay is ironic and when it is not.

Brander, Laurence. E.M. FORSTER: A CRITICAL STUDY. Lewisburg, Pa.: Bucknell Univ. Press, 1968.

This contains lengthy treatments of the nonfiction, but unfortunately these are essentially descriptive rather than analytic. A useful guide but hardly a "critical study."

Britten, Benjamin. "Some Notes on Forster and Music." In ASPECTS OF E.M. FORSTER: ESSAYS AND RECOLLECTIONS WRITTEN FOR HIS NINETIETH BIRTHDAY JANUARY 1, 1969. Ed. Oliver Stallybrass. New York: Harcourt, 1969. Pp. 81-86.

A brief review of EMF's opinions about music by his collaborator in the opera BILLY BUDD. In "The C Minor of That Life" (TWO CHEERS) EMF explores the connection between musical key and meaning; in "Not Listening to Music" (TWO CHEERS) he mocks the expert approach to music.

E.M. Forster

Colmer, John. E.M. FORSTER: THE PERSONAL VOICE. London: Routledge and Kegan Paul, 1975.

> Probably the best-written work of those summarizing the nonfiction.

Furbank, P.N. "Forster and 'Bloomsbury' Prose." In E.M. FORSTER: A HUMAN EXPLORATION: CENTENARY ESSAYS. Ed. G.K. Das and John Beer. New York: New York Univ. Press, 1979. Pp. 161-66.

> EMF's prose exhibits the Bloomsbury traits of obliqueness and amusingness.

Gardner, Philip, ed. E.M. FORSTER: THE CRITICAL HERITAGE. London: Routledge and Kegan Paul, 1973.

> Reprints contemporary reviews of ASPECTS, ABINGER, TWO CHEERS, THE HILL OF DEVI, and MARIANNE THORNTON.

Godshalk, William Leigh. "Some Sources of Durrell's ALEXANDRIA QUARTET." MFS, 13 (1967), 361-74.

> A brief noting of material, such as a passage on Gnosticism, Durrell took from ALEXANDRIA.

Goldman, Mark. "Virginia Woolf and E.M. Forster: A Critical Dialogue." TSLL, 7 (1966), 387-400.

> An excellent discussion of these authors' conflicting views. In "The Early Novels of Virginia Woolf" (ABINGER) and, indirectly, in ASPECTS, EMF rejects Woolf's formal experimentalism. In "The Raison d'Etre of Criticism in the Arts" (TWO CHEERS), EMF suggests that criticism is worthless, and thus again disagrees with Woolf.

Hanquart, Evelyn. "E.M. Forster's Manuscript of MARIANNE THORNTON." N&Q, 20 (1973), 336-40.

> A description of an early draft in King's College Library.

Herz, Judith Sherer. "Forster's Three Experiments in Autobiographical Biography." SLitI, 13, No. 1 (1980), 51-67.

> Argues that GOLDSWORTHY LOWES DICKINSON, MARIANNE THORNTON, and HILL OF DEVI contain personae of EMF and are imaginative reconstructions of autobiographical experience.

Irwin, W.R. "Help from the Critics." In THE GAME OF THE IMPOSSIBLE: A RHETORIC OF FANTASY. Urbana: Univ. of Illinois Press, 1976. Pp. 39-43.

> A good summary of EMF's comments about fantasy in ASPECTS.

Johnstone, J. K. THE BLOOMSBURY GROUP: A STUDY OF E.M. FORSTER, LYTTON STRACHEY, VIRGINIA WOOLF, AND THEIR CIRCLE. New York: Noonday, 1954.

>Johnstone paraphrases and quotes from the nonfiction a great deal in discussing EMF's aesthetics (pp. 62-76) and his values (pp. 100-113). A handy review.

Joseph, David I. THE ART OF REARRANGEMENT: E.M. FORSTER'S ABINGER HARVEST. New Haven, Conn.: Yale Univ. Press, 1964.

>A revised Yale honors thesis. Joseph takes up the five sections of ABINGER in order and emphasizes their interrelationships and artful arrangement. "ABINGER HARVEST falls somewhere between the realm of pure fiction and pure exposition."

Kelvin, Norman. E.M. FORSTER. Crosscurrents. Carbondale and Edwardsville: Southern Illinois Univ. Press, 1967.

>Chapter 8 is a brief summary of the nonfiction.

Klingopulos, G.D. "E.M. Forster's Sense of History: and Cavafy." EIC, 8 (1958), 156-65.

>A meandering discussion of EMF's "hellenism" which involves essays on Alexander and Cavafy in PHAROS.

Lakshmi, Vijay. "Virginia Woolf and E.M. Forster: A Study of Their Critical Relations." LHY, 12, No. 2 (1971), 34-49.

>A sloppily written review of the authors' attitudes toward each other. In his two essays on Woolf (in ABINGER and TWO CHEERS) EMF argues she does not construct life-like characters.

Macaulay, Rose. THE WRITINGS OF E.M. FORSTER. New York: Harcourt, 1938.

>This contains lengthy descriptions of the nonfictional prose written by 1938.

McDowell, Frederick P.W. E.M. FORSTER. Twayne's English Author Series. New York: Twayne, 1969.

>The concluding chapter is a useful, basic review of the nonfictional prose.

_____. "E.M. Forster and Goldsworthy Lowes Dickinson." SNNTS, 5 (1973), 441-56.

>A broadly focused article treating Dickinson, his autobiography, and EMF's GOLDSWORTHY LOWES DICKINSON. EMF's biog-

raphy eschews Dickinson's sex life; it is "most noteworthy for its characteristic Forsterian touches, for the felicity and spiritual poise of the style," and so forth.

_____. E.M. Forster's Conception of the Critic." TSL, 10 (1965), 93-100.

A good summary of EMF's ideas about the place of criticism; the article cites his essays on the subject throughout, such as "The Raison d'Etre of Criticism in the Arts" (TWO CHEERS). EMF loathed systematic criticism, favoring instead his own impressionistic responses. Although he thought the usefulness of the critic overrated, the critic could expose the fraudulent and keep the artist up to superior ideas.

_____. E.M. Forster's Theory of Literature." CRITICISM, 8 (1966), 19-43.

A valuable article which pulls together EMF's various pronouncements on literature in the nonfiction; he is seen to display "a remarkable intellectual consistency throughout his career."

Moore, Harry T. E.M. FORSTER. Columbia Essays in Modern Writers. New York: Columbia Univ. Press, 1965.

This contains a brief description of the nonfictional prose volumes.

Muir, Edwin. "Conclusion." In his THE STRUCTURE OF THE NOVEL. London: Hogarth, 1928. Pp. 134-46.

In his final chapter, Muir takes EMF to task for denigrating "flat" characters in ASPECTS.

Pinchin, Jane Lagoudis. ALEXANDRIA STILL: FORSTER, DURRELL, AND CAVAFY. Princeton, N.J.: Princeton Univ. Press, 1977.

Chapter 3 is a very full treatment of PHAROS AND PHARILLON and ALEXANDRIA, discussing the background to their composition, the influence of Cavafy in them, and how they function as preliminaries to PASSAGE TO INDIA.

Rawlings, Donn. "E.M. Forster, 'Prophecy,' and the Subversion of Myth." PAUNCH, 30 (1967), 17-36.

As involved discussion of EMF's ambivalence about "prophetic" fiction in ASPECTS. He is divided by "the claims of an attractive but potentially destructive transcendental myth . . . [and] . . . those of valued personal realities in 'life as it actually is,' a life in which experience is nevertheless frustratingly mutilated and fragmentary."

Schmerl, Rudolf B. "Fantasy as Technique." VQR, 43 (1967), 644-56.

Includes a very brief review of the section in ASPECTS on fantasy.

Shaheen, M.Y. "Forster on Meredith." RES, 24 (1973), 185-91.

> A review of EMF's remarks on Meredith in ASPECTS and elsewhere. "Forster's chief fault as a critic of Meredith is that he treats him mainly as a comic writer. . . . "

———. "Forster's Alexandria: The Transitional Journey." In E.M. FORSTER: A HUMAN EXPLORATION: CENTENARY ESSAYS. Ed. G.K. Das and John Beer. New York: New York Univ. Press, 1979. Pp. 79-88.

> On how EMF's review of religious history in ALEXANDRIA influences the religious speculation and even the narrative technique in PASSAGE TO INDIA.

Singh, Frances B. "The Centrality of Alexandria: A History and a Guide to Forster's Fiction." In APPROACHES TO E.M. FORSTER: A CENTENARY VOLUME. Ed. Vasant A. Shahane. Atlantic Highlands, N.J.: Humanities Press, 1981. Pp. 118-26.

> The city in ALEXANDRIA embodies the ideal of human connectedness that EMF's characters strive for in his fiction.

Stallybrass, Oliver. "Editor's Introduction." In his GOLDSWORTHY LOWES DICKINSON AND RELATED WRITINGS. Abinger Edition. London: Arnold, 1973. Pp. xi-xix.

> A brief, informative review of the book's writing history and reception.

———. "Editor's Introduction." In his TWO CHEERS FOR DEMOCRACY. Abinger Edition. London: Arnold, 1972.

> A brief discussion of the publishing history and revisions of the essays in TWO CHEERS.

Stone, Wilfred. THE CAVE AND THE MOUNTAIN: A STUDY OF E.M. FORSTER. Stanford, Calif.: Stanford Univ. Press, 1966.

> The best critical study of EMF, which refers to the nonfiction throughout. ASPECTS is analyzed at some length in the chapter "Forster's Esthetics," ALEXANDRIA in "A Passage to Alexandria," and the essays in "Criticism: The Near and the Far."

Thomson, George H. "A Forster Miscellany: Thoughts on the Uncollected Writings." In ASPECTS OF E.M. FORSTER: ESSAYS AND RECOLLECTIONS WRITTEN FOR HIS NINETIETH BIRTHDAY JANUARY 1, 1969. Ed. Oliver Stallybrass. New York: Harcourt, 1969. Pp. 155-75.

> A handy review of EMF's (then) uncollected nonfiction under the headings "Early Writings," "India and Egypt," "History, Society, and the Arts," "Literature," and "Autobiography." Some of the essays were reprinted in ALBERGO EMPEDOCLE.

Thumboo, Edwin. "E.M. Forster's Inner Passage to India; Dewas, Alexandria and the Road to Mau." In APPROACHES TO E.M. FORSTER: A CENTENARY VOL-

UME. Ed. Vasant A. Shahane. Atlantic Highlands, N.J.: Humanities Press, 1981. Pp. 35-58.

> Partly on how EMF's experiences of new philosophies and religions in Egypt, as recorded in PHAROS AND PHARILLON and ALEXANDRIA, prepared him for Indian life and PASSAGE TO INDIA.

Trevelyan, G.M. "Lecture V." In his A LAYMAN'S LOVE OF LETTERS. London: Longmans, 1954. Pp. 85-105.

> A defense of Scott against EMF's criticism expressed in ASPECTS that Scott's style and characterization were poor.

Trilling, Lionel. E.M. FORSTER: A STUDY. London: Hogarth, 1944.

> Chapter 9 begins as an assault on EMF's overly relaxed literary criticism and expands into a good discussion of his "relaxed will," the product or cause of his historical pessimism, for example. Trilling covers a great many essays.

―――. "The Great-Aunt of Mr. Forster." In his A GATHERING OF FUGITIVES. Boston: Beacon Press, 1956. Pp. 1-11.

> A review of MARIANNE THORNTON that places the Thorntons in the tradition of Britain's intellectual families.

Trivedi, H.K. "Forster and Virginia Woolf: The Critical Friends." In E.M. FORSTER: A HUMAN EXPLORATION: CENTENARY ESSAYS. Ed. G.K. Das and John Beer. New York: New York Univ. Press, 1979. Pp. 216-30.

> Cites the nonfiction in noting EMF found Woolf's fiction too radical technically, while she found his too "Edwardian."

Truitt, Willis H. "Thematic and Symbolic Ideology in the Works of E.M. Forster: In Memoriam." JAAC, 30 (1971), 101-09.

> A Marxist sees Marxist ideas in EMF and addresses such essays as "My Wood" (ABINGER), which deals with the evils of ownership, and "Me, Them and You" (ABINGER), which deals with class conflict.

Watt, Donald J. "G.E. Moore and the Bloomsbury Group." ELT, 12 (1969), 119-34.

> Notes that the doctrine expressed in "Art for Art's Sake" (TWO CHEERS) corresponds to Moore's "intrinsic good."

Woolf, Virginia. "The Art of Fiction." In THE MOMENT AND OTHER ESSAYS. Ed. Leonard Woolf. London: Hogarth, 1947. Pp. 89-93.

> Criticizes EMF's "unaesthetic attitude" toward the novel demonstrated in ASPECTS; he is more interested in characters than formal patterns.

EDMUND GOSSE (1849-1928)

NONFICTIONAL PROSE

ASPECTS AND IMPRESSIONS. London: Cassell; New York: Scribner's, 1922.

    Critical portraits of such figures as Samuel Butler, Henry James, and George Eliot as well as essays on French criticism and Norwegian writers. EG is more sympathetic to James than to Eliot.

BOOKS ON THE TABLE. London: Heinemann; New York: Scribner's, 1921.

    Forty brief critical essays mainly on literary figures, including Disraeli, Tolstoi, Poe, Clough, Massinger, Locker-Lampson, Saintsbury, Fielding, Carlyle, and Goethe.

COLLECTED ESSAYS OF EDMUND GOSSE. London: Heinemann, 1913. New York: Scribner's, 1914.

    The five-volume set includes: vol. 1, SEVENTEENTH CENTURY STUDIES; vol. 2, GOSSIP IN A LIBRARY; vol. 3, CRITICAL KIT-KATS; vol. 4, FRENCH PROFILES; and vol. 5, PORTRAITS AND SKETCHES.

COVENTRY PATMORE. London: Hodder and Stoughton; New York: Scribner's, 1905.

    A full-length treatment of a minor Victorian poet and friend of EG's. Some use of psychological method. Includes critical analysis of Patmore's best poetry.

CRITICAL KIT-KATS. London: Heinemann; New York: Dodd, Mead, 1896.

    Engaging personal portraits of and critical commentary on such figures as Pater, Christina Rossetti, Stevenson, and Whitman. Judges Whitman to be a near-great poet "for want of a definite shape and fixity."

ENGLISH LITERATURE: AN ILLUSTRATED RECORD. 4 vols. London: Heinemann; New York: Macmillan, 1905.

> Volume 1 was written by Richard Garnett; volume 2 by Garnett and EG; volumes 3 and 4 by EG. In volume 3, EG surveys the period from Milton to Johnson; in volume 4, he treats the period from Johnson to Tennyson. Generous illustrations of major literary figures, their haunts, their manuscripts, and their published works.

FATHER AND SON: A STUDY OF TWO TEMPERAMENTS. London: Heinemann, 1907. As FATHER AND SON: BIOGRAPHICAL RECOLLECTIONS. New York: Scribner's, 1907.

> Partly a biography of his Puritanical scientist father, and partly an autobiography. An outstanding and famous Victorian masterpiece. EG's greatest use of psychological analysis as he shows his father's depression and insanity over the religion-evolution controversy between the years 1850 and 1865. EG vividly records his own struggles to escape the rigorous narrowness of evangelical religion.

FRENCH PROFILES. London: Heinemann, 1904.

> Personal portraits of and critical commentary on such French writers as Daudet, Mallarmé, Samain, and Verlaine. The works of Zola are also discussed in a separate essay.

FROM SHAKESPEARE TO POPE: AN INQUIRY INTO THE CAUSES AND PHENOMENA OF THE RISE OF CLASSICAL POETRY IN ENGLAND. Cambridge: The Univ. Press, 1885.

> Critical essays which often emphasize historical milieu over close analysis of individual works. EG traces classical and Romantic movements in English poetry. The essay on Edmund Waller and his use of the heroic couplet is original and important.

GOSSIP IN A LIBRARY. London: Heinemann, 1891.

> Twenty-six wide-ranging essays, many of which deal with literary taste and reputations. Some of the more significant essays treat the reception of Wordsworth's poem "Peter Bell," the poetic achievement of Lady Winchilsea, and the compilation of early French dictionaries.

GRAY. English Men of Letters. London: Macmillan; New York: Harper, 1882.

> EG's first full-length biography which contains some critical analysis of Thomas Gray's works. Analyzes the strain of melancholy in Gray's personality. Concludes with a useful survey of

the critical reputation of Gray in the eighteenth to nineteenth centuries.

A HISTORY OF EIGHTEENTH CENTURY LITERATURE, 1660-1780. London and New York: Macmillan, 1889.

>Essays in literary history and judgment, covering such figures as Dryden, Pope, Swift, Fielding, and Johnson. Organized by genres. Good in tracing the origins of the novel.

IBSEN. London: Hodder and Stoughton; New York: Scribner's, 1907.

>Early and important comprehensive evaluation of the Norwegian playwright's works against the "intellectual life" of his times. Analyzes three categories of plays: studies in satire, realism, and imagination.

INTER ARMA: BEING ESSAYS WRITTEN IN TIME OF WAR. London: Heinemann; New York: Scribner's, 1916.

>Collects seven essays on the theme of war and literature, with specific reference to England, France, and Sweden. Speculates on how wars change the function and character of literature.

THE JACOBEAN POETS. London: Murray; New York: Scribner's, 1894.

>Essays in literary history and criticism covering English poetry written between 1603 and 1625. Examines Romantic and classical elements in poetry and drama of such writers as Robert Southwell, Ben Jonson, Thomas Campion, Michael Drayton, and Beaumont and Fletcher. The essay on "John Donne" is significant.

JEREMY TAYLOR. English Men of Letters. London and New York: Macmillan, 1904.

>Examines the prose, politics, and religion of the seventeenth-century Anglican clergyman. Includes critical evaluation of Taylor's writings; good analysis of his prose style.

LEAVES AND FRUIT. London: Heinemann, 1927.

>Thirty-seven informed and perceptive critical essays on such figures as Mallarmé, Edith Sitwell, Sassoon, Strachey, Montaigne, Whitman, Gissing, and Johnson. EG also discusses "The Agony of the Middle Ages" and "The Physiology of Taste."

THE LIFE AND LETTERS OF JOHN DONNE. 2 vols. London: Heinemann, 1899.

>One of the very first and best scholarly studies in the modern

revival of interest in the metaphysical poets. Some reliance on the psychological approach and good critical commentary on Donne's poetry and sermons.

THE LIFE OF ALGERNON CHARLES SWINBURNE. London: Macmillan, 1917.

EG's final critical biography of his long-time friend. Includes information and insights not available elsewhere. Good on literary milieu. Some of the critical analysis betrays EG's ethical bias.

THE LIFE OF PHILIP HENRY GOSSE, F.R.S. London: Kegan Paul, Trench, Trubner, 1890.

EG's first biography of his scientist father; a precursor to FATHER AND SON. Details P.H. Gosse's zoological studies in Canada, Jamaica, and the United States. Valuable insights into Victorian controversy over religion and science.

LIFE OF WILLIAM CONGREVE. London: Scott; New York: Whittaker, 1888.

Helped establish EG's renown as a legitimate eighteenth-century scholar. First full-length biography of the Restoration dramatist. Includes critical discussion of his works. EG published a revised and enlarged edition in 1924.

MORE BOOKS ON THE TABLE. London: Heinemann, 1923.

A collection of forty-one brief critical essays on such figures as Matthew Arnold, Queen Victoria, Mark Akenside, Leigh Hunt, Blake, and Gray. Also discusses the art of parody, burlesque, Georgian poetry, life at Oxford, and how to read the Bible.

NORTHERN STUDIES. London: Scott, 1890.

A revised edition of STUDIES IN THE LITERATURE OF NORTHERN EUROPE. Adds a chapter on Ibsen; deletes chapters on Germany and Holland.

PORTRAITS AND SKETCHES. London: Heinemann; New York: Scribner's, 1912.

Essential collection of thirteen critical essays on such figures as Gide, Lang, Swinburne, Tennyson, Whittier, and some of the Spasmodic poets. Mandell Creighton, clergyman, is the only nonliterary figure treated.

QUESTIONS AT ISSUE. London: Heinemann; New York: Appleton, 1893.

Collects fourteen lightweight reviews on such topics as nature

and future of poetry, influence of democracy on literature,
fictional realism, French symbolism, Shelley, Tennyson, Kipling,
and Stevenson. The essay "Has America Produced a Poet?" is
a lively item in the annals of literary history--Poe comes closest
to the honor according to EG.

RALEIGH. London: Longmans; New York: Appleton, 1886.

Biography of famed Elizabethan adventurer. The last three
chapters treat Raleigh's prose writings.

ROBERT BROWNING: PERSONALIA. London: Unwin; Boston and New
York: Houghton Mifflin, 1890.

A brief biography of the Victorian poet divided into two parts:
"The Early Career of Robert Browning, 1812-1846" and "Personal
Impressions." Much of the information EG obtained from Browning
himself. EG provides some critical analysis of his poetry.

SELECTED ESSAYS, FIRST SERIES. London: Heinemann, 1928. Freeport,
N.Y.: Books for Libraries, 1968.

Selects fourteen essays which convey EG's pleasure in reading
literature written by Pater, Sterne, Christina Rossetti, Tennyson,
Poe, Hardy, and others.

SELECTED ESSAYS, SECOND SERIES. London: Heinemann, 1928. Freeport,
N.Y.: Books for Libraries, 1968.

Selects twelve essays dealing with such figures as George Moore,
Wycherley, and the Brontës, as well as such topics as cats, dogs,
and the Bible.

SEVENTEENTH CENTURY STUDIES: A CONTRIBUTION TO THE HISTORY OF
ENGLISH POETRY. London: Kegan Paul, Trench and Co., 1883. New
York: Dodd, Mead, 1897.

Ten critical-historical essays on such English authors as Thomas
Lodge, John Webster, Robert Herrick, Richard Crashaw, Abraham
Cowley, and Thomas Otway.

A SHORT HISTORY OF MODERN ENGLISH LITERATURE. London: Heinemann;
New York: Appleton, 1897.

Literary history in summary form, from Chaucer to the 1890's.
EG strives to present "a feeling of the evolution of English
literature." More commentary on poetry than on prose. Covers
some figures not treated in EG's other works--especially good
on Victorian writers.

Edmund Gosse

SILHOUETTES. London: Heinemann; New York: Scribner's, 1925.

> A collection of forty-one critical essays on such writers as Wycherley, Andrew Lang, Melville, Austin Dobson, W.D. Howells, Mrs. Humphry Ward, George Saintsbury, Leslie Stephen, and on such topics as nature in poetry, Roman pictures, and American folk songs.

SIR THOMAS BROWNE. English Men of Letters. London and New York: Macmillan, 1905.

> EG concentrates on the uniqueness of Browne's ideas and prose style in such works as RELIGIO MEDICI, VULGAR ERRORS, and URN-BURIAL. The seventeenth-century physician's life is also treated, including his interests in astrology and witchcraft.

SOME DIVERSIONS OF A MAN OF LETTERS. London: Heinemann; New York: Scribner's, 1919.

> Collects seventeen significant critical essays, including discussions of literary taste, Shakespeare's songs, the Brontës' novels, Disraeli's novels, Hardy's poetry, and World War I poetry. EG ends with some perceptive musings on the Victorian Age and the future of English poetry.

STUDIES IN THE LITERATURE OF NORTHERN EUROPE. London: Kegan Paul, 1879.

> EG's first effort at literary history and criticism. Collects ten uneven essays on Scandinavian literature, covering such topics as Norwegian poetry, Ibsen, Danish poetry, and a Dutch poetess.

SWINBURNE. Edinburgh: Riverside Press, 1925.

> EG wrote this eighty-one page essay in 1875 and first published it in 1925.

THREE FRENCH MORALISTS, AND THE GALLANTRY OF FRANCE. London: Heinemann; New York: Scribner's, 1918.

> A tribute to young French soldiers killed in World War I; a discussion of three French moralists--La Rochefoucauld, La Bruyère, and Vauvenaragues.

TWO VISITS TO DENMARK: 1872, 1874. London: Smith, Elder, 1911. New York: Dutton, 1912.

> Valuable for its autobiographical insights. Offers sketches of notable Danes, including Hans Christian Andersen and Georg Brandes.

WORKS EDITED BY OTHERS

AMERICA: THE DIARY OF A VISIT, WINTER 1884-1885. Ed. Robert L. Peters and David G. Halliburton. Lafayette, Ind.: ELT Special Series, No. 2 (1966). Pp. 1-30.

> EG records his impressions of the United States and of such literary figures as Poe, Whitman, and Whittier. Some of the entries were later expanded into fuller critical portraits.

FATHER AND SON. Ed. William Irvine. Boston: Houghton Mifflin, 1965.

> An annotated text with helpful scholarly apparatus.

FATHER AND SON: A STUDY OF TWO TEMPERAMENTS. Ed. James Hepburn. London: Oxford Univ. Press, 1974.

> A useful and attractive edition, which includes explanatory notes, chronology, select bibliography, and illustrations.

BIBLIOGRAPHY

"Bibliographies of Modern Authors. Edmund William Gosse." LONDON MERCURY, 3, No. 14 (1920), 212-13.

> Included in this early primary bibliography is a checklist--selective and chronologically arranged--of EG's prose, 1870-1919.

Bredsdorff, Elias, comp. "Bibliographical Supplements." In SIR EDMUND GOSSE'S CORRESPONDENCE WITH SCANDINAVIAN WRITERS. Copenhagen: Gyldendal, 1960. Pp. 316-46.

> Chronologically arranged listing of EG's contributions in English to books, periodicals, and newspapers on Scandinavian topics. Also includes a brief secondary bibliography.

Gullick, Norman, comp. "Bibliography." In THE LIFE AND LETTERS OF SIR EDMUND GOSSE. Ed. Evan Charteris. London: Heinemann, 1931. Pp. 511-18.

> A selected, but fairly comprehensive list of EG's "most important" primary works. Arranged chronologically, with some brief annotations. Although incomplete, the best primary bibliography available.

Woolf, James D., comp. "Selected Bibliography." In SIR EDMUND GOSSE. New York: Twayne, 1972. Pp. 166-71.

> Includes chronological listing of EG's books. Lists editions of

his letters. Selective listing of secondary sources arranged alphabetically by author, with helpful annotations.

Woolf, James D., ed. "Sir Edmund Gosse: An Annotated Bibliography of Writings about Him." ELT, 11 (1968), 126-72. Continued in later volumes of ELT (12-18).

A nearly exhaustive (almost 300 items) secondary bibliography of items about EG. The entries are arranged alphabetically by author and nearly all are superbly annotated. In several items, however, Woolf's pro-Gosse bias hinders a judicious assessment. Includes some foreign-language scholarship and dissertations.

BIOGRAPHY

Charteris, Evan. THE LIFE AND LETTERS OF SIR EDMUND GOSSE. London: Heinemann, 1931.

The official biography. Several chapters deal with EG as literary critic and biographer. Focuses on the principles of "appreciation" and "illumination" in EG's criticism. Heavy reliance on EG's letters to trace his life story. Includes essential primary bibliography prepared by Norman Gullick.

Drinkwater, John. "Edmund Gosse." BOOKMAN (New York), 73 (1931), 463-72.

Offers some biographical information not found in Charteris' official biography. Drawing on letters from EG to Drinkwater, such areas as EG's interest in young writers, his tolerance, and the religious dimension in FATHER AND SON are explored.

CRITICISM

Adcock, Arthur St. John. "Sir Edmund Gosse, C.B." In his THE GLORY THAT WAS GRUB STREET. London: Sampson Low, Marston, 1928. Pp. 63-72.

Impressionistic evaluation of FATHER AND SON; praises the work for its "imaginative realism."

Arana, R. Victoria. "Sir Edmund Gosse's FATHER AND SON: Autobiography as Comedy." GENRE, 10 (1977), 63-76.

Well-argued and original essay which stresses the essentially comic and autobiographical elements in EG's masterpiece.

Arthur, Anthony. "Gosse's FATHER AND SON: Escape from 'The Prison of Puritanism.'" MBL, 3 (1978), 73-77.

Offers a rather simplified analysis of the style and method of
FATHER AND SON. Arthur appreciates the poetic style and
emotional ambience of childhood in the work as well as its use
of comedy.

Baylen, Joseph O. "Edmund Gosse, William Archer, and Ibsen in Victorian
Britain." TSL, 20 (1975), 124-37.

> By examining some unpublished correspondence between William
> Archer, Edward Tyas Cook, and EG, Baylen illuminates the
> complex literary relationships and shows how the men helped
> establish Ibsen's reputation in England. Baylen provides a
> balanced assessment of EG's reputation as a critic.

Beerbohm, Max. "A Recollection by Edm*nd G*sse." In his A CHRISTMAS
GARLAND. London: Heinemann, 1912. Pp. 135-46.

> Unparalleled parody of both the style and substance of a typical
> EG personal portrait of a literary figure. Conveys the smooth
> touch of his dramatic realism.

Binyon, Laurence. "Edmund Gosse." BOOKMAN, 57 (1919), 9-12.

> Appreciative comments on EG's accomplishments as biographer
> and literary historian.

Bissell, E. E. "Gosse, Wise, and Swinburne." BOOK COLLECTOR, 8 (1959), 297-99.

> Whether or not EG was involved in T. J. Wise's forgeries of
> Swinburne juvenilia, there are other examples of his "carelessness
> in literary matters."

Block, Haskell M. "The Alleged Parallel of Metaphysical and Symbolist
Poetry." CLS, 4 (1967), 145-59.

> Clarifies exactly what kinds of similarities EG saw between
> seventeenth-century metaphysical poetry and late nineteenth-
> century French symbolist poetry. Refers to EG's essay "The
> Poetry of John Donne" (JACOBEAN POETS) and LIFE OF
> DONNE.

Braybrooke, Patrick. CONSIDERATIONS ON EDMUND GOSSE. London:
Drane's, 1925.

> High praise for EG's outstanding work as a literary critic.
> Provides superficial and erratic surveys of many of EG's critical
> studies; estimates his reputation in the future.

Bredsdorff, Elias. "Introduction." In his SIR EDMUND GOSSE'S CORRE-

SPONDENCE WITH SCANDINAVIAN WRITERS. Copenhagen: Gyldendal, 1960. Pp. 1-23.

> Outlines EG's interest in Scandinavian literature, politics, and religion. Describes how EG was a pioneer in bringing Ibsen to British attention.

Buckley, Jerome Hamilton. SEASON OF YOUTH: THE BILDUNGSROMAN FROM DICKENS TO GOLDING. Cambridge, Mass.: Harvard Univ. Press, 1974. Pp. 25, 116-19, 302.

> Calls EG's struggle with faith "the dominant concern" of FATHER AND SON. Notes the ironic undercuttings in the book, but admires the father's "extra-ordinary intensity."

Burkhart, Charles. "George Moore and FATHER AND SON." NCF, 15 (1960), 71-77.

> Letters reveal Moore's inspiring influence on the composition stage of EG's masterpiece. Later EG rejected some of Moore's advice.

Clutton-Brock, Arthur. "The Wonderful Visitor." In ESSAYS ON BOOKS. London: Methuen, 1920. Pp. 67-77.

> Welcomes EG's LIFE OF SWINEBURNE for its mature, balanced handling of the poet and his poetry.

Collins, John Churton. "English Literature at the Universities." QR, 163 (1886), 289-329.

> Famous attack on EG's FROM SHAKESPEARE TO POPE. Collins found "blunders" in fact and judgment throughout the study; he dealt a damaging blow to EG's reputation as a scholar and critic.

Dodd, Philip. "The Nature of Edmund Gosse's FATHER AND SON." ELT, 22 (1979), 270-80.

> Reads FATHER AND SON as EG's personal (including sexual) exploration of "the conflict within him of pagan and Christian values." Shows how Matthew Arnold influenced EG's thoughts concerning paganism and puritanism. Comprehensive, but belabored discussion.

Duncan, Joseph E. "The Revival of Metaphysical Poetry, 1872-1912." PMLA, 68 (1953), 658-71.

> Analyzes EG's significant role in reviving interest in metaphysical poets with his LIFE OF DONNE. EG's study is the most influential in its period.

Eliot, T. S. "Donne in Our Time." In A GARLAND FOR JOHN DONNE. Ed. Theodore Spencer. Gloucester, Mass.: Smith, 1931. Pp. 1-19.

> Eliot cannot accept EG's interpretation of Donne's ELEGIES as autobiographical.

Elwin, Malcolm. OLD GODS FALLING. New York: Macmillan, 1939.

> Contains an unflattering depiction of EG as journalistic critic. Says EG had a "feline flair for satire." Praises his interest in Ibsen.

Folkenflik, Vivian, and Robert Folkenflik. "Words and Language in FATHER AND SON." BIOGRAPHY, 2 (1979), 157-74.

> A curious analysis of EG's masterpiece that stresses the tension between perception of the world through language and recognition of the Word of God.

Freeman, John. "Edmund Gosse." In his ENGLISH PORTRAITS AND ESSAYS. London: Hodder and Stoughton, 1924. Pp. 149-74.

> Values EG as a critical guide who is especially fine as a biographer. Good discussion of FATHER AND SON as a struggle between Calvinism and humanism.

──────. "Edmund Gosse: A Man of Letters." BOOKMAN, 67 (1925), 246-48.

> High praise for EG's critical and biographical studies of JEREMY TAYLOR and COVENTRY PATMORE as well as of "Samuel Butler" and "George Eliot" in ASPECTS. Admires candor in FATHER AND SON.

Fussell, Paul. "'My Dear Siegfried': Gosse to Sassoon." JRUL, 38 (1976), 85-97.

> Examines and quotes from a dozen of EG's letters not published in Charteris' biography. Fussell concludes that EG helped to refine Sassoon's prose style and provided him with the idea for MEMOIRS OF GEORGE SHERSTON.

Gardner, Helen. "The Argument about 'The Ecstacy.'" In ELIZABETHAN AND JACOBEAN STUDIES PRESENTED TO F. P. WILSON. Ed. Herbert Davis and Helen Gardner. Oxford, Engl.: Clarendon Press, 1959. Pp. 279-306.

> A noted scholar praises EG's accurate and perceptive insights concerning Donne's poetry.

Garnett, Richard. "Edmund Gosse." ENGLISH ILLUSTRATED MAGAZINE, 29 (1903), 641-42, 648-50.

Argues that EG's shorter critical portraits best display his talents as a writer.

Gordon, George S. "The Art and Ethics of Modern Biography." In his THE LIVES OF AUTHORS. London: Chatto and Windus, 1950. Pp. 12-22.

Discusses EG's portrait of "Queen Victoria" (MORE BOOKS ON THE TABLE) and FATHER AND SON as examples of new innovations in the art of biography which appeared before Lytton Strachey's studies.

Gracie, William J., Jr. "Truth of Form in Edmund Gosse's FATHER AND SON." JNT, 4 (1974), 176-87.

Suggestive essay which focuses on the book's symbolism and imagery as well as the importance of EG's "unconscious revelations" concerning his father.

Greenberg, Robert A. "Gosse's SWINBURNE, 'The Triumph of Time,' and the Context of 'Les Noyades.'" VP, 9 (1971), 95-110.

Discusses the merits and demerits of EG's biography, LIFE OF SWINBURNE. Greenberg clarifies some facts of the poet's life and relates them to the proper ordering and understanding of three poems in POEMS AND BALLADS.

Grosskurth, Phyllis. "Churton Collins: Scourge of the Late Victorians." UTQ, 34 (1965), 254-68.

Good background discussion of Collins' famous attack on EG. Treats the personality and positions of both men.

Helsinger, Howard. "Credence and Credibility: The Concern for Honesty in Victorian Autobiography." In APPROACHES TO VICTORIAN AUTOBIOGRAPHY. Ed. George P. Landow. Athens: Ohio Univ. Press, 1979. Pp. 56-63.

Makes subtle distinctions concerning EG's use of fact and fiction, or truth and imagination in FATHER AND SON. EG becomes an "artificer" who relies on imaginative creation to shape his inner life.

Hepburn, James. "Introduction." In his FATHER AND SON: A STUDY OF TWO TEMPERAMENTS. London: Oxford Univ. Press, 1974. Pp. xi-xvii.

Hepburn calls EG's scholarship and criticism "facile," but he values FATHER AND SON as a "poetic and profound" masterpiece, "his best work." Hepburn also summarizes contemporary reviews of the book.

Hind, C. Lewis. "Edmund Gosse." In AUTHORS AND I. London: Lane, 1921. Pp. 99-103.

Praises FATHER AND SON as EG's greatest work; analyzes some of the book's stylistic devices.

Hobson, Harold, Philip Knightly, and Leonard Russell. THE PEARL OF DAYS: AN INTIMATE MEMOIR OF THE SUNDAY TIMES. London: Hamilton, 1972.

Discusses the significance of the critical essays about literature that EG wrote for the SUNDAY TIMES: he helped establish a standard and a tradition. Calls for greater respect for his diverse talents.

Huntley, Frank L. SIR THOMAS BROWNE: A BIOGRAPHICAL AND CRITICAL STUDY. Ann Arbor: Univ. of Michigan Press, 1962.

Includes some harsh condemnation of EG's interpretation of selected works by Browne.

Irvine, William. "Introduction." In his FATHER AND SON. Boston: Houghton Mifflin, 1965. Pp. v-xlii.

Provides useful background information concerning religion and science in the nineteenth century. Ranks EG as a better biographer than critic.

Lewisohn, Ludwig. "The Agony of a Victorian." In his CITIES AND MEN. New York: Harper, 1927. Pp. 50-55.

Provocative discussion of the aesthetics behind EG's SOME DIVERSIONS. Interesting analysis of how Victorian critical taste fostered feelings of agony and despair.

Litzenberg, Karl. "The Victorians and the World Abroad." In THE REINTERPRETATION OF VICTORIAN LITERATURE. Ed. Joseph E. Baker. Princeton, N.J.: Princeton Univ. Press, 1950. Pp. 169-96.

Concentrates on EG's international outlook and praises his introduction of Ibsen to British culture. Values his Scandinavian scholarship.

MacColl, D.S. "Edmund Gosse." LONDON MERCURY, 24 (June 1931), 152-59.

Useful overview of EG's life and works. Praises EG's "cameos in print." Discusses the attack by Churton Collins.

Mais, S.P.B. "Edmund Gosse." In his SOME MODERN AUTHORS. London: Richards, 1923. Pp. 204-10.

Superficial summary of FATHER AND SON. Emphasizes how Calvinism tragically "enmeshed" EG's father.

Mandel, Barrett J. "Full of Life Now." In AUTOBIOGRAPHY: ESSAYS THEORETICAL AND CRITICAL. Ed. James Olney. Princeton, N.J.: Princeton Univ. Press, 1980. Pp. 49-72.

> Asserts that autobiography is "a genuine literary genre"; offers close analysis of some passages from FATHER AND SON to show that autobiography is "neither memory nor fiction."

Mattheisen, Paul F. "An Account of Queen Victoria." JRUL, 21 (1957), 7-32.

> Shows how Lady Mary Ponsonby of the Queen's Court provided background information for EG's essay "The Character of Queen Victoria" (MORE BOOKS ON THE TABLE).

Mattheisen, Paul F., and Michael Millgate. "Introduction: Edmund Gosse (1849-1928)." In their TRANSATLANTIC DIALOGUE: SELECTED AMERICAN CORRESPONDENCE OF EDMUND GOSSE. Austin: Univ. of Texas Press, 1965. Pp. 3-55.

> Biographical sketch with some critical analysis of EG's literary opinions. Useful commentary on EG's estimation of Walt Whitman.

Moore, George. AVOWALS. London: Heinemann, 1919. Pp. 1-96.

> A tour de force in which a long-time friend imagines an extended conversation with EG focusing on critical estimates of the English novel. Offers good insights concerning FATHER AND SON and works by Robert Louis Stevenson.

Morrissette, Bruce. "Early English and American Critics of French Symbolism." In STUDIES IN HONOR OF FREDERICK W. SHIPLEY BY HIS COLLEAGUES. St. Louis, Mo.: Washington Univ. Studies, 1942. Pp. 159-80.

> Points out some inadequacies of EG's critical interpretations of the French symbolists, especially Mallarmé.

O'Leary, John Gerard. ENGLISH LITERARY HISTORY AND BIBLIOGRAPHY. London: Grafton, 1928. Pp. 70-73.

> Concentrates on EG's work in literary history. Poses some interesting questions concerning EG's theory of literature and the concept of historical evolution.

Pearlman, E. "Father and Mother in FATHER AND SON." VN, No. 55 (Spring 1979), 19-23.

> A focused attempt to describe and set EG's upbringing in its context of psychological history. Good insights concerning Victorian concepts of God, father, and children.

Peters, Robert L. "Edmund Gosse's Two Whitmans." WWR, 11 (1965), 19-21.

> Accuses EG of distorting the facts of his 1885 visit to Whitman; it "reveals Gosse the litterateur at his worst."

Phelps, Gilbert. "Russian Realism and English Fiction." CAMBRIDGE JOURNAL, 3 (1950), 277-91.

> Refers to EG's opinions on Zola and the realistic novel in his critical essay "The Tyranny of the Novel" (FRENCH PROFILES).

Porter, Roger J. "Edmund Gosse's FATHER AND SON: Between Form and Flexibility." JNT, 5 (1975), 174-95.

> Insightful article which analyzes EG's balanced tone and "artfully cautious" path throughout FATHER AND SON. He toned down antagonisms and muted revelations for the public eye, but stopped short of full accommodation.

Pound, Ezra. "Swinburne Versus Biographers." POETRY: A MAGAZINE OF VERSE, 11 (1918), 322-29.

> A devastating ad hominem attack on EG and his euphemistic treatment of the notorious poet in LIFE OF SWINBURNE.

Pritchett, V. S. "A Plymouth Brother." In his THE LIVING NOVEL. New York: Reynal and Hitchcock, 1947. Pp. 116-21.

> Interesting analysis of EG's father in FATHER AND SON: argues that his brand of Calvinism is not the Victorian religious outlook but the seventeenth-century variety of John Bunyan and Jeremy Taylor.

Ralston, W. R. S. "THE QUARTERLY REVIEW and Mr. Gosse." ATHENAEUM, No. 3080 (6 November 1886), 601-02.

> Condemns Collins' attack on EG; defends EG's scholarship by surveying his previous works. Praises GRAY especially.

Rascoe, Burton. "Those Who Can, Criticize." BOOKMAN (NY), 66 (1928), 670-76.

> Praises EG's LEAVES AND FRUIT for its "natural" style and perceptive critical insights.

Robinson, James K. "A Neglected Phase of the Aesthetic Movement: English Parnassianism." PMLA, 67 (1953), 733-54.

> An important article which presents EG as a practitioner and critic of neglected, but significant innovations in English poetry between 1870 and 1890.

Edmund Gosse

Ross, Fredric R. "Philip Gosse's OMPHALOS, Edmund Gosse's FATHER AND SON, and Darwin's Theory of Natural Selection." ISIS, 68 (1977), 85-96.

> Warns that FATHER AND SON must be read as "literary rather than literal biography." Uses OMPHALOS incident to show in what ways EG distorted his father's intentions and circumstances. Valiant attempt to restore Philip Gosse's good name as an "honest laborer."

San Juan, E., Jr. "Gosse and Gibbon: Two Witnesses of Interior Reality." DISCOURSE, 7 (1964), 399-403.

> Interprets FATHER AND SON as an archetypal conflict between dynamic growth and a static culture of the past.

Seccombe, Thomas. "Edmund Gosse, C.B." BOOKMAN (London), 44 (June 1913), 109-13.

> Early assessment of EG's achievement. Values his essay portraits of contemporaries over the longer historical biographies. Includes a discussion of TWO VISITS TO DENMARK.

Shepherd, Henry F. "A Review of Edmund Gosse's FROM SHAKESPEARE TO POPE." PMLA, 1 (1884-85), 149-55.

> Early and important critical assessment of EG's controversial study. Shepherd enumerates his disagreements with EG's interpretations and links the changes in literature to broader developments in science and politics.

Sherman, Stuart P. "Like a Fine Old English Gentleman: The Essays of Edmund Gosse." In his THE EMOTIONAL DISCOVERY OF AMERICA AND OTHER ESSAYS. New York: Farrar and Rinehart, 1932. Pp. 213-17.

> A debunking indictment of EG as a lightweight Victorian craftsman. Complains that SOME DIVERSIONS OF A MAN OF LETTERS lacks focus and penetrating insights.

Shorter, Clement. "Mr. Edmund Gosse--An Impression." GOOD WORDS, 44 (April 1903), 250-55.

> Early, favorable survey of EG's work as biographer, essayist, and literary historian.

Sitwell, Sir Osbert. "Sir Edmund Gosse." In his NOBLE ESSENCES: A BOOK OF CHARACTERS. Boston: Little, Brown, 1950. Pp. 40-76.

> A close associate provides a string of rather unfavorable and sometimes distorted impressions of EG's personality; however, the assertion concerning the blend of Romantic and Victorian elements in EG's writing is provocative.

Squire, J.C. "Mr. Gosse's Criticisms." In his BOOKS REVIEWED. London: Heinemann, 1922. Pp. 109-15.

> Close examination of BOOKS ON THE TABLE as an indication of EG's style and interests as a literary critic. Original estimate in emphasizing the qualities of restraint and detachment in EG's writings.

Stephen, Leslie. "Life of John Donne." NATIONAL REVIEW, 34 (December 1899), 595-613.

> Thorough discussion of EG's LIFE OF DONNE. Praises the study for its many fresh insights, but disagrees with EG's autobiographical interpretation of some of Donne's love poems.

Strachey, Lytton. "Sir Thomas Browne." In his BOOKS AND CHARACTERS: FRENCH AND ENGLISH. New York: Harcourt, Brace, 1922. Pp. 31-47.

> Harsh indictment of EG's analysis of Browne's prose style in his study, SIR THOMAS BROWNE.

Symons, Arthur. "John Donne." FORTNIGHTLY REVIEW, N.S. 66 (1899), 734-45.

> An important man of letters elaborates the significant insights in EG's LIFE OF DONNE: his new prosody, his subtle intelligence, and his realism on the themes of love and death.

Temple, Ruth Z. "Sir Edmund Gosse." In her THE CRITIC'S ALCHEMY. New York: Twayne, 1953. Pp. 185-228.

> A thoughtful survey of EG's criticism written before 1900, which finds much of it inadequate or dilettantish. Accuses EG of misapplying the principles of French criticism and often degenerating to the level of gossip.

Tierney, Frank M. "Sir Edmund Gosse and the Revival of French Fixed Forms in the Age of Transition." ELT, 14 (1971), 191-99.

> Analyzes the content and influence of EG's essay, "A Plea for Certain Exotic Forms of Verse" (FRENCH PROFILES).

Traubitz, Nancy Baker. "Heavenly Mother: The Trinity as Structural Device in Edmund Gosse's FATHER AND SON." JNT, 6 (1976), 147-54.

> Original analysis of the tempering, humanizing influence of the three mother-figures (influenced by Ibsen's dramas) on the tyrannical father-figure in FATHER AND SON.

Waugh, Alec. "Edmund Gosse." VQR, 32 (1956), 69-78.

Examines the profound effect of Collins' famous attack (1886) on EG's subsequent life and writings: EG became "hypersensitive to criticism."

Waugh, Arthur. "Living Critics: Mr. Edmund Gosse." BOOKMAN (London), 10 (September 1896), 164-67.

Examines the influence of Matthew Arnold, Lang, Sainte-Beuve, Saintsbury, and Symonds on EG's critical method. Analyzes some of the disadvantages of EG's reliance on figurative language and discusses other features of his prose style. Useful essay.

Welby, T. Earle. "Sir Edmund Gosse: A Recovered Reputation." BOOKMAN (London), 80 (May 1931), 114-15.

Makes some generalized but interesting remarks concerning the differences between EG's early studies and the masterful later works. Especially praises his literary portraits.

Wertheimer, Douglas. "Gosse's Corrections to FATHER AND SON, 1907-1928." N&Q, N.S. 25 (1978), 327-32.

Lists and discusses fifty corrections to the first impression copy by EG over a number of years. Most changes were minor in nature.

──────. "The Identification of Some Characters and Incidents in Gosse's FATHER AND SON." N&Q, N.S. 23 (1976), 4-11.

Useful index to the identities of twenty-five pseudonymous characters in FATHER AND SON. Research based on papers held by Jennifer Gosse.

White, William. "Sir Edmund Gosse on Walt Whitman." VS, 1 (1957), 180-82.

Compares the tone and content of two letters EG wrote to Whitman with his sketch of the American bard in KIT-KATS. White regrets the disparity.

Williams, Orlo. CONTEMPORARY CRITICISM OF LITERATURE. London: Parsons, 1924. Pp. 182-87.

High praise for EG's work (ASPECTS AND IMPRESSIONS, BOOKS ON TABLE, and FATHER AND SON) and his assured reputation as an important critic. Admires his intelligence and urbanity.

Williams, Stanley T. "Two Victorian Boyhoods." In his STUDIES IN VICTORIAN LITERATURE. New York: Dutton, 1923. Pp. 57-70.

Illuminating study which compares the outlooks of the child and
his parents in EG's FATHER AND SON with those in John Stuart
Mill's AUTOBIOGRAPHY. Good on Victorian beliefs.

Wolf, Howard R. "British Fathers and Sons, 1773-1913: From Filial Sub-
missiveness to Creativity." PSYCHOANALYTICAL REVIEW, 52 (1965), 53-70.

> Worthwhile article which provides many stimulating insights into
> EG's psychological struggle for identity in FATHER AND SON.
> Impressive discussion of both psychology and literature.

Woolf, James D. "'In the Seventh Heaven of Delight': The Aesthetic Sense
in Gosse's FATHER AND SON." In INTERSPACE AND THE INWARD SPHERE:
ESSAYS ON ROMANTIC AND VICTORIAN SELF. Ed. Norman A. Anderson
and Margene E. Weiss. Macomb: Western Illinois Univ., 1978. Pp. 134-44.

> Woolf examines the tensions in FATHER AND SON between EG's
> inner and outer selves; he concludes that EG discovers a unified
> self through an expanded aesthetic. Woolf offers fresh and in-
> teresting insights on EG's use of aesthetic distancing in the auto-
> biography.

―――. SIR EDMUND GOSSE. Twayne's English Author Series. New York:
Twayne, 1972.

> Excellent and enthusiastic critical study of EG's works, which
> includes basic biographical details. Focuses on EG as literary
> critic and on the major ways that he falls within the tradition
> of Matthew Arnold and Sainte-Beuve. Includes chapters which
> provide perceptive analyses of EG's theory of criticism and his
> prose style. Also treats most of EG's biographies and critical
> portraits.

―――. "Tragedy in Gosse's FATHER AND SON." ELT, 9, No. 3 (1966),
137-44.

> Analyzes tragic and humorous elements in FATHER AND SON
> by comparing it with KING LEAR. A provocative and well-
> written article.

Woolf, Virginia. "The Art of Biography." In DEATH OF THE MOTH AND
OTHER ESSAYS. London: Hogarth, 1942. Pp. 119-26.

> Welcomes EG's FATHER AND SON and Strachey's pioneering
> studies as hopeful signs of new freedoms for the art of biography.

―――. "Edmund Gosse." In THE MOMENT AND OTHER ESSAYS. Ed.
Leonard Woolf. New York: Harcourt, Brace, 1942. Pp. 84-92.

> Regrets that EG's critical portraits and FATHER AND SON some-
> times lack incisive judgment. He falls short of a Boswell.

Wyke, Clement H. "Edmund Gosse as Biographer and Critic of Donne: His Fallible Role in the Poet's Rediscovery." TSLL, 17 (1976), 805-19.

> The fullest rehearsal available of EG's errors in his LIFE AND LETTERS OF DONNE; however, Wyke stresses the pioneering significance of EG's work.

R.B. CUNNINGHAME GRAHAM (1852-1936)

NONFICTIONAL PROSE

BERNAL DIAZ DEL CASTILLO: BEING SOME ACCOUNT OF HIM, TAKEN FROM HIS TRUE HISTORY OF THE CONQUEST OF NEW SPAIN. London: Nash; New York: Dodd, Mead, 1915.

> An interesting biography of a soldier under Cortes, which employs passages from Diaz's own memoir written about 1568 with commentary by CG. The result is a vivid portrait of a common soldier's experience.

A BRAZILIAN MYSTIC: BEING THE LIFE AND MIRACLES OF ANTONIO CONSELHEIRO. London: Heinemann; New York: Dodd, Mead, 1920.

> CG's most interesting biography, on a Gnostic fanatic who flourished in Brazil in the 1890's and established his own "holy city." CG admires the "Counsellor's" courage but deplores his irrationality.

BROUGHT FORWARD. London: Duckworth; New York: Stokes, 1916.

> A collection of fifteen stories and sketches. Several deal with the impact of WWI, both in Britain and on CG procuring horses in Argentina for the army.

CARTAGENA AND THE BANKS OF THE SINU. London: Heinemann; New York: Doran, 1921.

> Partly a history, partly a travel volume on the Columbian region to which CG was sent to obtain horses for the British army in WWI.

CHARITY. London: Duckworth, 1912.

> Seventeen of the usual tales and sketches set in exotic locales. The most interesting of the sketches, "Immortality," expresses CG's pessimistic view that nothing endures.

R.B. Cunninghame Graham

THE CONQUEST OF NEW GRANADA: BEING THE LIFE OF GONZALO JIMENEZ DE QUESADA. London: Heinemann; Boston: Houghton Mifflin, 1922.

>A history of the conquest of Columbia by Quesada, whom CG considers more merciful than Cortes and Pizarro but their equal in achievement.

THE CONQUEST OF THE RIVER PLATE. London: Heinemann; Garden City, N.Y.: Doubleday, 1924.

>A history of Spanish campaigns in the area of Argentina, Uruguay, and Paraguay. CG emphasizes both the courage and ruthlessness of the Conquistadors, and notes numerous parallels between them and twentieth-century British colonists: "The Spaniards believed themselves, just as we do today, to be a chosen people, having a mission to spread the truth. . . . "

DOUGHTY DEEDS: AN ACCOUNT OF THE LIFE OF ROBERT GRAHAM OF GARTMORE, POET AND POLITICIAN, 1735-1797, DRAWN FROM HIS LETTERBOOKS & CORRESPONDENCE. London: Heinemann; New York: Dial, 1925.

>CG's memoirs of his ancestor, who resembled CG in his travels and politics. Although the book is factually weak, it does afford interesting portraits of eighteenth-century life in Jamaica and Scotland.

FAITH. London: Duckworth, 1909.

>A collection of eighteen short stories and travel sketches; several of the latter are set in Europe. The most interesting of these, entitled "Andorra" after the tiny European state, vividly depicts a wild and beautiful region that reminds CG of South America.

A HATCHMENT. London: Duckworth, 1913.

>A collection of sixteen sketches and stories; one of the most memorable essays, "Loose and Broken Men," depicts the rough life of the Highlanders.

HERNANDO DE SOTO: TOGETHER WITH AN ACCOUNT OF ONE OF HIS CAPTAINS, GONCALO SILVESTRE. London: Heinemann, 1903. New York: Dial, 1924.

>A history of de Soto emphasizing his last years.

R.B. Cunninghame Graham

HIS PEOPLE. London: Duckworth, 1906.

A collection of eighteen tales and sketches. One of the most interesting renders CG's impression of Parnell as a politician in the House of Commons.

HOPE. London: Duckworth, 1910.

A collection of nineteen essays and stories, including some sketches of CG's ancestors.

THE HORSES OF THE CONQUEST. London: Heinemann, 1930.

A learned but anecdotal history of the role of the horse in the Spanish conquest of South America.

THE IPANE. London: Unwin, 1899. New York: Boni, 1925.

A collection of fifteen stories and essays. The most important are "Bristol Fashion," a bitter denunciation of colonialism, and "A Survival," an assault on the Kailyard School in Scottish literature.

JOSE ANTONIO PAEZ. London: Heinemann; Philadelphia: Macrae-Smith, 1929.

A biography of Paez, the Venezuelan general and president too long overshadowed by Bolivar, according to CG.

MIRAGES. London: Heinemann, 1936.

CG's final essay collection.

MOGREB-EL-ACKSA: A JOURNEY IN MOROCCO. London: Heinemann, 1898. New York: Viking, 1930.

CG's best book. It depicts his fantastic attempt to reach the forbidden city of Tarudant in Morocco in 1897 while disguised as Sheikh Mohammed El Fasi. He was caught just short of his goal and detained for some time by the local kaid. The volume was the inspiration for Shaw's CAPTAIN BRASSBOUND'S CONVERSION.

NOTES ON THE DISTRICT OF MENTEITH FOR TOURISTS AND OTHERS. London: Black, 1895.

CG's first book, on his home region in Scotland. It is a brief, amusing account of historical figures of the district. An illustrated edition was published by CG in 1930.

R.B. Cunninghame Graham

PEDRO DE VALDIVIA: CONQUEROR OF CHILE. London: Heinemann, 1926. New York: Harper, 1927.

> Another of CG's series on the Conquistadors. It is probably the weakest because CG is not well-informed about Valdivia and because, as CG admits in his preface, Valdivia possesses no traits unusual to his fellows.

PORTRAIT OF A DICTATOR: FRANCISCO SOLANO LOPEZ (PARAGUAY, 1865-1870). London: Heinemann, 1933.

> A biography of the monstrous Paraguayan dictator, written in appalled reaction to the posthumous admiration of him. CG was himself in Paraguay shortly after Lopez was killed by Brazilian troops. Paraguay under Lopez bears a striking resemblance to the South American country in Conrad's NOSTROMO; CG seems to have supplied his friend with factual information for that novel.

PROGRESS AND OTHER SKETCHES. London: Duckworth, 1905.

> A collection of eighteen pieces, most of them fiction. The volume is noteworthy for its sexual frankness; in the sketch "A Vestal" CG berates the hypocrisy of European society on sexual matters.

REDEEMED AND OTHER SKETCHES. London: Heinemann, 1927.

> A collection of sixteen pieces, including memorial (and overwritten) tributes to Wilfrid Blunt and Joseph Conrad.

FATHER ARCHANGEL OF SCOTLAND AND OTHER ESSAYS. London: Black, 1896.

> CB's first essay and story collection; the second, tenth, eleventh, and twelfth pieces were written by his wife Gabriela. The volume treats Spanish themes and has several sketches on Catholic priests. The title essay, for example, is an amusing account of a Capuchin friar attempting to convert the Scots.

SCOTTISH STORIES. London: Duckworth, 1914.

> A collection of sixteen sketches, all previously published in CG's books.

SUCCESS. London: Duckworth, 1902.

> Along with the usual studies of exotic locales, this collection of seventeen sketches includes several on the tawdriness of modern London life. Their theme is introduced by the title essay, decrying the vulgarity of success; the sterility of the Empire's capital

is demonstrated in such pieces as "The Pyramid" (on music halls), "Terror" (on London street life), and "Might, Majesty, and Dominion" (on the funeral of Victoria).

THIRTEEN STORIES. London: Heinemann, 1900.

> A story and essay collection, mostly on north Africa and South America. Many of the sketches contrast the epic past with the sordid, commercial present. "Victory," for example, plays the vulgarity of the United States at the time of the Spanish-American War against the dignity of old Spain.

A VANISHED ARCADIA: BEING SOME ACCOUNT OF THE JESUITS IN PARAGUAY, 1607 TO 1767. London: Heinemann; New York: Macmillan, 1901.

> A defense of the Jesuits, whose paternalistic treatment of the Indians is seen as preferable to that of the plantation owners who followed them.

WRIT IN SAND. London: Heinemann, 1932.

> A collection of six pieces, the most interesting of which, "Writ in Sand," likens life to a circus in town for one performance.

WORKS EDITED BY OTHERS

THE ESSENTIAL R.B. CUNNINGHAME GRAHAM. Ed. Paul Bloomfield. London: Cape, 1952.

> This contains generous selections from MOGREB-EL-ACKSA, from "Stories and Sketches," and from "The Latin American Histories."

GAUCHOS OF THE PAMPAS AND THEIR HORSES: BY W.H. HUDSON AND R.B. CUNNINGHAME GRAHAM. Comp. J. Frank Dobie. Hanover, N.H.: Westholm Publications, 1963.

> Collects "The Horse of the Pampas" and "San Jose" from CG and "Story of a Piebald Horse" and "Cristiano: The Sentinel Horse" from Hudson.

THE HORSES OF THE CONQUEST. Ed. Robert Moorman Denhardt. Norman: Univ. of Oklahoma Press, 1949.

> An annotated edition of the 1930 work.

RODEO: A COLLECTION OF TALES AND SKETCHES OF R.B. CUNNINGHAME GRAHAM. Ed. A[ime] F[elix] Tschiffely. London: Heinemann, 1936.

> Forty-seven are included.

R.B. Cunninghame Graham

SELECTED WRITINGS OF CUNNINGHAME GRAHAM. Ed. Cedric Watts. Rutherford, N.J.: Fairleigh Dickinson Univ. Press, 1981.

   This contains a selection of eight political pieces and eleven literary ones.

THE SOUTH AMERICAN SKETCHES OF R.B. CUNNINGHAME GRAHAM. Ed. John Walker. Norman: Univ. of Oklahoma Press, 1978.

   A selection of thirty sketches, grouped according to the countries they treat.

THIRTY TALES AND SKETCHES. Ed. Edward Garnett. London: Duckworth, 1929.

   A selection from IPANE, THIRTEEN STORIES, SUCCESS, PROGRESS, HIS PEOPLE, FAITH, HOPE, CHARITY, HATCHMENT, BROUGHT FORWARD, and REDEEMED.

BIBLIOGRAPHY

Chaundy, Leslie, ed. A BIBLIOGRAPHY OF THE FIRST EDITIONS OF THE WORKS OF ROBERT BONTINE CUNNINGHAME GRAHAM. London: Dulau, 1924.

   The rare primary bibliography, covering up to 1924, with sections on books and introductions.

Walker, John, comp. "A Chronological Bibliography of Works on R.B. Cunninghame Graham (1852-1936)." BIBLIOTHECK, 9 (1978), 47-64.

   A fifteen-page list, unannotated and chronologically arranged.

_____. "R.B. Cunninghame Graham and THE LABOUR ELECTOR." BIBLIOTHECK, 7 (1974), 72-75.

   An addendum to Watts's BIBLIOTHECK piece.

_____, ed. "R.B. Cunninghame Graham: An Annotated Bibliography of Writings about Him." ELT, 22 (1979), 78-156.

   A heavily annotated listing of criticism arranged alphabetically by author.

Watts, C[edric] T., comp. "R.B. Cunninghame Graham (1852-1936): A List of His Contributions to Periodicals." BIBLIOTHECK, 4 (1965), 186-99.

   A listing of CG's essays, stories, reviews, and letters published in periodicals.

R.B. Cunninghame Graham

Watts, Cedric, and Laurence Davies, eds. CUNNINGHAME GRAHAM: A CRITICAL BIOGRAPHY. London: Cambridge Univ. Press, 1979.

> This contains by far the fullest readily available listing of CG's works. A selective secondary listing is also included.

BIOGRAPHY

Bloomfield, Paul. "Introduction." In his THE ESSENTIAL R.B. CUNNINGHAME GRAHAM. London: Cape, 1952. Pp. 13-27.

> Contains a brief biographical sketch with some critical evaluation.

MacDiarmid, Hugh. CUNNINGHAME GRAHAM: A CENTENARY STUDY. Glasgow: Caledonian Press, 1952.

> A slight volume, discussing CG's relation to Scottish nationalism and reviewing briefly his life and career.

Tschiffely, Aime Felix. DON ROBERTO: BEING THE ACCOUNT OF THE LIFE AND WORKS OF R.B. CUNNINGHAME GRAHAM, 1852-1936. London: Heinemann, 1937.

> A long anecdotal biography by an acquaintance. Chapter 15 quotes heavily from correspondence between CG and writers such as Hudson and Conrad.

Watts, Cedric, and Laurence Davies. CUNNINGHAME GRAHAM: A CRITICAL BIOGRAPHY. London: Cambridge Univ. Press, 1979.

> The best biography to date, with useful chapters analyzing CG's works and literary friendships.

West, Herbert Faulkner. A MODERN CONQUISTADOR: ROBERT BONTINE CUNNINGHAME GRAHAM: HIS LIFE AND WORKS. London: Cranley and Day, 1932.

> West's view of the life was deeply influenced by CG himself, but his book provides a quite useful and extensive rehashing of the prose.

CRITICISM

Davies, Laurence. "Cunninghame Graham's South American Sketches." CLS, 9 (1972), 253-65.

> An excellent discussion of the artistry of CG's sketches. In them he seeks ways to "combine the authenticity of personal observation and narration with the suggestive and unsettling effects of short fiction."

_____. "R.B. Cunninghame Graham: The Kailyard and After." SSL, 11 (1974), 156-77.

> A good discussion of GC's criticism of the Kailyard School in periodical publications and IPANE.

Graham, Stephen. "Laird and Caballero: Cunninghame Graham." In his THE DEATH OF YESTERDAY. London: Benn, 1930. Pp. 36-52.

> A casual appreciation that argues for CG "reality is Scotland; romance is South America."

Haymaker, Richard E. PRINCE-ERRANT AND EVOCATOR OF HORIZONS: A READING OF R.B. CUNNINGHAME GRAHAM. Kingsport, Tenn.: Kingsport Press, 1967.

> Reviews the writings at length (without much analysis) and then presents chapters on CG's social thought and world view (with which the author often takes issue); for example, "The moral element is probably more deeply rooted in life and in the universe than Graham's utterances would lead us to believe."

MacShane, Frank. "R.B. Cunninghame Graham." SAQ, 58 (1969), 198-207.

> A brief, useful review of CG's works and literary techniques.

Meyers, Jeffrey. "The Genius of Failure: R.B. Cunninghame Graham." LONDON MAGAZINE, 15, No. 4 (1975), 54-73.

> An antagonistic review of CG's life and works which bucks the tide in terming his histories boring. "Graham creates his finest work when he abandons the disastrously arch and posturing persona of a rakish yet somewhat sentimental literary gaucho," says Meyers.

Parker, W.M. "A Modem Elizabethan: R.B. Cunninghame Graham." In his MODERN SCOTTISH WRITERS. Edinburgh: Hodge, 1917. Pp. 197-219.

> An early, admiring review which neglects to emphasize the Scottish writings. Parker does note the connections with Hudson and Conrad.

Stallman, Robert W. "Robert Cunninghame Graham's South American Sketches." HISPANIA, 28 (1945), 69-75.

> Essentially a comparison of Hudson and CG, noting their sympathy for the animals and natives of the pampas.

Walker, John. "Introduction." In his THE SOUTH AMERICAN SKETCHES OF R.B. CUNNINGHAME GRAHAM. Norman: Univ. of Oklahoma Press, 1978. Pp. 3-19.

> Contains a brief survey of CG's themes and techniques.

Watts, Cedric. "Conrad and Cunninghame Graham: A Discussion with Addenda to their Correspondence." YES, 7 (1977), 157-65.

    Suggests the influence of VANISHED ARCADIA and HERNANDO DE SOTO on Conrad's NOSTROMO.

ROBERT GRAVES (1895-   )

NONFICTIONAL PROSE

BUT IT STILL GOES ON: AN ACCUMULATION. London: Cape, 1930. New York: Cape, 1931.

> A sequel to GOOD-BYE. RG presents autobiographical anecdotes "of a less valedictory nature."

THE COMMON ASPHODEL: COLLECTED ESSAYS ON POETRY, 1922-1949. London: Hamilton, 1949.

> A collection of forty-four essays on poetry, including material from OBSERVATIONS, FUTURE OF POETRY, MODERNIST POETRY, ANTHOLOGIES, with the addition of "Poetry and Politics," "How Poets See," "'Mad Mr. Swinburne,'" and "The Common Asphodel."

CONTEMPORARY TECHNIQUES OF POETRY: A POLITICAL ANALOGY. Hogarth Essays. London: Hogarth, 1925.

> A brief survey of the spectrum of contemporary approaches to poetic diction, meter, texture, rhyme, and structure.

THE CRANE BAG, AND OTHER DISPUTED SUBJECTS. London: Cassell, 1969.

> A collection of some of RG's less famous lectures, essays, and reviews on a variety of subjects, including reincarnation, bullfighting, mass tourism, witches, and superstitions.

THE CROWNING PRIVILEGE: THE CLARK LECTURES 1954-1955, ALSO VARIOUS ESSAYS ON POETRY AND SIXTEEN NEW POEMS. London: Cassell, 1955. As THE CROWNING PRIVILEGE: COLLECTED ESSAYS ON POETRY. Garden City, N.Y.: Doubleday, 1956.

> A collection of sixteen essays on poetry and prosodic laws, including "The Crowning Privilege," "The Road to Rydal Mount," "The Essential E. E. Cummings," "The Poet and His Public," and

the controversial "Dr. Syntax and Mr. Pound." The American edition adds nine more essays from COMMON ASPHODEL.

DIFFICULT QUESTIONS, EASY ANSWERS. London: Cassell, 1972. Garden City, N.Y.: Doubleday, 1973.

    A collection of twenty-five of RG's shorter prose-pieces, including "Genius," "Poetry and Obscenity," "Goddesses and Obosoms," "Rationality," "The Greek Tradition," "The Inner Ear," and "Speaking Freely" (a 1970 interview with Edwin Newman).

5 PENS IN HAND. Garden City, N.Y.: Doubleday, 1958.

    A collection of thirteen essays, including "Why I Live in Majorca," "Legitimate Criticism of Poetry," "The White Goddess," "Diseases of Scholarship, Clinically Considered," and "Answer to a Religious Questionnaire."

FOOD FOR CENTAURS: STORIES, TALKS, CRITICAL STUDIES, POEMS. Garden City, N.Y.: Doubleday, 1960.

    Contains three essays on poetry, "Sweeney among the Blackbirds," "The Making and Marketing of Poetry," "Pulling a Poem Apart," as well as some studies in history and reviews of new books.

GOODBYE TO ALL THAT: AN AUTOBIOGRAPHY. London: Cape, 1929. New York: Cape, 1930.

    RG's autobiography, written at age thirty-three and covering his early years to 1929. The book is a burial of the horrible memories of World War I, a bitter leave-taking of England, and an attack on English conventions.

GOODBYE TO ALL THAT: AN AUTOBIOGRAPHY. Garden City, N.Y.: Doubleday; London: Cassell, 1957.

    A new edition with substantial revisions, including omission of "dull or foolish patches" and restoration of "a few suppressed anecdotes"; a prologue and an epilogue are added to provide a brief sketch of his life since 1929.

THE GREEK MYTHS. 2 vols. London and Baltimore: Penguin, 1955.

    In an impressive display of scholarship, RG retells the legends of ancient Greece and interweaves his own commentary, which takes into consideration variant sources and modern anthropological studies. Well-documented and interesting.

THE HEBREW MYTHS: THE BOOK OF GENESIS. Garden City, N.Y.: Doubleday; London: Cassell, 1964.

Written with Raphael Patai, this study is a companion volume to GREEK MYTHS. Criticism and interpretation of Genesis stories for "the intelligent general reader."

LARS PORSENA: OR THE FUTURE OF SWEARING AND IMPROPER LANGUAGE. London: Kegan Paul; New York: Dutton, 1927.

RG defends the liveliness, purity, and simplicity of the English language, complete with blasphemous and taboo words.

LAWRENCE AND THE ARABS. London: Cape, 1927. As LAWRENCE AND THE ARABIAN ADVENTURE. Garden City, N.Y.: Doubleday, 1928.

An extensive biography of T.E. Lawrence, with supporting maps of his Near East campaigns in World War I. RG had permission to use Lawrence's copyrighted material and he corresponded with him.

THE LONG WEEK-END: A SOCIAL HISTORY OF GREAT BRITAIN 1918-1939. With Alan Hodge. London: Faber, 1940. New York: Macmillan, 1941.

This is a social history of Great Britain--especially London and its environs--between the two World Wars. No part of the social scene escapes RG's eye as he covers such varied topics as women, reading matter, sex, stage and screen, hiking, nudism, and pacifism.

MAJORCA OBSERVED. With Paul Hogarth. London: Cassell; Garden City, N.Y.: Doubleday, 1965.

A travel book describing the social life and customs of Majorca. Some topics covered are: "Why I Live in Majorca 1953," "Postscript, 1965," "School Life in Majorca 1955," "Ditching in a Fishless Sea," and "George Sand in Majorca."

MAMMON AND THE BLACK GODDESS. London: Cassell; Garden City, N.Y.: Doubleday, 1965.

A survey of what forces stimulate and inhibit the creation of poetry. Some topics include: "Mammon," "The Poet in a Valley of Dry Bones," "Real Women," and "Intimations of the Black Goddess."

THE MEANING OF DREAMS. London: Palmer, 1924. New York: Greenberg, 1925.

A basic survey and discussion of various theories that offer explanations of the value and variety of dreams. The last chapter deals with "Dreams and Poetry."

MRS. FISHER: OR THE FUTURE OF HUMOUR. London: Kegan Paul; New York: Dutton, 1928.

    RG discriminates various types of humor and predicts that with the spread of inventions and antipoetic tendencies, humor will become increasingly "goddawful."

THE NAZARENE GOSPEL RESTORED. London: Cassell, 1953. Garden City, N.Y.: Doubleday, 1954.

    A scholarly study written with Joshua Podro of some of the "curiosities" of New Testament criticism and the principles of gospel-making. Specific examples of parallel texts of some of the Gospels along with commentary and reconstruction are also provided.

OCCUPATION: WRITER. New York: Creative Age Press, 1950. London: Cassell, 1951.

    A selection of some of RG's miscellaneous essays, including "Lars Porsena," "Mrs. Fisher," and "Occupation: Writer."

ON ENGLISH POETRY: BEING AN IRREGULAR APPROACH TO THE PSYCHOLOGY OF THIS ART, FROM EVIDENCE MAINLY SUBJECTIVE. London: Heinemann; New York: Knopf, 1922.

    A collection of sixty-one essays about the many aspects of poetry or of being a poet. Some essays included are: "Poetry and Primitive Magic," "Connection of Poetry and Humor," "The God Called Poetry," "The Use of Poetry," "Histories of Poetry," "The Poet as Outsider," and "Poetry as Labour." Definitions of types and techniques of poetry are also discussed.

ON POETRY: COLLECTED TALKS AND ESSAYS. Garden City, N.Y.: Doubleday, 1969.

    A collection of thirty essays and lectures about poetry, including "The Crowning Privilege," "The Road to Rydal Mount," "These Be Your Gods, O Israel!," the provocative "Dr. Syntax and Mr. Pound," "Legitimate Criticism of Poetry," "The Anti-Poet," and "Muntu, Mammon, Marxism."

OXFORD ADDRESSES ON POETRY. London: Cassell, 1961. Garden City, N.Y.: Doubleday, 1962.

    A collection of lectures delivered by RG as professor of poetry at Oxford University. The addresses included are: "The Dedicated Poet," "The Personal Muse," "Poetic Gold," "The Word 'Báraka,'" and "The Poet's Paradise." RG develops the theme that "thwarted passion stimulates poetic insight" and discusses English poetic heritage.

Robert Graves

A PAMPHLET AGAINST ANTHOLOGIES. With Laura Riding. London: Cape; Garden City, N.Y.: Doubleday, 1928.

> This is a wide-ranging discussion of the different types of anthologies with an attempt to define what is "the popular poem" and the "popular reader."

POETIC CRAFT AND PRINCIPLE: LECTURES AND TALKS. London: Cassell, 1967.

> Selected essays dealing with poetic technique.

POETIC UNREASON AND OTHER STUDIES. London: Palmer, 1925.

> Contains some important delineations of RG's fundamental ideas about poetic theory, including "A Theory of Consciousness," "The Illogical Element in Poetry," "Classical and Romantic," and "Sensory Vehicles of Poetic Thought."

THE READER OVER YOUR SHOULDER: A HANDBOOK FOR WRITERS OF ENGLISH PROSE. With Alan Hodge. London: Cape; New York: Macmillan, 1943.

> This is an informative discussion of "the principles of clear statement" as well as the history and types of English prose styles, followed by representative selections from T.S. Eliot, Ernest Hemingway, Aldous Huxley, Bertrand Russell, G.B. Shaw, and many others.

STEPS: STORIES, TALKS, ESSAYS, POEMS, STUDIES IN HISTORY. London: Cassell, 1958.

> Reprints many of the essays found in 5 PENS and adds "Sweeney among the Blackbirds," "The Making and Marketing of Poetry," "Pulling a Poem Apart," and several others on historical and religious topics.

A SURVEY OF MODERNIST POETRY. With Laura Riding. London: Heinemann, 1927. Garden City, N.Y.: Doubleday, 1928.

> This work is an excellent general introduction to the many facets and problems of modernist poetry. RG is particularly concerned with the "Plain Reader's Rights" in regard to form and subject matter in modernist poetry.

THE WHITE GODDESS: A HISTORICAL GRAMMAR OF POETIC MYTH. London: Faber; New York: Creative Age Press, 1948.

> RG's most important work--the result of forty years of independent reading--is a study of the sources of poetry and truth. He asserts that "the single grand theme of poetry" should be the refinement of the language of poetic myth to describe the poet's

relationship to the Moon-goddess or Muse: "The function of poetry is religious invocation of the Muse; its use is the experience of mixed exaltation and horror that her presence excites." RG views philosophy, science, and industry as enemies of poetry, myth, and matriarchal society. RG published revised editions in 1952 and 1961.

WORKS EDITED BY OTHERS

SELECTED POETRY AND PROSE OF ROBERT GRAVES. Ed. James Reeves. London: Hutchinson, 1961.

>Reprints selections from OCCUPATION and GOOD-BYE. Some useful annotations are provided.

BIBLIOGRAPHY

Edwards, A. S. G., and Diane Tolomeo, comps. "Robert Graves: A Check-List of His Publications, 1965-1974." MHR, 35 (1975), 168-79.

>This checklist supplements Higginson's bibliography by listing books and pamphlets as well as contributions to books and periodicals published by RG during the period 1965-74.

Higginson, Fred Hall, ed. A BIBLIOGRAPHY OF THE WORKS OF ROBERT GRAVES. London: Vane, 1966.

>The best primary bibliography, which lists the works of RG, including books and pamphlets, contributions to books, press, and periodicals. Also includes miscellanea and a selective list of works about RG.

Mason, Ellsworth, comp. "Emendations and Extensions of the Bibliography of Robert Graves." AEB, 2 (1978), 265-315.

>An important update.

Pownall, David E., ed. "An Annotated Bibliography of Articles on Robert Graves." FRG, No. 2 (1973), 17-23.

>An annotated bibliography of scholarly and critical articles on RG. "This listing from 1954 to 1970 is not exhaustive. . . ."

BIOGRAPHY

Skelton, Robin, and William David Thomas, eds. MHR, No. 35 (1975), 1-188, Graves Special Number.

Deals with RG's life and the general themes of his works, especially the poetry. The issue does not include a detailed exploration of RG's work as a critic or prose writer. There are, however, interesting personal reminiscences of RG by Susan Musgrave, James Reeves, Anthony Kerrigan, and John Auerbach.

CRITICISM

Adams, Hazard. "Criticism: Whence and Whither?" ASCH, 28 (1959), 226-38.

>Adams argues that in recent years RG's criticism has been "pretty consistently wrong." The essay "These Be Your Gods, O Israel!" in CROWNING PRIVILEGE is an unfair attack on modern poets based on irrational grounds, "the most remarkable example of professional jealousy."

Boyle, Ted E., and Richard F. Peterson. "The Robert Graves Collection: The Artist and the Personality." I CARBS, 1 (1973), 52-60.

>A cursory examination of the RG papers in Morris Library (Southern Illinois University--Carbondale) reveals interesting conclusions about RG's prose works: he is "an extremely careful planner" but he holds "his prose in rather low repute" because "he uses the verso of both the holograph and typescript of his prose pieces" when he does new writing.

Cohen, John Michael. ROBERT GRAVES. Writers and Critics. Edinburgh: Oliver and Boyd, 1960.

>An introductory study of RG's work. Discusses WHITE GODDESS as a "source-book" for RG's poetry.

Day, Douglas. SWIFTER THAN REASON: THE POETRY AND CRITICISM OF ROBERT GRAVES. Chapel Hill: Univ. of North Carolina Press, 1963.

>An impressive full-length study of four distinct periods of RG's work as poet and critic. Day presents changes in RG's thinking in a clear and informative manner, including substantial discussions of ON ENGLISH POETRY, SURVEY OF MODERNIST POETRY, and WHITE GODDESS.

DeBell, Diane. "Strategies of Survival: David Jones, IN PARENTHESIS, and Robert Graves, GOOD-BYE TO ALL THAT." In THE FIRST WORLD WAR IN FICTION: A COLLECTION OF CRITICAL ESSAYS. Ed. Holger Klein. London: Macmillan, 1976. Pp. 160-73.

>Comparison of two writers' recountings of World War I experiences.

GOOD-BYE is "perhaps the most valuable source in English for the individual and collective experience of trench warfare." However, because it is an emotionally charged, personal account filled with anecdotal information, its factual content is hard to validate.

Enright, D. J. "Robert Graves and the Decline of Modernism." EIC, 11 (1961), 319-37.

> Enright argues that RG's rise in reputation coincides with the decline of modernism. Various essays on poetry and culture by RG are examined--from COMMON ASPHODEL, CROWNING PRIVILEGE, POETIC UNREASON, STEPS, and SURVEY--and Enright is impressed that RG is never a dogmatic molder of taste.

Frank, Frederick S. "The Cool Web of Memory: An Initiatory Reading of Robert Graves's GOOD-BYE TO ALL THAT." FRG, 5 (1976), 74-82.

> Intelligent discussion of the narrator and narrative pattern of GOOD-BYE. Frank discusses the complex methods whereby RG as autobiographer "controls and uses his past by subjecting it to the rigors of artistic form."

FRG (FOCUS ON ROBERT GRAVES). Boulder: University of Colorado Libraries, 1972-- . 2 per year.

> Purpose of journal is "to develop a fruitful interrelationship between scholars, collectors, and libraries interested in Graves."

Grant, Patrick. "The Dark Side of the Moon: Robert Graves as Mythographer." MHR, 35 (1975), 143-65.

> An instructive essay with extensive discussion of GREEK MYTHS and WHITE GODDESS. Grant argues that RG perceives the problems of modern mythography with clarity and he offers "a distinctive and original solution."

Hijmans, Ben L. "Robert Graves, The White Goddess, and Vergil." MOSAIC, 2, No. 2 (1969), 58-73.

> An ingenious and instructive essay which compares the contrary approaches to poetry of RG and Vergil. Hijmans contends that "Graves's own poetic practice may have gained much from his notion of what 'poetry' ought to be, but that the same notion defeats him as a critic. . . . "

Hoffman, Daniel. BARBAROUS KNOWLEDGE: MYTH IN THE POETRY OF YEATS, GRAVES, AND MUIR. New York: Oxford Univ. Press, 1967.

> Includes treatment of RG's life, poetic theory, and philosophy of composition as in GOOD-BYE, ON ENGLISH POETRY, POETIC UNREASON, and WHITE GODDESS.

Jarrell, Randall. "Graves and the White Goddess Part II." YR, 45 (1956), 467-78.

> A psychoanalytical and anthropological interpretation of GOOD-BYE and WHITE GODDESS. Drawing on theories of Freud and Jung, Jarrell argues that "Graves' world-picture is a projection upon the universe of his own unconscious."

Kirkham, Michael. "The 'Poetic Liberation' of Graves." MINNR, 6 (1966), 244-54.

> Kirkham argues that in working out the White Goddess mythology, RG secured a "body of precisely meaningful symbols" that influenced the content, language, and emotional content of his later poetry.

Lucas, F.L. "Critical Unreason: Or Dr. Cottard's Saturday Night." In his AUTHORS DEAD AND LIVING. London: Chatto and Windus, 1926. Pp. 255-63.

> Lucas objects strongly to RG's "sweeping" generalizations and the application of psychoanalysis to poetry in POETIC UNREASON.

Mehoke, James S. ROBERT GRAVES: PEACE-WEAVER. The Hague: Mouton, 1975.

> A useful but complex study of RG's work and his revered values--"patience, dignity, love." Good discussion of RG's autobiography, expository, and mythic prose. Mehoke demonstrates that "the Myth is neither doctrinal, national, racial"; RG's vision is social and not exclusively personal.

Peschmann, Hermann. "Salute to Robert Graves." ENGLISH, 14 (1962), 2-8.

> Brief discussion of WHITE GODDESS, especially how it connects intimately with RG's later poetry.

Reeves, James. "Introduction." In his SELECTED POETRY AND PROSE. London: Hutchinson, 1961. Pp. 11-20.

> Praises RG's work as a poet; sees the prose works as mainly RG's diversified attempts "to make a living." However, Reeves admires RG's lucid, objective, and antiromantic prose style.

Seymour-Smith, Martin. ROBERT GRAVES. British Council Pamphlet. London: Longmans, 1956.

> Early, highly admiring biocritical study of RG, "one of the most versatile English prose writers of our time." Brief discussion of GOOD-BYE, POETIC UNREASON, and WHITE GODDESS.

Sossaman, Stephen. "Sassoon and Blunden's Annotation of GOOD-BYE TO ALL THAT." FRG, 5 (1976), 87.

> Brief discussion of the many comments and "corrections" made by Sassoon and Blunden in a copy of GOOD-BYE. Sassoon remarks on RG's style; Blunden questions RG's historical accuracy and attacks RG's motives as self-seeking in writing the autobiography.

Stade, G. ROBERT GRAVES. Columbia Essays on Modern Writers. New York: Columbia Univ. Press, 1967.

> A useful basic introduction to RG's work and career.

Steiner, George. "The Genius of Robert Graves." KR, 22 (1960), 340-65.

> A cursory, appreciative essay on RG's works. Steiner relates RG's great speed in writing some of the prose works "to make money." Particular attention is given to WHITE GODDESS, GREEK MYTHS, and NAZARENE GOSPEL.

Trilling, Lionel. "A Ramble on Graves." In his A GATHERING OF FUGITIVES. Boston: Beacon Press, 1956. Pp. 20-30.

> A brief survey of RG's prose works leads Trilling to conclude that RG "as a prose writer is a first-rate secondary figure in our literature." Trilling praises the prose for its intelligence, "wide and curious scholarship," and "gracefulness and verve."

Vickery, John B. ROBERT GRAVES AND THE WHITE GODDESS. Lincoln: Univ. of Nebraska Press, 1972.

> A concise introductory discussion to RG's mythopoeic thought. Vickery argues that the source of RG's goddess figure lies in Frazer's THE GOLDEN BOUGH and in the work of Jane Harrison and the Cambridge anthropologists.

Warmsley, Nigel. "Graves Where Is Thy Sting?" TWENTIETH CENTURY, 176, No. 1033 (1967), 47-48.

> Brief discussion of POETIC CRAFT. Warmsley regrets that RG's Oxford lectures on poetry "use the rhetorical trick of setting up non-existent targets in order to knock them down" but welcomes RG's informed comments on poetic craft now in book form.

Weisinger, Herbert. "'A Very Curious and Painstaking Person'--Robert Graves as Mythographer." In his THE AGONY AND THE TRIUMPH. East Lansing: Michigan State Univ. Press, 1964. Pp. 146-58.

> Explores the question of how critics should respond to RG's scholarly methods in GREEK MYTHS. Weisinger concludes that RG's attitude toward myth is "essentially romantic . . . passion congealed in form."

Wilson, Colin. "Some Notes on Graves's Prose." SHENANDOAH 13, No. 2 (1962), 55-62.

>Impressionistic criticism. Wilson examines some of RG's essays and WHITE GODDESS and concludes that RG is "a born writer" who is often wrong-headed and exasperating. Further, "Graves is not a writer of ideas" and the love of classical antiquity is the "unifying emotion" of all his prose work.

PHILIP GUEDALLA (1889-1944)

NONFICTIONAL PROSE

ARGENTINE TANGO. London: Hodder and Stoughton, 1932. New York, London: Harper, 1933.

Descriptions of and travels in the Argentine republic.

BONNET AND SHAWL: AN ALBUM. London: Hodder and Stoughton; New York: Putnam's, 1928.

A collection of biographical sketches of six Victorian women-- Jane Welsh Carlyle, Catherine Gladstone, Mary Arnold, Mary Anne Disraeli, Emily Tennyson, and Emily Palmerston.

CONQUISTADOR, AMERICAN FANTASIA. London: Benn, 1927. New York: Harper, 1928.

Descriptive travelog of the United States during three months of the late 1920's. PG records his romantic impressions of such places as New York City, Niagra Falls, Gettysburg, Grand Canyon, and San Francisco. Indians, young people, and a southern gentleman are also described.

THE DUKE. London: Hodder and Stoughton, 1931. As WELLINGTON. New York: Harper, 1931.

A notable, full-length study of the Duke of Wellington's life and times. PG's best-known biography, full of resonant prose passages. Maps and extensive references are included in the English edition only.

A GALLERY. London: Constable; New York: Putnam's, 1924.

Biographical essays on twenty-four contemporary authors and politicians, including such figures as Anatole France, Thomas Hardy, Bernard Shaw, Arnold Bennett, Joseph Conrad, Ramsay MacDonald, Winston Churchill, and Marcel Proust.

Philip Guedalla

THE HUNDRED DAYS. London: Davies; New York: Putnam, 1934.

    Study of the historical times of Napoleon I, concentrating on Elba and the one hundred days before Waterloo.

THE HUNDREDTH YEAR. New York: Doubleday, 1939. London: Butterworth, 1940.

    A record of the year 1936 by "a contemporary who lived in the very centre of it." The year is chosen because it marks the transition from postwar conditions to the then present situation.

THE HUNDRED YEARS. London: Hodder and Stoughton, 1936. New York: Doubleday, 1937.

    Covers the period 1837 to 1936. PG says the book is "an attempt to describe the leading moments of the century as they affected the leading units of the Western world." Significant events that occurred in Great Britain, France, Russia, Germany, and the United States are examined.

IDYLLS OF THE QUEEN. London: Hodder and Stoughton, 1937.

    Collection of Victorian studies with specific treatment of such figures as Queen Victoria, Gladstone, and Disraeli. Also reprints sketches from BONNET AND SHAWL.

IGNES FATUI, A BOOK OF PARODIES. Oxford: Blackwell, 1911.

    Juvenilia. Parodies written by PG as an undergraduate at Balliol College.

INDEPENDENCE DAY, A SKETCH BOOK. London: Murray, 1926. As FATHERS OF THE REVOLUTION. New York: Putnam, 1926.

    Essays on key figures involved in the American Revolution, including sketches of unwilling participants such as George III and Cornwallis. In his sketch of Washington, PG states his fundamental precept: "The first essential of sound portraiture is background." Some other figures treated include Louis XVI, Lafayette, Burke, and Franklin. The sketches "make no pretence of completeness or finality" and avoid the contemporary affliction of "tittering denigration."

THE LIBERATORS, WITH PORTRAITS BY F. J. KORMIS. London: Hodder and Stoughton, 1942.

    Sketches of fourteen statesmen.

MASTERS AND MEN. London: Constable; New York: Putnam, 1923.

Twenty-seven casual and often witty essays on various subjects, including "The Critics," "Mr. Disraeli, Poet," "Mr. George Saintsbury," "Mr. G. K. Chesterton," and "Mr. Pitt."

MEN OF AFFAIRS: COLLECTED ESSAYS II. London: Hodder and Stoughton, 1927.

Sketches of British statesmen.

MEN OF LETTERS: COLLECTED ESSAYS I. London: Hodder and Stoughton, 1927.

Historical and critical essays on English and French literature.

MEN OF WAR: COLLECTED ESSAYS III. London: Hodder and Stoughton, 1927.

Volume 3 of COLLECTED ESSAYS. These essays were first published in SUPERS, MASTERS, and GALLERY. Some of the reprinted essays included are "The Soldiery," "The Huns," "The Normans," "King Alfred," and "King Frederick the Great."

METRI GRATIA: VERSE AND PROSE. Oxford, Engl.: Blackwell, 1911.

Juvenilia. Written by PG in his undergraduate days at Balliol College.

MIDDLE EAST, 1940-1942, A STUDY IN AIR POWER. London: Hodder and Stoughton, 1944.

The reconstructed story of the air war in the Middle East through the eyes of an amateur. Includes maps.

THE MISSING MUSE AND OTHER ESSAYS. London: Hodder and Stoughton, 1929. As THE MISSING MUSE. New York: Harper, 1930.

PG laments the disappearance of Clio, the muse of history. In the prefatory essay "Conversation with a Caller" the author maintains that essays "are only studies casually detached from a prose-writer's sketchbook." Important essays in the volume include "The Missing Muse," "Edwardian Nocturne" (a period piece), "Mr. Belloc: A Panorama," "Portrait of a Lady" (Lady Astor, an early feminist), and "The Death of the Novel" (a critical discussion).

MR. CHURCHILL, A PORTRAIT. London: Hodder and Stoughton, 1941. New York: Reynal and Hitchcock, 1942.

Biography of Winston Churchill, from early education to beginning of World War II. Includes an interesting chapter on the leader as jeremiad in the 1930's.

Philip Guedalla

PALMERSTON, 1784-1865. London: Benn, 1926. New York: Putnam, 1927.

> PG's first successful biography is a notable full-length study of Palmerston's life and times. In his research PG drew extensively on unpublished source material. PG calls the Prime Minister "the last fragment of the Eighteenth Century."

THE PARTITION OF EUROPE, A TEXTBOOK OF EUROPEAN HISTORY, 1715-1815. Oxford, Engl.: Clarendon Press, 1914.

> PG's first historical work. Discusses the European balance of power system that was in effect for a century and focuses specifically on the rise of Prussia and various political upheavals in France.

RAG-TIME AND TANGO. London: Hodder and Stoughton, 1938.

> Collects CONQUISTADOR, ARGENTINE TANGO, and some revised versions of previously uncollected articles.

THE SECOND EMPIRE: BONAPARTISM, THE PRINCE, THE PRESIDENT, THE EMPEROR. London: Constable; New York: Putnam, 1922.

> Treats Napoleon III as a comic opera figure in the frivolous, gas-lit age of the Second Empire, 1852-1870.

STILL LIFE: COLLECTED ESSAYS IV. London: Hodder and Stoughton, 1927.

> Volume 4 of COLLECTED ESSAYS reprints essays from SUPERS, MASTERS, and GALLERY.

SUPERS AND SUPERMEN: STUDIES IN POLITICS, HISTORY, AND LETTERS. London: Unwin, 1920. New York: Putnam, 1924.

> Biographical essays on such figures from European history as King Alfred, Frederick the Great, Louis Philippe, and Disraeli. In the memorial essay on Lord Kitchener, PG reaffirms his belief in the importance of historical background for biography to elevate it above "mere anecdote."

THE TWO MARSHALS: BAZAINE, PÉTAIN. London: Hodder and Stoughton; New York: Reynal and Hitchcock, 1943.

> Biographies of the two military figures, Achille François Bazaine and Henri Philippe Pétain. Includes maps of campaigns and extensive references.

CRITICISM

Applejoy, Petronius. "Philip Guedalla." CATHW, 142 (1936), 719-22.

Applejoy criticizes PG's "glitter of style" and argues that PG is essentially a shrewd political historian who lacks the "broad grasp of social and economic history that Chesterton and Belloc have."

Lock, D.R. "Philip Guedalla Writes History." NEW HUMANIST, 9 (1936), 151-53.

> High praise for PG's historical books. Lock applauds their scholarship and admires the "vivacious" pace of the narratives. Lock also distinguishes between PG's and Strachey's approaches.

Murray, D.L. "Mr. Philip Guedalla." LONDON MERCURY, 14 (1926), 272-81.

> Generally appreciative discussion of PG's SUPERMEN, SECOND EMPIRE, GALLERY, and INDEPENDENCE DAY. Murray applauds PG's "keen sensitiveness to the visible detail of life," his effective irony, his fairness and objectivity, and his liberal skepticism.

Ritchie, Charles. "Strachey and Guedalla: An Essay in Comparison." DR, 12 (1933), 49-502.

> Compares the achievements of the two founders of the "new biography." Ranks PG as "far the inferior as a literary artist," but superior as an historian. Regrets the influence they have on their shoddy imitators.

Woolf, Leonard. "The World of Books: PALMERSTON." NATION AND ATHENAEUM, 40 (1926), 339.

> Praises PG's "gallant effort" and then analyzes the causes of the book's failure as biography: excessive verbal cleverness and a flawed conception of history.

W.H. HUDSON (1841-1922)

THE COLLECTED WORKS OF W.H. HUDSON (London: Dent; New York: Dutton, 1923), runs to twenty-four volumes.

NONFICTIONAL PROSE

ADVENTURES AMONG BIRDS. London: Hutchinson, 1913. New York: Kennerley, 1915.

    A volume dealing primarily with birds--their singing, their capacity for friendship--but also depicting various rustics WH has met in his ramblings in England.

AFOOT IN ENGLAND. London: Hutchinson, 1909. New York: Knopf, 1922.

    Opening with the advice "not to look at a guide-book until the place it treats of has been explored and left behind," this travel book records WH's fresh encounters with people and ruins throughout England. Cobbett is praised in the chapter "Rural Rides."

ARGENTINE ORNITHOLOGY: A DESCRIPTIVE CATALOGUE OF THE BIRDS OF THE ARGENTINE REPUBLIC. With P.L. Sclater. 2 vols. London: Porter, 1888-89. Rev. ed. as BIRDS OF LA PLATA. 2 vols. London: Dent; New York: Dutton, 1920.

    WH's first book, written in collaboration with Sclater of the London Zoological Society with whom WH had earlier corresponded from Argentina about birds. WH employed numerous passages from his own letters in his contribution to the volume: detailed descriptions of the birds and their habits.

BIRDS AND MAN. London and New York: Longmans, 1901.

    A study of man's varying response to birds, adducing WH's

personal experiences and those of people he has encountered. The seventh chapter discusses man's delight in personification. John Burroughs and Gilbert White are frequently cited.

BIRDS IN A VILLAGE. London: Chapman and Hall; Philadelphia: Lippincott, 1893. Rev. ed. as BIRDS IN TOWN AND VILLAGE. London: Dent; New York: Dutton, 1919.

> WH's first book on British birds. It contains a bitter chapter on killing birds for their feathers and a less bitter one on caging them. Thoreau is mentioned several times.

BIRDS IN LONDON. London and New York: Longmans, 1898.

> A tour of London locales and the birds in them which continues the protest against the extermination of birds voiced in BIRDS IN A VILLAGE. There is a chapter on the evil of stray cats.

THE BOOK OF A NATURALIST. London and New York: Hodder and Stoughton, 1919.

> A collection of diverse essays, mostly reprinted and mostly on animals. Among them is WH's notorious essay "The Great Dog-Superstition" which says that dogs are stupid.

BRITISH BIRDS. London and New York: Longmans, 1895.

> Most of this consists of descriptions of the "appearance, language, and life-habits" of all the bird species in Britain.

FAR AWAY AND LONG AGO: A HISTORY OF MY EARLY LIFE. London: Dent; New York: Dutton, 1918.

> WH's superb autobiography of his boyhood in Argentina, full of natural description but most memorable for the series of vivid human portraits: a captured murderer, a drunken tutor, a gaucho duelist, a patriarchal polygamist, and the like. Fundamentally, the book records WH's spiritual development: his early animism and terror of death, his near-fatal illness, and his encounter with Darwinism.

HAMPSHIRE DAYS. London and New York: Longmans, 1903.

> WH's second regional study, focusing somewhat less on humanity than NATURE IN DOWNLAND and containing many examples of, and some meditation on, violence in nature.

A HIND IN RICHMOND PARK. London: Dent, 1922. New York: Dutton, 1923.

W.H. Hudson

A witty (at times acerbic) treatment of senses in animals and humans, including the "wind sense," the sense of direction, and telepathy. There are numerous literary references; for example, WH discusses music in English poets.

IDLE DAYS IN PATAGONIA. London: Chapman and Hall; New York: Appleton, 1893.

WH's first autobiographical volume, based on his ornithological expedition to Patagonia (southern Argentina) in 1871. The book is less focused on people than FAR AWAY and more focused on nature; several chapters, such as "Bird Music in South America," are written in a scientific vein. The book depicts, however, WH's abandonment of the scientific approach to nature in favor of an animistic one. The penultimate chapter, "The Plains of Patagonia," treats his new philosophy most directly.

THE LAND'S END: A NATURALIST'S IMPRESSIONS IN WEST CORNWALL. London: Hutchinson; New York: Appleton, 1908.

WH's third regional study of England, centering on the customs and morals of the Cornish, a sober, humorless, tough people according to WH.

THE NATURALIST IN LA PLATA. London: Chapman and Hall; New York: Appleton, 1892.

A collection of essays on the insect, bird, and animal life in Argentina. The book is based on first-hand observation and on the work of previous naturalists cited throughout. WH frequently disagrees with Darwin; for example, "Darwin's conjecture that the extreme violence of the pampero, or south-west wind, prevented trees from growing, is now proved to have been ill-founded. . . ."

NATURE IN DOWNLAND. London and New York: Longmans, 1900.

WH's first regional study of England, focusing on the Sussex Downs. The geography, vegetation, and animal life are vividly depicted, and the rustics are seen as part of them. WH prides himself on "the mental attitude of the naturalist, whose proper study is not mankind but animals, including man." The Downs are contrasted to ugly Chichester which smells, says WH, like a cesspool.

A SHEPHERD'S LIFE: IMPRESSIONS OF THE SOUTH WILTSHIRE DOWNS. London: Methuen; New York: Dutton, 1910.

WH's fourth and greatest English regional study, set in the Wiltshire Downs. Unlike the others, it focuses upon a central

character, the shepherd Caleb Bawcombe. The narration of his
and his father's experiences constitutes a large part of the book;
they treat both the timeless shepherd's customs and the social
history of the area from about 1800.

A TRAVELLER IN LITTLE THINGS. London: Dent; New York: Dutton, 1921.

A collection of diverse essays, most reprinted, and focusing
more on people than BOOK OF A NATURALIST. Several pieces
are whimsical portraits of children.

WORKS EDITED BY OTHERS

THE BEST OF W.H. HUDSON. Ed. Odell Shepard. New York: Dutton, 1949.

Contains studies from IDLE DAYS, NATURE IN DOWNLAND,
BIRDS AND MAN, HAMPSHIRE DAYS, LAND'S END, AFOOT
IN ENGLAND, SHEPHERD'S LIFE, FAR AWAY, BOOK OF A
NATURALIST, BIRDS IN TOWN AND VILLAGE, A TRAVELLER
IN LITTLE THINGS, and A HIND.

GAUCHOS OF THE PAMPAS AND THEIR HORSES: BY W.H. HUDSON AND
R.B. CUNNINGHAME GRAHAM. Comp. J. Frank Dobie. Hanover, N.H.:
Westholm Publications, 1963.

Collects "Story of a Piebald Horse" and "Cristiano: The Sentinel
Horse" from WH and "The Horse of the Pampas" and "San Jose"
from Graham.

A HUDSON ANTHOLOGY. Ed. Edward Garnett. London: Dent, 1924.

A generous selection of usually brief passages culled from the
American nature books, the British nature books, and the fiction.

RARE, VANISHING AND LOST BRITISH BIRDS: COMPILED FROM NOTES
BY W.H. HUDSON. Ed. Linda Gardiner. London: Dent, 1923.

Employing WH's notes, this posthumously carries out his proposed
expansion of his 1894 pamphlet LOST BRITISH BIRDS. Twenty-
five endangered species are discussed.

BIBLIOGRAPHY

Payne, John R., ed. W.H. HUDSON: A BIBLIOGRAPHY. Folkestone,
Kent: Dawson, 1977.

Supersedes Wilson as the best primary bibliography, with sections
on books, contributions to books and periodicals, and translations.
There is also a useful listing of books on WH.

Wilson, George F., ed. A BIBLIOGRAPHY OF THE WRITINGS OF W.H. HUDSON. London: Bookman's Journal, 1922.

> The early, primary descriptive bibliography, with a section on books and a very brief section on essays.

BIOGRAPHY

Looker, Samuel J., ed. WILLIAM HENRY HUDSON: A TRIBUTE BY VARIOUS WRITERS. Worthing, Sussex: Worthing Art Development Scheme, 1947.

> A rare, informative hodgepodge of photographs and brief essays. Some are memoirs of WH by acquaintances; several discuss his authorial connections with various regions in Britain.

Roberts, Morley. W.H. HUDSON: A PORTRAIT. London: Dutton, 1924.

> A long-winded anecdotal memoir by a friend, with some casual commentary on the works.

Shrubsall, Dennis. W.H. HUDSON: WRITER AND NATURALIST. Tisbury, Wiltshire: Compton, 1978.

> A good, if short, biography that pays some attention to the critical reception of the works.

Tomalin, Ruth. W.H. HUDSON. New York: Greenwood, 1954.

> A popular biography with superficial commentary on the works.

West, Herbert Faulkner. FOR A HUDSON BIOGRAPHER. Hanover, N.H.: Westholm Publications, 1958.

> A hodgepodge of minor Hudsoniana, including obituary notices on him and a copy of his Last Will.

_____. W.H. HUDSON'S READING. Privately printed, 1947.

> A slight, casually organized review of WH's literary opinions, based only on his published letters.

CRITICISM

Brown, Christopher. "Hudson's FAR AWAY AND LONG AGO: The Uses of the Past." RS, 49 (1981), 221-30.

Argues that WH's rendering of the past in FAR AWAY is motivated and organized by his present fear of disease and death.

Cahoon, Herbert. "Herman Melville and W.H. Hudson." AN&Q, 8 (1949), 131-32.

> Notes reference in IDLE DAYS and AFOOT IN ENGLAND to "The Whiteness of the Whale" chapter in MOBY DICK.

Charles, R.H. "The Writings of W.H. Hudson." E & S, 20 (1935), 135-51.

> A general survey, containing a brief discussion of WH's mysticism.

De La Mare, Walter. "Naturalists." In his PLEASURES AND SPECULATIONS. London: Faber, 1940. Pp. 47-65.

> An informed and amusing discussion of WH as "field naturalist," "human-naturalist," and "super-naturalist."

Fletcher, James V. "The Creator of Rima: W.H. Hudson: A Belated Romantic." SR, 41 (1933), 24-40.

> An antagonistic study presenting WH as a confused antihumanist. His natural philosophy is a "crazy-quilt of ideas in which the pantheistic mysticism of Wordsworth, the Rousselian doctrine of natural education, the romantic conception of the noble savage, and the Meredithian glorification of the struggle for existence are all pieced together."

Ford, Ford Madox. "W.H. Hudson." AMERICAN MERCURY, 37 (1936), 307-17.

> An amusing memoir which praises WH's capacity to make the reader visualize natural scenes.

Frederick, John T. WILLIAM HENRY HUDSON. Twayne's English Author Series. New York: Twayne, 1972.

> A useful survey of the works, organized in roughly chronological fashion. Frederick emphasizes WH's abilities as an essayist, terming him "one of the greatest masters of the personal essay in any literature and of all time."

Garnett, Edward. "W.H. Hudson." DIAL, 62 (1917), 83-87.

> An admiring review that judges WH superior to Richard Jefferies, "in the way he weaves his frankly human interests in the characters and life of countrymen he meets into the texture of his nature study."

_____. "W.H. Hudson: An Appreciation." THE ACADEMY AND LITERATURE, 62 (1902), 632-34.

> Wishes WH had spent less effort on nature writing and more on fiction.

Hamilton, Robert. "The Spirit of W.H. Hudson: An Evaluation." QR, 275 (1940), 239-48.

> Argues WH's style mixes simplicity and strangeness.

_____. W.H. HUDSON: THE VISION OF EARTH. London: Dent, 1946.

> Three chapters review the contents of the essay volumes, FAR AWAY AND LONG AGO, and A HIND IN RICHMOND PARK. The author's approach to WH from a Christian standpoint occasionally proves irritating.

Haymaker, Richard E. FROM PAMPAS TO HEDGEROWS AND DOWNS: A STUDY OF W.H. HUDSON. New York: Bookman Associates, 1954.

> The best critical study. It contains an excellent review of the nature essay tradition behind WH and a discussion of his "artistry" (keen senses, the "mythical faculty," tone). A long central chapter treats WH's use of "landscape backgrounds," "animal portraiture," and the like. The final chapter discusses his philosophy.

Massingham, H.J. "W.H. Hudson." In his UNTRODDEN WAYS. New York: Dutton, 1923. Pp. 11-37.

> An impressionistic account of WH's personal and artistic qualities.

Pound, Ezra. "Hudson: Poet Strayed into Science." LITTLE REVIEW, 7, No. 1 (1920), 13-17.

> An amusingly fierce extension of WH's anti-industrial ideas: "for the same system man is degraded, and the wild beasts destroyed."

R.,E. "The Work of W.H. Hudson." ENGLISH REVIEW, 2 (1909), 157-64.

> An early appreciation, praising the simplicity of WH's style.

Rodker, John. "W.H. Hudson." LITTLE REVIEW, 7, No. 1 (1920), 18-28.

> WH's affinity with nature is both a source of his appeal and of his artistic imperfection.

T.E. HULME (1883-1917)

NONFICTIONAL PROSE

All of TEH's nonfictional books are posthumous.

WORKS EDITED BY OTHERS

"Appendices." In T. E. HULME. Ed. Michael Roberts. London: Faber, 1938. Pp. 255-303.

> Contains three poems, "Lecture on Modern Poetry," and "Notes on Language and Style."

FURTHER SPECULATIONS BY T. E. HULME. Ed. Samuel Hynes. Minneapolis: Univ. of Minnesota Press, 1955.

> A further collection of TEH's writings on philosophy and art, along with several pro-militarist essays and his hitherto unpublished "Diary from the Trenches" on his vivid experiences as an enlisted man. One of the more important pieces, "A Lecture on Modern Poetry," calls for a new irregular verse form.

THE LIFE AND OPINIONS OF T. E. HULME. Ed. Alun R. Jones. Boston: Beacon Press, 1960.

> Collects two pseudonymous articles: "A Tory Philosophy" and "A Personal Impression of Bergson." The former asserts that man's intellectual and ethical capacity is unchanging in time.

"Notes on Language and Style." Ed. Herbert Read. CRITERION, 3 (1925), 485-97. Rpt. Seattle: Univ. of Washington Chapbooks, 1925.

> Fragmentary notes to the effect that literary style should stress images and analogies because thought does.

SPECULATIONS: ESSAYS ON HUMANISM AND THE PHILOSOPHY OF ART.
Ed. Herbert Read. London: Kegan Paul; New York: Harcourt, 1924.

    The famous posthumous collection expressing TEH's antihumanism and antiromanticism and celebrating the philosophy of Bergson and the modernist art of Jacob Epstein. Read pieced the volume together both from published articles and from unpublished notes. An example of the former, "Romanticism and Classicism," denounces romantic "sloppiness" in favor of the "dry hardness" of classical verse. "Cinders," constructed from notes, depicts a chaotic universe given structure only by the mind of man.

BIBLIOGRAPHY

Hynes, Samuel, ed. FURTHER SPECULATIONS BY T.E. HULME. Minneapolis: Univ. of Minnesota Press, 1955.

    Contains chronological listings of TEH's publications and criticism on them; superseded by Jones.

Jones, Alun R., ed. THE LIFE AND OPINIONS OF T.E. HULME. Boston: Beacon Press, 1960.

    This contains a chronologically ordered listing of TEH's publications and a selected list of secondary sources.

Martin, W., comp. "T.E. Hulme: A Bibliographical Note." N&Q, 9 (1962), 307.

    Adds twelve primary items to Jones (above).

BIOGRAPHY

Epstein, Jacob. "T.E. Hulme and His Friends." In his EPSTEIN: AN AUTOBIOGRAPHY. New York: Dutton, 1955. Pp. 59-68.

    This contains a brief, admiring sketch by a close friend and reprints TEH's "Mr. Epstein and the Critics."

Jones, Alun R. THE LIFE AND OPINIONS OF T.E. HULME. Boston: Beacon Press, 1960.

    Most of this (pp. 17-143) is a fine critical biography, with chapters on TEH's poetic theory, his views on humanism, and the like.

T.E. Hulme

CRITICISM

Belgion, Montgomery. "In Memory of T.E. Hulme." SATR (USA), 4 (1927), 154-55.

    A brief tracing of TEH's ideas and their continuation in such figures as Eliot and Wyndham Lewis.

Brandabur, Edward. "The Eye in the Ceiling and the Eye in the Mud: T.E. Hulme's Comedy of Perception." PLL, 9 (1973), 420-27.

    Argues that TEH's attempt to avoid abstract poetic description is motivated by sexual impulses.

Coffman, Stanley K., Jr. "T.E. Hulme as Imagist." In his IMAGISM: A CHAPTER FOR THE HISTORY OF MODERN POETRY. Norman: Univ. of Oklahoma Press, 1951. Pp. 47-73.

    A survey of TEH's poetic theories.

Daiches, David. "T.E. Hulme and T.S. Eliot." In his POETRY AND THE MODERN WORLD: A STUDY OF POETRY IN ENGLAND BETWEEN 1900 AND 1939. Chicago: Univ. of Chicago Press, 1940. Pp. 90-105.

    Notes both Eliot and TEH associate classicism with antihumanism.

Daniells, J.R. "T.S. Eliot and His Relation to T.E. Hulme." UTQ, 2 (1933), 380-96.

    Without claiming influence, this study notes how Eliot fills out many of TEH's notions about philosophy and poetry.

Davie, Donald. "Syntax as Unpoetical: T.E. Hulme." In his ARTICULATE ENERGY: AN INQUIRY INTO THE SYNTAX OF ENGLISH POETRY. London: Routledge and Kegan Paul, 1955. Pp. 1-13.

    On the importance of TEH's rejection of syntax in poetry.

Fairchild, Hoxie Neale. "Hulme and the Imagists." In his RELIGIOUS TRENDS IN ENGLISH POETRY: VOLUME V: 1880-1920: GODS OF A CHANGING POETRY. New York: Columbia Univ. Press, 1962. Pp. 427-85.

    A hostile discussion of TEH's failure to posit a redemptive Christian God.

Flint, F.S. "The History of Imagism." THE EGOIST, 2 (1915), 70-71.

    Presents TEH as the initiating figure of the movement.

Hansen, Miriam. "T.E. Hulme, Mercenary of Modernism, or, Fragments of Avantgarde Sensibility in Pre-World War I Britain." ELH, 47 (1980), 355-85.

A learned, complex discussion of the relationship between TEH's aesthetics and his political ideals of "order, discipline, hierarchy, and tradition."

Hendry, J.F. "Hulme as Horatio." LIFE AND LETTERS TODAY, 35 (1942), 136-47.

Finds TEH's philosophy too abstract, a "mechanist idealism" lacking bridges to intuition.

Hughes, Glenn. IMAGISM AND THE IMAGISTS: A STUDY IN MODERN POETRY. London: Oxford Univ. Press, 1931.

This contains a brief summary (pp. 9-23) of TEH's poetic theory.

Hynes, Samuel. "Introduction." In his FURTHER SPECULATIONS BY T.E. HULME. Minneapolis: Univ. of Minnesota Press, 1955. Pp. vii-xxxi.

A useful survey of the career that makes the point that TEH was not an organized thinker but a propagandist.

Jones, A.R. "Notes toward a History of Imagism: An Examination of Literary Sources." SAQ, 60 (1961), 262-85.

Cites some of TEH's writings in arguing that he, not Pound or Ford, was the key figure of Imagism.

―――. "T.E. Hulme, Wilhelm Worringer, and the Urge to Abstraction." BJA, 1 (1960), 1-7.

Although TEH speaks positively of Worringer, his position on the place of empathy in the aesthetics of abstract art is antithetical to Worringer's position.

Kamerbeek, J., Jr. "T.E. Hulme and German Philosophy: Dilthey and Scheler." CL, 21 (1969), 193-212.

A study of how Dilthey's conception of Weltanschauung and Scheler's critique of social progressivism influenced TEH.

Kermode, Frank. "T.E. Hulme." In his ROMANTIC IMAGE. London: Routledge and Kegan Paul, 1957. Pp. 119-37.

A hostile but useful survey of TEH's aesthetics. He was more romantic than he knew.

Krieger, Murray. "The Ambiguous Anti-Romanticism of T.E. Hulme." ELH, 20 (1953), 300-314.

Citing SPECULATIONS throughout, Krieger notes that despite
TEH's rejection of romanticism his concept of intuition is close
to the Coleridgean imagination.

Lewis, Wyndham. "Hulme of Original Sin." In BLASTING AND BOMBAR-
DIERING. London: Eyre and Spottiswoode, 1937. Pp. 99-104.

Praises TEH as the first person of his generation to have heard
of Original Sin.

Martin, Wallace. THE NEW AGE UNDER ORAGE: CHAPTERS IN ENGLISH
CULTURAL HISTORY. Manchester, Engl.: Manchester Univ. Press, 1967.

Notes TEH's connection with the journal throughout.

Nelson, Francis W. VALET TO THE ABSOLUTE: A STUDY OF THE PHILOSOPHY
OF T. E. HULME. Wichita, Kans.: Univ. of Wichita Bulletin No. 22, 1950.

Little more than a close rehash of the contents of SPECULATIONS.

Nott, Kathleen. "Mr. Hulme's Sloppy Dregs." In her THE EMPEROR'S
CLOTHES. London: Heinemann, 1953. Pp. 56-104.

A detailed defense of logical thought against the strictures of
TEH and Bergson.

Pondrom, Cyrena N. "Hulme's 'A Lecture on Modern Poetry' and the Birth
of Imagism." PLL, 5 (1969), 465-70.

Suggests this essay (FURTHER SPECULATIONS) is not the initiating
document of Imagism, as often claimed, because written too late.

Pound, Ezra. "This Hulme Business." 1938. Rpt. Hugh Kenner. THE POETRY
OF EZRA POUND. Norfolk, Conn.: New Directions, 1951. Pp. 307-09.

Pound argues that Ford was more important than TEH as a
literary influence in pre-war London.

Primeau, Ronald. "On the Discrimination of Hulme: Toward a Theory of the
'Anti-romantic' Romanticism of Modern Poetry." JML, 3 (1974), 1104-22.

A close examination of the tension in TEH's thought between
romantic and antiromantic ideas, one typical of modernist poetry,
according to Primeau.

Pulos, C E. "T. E. Hulme." In his THE NEW CRITICS AND THE LANGUAGE
OF POETRY. Lincoln: Univ. of Nebraska Press, 1958. Pp. 15-24.

A discussion of the areas in which TEH's aesthetics agree and
disagree with Bergson's.

Rackin, Phyllis. "Hulme, Richards, and the Development of Contextualist Poetic Theory." JAAC, 25 (1967), 413-25.

> A complex study of Richard's objections to TEH's doctrine of concreteness in poetry.

Read, Herbert. "The Isolation of the Image: T. E. Hulme." In THE TRUE VOICE OF FEELING: STUDIES IN ENGLISH ROMANTIC POETRY. London: Faber, 1952. Pp. 101-15.

> A general review of TEH's ideas on poetry that cites SPECULATIONS, "Lecture on Modern Poetry," and "Notes on Language and Style" (Roberts' T. E. HULME).

Riding, Laura. "T. E. Hulme, the New Barbarism, and Gertrude Stein." In her CONTEMPORARIES AND SNOBS. New York: Doubleday, 1928. Pp. 123-99.

> Finds TEH's absolutist mental tendency and his antihumanism "barbaric."

Roberts, Michael. T. E. HULME. London: Faber, 1938.

> A good, full-length explication of TEH's ideas that places them in the context of western philosophy. Though not an original thinker, TEH expresses important ideas clearly and less contradictorily than often assumed.

Robinson, A. D. "New Sources for Imagism." N&Q, 27 (1980), 238-40.

> Mainly on how TEH's criticism of prose in "Lecture on Modern Poetry" (FURTHER SPECULATIONS) is indebted to the psychological concept of "reflex speech."

Schuchard, Ronald. "Eliot and Hulme in 1916: Toward a Revaluation of Eliot's Critical and Spiritual Development." PMLA, 88 (1973), 1083-94.

> A detailed study of Eliot's knowledge of TEH that argues Eliot's classicist-royalist-Catholic sentiments were developed earlier than supposed and were influenced by TEH.

Shapiro, Karl. "T. S. Eliot: The Death of Literary Judgment." In his DEFENSE OF IGNORANCE. New York: Random, 1960. Pp. 35-60.

> In this lambasting of Eliot, Shapiro sees his deplorable notions springing from SPECULATIONS, "the MEIN KAMPF of modern criticism and a thoroughly evil work."

Tate, Allen. "Poetry and the Absolute." SR, 35 (1927), 41-52.

> Cites "Critique of Satisfaction" (SPECULATIONS) in arguing TEH goes too far in denigrating subject matter in poetry.

Ward, Anne. "Speculations on Eliot's Time-World: An Analysis of THE FAMILY REUNION in Relation to Hulme and Bergson." AL, 21 (1949), 18-34.

> Argues that the play employs three Bergsonian time categories modified by Hulme: clock time, duration, and a realm of timeless absolutes.

Wecter, Dixon. "Hulme and the Tragic View." SOR, 5 (1939), 141-52.

> Raises problems with TEH's thinking--the tension between his "will to believe and the fear of believing too much," for example.

Williams, Raymond. "T. E. Hulme." In his CULTURE AND SOCIETY: 1780-1950. New York: Columbia Univ. Press, 1958. Pp. 190-95.

> Accuses TEH of belief in the "pseudo-category. . . . of an ultimate, essential condition of man."

ALDOUS HUXLEY (1894-1963)

THE COLLECTED WORKS OF ALDOUS HUXLEY (London: Chatto and Windus, 1946--) contains nearly all the nonfiction volumes.

NONFICTIONAL PROSE

ADONIS AND THE ALPHABET AND OTHER ESSAYS. London: Chatto and Windus, 1956. As TOMORROW AND TOMORROW AND TOMORROW AND OTHER ESSAYS. New York: Harper, 1956.

> A collection of wide-ranging essays. Two of the more important, "The Education of an Amphibian" and "Knowledge and Understanding," argue that man's tendency toward verbal expression and abstract thought has dissociated him from life. AH supports "the rediscovery within ourselves of a virgin not-mind capable of non-verbally not-thinking in response to immediate experience."

ALDOUS HUXLEY'S STORIES, ESSAYS, AND POEMS. London: Dent, 1937.

> Contains chapters from the travel books, and representative essays from ON THE MARGIN, PROPER STUDIES, MUSIC AT NIGHT, and OLIVE TREE. The collection also includes "What Are You Going to Do About It?," AH's pacifist essay written for the Peace Pledge Union in 1936.

ALONG THE ROAD: NOTES AND ESSAYS OF A TOURIST. London: Chatto and Windus; New York: Doran, 1925.

> AH's first travel book, descriptive primarily of Italy and Holland but also discussing such topics as the mentality of the tourist and great paintings. AH reveals himself to be a clever, detached observer of foreign scenes, admiring Holland's landscape for its geometric precision and Piero della Francesca for his intellectual mastery rather than for emotional fervor.

THE ART OF SEEING. New York: Harper, 1942. London: Chatto and Windus, 1943.

Aldous Huxley

On the eye exercises of Dr. W.H. Bates that improved AH's terrible vision in 1939.

BEYOND THE MEXIQUE BAY. London: Chatto and Windus; New York: Harper, 1934.

> A record of AH's trip to Central America. It includes both vivid scenes and meditation on such matters as time and the evils of nationalism. In explicit disagreement with D.H. Lawrence, AH concludes that "the attempt to return to primitiveness is both impractical and, I believe, wrong."

BRAVE NEW WORLD REVISITED. London: Chatto and Windus; New York: Harper, 1958.

> The nonfictional sequel to AH's anti-utopian novel BRAVE NEW WORLD. AH argues that overpopulation and improved techniques of propaganda are the principal threats to liberty. Somewhat despairingly, he advocates training in the analysis of language, and small, self-governing social units as antidotes.

COLLECTED ESSAYS. New York: Harper, 1959. London: Chatto and Windus, 1960.

> An extensive selection, under the headings "Nature," "Travel," "Love, Sex, and Physical Beauty," "Literature," "Painting," "Music," "Matters of Taste and Style," "History," "Politics," "Psychology," "Rx for Sense and Psyche," and "Way of Life."

A DAY IN WINDSOR. With J.A. Kings. London: Britannicus Liber, 1953.

> Not seen.

THE DEVILS OF LOUDON. London: Chatto and Windus; New York: Harper, 1952.

> A fascinating account of demonically possessed nuns in seventeenth-century France. AH focuses on three figures in the case: a salacious priest burned at the stake for witchcraft, a sexually frustrated nun who accuses him of causing her possession, and an ascetic Jesuit who tries to exorcise her. Theirs is a tragedy of religious and psychological extremism. AH suggests that the attempt to escape the self either by extreme sensual indulgence or denial is fatal.

DO WHAT YOU WILL: ESSAYS. London: Chatto and Windus; Garden City, N.Y.: Doubleday, 1929.

> AH's second treatise on man, written under the (misunderstood) influence of D.H. Lawrence. In PROPER STUDIES, AH had stressed the need to unify the personality; in this volume he stresses the importance of recognizing the conflicting elements

of the personality, including the sexual, and of indulging each fully. He upbraids numerous writers for failing to grasp the multiplicity of the self: Pascal's religious extremism is attacked as is Wordsworth's idealizing tendency in the famous essay "Wordsworth in the Tropics."

THE DOORS OF PERCEPTION. London: Chatto and Windus; New York: Harper, 1954.

AH experiences something like mystical vision engendered not by mortification (as suggested in PERENNIAL PHILOSOPHY) but by a mescaline trip in 1953.

ENDS AND MEANS: AN ENQUIRY INTO THE NATURE OF IDEALS AND INTO THE METHODS EMPLOYED FOR THEIR REALIZATION. London: Chatto and Windus; New York: Harper, 1937.

AH's third major philosophical effort (after PROPER STUDIES and DO WHAT YOU WILL). Under the influence of the pacifist Gerald Heard, AH now presents the charitable man, "non-attached" from selfish drives, as the salvation of society. AH offers a series of rather naive "recipes" for social reform based on the ethics of nonattachment, which he correlates in the final sections of the book with mystical experience.

ESSAYS NEW AND OLD. London: Chatto and Windus, 1926. New York: Doran, 1927.

A collection of essays, some hitherto uncollected, some drawn from ON THE MARGIN and the travel volumes. Two of the more interesting pieces in the former category are "Sincerity in Art" (a matter of talent, not will) and "Where Are the Movies Moving?" (toward surreal expression).

GREY EMINENCE: A STUDY IN RELIGION AND POLITICS. London: Chatto and Windus; New York: Harper, 1941.

A companion volume to DEVILS OF LOUDON, also set in seventeenth-century France and also depicting religion gone wrong. The biography treats Father Joseph, a strict contemplative who for seemingly the best of motives becomes Richelieu's dreaded lieutenant in foreign affairs. Written when AH was under the influence of pacifism, the book indicates that ethics are corrupted by politics.

HEAVEN AND HELL. London: Chatto and Windus; New York: Harper, 1956.

A companion volume to DOORS OF PERCEPTION. It focuses on "visionary" art, such as stained glass windows and Islamic arabesques: "Bright, pure colours are characteristic of the Other World."

Aldous Huxley

HOLY FACE AND OTHER ESSAYS. London: Fleuron, 1929.

> A collection of six essays including "Wordsworth in the Tropics" and "Swift."

JESTING PILATE: THE DIARY OF A JOURNEY. London: Chatto and Windus, 1926. As JESTING PILATE: AN INTELLECTUAL HOLIDAY. New York: Doran, 1926.

> AH's second travel book, based on a tour of the Far East in 1925. AH is an unsympathetic observer of India and the Orient finding these regions confusing and uncivilized. He is attracted, however, to the eastern mysticism that becomes so important in his later years.

LITERATURE AND SCIENCE. London: Chatto and Windus; New York: Harper, 1963.

> AH's last book, which addresses the "two cultures" debate.

MUSIC AT NIGHT AND OTHER ESSAYS. London: Chatto and Windus; Garden City, N.Y.: Doubleday, 1931.

> An essay collection treating various artistic and cultural topics. Some of the more important essays, such as "Notes on Liberty and the Boundaries of the Promised Land" and "On the Charms of History and the Future of the Past" warn of the dangers of mechanization and specialization AH would depict in BRAVE NEW WORLD (1932).

THE OLIVE TREE AND OTHER ESSAYS. London: Chatto and Windus, 1936. New York: Harper, 1937.

> Written when AH's interest in pacifism was growing, this collection generally deals with man's tendency to rationalize his immoral desires such as war. There is extensive discussion of propaganda and euphemistic language. There is also a lengthy essay on D.H. Lawrence.

ON THE MARGIN: NOTES AND ESSAYS. London: Chatto and Windus; New York: Doran, 1923.

> AH's first volume of essays, which deal with literary and cultural topics. The most significant essays are about the horror of mass culture (e.g., "Democratic Art") and the inadequacies of contemporary literature (e.g., "Subject-Matter of Poetry," which argues modern poets have failed to treat science as a worthy subject).

THE PERENNIAL PHILOSOPHY. New York: Harper, 1945. London: Chatto and Windus, 1946.

Aldous Huxley

Like TEXTS AND PRETEXTS, this is an anthology of great writings with commentary by AH. In this case the writings are by mystics of various faiths who have shared the underlying philosophy of all religions: mortification of the ego to facilitate union with the Godhead. The book emphasizes the same theme found in ENDS AND MEANS.

PROPER STUDIES. London: Chatto and Windus, 1927. Garden City, N.Y.: Doubleday, 1928.

AH's first book of philosophical speculation. Although the chapter "Personality and the Discontinuity of the Mind" stresses the need of the individual to mold inherited traits, the thrust of PROPER STUDIES is that people inherit different characteristics and that the institutions of education and religion must be flexible enough to meet various needs. Noting the manifest fact that all men are not created equal, AH argues that in the field of government an intellectual aristocracy should rule.

ROTUNDA: A SELECTION FROM THE WORKS OF ALDOUS HUXLEY. London: Chatto and Windus, 1932.

Reprints sections of ALONG THE ROAD, DO WHAT YOU WILL, JESTING PILATE, and MUSIC AT NIGHT.

SCIENCE, LIBERTY AND PEACE. New York: Harper, 1946. London: Chatto and Windus, 1947.

A brief treatise on the threat of advanced weaponry and mass technology to freedom that anticipates BRAVE NEW WORLD REVISITED.

TEXTS AND PRETEXTS: AN ANTHOLOGY WITH COMMENTARIES. London: Chatto and Windus, 1932. New York: Harper, 1933.

An anthology mostly of great poetry, with explications by AH. This odd volume was the product of AH's belief that art has taken the place of religion in society; we must imitate good rather than popular art.

THEMES AND VARIATIONS. London: Chatto and Windus; New York: Harper, 1950.

The first half of this is a long essay on the eighteenth-century French philosopher Maine de Biran who, AH tells us, ultimately failed to acquire the perennial philosophy. The second part consists of essays on art and literature. One of the more interesting, "Variations on a Baroque Tomb," is about the ability of art to ruin human smugness by presenting the "un-rationalizable facts" of sex and death.

VULGARITY IN LITERATURE: DIGRESSIONS FROM A THEME. London: Chatto and Windus, 1930.

> An examination of vulgarity in form (Poe is an example) and in emotion (Dickens is an example).

WORKS EDITED BY OTHERS

ALDOUS HUXLEY: ON ART AND ARTISTS. Ed. Morris Philipson. New York: Harper, 1960.

> A copious collection of essays on various arts and artists. All were previously collected.

GREAT SHORT WORKS OF ALDOUS HUXLEY. Ed. Bernard Bergonzi. New York: Harper, 1969.

> Collects "Centenaries" (ON THE MARGIN), "Beauty in 1920" (ON THE MARGIN), "The Palio at Siena" (ALONG THE ROAD), "The Best Picture" (ALONG THE ROAD), "Books for the Journey" (ALONG THE ROAD), "Wordsworth in the Tropics" (DO WHAT YOU WILL), and "Variations on a Philosopher" (THEMES AND VARIATIONS).

THE WORLD OF ALDOUS HUXLEY: AN OMNIBUS OF HIS FICTION AND NON-FICTION OVER THREE DECADES. Ed. Charles J. Rolo. New York: Harper, 1947.

> Collects "Jaipur" and "Cawnpore" (JESTING PILATE), "Fashions in Love" (DO WHAT YOU WILL), "Meditation on El Greco," "Sermons in Cats," extracts from "Vulgarity in Literature" (all three from MUSIC AT NIGHT), "Decentralization and Self-Government" (ENDS AND MEANS), "Politics and Religion" (GREY EMINENCE), and "What Can the Scientist Do?" (SCIENCE, LIBERTY AND PEACE).

BIBLIOGRAPHY

Clareson, Thomas D., and Carolyn S. Andrews, comps. "Aldous Huxley: A Bibliography, 1960-1964." EXTRAPOLATION, 6 (1964), 2-21.

> An updating of Eschelbach and Shober (p. 244).

Davis, Dennis D., comp. "Aldous Huxley: A Bibliography, 1965-1973." BB, 31 (1974), 67-70.

> A listing of secondary articles and books (alphabetically arranged by author) and of posthumous primary selections.

Aldous Huxley

Duval, Hanson R., ed. ALDOUS HUXLEY: A BIBLIOGRAPHY. New York: Arrow, 1939.

> The best descriptive bibliography of AH's work published before October 1939, with sections on books, prefaces, articles, reprints, and miscellanea.

Eschelbach, Claire J., and Joyce Lee Shober, comps. ALDOUS HUXLEY: A BIBLIOGRAPHY, 1916-1959. Berkeley and Los Angeles: Univ. of California Press, 1961.

> The necessary supplement to Duval's bibliography. Although the primary section is not nearly as descriptive as Duval's, this bibliography does contain a secondary section, including "Criticism of Individual Works."

Eschelbach, Claire J., and Joyce S[hober] Marthaler, comps. "Aldous Huxley: A Bibliography, 1914-1964 (A Supplementary Listing)." BB, 28 (1971), 114-17.

> Updates Eschelbach and Shober (above).

BIOGRAPHY

Bedford, Sybille. ALDOUS HUXLEY: A BIOGRAPHY. 2 vols. London: Chatto and Windus, 1973-74.

> The best biography, with information on the writing history of the nonfiction and some useful summaries of it.

Clark, Ronald W. THE HUXLEYS. London: Heinemann, 1968.

> A biography of the family which briefly discusses the nonfiction in tracing the development of AH's ideas.

CRITICISM

Atkins, John. ALDOUS HUXLEY: A LITERARY STUDY. [1956]. Rev. ed. New York: Orion, 1967.

> A study of AH's ideas that refers in passing to many of the nonfiction volumes. There is no index.

Bentley, Joseph. "Huxley's Ambivalent Responses to the Ideas of D. H. Lawrence." TCL, 13 (1967), 139-53.

> Cites AH's essays on Swift (DO WHAT YOU WILL) and Lawrence (OLIVE TREE) in arguing that Lawrence finally failed to cure AH of his manichaenism.

Birnbaum, Milton. "Aldous Huxley: An Aristocrat's Comments on Popular Culture." JPC, 2 (1968), 106-12.

> Cites passages in several prose volumes in outlining AH's disgust with movies, jazz, and the like.

──────. "Aldous Huxley's Animadversions Upon Sexual Love." TSLL, 8 (1966), 285-96.

> Notes passages in DO WHAT YOU WILL, OLIVE TREE, TEXTS AND PRETEXTS, ENDS AND MEANS, and DEVILS OF LOUDON in describing AH's distaste for sex.

──────. "Aldous Huxley's Conception of the Nature of Reality." PERSONALIST, 47 (1966), 297-314.

> The conception evolves from a conventional one to that of Buddhistic mysticism to one merging mysticism and science.

──────. ALDOUS HUXLEY'S QUEST FOR VALUES. Knoxville: Univ. of Tennessee Press, 1971.

> This cites the nonfiction throughout in laying out AH's ideas. It includes Birnbaum's many articles on AH "revised slightly."

──────. "Aldous Huxley's Quest for Values: A Study in Religious Syncretism." CLS, 3 (1966), 169-82.

> A useful summary of AH's religious views--his dislike of Judaism and Christianity, his gradual embracing of mysticism--which cites the nonfictional prose throughout.

──────. "Aldous Huxley's Views on Education." XAVIER UNIVERSITY STUDIES, 6 (1967), 81-91.

> A summary that quotes from several nonfiction works.

Brander, Laurence. ALDOUS HUXLEY: A CRITICAL STUDY. Lewisburg, Pa.: Bucknell Univ. Press, 1970.

> A quite thorough treatment (pp. 117-237) of the nonfiction, which, however, does little else than summarize the contents.

Cary, Richard. "Aldous Huxley, Vernon Lee and the Genius Loci." CLQ, Series 5 (1960), 128-40.

> A comparison of the travel books of the two authors. AH is the more jaundiced traveller.

Conner, Frederick W. "'Attention'!: Aldous Huxley's Epistemological Route to Salvation." SR, 81 (1973), 282-308.

A good review of those prose works, from DO WHAT YOU WILL to DOORS OF PERCEPTION, that mark AH's acceptance of intuitive knowledge as opposed to cognition.

Estrich, Helen Watts. "Jesting Pilate Tells the Answer." SR, 47 (1939), 63-81.

> Quotes heavily from ENDS AND MEANS in laying out AH's "new" philosophy of mysticism.

Gunn, Drewey W. AMERICAN AND BRITISH WRITERS IN MEXICO, 1556-1973. Austin: Univ. of Texas Press, 1974. Pp. 160-63.

> A brief review of BEYOND THE MEXIQUE BAY, emphasizing AH's speculations on "the nature of art and the nature of the primitive."

Häusermann, Hans Walter. "Aldous Huxley as Literary Critic." PMLA, 48 (1933), 908-18.

> A useful review of AH's critical likes and dislikes; the latter include Gide, Proust, Conrad, and Mansfield. Drawing on PROPER STUDIES, ON THE MARGIN, VULGARITY IN LITERATURE and uncollected essays, Häusermann concludes that to AH "the essential function of literature is . . . to give a picture of life in its totality, excluding neither its spiritual nor its material aspects."

Henderson, Alexander. ALDOUS HUXLEY. London: Chatto and Windus, 1935.

> The first critical book on AH. It contains brief chapters on "Man Alone" (treating DO WHAT YOU WILL), "Man in Society" (PROPER STUDIES), "Travel Books" (JESTING PILATE, BEYOND THE MEXIQUE BAY), and "Criticism" (MUSIC AT MIGHT and others). An intelligent study.

Holmes, Charles M. ALDOUS HUXLEY AND THE WAY TO REALITY. Bloomington: Indiana Univ. Press, 1970.

> Refers to most of the nonfiction volumes, especially DO WHAT YOU WILL, ENDS AND MEANS and PERENNIAL PHILOSOPHY, in tracing the evolution of AH's values. Very useful.

Joad, C.E.M. "Aldous Huxley and the Dowagers." In his RETURN TO PHILOSOPHY: BEING A DEFENCE OF REASON, AN AFFIRMATION OF VALUES, AND A PLEA FOR PHILOSOPHY. London: Faber, 1935. Pp. 78-94.

> A philosopher assaults AH's skepticism expressed in "Pascal" (DO WHAT YOU WILL).

King, Carlyle. "Aldous Huxley and Music." QQ, 70 (1963), 336-51.

> A review of AH's comments on music in the fiction and nonfiction such as MEXIQUE BAY and ADONIS AND THE ALPHABET.

Kirkwood, M.M. "The Thought of Aldous Huxley." UTQ, 6 (1937), 189-98.

> Cites several nonfiction volumes in noting that AH rejects skepticism for a more affirmative approach to life.

Kuehn, Robert E., ed. ALDOUS HUXLEY: A COLLECTION OF CRITICAL ESSAYS. Englewood Cliffs, N.J.: Prentice-Hall, 1974.

> Reprints Peter Quennell's "Electrifying the Audience: MUSIC AT NIGHT and BEYOND THE MEXIQUE BAY," Milton Birnbaum's "Aldous Huxley's Quest for Values: A Study in Religious Syncretism," and the chapter on GREY EMINENCE and the DEVILS OF LOUDON in Harold Watt's Twayne volume.

Lothian, John M. "Wordsworth North of Forty-Nine." ABERDEEN UNIVERSITY REVIEW, 33 (1950), 245-51.

> Argues that in "Wordsworth in the Tropics" (DO WHAT YOU WILL) AH shows that it is he (not Wordsworth) who wants nature easy and pretty.

McCormack, Arthur. "Mr. Huxley and Overpopulation." MONTH, 22 (1959), 84-91.

> A Catholic argues that AH's fear of overpopulation expressed in BRAVE NEW WORD REVISITED is needless.

Marovitz, Sanford E. "Aldous Huxley and the Visual Arts." PLL, 9 (1973), 172-88.

> A thorough study of AH's changing attitudes toward painting as expressed in books such as ADONIS AND THE ALPHABET and THEMES AND VARIATIONS. He began by assuming art was "a kind of intellectual exercise," and ended recognizing its "religious and visionary implications."

Martin, Kingsley. "The Pacifist's Dilemma To-Day." POLITICAL QUARTERLY, 9 (1938), 155-72.

> An attack on what Martin views as the contradictions of AH's pacifism expressed in ENDS AND MEANS.

Meckier, Jerome. "A Neglected Huxley 'Preface': His Earliest Synopsis of BRAVE NEW WORLD." TCL, 25 (1979), 1-20.

>AH's preface to J.H. Burns's A VISION OF EDUCATION outlines the ideas on education and genetics found four years later in BRAVE NEW WORLD.

Quennell, Peter. "Electrifying the Audience." LONDON MAGAZINE, 2, No. 7 (1955), 62-64.

>MUSIC AT NIGHT and MEXIQUE BAY are composed in too flippant and clever a manner.

Schmerl, Rudolf B. "Aldous Huxley's Social Criticism." CHIR, 13, No. 1 (1959), 37-58.

>An excellent survey of AH's social thought as expressed in PROPER STUDIES, DO WHAT YOU WILL, ENDS AND MEANS, SCIENCE, LIBERTY AND PEACE, and BRAVE NEW WORLD REVISITED. In them, AH progresses from a distaste for democracy to a fear of totalitarianism.

Sharma, Arvind. "Mescaline and Hindu Mystical Experience." STUDIES IN RELIGION, 5 (1975), 171-76.

>Discusses AH's claim in DOORS OF PERCEPTION that a mescaline trip is like a Hindu mystical experience.

Thody, Philip. ALDOUS HUXLEY: A BIOGRAPHICAL INTRODUCTION. London: Studio Vista, 1973.

>Contains brief discussion of the nonfiction in light of the thesis that AH is obsessed with suffering and decay and the dichotomy between the ideal and the actual for biographical reasons.

Vitoux, Pierre. "Aldous Huxley and D.H. Lawrence: An Attempt at Intellectual Sympathy." MLR, 69 (1974), 501-22.

>Although the article focuses on POINT COUNTER POINT, which Vitoux finds more interesting than AH's essays, the influence of D.H. Lawrence on the idea of "life worship" in DO WHAT YOU WILL is discussed.

Watkin, E.I. "Aldous Huxley: A Philosophy of Moods." In MEN AND TENDENCIES. London: Sheed and Ward, 1937. Pp. 29-48.

>A learned, Christian attack on AH's skepticism expressed in "Pascal" (DO WHAT YOU WILL).

Watt, Donald, ed. ALDOUS HUXLEY: THE CRITICAL HERITAGE. London: Routledge and Kegan Paul, 1975.

>Contains contemporary reviews of JESTING PILATE, DO WHAT

YOU WILL, MUSIC AT NIGHT, ENDS AND MEANS, GREY
EMINENCE, PERENNIAL PHILOSOPHY, DEVILS OF LOUDON
THE GENIUS AND THE GODDESS, and COLLECTED ESSAYS.

Watts, Harold H. ALDOUS HUXLEY. TEAS. New York: Twayne, 1969.

> The only extended discussion of the nonfiction occurs in chapter 6, which deals with GREY EMINENCE and DEVILS OF LOUDON. Both books depict "the cost in misery and the sadness of neglected possibilities that come from faulty estimates of man's position."

Webster, H.T. "Aldous Huxley: Notes on a Moral Evolution." SAQ, 45 (1946), 372-83.

> This includes a brief attack on the impracticality of the ideas in ENDS AND MEANS.

Woodcock, George. DAWN AND THE DARKEST HOUR: A STUDY OF ALDOUS HUXLEY. London: Faber, 1972.

> An excellent survey of AH's works that emphasizes the later nonfiction, more significant than the late fiction, according to Woodcock. There are sizable discussions of the political writings of the late thirties, such as ENDS AND MEANS, of the biographies GREY EMINENCE and DEVILS OF LOUDON, and of the religious writings, such as PERENNIAL PHILOSOPHY.

Woods, Richard D. "SANGRE PATRICIA and THE DOORS OF PERCEPTION." ROMN, 12 (1971), 302-6.

> Notes the similarity of the drug experiences in the two books, without suggesting influence.

Yoder, Edwin M. "Aldous Huxley and His Mystics." VQR, 42 (1966), 290-94.

> Traces AH's interest in mysticism, in the unseen (evinced in works like PERENNIAL PHILOSOPHY), back to his poor sight.

Zaehner, Robert C. "Mescalin" and "Mescalin Interpreted." In MYSTICISM, SACRED AND PROFANE: AN INQUIRY INTO SOME VARIETIES OF PRAETERNATURAL EXPERIENCE. London: Oxford Univ. Press, 1957. Pp. 1-29.

> An antagonistic review of DOORS OF PERCEPTION finding AH's mescalin visions not the equivalent of religious mystical vision.

Zahner, Lilly. DEMON AND SAINT IN THE NOVELS OF ALDOUS HUXLEY. Swiss Studies in English. Bern, Switz.: Francke, 1975.

> Includes a lengthy rehash of GREY EMINENCE and DEVILS OF LOUDON (pp. 89-123) that is awkwardly written and rendered in microscopic print.

Zeitlin, Jacob Israel. [untitled address]. In ALDOUS HUXLEY 1894-1963: A MEMORIAL VOLUME. Ed. Julian Huxley. London: Chatto and Windus, 1965. Pp. 129-34.

    A casual review of AH's art criticism, which cites passages in ALONG THE ROAD and GREY EMINENCE.

D.H. LAWRENCE (1885-1930)

The "Phoenix Edition" (London: Heinemann, 1954--) contains most of the nonfiction volumes but is textually corrupt. Cambridge University Press is now issuing the standard edition, of which APOCALYPSE AND THE WRITINGS ON REVELATION (p. 253) is the first fruit.

NONFICTIONAL PROSE

APOCALYPSE. Florence: Orioli; New York: Viking, 1931. London: Secker, 1932.

> A digressive, anthropologically informed interpretation of "Revelations," the work first encountered by DHL in Chapel as a boy. He discusses its pagan origins and discerns "true cosmic worship" in its first part. In general, however, the book expresses the dark side of Christianity: the desire of the weak for revenge on the successful.

ASSORTED ARTICLES. London: Secker; New York: Knopf, 1930.

> Reprinted in PHOENIX II, below, this title contains essays on assorted topics which were written in DHL's final years. "Autobiographical Sketch" is among them.

ETRUSCAN PLACES. London: Secker; New York: Viking, 1932.

> DHL's final travel book, based on his 1927 visit to Etruscan sites. The sensitive vitality of the Etruscans is contrasted to the destructive power of ancient Rome and modem Italy under Mussolini.

FANTASIA OF THE UNCONSCIOUS. New York: Seltzer, 1922. London: Secker, 1923.

> The sequel to PSYCHOANALYSIS AND THE UNCONSCIOUS (p. 252) which, in the course of describing how children should

D.H. Lawrence

and should not be raised, presents the Laurentian "system" of bodily planes, nexi, and currents. Of special interest are DHL's extension of his views into cosmology and his argument that the mother is responsible for the Oedipal longings of the son. An epilogue addressed to Americans is appended to the Seltzer edition.

MORNINGS IN MEXICO. London: Secker; New York: Knopf, 1927.

DHL's third travel book, based on his experiences both in Mexico and the southwestern United States. Particularly noteworthy are three pieces on the import of Indian dances: "Indians and Entertainment," "The Dance of the Sprouting Corn," and "The Hopi Snake Dance."

MOVEMENTS IN EUROPEAN HISTORY. London: Oxford Univ. Press, 1921.

DHL's history textbook, published (at Oxford's insistence) under the pseudonym "Lawrence H. Davison." DHL emphasizes the inner dynamic of European history and perceives a central tension between the impulses to conquest and production. The need for a strong leader is also stressed.

PORNOGRAPHY AND OBSCENITY. Criterion Miscellany. London: Faber, 1929. New York: Knopf, 1930.

Written by the Home Secretary, volume 6 of the Miscellany series is entitled DO WE NEED A CENSOR? (he thinks we do). Volume 5 constitutes DHL's side of the debate-by-essay that Faber contrived. It argues that the modern failure to think of sex "cleanly" leads to true pornography and the sin of masturbation.

A PROPOS OF LADY CHATTERLEY'S LOVER: BEING AN ESSAY EXTENDED FROM "MY SKIRMISH WITH JOLLY ROGER." London: Mandrake, 1930.

Longer, revised version of "My Skirmish with Jolly Roger" that decries the cheapening of sex into mental sensationalism and includes an ad hominem attack on Bernard Shaw.

PSYCHOANALYSIS AND THE UNCONSCIOUS. New York: Seltzer, 1921. London: Secker, 1923.

A frontal assault on Freud's rationalistic approach to such matters as sexuality and the unconscious.

REFLECTIONS ON THE DEATH OF A PORCUPINE. Philadelphia: Centaur Press, 1925. London: Secker, 1934.

A volume of seven essays including "The Crown" and "The Novel."

D.H. Lawrence

SEA AND SARDINIA. New York: Seltzer, 1921. London: Secker, 1923.

> DHL's second travel volume, based on his brief visit to Sardinia in 1921 with his wife, Frieda, the "queen bee." The book records one of his many retreats to an earlier world, which proves, however, less than Edenic. DHL at his most engaging.

STUDIES IN CLASSIC AMERICAN LITERATURE. New York: Seltzer, 1923. London: Secker, 1924.

> Among the sharpest commentaries ever written on the American Romantics and often wickedly funny. That American literature records a hatred of the instinctual and the result of that hatred is the thesis of twelve essays: "The Spirit of Place," "Benjamin Franklin," "Hector St. John de Crevecoeur," "Fenimore Cooper's White Novels," "Fenimore Cooper's Leatherstocking Novels," "Edgar Allan Poe," "Nathanial Hawthorne and THE SCARLET LETTER," "Hawthorne's BLITHEDALE ROMANCE," "Dana's TWO YEARS BEFORE THE MAST," "Herman Melville's TYPEE and OMOO," "Herman Melville's MOBY DICK," and "Whitman." A foreword is included in the American edition only.

TWILIGHT IN ITALY. London: Duckworth; New York: Heubsch, 1916.

> DHL's first travel book, based on his Italian experiences of 1912-13. It consists of ten vivid prose sketches (seven under the general title "On the Lago di Garda") and represents one of DHL's first attacks on "northern" industrialism.

WORKS EDITED BY OTHERS

APOCALYPSE AND THE WRITINGS ON REVELATION. Ed. Mara Kalnins. Cambridge: The Univ. Press, 1980.

> The first production of THE CAMBRIDGE EDITION OF THE LETTERS AND WORKS OF D.H. LAWRENCE. It includes a fully annotated APOCALYPSE plus a review and an introduction DHL wrote on the subject.

ART AND PAINTING: D.H. LAWRENCE. London: Bureau of Current Affairs, 1951.

> Collects "Making Pictures," "Art and Morality," "Pictures on the Walls," and excerpts from "Introduction to These Paintings."

D.H. LAWRENCE: SELECTED ESSAYS. Ed. Richard Aldington. Harmondsworth: Penguin, 1950.

> Includes essays drawn from ASSORTED ARTICLES, PORCUPINE, TWILIGHT IN ITALY, MORNINGS IN MEXICO, STUDIES, PHOENIX, and pieces since collected in PHOENIX II.

D.H. Lawrence

D.H. LAWRENCE: SELECTED LITERARY CRITICISM. Ed. Anthony Beal. London: Heinemann, 1956.

> Section headings are "Autobiographical," "Puritanism and the Arts," "Verse," "Contemporaries and the Importance of the Novel," "Continentals," and "Americans."

D.H. LAWRENCE AND ITALY: TWILIGHT IN ITALY, SEA AND SARDINIA, ETRUSCAN PLACES. Ed. Anthony Burgess. New York: Viking, 1972.

D.H. LAWRENCE ON EDUCATION. Ed. Joy Williams and Raymond Williams. Harmondsworth: Penguin, 1973.

> Excellent compilation of DHL's writings on the subject. The book includes "Education of the People" and "Education and Sex in Man, Woman and Child."

THE LATER D.H. LAWRENCE. Ed. William York Tindall. New York: Knopf, 1952.

> Reprints selections from PORCUPINE, MORNINGS IN MEXICO, and ASSORTED ARTICLES.

LOVE AMONG THE HAYSTACKS AND OTHER PIECES. Ed. David Garnett. London: Nonesuch Press, 1930.

> Pieces written in 1912, later sent to Edward Garnett who was unable to place them in publications. The volume includes "A Chapel among the Mountains" and "A Hay Hut among the Mountains."

PHOENIX: THE POSTHUMOUS PAPERS OF D.H. LAWRENCE. Ed. Edward D. McDonald. New York: Viking, 1936.

> An invaluable compilation of prefaces, essays, and sketches under the headings "Nature and Poetical Pieces," "Peoples, Countries, Races," "Love, Sex, Men and Women," "Literature and Art," "Education," "Ethics, Psychology, Philosophy," and "Personalia and Fragments." Some of the most important works contained are "Nottingham and the Mining Countryside," "Study of Thomas Hardy," "Morality and the Novel," and "The Flying Fish."

PHOENIX II: UNCOLLECTED, UNPUBLISHED, AND OTHER PROSE WORKS BY D.H. LAWRENCE. Ed. Warren Roberts and Harry T. Moore. New York: Viking, 1968.

> The second Phoenix collection. It includes numerous essays and reprints A PROPOS OF LADY CHATTERLEY'S LOVER, PORCUPINE, and ASSORTED ARTICLES. Of special interest is the first section,

"Stories and Sketches," which includes very early pieces on DHL's experiences during his years as a school teacher in the London suburb of Croydon and "Prologue to WOMEN IN LOVE."

THE PORTABLE D.H. LAWRENCE. Viking Portable Library. Ed. Diana Trilling. New York: Viking, 1947.

This contains very modest selections from the travel books and essays.

PSYCHOANALYSIS AND THE UNCONSCIOUS AND FANTASIA OF THE UNCONSCIOUS. Ed. Philip Rieff. New York: Viking, 1960.

SEX, LITERATURE AND CENSORSHIP: ESSAYS BY D.H. LAWRENCE. Ed. Harry T. Moore. London: Heinemann, 1955.

Collects eleven titles including "The Novel," "Sex versus Loveliness," and A PROPOS OF LADY CHATTERLEY'S LOVER.

THE SYMBOLIC MEANING: THE UNCOLLECTED VERSIONS OF STUDIES IN CLASSIC AMERICAN LITERATURE. Ed. Armin Arnold. Fontwell, Arundel, Engl.: Centaur, 1962.

A valuable collection of the early versions of the American literature essays, which differ markedly from those published in book form in 1923; the earlier are more objective, less hysterical.

BIBLIOGRAPHY

Arnold, Armin. "D.H. Lawrence's First Critical Essays: Two Anonymous Reviews Identified." PMLA, 79 (1964), 185-88.

They are on German poetry and are published in the ENGLISH REVIEW of January 1912; Arnold reprints both.

Beards, Richard D., comp. "D.H. Lawrence: Ten Years of Criticism, 1959-68, A Checklist." DHLR, 1 (1968), 245-85. Continued in subsequent volumes.

The best listing of criticism. Appearing yearly, it contains a general section and sections on each of the primary works.

Beebe, Maurice, and Anthony Tommasi, comps. "Criticism of D.H. Lawrence: A Selected Checklist with an Index to Studies of Separate Works." MFS, 5 (1959), 83-98.

McDonald, Edward D., ed. A BIBLIOGRAPHY OF THE WRITINGS OF D.H. LAWRENCE. Philadelphia: Centaur Book Shop, 1925.

D.H. Lawrence

    The first important attempt at an annotated primary bibliography of DHL. DHL himself assisted McDonald in compiling it.

─────. THE WRITINGS OF D.H. LAWRENCE 1925-30: A BIBLIOGRAPHICAL SUPPLEMENT. Philadelphia: Centaur Book Shop, 1931.

Roberts, Warren, ed. A BIBLIOGRAPHY OF D.H. LAWRENCE. Soho Bibliographies. London: Rupert Hart-Davis, 1963.

    The major primary bibliography of DHL. This excellent work contains sections entitled "Books and Pamphlets," "Contributions to Books," "Contributions to Periodicals," "Translations" (of DHL's writings by others), "Manuscripts," and "Books and Pamphlets about D.H. Lawrence" (a five-page listing).

White, William, comp. D.H. LAWRENCE, A CHECKLIST: WRITINGS ABOUT D.H. LAWRENCE, 1931-1950. Detroit: Wayne State Univ. Press, 1950.

    Organized chronologically.

BIOGRAPHY

Several memoirs focus on DHL's experiences in Mexico and the American southwest; those are tangentially relevant, therefore, to MORNINGS IN MEXICO. See Dorothy Brett, LAWRENCE AND BRETT: A FRIENDSHIP, Philadelphia: Lippincott, 1933; Witter Bynner, JOURNEY WITH GENIUS: RECOLLECTIONS AND REFLECTIONS CONCERNING THE D.H. LAWRENCES, New York: John Day, 1951; Eliot Fay, LORENZO IN SEARCH OF THE SUN: D.H. LAWRENCE IN ITALY, MEXICO, AND THE AMERICAN SOUTHWEST, New York: Bookman Associates, 1953; Joseph Foster, D.H. LAWRENCE IN TAOS, Albuquerque: Univ. of New Mexico Press, 1972; Mabel Dodge Luhan, LORENZO IN TAOS, New York: Knopf, 1932.

Delany, Paul. D.H. LAWRENCE'S NIGHTMARE: THE WRITER AND HIS CIRCLE IN THE YEARS OF THE GREAT WAR. New York: Basic Books, 1978.

    A critical biography that discusses the nonfiction of 1914-18 in the course of showing how DHL wrote WOMEN IN LOVE and broke permanently with England.

Hamalian, Leo. D.H. LAWRENCE IN ITALY. New York: Taplinger, 1981.

    A biography of DHL's Italian experience that draws on nonfiction.

Moore, Harry T. POSTE RESTANTE: A LAWRENCE TRAVEL CALENDAR. Berkeley and Los Angeles: Univ. of California Press, 1956.

    A calendar of DHL's journeys throughout his life, which provides information useful for the study of the travel books.

D.H. Lawrence

———. THE PRIEST OF LOVE: A LIFE OF D.H. LAWRENCE. New York: Farrar, 1974.

> The finest biography of DHL, well-informed and unbiased. An expansion of Moore's THE INTELLIGENT HEART, it provides factual information on the writing of the nonfiction and some interpretation of it.

CRITICISM

Allendorf, Otmar. "The Origin of Lawrence's 'Study of Thomas Hardy.'" N&Q, 17 (1970), 466-67.

> DHL may have been commissioned to write the piece for Nisbet and Co.'s "Writers of the Day" Series.

Arnold, Armin. D.H. LAWRENCE AND AMERICA. London: Linden Press, 1958.

> A thorough treatment of DHL's biographical and literary relations with America. Arnold briefly explicates each of the American literature essays, comparing early and final versions.

———. "Introduction." In his THE SYMBOLIC MEANING: THE UNCOLLECTED VERSIONS OF STUDIES IN CLASSIC AMERICAN LITERATURE. Fontwell, Arundel, Engl.: Centaur, 1962. Pp. 1-11.

> A useful review of the publishing history of these essays.

Bantock, Geoffrey H. "D.H. Lawrence and the Nature of Freedom." In his FREEDOM AND AUTHORITY IN EDUCATION: A CRITICISM OF MODERN CULTURAL AND EDUCATIONAL ASSUMPTIONS. London: Faber, 1952. Pp. 133-81.

> A conservative educator praises DHL's writings on education, from which he quotes without adequate citation.

Beards, Richard D. "D.H. Lawrence and the 'Study of Thomas Hardy,' His Victorian Predecessor." DHLR, 2 (1969), 210-29.

> Employs the "Study" (PHOENIX) to suggest Hardy's influence on DHL in three respects: the relationship of characters to their natural environment, the importance of sexuality, and the tendency to depict the isolated hero.

Beker, Miroslav. "'The Crown,' 'The Reality of Peace,' and WOMEN IN LOVE." DHLR, 2 (1969), 254-64.

> Passages on corruption in "The Crown" (PORCUPINE) and "The Reality of Peace" (PHOENIX) applied to the novel.

Boulton, James T. "Introduction to the New Edition." In his MOVEMENTS IN EUROPEAN HISTORY. London: Oxford Univ. Press, 1971.

D.H. Lawrence

A useful review of the writing and publishing history of MOVEMENTS.

Burns, Aidan. NATURE AND CULTURE IN D.H. LAWRENCE. London: Macmillan, 1980.

Chapter 2 presents STUDIES as the key nonfictional expression of DHL's ideas about the self.

Cavitch, David. D.H. LAWRENCE AND THE NEW WORLD. New York: Oxford Univ. Press, 1969.

An important book which demonstrates how DHL's quest for the good place is informed by his psychological difficulties. Includes brief discussions of the travel books and a chapter on STUDIES (ch. 4).

Clark, L.D. "The Apocalypse of Lorenzo." DHLR, 3 (1970), 141-60.

According to Clark, DHL tended toward Apocalyptic expression during the war and at the end of his life; his writings (e.g., APOCALYPSE) are rather literally reviewed.

_____. "D.H. Lawrence and the American Indian." DHLR, 9 (1976), 305-72.

Contains numerous references to the MORNINGS IN MEXICO essays and analyzes at some length the "Cooper" section of STUDIES.

_____. THE MINOAN DISTANCE: THE SYMBOLISM OF TRAVEL IN D.H. LAWRENCE. Tucson: Univ. of Arizona Press, 1980.

A major study of the travel motif in DHL's fiction, poetry, and nonfiction showing how travel constitutes a spiritual quest for identity. Clark examines TWILIGHT IN ITALY in chapter 6, SEA AND SARDINIA in chapter 9, MORNINGS IN MEXICO in chapter 12, ETRUSCAN PLACES in chapter 14, and STUDIES in chapters 8 and 11.

Corke, Helen. D.H. LAWRENCE: THE CROYDON YEARS. Austin: Univ. of Texas Press, 1965.

A collection of essays by a teaching colleague of DHL at Croydon. The book is most notable for a memoir of Jessie Chambers but also contains a long, casual essay protesting DHL's extreme views in APOCALYPSE.

Cornwell, Ethel F. "The Sex Mysticism of D.H. Lawrence." In THE STILL POINT: THEME AND VARIATIONS IN THE WRITINGS OF T.S. ELIOT, COLERIDGE, YEATS, HENRY JAMES, VIRGINIA WOOLF AND D.H. LAWRENCE. New Brunswick, N.J.: Rutgers Univ. Press, 1962. Pp. 208-41.

Covers most of the important theoretical writings in discussing
DHL's desire to reach beyond his antinomies toward "fullness
of being." A good basic survey.

Cowan, James C. D.H. LAWRENCE'S AMERICAN JOURNEY: A STUDY IN
LITERATURE AND MYTH. Cleveland, Ohio: The Press of Case Western Reserve Univ., 1970.

> DHL's American journey is a "quest for the symbols and myths"
> with which to revivify western civilization. The first three
> chapters feature brief treatments of major nonfictional prose
> works, including MOVEMENTS IN EUROPEAN HISTORY.

──────. "Lawrence's Romantic Values: STUDIES IN CLASSIC AMERICAN LITERATURE." BSUF, 8, No. 1 (1967), 30-35.

> DHL rejects American idealism in favor of "dynamic organicism."
> An elementary study.

Dahlberg, Edward, and Herbert Read. "On D.H. Lawrence." In their TRUTH
IS MORE SACRED: A CRITICAL EXCHANGE ON MODERN LITERATURE. New
York: Horizon Press, 1961. Pp. 69-117.

> Contains a brief review of the antiarcadian theme in STUDIES.

Dawson, E.W. "Lawrence's Pollyanalytic Esthetic for the Novel." PAUNCH,
No. 26 (1966), 60-68.

> A handy paraphrase of DHL's writings about the novel, which
> should be vital rather than idea-ridden.

Deakin, William. "D.H. Lawrence's Attacks on Proust and Joyce." EIC, 7
(1957), 383-403.

> Defends Proust and Joyce against the charge of triviality voiced
> in "Surgery for the Novel" (PHOENIX).

Draper, R.P., ed. D.H. LAWRENCE: THE CRITICAL HERITAGE. London:
Routledge and Kegan Paul, 1970.

> Contains contemporary reviews of SEA AND SARDINIA,
> FANTASIA, STUDIES, PORCUPINE, and PORNOGRAPHY AND
> OBSCENITY.

Eliot, T.S. AFTER STRANGE GODS: A PRIMER OF MODERN HERESY.
London: Faber, 1934.

> Commends FANTASIA as "a criticism of the modern world" in
> an otherwise antagonistic treatment of DHL.

D.H. Lawrence

Ellis, David. "Reading Lawrence: The Case of SEA AND SARDINIA." DHLR, 10 (1977), 52-63.

> A study of the artful use of narrative technique and narrative persona in the book.

Elsbree, Langdon. "D.H. Lawrence, Homo Ludens, and the Dance." DHLR, 1 (1968), 1-30.

> While discussing DHL's novelistic use of dancing in terms of Huizinga's theories of play, Elsbree briefly notes DHL's "Making Love to Music" (PHOENIX). Etruscan dancing preserves "integrity of self"; modern dancing reflects diseased attitudes toward sex.

Fahey, William A. "Lawrence's San Gaudenzio Revisited." DHLR, 1 (1968), 51-59.

> Argues the four "San Gaudenzio" chapters in TWILIGHT IN ITALY feature characters who represent various stages of primitivism and modernism. DHL does not find any of these stages fully satisfactory.

Foster, Richard. "Criticism as Rage: D.H. Lawrence." In A D.H. LAWRENCE MISCELLANY. Ed. Harry T. Moore. Carbondale: Southern Illinois Univ. Press, 1959. Pp. 312-25.

> Surveys the major recipients of DHL's critical ire. "This is, of course, only the barest sort of summary," Foster notes.

Freeman, Mary. D.H. LAWRENCE: A BASIC STUDY OF HIS IDEAS. Gainesville: Univ. of Florida Press, 1959.

> A survey of DHL's social thought based primarily on the fiction. Useful interchapters called "Cross Sections," however, involve the nonfictional prose, and treat such topics as DHL's relation to futurism and fascism.

Gersh, Gabriel. "In Search of D.H. Lawrence's SEA AND SARDINIA." QQ, 80 (1973), 581-88.

> Retraces DHL's footsteps in Sardinia.

Getti, Hilary. "D.H. Lawrence and the Idea of Education." EM, 21 (1970), 207-31.

> A summary of "The Education of the People" (PHOENIX).

Glicksberg, Charles I. "D.H. Lawrence and Science." SCIENTIFIC MONTHLY, 78 (1951), 99-104.

> Briefly cites APOCALYPSE and the psychological volumes in a general, and antagonistic, survey.

Goodheart, Eugene. "Lawrence and Christ." In his THE CULT OF THE EGO: THE SELF IN MODERN LITERATURE. Chicago: Univ. of Chicago Press, 1968. Pp. 161-82.

    Briefly cites APOCALYPSE, "Study of Thomas Hardy" and DHL's introduction to THE BROTHERS KARAMAZOV (PHOENIX) in making the obvious point that DHL is not Christian.

_____. THE UTOPIAN VISION OF D.H. LAWRENCE. Chicago: Univ. of Chicago Press, 1963.

    Notes the utopian aspect of DHL's ideas and contains a brief review (pp. 103-15) of the two psychological treatises.

Gordon, D[avid] J. D.H. LAWRENCE AS A LITERARY CRITIC. Yale Studies in English. New Haven, Conn.: Yale Univ. Press, 1966.

    A 172-page analysis of DHL's aesthetic and critical ideas and of the ideas expressed in the criticism. As a critic, DHL was "emotionally very alive, intellectually capable and skillful in essential logic, and morally very honest." The chapters are organized by subject (e.g., "The Quarrel with Tragedy") rather than by work.

Green, Martin. "Studies in Classic American Literature." In his RE-APPRAISALS: SOME COMMONSENSE READINGS IN AMERICAN LITERATURE. New York: Norton, 1965. Pp. 231-47.

    STUDIES is too eccentric and unbalanced.

Gurling, Freda E. "D.H. Lawrence's Apology for the Artist." LONDON MERCURY, 33 (1936) 596-603.

    In his critical pronouncements DHL downplays the quality of high artistry which is, however, evident in his own works.

Gutierrez, Donald. "D.H. Lawrence's Golden Age." DHLR, 9 (1976), 377-408.

    A survey of the ideas in ETRUSCAN PLACES that ranges into DHL's world-view and the theories of professional Etruscologists.

_____. "A New Heaven and an Old Earth: D.H. Lawrence's APOCALYPSE, Apocalyptic, and the BOOK OF REVELATION." REVIEW OF EXISTENTIAL PSYCHOLOGY AND PSYCHIATRY, 15 (1977), 61-85.

    A learned study of the reasons--such as his vitalism and his dislike of the linear conception of time--that DHL assaults the BOOK OF REVELATION.

Harper, Howard M., Jr. "FANTASIA and the Psychodynamics of WOMEN IN LOVE." In his THE CLASSIC BRITISH NOVEL. Athens: Univ. of Georgia Press, 1972. Pp. 202-19.

>The ideas of "polarity" and the four bodily centers in FANTASIA serve as a gloss to the relationships in the novel.

Harrison, John R. "D.H. Lawrence." In his THE REACTIONARIES: A STUDY OF THE ANTI-DEMOCRATIC INTELLIGENTSIA. New York: Schocken Books, 1966. Pp. 163-89.

>Briefly cites several of the nonfictional works in discussing DHL's social ideas.

Hassall, Christopher. "D.H. Lawrence and the Etruscans." EDH, 31 (1962), 61-78.

>A rambling discourse which asserts that the naturalness DHL perceived in the Etruscans (and recorded in ETRUSCAN PLACES) influenced his late poetic style.

Hinz, Evelyn J. "The Beginning and the End: D.H. Lawrence's PSYCHO-ANALYSIS and FANTASIA." DR, 52 (1972), 251-65.

>In PSYCHOANALYSIS, DHL attempts to refute Freud with scientific discourse; FANTASIA, in contrast, manifests "an archetypal perspective and an artistic structure."

―――. "History as Education and Art: D.H. Lawrence's MOVEMENTS IN EUROPEAN HISTORY." MBL, 2 (1977), 139-52.

>In writing MOVEMENTS, DHL was initially motivated to discover the origins of WWI in political failures of the past; ultimately, however, he emphasizes the archetypal quality of history, seeing events as "manifestations of a life force."

Hochman, Baruch. ANOTHER EGO: THE CHANGING VIEW OF SELF AND SOCIETY IN THE WORK OF D.H. LAWRENCE. Columbia: Univ. of South Carolina Press, 1970.

>The most thorough analysis of DHL's ideas about the self and society. In arguing that "Lawrence moves from a radical individualism to . . . a radical (if qualified) communalism," Hochman refers throughout to the nonfictional prose works, particularly to "The Crown" (PORCUPINE), "Study of Thomas Hardy" (PHOENIX), and FANTASIA.

Hoffman, Frederick J. "From Surrealism to the Apocalypse: A Development in Twentieth Century Irrationalism." ELH, 5 (1948), 147-65.

>Discusses the psychological treatises and APOCALYPSE in pre-

senting DHL as a link between the surrealists and the WWII "Poets of the Apocalypse" (e.g., G. S. Fraser). Excellent.

――――. "Lawrence's Quarrel with Freud." In his FREUDIANISM AND THE LITERARY MIND. Baton Rouge: Louisiana State Univ. Press, 1945. Pp. 151-76.

    Cites PSYCHOANALYSIS and FANTASIA in an excellent survey of DHL's disagreements with and misunderstandings of Freud on such matters as incest and the unconscious.

Hough, Graham. THE DARK SUN: A STUDY OF D. H. LAWRENCE. New York: Macmillan, 1957.

    Perhaps the finest survey of DHL's work. Hough emphasizes the novels but includes chapters on tales and poems as well. A final chapter on DHL's philosophy, which draws upon the non-fictional prose, is excellent.

Irwin, W. R. "The Survival of Pan." PMLA, 76 (1961), 159-67.

    Briefly paraphrases "Pan in America" (PHOENIX).

Janik, Del Ivan. "The Two Infinites: D. H. Lawrence's TWILIGHT IN ITALY." DHLR, 7 (1974), 179-98.

    Argues that the book's style, vacillating between vivid description and exposition, reflects the thematic antinomies of South and North, past and future, body and mind.

Jarrett-Kerr, Martin. "D. H. Lawrence and 'The Spirit of Place.'" In DER ENGLISCHE ESSAY: ANALYSEN. Ed. Horst Weber. Darmstadt, Ger.: Wissenschaftliche Buchgesellschaft, 1975. Pp. 308-19.

    Divides DHL's essays into three kinds: critical, philosophical, and descriptive.

Kalnins, Mara. "Introduction." In her APOCALYPSE AND THE WRITINGS ON REVELATION. Cambridge: The Univ. Press, 1980. Pp. 3-38.

    A very full survey of the sources of DHL's last book, of its writing and publication history, and of its reception.

Keith, W. J. "Spirit of Place and Genius Loci: D. H. Lawrence and Rolf Gardiner." DHLR, 7 (1974), 127-38.

    Contains a brief reference to A PROPOS OF LADY CHATTERLEY'S LOVER as evincing Gardiner's influence.

Kermode, Frank. "Lawrence and the Apocalyptic Types." CRITQ, 10 (1968), 14-38.

    Contains a brief discussion of APOCALYPSE.

_____. "Spenser and the Allegorists." PBA, 48 (1962), 261-79.

>Contains an interesting section on the occult sources that inform APOCALYPSE.

Kessler, Jascha. "D.H. Lawrence's Primitivism." TSLL, 5 (1964), 467-88.

>A lengthy and learned assault on the doctrines espoused in FANTASIA. While attacking the mechanistic approach to life DHL embodies it.

Kinkead-Weekes, Mark. "Lawrence on Hardy." In THOMAS HARDY AFTER FIFTY YEARS. Ed. Lance St. John Butler. Totowa, N.J.: Rowman and Littlefield, 1977. Pp. 90-103.

>In explicating "Study of Thomas Hardy" (PHOENIX), Kinkead-Weekes notes that DHL's periodic digressions from and returns to Hardy dramatize DHL's deepening comprehension of his subject.

_____. "The Marble and the Statue: The Exploratory Imagination of D.H. Lawrence." In IMAGINED WORLDS: ESSAYS ON SOME ENGLISH NOVELS AND NOVELISTS IN HONOUR OF JOHN BUTT. Ed. Maynard Mack and Ian Gregor. London: Methuen, 1969. Pp. 371-418.

>An excellent study of the impact of the "Study of Thomas Hardy" (PHOENIX) and "The Crown" (PORCUPINE) on DHL's writing of THE RAINBOW and WOMEN IN LOVE. "As the 'Study' was the growing point between THE WEDDING RING and THE RAINBOW, so 'The Crown' links THE RAINBOW with WOMEN IN LOVE."

Klingopulos, G.D. "Lawrence's Criticism." EIC, 7 (1957), 294-303.

>A well-written survey of the material collected in D.H. LAWRENCE: SELECTED LITERARY CRITICISM, p. 254.

Lee, Brian. "America, My America." In RENAISSANCE AND MODERN ESSAYS: PRESENTED TO VIVIAN DE SOLA PINTO IN CELEBRATION OF HIS SEVENTIETH BIRTHDAY. Ed. G.R. Hibbard. London: Routledge and Kegan Paul, 1966. Pp. 181-88.

>Bucks the tide in asserting that the final versions of the American literature essays are finer than the earlier; that "the white heat of anger and excitement . . . is anyway preferable to the affected academicism of his first attempt."

Longville, Timothy. "The Longest Journey: D.H. Lawrence's PHOENIX." CRITQ, 4 (1962), 82-87.

>PHOENIX reveals DHL more convinced of physical and social destruction than of rebirth.

McDonald, Edward D. "Introduction." In his PHOENIX: THE POSTHUMOUS PAPERS OF D.H. LAWRENCE. New York: Viking, 1936. Pp. ix-xxvii.

    A useful account of the background of these various works.

Mann, Charles W. "D.H. Lawrence: Notes on Reading Hawthorne's THE SCARLET LETTER." NHJ, (1973), Pp. 9-25.

    Prints DHL's reading notes to THE SCARLET LETTER which were the basis for his "Nathaniel Hawthorne" in THE ENGLISH REVIEW.

Martin, Dexter. "D.H. Lawrence and Pueblo Religion: An Inquiry into Accuracy." ARQ, 9 (1953), 219-34.

    Cites MORNINGS IN MEXICO and other works in arguing that DHL is "more right than wrong."

Maud, Ralph N. "D.H. Lawrence: True Emotion as the Ethical Control in Art." WHR, 9 (1955), 233-40.

    A comparison of DHL and Irving Babbitt. DHL's nonfiction indicates that, like Babbitt, he rejects extreme Romantic emotionalism.

Merivale, Patricia. "D.H. Lawrence and the Modern Pan Myth." TSLL, 6 (1964), 297-305.

    Discusses "Pan in America" (PHOENIX). Pan embodies both the beauty and the terror of nature.

Miko, Stephen J. TOWARD WOMEN IN LOVE: THE EMERGENCE OF A LAWRENTIAN AESTHETIC. Yale Studies in English. New Haven, Conn.: Yale Univ. Press, 1972.

    Miko's chapter 5 consists of a close reading of "Study of Thomas Hardy" (PHOENIX) and "The Crown" (PORCUPINE). In them DHL envisions life as essentially dualistic.

Mitchell, Peter Todd. "Lawrence's SEA AND SARDINIA Revisited." TQ, 8, No. 1 (1965), 67-72.

    An informal piece retracing the Lawrences' journey through Sardinia; illustrated with paintings by Mitchell.

Morris, Tom. "On ETRUSCAN PLACES." PAUNCH, 40-41 (1975), 8-39.

    The first part of this is a lengthy rehash of DHL's impressions of Etruscan art; the second discusses the political distinctions in the book, contrasting the Etruscans to the power-hungry Romans, predecessors of the Fascists.

Nehls, Edward. "D.H. Lawrence: The Spirit of Place." In THE ACHIEVEMENT OF D.H. LAWRENCE. Ed. Frederick J. Hoffman and Harry T. Moore. Norman: Univ. of Oklahoma Press, 1953. Pp. 268-90.

    A superficial rehearsal of the three Italian travel books.

Nichols, Ann Eljenholm. "Syntax and Style: Ambiguities in Lawrence's TWILIGHT IN ITALY." CCC, 16 (1965), 261-66.

    A syntactical analysis of TWILIGHT IN ITALY; the syntax is "epic."

Palmer, Paul R. "D.H. Lawrence and the 'Q.B.' in Sardinia." CLC, 18, No. 1 (1968), 3-9.

    A brief, admiring paraphrase of SEA AND SARDINIA.

Panichas, George A. "E.M. Forster and D.H. Lawrence: Their Views on Education." In RENAISSANCE AND MODERN ESSAYS: PRESENTED TO VIVIAN DE SOLA PINTO IN CELEBRATION OF HIS SEVENTIETH BIRTHDAY. Ed. G.R. Hibbard. London: Routledge and Kegan Paul, 1966. Pp. 199-213.

    Briefly mentions A PROPOS OF LADY CHATTERLEY'S LOVER, "Education of the People" (PHOENIX), and FANTASIA. According to DHL, "There should be no effort made to teach children to think, to have ideas. Only to lift them and urge them into dynamic activity."

Paterson, John. "D.H. Lawrence: The One Bright Book of Life." In THE NOVEL AS FAITH: THE GOSPEL ACCORDING TO JAMES, HARDY, CONRAD, JOYCE, LAWRENCE AND VIRGINIA WOOLF. Boston: Gambit, 1973. Pp. 143-83.

    A useful summation of DHL's theories on the novel.

Pierle, Robert C. "D.H. Lawrence's STUDIES IN CLASSIC AMERICAN LITERATURE: An Evaluation." SOQ, 6 (1968), 333-40.

    A superficial review.

Pinion, F.B. A D.H. LAWRENCE COMPANION: LIFE, THOUGHT, AND WORKS. London: Macmillan, 1978.

    This contains sections affording handy, intelligent surveys of DHL's principal ideas, his travel writings, and his literary criticism.

Pinto, Vivian de Sola. "Lawrence and the Nonconformist Hymns." In A D.H. LAWRENCE MISCELLANY. Ed. Harry T. Moore. Carbondale: Southern Illinois Univ. Press, 1959. Pp. 103-13.

    Prints the draft of "Hymns in a Man's Life" (ASSORTED ARTICLES).

Richardson, John Adkins, and John I. Ades. "D.H. Lawrence on Cézanne: A Study in the Psychology of Critical Intuition." JAAC, 28 (1970), 441-53.

>Approaches Cézanne through DHL's pronouncement on him in the introduction to THE PAINTINGS OF D.H. LAWRENCE (PHOENIX). DHL appreciates Cézanne's "direct, instinctive grasp of the objective contents of reality."

Rieff, Philip. "Introduction." In his PSYCHOANALYSIS AND THE UNCONSCIOUS AND FANTASIA OF THE UNCONSCIOUS. New York: Viking, 1960. Pp. vii-xxiii.

>Intelligent and balanced overview of the relation of DHL's psychological theories to the cultural trends of his century.

――――. "The Therapeutic as Mythmaker: Lawrence's True Christian Philosophy." In his THE TRIUMPH OF THE THERAPEUTIC: USES OF FAITH AFTER FREUD. New York: Harper, 1966. Pp. 189-231.

>Refers to PSYCHOANALYSIS and FANTASIA throughout in contrasting Freud and DHL as "post-Christian" philosophers. DHL's emphasis on "the irrational power of love" is, however, essentially religious. Excellent.

Roberts, Mark. "D.H. Lawrence and the Failure of Energy." In his THE TRADITION OF ROMANTIC MORALITY. London: Macmillan, 1973. Pp. 322-48.

>Notes DHL calls for a balance of faculties in PSYCHOANALYSIS and FANTASIA, not the dominance of the unconscious.

Salgado, Gamini. "D.H. Lawrence as Literary Critic." LONDON MAGAZINE, 7, No. 2 (1960), 49-57.

>A brief overview. DHL's criticism exhibits a tension between objectivity and emotional reaction.

Saxena, H.S. "The Critical Writings of D.H. Lawrence." INDIAN JOURNAL OF ENGLISH STUDIES, 2 (1961), 130-37.

>Cites various prose passages in setting forth DHL's ideas on the novel. Slight.

Schneiderman, Leo. "Notes on D.H. Lawrence's STUDIES IN CLASSIC AMERICAN LITERATURE." CONNR, 1, No. 2 (1968), 57-71.

>Argues STUDIES reveals more about DHL himself than it does about American life and letters. Jeeringly antagonistic.

Schorer, Mark. "Lawrence and the Spirit of Place." In A D.H. LAWRENCE MISCELLANY. Ed. Harry T. Moore. Carbondale: Southern Illinois Univ. Press, 1959. Pp. 280-94.

>Mentions the travel books in passing.

Sitesh, Aruna. D.H. LAWRENCE: THE CRUSADER AS CRITIC. Delhi: Macmillan Co. of India, 1975.

> Not seen.

Small, Michel. "The Tale the Critic Tells: D.H. Lawrence on Nathaniel Hawthorne." PAUNCH, No. 40-41 (1975), 40-58.

> "But in the process of separating the tale from the teller, the tale becomes more and more Lawrence's and less and less Hawthorne's. . . ."

Spender, Stephen. "Pioneering the Instinctive Life." In his THE CREATIVE ELEMENT: A STUDY OF VISION, DESPAIR AND ORTHODOXY AMONG SOME MODERN WRITERS. London: Hamilton, 1953. Pp. 92-107.

> Cites FANTASIA in an elementary review of DHL's ideas.

Stavrou, Constantine N. "D.H. Lawrence's 'Psychology' of Sex." L&P, 6 (1956), 90-95.

> Contains a rudimentary explication of the four body centers posited by DHL in PSYCHOANALYSIS and FANTASIA.

Stewart, John L. "D.H. Lawrence: 'The Dance of the Sprouting Corn.'" In DER ENGLISCHE ESSAY: ANALYSEN. Ed. Horst Weber. Darmstadt, Ger.: Wissenschaftliche Buchgesellschaft, 1975. Pp. 304-07.

> A brief analysis of the imagery and organization of "The Dance of the Sprouting Corn" (MORNINGS IN MEXICO).

Swan, Michael. "D.H. Lawrence: Italy and Mexico." In his A SMALL PART OF TIME: ESSAYS ON LITERATURE, ART AND TRAVEL. London: Cape, 1957. Pp. 279-87.

> DHL's travel writings on Italy and Mexico are unbalanced and uninformed.

Swigg, Richard. LAWRENCE, HARDY, AND AMERICAN LITERATURE. New York: Oxford Univ. Press, 1972.

> Involves DHL's conception of tragedy as influenced by Hardy, Poe, Hawthorne, Melville, and Cooper. Swigg writes close and lengthy analyses of the impact of "Study of Thomas Hardy" (PHOENIX) on THE RAINBOW and of STUDIES on THE RAINBOW and WOMEN IN LOVE.

Tracy, Billy T. "D.H. Lawrence and the Travel Book Tradition." DHLR, 11 (1978), 272-93.

> A lengthy, highly informative treatment. Tracy compares DHL

to travel-writing contemporaries (especially Hudson), places him as an "ethnologist" travel writer (primarily concerned with the "daily life of a people"), and notes that DHL's desire to discover Eden is typical of the genre's practitioners.

――――. "'Reading Up the Ancient Etruscans': Lawrence's Debt to George Dennis." TCL, 23 (1977), 437-50.

> In composing ETRUSCAN PLACES, DHL borrowed from and reacted against Dennis' nineteenth-century travel book CITIES AND CEMETERIES OF ETRURIA.

Wagner, Jeanie. "D.H. Lawrence's Neglected 'Italian Studies.'" DHLR, 13 (1980), 260-74.

> Compares three essays published in the ENGLISH REVIEW in September 1913, with their revised versions in TWILIGHT IN ITALY.

Walsh, William. THE USE OF IMAGINATION: EDUCATIONAL THOUGHT AND THE LITERARY MIND. New York: Barnes and Noble, 1960.

> Walsh's chapter 9 summarizes "Education of the People" (PHOENIX).

Weiner, S. Ronald. "The Rhetoric of Travel: The Example of SEA AND SARDINIA." DHLR, 2 (1969), 230-44.

> An illuminating examination of the book's symbolism and style, which, Weiner argues, have homiletic designs upon the reader.

Wert, Paul. "D.H. Lawrence: Mystical Critic." SORA, 1 (1965), 210-28.

> Contains a close review of the original versions of the American literature essays as published by Armin Arnold in THE SYMBOLIC MEANING, above: "The first two versions are good-tempered, explain at greater length, are less subjective, quote more. . . ."

Whitaker, Thomas R. "Lawrence's Western Path: MORNINGS IN MEXICO." CRITICISM, 3 (1961), 219-36.

> The narrator of the essays is a deliberately constructed character on a pilgrim's progress toward "otherness."

White, Richard L. "D.H. Lawrence the Critic: Theories of English and American Fiction." DHLR, 11 (1978), 156-74.

> Argues that Richard Chase's thesis in THE AMERICAN NOVEL AND ITS TRADITION about the isolation of the American protagonist and the social integration of the British protagonist is also present in DHL's fiction criticism.

Wildi, Max. "The Birth of Expressionism in the Work of D.H. Lawrence." ES, 19 (1937), 241-59.

>Covers "Foreword to Sons and Lovers," "Study of Thomas Hardy" (PHOENIX), and "The Crown" (PORCUPINE) in asserting DHL shows an increasing tendency toward symbolic representation, "deforming in that process the conventional shape of things in the attempt to give them an essential one."

Williams, Raymond. "D.H. Lawrence." In his CULTURE AND SOCIETY, 1780-1950. New York: Columbia Univ. Press, 1958. Pp. 199-215.

>Employs DHL's essays "Democracy" (PHOENIX) and "Nottingham and the Mining Country" (PHOENIX) to present DHL as having "much in common with a socialist like Morris."

Worthen, John. D.H. LAWRENCE AND THE IDEA OF THE NOVEL. London: Macmillan, 1979.

>Cites nonfiction such as FANTASIA OF THE UNCONSCIOUS and PHOENIX in a highly informative study of the novels' writing histories and the evolution of DHL's generic views.

T.E. LAWRENCE (1888-1935)

NONFICTIONAL PROSE

TEL's technical reports for the RAF are not listed here.

CARCHEMISH: A REPORT ON THE EXCAVATIONS OF DJERABIS ON BEHALF OF THE BRITISH MUSEUM. London: British Museum, 1914.

> Coauthored by C. Leonard Woolley, this is the companion volume to WILDERNESS OF ZIN (see p. 272).

THE MINT: A DAY BOOK OF THE R.A.F. DEPOT BETWEEN AUGUST AND DECEMBER 1922 WITH LATER NOTES. London: Cape; New York: Doubleday, 1955.

> An account of the rigorous life of an enlisted man in the RAF. In 1922 TEL retreated into this life under the pseudonym "J.H. Ross." The book was published in a very limited edition in America in 1936.

REVOLT IN THE DESERT. London: Cape; New York: Doran, 1927.

> An abridgement of SEVEN PILLARS (below) which retains the military aspects and omits the reflective.

SEVEN PILLARS OF WISDOM: A TRIUMPH. London: Cape; Garden City, N.Y.: Doubleday, 1935.

> TEL's major work, which runs to over 600 pages. Beautifully written, it recounts his struggles with British stupidity and Arab in-fighting to forge the Arab campaign against the Turks in WWI that culminated in the capture of Damascus. The narrative also presents evocative portraits of the Arab land and culture and their psychological effect on the self-conflicted idealist, Lawrence of Arabia. The volume's publishing history is extremely complex: limited editions of it were issued in 1922 and 1926.

T.E. Lawrence

THE WILDERNESS OF ZIN. London: Cape; New York: Scribner's, 1936.

> A report written in conjunction with C. Leonard Woolley and privately printed in 1915 by the Palestine Exploration Fund. The work surveys desert life and ruins seen by TEL in early 1914; he was probably spying on the Turks at the time.

WORKS EDITED BY OTHERS

CRUSADER CASTLES. Ed. A.W. Lawrence. 2 vols. London: Golden Cockerel Press, 1936.

> The first volume is TEL's Oxford thesis demonstrating that Crusader castles were built on western patterns. The second volume is a collection of letters from TEL to his mother, written while on various tours of European fortifications.

THE ESSENTIAL T.E. LAWRENCE. Ed. David Garnett. London: Cape, 1951.

> Numerous letters and passages from TEL's works arranged chronologically.

EVOLUTION OF A REVOLT: EARLY POSTWAR WRITINGS OF T.E. LAWRENCE. Ed. Stanley Weintraub and Rodelle Weintraub. University Park: Pennsylvania State Univ. Press, 1968.

> Newspaper and journal articles dating between 1918 and 1921 on various Arab and military affairs. Some of these were extracted by TEL from the manuscript of SEVEN PILLARS.

MEN IN PRINT: ESSAYS IN LITERARY CRITICISM. Ed. A.W. Lawrence. London: Golden Cockerel Press, 1940.

> Brief reviews by TEL of James Fletcher, D.H. Lawrence, H.G. Wells, Henry Williamson, Doughty, and Walter Savage Landor.

ORIENTAL ASSEMBLY. Ed. A.W. Lawrence. London: Williams and Norgate, 1939.

> A collection of TEL's writings on Arabia. These include a diary of his 1911 walking tour and the suppressed first chapter of SEVEN PILLARS, which accuses the British of betraying the cause of Arab nationalism.

SECRET DISPATCHES FROM ARABIA. Ed. A.W. Lawrence. London: Golden Cockerel Press, 1939.

> TEL's contribution to the ARAB BULLETIN, a secret intelligence magazine he founded in 1916 for disseminating political and military news to British officials in the Middle East.

T.E. Lawrence

BIBLIOGRAPHY

Armstrong, Terence Ian Fytton, ed. ANNOTATIONS ON SOME MINOR WRITINGS OF "T.E. LAWRENCE." London: Partridge, 1935.

> Issued under the pseudonym "G," this is an early attempt at a primary bibliography; it does not treat SEVEN PILLARS or REVOLT IN THE DESERT.

Baxter, Frank C., ed. AN ANNOTATED CHECK-LIST OF A COLLECTION OF WRITINGS BY AND ABOUT T.E. LAWRENCE. Los Angeles: Univ. of Southern California, 1968.

> A rare hodge-podge that lists and heavily annotates materials in a private collection. These include extensive primary holdings, extensive works on the Arabia of TEL's time, and lots of miscellanea.

Clements, Frank, ed. T.E. LAWRENCE: A READER'S GUIDE. Hamden, Conn.: Archon Books, 1973.

> A primary and secondary bibliography with numerous annotations.

Duval, Elizabeth W., ed. T.E. LAWRENCE: A BIBLIOGRAPHY. New York: Arrow Editions, 1938.

> A good primary bibliography, with sections on TEL's books, introductions, periodical publications, letters, and miscellanea.

German-Reed, T., ed. BIBLIOGRAPHICAL NOTES ON T.E. LAWRENCE'S SEVEN PILLARS OF WISDOM AND REVOLT IN THE DESERT. London: Foyle, 1928.

> Sixteen pages on the complex matter.

Meyers, Jeffrey, comp. "T.E. Lawrence." BB, 29, No. 1 (1972), 25-36.

> Valuable for its extensive listing of secondary works on TEL, arranged alphabetically.

_____. T.E. LAWRENCE: A BIBLIOGRAPHY. New York: Garland, 1974.

> An unannotated primary and secondary listing of forty-eight pages.

_____. "T.E. Lawrence: A Supplement." BB, 35 (1978), 84-87.

> A supplement to Meyers' 1974 bibliography, this lists five primary items and numerous secondary items, arranged alphabetically by author's name and unannotated.

T.E. Lawrence

BIOGRAPHY

Aldington, Richard. LAWRENCE OF ARABIA: A BIOGRAPHICAL ENQUIRY. London: Collins, 1955.

> A bitter debunking of the TEL myth which presents SEVEN PILLARS as largely fictitious.

Graves, Robert. LAWRENCE AND THE ARABIAN ADVENTURE. Garden City, N.Y.: Doubleday, 1928.

> The first major biography. Graves calls SEVEN PILLARS a great book but finds its style overwrought.

Hyde, H. Montgomery. SOLITARY IN THE RANKS: LAWRENCE OF ARABIA AS AIRMAN AND PRIVATE SOLDIER. London: Constable, 1977.

> A history of TEL's enlisted service, about which he wrote in MINT.

Lawrence, A.W., ed. T.E. LAWRENCE BY HIS FRIENDS. London: Cape, 1937.

> Includes brief pieces by Edward Garnett on TEL as a keen literary critic and by Jonathan Cape on his publishing relationship with TEL. An interesting list of the books owned by TEL at his death is also included.

Mack, John E. A PRINCE OF OUR DISORDER: THE LIFE OF T.E. LAWRENCE. Boston: Little, Brown, 1976.

> The best biography. It has a psychological bent and refers to TEL's prose works only to elucidate the life.

Marriott, Paul J. OXFORD'S LEGENDARY SON: THE YOUNG LAWRENCE OF ARABIA, 1888-1910. Oxford, Engl.: Marriott, 1977.

> A brief work affording details of TEL's cycling tours that produced CRUSADER CASTLES.

Payne, Robert. LAWRENCE OF ARABIA: A TRIUMPH. Rev. ed. London: Hale, 1966.

> This biography includes an appreciative chapter on SEVEN PILLARS, centering on style.

Stewart, Desmond. T.E. LAWRENCE. New York: Harper, 1977.

> A debunking biography that argues that some of SEVEN PILLARS, such as the Deraa episode, is not factual but rather the "mythic" expression of TEL's psychological quirks.

Villars, Jean Beraud. T. E. LAWRENCE: THE SEARCH FOR THE ABSOLUTE. Trans. Peter Dawnay. London: Sidgwick and Jackson, 1958.

> This biography contains a section on SEVEN PILLARS which indicates TEL's inaccuracies in the volume.

Weintraub, Stanley. PRIVATE SHAW AND PUBLIC SHAW: A DUAL PORTRAIT OF LAWRENCE OF ARABIA AND G. B. S. New York: Braziller, 1963.

> A history of TEL's friendship with Shaw. Shaw acted as TEL's literary advisor in connection with SEVEN PILLARS and MINT.

CRITICISM

Blackmur, R. P. "The Everlasting Effort: A Citation of T. E. Lawrence." In his THE EXPENSE OF GREATNESS. Gloucester, Mass.: Smith, 1958. Pp. 1-36.

> A sophisticated study of TEL's personality, based in part on analysis of prose techniques in SEVEN PILLARS and MINT. TEL was one for whom "mastery is felt as self-nullity."

Forster, E. M. "T. E. Lawrence." In his ABINGER HARVEST. New York: Meridian, 1955. Pp. 134-40.

> A brief admiration of SEVEN PILLARS, emphasizing its reflective side.

Henighan, T. J. "T. E. Lawrence's SEVEN PILLARS OF WISDOM: Vision as Pattern." DR, 51 (1971), 49-59.

> An interesting reading of SEVEN PILLARS as a pastoral work featuring the city-country contrast.

Howe, Irving. "T. E. Lawrence: The Problem of Heroism." HUDR, 15 (1962), 333-64.

> Terms SEVEN PILLARS "the model for a genre that would become all too characteristic of the age: a personal narrative through which a terrible experience is relived, burned out, perhaps transcended."

Hull, Keith N. "Creeds, History, Prophets, and Geography in SEVEN PILLARS OF WISDOM." TQ, 18, No. 3 (1975), 15-28.

> Traces how the topics listed in the title (and discussed by TEL in the first seven chapters of SEVEN PILLARS) underlie the book's "thematic and dramatic organization." For instance, the breaking of TEL's will in the northern town of Deraa reflects the tendency of Arab faiths to collapse outside the desert, as discussed in chapter 3.

———. "Lawrence of THE MINT, Ross of the RAF." SAQ, 74 (1975), 340-48.

> Argues that while SEVEN PILLARS depicts the disintegration of TEL's personality, MINT depicts his attempt to achieve a "corporate identity" in the RAF. TEL's sexuality and self-consciousness made this difficult.

———. "T. E. Lawrence's Perilous Parodies." TQ, 15, No. 2 (1972), 56-61.

> A slight piece on the reasons for TEL's parodic stance in one episode of SEVEN PILLARS.

Macphail, Andrew. THREE PERSONS. London: Murray, 1929.

> One is TEL, and Macphail writes an early, shrewd appraisal of SEVEN PILLARS, noting its poetic quality and the ascetic side of TEL shown in it.

Malraux, Andre. "Lawrence and the Demon of the Absolute." HUDR, 8 (1956), 519-32.

> A reading of TEL's personality through SEVEN PILLARS; Malraux notes the absence of adequate characterization in the book and the failure to achieve a tragic quality.

Meyers, Jeffrey. "E.M. Forster and T.E. Lawrence: A Friendship." SAQ, 69 (1970), 206-16.

> A description of the close relationship between TEL and Forster, including a summary of Forster's criticism of SEVEN PILLARS and MINT.

———. "The Revisions of SEVEN PILLARS OF WISDOM." PMLA, 88 (1973), 1066-82.

> A thorough study of the volume's textual history: "with each version of SEVEN PILLARS Lawrence moved further from actual history and closer to an imaginative recreation of it."

———. THE WOUNDED SPIRIT: A STUDY OF SEVEN PILLARS OF WISDOM. London: Brian and O'Keeffe, 1973.

> An examination of the book in various historical and psychological contexts. Most interesting are three chapters on the influence of Doughty (TRAVELS IN ARABIA DESERTA, 1888), Tolstoy, and Nietzsche on the volume.

Mills, Gordon. "T.E. Lawrence as a Writer." TQ, 5, No. 3 (1962), 35-45.

> Sees SEVEN PILLARS as essentially a work of fiction, complete with motifs and a deliberately contrived style achieving objectivity through restraint.

Notopoulos, James A. "The Tragic and the Epic in T. E. Lawrence." YR, 54 (1965), 331-45.

>A good discussion of epic themes and motifs in SEVEN PILLARS.

O'Donnell, Thomas J. THE CONFESSIONS OF T. E. LAWRENCE: THE ROMANTIC HERO'S PRESENTATION OF SELF. Athens: Ohio Univ. Press, 1979.

>An expansion of his article. O'Donnell sees SEVEN PILLARS and MINT as presenting a vacillation between TEL's expansive, imperialistic, sadistic self and his introspective, masochistic self. The third part of MINT is an unsuccessful attempt at resolution.

_____. "T. E. Lawrence and the Confessional Tradition: Either Angel or Beast." GENRE, 9 (1976), 135-51.

>Sees in SEVEN PILLARS and MINT features characteristic of the modern secular confession, such as the failure to present the life in terms of coherent myth.

Payne, Robert. "On the Prose of T. E. Lawrence." PROSE, 4 (Spring 1972), 91-108.

>The epical style of SEVEN PILLARS matches its subject; TEL's prose was influenced by Malory, Charles Doughty, and Wyndham Lewis.

Rota, Bertram. "Lawrence of Arabia and SEVEN PILLARS OF WISDOM." TQ, 5, No. 3 (1962), 46-53.

>Brings new evidence to bear on the identity of "S. A.," the mysterious dedicatee of the initial poem in SEVEN PILLARS.

Tabachnick, Stephen Ely. T. E. LAWRENCE. Twayne's English Author Series. Boston: Twayne, 1978.

>A thorough discussion of SEVEN PILLARS, which Tabachnick assigns to the subgenre of "poetic autobiography," emphasizing inner explorations and unsettled personalities. The book is especially useful for its discussion of the travel literature tradition lying behind SEVEN PILLARS.

_____. "The T. E. Lawrence Revival in English Studies." RS, 44 (1976), 190-98.

>A highly useful review article of recent secondary works.

_____. "Two 'Arabian' Romantics: Charles Doughty and T.E. Lawrence." ELT, 16 (1973), 11-25.

An informative comparison of the two travel writers. Both tended to romanticize Arabia.

Weintraub, Rodelle, and Stanley Weintraub. LAWRENCE OF ARABIA: THE LITERARY IMPULSE. Baton Rouge: Louisiana State Univ. Press, 1975.

A useful volume surveying all of TEL's writings. His literary relationships and critical reception are emphasized.

_____. "MOBY-DICK and SEVEN PILLARS OF WISDOM." SAF, 2 (1974), 238-40.

Briefly treats the influence of Melville's novel on SEVEN PILLARS.

F.R. LEAVIS (1895-1978)

FRL both contributed to and edited SCRUTINY between 1932 and 1953. There is a reprint of the entire set, which includes a "Retrospect" by FRL (1963); there are several volumes of selections from the journal (1948, 1964, and 1968).

NONFICTIONAL PROSE

ANNA KARENINA AND OTHER ESSAYS. London: Chatto and Windus, 1967.

> Includes the title essay as well as fifteen others on works by such figures as Johnson, Bunyan, Henry James, Twain, and Pound. Several of the essays focus on American literature and the nature of scholarly criticism.

THE COMMON PURSUIT. London: Chatto and Windus; New York: Stewart, 1952.

> One of FRL's most important works. Includes twenty-four essays on such general topics as "Literature and Society," "Sociology and Literature," "Literary Criticism and Philosophy," and "The Progress of Poesy" as well as on such specific literary figures as Bunyan, Shakespeare, Milton, Swift, Pope, Hopkins, D.H. Lawrence, James, and Forster.

CULTURE AND ENVIRONMENT: THE TRAINING OF CRITICAL AWARENESS. With Denys Thompson. London: Chatto and Windus, 1933.

> Fourteen essays on such topics as advertising's appeals and status, the implications of leisure and standardization for culture, and the loss of tradition and organic community.

D.H. LAWRENCE. Minority Pamphlets. Cambridge, Engl.: Fraser, 1930.

> FRL defines exactly what he means by ascribing "genius" to Lawrence: his honest power of distinguishing his own feelings. Compares his importance to Blake in the search for inner reality.

Finds SONS AND LOVERS and RAINBOW "difficult to get
through" and praises the "intense concentration" of later works,
such as LADY CHATTERLEY'S LOVER and ST. MAWR.

D.H. LAWRENCE, NOVELIST. London: Chatto and Windus, 1955. New
York: Knopf, 1956.

Favorable discussion of D.H. Lawrence's novels and tales in
relation to the concepts of art, class, and tradition. Includes
an appendix on "Mr. Eliot and Lawrence."

DICKENS THE NOVELIST. With Q.D. Leavis. London: Chatto and Windus,
1970.

FRL revises and upgrades his previous opinions of DOMBEY
AND SON, HARD TIMES, and LITTLE DORRIT.

EDUCATION AND THE UNIVERSITY: A SKETCH FOR AN 'ENGLISH SCHOOL.'
London: Chatto and Windus, 1943. New York: Stewart, 1948.

Includes essays entitled, "The Idea of a University," "A Sketch
for an 'English School,'" and "Literary Studies" as well as an
appendix on "T.S. Eliot's Later Poetry" and "How To Teach
Reading."

ENGLISH LITERATURE IN OUR TIME AND THE UNIVERSITY. London: Chatto
and Windus, 1969.

Contains six essays as well as an introduction and brief appendixes.
Three essays deal with his general approaches to literary study
and criticism; three essays deal with specific aspects of T.S.
Eliot's achievement. The most famous is "Why FOUR QUARTETS
Matters in a Technologico-Benthamite Age."

FOR CONTINUITY. Cambridge, Engl.: Minority Press, 1933. Freeport,
N.Y.: Books for Libraries Press, 1968.

Collects thirteen essays which treat such general topics as
Marxism, civilization and culture, state of criticism and the
literary mind, as well as such specific figures as Arnold Bennett,
Dos Passos, D.H. Lawrence, and Joyce.

GERARD MANLEY HOPKINS: REFLECTIONS AFTER FIFTY YEARS. London:
Ruddock, 1971.

Annual lecture before the Hopkins Society (1971). FRL expresses
his regret that Hopkins has been made into "a minor academic
industry." However, he analyzes some of the techniques and
effects which serve as clear proof of his "rare poetic gift."

F.R. Leavis

THE GREAT TRADITION: GEORGE ELIOT, HENRY JAMES, JOSEPH CONRAD. London: Chatto and Windus; New York: Stewart, 1948.

> Very likely FRL's most important and influential book. The aesthetic and moral continuity among Austen, Eliot, James, and Conrad is demonstrated (though Austen is not treated fully here). He praises their adult themes and their "awareness of the possibilities of life." Dickens is dismissed as a "great entertainer" and others such as Fielding and Smollett are excluded from the pantheon in brief footnotes.

HOW TO TEACH READING: A PRIMER FOR EZRA POUND. Cambridge, Engl.: Fraser, 1932.

> FRL is critical of Ezra Pound's prescriptions in HOW TO READ and offers some of his own positive suggestions, such as the training of a reader's sensibility, appreciation for models of critical method, and the idea of tradition.

LECTURES IN AMERICA. With Q.D. Leavis. London: Chatto and Windus; New York: Pantheon, 1969.

> The three essays by FRL deal with T.S. Eliot, Yeats, and the nature of culture in an industrial society.

THE LIVING PRINCIPLE: 'ENGLISH' AS A DISCIPLINE OF THOUGHT. London: Chatto and Windus, 1975.

> Eight essays which explore the nature of such abstract concepts as thought, language, objectivity, and sincerity. The essays "Judgment and Analysis" and "Prose" are useful to students of literature.

MASS CIVILIZATION AND MINORITY CULTURE. Minority Pamphlets. Cambridge, Engl.: Fraser, 1930.

> Thirty pages of documented despair (references to Arnold, Richards, and Spengler) with one paragraph of questionable hope for the future. Only a dwindling minority are capable of appreciating art and literature in an increasingly mechanized world. However, he strongly rejects "an isolated aesthetic realm." Reprinted in the second edition of EDUCATION AND THE UNIVERSITY (1948).

NEW BEARINGS IN ENGLISH POETRY: A STUDY OF THE CONTEMPORARY SITUATION. London: Chatto and Windus, 1932. New York: Stewart, 1950.

> One of FRL's most important works. Sketches the relationships between poetry, past tradition, and early twentieth-century conditions; analyzes the poetic achievements of T.S. Eliot, Ezra Pound, and G.M. Hopkins in detail. The Victorian and Georgian poets are judged inferior and break the tradition.

NOR SHALL MY SWORD: DISCOURSES ON PLURALISM, COMPASSION AND SOCIAL HOPE. London: Chatto and Windus; New York: Barnes and Noble, 1972.

> Includes seven late and rather cantankerous essays, including "Literarism versus Scientism," "The Misconception and the Menace," "Elites, Oligarchies and an Educated Public," and one on C.P. Snow.

REVALUATION: TRADITION AND DEVELOPMENT IN ENGLISH POETRY. London: Chatto and Windus, 1936. New York: Stewart, 1947.

> One of FRL's most important works. Includes important and insightful new estimates of the literary achievements of Milton, Pope, Wordsworth, Blake, Coleridge, Byron, Shelley, and Keats.

THOUGHT, WORDS AND CREATIVITY: ART AND THOUGHT IN LAWRENCE. London: Chatto and Windus; New York: Oxford Univ. Press, 1976.

> Provides close and integrated analyses of D.H. Lawrence's PLUMED SERPENT, WOMEN IN LOVE, CAPTAIN'S DOLL, and RAINBOW. FRL focuses on how thought and industrial work are related to "art, being and culture."

TWO CULTURES? THE SIGNIFICANCE OF C.P. SNOW. London: Chatto and Windus, 1962. New York: Random House, 1963.

> Contains FRL's famous Richmond Lecture (1962)--an attack on C.P. Snow--with an essay by Michael Yudkin on Sir Charles Snow's 1959 Rede Lecture. Touched off a heated controversy over the split between the arts and sciences in the 1960's.

BIBLIOGRAPHY

Baker, William, comp. "F.R. Leavis, 1965-1979, and Q.D. Leavis, 1922-1979: A Bibliography of Writings by and about Them." BB, 37 (1980), 185-208.

> A worthwhile, lightly annotated compilation divided into five sections: "Chronological List of the Writings of F.R. Leavis, 1965-1979"; "Chronological List of the Writings of Q.D. Leavis"; "A Checklist of Reviews of F.R. Leavis' Books, 1965-1978, and of Q.D. Leavis' Books, 1932-1970"; "A Checklist of Writings About F.R. Leavis, 1965-1979, and Q.D. Leavis, 1944-1979"; "F.R. Leavis: Obituaries and Tributes."

Bilan, R.P., comp. "Bibliography." In his THE LITERARY CRITICISM OF F.R. LEAVIS. Cambridge: The Univ. Press, 1979. Pp. 320-32.

Extensive listing in chronological order of books, uncollected
essays, and uncollected reviews by FRL. Also lists many articles
and books on FRL. Not annotated.

Greenwood, Edward, comp. "A Select Bibliography." In his F.R. LEAVIS.
Harlow, Engl.: Longman, 1978. Pp. 54-58.

Lists FRL's books, uncollected essays and reviews, and some
critical studies on FRL. Brief annotations.

Hayman, Ronald, comp. "Bibliographies." In his LEAVIS. London: Heinemann,
1976. Pp. 147-53.

Includes an analytical bibliography of FRL's books, a select
list of FRL's uncollected essays and reviews, and a selected list
of criticism on FRL. All lists are unannotated and in chronological order.

McKenzie, D.F., and M.P. Allum, comps. F.R. LEAVIS: A CHECK-LIST,
1924-1964. London: Chatto and Windus, 1966.

A chronological list of FRL's books, articles, reviews, and
published letters which is complete to the end of 1964. Some
of the many reprints are noted. A selective secondary bibliography is also included. Includes a helpful index.

BIOGRAPHY

Hayman, Ronald. LEAVIS. London: Heinemann, 1976.

First full-length study of FRL is a mixture of biography and
criticism. Provides basic facts of FRL's life and stresses the
professional difficulties of his early career years as an educational revolutionary. Q.D. Leavis viewed as a decisive
helpmate. Traces history of SCRUTINY and provides often
superficial analyses of the critical works. Slight documentation
and fussy tone throughout.

CRITICISM

Aithal, S. Krishnamoorthy. "The Use of Interpretation in the Criticism of
F.R. Leavis." BJA, 18 (1978), 342-44.

Faults FRL's method of interpretation which conveys the impression that he explains a given work of art completely.
Brief, but provocative argument on the nature of twentieth-century criticism.

Anderson, Perry. "Components of the National Culture." NEW LEFT REVIEW, 50 (1968), 3-57.

> Thoughtful commentary on FRL's work and the assumptions behind it. Argues that as philosophy became technical, literary criticism became ethical; points out the difficulties of FRL's critical method presupposing "a morally and culturally unified audience."

Bateson, F.W. "F.R.L. and E in C: A Retrospect." EIC, 28 (1978), 353-61.

> A colleague reminisces on SCRUTINY and on some articles by and about FRL in EIC; he ranks FRL as one of England's "most effective propagandists for criticism."

Bedford, William. "Leavis and the Wittgensteinians." EIC, 27 (1977), 86-89.

> Complains that FRL in LIVING PRINCIPLE has ignored or misrepresented Wittgenstein's discussions of the question of dualism and the nature of meaning.

Bergonzi, Bernard. "Criticism and the Milton Controversy." In THE LIVING MILTON. Ed. Frank Kermode. London: Routledge and Kegan Paul, 1960. Pp. 162-80.

> Summarizes FRL's anti-Miltonic arguments and finds them "unanswerable" within the confines of the critical terms he sets up. However, Bergonzi shows why FRL's criteria are insufficient; thus, his argument is "unsatisfactory."

Bethell, Samuel Leslie. ESSAYS ON LITERARY CRITICISM AND THE ENGLISH TRADITION. Folcroft, Pa.: Folcroft Press, 1969.

> Examines FRL's opinions (on pages 53-87) on the Shakespeare-Donne as well as the Spenser-Milton-Tennyson traditions. Bethell argues and disagrees with some of FRL's points in an effort to establish "a more comprehensive" critical position.

Bilan, R.P. "The Basic Concepts and Criteria of F.R. Leavis' Novel Criticism." NOVEL, 9 (1976), 197-216.

> A worthwhile discussion of the basic tenets of FRL's fiction criticism. Implicitly, Bilan sees FRL insisting that there is a "close relation between the novel and morality" and that great novels "present an affirmation of life." Bilan carefully defines FRL's concepts of fiction form, moral fable, moral enactment, and moral exploration.

──────. "F.R. Leavis on the Novel: Problems in Evaluation." CE, 38 (1976), 325-41.

> Admires the "real originality" of FRL's evaluations of prose

fiction but argues for "a clear hierarchy" for assessing his different kinds of judgments. Inappropriate, questionable, and especially unsupported judgments preclude a critical response.

_____. "F.R. Leavis's Revaluation of T.S. Eliot." UTQ, 47 (1977-78), 151-62.

Useful survey of FRL's changing attitude toward Eliot's work. Praises the critique of FOUR QUARTETS in LIVING PRINCIPLE and calls it the culmination of FRL's "disengagement from Eliot."

_____. "Leavis on Lawrence: The Problem of the Normative." DHLR, 11 (1978), 38-49.

A thoughtful discussion which agrees with FRL's argument in D.H. LAWRENCE: NOVELIST that Lawrence's work is essentially affirmative, but questions "the normative bearings" of that art. Bilan carefully defines the technical terms and insightfully relates FRL's interpretations to his own readings of Lawrence's novels.

_____. THE LITERARY CRITICISM OF F.R. LEAVIS. Cambridge: The Univ. Press, 1979.

An excellent and extended study of FRL's views of society, culture, and criticism. Includes detailed analysis of his poetry and novel criticism, with special attention to his studies of D.H. Lawrence's fiction. Provides slight commentary on FRL's later criticism. Includes extensive bibliography.

Black, Michael. "A Kind of Valediction: Leavis on Eliot, 1929-1975." THE NEW UNIVERSITIES QUARTERLY, 30 (1975), 78-93.

A valuable survey--with some insightful analysis--of FRL's "focal concern" with T.S. Eliot's ideas and poetry from 1929 to 1975.

_____. "The Reputation of F.R. Leavis." BFORUM, 3 (1977), 534-38.

Argues that if FRL's true importance is to be preserved, he must be seen as an international figure and part of "a long tradition" of prophetic criticism.

Bourne, John. "The Loneliness of the Long Distance Runner." THE GUARDIAN, 8 April 1960, p. 11.

FRL explains to Bourne his reluctance to comment on modern British and American writers.

Boyers, Robert. F.R. LEAVIS, JUDGMENT AND THE DISCIPLINE OF THOUGHT. Literary Frontiers. Columbia: Univ. of Missouri Press, 1978.

> A brief study which explains FRL's key ideas and shows how he differs from many modern critics. Discusses the qualities of "meanness and forthrightness" in FRL's work and concludes that the influence of T.S. Eliot's criticism has been greater than that of FRL's.

Bradbury, Malcolm. "The Rise of the Provincials." AR, 16 (1956), 469-77.

> Although FRL's criticism elucidates the text, it is informed by both a moral outlook and an aggressive attack on the "literary attitude" of dilettantism.

Bradshaw, Graham. "Leavis, OTHELLO, and Self-Knowledge." DQR, 9 (1979), 218-31.

> Explains at some length why he finds FRL's influential but hostile account of Othello's character to be "wrong-headed" and "uncharacteristic." Offers his own reading as a compromise.

Browne, Wynyard. "The Culture-Brokers." LONDON MERCURY, 28 (1933), 436-45.

> Condemns FRL's position in HOW TO TEACH READING that poetry must be protected "by a minority of the cultivated."

Buckley, Vincent. "Leavis and His 'Line.'" CR, 8 (1965), 110-20.

> Interesting discussion of the relationship between being a creative artist and a creative critic. FRL succeeds in his studies because he understands fully the workings of the creative process.

_____. POETRY AND MORALITY: STUDIES ON THE CRITICISM OF MATTHEW ARNOLD, T.S. ELIOT AND F.R. LEAVIS. London: Chatto and Windus, 1959. Pp. 158-213, 227-33.

> Refers to many of FRL's critical works; offers extended discussion of his ideas on impersonality and values as well as poetic reality and artistic sincerity. Buckley argues that in the criticism of FRL there are "self-imposed limitations" because he stresses relevance and always has an eye on audience. Good on FRL's procedures of analysis and evaluation.

Butler, Colin. "F.R. Leavis: Some General Considerations and Some Comparisons with Nietzsche." ES, 61 (1980), 507-19.

> Intelligent and valuable article which examines FRL's critical premises and representations of human values against the background of Nietzsche's philosophical writings.

Byrne, Peter. "Leavis, Literary Criticism, and Philosophy." BJA, 19 (1979), 263-73.

> A thoughtful philosophical analysis of the basic assumptions made about the nature of literary criticism by both FRL and Wellek during their famous controversial exchange. Byrne ends by suggesting three additional issues, such as "how Leavis's rejection of theory in criticism is compatible with his moralism."

Colbert, Robert Edward. "F.R. Leavis and THE GREAT TRADITION." RS, 47 (1979), 59-66.

> Colbert repeats the old charge of FRL's "strong Puritan streak"; however, his analysis of FRL's inability to appreciate comedy and satire in English novels is of some interest.

Cornelius, David Krause, and Edwin St. Vincent, comps. CULTURES IN CONFLICT: PERSPECTIVES ON THE SNOW-LEAVIS CONTROVERSY. Chicago: Scott, Foresman, 1964.

> Includes a collection of ten previously published essays that represent the main outlines of "The Snow-Leavis Controversy." Offers study questions and suggested topics for students.

Coulson, Peter. "The Attack on Leavis." EIC, 13 (1963), 107-12.

> Invokes the spirit of Matthew Arnold to explain the limitations of FRL's many opponents as a sign of the limitations of the age.

Cronin, Anthony. "A Massacre of Authors." ENCOUNTER, 6, No. 4 (1956), 25-32.

> Cronin condemns FRL's criticism of poetry for its vague and narrow-minded approach. He regrets that FRL appreciates very few authors. Maintains that the creative artist also writes the best criticism.

Daniel, John. "Pride, Prejudice and Wit." NATION, 198 (1964), 170-71.

> A brief but interesting sketch of the temper of FRL's outlook as a literary critic. Daniel values his work on individual writers but resists extending his theoretical framework to the larger society.

Davie, Donald. "F.R. Leavis's 'How to Teach Reading.'" EIC, 7 (1957), 231-41.

> A rambling attack on FRL's treatment of artistic technique and his neglect of foreign (especially European) literatures. Davie recommends Pound's essay "How to Read" over FRL's opinions.

_____. "Winters and Leavis: Memories and Reflections." SR, 87 (1979), 727-39.

> Provides a personal defense of his admiration for the two critics and their unrelenting zealotry. In the arts, the pair have done much to help distinguish between "the genuine and the fake, or between the achieved and the unachieved."

"F.R. Leavis; b. 1895: Stability and Growth." THE NEW UNIVERSITIES QUARTERLY, 30 (1975), 24-106.

> Contributions by Michael Tanner, Andor Gomme, Michael Black, Fred Inglis, David Holbrook, and others. Most focus on aspects of FRL's LIVING PRINCIPLE.

Fisher, Philip. "Questions of English." CE, 40 (1979), 727-39.

> Surveys FRL's increasingly futile concern with judging over his career. Argues that in his critical positions, FRL "progressively abandoned" the actual world and his works displayed invective and indignation.

Fraser, John. "Leavis, Winters, and 'Concreteness.'" FWF, 1 (1974), 249-66.

> A well-organized comparison of the two critics' concern with concreteness, or "a secure grasp of the actual," in their psychologically integrated interpretations of literature.

_____. "Leavis, Winters, and Poetry." SORA, 5 (1972), 179-96.

> Includes a precise examination of the limitations of FRL's critical writings on poetry. Shows how in several important ways Winters is "more correct than Leavis about poetry."

_____. "Leavis, Winters, and 'Tradition.'" SOR, N.S. 7 (1971), 963-85.

> A rambling discussion which demonstrates how the two critics have "implicitly redefined the idea of 'tradition' for us." Fraser ends with a philosophical twist.

_____. "Leavis and Winters: A Question of Reputation." WHR, 26 (1972), 1-16.

> Provides a good examination of why "incongruities and discrepancies" exist concerning the reputations of the two controversial critics. Political and personal bias have blinded some in acknowledging their true merits.

_____. "Leavis and Winters: Professional Manners." CQ, 5 (1970-71), 41-71.

> A controversial discussion which rebukes the inconsistency of the academic establishment and argues that in their critical works, FRL and Yvor Winters are "truly professional" and they display the "proper professional manners" of intensity and curiosity.

____. "A Tribute to Dr. F.R. Leavis." WR, 23 (1959), 139-47.

> A sympathetic survey which ranges over FRL's writings and activities to point out some undervalued features. Fraser regrets that the "depth" and "soundness" of FRL's work have not received fuller attention because his influence is "health-promoting."

French, Philip. "Leavis at 80--What Has His Influence Been?" THE LISTENER, 94 (1975), 107-10.

> A symposium edited by Philip French with contributions from D.W. Harding, L.C. Knights, M.C. Bradbrook, William Walsh, Christopher Ricks, and others. Includes interesting assessments of FRL's place in the English critical tradition and offers insightful comparisons of FRL's work to Coleridge's, Arnold's, Richard's, Empson's, and Eliot's.

Gerhardi, William, Stephen Toulmin, Lord Boothby, G.S. Fraser et al. "Sir Charles Snow, Dr. F.R. Leavis, and the Two Cultures." SPECTATOR, 208 (1962), 329-33.

> Interesting collection of some immediate negative reactions to FRL's Richmond lecture. Most agree that he "overstates his case" and makes vast "ill-mannered" generalizations concerning C.P. Snow's work.

Gersh, Gabriel. "The Moral Imperatives of F.R. Leavis." AR, 28 (1968), 520-28.

> A somewhat narrow appreciation of FRL's study of literature as a discipline and "as a moral and social force."

Goldberg, S.L. "Augustanism and the Tragic." CR, 17 (1974), 21-37.

> A careful examination of the grounds and implications of FRL's denial of the Augustan Age's capacity for the tragic in several essays in THE COMMON PURSUIT and in REVALUATION.

Gomme, Andor. ATTITUDES TO CRITICISM. Carbondale: Southern Illinois Univ. Press, 1966.

> Because he thinks that explicit theory should not direct criticism, Gomme ranks FRL's early works high above books by Ransom, Burke, and Winters. Examines FRL's concrete critical method of dealing immediately with both poetry and fiction. Also treats his ideas on culture and tradition.

____. "Why Literary Criticism Matters in a Technologico-Benthamite Age." THE NEW UNIVERSITIES QUARTERLY, 30 (1975), 36-53.

> An informed and fairly extensive discussion of FRL's LIVING PRINCIPLE.

Green, Martin. "A Literary Defence of 'The Two Cultures.'" CRITQ, 4 (1962), 155-62.

> An intelligent essay which finds value in C.P. Snow's lecture "The Two Cultures" and offers a point-by-point refutation of FRL's attack on it. To Martin, FRL's idea of culture is ungenerous and backward-looking.

Greenberg, Martin. "The Influence of Mr. Leavis." PR, 16 (1949), 856-59.

> Although sometimes wrongheaded, FRL is a critic "of genuine personal taste and independent conviction"; his writing conveys "a genuine experiencing of the literary work."

Greenwood, Edward Baker. F.R. LEAVIS. Writers and Their Work. Harlow: Longman, 1978.

> Offers a good assessment of true significance of FRL's criticism of both poetry and fiction. However, in explaining intellectual influences on FRL's thought the study often becomes too complex in its discriminations to serve as a useful introduction to FRL's work.

Gribble, James. "Logical and Psychological Considerations in the Criticism of F.R. Leavis." BJA, 10 (1970), 39-57.

> Attempts a philosophical analysis of FRL's literary critical argument. Examines how he organically relates such key poetic concepts as "imagery," "movement," "rhythm," "thought," and "feeling" in several of his works.

Grigson, Geoffrey. "Leavis against Eliot." ENCOUNTER, 12, No. 4 (1959), 68-69.

> Harsh condemnation of FRL's undignified criticism of the poet-critic's personal behavior in the latest "revaluation" of T.S. Eliot's achievement. Also criticizes FRL's tortuous prose style.

Hand, Harry E. "The Paper Curtain: The Divided World of Snow and Leavis Revisited." JOURNAL OF HUMAN RELATIONS, 14 (1966), 351-63.

> Argues that increasing specialization has obscured the traditional differences between science and the humanities. Restates both Snow's and FRL's original positions, which have been distorted.

Harvey, J. "F.R. Leavis: An Appreciation." ENCOUNTER, 52, No. 5 (1979), 59-67.

> Although Harvey offers the expected anecdotes about FRL's personality, his comments about some of the works are insightful. Shows how FRL developed "a language for evaluating emotion" and returned often to the two antithetical themes of "ego" and "civilisation."

_____. "The Leavises' Dickens." CQ, 6, No. 1 (1972), 77-93.

> An original review of DICKENS THE NOVELIST which stresses the different approaches and even disagreements in interpretation between FRL and his wife. Focuses on Q.D. Leavis' contributions to the book.

Heyl, Bernard. "The Absolutism of F.R. Leavis." JAAC, 13 (1954), 249-55.

> Warns against the "baneful" effects of FRL's "critical dogmatism" which implicitly accepts the value theory of absolutism. Recommends the alert reader embrace relativist theory in experiencing works of art.

Hirsch, David. "HARD TIMES and F.R. Leavis." CRITICISM, 6 (1964), 1-16.

> Regrets FRL's high praise of Dickens' novel HARD TIMES. Hirsch argues that FRL misunderstands the book's imagery and symbolism; detects a real weakness and confusion in both "his aesthetic and moral criticism."

Holbrook, David. "F. R. Leavis and 'Creativity.'" THE NEW UNIVERSITIES QUARTERLY, 30 (1975), 66-77.

> Questions the "unsubstantial" grounds of psychology and philosophy that FRL employs in analyzing Eliot's FOUR QUARTETS in LIVING PRINCIPLE. Also his criticism is often too creative.

Holloway, John. THE CHARTED MIRROR: LITERARY AND CRITICAL ESSAYS. London: Routledge and Kegan Paul, 1960. Pp. 204-26.

> Superficial analysis of THE GREAT TRADITION. Holloway objects to the "cryptic quality" of several passages and regrets the critical establishment's move toward "a narrower and narrower range of interests."

Inglis, Fred. "Attention to Education: Leavis and the Leavisites." THE NEW UNIVERSITIES QUARTERLY, 30 (1975), 94-106.

> Interesting study of the historical and intellectual background that evoked FRL's moral and pedagogical response.

Jackson, R.L.P. "Leavis at 80." QUADRANT, 104 (1976), 40, 70-79.

> A good essay which shows how FRL's greatness consists of an ability to "combine stability with growth." Focuses on the philosophical elements in THE LIVING PRINCIPLE to elaborate his thesis.

James, Clive. THE METROPOLITAN CRITIC. London: Faber, 1974. Pp. 150-58.

> Discusses LECTURES IN AMERICA and shows how FRL's view of society is "seriously hurt by pessimism."

Jarrett-Kerr, Martin. "The Literary Criticism of F.R. Leavis." EIC, 2 (1952), 351-68.

> A highly impressionistic and appreciative survey of FRL's criticism through COMMON PURSUIT. Offers a rebuttal to those who have objected to FRL's prose style.

Johnson, Lesley. "F.R. Leavis." In her THE CULTURAL CRITICS: FROM MATTHEW ARNOLD TO RAYMOND WILLIAMS. London: Routledge and Kegan Paul, 1979. Pp. 93-115.

> Summarizes FRL's ideas on literature, society, and education; discusses reactions to his ideas and his influence on other critics. She argues that FRL's "concept of culture" is unclear in his later writings, which display a shrill tone and a "note of desperation." Views Arnold as more charitable and less elitist than FRL.

Jones, Alun. "F.R. Leavis and After." CRITQ, 1 (1959), 253-57.

> Argues that FRL's followers apply his methods with mechanical rigor and lack his creative variability.

Kenner, Hugh. "A Monument to a Great Critic." VQR, 40 (1964), 295-98.

> Includes a brief analysis of FRL's prose style and calls REVALUATION "his finest book."

Killham, John. "The Use of 'Concreteness' as an Evaluative Term in F.R. Leavis's THE GREAT TRADITION." BJA, 5 (1965), 14-24.

> A lucid and informed discussion of how the limited touchstone of "concreteness" relates to realism and moral seriousness. Killham disagrees with FRL's charge that James's last novels show a lack of specificity.

Liddell, Robert. "Lawrence and Dr. Leavis: The Case of ST. MAWR." EIC, 4 (1954), 321-27.

> Finds fault with FRL's "eulogy" of St. Mawr and claims that he has "abandoned criticism for uncritical adoration."

Lodge, David. LANGUAGE OF FICTION: ESSAYS IN CRITICISM AND VERBAL ANALYSIS OF THE ENGLISH NOVEL. London: Routledge and Kegan Paul, 1966.

Discusses FRL's ideas on the moral dimension of fiction. Lodge explains the extent to which he dissents from FRL's approach.

McAlister, F. L.   "Milton and the Anti-Academics."   JEGP, 61 (1962), 779-87.

Analyzes the nature of FRL's reaction against Milton by placing it in the context of a larger background which has brought changes in poetic theory and new critical approaches. Because FRL hates the academy, he denigrates Milton's traditional greatness.

McLuhan, H. M.   "Poetic v. Rhetorical Exegesis: The Case for Leavis against Richards and Empson."   SR, 52 (1944), 266-76.

A valuable and balanced discussion of the three critics' methods of evaluating poems. McLuhan argues that FRL's method has "superior relevance" to that of Empson and Richards because he believes a poem should refine "moral perception" and extend "dramatic awareness."

Mills, A. R.   "THE PORTRAIT OF A LADY and Dr. Leavis."   EIC, 14 (1964), 380-87.

Criticizes the superlatives FRL has applied to James's novel in THE GREAT TRADITION. Also finds FRL's only stricture--"that James demands homage for Isabel"--to be incorrect.

Milner, Andrew.   "Leavis and English Literary Criticism."   PRAXIS 1, No. 2 (1976), 91-106.

An excellent article. Milner demonstrates that the development of "Leavisian" literary criticism must be viewed within the context of the English Marxist school's "challenge to traditional English cultural values." Milner provides clear and well-documented explanations of the critical debate between FRL and the Marxists during the thirties.

Most, Glenn W.   "Principled Reading."   DIACRITICS, 9, No. 2 (1979), 53-64.

Praises and analyzes the significance of FRL's close reading of Eliot's FOUR QUARTETS in LIVING PRINCIPLE. Views the book as a culmination of a life's work.

Mudrick, Marvin.   "Leavis, Dickens, and the Last Days."   HUDR, 24 (1971), 346-54.

A sparkling but resounding condemnation of DICKENS THE NOVELIST. Objects to the book's "insufferable moral tone," its inability to persuade, and its pedestrian categorizing of Dickens' themes.

Mulhern, Francis. THE MOMENT OF SCRUTINY. London: New Left Books, 1979.

> A Marxist study in the sociology of literature which analyzes in historical form the "whole cultural current"--rather than just FRL's leadership--that formed the continuing phenomenon of SCRUTINY between 1932 and 1953. The analyses of the journal's aesthetics as well as its literary and music criticism are admittedly "incomplete." Includes a useful bibliography of writings on SCRUTINY and its contributors.

Nichols, William. "Skeptics and Believers: The Science-Humanities Debate." ASCH, 45 (1976), 377-86.

> Finds FRL's larger points about science, literature, and culture in his response to C.P. Snow to be valid; however, his "brilliant invective" obscures his argument. Relates FRL's skepticism to ideas of Carlyle and Arnold.

Panichas, George A. "The Leavisite Rubrics." In his THE REVERENT DISCIPLINE: ESSAYS IN LITERARY CRITICISM AND CULTURE. Knoxville: Univ. of Tennessee Press, 1974. Pp. 378-93.

> Good sketch of the form and method of FRL's criticism, which also notes some recent objections to his work. Focuses mainly on defining FRL's "Puritanism" and lack of magnanimity. Values FRL "for disciplining us in how to read."

Poole, Roger C. "Life versus Death in the Later Criticism of F.R. Leavis." RMS, 16 (1972), 112-41.

> An intelligent and well-documented essay which ranges over most of FRL's works to explore his changing views on how various writers convey the "values of life" and promote the creative spirit in a world threatened by the life-denying forces of quantification and industrialism. Shows how his interests are teleological in their concern with the "aims and ends of literature in society." Compares FRL to the Realist critic Georg Lukacs.

Pradhan, S.K. "Literary Criticism and Cultural Diagnosis: F.R. Leavis on W.H. Auden." BJA, 12 (1972), 384-94.

> Interesting analysis of how FRL detects Auden's "disabilities" through both close literary analysis and sociocultural criticism.

Priestley, J.B. THOUGHTS IN THE WILDERNESS. London: Heinemann, 1957.

> Harsh indictment (pages 202-08) of FRL's critical mutilations of literary giants such as Fielding. Dismisses FRL as "a sort of Calvinist theologian of contemporary culture."

Putt, S. Gorley. "The Snow-Leavis Rumpus." AR, 23 (1963), 299-312.

> Fresh examination of the Snow-Leavis controversy which concludes that they are "both radical evangelists of the old-fashioned non-conformist type."

──────. "Technique and Culture: Three Cambridge Portraits." E&S, N.S. 14 (1961), 17-34.

> Charges that FRL's critical technique is an enemy to the reconciliation of the two cultures. Also criticizes the approaches of Snow and Quiller-Couch.

Rahv, Phillip. "On F.R. Leavis and D.H. Lawrence." In his LITERATURE AND THE SIXTH SENSE. Boston: Houghton-Mifflin, 1969. Pp. 289-306.

> Argues that FRL's critical pronouncements are marred by "a kind of provincial moralism" and "a protestant narrowness of sensibility."

Ricks, Christopher. MILTON'S GRAND STYLE. Oxford, Engl.: Clarendon, 1963.

> Chapter 1 defends Milton's powerful style against such detractors as FRL who called it monotonous in an essay in REVALUATION. Ricks argues that "delicacy and subtlety" as well as strength characterize Milton's style.

Ringrose, C.X. "F.R. Leavis and Yvor Winters on G.M. Hopkins." ES, 55 (1974), 32-42.

> Contrasts the two critics' estimates of Hopkins' poetry. Ringrose calls FRL's chapter on Hopkins "the weakest part of NEW BEARINGS" and shows how later he revised his approach significantly in an essay in COMMON PURSUIT.

Robinson, Ian. THE SURVIVAL OF ENGLISH: ESSAYS IN CRITICISM OF LANGUAGE. Cambridge: The Univ. Press, 1973.

> High praise for FRL's work (pages 217-42) because it values the "important place of imaginative literature in our world." Calls NOR SHALL MY SWORD "the great creative work of our generation"; it applies critical standards to human problems.

Robson, W.W. "F.R. Leavis 1895-1978." SR, 87 (1979), 507-14.

> A pedestrian survey of FRL's career; Robson offers only brief summaries of some of the more important works.

──────. "Mr. Leavis on Literary Studies." UNIVERSITIES QUARTERLY, 11 (1957), 164-71.

Draws some distinctions between history and criticism and also between understanding and valuing in light of FRL's statements. Calls REVALUATION "an experiment in historical method."

Sadock, Geoffrey. "Dickens and Dr. Leavis: A Critical Commentary on HARD TIMES." DSA, 2 (1972), 208-16.

Argues that FRL's interpretation of the novel as a denunciation of Benthamism is too limited because it ignores the more significant dimension of psychological problems. Also accuses FRL of making an "arbitrary choice" in singling out the book for praise.

Shrubb, Peter. "F.R. Leavis (1895-1978)." QUADRANT, 131 (1978), 17-20.

A brief account of FRL's importance as a critic and teacher. Shrubb most appreciates his "Englishness," which makes his prose style "knotty," strenuous, and independent.

Singh, G.S. "Better History and Better Criticism: The Significance of F.R. Leavis." EM, 16 (1965), 215-79.

A long appreciative essay on FRL's achievement: his criticism is "provocative," "constructive," and "creatively effective" for the modern world and he offers "a major revaluation" of past British literature.

Sitwell, Edith. ASPECTS OF MODERN POETRY. London: Duckworth, 1934. Pp. 21-32.

Harsh criticism of FRL's analyses of such poets as Pound and Milton.

Snow, C.P. "The Two Cultures: A Second Look." TLS, no. 3217 (25 October 1963), pp. 839-44.

Announces his intention to rise above level of "personal abuse" to restate and redefine some of the key issues in the science versus the humanities debate.

Stein, Walter. "Christianity and the Common Pursuit." In his CRITICISM AS DIALOGUE. Cambridge: The Univ. Press, 1969. Pp. 32-58.

Enumerates the fundamental principles of agreement and disagreement between the Christian critic and FRL. Admires his "disciplining of literary judgments."

Steiner, George. "Men and Ideas: F.R. Leavis." ENCOUNTER, 18, No. 5 (1962), 37-45.

A balanced and cogent assessment of FRL's work as a literary critic. Shows how his early criticism is "a plea for a live, humane social order"; calls his critique of the English novel his "principal achievement." Yet his late works are marred by a harsh insensitivity.

Strickland, Geoffrey. "The Question of Tone: Reflections on the Leavis-Snow Controversy." DELTAES, 30 (1963), 16-21.

> Defends FRL's criticisms of C.P. Snow and argues that they are based on clear understanding and full evidence. Summarizes and dismisses the protests against FRL's Richmond lecture.

"Symposium: F.R. Leavis 1895-1978." NEW STATESMAN, 95, No. 2457 (1978), 536-37.

> Very brief assessments of FRL's life and work by George Steiner, Geoffrey Grigson, Kingsley Amis, David Lodge, D.J. Enright, Ian Hamilton, John Bayley, Clive James, and Malcolm Bradbury. A sample statement: "All good critics are natural authoritarians. . . ."

Tanner, Michael. "Literature and Philosophy." THE NEW UNIVERSITIES QUARTERLY, 30 (1975), 54-64.

> A philosopher ranges over FRL's career and concludes that his views on philosophy in LIVING PRINCIPLE have reached a higher and more complex level, yet distrust of the discipline lingers.

―――. "The Middle Way in Literary Criticism." THE LISTENER, 68 (1962), 713-14.

> Argues that FRL is "the greatest literary critic of this century" because he mediates between the opposing extremes of aestheticism and didacticism. Tanner focuses specifically on FRL's discussions of ST. MAWR and ANNA KARENINA.

Traversi, Derek. "Leavis and the Case of D.H. Lawrence." MONTH, N.S. 15 (1956), 166-71.

> Praises FRL's "close and penetrating analysis" of Lawrence's novels in D.H. LAWRENCE: NOVELIST. Traversi would stress Lawrence's religious spirit even more than FRL does.

Trilling, Lionel. "Dr. Leavis and the Moral Tradition." In his A GATHERING OF FUGITIVES. Boston: Beacon, 1956. Pp. 101-06.

> Finds FRL's critical judgment in THE GREAT TRADITION to be "of the first order" but regrets his arrogant exclusion of Dickens and the Bloomsbury group of writers.

_____. "The Leavis-Snow Controversy." In his BEYOND CULTURE: ESSAYS ON LITERATURE AND LEARNING. New York: Viking, 1965. Pp. 145-77.

> An interesting summary of the Victorian background and immediate circumstances of the famous debate. Trilling sees flaws in Snow's position. He condemns harshly FRL's tone for its "excess and distortion" but endorses his ideas on literary tradition.

Vivas, Eliseo. "Mr. Leavis on D.H. Lawrence." SR, 65 (1957), 123-36.

> Negative review of D.H. LAWRENCE: NOVELIST. Although FRL's book is valuable for demonstrating that Lawrence is an artist, FRL's claims for him are "excessive" and often unsupportable.

Walsh, William. F.R. LEAVIS. London: Chatto and Windus, 1980.

> A very fine, appreciative study of FRL's "positive achievement." Walsh relates phases of FRL's career to three predecessors: "Leavis was Johnsonian in temperament, Arnoldian in the practice of criticism, and Coleridgean in his conclusions." Also provides good commentary on FRL's ideas on education and work with SCRUTINY.

_____. "A Sharp Unaccommodating Voice: The Criticism of F.R. Leavis." In his A HUMAN IDIOM: LITERATURE AND HUMANITY. New York: Barnes and Noble, 1964. Pp. 106-27.

> Suggestive analysis of the method and influence of NEW BEARINGS, REVALUATIONS, GREAT TRADITION, and CULTURE AND ENVIRONMENT. High praise for FRL as a pioneer who established a mode of criticism that was "integral, coherent and decisively in a modern idiom."

Watson, Garry. THE LEAVISES, THE 'SOCIAL,' AND THE LEFT. Swansea, Wales: Brynmill, 1977.

> A curious, bitter attack on the "London literary world" plus all others who ignore or condemn FRL's work. The book is about as lucid as its title, though it does repeatedly insist that "the critical practice of the Leavises represents the only valid critical alternative."

Wellek, René. "Literary Criticism and Philosophy." SCRUTINY, 5 (1937), 375-83.

> The opening round of a war with FRL that Wellek lost. Wellek accuses FRL of ignoring questions of belief in his discussions of writers in REVALUATION; further, his "realist philosophy" makes him insensitive to romanticism and idealism.

_____. "The Literary Criticism of Frank Raymond Leavis." In LITERARY VIEWS: CRITICAL AND HISTORICAL ESSAYS. Ed. Carroll Camden. Chicago: Univ. of Chicago Press, 1964. Pp. 175-93.

> Attempts a balanced appraisal. However, Wellek dwells on the conventional list of FRL's limitations: that his critical favorites are few; that he neglects literary history or scholarship; that his critical theories are vague because his "main concern is always with the concrete"; and that he overlooks world literature.

Williams, Raymond. CULTURE AND SOCIETY, 1780-1950. New York: Harper and Row, 1958. Pp. 252-63.

> Praises FRL's "valuable" educational proposals but finds "dangers" in his concept of a defensive, cultivated minority. Most of Williams' references are to MASS CIVILIZATION and CULTURE AND ENVIRONMENT.

Williams, Raymond, R. J. Kaufmann, and Alun Jones. "Our Debt to Dr. Leavis--A Symposium." CRITQ, 1 (1959), 245-57.

> Several critics of a younger generation assess FRL's influence on critical theory, educational practice, and a whole generation.

Wilson, Angus. "If It's New and Modish Is It Good?" NYTBR, 2 July 1961, pp. 1, 12.

> Provocative analysis of the positive and negative implications of FRL's influence on the writing and study of modern fiction.

Wright, Iain. "F. R. Leavis, the SCRUTINY Movement and the Crisis." In CULTURE AND CRISIS IN BRITAIN IN THE THIRTIES. Ed. Jon Clark, Margot Heinemann, David Margolies, and Carole Snee. London: Lawrence and Wishart, 1979. Pp. 37-65.

> A well-documented, comprehensive study of the positive and negative effects of FRL's critical journal. Also makes integrated references to FRL's book-length studies from the period.

Zak, William F. "Conrad, F. R. Leavis, and Whitehead: HEART OF DARKNESS and Organic Holism." CONRADIANA, 4, No. 1 (1972), 5-24.

> Shows how the ending of Conrad's novel brilliantly refutes FRL's strictures in GREAT TRADITION that a dramatic action cannot be both precise and mysterious.

C.S. LEWIS (1898-1963)

NONFICTIONAL PROSE

THE ABOLITION OF MAN: OR REFLECTIONS ON EDUCATION WITH SPECIAL REFERENCE TO THE TEACHING OF ENGLISH IN THE UPPER FORMS OF SCHOOLS. London: Oxford Univ. Press, 1943. New York: Macmillan, 1947.

> Originally the Riddell Memorial Lectures delivered in 1942. It is a closely reasoned defense of the existence of moral law, "of objective value," against the trends toward a radical subjectivism in modern education.

THE ALLEGORY OF LOVE: A STUDY IN MEDIEVAL TRADITION. Oxford, Engl.: Clarendon Press; New York: Oxford Univ. Press, 1936.

> CSL's first major work of nonfiction. It is a treatise on the allegorical mode and the courtly love conventions it expresses in medieval and renaissance literature. The work features THE ROMANCE OF THE ROSE, Chaucer, and Spenser as CSL traces the evolution of adulterous courtly love to the conception of romantic marriage in THE FAERIE QUEENE.

ARTHURIAN TORSO: CONTAINING THE POSTHUMOUS FRAGMENT OF THE FIGURE OF ARTHUR BY CHARLES WILLIAMS AND A COMMENTARY ON THE ARTHURIAN POEMS OF CHARLES WILLIAMS BY C.S. LEWIS. London and New York: Oxford Univ. Press, 1948.

> The commentary, "Williams and the Arthuriad," explicates Williams' cycle.

BEYOND PERSONALITY: THE CHRISTIAN IDEA OF GOD. London: Geoffrey Bles, 1944. New York: Macmillan, 1945.

> A collection of radio talks on the conception of the Trinity.

BROADCAST TALKS. London: Geoffrey Bles, 1942. As THE CASE FOR CHRISTIANITY. New York: Macmillan, 1943.

Talks delivered in 1941 and 1942, entitled "Right and Wrong: A Clue to the Meaning of the Universe" and "What Christians Believe." The former points to an innate moral sense in humanity as proof of the existence of God. The latter starts with that argument and proceeds to outline basic Christian beliefs.

CHRISTIAN BEHAVIOUR: A FURTHER SERIES OF BROADCAST TALKS. London: Geoffrey Bles; New York: Macmillan, 1943.

A collection of eight BBC addresses. "Morality and Psychoanalysis" argues the two are not irreconcilable since the latter may improve man's capacity to make free choices.

THE DISCARDED IMAGE: AN INTRODUCTION TO MEDIEVAL AND RENAISSANCE LITERATURE. Cambridge: The Univ. Press, 1964.

On the classical and Christian sources of the medieval world view and the outlines of it. In the epilogue CSL suggests that the twentieth-century model is likewise only metaphorically truthful.

ENGLISH LITERATURE IN THE SIXTEENTH CENTURY EXCLUDING DRAMA. The Oxford History of English Literature, vol. 3. Oxford, Engl.: Clarendon Press, 1954.

The fruit of many years labor, this study examines first the end of the Middle Ages, then the "drab" literature of mid-century, then the "golden" period of Sidney and Spenser. CSL stresses the continuities with the Middle Ages and downplays the classical impact on the Renaissance.

AN EXPERIMENT IN CRITICISM. Cambridge: The Univ. Press, 1961.

An interesting discourse on kinds of readers and proper and improper motives for reading. The most proper, according to CSL, is to share the vantage points of others and to experience the harmony of art.

THE FOUR LOVES. London: Geoffrey Bles; New York: Harcourt, 1960.

An attempt to define the proper Christian attitude toward affection, friendship, eros, and charity--as well as "Loves for the Sub-human."

A GRIEF OBSERVED. London: Faber, 1961. Greenwich, Conn.: Seabury Press, 1963.

Issued under the pseudonym "N.W. Clerk," this is a frank, intimate record of CSL's thoughts upon his wife's death from cancer. They include questioning the nature of God and the consolations of religion.

C.S. Lewis

LETTERS TO MALCOLM: CHIEFLY ON PRAYER. London: Geoffrey Bles; New York: Harcourt, 1964.

> Twenty-two "letters" to a fictitious recipient on such ecclesiastical topics as the validity of petitionary prayer and the revision of the liturgy.

MERE CHRISTIANITY: A REVISED AND AMPLIFIED EDITION, WITH A NEW INTRODUCTION, OF THE THREE BOOKS BROADCAST TALKS, CHRISTIAN BEHAVIOUR AND BEYOND PERSONALITY. London: Geoffrey Bles; New York: Macmillan, 1952.

MIRACLES: A PRELIMINARY STUDY. London: Geoffrey Bles; New York: Macmillan, 1947.

> A closely reasoned defense of the possibility of miracles. It involves an attack on the naturalist conception of the universe and the pantheistic conception of God, and argues miracles do not entail a "breaking" of nature's laws. CSL appeals to our "innate sense of the fitness of things" in judging the probability of specific miraculous reports.

THE PERSONAL HERESY: A CONTROVERSY. London and New York: Oxford Univ. Press, 1939.

> A debate, taking the form of alternating essays, between CSL and E.M.W. Tillyard over what a New Critic would term the biographical fallacy. CSL takes the New Critical stance, Tillyard the romantic.

A PREFACE TO PARADISE LOST: BEING THE BALLARD MATTHEWS LECTURES DELIVERED AT UNIVERSITY COLLEGE, NORTH WALES, 1941. London: Oxford Univ. Press, 1942.

> A learned study--and defense--of PARADISE LOST. The first half examines the form and style of Milton's work in terms of the epic tradition; the second half discusses the content of the poem in terms of the Augustinian conception of the Fall.

THE PROBLEM OF PAIN. London: Centenary Press, 1940. New York: Macmillan, 1943.

> CSL's first major work of theological nonfiction, and one of his more controversial books. In his attempt to reconcile the fact of pain with the Christian God, CSL adduces arguments ranging from the necessity of a universe of natural laws to include the possibility of pain to the notion that the lower animals do not suffer.

REFLECTION ON THE PSALMS. London: Geoffrey Bles; New York: Harcourt, 1958.

An examination of the Psalms that addresses such topics as the presence of hatred in them and the allegorical level of them.

REHABILITATIONS AND OTHER ESSAYS. London and New York: Oxford Univ. Press, 1939.

A collection of nine essays on various literary topics, including a defense of Shelley from Eliot, a discussion of the English syllabus at Oxford, and an analysis of alliterative poetry. "Christianity and Literature" argues that imitation rather than originality should be the aim of authors.

STUDIES IN WORDS. Cambridge: The Univ. Press, 1960.

A study of the meanings and derivations of the words "nature," "sad," "wit," "free," "sense," "simple," "conscience," and "conscious" that addresses "the history of thought and sentiment which underlies the semantic biography of a word. . . ." CSL issued a revised edition in 1967.

SURPRISED BY JOY: THE SHAPE OF MY EARLY LIFE. London: Geoffrey Bles, 1955. New York: Harcourt, 1956.

A record of CSL's spiritual development up to his conversion in 1929. Although sidetracked by such temptations as the occult and intellectual pride, CSL finally decides that joy resides in surrender to God.

THEY ASKED FOR A PAPER: PAPERS AND ADDRESSES. London: Geoffrey Bles, 1962.

A collection of twelve pieces on religious and literary topics. There are essays on Hamlet, Kipling, and Scott; "The Literary Impact of the Authorised Version" is a learned address on that topic.

TRANSPOSITION AND OTHER ADDRESSES. London: Geoffrey Bles, 1949. As THE WEIGHT OF GLORY AND OTHER ADDRESSES. New York: Macmillan, 1949.

A collection of five addresses on religious topics. The most interesting, "Transposition," discusses speaking in tongues.

THE WORLD'S LAST NIGHT AND OTHER ESSAYS. New York: Harcourt, 1960.

A collection of seven pieces on religious topics. One of the more interesting, "On Obstinacy in Belief," defends Christians against the charge of irrationality leveled by some scientists.

C.S. Lewis

WORKS EDITED BY OTHERS

C.S. LEWIS ON SCRIPTURE: HIS THOUGHTS ON THE NATURE OF BIBLICAL INSPIRATION, THE ROLE OF REVELATION AND THE QUESTION OF INERRANCY. Ed. Michael J. Christensen. Waco, Tex.: Word Books, 1979.

> The editor paraphrases CSL.

CHRISTIAN REFLECTIONS. Ed. Walter Hooper. Grand Rapids, Mich.: Eerdmans, 1967.

> A collection of fourteen essays and addresses produced in CSL's last twenty years. Among those appearing for the first time, "The Funeral of a Great Myth" derides Evolutionism as a "work of the folk imagination."

FERN-SEED AND ELEPHANTS AND OTHER ESSAYS ON CHRISTIANITY. Ed. Walter Hooper. London: Collins-Fontana Books, 1975.

> A collection of eight essays and addresses on religion.

GOD IN THE DOCK: ESSAYS ON THEOLOGY AND ETHICS. Ed. Walter Hooper. Grand Rapids, Mich.: Eerdmans, 1970.

> A collection of numerous essays and letters on theological and ethical topics.

THE JOYFUL CHRISTIAN: 127 READINGS FROM C.S. LEWIS. Ed. William Griffin. New York: Macmillan, 1977.

> A MIND AWAKE redux.

A MIND AWAKE: AN ANTHOLOGY OF C.S. LEWIS. Ed. Clyde S. Kilby. London: Geoffrey Bles, 1968.

> A collection of brief passages drawn from CSL's nonfiction on various religious and ethical topics.

OF OTHER WORLDS: ESSAYS AND STORIES. Ed. Walter Hooper. London: Geoffrey Bles, 1966.

> A collection of four fictional works and nine essays on fantasy and science fiction themes.

SELECTED LITERARY ESSAYS. Ed. Walter Hooper. Cambridge: The Univ. Press, 1969.

> A collection of most of CSL's literary essays (excluding those in Hooper's STUDIES IN MEDIEVAL AND RENAISSANCE LITERATURE). Ordered by the chronology of their subjects, they range

from studies of alliterative meter to studies of Freudian and anthropological approaches to literature.

SPENSER'S IMAGES OF LIFE. Ed. Alastair Fowler. Cambridge: The Univ. Press, 1967.

> The editor has expanded CSL's rough lecture notes on THE FAERIE QUEENE into ten essays on it.

STUDIES IN MEDIEVAL AND RENAISSANCE LITERATURE. Ed. Walter Hooper. London: Cambridge Univ. Press, 1966.

> Fourteen essays in the area, either hitherto unpublished or difficult to obtain. They include five pieces on Spenser, and "Imagination and Thought in the Middle Ages," which emphasizes the orderliness of the medieval mind and world view.

BIBLIOGRAPHY

Christopher, Joe R., and Joan K. Ostling, eds. C.S. LEWIS: AN ANNOTATED CHECKLIST OF WRITINGS ABOUT HIM AND HIS WORKS. Kent, Ohio: Kent State Univ. Press, n.d.

> An inclusive and well-annotated secondary bibliography that has lengthy sections on the writings about CSL's "Religion and Ethics" and his "Literary Criticism."

Hooper, Walter, ed. "A Bibliography of the Writings of C.S. Lewis." In LIGHT ON C.S. LEWIS. Ed. Jocelyn Gibb. London: Geoffrey Bles, 1965. Pp. 117-60.

> A chronologically ordered primary bibliography by a secretary of CSL. It is divided into sections on books, short stories, prefaces, essays, poems, reviews, and letters.

BIOGRAPHY

Carpenter, Humphrey. THE INKLINGS: C.S. LEWIS, J.R.R. TOLKIEN, CHARLES WILLIAMS, AND THEIR FRIENDS. London: Unwin, 1978.

> A history of the Inklings, an informal Oxford group of which CSL was a central figure. It traces their intellectual and personal relationships.

Como, James T., ed. C.S. LEWIS AT THE BREAKFAST TABLE AND OTHER REMINISCENCES. New York: Macmillan, 1979.

> In the vein of LIGHT ON C.S. LEWIS, a collection of twenty-four essays by acquaintances on CSL as a tutor, orator, and the like.

Gibb, Jocelyn, ed. LIGHT ON C.S. LEWIS. London: Geoffrey Bles, 1965.

> A collection of nine essays on various aspects of CSL's character and career. The most interesting on his character, by fellow Oxford undergraduate Nevill Coghill, likens it to Samuel Johnson's.

Gilbert, Douglas, and Clyde S. Kilby, eds. C.S. LEWIS: IMAGES OF HIS WORLD. Grand Rapids, Mich.: Eerdmans, 1973.

> A picture book of Oxford, Cambridge, and elsewhere.

Green, Roger Lancelyn, and Walter Hooper. C.S. LEWIS: A BIOGRAPHY. New York: Harcourt, 1974.

> An admiring biography by friends of CSL that draws heavily on his letters. Some attention is given to the writing history of his more important volumes.

Keefe, Carolyn, ed. C.S. LEWIS: SPEAKER AND TEACHER. Grand Rapids, Mich.: Zondervan Publishing House, 1971.

> A collection of seven brief memoirs of CSL as conversationalist and public speaker at Oxford and elsewhere.

CRITICISM

Adams, E.W. "The Problem of Pain as a Doctor Sees It." HIBBERT JOURNAL, 42 (1944), 145-51.

> An attack on PROBLEM OF PAIN questioning CSL's arguments on such topics as the limited nature of human and animal suffering.

Barfield, Owen. "C.S. Lewis and Historicism." In MAN'S NATURAL POWERS: ESSAYS FOR AND ABOUT C.S. LEWIS. Ed. Raymond P. Tripp, Jr. N.p.: Society for New Language Study, 1975. Pp. 1-8.

> Notes a basic contradiction between CSL's debunking of historical patterns, as voiced in such essays as "Historicism" (CHRISTIAN REFLECTIONS) and his faith in Christianity, preeminently a "historical" religion.

Barrington-Ward, Simon. "The Uncontemporary Apologist." THEOLOGY, 68 (1965), 103-08.

> Complains about CSL's remoteness from contemporary life and the distant tone of his theology.

Bennett, Joan. "The Love Poetry of John Donne: A Reply to Mr. C.S. Lewis." In SEVENTEENTH-CENTURY ENGLISH POETRY: MODERN ESSAYS IN CRITICISM. Ed. William R. Keast. New York: Oxford Univ. Press, 1962. Pp. 111-31.

Refutes CSL's view expressed in ALLEGORY OF LOVE that John
Donne holds a medieval view of the sinfulness of sex and women.

Brandt, William J. "A Textual Analysis." In his THE RHETORIC OF ARGU-
MENTATION. Indianapolis: Bobbs-Merrill, 1970. Pp. 172-97.

An analysis of the rhetorical tactics in a section of ABOLITION
OF MAN.

Brooke, N.S. "C.S. Lewis and Spenser: Nature, Art and the Bower of Bliss."
CAMBRIDGE JOURNAL, 2 (1949), 420-34.

Disagrees with CSL's interpretation in ALLEGORY OF LOVE of
the bower of bliss.

Carnell, Corbin Scott. BRIGHT SHADOW OF REALITY: C.S. LEWIS AND
THE FEELING INTELLECT. Grand Rapids, Mich.: Eerdmans, 1974.

A tracing in CSL's works of his idea of sehnsucht (romantic
nostalgia).

──────. "C.S. Lewis on Eros as a Means of Grace." In IMAGINATION AND
THE SPIRIT: ESSAYS IN LITERATURE AND THE CHRISTIAN FAITH PRESENTED
TO CLYDE S. KILBY. Ed. Charles A. Huttar. Grand Rapids, Mich.: Eerd-
mans, 1971. Pp. 341-51.

Reviews CSL's ideas on sexuality and marriage as expressed in
FOUR LOVES and elsewhere.

Como, James. "The Critical Principles of C.S. Lewis." CSLBULL, 2 (1971),
5-10.

Terms CSL a critical Platonist who believes poetry should reflect
ideal forms.

Conn, Harvie M. "Literature and Criticism." WESTMINISTER THEOLOGICAL
JOURNAL, 23 (1960), 26-31.

Argues that CSL does not sufficiently posit a "Christian ground-
motive" for literary criticism in ABOLITION OF MAN.

Conquest, Robert. "The Art of the Enemy." EIC, 7 (1957), 42-55.

Perceives tendencies toward totalitarianism and sadism in both
Charles Williams' Arthurian poem cycle and CSL's gloss of it
in ARTHURIAN TORSO.

Cunningham, Richard B. C.S. LEWIS: DEFENDER OF THE FAITH. Philadelphia:
Westminster Press, 1967.

>   A learned study of CSL's tactics as Christian Apologist, with discussion of PROBLEM OF PAIN, MIRACLES, and "The Case for Christianity" (MERE CHRISTIANITY).

Davies, Horton. "Distinguished Lay Preaching: B.L. Manning and C.S. Lewis." In his VARIETIES OF ENGLISH PREACHING: 1900-1960. Englewood Cliffs, N.J.: Prentice-Hall, 1963. Pp. 164-93.

>   Reviews the contents of three of CSL's sermons printed in TRANSPOSITION.

Donaldson, E. Talbot. "The Myth of Courtly Love." VENTURES, 6 (1965), 16-23.

>   Disagrees with CSL's opinion, expressed in ALLEGORY OF LOVE, that courtly love necessarily involves adultery.

Farrer, Austin. "The Christian Apologist." In LIGHT ON C.S. LEWIS. Ed. Jocelyn Gibb. London: Geoffrey Bles, 1965. Pp. 23-43.

>   A close analysis of the argumentative tactics in PROBLEM OF PAIN.

Fichte, Joerg O. "The Reception of C.S. Lewis' Scholarly Works in Germany." In MAN'S NATURAL POWERS: ESSAYS FOR AND ABOUT C.S. LEWIS. Ed. Raymond P. Tripp, Jr. N.p.: Society for New Language Study, 1975. Pp. 17-21.

Gilbert, Allan H. "Critics of Mr. C.S. Lewis on Milton's Satan." SAQ, 47 (1948), 216-25.

>   A defense of CSL's negative opinion of Milton's Satan voiced in PREFACE TO PARADISE LOST. This is a reply to Stoll (see p. 311).

Goldberg, S.L. "C.S. Lewis and the Study of English." MELBOURNE CRITICAL REVIEW, 5 (1962), 119-27.

>   Attacks EXPERIMENT IN CRITICISM for undervaluing the efficacy of evaluative criticism.

Haldane, J.B.S. "God and Mr. C.S. Lewis." In RATIONALIST ANNUAL FOR THE YEAR 1948. Ed. Frederick Watts. London: Watts, 1948. Pp. 78-85.

>   An attempt to refute CSL's argument in BROADCAST TALKS that man's sense of moral obligation demonstrates a supernatural standard.

Hamilton, Carol J. "Christian Myth and Modern Man." ENCOUNTER (Butler Univ. College of Religion, Indiana), 29 (1968), 246-55.

Contrasts the attitudes of CSL and the theologian Bultmann on myth: Bultmann seeks to "remove the stumbling block of mythological expression" while CSL has embraced myth.

Hamilton, George Rostrevor. HERO OR FOOL? A STUDY OF MILTON'S SATAN. London: Unwin, 1944.

Satan is heroic rather than ludicrous, as CSL would have him in PREFACE TO PARADISE LOST.

Hannay, Margaret Patterson. C.S. LEWIS. New York: Ungar, 1981.

Chapter 4 on literary criticism and chapter 5 on Christian apologetics provide handy summaries of CSL's books in these fields and conclude with overviews of his critical and apologetic tendencies.

Hartshorne, Charles. "Philosophy and Orthodoxy." ETHICS, 54 (1944), 295-98.

A brief discussion of PROBLEM OF PAIN and CASE FOR CHRISTIANITY that raises several objections to CSL's orthodox views on God's relationship with man.

Holmer, Paul L. C.S. LEWIS: THE SHAPE OF HIS FAITH AND THOUGHT. New York: Harper, 1976.

A study of CSL that finds him "a moralist without a definitive moral thesis, a theologian without being a schoolish type, a critic without having quite a critical theory."

Hooper, Walter. "Oxford's Bonny Fighter." In C.S. LEWIS AT THE BREAKFAST TABLE AND OTHER REMINISCENCES. Ed. James T. Como. New York: Macmillan, 1979. Pp. 137-85.

A lengthy history of CSL's career as president of the Oxford Socratic Club. Hooper supplies information about several of CSL's papers, later printed in such collections as GOD IN THE DOCK and WORLD'S LAST NIGHT.

Kilby, Clyde S. THE CHRISTIAN WORLD OF C.S. LEWIS. Grand Rapids, Mich.: Eerdmans, 1964.

A handy, clearly organized review of CSL's fictional and nonfictional religious books.

Kreeft, Peter. C.S. LEWIS: A CRITICAL ESSAY. Contemporary Writers in Christian Perspective. Grand Rapids, Mich.: Eerdmans, 1969.

A slight overview, stressing CSL's theology.

Kuhn, Daniel K. "The Joy of the Absolute: A Comparative Study of the Romantic Visions of William Wordsworth and C. S. Lewis." In IMAGINATION AND THE SPIRIT: ESSAYS IN LITERATURE AND THE CHRISTIAN FAITH PRESENTED TO CLYDE S. KILBY. Ed. Charles Huttar. Grand Rapids, Mich.: Eerdmans, 1971. Pp. 189-214.

> Quotes SURPRISED BY JOY in preferring CSL's Christian romanticism to Wordsworth's "anthropocentric romanticism."

Lawlor, John. "On Romanticism in the CONFESSIO AMANTIS." In PATTERNS OF LOVE AND COURTESY: ESSAYS IN MEMORY OF C. S. LEWIS. Ed. John Lawlor. Evanston, Ill.: Northwestern Univ. Press, 1966. Pp. 122-40.

> Argues against CSL's claim in ALLEGORY OF LOVE that Gower is romantic.

_____. "'Rasselas,' Romanticism and the Nature of Happiness." In FRIENDSHIP'S GARLAND: ESSAYS PRESENTED TO MARIO PRAZ ON HIS SEVENTIETH BIRTHDAY. Ed. Vittorio Gabrieli. Rome: Edizioni di Storia e Letteratura, 1966. Pp. 243-70.

> On CSL's union of theology and the romantic impulse, as discussed in SURPRISED BY JOY.

_____, ed. PATTERNS OF LOVE AND COURTESY: ESSAYS IN MEMORY OF C. S. LEWIS. Evanston, Ill.: Northwestern Univ. Press, 1966.

> A collection of ten scholarly essays on courtesy and courtly love, most of which give a respectful nod to ALLEGORY OF LOVE. That by Lawlor, involving CSL more fully, is listed above.

Lee, Ernest George. C. S. LEWIS AND SOME MODERN THEOLOGIANS. London: Lindsey Press, 1944.

> Perceives failures of logic in PROBLEM OF PAIN.

Masterman, Margaret. "C. S. Lewis: The Author and the Hero." TWENTIETH CENTURY, 158 (1955), 539-48.

> SURPRISED BY JOY, while unmystical in its dour and hectoring persona/hero, does conform to the mystical conception of joy.

Meilaender, Gilbert. THE TASTE FOR THE OTHER: THE SOCIAL AND ETHICAL THOUGHT OF C. S. LEWIS. Grand Rapids, Mich.: Eerdmans, 1978.

> A study of CSL's conception of Christian community that attempts to deduce his ideas on such topics as economics and sexuality.

Myers, W.A. "C. S. Lewis's Argument for Natural Law Ethics." In MAN'S NATURAL POWERS: ESSAYS FOR AND ABOUT C. S. LEWIS. Ed. Raymond P. Tripp, Jr. N.p.: Society for New Language Study, 1975. Pp. 43-46.

An admiring discussion of CSL's theory, voiced in ABOLITION OF MAN, that "values are primary and cannot be justified."

Norwood, W.D., Jr. "C.S. Lewis, Owen Barfield and the Modern Myth." MQ, 8 (1967), 279-91.

Draws on DISCARDED IMAGE and ENGLISH LITERATURE IN THE SIXTEENTH CENTURY in noting CSL believes the Copernican universe should only be considered metaphor, not fact.

Nott, Kathleen. "Lord Peter Views the Soul." In her THE EMPEROR'S CLOTHES. London: Heinemann, 1953. Pp. 253-98.

A lengthy assault on the anti-scientific bias of CSL and Dorothy Sayers. In MIRACLES, CSL is guilty of positing a Cartesian split between the reason and nature.

Rodway, Allan, and Mark Roberts. "English in the University, II: 'Practical Criticism' in Principle and Practice." EIC, 10 (1960), 1-17.

Takes CSL to task for valuing learning for its own sake in REHABILITATIONS.

Sale, Roger. "England's Parnassus: C.S. Lewis, Charles Williams and J.R.R. Tolkien." HUDR, 17 (1964), 203-25.

A penetrating discussion of CSL's theological and critical amateurishness. His Christian writings "are only for the intellectually slack, would-be believer"; he stirs up enthusiasm for reading, but his analyses of specific works are second-rate.

Sharrock, Roger. "Second Thoughts: C.S. Lewis on Chaucer's TROILUS." EIC, 8 (1958), 123-37.

Argues that CSL overemphasizes the courtly love element in his discussion of Chaucer's poem in ALLEGORY OF LOVE.

Starkman, M.K. "The Militant Miltonist; or, the Retreat from Humanism." ELH, 26 (1959), 209-28.

Accuses CSL in PREFACE TO PARADISE LOST of ignoring Milton's heterodoxy and emphasizing the Christian aspects of the poem at the expense of the aesthetic.

Stoll, Elmer Edgar. "Give the Devil His Due: A Reply to Mr. Lewis." RES, 20 (1944), 108-24.

Protests CSL's interpretation of Milton's Satan (expressed in PREFACE TO PARADISE LOST) as oversimplified and overderogatory.

Sundaram, P. S. "C. S. Lewis: Literary Critic." QUEST (Bombay), 60 (1969), 58-66.

>An odd jumble of anecdote and career survey. CSL avoided judgmental criticism according to Sundaram.

Tamaizumi, Yasuo. "The Conditions of Happiness in Our Age--A Japanese Impression of C. S. Lewis." In MAN'S NATURAL POWERS: ESSAYS FOR AND ABOUT C. S. LEWIS. Ed. Raymond P. Tripp, Jr. N. p.: Society for New Language Study, 1975. Pp. 47-54.

>Argues that in criticism CSL's feelings often warp his judgment.

Tripp, Raymond P., Jr. "Chiliastic Agnosticism and the Style of C. S. Lewis." In his MAN'S NATURAL POWERS: ESSAYS FOR AND ABOUT C. S. LEWIS. N. p.: Society for New Language Study, 1975. Pp. 27-34.

>An exceedingly complex essay that attempts to trace the illogic in much of CSL's prose back to the illogic of Christianity.

_____, ed. MAN'S NATURAL POWERS: ESSAYS FOR AND ABOUT C. S. LEWIS. N. p.: Society for New Language Study, 1975.

>A collection of ten essays on CSL's fiction and nonfiction.

Utley, Francis Lee. "Anglicanism and Anthropology: C. S. Lewis and John Speirs." SFQ, 31 (1967), 1-11.

>Regrets CSL's view that anthropology is irrelevant to literary criticism.

Vinaver, Eugene. "On Art and Nature: A Letter to C. S. Lewis." In ESSAYS ON MALORY. Ed. J. A. W. Bennett. Oxford, Engl.: Clarendon Press, 1963. Pp. 29-40.

>A defense of Malory against certain strictures CSL raises in his essay "The English Prose 'Morte'" (appearing in the same book).

Wain, John. "A Great Clerke." In C. S. LEWIS AT THE BREAKFAST TABLE AND OTHER REMINISCENCES. Ed. James T. Como. New York: Macmillan, 1979. Pp. 68-76.

>Judges CSL's most scholarly works, such as ENGLISH LITERATURE IN THE SIXTEENTH CENTURY, to be his best. In them, CSL downplays his persona of the Old Western Man and the rhetorical tricks often produced by that character.

Walsh, Chad. C. S. LEWIS: APOSTLE TO THE SKEPTICS. New York: Macmillan, 1949.

An early treatment of CSL's works; discussion of them in the first half is usefully organized by genre.

_____. THE LITERARY LEGACY OF C.S. LEWIS. New York: Harcourt, 1979.

A rework of Walsh's early study that covers all of CSL's literary career and focuses more on the literary rather than the religious attribute of it.

Weatherby, H.L. "Two Medievalists: Lewis and Eliot on Christianity and Literature." SR, 78 (1970), 330-47.

Drawing on DISCARDED IMAGE and SURPRISED BY JOY, Weatherby argues that, in contrast to Eliot, CSL finds the medieval mentality fully as "dissociated" as the modern.

Weathers, Winston. "The Rhetoric of Certitude." SHR, 2 (1968), 213-22.

Sees CSL's style as expressing surety through his "rhetoric of certitude," involving simple diction, pejorative diction, word repetition, and so forth.

White, William Luther. THE IMAGE OF MAN IN C.S. LEWIS. Nashville: Abingdon Press, 1969.

Cites the nonfiction throughout in discussing CSL's views of the human condition and the myths he discovered to express those views.

WYNDHAM LEWIS (1882-1957)

NONFICTIONAL PROSE

AMERICA, I PRESUME. New York: Howell, Soskin, 1940.
>Comic impressions of the United States through an Englishman's eyes.

AMERICA AND COSMIC MAN. London: Nicholson and Watson, 1948. Garden City, N.Y.: Doubleday, 1949.
>Hails America's promise as a utopia that will transcend narrow individualism and nationalism. WL enters a strong plea for an "internationalist" outlook. Examines American culture and traces political ideas back to the polarity of Hamilton and Jefferson.

ANGLOSAXY: A LEAGUE THAT WORKS. Toronto: Ryerson Press, 1941.
>In contrast to Germany, England is praised as a formidable sea power and a haven for democracy.

THE ART OF BEING RULED. London: Chatto and Windus; New York: Harper, 1926.
>Important genesis of WL's subsequent polemical studies. Discusses such social issues as the family and feminism; examines the political doctrines of socialism.

BLASTING AND BOMBARDIERING. London: Eyre and Spottiswoode, 1937. Berkeley and Los Angeles: Univ. of California Press, 1967.
>WL's autobiography from 1914 to 1926. Provides often sardonic reactions to the World War I experience at home and at the front; presents the mood of post-war disillusion. WL also recalls his meetings with the Sitwells, Joyce, Pound, and Eliot. Anne Wyndham Lewis deleted and modified some passages in the 1967 edition.

THE CALIPH'S DESIGN. ARCHITECTS! WHERE IS YOUR VORTEX? London: The Egoist Ltd., 1919.

> A pamphlet consisting of four essays of art criticism. Examines the shortcomings of modern painting that may "infect succeeding generations." Condemns the "listlessness" and "dilettantism" of studio art.

COUNT YOUR DEAD: THEY ARE ALIVE! OR A NEW WAR IN THE MAKING. London: Dickson, 1937. New York: Gordon Press, 1972.

> An impassioned plea in dialog form for peace. WL satirizes British reactions to the Spanish Civil War and to Hitler. Political commentary on communism and fascism.

THE DEMON OF PROGRESS IN THE ARTS. London: Methuen, 1954. Chicago: Regnery, 1955.

> WL depicts art as at the mercy of revolution and technology. These forces push modern art to experimental "extremes which end in an insane zero." Thus, abstract art is condemned, along with the visual artist's irresponsible freedom.

THE DIABOLICAL PRINCIPLE AND THE DITHYRAMBIC SPECTATOR. London: Chatto and Windus, 1931. New York: Haskell House, 1971.

> WL attacks such schools as the Joycean TRANSITION group based in Paris and Cambridge anthropologists who reduce art to the level of folk product. WL discusses the origins, rituals, and status of art. Relates art to social problems; defines the new philistinism and the new nihilism.

DOOM OF YOUTH. London: Chatto and Windus, 1932. As THE DOOM OF YOUTH. New York: McBride, 1932.

> WL attacks "youth-politics" or the cult of youth as it is exploited by journalists and advertisers for both political and economic purposes. Bemoans the decay of European traditions.

FILIBUSTERS IN BARBARY. London: Grayson; New York: National Travel Club, 1932.

> A travel book about the land and people in North Africa, based on WL's visit to Morocco, 1931-32. Interesting comments on Islam, oil, and outlooks. WL even describes a visit to the brothel of Agadir.

HITLER. London: Chatto and Windus, 1931. New York: Gordon Press, 1972.

> Controversial study of Hitler's life and doctrines. The book damaged WL's reputation in the thirties.

Wyndham Lewis

THE HITLER CULT. London: Dent, 1939. New York: Gordon Press, 1972.

> WL indicts Hitler as a charlatan and eschews any sympathy with mass murders by the state.

THE JEWS: ARE THEY HUMAN? London: Allen and Unwin, 1939. New York: Gordon Press, 1972.

> Despite its ironic title, WL presents a balanced discussion of anti-Semitism.

LEFT WINGS OVER EUROPE: OR, HOW TO MAKE A WAR ABOUT NOTHING. London: Cape, 1936. New York: Gordon Press, 1972.

> Highly controversial polemic in which WL maintains that Hitler is a mere pretext for a war that "internationalists" have planned for their own sordid ends. Outrageous depiction of a wronged Germany at the hands of a persecuting England-Europe.

THE LION AND THE FOX: THE RÔLE OF THE HERO IN THE PLAYS OF SHAKESPEARE. London: Richards; New York: Harper, 1927.

> A critical-historical study of Shakespeare's and Machiavelli's concepts of heroes. This wide-ranging study deals with the many sides of Shakespeare's genius--as showman, executioner, nihilist--and analyzes characters from jester to king.

MEN WITHOUT ART. London: Cassell, 1934. New York: Russell, 1964.

> Fifteen critical essays on such figures as T.S. Eliot, Faulkner, Flaubert, and Hemingway and such topics as satire and the status of the artist. Although WL gloomily predicts the demise of art and taste, he offers insightful commentary on art's relation to industrialism, classicism, politics, and humor.

THE MYSTERIOUS MR. BULL. London: Hale, 1938.

> A popular depiction of the British character. WL examines the Englishman's (or John Bull's) origins and traditions and delineates his characteristics as artist, lover, humorist, and politician.

THE OLD GANG AND THE NEW GANG. London: Harmsworth, 1933. New York: Haskell House, 1972.

> WL offered this sixty-four page pamphlet as a substitute for DOOM OF YOUTH, which was suppressed. WL sees new political tyrants replacing the obsolete capitalist leaders.

PALEFACE: THE PHILOSOPHY OF THE "MELTING-POT." London: Chatto and Windus, 1929. New York: Haskell House, 1969.

Includes famous attacks on Anderson, Lawrence, and the theme of the "dark within."

RUDE ASSIGNMENT: A NARRATIVE OF MY CAREER UP-TO-DATE. London and New York: Hutchinson, 1950.

WL offers a valuable reassessment of his personal, artistic, and literary career, with special emphasis on his polemical writings. Valuable reflections on the status of the intellectual and the function of satire and politics.

TIME AND WESTERN MAN. London: Chatto and Windus, 1927. New York: Harcourt, 1928.

WL's most important nonfictional work. The essay "The Revolutionary Simpleton" is especially brilliant. Includes philosophical discussion of the concepts of time and romance, plus important critical estimates of modern literature and history. Specific figures treated are: Ezra Pound, Gertrude Stein, Charlie Chaplin, and James Joyce.

THE WILD BODY. London: Chatto and Windus, 1927. New York: Harcourt, Brace, 1928.

Primarily a collection of short stories, but includes the essays "Inferior Religions" and "The Meaning of the Wild Body," in which WL outlines his theory of the comic.

THE WRITER AND THE ABSOLUTE. London: Methuen, 1952.

Examines the effects of politics on such writers as Camus, Malraux, Orwell, and Sartre. Also treats the issue of freedom of the press and speculates on a Utopian republic of letters.

WYNDHAM LEWIS THE ARTIST, FROM BLAST TO BURLINGTON HOUSE. London: Laidlaw, 1939. New York: Haskell House, 1971.

Important collection of WL's writings on contemporary art from BLAST and THE TYRO, plus THE CALIPH'S DESIGN. Also WL discusses his work as a painter and outlines his aesthetic in "Essay on the Objective of Art in Our Time."

WORKS EDITED BY OTHERS

ENEMY SALVOES: SELECTED LITERARY CRITICISM. Ed. C.J. Fox. London: Vision, 1975.

An important collection of twenty-nine essays of WL's literary criticism, including discussions of satire and the writer and politics as well as valuable assessments of Henry James, G.B.

Shaw, D. H. Lawrence, T. S. Eliot, and many other writers. Unfortunately, some of the essays appear in abridged form.

A SOLDIER OF HUMOR AND SELECTED WRITINGS. Signet Classics. Ed. Raymond Rosenthal. New York: New American Library, 1966.

> Besides short stories, this collection includes miscellaneous essays from BLAST and WL's books.

WYNDHAM LEWIS: AN ANTHOLOGY OF HIS PROSE. Ed. E.W.F. Tomlin. London: Methuen, 1969.

> Excellent collection which includes valuable headnotes and some footnotes to the various selections. Draws from WL's writings on sociology, philosophy, literature, the arts, his own life, and travel to such countries as Morocco and America.

WYNDHAM LEWIS ON ART: COLLECTED WRITINGS 1913-1956. Ed. Walter Michel and C. J. Fox. London: Thames and Hudson, 1969.

> Arranged in chronological order, this collection includes useful explanatory headnotes to the four-part divisions: "The 'Blast' Period," "World War I and the Early Twenties," "The Trough between the Wars," and "The Forties and After." Most of the essays are reprinted in full. Also includes helpful endnotes, bibliography, and index.

BIBLIOGRAPHY

Daniels, Mary F., ed. WYNDHAM LEWIS: A DESCRIPTIVE CATALOGUE OF THE MANUSCRIPT MATERIAL IN THE DEPARTMENT OF RARE BOOKS CORNELL UNIVERSITY LIBRARY. Ithaca, N.Y.: Cornell Univ. Library, 1972.

> An updated listing of important WL holdings at Cornell University Library.

Kenner, Hugh, comp. "Bibliography." In his WYNDHAM LEWIS. Norfolk, Conn.: New Directions, 1954. Pp. 159-64.

> Chronological list of WL's writings includes all books and a few periodical essays. Most items are briefly annotated.

Meyers, Jeffrey, comp. "Wyndham Lewis: A Bibliography of Criticism, 1912-1980." BB, 37 (1980), 33-52.

> Excellent list of over 900 books, articles, and reviews in English, French, Italian, German, and Swedish about WL's works as both writer and painter. Arranged alphabetically by author. Few annotations, but most important studies designated by an asterisk.

Morrow, Bradford, and Bernard Lafourcade, eds. A BIBLIOGRAPHY OF THE WRITINGS OF WYNDHAM LEWIS. Santa Barbara, Calif.: Black Sparrow Press, 1978.

> The best and most extensive primary and secondary bibliography available on WL. Nearly comprehensive listings of books and articles by and about WL. Chronological arrangement within sections with accurate descriptions and helpful, concise annotations.

Pound, Omar S., and Philip Grover, eds. WYNDHAM LEWIS: A DESCRIPTIVE BIBLIOGRAPHY. Folkestone, Engl.: Dawson, 1978.

> Comprehensive descriptive primary bibliography which lists books, pamphlets, portfolios, periodical contributions, and other miscellaneous items by WL. Arranged chronologically within sections.

Pritchard, William H., comp. "Selected Bibliography." In his WYNDHAM LEWIS. New York: Twayne, 1968. Pp. 170-75.

> Includes selected list of primary sources, with some annotations and a helpful listing of some secondary sources that are more fully annotated. Alphabetical arrangement by title and by author.

Rose, William K., comp. WYNDHAM LEWIS AT CORNELL. A REVIEW OF THE LEWIS PAPERS PRESENTED TO THE UNIVERSITY BY WILLIAM G. MENNEN. Ithaca, N.Y.: Cornell Univ. Library, 1961.

> Describes holdings in Cornell University Library collection.

Wagner, Geoffrey, comp. "Bibliography." In WYNDHAM LEWIS: A PORTRAIT OF THE ARTIST AS THE ENEMY. New Haven, Conn.: Yale Univ. Press, 1957. Pp. 315-48.

> Includes a very nearly complete chronological checklist of WL's written work--including many periodical contributions--with a selected list of secondary sources arranged alphabetically by author. Spotty annotations.

BIOGRAPHY

Kenner, Hugh. WYNDHAM LEWIS. Makers of Modern Literature. Norfolk, Conn.: New Directions, 1954.

> Not a full-length biography, but "an account" of WL's career. A balanced and extremely perceptive study of WL's personality and writings. Explains the intricacies of WL's creative intelligence, sometimes in a complex manner.

Wyndham Lewis

Meyers, Jeffrey. THE ENEMY: A BIOGRAPHY OF WYNDHAM LEWIS. London: Routledge and Kegan Paul, 1980.

> The most comprehensive biography of WL follows in chronological order the phases of his life. Scrupulously documented with many references to various personal letters and interviews. Passionately argued throughout, Meyers concludes that WL's reputation should be greater than it is and he blames this fate on the unfortunate political tracts.

Tomlin, E. W. F. WYNDHAM LEWIS. Writers and Their Work. London: Longmans, Green, 1955.

> A pamphlet which serves as a useful introduction to WL's life and works. As a friend and admirer, Tomlin focuses on WL's philosophical speculations.

Woodcock, George, ed. WYNDHAM LEWIS IN CANADA. Canadian Literature Series. Vancouver: Univ. of British Columbia Publications Centre, 1971.

> A collection of thirteen essays which treat the many sides of WL's rather sad stay in Canada during the early 1940s. Most of the contributions are more biography than criticism. Good general background on the influence of art, nature, and culture on WL.

CRITICISM

Bates, Ralph. "Wyndham Lewis." TIME AND TIDE, 16, No. 2 (1935), 35-37; No. 3 (1935), 90-91.

> Appreciative survey of WL's work, but criticizes his overemphasis of theory.

Beckett, Samuel, et al. OUR EXAMINATION ROUND HIS FACTIFICATION FOR INCAMINATION OF WORK IN PROGRESS. Paris: Shakespeare and Co., 1929.

> Deals with WL's criticism of Joyce in TIME AND WESTERN MAN.

Bridson, D. G. THE FILIBUSTER. A STUDY OF THE POLITICAL IDEAS OF WYNDHAM LEWIS. London: Cassell, 1972.

> Excellent and comprehensive analysis of WL's political philosophy.

Burke, Kenneth. ATTITUDES TOWARD HISTORY. 2nd ed., rev. Los Altos, Calif.: Hermes Publications, 1959.

> Discussion of satirical and grotesque elements in WL's works.

Carter, Huntly. "'Sociology' in the New Literature." THE SOCIOLOGICAL REVIEW, 20 (1928), 250-55.

>Sees in WL's thought patterns both individualistic and Thomist strains.

Carter, Thomas H., ed. "Wyndham Lewis Number." SHENANDOAH, 4, Nos. 2-3 (1953).

>Includes contributions by Pound, Kenner, Eliot and several others. However, only H.M. McLuhan's article, "Wyndham Lewis: His Theory of Art and Communication" (pp. 77-88), deals extensively with WL's nonfiction prose.

Chace, William M. "On Lewis's Politics: The Polemics Polemically Answered." In WYNDHAM LEWIS: A REVALUATION. Ed. Jeffrey Meyers. London: Athlone, 1980. Pp. 149-65.

>Revaluates WL's controversial political tracts of the 1930s. Posits that the writings are insensitive because WL was "shielded from the obvious vulgarity of his surroundings." Includes interesting comparisons to Orwell and Pound.

Chapman, Robert. "Lawrence, Lewis and the Comedy of Literary Reputation." STC, No. 6 (1970), 85-95.

>Analyzes the combination of factors that damaged WL's reputation, including his controversial political views and his "concept and practice of satire."

_____. "Letters and Autobiographies." In WYNDHAM LEWIS: A REVALUATION. Ed. Jeffrey Meyers. London: Athlone, 1980. Pp. 15-28.

>Values WL's letters more than BLASTING AND BOMBARDIERING and RUDE ASSIGNMENT because the two books show "strains of hasty composition." Good analysis of the tone and significance of WL's autobiographical writings.

_____. WYNDHAM LEWIS: FICTIONS AND SATIRES. London: Vision Press, 1973.

>Includes detailed discussions of WL's satiric works.

Chesterton, G.K. "The Doom of Doom. A Reply to Mr. Wyndham Lewis's Articles on Youth-Politics." TIME AND TIDE, 12 (1931), 910-13, 935-36.

>Admiring discussion of WL as a controversial genius.

Coffey, Warren. "Wyndham Lewis: Enemy of the Rose." RAMPARTS, 2, No. 1 (1963), 70-76.

> Outlines WL's accomplishments and ranks him as the leading figure of his time.

Cookson, William. AGENDA, 7-8 (1969-70). Special Wyndham Lewis Issue.

> Articles by Pritchard, Seymour-Smith, Sisson, and Tomlin deal with WL's nonfiction prose and criticism and are annotated separately. Twenty-two other articles deal with WL's fiction and paintings.

Dohmen, William F. "Chilly Spaces: Wyndham Lewis as Ondt." JJQ, 11 (1974), 368-86.

> Well-documented essay which traces Joyce's relationship with WL and outlines Joyce's responses to WL's criticisms of his ideas and techniques.

Dupee, F.W. "The English Literary Left." PR, 5, No. 3 (1938), 11-21.

> Interesting portrait of Britain in the 1920's: WL was one of many "modern" individuals who never unified to form a "modern" movement.

Eliot, T.S. "A Commentary: The Politics of Men of Letters." THE CRITERION, 8 (1929), 378-80.

> WL and several other writers are labelled Fascists.

_____. "A Note on Monster Gai." HUDR, 7 (1955), 522-26.

> Examines some of WL's prose and ranks him as "the greatest prose master of style" in his times.

_____. "Wyndham Lewis." HUDR, 10 (1957), 167-71.

> Offers some personal recollections and analyzes several of WL's late works.

Fjelde, Rolf. "Time, Space, and Wyndham Lewis." WR, 15 (1951), 201-12.

> A serious attempt to trace a unifying pattern in WL's diverse works. Fjelde finds some of the following recurrent themes: the cult of the child, the cult of the artist, and the cult of time in philosophy and the arts.

Fox, C.J. "Lewis as Travel Writer: The Forgotten FILIBUSTERS IN BARBARY." In WYNDHAM LEWIS: A REVALUATION. Ed. Jeffrey Meyers. London: Athlone, 1980. Pp. 166-80.

> Illuminating analysis of style and theme of WL's longest travel book, which records his visit to Morocco. Fox regrets that WL didn't write more in this genre.

Fraser, G. S. EZRA POUND. London: Oliver and Boyd, 1960. Pp. 86-93.
>Offers several insights into WL's criticism on Pound.

―――― . "Wyndham Lewis: An Energy of Mind (an Appreciation)." TWENTIETH CENTURY, 161 (1957), 386-92.
>Brief, but useful overview of WL's literary output.

Frye, Northrop. "Neo-Classical Agony." HUDR, 9 (1957), 592-98.
>Primarily negative criticism of WL's works.

Gawsworth, John. [Terence Ian Fytton Armstrong]. APES, JAPES, AND HITLERISM. A STUDY AND BIBLIOGRAPHY OF WYNDHAM LEWIS. London: Unicorn Press, 1932.
>An early critical study of WL. Includes an early bibliography.

Glasheen, Adeline. "Rough Notes on Joyce and Wyndham Lewis." WN, 8, No. 5 (1971), 67-75.
>Interesting discussion which touches on paradoxical relationships between ULYSSES and TIME AND WESTERN MAN.

Glicksberry, Charles I. "Wyndham Lewis: The Artist in Revolt." CALR, 66 (1938), 263-79.
>Surveys WL's political ideas in his own writings.

Goldring, Douglas. REPUTATIONS. ESSAYS IN CRITICISM. New York: Seltzer, 1920. Pp. 135-44.
>Concise overview of WL's literary career.

Graham, C. "Wyndham Lewis and the Fanatical Celt." THE MODERN SCOT, 6 (1935), 210-18.
>Interesting comments on the recurring portraits of Celts as extremists in WL's writings.

Gregory, Horace. "Wyndham Lewis: The Artist at War with Himself." In his THE DYING GLADIATORS AND OTHER ESSAYS. New York: Grove, 1961. Pp. 21-27.
>Outlines the controversial dimensions of WL's career and renders an affirmative estimation.

Grigson, Geoffrey. A MASTER OF OUR TIME: A STUDY OF WYNDHAM LEWIS. London: Methuen, 1951.

An admiring pamphlet which pays enthusiastic tribute to WL's singular achievement.

Hamilton, Alastair. THE APPEAL OF FASCISM, 1919-1945. London: Blond, 1971. Pp. 281-85.

Estimates WL's achievement by divorcing his ideas from his politics.

Harrison, John R. THE REACTIONARIES, A STUDY OF THE ANTI-DEMOCRATIC INTELLIGENTSIA, W.B. YEATS, WYNDHAM LEWIS, EZRA POUND, T.S. ELIOT, D.H. LAWRENCE. London: Gollancz, 1966.

One chapter analyzes WL's political positions.

Hoffman, Frederick J. THE TWENTIES. New York: Viking, 1949.

Evaluates the importance of WL's TIME AND WESTERN MAN in its time period.

Holloway, John. "Wyndham Lewis: The Massacre and the Innocents." HUDR, 10 (1957), 171-88.

A superb essay on the themes in WL's works. Holloway analyzes WL's "massive or violent insight" into twentieth-century reality and argues that his reputation is equal to Yeats's, Eliot's, and Lawrence's.

Howarth, Herbert. NOTES ON SOME FIGURES BEHIND T.S. ELIOT. Boston: Houghton Mifflin, 1964.

Includes an analysis of the relationship between WL and T.S. Eliot.

Jameson, Frederic. FABLES OF AGGRESSION: WYNDHAM LEWIS, THE MODERNIST AS FASCIST. Berkeley and Los Angeles: Univ. of California Press, 1979.

Freudian-Marxist analysis of WL by a brilliant critic. Includes significant commentary on ART OF BEING RULED, HITLER, MEN WITHOUT ART, and TIME AND WESTERN MAN. Provides fresh insights into WL's philosophy and politics.

———. "Wyndham Lewis as Futurist." HUDR, 26 (1973), 295-329.

Analyzes WL's "energetic" prose style.

Kenedy, R.C. "Wyndham Lewis or the Stand against Aphrodite's Sunset-Struck Star." ART INTERNATIONAL, 15, No. 9 (1971), 71-77, 80.

A wide-ranging and impassioned essay which measures WL's

greatness against the "artistic and political concepts of Right and Left." Kenedy urges an enlarged view that encompasses both WL's literary and artistic works.

Kenner, Hugh. "Vortex Lewis." In his THE POUND ERA. Berkeley and Los Angeles: Univ. of California Press, 1971. Pp. 232-47.

> Concise discusssion of the relationship between WL and Ezra Pound between 1910 and 1919. Concentrates on the Vorticism movement.

Kirk, Russell. "Wyndham Lewis's First Principles." YR, 44 (1955), 520-34.

> Valuable analysis of WL's political ideas and satirical techniques.

Leavis, F. R. THE COMMON PURSUIT. London: Chatto and Windus, 1952.

> Leavis compares Eliot, Lawrence, and WL. Without offering too many specific reasons, Leavis renders a negative assessment of WL.

THE LEWIS LETTER. Glasgow: Wyndham Lewis Society, nos. 1-8 Dec. 1974-Aug. 1978. 2 per year. Name changed to: ENEMY NEWS: NEWSLETTER OF THE WYNDHAM LEWIS SOCIETY, Twichenham, Middlesex: no. 9, Dec. 1978-- . 2 per year.

> Critical and biographical articles as well as brief biographical updates on WL. Sponsored by the WL Society, Glasgow, Scotland.

Lindsay, Jack. "The Modern Consciousness. An Essay Towards an Integration." THE LONDON APHRODITE, No. 1 (1928), 3-24.

> Explains WL's reactions against D.H. Lawrence and Nietzsche's philosophies.

MacShane, Frank. "The English Review." SAQ, 60 (1961), 311-20.

> High praise for WL as a "spectacular" essay writer.

Materer, Timothy. "Lewis and the Patriarchs: Augustus John, W. B. Yeats, T. Sturge Moore." In WYNDHAM LEWIS: A REVALUATION. Ed. Jeffrey Meyers. London: Athlone, 1980. Pp. 47-63.

> Outlines WL's friendship with these figures and analyzes their reactions to such works as TIME AND WESTERN MAN.

_____. VORTEX: POUND, ELIOT, AND LEWIS. Ithaca, N.Y.: Cornell Univ. Press, 1979.

> Includes helpful discussions of WL's aesthetics as well as his social and political opinions. Extensive treatment of TIME AND WESTERN MAN.

Mayne, Richard. "Wyndham Lewis." ENCOUNTER, 38, No. 2 (1972), 42-51.

> General survey of WL's life and works.

Melville, Cecil F. THE TRUTH ABOUT THE NEW PARTY (AND MUCH ELSE BESIDES CONCERNING SIR OSWALD MOSLEY'S POLITICAL AIMS, THE "NAZI" MOVEMENT OF HERR ADOLPH HITLER, AND THE ADVENTURE IN POLITICAL PHILOSOPHY OF MR. WYNDHAM LEWIS). London: Wishart, 1931. Passim.

> A curious early discussion which weighs the "right" and "wrong" elements in WL's political ideas.

Meyers, Jeffrey, ed. WYNDHAM LEWIS: A REVALUATION. London: Athlone, 1980.

> Eighteen distinguished scholars revaluate the many sides of WL's achievement. The essays by Chapman, Chace, Fox, Materer, Pritchard, and Tomlin are annotated separately.

Michel, Walter. "Tyros and Portraits: The Early Twenties and Wyndham Lewis." APOLLO, 82 (1965), 128-33.

> Well-focused discussion of a phase of WL's career.

Michel, Walter, and C. J. Fox. "Introduction." In their WYNDHAM LEWIS ON ART: COLLECTED WRITINGS, 1913-1956. New York: Funk and Wagnalls, 1969. Pp. 11-17.

> Explains the connections between WL's talents as writer and painter. Finds "intelligence, wit, and sensibility" in his critical essays. Judges WL's essays of the twenties to be his best.

Munton, Alan. "The Politics of Wyndham Lewis." PNR, 4, No. 1 (1976), 34-39.

> Original and informed discussion which sees a "revolutionary" dimension to WL's political ideas.

Orage, A. R. THE ART OF READING. New York: Farrar and Rinehart, 1930.

> Negative estimate of WL and Vorticism.

_____. READERS AND WRITERS (1917-1921). New York: Knopf, 1922.

> Mocks and derides WL's presumed "cleverness."

Porteus, Hugh Gordon. WYNDHAM LEWIS: A DISCURSIVE EXPOSITION. London: Harmsworth, 1932.

> An early--and now dated--critical study on WL's work. Views DIABOLICAL PRINCIPLE and HITLER in favorable terms.

Pound, Ezra. "D'Artagnan Twenty Years After." THE CRITERION, 16 (1937), 606-17.

>Reviews WL's vitality and creativity as an important writer for the past twenty-five years.

──────. "Data." THE EXILE, 4 (1928), 104-17.

>Part of this rambling essay is a defense of WL: "I am for Mr. Lewis, even when he is wrong, and I am against the abominable public and race amongst which he lives."

──────. "Vorticism." THE FORTNIGHTLY REVIEW, 46 (1914), 461-71.

>Explains WL's contributions to the literary movement.

Praz, Mario. "Wyndham Lewis." ES, 10, No. 1 (1928), 1-8.

>Brief discussion of TIME AND WESTERN MAN and LION AND THE FOX, with especially unfavorable estimation of the latter title.

Pritchard, William H. "Lawrence and Lewis." AGENDA, 7-8 (1969-70), 140-47.

>Refutes earlier estimations of the pair by T.S. Eliot and F.R. Leavis. Provides a well-organized comparison of both Lawrence's and WL's accomplishments as critics and novelists.

──────. "Literary Criticism as Satire." In WYNDHAM LEWIS: A REVALUATION. Ed. Jeffrey Meyers. London: Athlone, 1980. Pp. 196-210.

>Focuses on MEN WITHOUT ART and THE WRITER AND THE ABSOLUTE. Insightful explanation and appreciation of WL's partial truths and satiric performances in his essays.

──────. "On Wyndham Lewis." PR, 35 (1968), 253-67.

>Perceptive discussion of WL's reputation and achievement as a literary critic. Pritchard grapples with the question of whether WL's politics or his satire and criticism of other men's works caused his reputation to decline.

──────. SEEING THROUGH EVERYTHING. ENGLISH WRITERS 1918-1940. New York: Oxford Univ. Press, 1977.

>Good general study which delineates WL's place against the background of his times. Estimates his role as satirist.

──────. WYNDHAM LEWIS. Profiles in Literature. London: Routledge and Kegan Paul, 1972.

Wyndham Lewis

Useful as an introductory critical study of WL's writings.

_____. WYNDHAM LEWIS. Twayne's English Author Series. New York: Twayne, 1968.

Valuable introductory study of WL's works--especially good on WL as a "critic of modern culture."

_____. "Wyndham Lewis and Lawrence." IOWAR, 2, No. 2 (1971), 91-96.

Disagrees with F. R. Leavis' estimations of WL and D. H. Lawrence.

Regnery, Henry. "Eliot, Pound and Lewis: A Creative Friendship." MODA, 16 (1972), 146-60.

Exhaustively detailed, but hardly original, outline of the important relationships among the three writers. Includes a brief critical analysis of TIME AND WESTERN MAN.

Rickword, Edgell. "Wyndham Lewis." In his SCRUTINIES II. London: Wishart, 1931. Pp. 139-61.

Rickword values the "energetic" WL as a philosopher, satirist, and critic of literature. Rickword sympathetically analyzes the ideas and techniques in CALIPH'S DESIGN, ART OF BEING RULED, and several other works.

Riding, Laura. ANARCHISM IS NOT ENOUGH. London: Cape, 1928.

Thorough and entertaining treatment (pages 41-133) of both WL's work and personality.

Rose, William K. "Ezra Pound and Wyndham Lewis: The Crucial Years." SORA, N. S. 4 (1968), 72-89.

Despite some egotistical differences, the pair agreed on the aristocracy of art and mind, aesthetic principles, and authoritarian politics. Includes good analysis of reciprocal influences in tone and style.

Seymour-Smith, Martin. "Wyndham Lewis as Imaginative Writer." AGENDA, 7-8 (1969-70), 9-15.

Explains why there is an apparent lack of emphasis of the unconscious and the imagination in WL's critical writings. Believes that WL valued restraint and polemical energy more than creativity.

_____. "Zero and the Impossible." ENCOUNTER, 9, No. 5 (1957), 38-51.

Deals partly with WL analyzing the "creative legitimacy" of his prose style.

Sisson, C. H. "Introduction." In ENEMY SALVOES: SELECTED LITERARY CRITICISM. Ed. C. J. Fox. New York: Barnes and Noble, 1976. Pp. 7-18.

    Good assessment of WL's contributions to twentieth-century criticism. Sisson compares WL with T. S. Eliot's influence and accomplishments. Concludes that WL's honest satire never sought "to diminish what is of value," but exposed "the weak or frivolous."

_____. "The Politics of Wyndham Lewis." AGENDA, 7-8 (1969-70), 109-16.

    Explains and defends most of WL's political stances.

_____. "Wyndham Lewis's Study of Himself." PNR, 7 (1978), 13-15.

    Balanced, perceptive analysis of WL's theory of himself and time in MEN WITHOUT ART and TIME AND WESTERN MAN.

Slater, Montagu. "Journalism and Art: VI--P. Wyndham Lewis." ARTS AND CRAFTS, 3, No. 1 (1929), 14-17.

    Examines and compares WL's accomplishments in the two fields.

Smith, Page. "Wyndham Lewis's AMERICA AND COSMIC MAN." JOURNAL OF RELIGION, 56 (1976), 255-62.

    Admiring and close analysis of AMERICA AND COSMIC MAN. Smith urges historians to recognize WL's perceptive insights into American history and culture.

Spanos, William V. "Modern Literary Criticism and the Spatialization of Time: An Existential Critique." JAAC, 29 (1970), 87-104.

    An existentialist traces the influence of Worringer's philosophy on WL and others.

Spender, Stephen. THE DESTRUCTIVE ELEMENT. London: Cape, 1935. Pp. 205-16.

    Valuable analysis of WL's theory of satire.

Stone, Geoffrey. "The Ideas of Wyndham Lewis." THE AMERICAN REVIEW, 1 (1933), 578-99.

    Early survey of WL's critical ideas. Explains, but does not judge, WL's positions in ART OF BEING RULED, and TIME AND WESTERN MAN. Part 2 appears in volume 2 (1933), 82-96; in part 2, Stone treats WL's controversial political writings of the early 1930s.

Stonier, G. W. "That Taxi-Driver." TWENTIETH CENTURY VERSE, No. 6-7 (1937), 22-24.

Brief discussion of WL's significance as a literary critic: as a counterrevolutionary, he is "indispensable" for the twentieth century.

Tomlin, E. W. F. "Introduction." In his WYNDHAM LEWIS. AN ANTHOLOGY OF HIS PROSE. London: Methuen, 1969. Pp. 1-20.

> Highly appreciative and impressionistic survey of WL's life and works written by a longtime friend of WL. Tomlin sees an essential Arnoldian "high seriousness" and integrity in WL's writings. Yet he also had a "keen and infectious sense of humour." Concludes with a brief assessment of WL's influence and reputation.

_____. "The Philosopher-Politician." TWENTIETH CENTURY VERSE, No. 6-7. (1937), 32-36.

> Brief but perceptive assessment of WL's philosophical and political ideas.

_____. "The Philosophical Influences." In WYNDHAM LEWIS: A REVALUATION. Ed. Jeffrey Meyers. London: Athlone, 1980. Pp. 29-46.

> Clear and carefully done study of the complex philosophical influences--both European and English--on WL. Covers WL's critique of contemporary historical and social thought, including religion. Values TIME AND WESTERN MAN as a "stimulating" book.

_____. "Reflections on TIME AND WESTERN MAN." AGENDA, 7-8 (1969-70), 97-108.

> Values TIME AND WESTERN MAN as a major work of the twentieth century and argues that it is central to understanding WL's other works.

TWENTIETH CENTURY VERSE, No. 6-7 (1937). Wyndham Lewis Double Number.

> Good but brief collection of essays which treat both WL's art and criticism.

Vines, Sherard. MOVEMENTS IN MODERN ENGLISH POETRY AND PROSE. London: Oxford Univ. Press, 1927. Pp. 200-208.

> Informed commentary on CALIPH'S DESIGN and THE LION AND THE FOX.

Wagner, Geoffrey. "The Fascist Mentality--Wyndham Lewis." THE WIENER LIBRARY BULLETIN, 22, No. 3 (1968), 35-40.

> Despite WL's later "obfuscations," WL's political outlook is essentially Fascist. Surveys WL's sixteen political books.

_____. WYNDHAM LEWIS: A PORTRAIT OF THE ARTIST AS THE ENEMY. New Haven, Conn.: Yale Univ. Press, 1957.

> A storehouse of details about WL's life and writings. The study, however, lacks a well-focused critical argument and often lacks enthusiasm for its subject. Includes an essential bibliography.

Watson, Sheila. "Wyndham Lewis and G. K. Chesterton." CREV, 6 (1980), 254-71.

> Traces WL's many remarks concerning G. K. Chesterton and concludes that he held an ambivalent attitude, mixed with rebuke and respect. Brief coverage of ART OF BEING RULED, TIME AND WESTERN MAN, RUDE ASSIGNMENT, and DIABOLICAL PRINCIPLE.

Wilson, Colin. "Wyndham Lewis: A Refracted Talent?" BOOKS AND BOOKMEN, 19 (1974), No. 5, 44-48; No. 6, 51-52; No. 7, 39-42.

> Interesting series of assessments of WL as a "failed" artistic genius who lacked self-discipline. Generally sees more merit in WL's critical studies than in his fiction.

Young, Vernon. "The Late Lamenting Wyndham Lewis." HUDR, 29 (1976), 464-70.

> Unrelenting condemnation of WL's narrow "animosity" in his critical essays.

Zable, Arnold. "Wyndham Lewis--Fascist? A Case Study." THE MELBOURNE JOURNAL OF POLITICS, 2 (1969), 36-49.

> Valuable case study of WL's overall authoritarian outlook toward society. Concludes that WL "made the mistake of equating fascism in politics with classicism in literature" in the 1930s.

JOHN MIDDLETON MURRY (1889-1957)

NONFICTIONAL PROSE

ADAM AND EVE: AN ESSAY TOWARDS A NEW AND BETTER SOCIETY. London: Dakers, 1944.

> Treats sexual relationships between men and women. It rejects Eliot's asceticism and Lawrence's idea of the antagonism between sex and Christianity.

ASPECTS OF LITERATURE. London: Collins, 1920. New York: Knopf, 1921.

> A collection of nineteen essays and reviews, most originally appearing in the ATHENAEUM. Three of the more interesting are "The Function of Criticism," which asserts the identity of the good life with the aesthetic; "Mr. Yeats's Swan Song," which charges Yeats with failure to develop an adequate mythology; and "The Problem of Keats," which asserts the importance of the revised introduction to "Hyperion."

THE BETRAYAL OF CHRIST BY THE CHURCHES. London: Dakers, 1940.

> Written under the impact of war, this accuses the Church of failing to address social issues and of failing to provide a code of behavior practical to normal men.

BETWEEN TWO WORLDS: AN AUTOBIOGRAPHY. London: Cape, 1935. As THE AUTOBIOGRAPHY OF JOHN MIDDLETON MURRY: BETWEEN TWO WORLDS. New York: Messner, 1936.

> A survey of JMM's life from infancy but emphasizing his experience with Lawrence and Mansfield. The book is marked by bathos and sexual frankness.

THE CHALLENGE OF SCHWEITZER. London: Jason Press, 1948.

> JMM prefers Christian ethics to Schweitzer's ethic of reverence for all life, too vague for JMM.

John Middleton Murry

CHRISTOCRACY. London: Dakers, 1942.
EUROPE IN TRAVAIL redux.

COMMUNITY FARM. London: Nevill, 1952.

A record of JMM's attempt to found a communalist utopian society at his Norfolk farm.

THE CONQUEST OF DEATH. London and New York: Nevill, 1951.

This odd volume consists of a translation of Benjamin Constant's love story ADOLPHE and a lengthy explication of it by JMM.

COUNTRIES OF THE MIND: ESSAYS IN LITERARY CRITICISM. London: Collins; New York: Dutton, 1922.

A collection of twelve periodical essays on literary topics. Among them are "Shakespeare and Love," "A Neglected Heroine of Shakespeare" (Virgilia in CORIOLANUS), and "'Arabia Deserta'" ("a direct enlargement of human experience").

COUNTRIES OF THE MIND: ESSAYS IN LITERARY CRITICISM: SECOND SERIES. London: Oxford Univ. Press, 1931.

Fourteen essays on literature, most originally published in THE TIMES LITERARY SUPPLEMENT. One of the most interesting, "Metaphor," is a penetrating analysis of the relation of imagery and metaphor.

THE DEFENCE OF DEMOCRACY. London: Cape, 1939.

In this volume, JMM parts ways with Marxism and calls for a Christian democracy. "It is plain that the efficacy of the primitive Marxist categories is exhausted," he argues.

DISCOVERIES: ESSAYS IN LITERARY CRITICISM. London: Collins, 1924.

A collection of thirteen essays including ones on Falstaff, Coriolanus, and Chekhov.

EUROPE IN TRAVAIL. London: Sheldon Press; New York: Macmillan, 1940.

Originally BBC talks, this short volume calls for a new order of Christian socialism to oppose totalitarianism.

THE EVOLUTION OF AN INTELLECTUAL. London: Cobden-Sanderson, 1920.

A collection of nineteen previously published essays on literature and politics. "The Honesty of Russia" and "The Dream of a Queer Fellow" deal with Russian writers; "Realism" is an interesting attempt to define the literary term.

John Middleton Murry

THE FREE SOCIETY. London: Dakers, 1948.

> This work expresses JMM's fear of a third world war and calls for a world ruled by a UN-like body; he also, however, fears Communist Russia and goes so far as to propose "preventive war" against her.

FYODOR DOSTOEVSKY: A CRITICAL STUDY. London: Secker; New York: Dodd, Mead, 1916.

> JMM's first book, celebrating Dostoevsky's "universal sympathy."

GOD: BEING AN INTRODUCTION TO THE SCIENCE OF METABIOLOGY. London: Cape; New York: Harper, 1929.

> A long treatise on the theological implications of mystical experience. JMM had undergone one when anaesthetized in an operation.

HEAVEN--AND EARTH. London: Cape, 1938. As HEROES OF THOUGHT. New York: Messner, 1938.

> A tracing of the development of Christian civilization through the writings of authors from Chaucer to Morris. JMM desires a rejection of Protestant individuality in favor of a unified Catholic church, "the re-recreation of an acknowledged spiritual authority."

JOHN CLARE AND OTHER STUDIES. London: Nevill, 1950.

> This consists of twenty-one previously published essays on authors, including five on Shakespeare.

JONATHAN SWIFT: A CRITICAL BIOGRAPHY. London: Cape, 1954. New York: Noonday Press, 1955.

> JMM's last critical biography. He chose as his subject "someone with whom I could not possibly identify myself" and the resulting biography is more objective than usual for JMM.

KATHERINE MANSFIELD AND OTHER LITERARY PORTRAITS. London: Nevill, 1949.

> A collection of seventeen essays on authors, including three on Keats and three on Mansfield, treating the importance of love in her writing, her personality as revealed in her letters, and one on her physicians.

KEATS. London: Cape; New York: Noonday Press, 1955.

> The final metamorphosis of STUDIES IN KEATS. It adds three

essays, including one concerning the poet's relationship with
Isabella Jones.

KEATS AND SHAKESPEARE: A STUDY OF KEATS' POETIC LIFE FROM 1816
TO 1820. London and New York: Oxford Univ. Press, 1925.

> JMM's best-known book, of major importance in the history of
> Keats studies. A critical biography, it traces Keats's rejection
> of Wordsworth and Milton in favor of Shakespeare and negative
> capability, an open acceptance of experience.

THE LIFE OF JESUS. London: Cape, 1926. As JESUS, MAN OF GENIUS.
New York: Harper, 1926.

> The life of Jesus from baptism to crucifixion, complete with extra-
> Biblical dialog.

LOOKING BEFORE AND AFTER: A COLLECTION OF ESSAYS. London:
Sheppard Press, 1948.

> A collection of 1940's essays arranged in three groups treating
> Christianity, pacifism, and literary authors.

LOVE, FREEDOM AND SOCIETY. London: Cape, 1957.

> A comparison of the social and religious views of Schweitzer
> and Lawrence.

THE MYSTERY OF KEATS. London: Nevill, 1949.

> The third version of STUDIES IN KEATS, with a new essay on
> Fanny Brawne.

THE NECESSITY OF COMMUNISM. London: Cape; New York: Smith, 1932.

> JMM argues for a Communist state, yet expresses dislike for
> materialism and Russian tyranny.

THE NECESSITY OF PACIFISM. London: Cape, 1937.

> Disenchanted with the stagnation of socialism in England, yet
> fearful of revolutionary violence, JMM now stresses the pacifistic
> "ideal of human brotherhood" as the means to social change.

PENCILLINGS: LITTLE ESSAYS ON LITERATURE. London: Collins, 1923.
New York: Seltzer, 1925.

> A collection of twenty-eight periodical essays on literary topics.
> Among them are "Chiaroscuro," which protests against the
> "esoteric" quality of modernist literature, and "Dickens," which
> notes with pleasure the Dickens revival.

John Middleton Murry

THE PLEDGE OF PEACE. London: Joseph, 1938.

> A collection of pacifist articles first published in PEACE NEWS.

THE PRICE OF LEADERSHIP. London: Student Christian Movement Press; New York: Harper, 1939.

> This calls for the education of a Christian ruling class and attempts to reconcile democracy with that idea. Arnold is frequently cited.

THE PROBLEM OF STYLE. London and New York: Oxford Univ. Press, 1922.

> One of JMM's most important works, consisting of six lectures delivered at Oxford in 1921. Rejecting a rhetorical conception of style, he defines it as "universal significance" communicated largely by way of metaphor.

REMINISCENCES OF D.H. LAWRENCE. London: Cape; New York: Holt, 1933.

> Most of this strange book consists of a defense by JMM against Catharine Carswell's criticism of his relationship with Lawrence, voiced in her THE SAVAGE PILGRIMAGE. He does this by a page-by-page refutation of her book and by reprinting his reviews of Lawrence's works.

SHAKESPEARE. London: Cape; New York: Harcourt, 1936.

> One of JMM's best-known books, which attempts "to give the 'sensation' of Shakespeare." This involves attempts to reconstruct his life from the works, a discussion of his historical vision, and a chapter on "The Shakespeare Man," of whom Hamlet is the type.

SON OF WOMAN: THE STORY OF D.H. LAWRENCE. London and New York: Cape, 1931.

> The early, controversial biography of D.H. Lawrence that sees both his works and life as determined by his Oedipal difficulties.

STUDIES IN KEATS. London and New York: Oxford Univ. Press, 1930.

> A collection of six essays. These include pieces on "Endymion," "On First Looking into Chapman's Homer," and "Ode on a Grecian Urn." There are three enlarged versions of this book, listed separately.

STUDIES IN KEATS: NEW AND OLD. London and New York: Oxford Univ. Press, 1939.

> This adds three new essays to STUDIES IN KEATS: "The Poet
> and the Dreamer" (on "The Fall of Hyperion"), "Keats and
> Milton," and "Keats and Wordsworth."

THINGS TO COME: ESSAYS. London: Cape; New York: Macmillan, 1928.

> A collection of twenty-six periodical essays on literature and
> religion. Among them is "Christ or Christianity?" which cele-
> brates Jesus as humanist hero while denying the existence of
> God the Father.

TO THE UNKNOWN GOD: ESSAYS TOWARDS A RELIGION. London: Cape, 1924. New York: Smith, 1930.

> A collection of ADELPHI pieces on religious topics. Among
> them is "Literature and Religion" that parallels literature and
> religion as products of "soul."

UNPROFESSIONAL ESSAYS. London: Cape, 1956.

> This consists of four essays on Fielding, Clare, Whitman, and
> the verse dramas of T. S. Eliot. Fielding's moral "generosity,"
> Whitman's democratic impulse, and Eliot's unhealthy asceticism
> are discussed.

WILLIAM BLAKE. London: Cape, 1933.

> An attempt through close textual study to define Blake's "gospel,"
> which involves the virtues of forgiveness and denial of the ego.

WORKS EDITED BY OTHERS

J. MIDDLETON MURRY: SELECTED CRITICISM: 1916-1957. Ed. Richard Rees. London: Oxford Univ. Press, 1960.

> Twenty-nine essays, mostly on literature.

KATHERINE MANSFIELD AND OTHER LITERARY STUDIES. London: Constable, 1959.

> Consists of essays on George Gissing, Henry Williamson, and
> Katherine Mansfield.

POETS, CRITICS, MYSTICS: A SELECTION OF CRITICISMS WRITTEN BETWEEN 1919 AND 1955 BY JOHN MIDDLETON MURRY. Crosscurrents. Ed. Richard Rees. Carbondale: Southern Illinois Univ. Press, 1970.

> A collection of twenty-four review essays arranged under the
> topics "Poets and Novelists," "Critics," and "Mystics." Most
> were written for THE TIMES LITERARY SUPPLEMENT.

BIBLIOGRAPHY

Lilley, George, ed. A BIBLIOGRAPHY OF JOHN MIDDLETON MURRY: 1889-1957. Folkestone, Kent: Dawson, 1974.
> The best primary bibliography, with sections on books, contributions to books, and contributions to periodicals.

BIOGRAPHY

Carswell, John. "The Adelphi Hero." In his LIVES AND LETTERS: A.R. ORAGE, BEATRICE HASTINGS, KATHERINE MANSFIELD, JOHN MIDDLETON MURRY, S.S. KOTELIANSKY: 1906-1957. London: Faber, 1978. Pp. 228-58.
> An antagonistic but certainly informed survey of JMM's life from 1925 that presents many of his works as influenced by his personal problems.

Heppenstall, Rayner. FOUR ABSENTEES. London: Barrie and Rockliff, 1960.
> An odd sequel to A STUDY IN EXCELLENT NORMALITY (see p. 340) that jumbles reminiscences of JMM with those of Eric Gill, George Orwell, and Dylan Thomas from 1934 on. There is no index.

Lea, F.A. THE LIFE OF JOHN MIDDLETON MURRY. London: Methuen, 1959.
> The only full-scale biography, which, despite its emphasis on JMM as "moralist" rather than as critic, does say a good deal about his literary relationships.

Murry, Mary Middleton. TO KEEP FAITH. London: Constable, 1959.
> An intimate memoir of JMM's last years by his (last) wife. It includes some background on COMMUNITY FARM.

CRITICISM

Beer, J.B. "John Middleton Murry." CRITQ, 3 (1961), 59-66.
> A balanced overview of JMM's strengths and weaknesses as a critic. Beer notes his "passive sensibility" and compares it to that of the later Coleridge.

Bennett, James R. "The Problem of Style." DHLR, 2 (1969), 32-46.

> A detailed, chapter-by-chapter analysis of THE PROBLEM OF STYLE that notes both its strengths and its weaknesses (e.g., the intentional fallacy).

Eliot, T.S. "Foreword." In KATHERINE MANSFIELD AND OTHER LITERARY STUDIES. London: Constable, 1959. Pp. vii-xii.

> Eliot praises the creativity and personal engagement in JMM's criticism.

Fogle, Richard Harter. "Beauty and Truth: John Middleton Murry on Keats." DHLR, 2 (1969), 68-75.

> Praises JMM's sensitive approach to Keats, but wishes for more discussion of the poems detached from the poet.

Glicksberg, Charles I. "John Middleton Murry: Christ among the Critics." SAQ, 38 (1939), 82-99.

> An examination of the intellectual-mystical tension in JMM's career.

Griffin, Ernest G. "The Circular and the Linear: The Middleton Murry-D.H. Lawrence Affair." DHLR, 2 (1969), 76-92.

> An even-handed account of JMM's troubled relationship with Lawrence that produced SON OF WOMAN and essays in ADAM AND EVE and LOVE, FREEDOM AND SOCIETY.

――――. JOHN MIDDLETON MURRY. Twayne's English Author Series. New York: Twayne, 1969.

> A most useful study. It reviews at length the major books and puts JMM in the intellectual milieu of his day.

Griffith, Philip Mahone. "Middleton Murry on Swift: 'The Nec Plus Ultra of Objectivity?'" DHLR, 2 (1969), 60-67.

> An examination of JONATHAN SWIFT that identifies women and scatology as its principal subjects and argues they have more to do with JMM than with Swift.

Heath, William W. "The Literary Criticism of John Middleton Murry." PMLA, 70, No. 1 (1955), 47-57.

> A useful review of JMM's idea on the function of the literary critic, expressed in such works as THE PROBLEM OF STYLE, "A Critical Credo" (COUNTRIES OF THE MIND), and "The Function of Criticism" (ASPECTS OF LITERATURE).

John Middleton Murry

Heppenstall, Rayner. MIDDLETON MURRY: A STUDY IN EXCELLENT NORMALITY. London: Cape, 1934.

> An early study of JMM's thought, praising his broad interests in contrast to the narrow intellectual cliques of his time. The book is especially good on JMM's differences with writers such as Eliot and Chesterton.

Jones, John. "Murry Revaluated." THE NEW STATESMAN, 58 (1959), 848.

> Jones claims JMM's criticism is undervalued, but notes his failings as a critic: insufficient self-possession and a "pervading soft confusion of life and art which leaves an overall impression of mess. . . ."

Kaufmann, R.J. "On Using an Obsessed Critic: John Middleton Murry." GRADUATE STUDENT OF ENGLISH, 3, No. 2 (1960), 4-8.

> A defense of the moralistic bias in JMM's criticism.

Knight, G. Wilson. "J. Middleton Murry." In OF BOOKS AND HUMANKIND: ESSAYS AND POEMS PRESENTED TO BONAMY DOBREE. Ed. John Butt. London: Routledge and Kegan Paul, 1964. Pp. 149-63.

> A history of critical disagreements between Knight and JMM that quotes heavily from TO THE UNKNOWN GOD and THINGS TO COME.

Lea, F.A. "Murry and Marriage." DHLR, 2 (1969), 1-21.

> A complicated discussion, involving several of the prose volumes, of how JMM's ideas on marriage affect his writings.

Mairet, Philip. JOHN MIDDLETON MURRY. Writers and Their Work. London: Longmans, Green, 1958.

> Briefly reviews the contents of JMM's books on Dostoevsky, Keats, Shakespeare, Lawrence, and Swift, and also THE PROBLEM OF STYLE.

Rees, Richard. "Politics of a Mystic." DHLR, 2 (1969), 24-31.

> Criticizes THE NECESSITY OF COMMUNISM for its naivete and emotive language.

_____. A THEORY OF MY TIME: AN ESSAY IN DIDACTIC REMINISCENCE. London: Secker and Warburg, 1963.

> An autobiography, written by a colleague on THE ADELPHI, that cites JMM throughout; his spirituality is amenable to Rees's disenchantment with materialism.

Seaver, George. ALBERT SCHWEITZER: A VINDICATION. Boston: Beacon Press, 1951.

> A reply to JMM's CHALLENGE OF SCHWEITZER that attempts to refute his argument point by point.

Seymour-Smith, Martin. "Zero and the Impossible: Roy Campbell, Wyndham Lewis, Joyce Cary, John Middleton Murry." ENCOUNTER, 9, No. 5 (1957), 38-51.

> A shrewd, hostile look at the sources of JMM's "unexamined emotion of compassion."

Stanford, Derek. "Middleton Murry as Literary Critic." EIC, 8 (1958), 60-67.

> An excellent short discussion of some of the sources of JMM's romantic criticism and of his critical likes and dislikes.

Thayer, C. G. "Murry's SHAKESPEARE." DHLR, 2 (1969), 47-59.

> A defense of JMM's SHAKESPEARE, which notes JMM is best on those plays that did not emotionally engage Shakespeare.

GEORGE ORWELL [ERIC BLAIR] (1903-50)

The four volumes of THE COLLECTED ESSAYS, JOURNALISM, AND LETTERS OF GEORGE ORWELL (London: Secker; New York: Harcourt, 1968) leave out fully two thirds of GO's shorter pieces and reviews, as well as the three books of reportage.

NONFICTIONAL PROSE

CRITICAL ESSAYS. London: Secker, 1946.

    A collection of ten of GO's essays, including "Charles Dickens," "Boys' Weeklies," "Rudyard Kipling," and "Benefit of Clergy."

DICKENS, DALI AND OTHERS: STUDIES IN POPULAR CULTURE. New York: Reynal and Hitchcock, 1946. As CRITICAL ESSAYS. London: Secker, 1951.

    A collection of ten essays, including "Charles Dickens," "Boys' Weeklies," "Wells, Hitler and World State," "The Art of Donald McGill," "Rudyard Kipling," "Benefit of Clergy," "W. B. Yeats," "Salvador Dali," "Arthur Koestler," "Ruffles and Miss Blandish," "In Defense of P. G. Wodehouse."

DOWN AND OUT IN PARIS AND LONDON, A NOVEL. London: Secker, 1949.

    A record of GO's experiences of living with tramps, dishwashers, and others in the filthy rooms of working-class districts. GO shows the rewards and discomforts of surviving in two metropolises with very little money or promise.

THE ENGLISH PEOPLE. London: Collins, 1947.

    A picture book with twenty-five illustrations in which GO discusses the moral and political outlook of the English people, their future, the English class system, and the English language.

George Orwell

HOMAGE TO CATALONIA. London: Secker, 1938. New York: Harcourt, 1952.

> Personal account of the Spanish Civil War. GO provides controversial details of the internal struggles of the revolutionary Leftist forces.

INSIDE THE WHALE AND OTHER ESSAYS. London: Gollancz, 1940.

> Includes "Charles Dickens," "Boys' Weeklies," "Inside the Whale," "Children's Periodicals," and "Henry Miller."

THE LION AND THE UNICORN: SOCIALISM AND THE ENGLISH GENIUS. London: Secker, 1941.

> An analysis of the English character. GO records his belief that World War II would bring about a social revolution to Britain.

THE ROAD TO WIGAN PIER. Left Book Club Collection. London: Gollancz, 1937.

> A report on the industrial North's poverty and depression, followed by an essay on class and socialism.

TALKING TO INDIA. Ed. George Orwell. London: Unwin, 1943.

> A selection of English-language broadcasts to India, written by E.M. Forster, Ritchie Calder, Cedric Dover, Hsiao Ch'ien, and others. Edited and with an introduction by GO.

WORKS EDITED BY OTHERS

ENGLAND, YOUR ENGLAND, AND OTHER ESSAYS. Ed. Sonia Orwell. London: Secker, 1953.

> A collection by his second wife of eleven essays, including "Why I Write," "Inside the Whale," "England, Your England," and two chapters from WIGAN PIER.

THE ORWELL READER: FICTION, ESSAYS, AND REPORTAGE BY GEORGE ORWELL. Ed. Richard H. Rovere. New York: Harcourt, 1956.

SHOOTING AN ELEPHANT AND OTHER ESSAYS. Ed. Sonia Orwell. London: Secker; New York: Harcourt, 1950.

> A collection by his second wife of eighteen essays, including "Shooting an Elephant," "A Hanging," "Politics vs. Literature," "Politics and the English Language," and a selection from a weekly column GO wrote for the British magazine TRIBUNE.

BIBLIOGRAPHY

McDowell, M. Jennifer. "George Orwell: Bibliographical Addenda." BB, 23 (1963), 224-29; BB, 24 (1963), 19-24, 36-40. Supplemented by I.R. Willison and Ian Angus: BB, 24 (1965), 180-87.

> Supplements the GO bibliography prepared by Zeke and White. Includes articles about GO from Poland, Yugoslavia, and the USSR, as well as from the American and English Communist press.

Meyers, Jeffrey. "George Orwell: A Bibliography." BB, 31 (1974), 117-21.

> Lists virtually every important article and book that has been written on GO in English and in foreign languages.

──────. "George Orwell: A Selected Checklist." MFS, 21 (1975), 133-36.

> Supplements Meyers' earlier list of criticism.

Meyers, Jeffrey, and Valerie Meyers, eds. GEORGE ORWELL: AN ANNOTATED BIBLIOGRAPHY OF CRITICISM. New York: Garland, 1977.

> The best secondary bibliography on GO which gives concise annotations for five hundred items.

Zeke, Zoltan G., and William White. "George Orwell: A Selected Bibliography." BB, 23 (1961), 110-14.

> Includes a list of GO's collected essays as well as essays and reviews in periodicals and books. "The authors make no claim to completeness in this first Orwell bibliography."

──────. "Orwelliana." BB, 23 (1961-1962), 140-44, 166-68.

> Checklist of books, chapters in books, periodical articles and reviews of books by and about GO, and addenda listing of essays and reviews by GO.

BIOGRAPHY

Buddicom, Jacintha. ERIC AND US: A REMEMBRANCE OF GEORGE ORWELL. London: Frewin, 1974.

> A childhood friend's recollections of GO, "a first-hand record of Orwell's home life in the early years." Presents some new material and anecdotes. Covers the years 1903-27.

Crick, Bernard. GEORGE ORWELL: A LIFE. New York: Little, Brown, 1980.

> The most complete biography of GO. Crick had full access to GO's papers; offers insights concerning how "the books came to be written and published." Good commentary on GO's politics and prose style.

Gross, Miriam, ed. THE WORLD OF GEORGE ORWELL. New York: Simon and Schuster, 1971.

> A collection of eighteen essays by different writers, covering all of GO's life, his reputation, and his historical period. GO's political positions are also discussed. Several personal reminiscences present new facts about GO. Social conditions of the period as well as events in GO's life are presented in photographs. Historically interesting, but of little value to critical study.

Stansky, Peter, and William Abrahams. THE UNKNOWN ORWELL. London: Constable, 1972.

> A biography of GO's first thirty years that culminates with the publication of DOWN AND OUT, his first book. The study is not as revealing as the title might suggest and the thesis that "Blair was the man to whom things happened; Orwell the man who wrote about them" is not entirely convincing.

CRITICISM

Alldritt, Keith. THE MAKING OF GEORGE ORWELL: AN ESSAY IN LITERARY HISTORY. New York: St. Martin's, 1969.

> Argues that GO "began to write as an adherent of symbolism" but soon worked out "a new sense of the writer's function" and relationship with the reader. Attempts to go beyond studies that have treated GO as an isolated figure and discuss him as part of the history of the 30's and 40's, specifically the literary history of these periods. Extensive treatment of GO's prose accounts (DOWN AND OUT, HOMAGE, WIGAN PIER), but only brief discussion of essays.

Atkins, John Alfred. GEORGE ORWELL: A LITERARY AND BIOGRAPHICAL STUDY. New York: Ungar, 1954.

> Quotes much of GO's journalism.

Bal, Sant Singh. GEORGE ORWELL: THE ETHICAL IMAGINATION. Atlantic Highlands, N.J.: Humanities Press, 1981.

> Argues that GO's ethical principles are a "moving force behind his aesthetic." Bal provides a useful survey of GO's works and includes an excellent chapter on imperialism.

George Orwell

Beadle, Gordon B. "George Orwell and the Death of God." COLORADO QUARTERLY, 23 (1974), 51-63.

> Compares GO to Charles Dickens and shows why GO was "a moral rather than an ideological critic of society." From the Victorian tradition, GO believed in an "underdog" Christianity, stripped of its mysticism and hope.

Brander, Laurence. GEORGE ORWELL. New York: Longmans, 1954.

> A basic survey of GO's work by a critic who knew GO in the forties.

Calder, Jenni. CHRONICLES OF CONSCIENCE: A STUDY OF GEORGE ORWELL AND ARTHUR KOESTLER. Pittsburgh: Univ. of Pittsburgh Press, 1968.

> Calder compares GO and Koestler as prophets and revolutionaries. A valuable study of GO's political and social ideas.

Chanda, S.M. "George Orwell's Sense of Responsibility." LCRIT, 11, No. 3 (1974), 68-75.

> A rather incoherent article that examines some of GO's essays and concludes that he had "a remarkably strong sense of responsibility" in social and literary matters.

Churchill, R.C. DISAGREEMENTS: A POLEMIC ON CULTURE IN THE ENGLISH DEMOCRACY. London: Secker, 1950.

> Discusses GO's sentimental outlook in WIGAN PIER.

Dooley, D.J. "The Limitations of George Orwell." UTQ, 28 (1958), 291-300.

> A provocative essay that presents GO as a victim of his own "doublethink." Dooley makes a case that GO's books are interesting "as portraits of the mind of a man who . . . imprisoned himself inside the game he played."

Espey, David B. "George Orwell vs. Christopher Caudwell: Politics and Literary Criticism." ILLINOIS QUARTERLY, 36, No. 4 (1974), 46-60.

> Outlines the striking parallels between GO's and Caudwell's careers, although neither man knew the other. The fundamental difference between the critical outlooks of GO and Caudwell is that "Orwell can separate political and aesthetic judgments on a work or artist" but Caudwell cannot.

Fitzgerald, John J. "George Orwell's Social Compassion." DISCOURSE, 9 (1966), 219-26.

George Orwell

Discusses GO's DOWN AND OUT and WIGAN PIER. Fitzgerald says that "a deep social compassion not only animated his books but also motivated GO's mature and complex life.

Fyvel, T.R. "George Orwell and Eric Blair: Glimpses of a Dual Life." ENCOUNTER, 13, No. 1 (1959), 60-65.

A chatty note which reveals some "private secrets" about GO through interviews with relatives who knew him. Brief discussion of WIGAN PIER and HOMAGE.

Glicksberg, Charles I. "The Literary Contribution of George Orwell." ARQ, 10 (1954), 234-45.

A superficial survey of GO's novels, accounts, and a few critical essays.

Griffin, C.W. "Orwell and the English Language." AUDIENCE, 7, No. 1 (1960), 63-76.

Discusses the current crisis of the English language and is only superficially related to GO. "Orwell reminds us we are not powerless in the fight against slovenly language."

Harris, Harold J. "Orwell's Essays and 1984." TCL, 4 (1959), 154-61.

Demonstrates that in GO's essays there can be found many of the raw materials which were later to be reworked into 1984.

Highet, Gilbert. "The Outsider." In A CLERK OF OXENFORD: ESSAYS ON LITERATURE AND LIFE. New York: Oxford Univ. Press, 1954. Pp. 62-68.

Briefly discusses GO's life and works. Highet sees GO as a displeased person: "Throughout much of his life he was on the outside looking in, and during the rest he was a prisoner yearning to escape."

Hodge, Bob, and Roger Fowler. "Orwellian Linguistics." In LANGUAGE AND CONTROL. Ed. Roger Fowler, Bob Hodge, Gunther Kress, and Tony Trew. London: Routledge, 1979. Pp. 6-25.

The authors downplay the significance of GO's essays "Politics and the English Language" (COLLECTED ESSAYS, IV) and "The English Language" (COLLECTED ESSAYS, III), and argue that his novel 1984 is his "major work on language."

Hoggart, Richard. "George Orwell and THE ROAD TO WIGAN PIER." CRITQ, 7 (1965), 72-85.

A thumbnail sketch of GO's life and class origins. "WIGAN PIER, more than any other books of Orwell's, shows a host of contradictions in his thinking" because socialism was, at that time, fairly new to him.

──────. "Introduction to THE ROAD TO WIGAN PIER." In GEORGE ORWELL: A COLLECTION OF CRITICAL ESSAYS. Twentieth Century Views. Ed. Raymond Williams. Englewood Cliffs, N.J.: Prentice-Hall, 1974. Pp. 34-51.

> Calls WIGAN PIER GO's "first directly political book." Hoggart attempts to reconstruct GO's political and social philosophy at the time that he wrote the book.

Hollis, Christopher. A STUDY OF GEORGE ORWELL: THE MAN AND HIS WORKS. Chicago: Regnery, 1956.

> A biographical-critical study of GO by a personal acquaintance. Sketchy treatment of GO's formative years, and an expressed unwillingness to "probe further into private secrets." Full discussion of essays and prose accounts: Hollis' main purpose is to criticize GO's writings and explain his ideas.

Hopkinson, Tom. GEORGE ORWELL. Writers and Their Work. London: Longmans, Green, 1962.

> A basic, sympathetic introduction to GO's life and works, which includes discussion of his social criticism. Hopkinson values the essays and DOWN AND OUT, but calls WIGAN PIER his "worst book." Includes a brief bibliography.

Ingle, Stephen J. "The Politics of George Orwell: A Reappraisal." QQ, 80 (1973), 22-33.

> An interesting, well-supported argument which covers most of GO's career. Ingle argues that GO's "sometimes contradictory views were more personal and moral than political, and that he was never really a socialist at any time in his life."

Jamal, Zahir. "Orwell in Spain." RMS, 20 (1976), 54-64.

> Detailed facts about militia life in the Spanish revolution as background information for HOMAGE. GO's book reveals the innocence and the "miasma" of lying that were part of the revolution.

Kalechofsky, Roberta. GEORGE ORWELL. Modern Literature Monograph Series. New York: Ungar, 1973.

> A general introduction to GO's life and works. Brief and sometimes superficial discussions of GO's essays and prose. The discussion of WIGAN PIER is helpful and more complete.

Katz, Wendy R. "Imperialism and Patriotism: Orwell's Dilemma in 1940." MSLC, 3 (1980), 99-105.

> Discusses in detail three of GO's wartime essays, "Culture and Democracy," "Fascism and Democracy," and "Patriots and Revolutionaries." These essays are not in COLLECTED ESSAYS, but they implicitly refute "his anti-war position" and show his turn of mind to support the war against Germany and Italy. All these essays stress the need for democratic socialism in Britain.

Keskinen, Kenneth. "'Shooting an Elephant'--an Essay to Teach." EJ, 55 (1966), 669-75.

> GO's style, tone and content are shown to be relevant for the 1960's classroom.

King, Carlyle. "The Politics of George Orwell." UTQ, 26 (1956), 79-91.

> A didactic essay valuable in that it links concisely many of GO's writings to the political experience of imperialism.

Kirk, Russell. "George Orwell's Despair." INTERCOLLEGIATE REVIEW, 5, No. 1 (1968), 21-25.

> A conservative's analysis of GO. Kirk argues that GO's socialism "scarcely can be called a position at all, but only an agonized leap in the dark." GO despaired over the conditions of modern society.

Kubal, David L. "DOWN AND OUT IN PARIS AND LONDON: The Conflict of Art and Politics." MQ, 12 (1971), 199-201.

> Justifies GO's dealing with politics in his works written in the 1930's. Yet GO also felt the need to raise political writing above propaganda to the level of art.

_____. OUTSIDE THE WHALE: GEORGE ORWELL'S ART AND POLITICS. Notre Dame, Ind.: Univ. of Notre Dame Press, 1972.

> A rather superficial study which attempts to relate the political and literary strains in GO's work. Kubal treats some of GO's essays as well as DOWN AND OUT, HOMAGE, and WIGAN PIER.

Land, Berel. "The Politics and Art of Decency: Orwell's Medium." SAQ, 75 (1976), 424-33.

> Discusses a few of GO's essays in detail. Land maintains that GO's essays show a "remarkable power" and are animated by "the principle of moral action."

George Orwell

Lee, Robert A. ORWELL'S FICTION. Notre Dame, Ind.: Univ. of Notre Dame Press, 1969.

>   Contains a chapter discussion of HOMAGE.

Lief, Ruth Ann. HOMAGE TO OCEANIA: THE PROPHETIC VISION OF GEORGE ORWELL. Columbus: Ohio State Univ. Press, 1969.

>   Superficial and unsatisfactory discussion of GO's critical and historical writing, including essays about automation, alienation, and totalitarianism. Lief concludes that GO was "remarkable for political passion and insight."

McNelly, Cleo. "On Not Teaching Orwell." CE, 38 (1977), 553-66.

>   GO's essays are prime examples of how not to teach composition because their levels of style and content do not meet the experience of today's students.

Mellichamp, Leslie. "George Orwell and the Ethics of Revolutionary Politics." MODA, 9 (1965), 272-78.

>   Discusses in labored detail three aspects of the ethical difficulty posed by revolutionary politics in a controversial passage from GO's late essay "Writers and Leviathan" (SUCH, SUCH WERE THE JOYS).

Meyers, Jeffrey. "'An Affirming Flame': Orwell's HOMAGE TO CATALONIA." ARQ, 27 (1971), 3-22.

>   Argues that GO's psychological motivations and needs as well as the pattern of historical events contributed to the mixed form that HOMAGE is. Meyers tries to show that the greatness of HOMAGE stems from its embodiment of GO's own honesty, idealism, and courage.

_____. "Orwell's Painful Childhood." ARIELE, 3, No. 1 (1972), 54-61.

>   Traces GO's guilt feelings and "masochistic strain" to traumatic experiences in his early childhood. Meyers argues that GO ultimately transcended his personal guilt by channelling it into "effective social and political thought and action."

_____. A READER'S GUIDE TO GEORGE ORWELL. Totowa, N.J.: Littlefield and Adams, 1977.

>   Concise but perceptive analysis, including discussions of GO's essays, DOWN AND OUT, WIGAN PIER, and HOMAGE.

_____, ed. GEORGE ORWELL: THE CRITICAL HERITAGE. Boston: Routledge and Kegan Paul, 1975.

Revealing collection of contemporary reviews which trace the
critical reputation of such works as DOWN AND OUT, WIGAN
PIER, HOMAGE, and GO's critical essay collections.

O'Flinn, J. P. "Orwell on Literature and Society." CE, 31 (1970), 603-12.

    Discusses GO's literary criticism, which has much to say
about how "society both influences and is influenced by its
writers."

Oxley, B. T. GEORGE ORWELL. Arco Literary Critiques Series. New York:
Arco, 1969.

    A brief, introductory guide for undergraduates studying GO
for the first time.

Pawling, Chris. "George Orwell and the Documentary in the Thirties." L&H,
No. 4 (Autumn 1976), 81-93.

    Examines the influence of Dickens' liberal humanism and GO's
own nostalgia for Edwardian England upon depictions of the
working class in WIGAN PIER and DOWN AND OUT.

Philmus, Robert M. "The Language of Utopia." SLITI, 6, No. 2 (1973),
61-78.

    Explores the discussion of Swift's GULLIVER'S TRAVELS in GO's
essay "Politics vs. Literature" (SHOOTING AN ELEPHANT).
Philmus argues that GO's outlook and language fit a closed
social order better than they did utopian or anti-utopian modes.

Ramsey, Roger. "'Down in Paris': Orwell's First Novel." ARQ, 32 (1976),
154-70.

    Sees DOWN AND OUT as only ostensibly an autobiographical
account that "partakes of a number of fictional techniques."
An interesting essay about the "nonfictional novel" and the
co-existence of autobiography and fiction.

Rank, Hugh. "Mr. Orwell, Mr. Schlesinger, and the Language." CCC, 28
(1977), 159-65.

    A provocative article that points out some "serious stylistic
flaws" and questionable assumptions in GO's classic essay on
politics and language (SHOOTING AN ELEPHANT).

Rees, Richard. GEORGE ORWELL: FUGITIVE FROM THE CAMP OF VICTORY.
Carbondale: Southern Illinois Univ. Press, 1962.

    Rees, an acquaintance of GO's, gives his "seasoned memories

of the man" as well as some penetrating critical analysis of GO's works and ideas.

Rieff, Philip. "George Orwell and the Post-Liberal Imagination." KR, 16 (1954), 49-70.

> Discusses GO's WIGAN PIER, DOWN AND OUT, and the essay "Inside the Whale" (INSIDE THE WHALE). Rieff argues that GO was the perfect liberal, but with a strain of "residual ambiguity."

Ringbom, Hakan. GEORGE ORWELL AS ESSAYIST: A STYLISTIC STUDY. Abo, Finland: Obo Akademi, 1973.

> Technical, but original study which provides concrete analysis of some characteristic stylistic features of GO's essays. Appendixes provide statistical tables.

Ross, William T. "'My Theme is Poverty': Orwell's DOWN AND OUT IN PARIS AND LONDON." MODERNIST STUDIES: LITERATURE AND CULTURE 1920-1940, 1, No. 2 (1974), 31-39.

> Argues that in DOWN AND OUT, GO "deliberately courted poverty . . . to expiate his own guilt" for having served "the cause of oppression and imperialism" as a policeman in Burma.

Sandison, Alan. THE LAST MAN IN EUROPE: AN ESSAY ON GEORGE ORWELL. London: Macmillan, 1974.

> Stressing religious tradition, Sandison describes GO's "fundamental moral sympathies" and in doing so exposes "the nature of his creative vision and the impulse behind it." Some discussion of DOWN AND OUT, WIGAN PIER, and HOMAGE along these lines.

Scruggs, Charles. "George Orwell and Jonathan Swift: A Literary Relationship." SAQ, 76 (1977), 177-89.

> Although GO criticized Swift's politics in an essay, a fuller comparison of the two writers' works reveals that their basic cause was the same: "to free man from the delusions of cant and hypocrisy."

Shapiro, Marjorie. "George Orwell's Criticism." CONNR, 6, No. 2 (1973), 70-75.

> Demonstrates that GO wrote practical criticism about literature, often about the relationship of literature to politics. Numerous essays by GO are discussed briefly.

Small, Christopher. THE ROAD TO MINILUV: GEORGE ORWELL, THE STATE, AND GOD. London: Gollancz, 1975.

> A comprehensive discussion of GO's works, which "exhibit a clear sequence, as linked parts of a continuous movement, or journey." Brief discussion of selected essays, DOWN AND OUT, HOMAGE, and WIGAN PIER, but valuable perspective for integrating these with GO's novels, poems, and career.

Smith, Malcolm. "George Orwell, War and Politics in the 1930's." L&H, 6 (1980), 219-34.

> A good background essay which examines the intellectual and emotional conceptions of war during the period 1910-1950 to show that GO's political writings on the topic are more typical than individualistic.

Smyer, Richard I. "Loss of Innocence in George Orwell's DOWN AND OUT IN PARIS AND LONDON." SOUTH DAKOTA REVIEW, 8, No. 4 (1970), 75-83.

> Smyer argues that DOWN AND OUT expresses GO's lost sexual innocence and growing antisensuality.

Sperber, Murray A. "'Marx: G.O.'s Dog': A Study of Politics and Literature in George Orwell's HOMAGE TO CATALONIA." Dr, 52 (1972), 236-36.

> Important Marxist analysis. Sperber argues that GO defined his political position on the Spanish Civil War after he returned from Spain. The dialectical structure of HOMAGE is helpful in conveying the many levels of reality in the Spanish Civil War.

Stevenson, John. "Myth and Reality: Britain in the 1930's." In CRISIS AND CONTROVERSY: ESSAYS IN HONOUR OF A.J.P. TAYLOR. Ed. Alan Sked and Chris Cole. New York: St. Martin's, 1976. Pp. 90-109.

> Drawing on economic statistics, Stevenson places GO's WIGAN PIER in perspective: the book was not wholly representative of Britain's 1930's depression.

Thomas, Edward Morely. ORWELL. New York: Barnes and Noble, 1968.

> Perceptive comments on GO's rhetorical style. The final chapter especially has concrete analysis and valuable observations. Thomas maintains that the body of GO's essays is equal to his finest work.

Thompson, E. P. "Inside Which Whale?" In GEORGE ORWELL: A COLLECTION OF CRITICAL ESSAYS. Twentieth Century Views. Ed. Raymond Williams. Englewood Cliffs, N.J.: Prentice-Hall, 1974. Pp. 80-88.

George Orwell

    Charges that GO's "Inside the Whale" (INSIDE THE WHALE AND OTHER ESSAYS) is "an apology for quietism." Because of GO's "profound political pessimism," he tended, after a certain point, simply to give up on a problem.

_____. "Outside the Whale." In his OUT OF APATHY. London: Stevens, 1960. Pp. 141-94.

    Discusses GO's HOMAGE, WIGAN PIER, and selected essays while developing the point that socialism "must grow from existing strengths."

Trilling, Lionel. "George Orwell and the Politics of Truth." In GEORGE ORWELL: A COLLECTION OF CRITICAL ESSAYS. Twentieth Century Views. Ed. Raymond Williams. Englewood Cliffs, N.J.: Prentice-Hall, 1974. Pp. 62-79.

    High praise for the significance of GO's HOMAGE. GO was both an intellectual and an activist; the book is both a record of personal experience and "a testimony to the nature of modern life."

Vorhees, Richard J. "George Orwell: Rebellion and Responsibility." SAQ, 53 (1954), 556-65.

    The contradictions in GO's life can be explained by the clash within him between a strong sense of responsibility and the feeling of rebellion which developed from his experiences with various social institutions.

_____. "George Orwell as Critic." PRS, 28 (1954), 105-12.

    An interesting and valuable article which treats the variety of GO's critical essays. GO was interested in the ordinary man as reader.

_____. THE PARADOX OF GEORGE ORWELL. Lafayette, Ind.: Purdue Univ. Press, 1961.

    An original and valuable study, pursuing three main lines of paradox running through GO's life and writing: 1) GO was a rebel with a remarkably strong sense of responsibility; 2) GO was horrified by large concentrations of power, but he was determined to resist them; 3) GO crusaded for a socialistic society, yet he had important reservations about socialism.

Wain, John. "George Orwell as a Writer of Polemic." In GEORGE ORWELL: A COLLECTION OF CRITICAL ESSAYS. Twentieth Century Views. Ed. Raymond Williams. Englewood Cliffs, N.J.: Prentice-Hall, 1974. Pp. 89-102.

An intelligent and stimulating essay which demonstrates that the Renaissance "kind" that GO's works belong to is the polemic. Various works are related to the definition of the writer as polemicist.

───────. "Orwell in Perspective." NEW WORLD WRITING, No. 12 (1957), 84-96.

A valuable essay in which Wain maintains that much of the criticism of GO has been misdirected because critics have not "understood what kinds of books he was writing."

Warburg, Fredric J. "From Wigan to Barcelona." In AN OCCUPATION FOR GENTLEMEN. Boston: Houghton Mifflin, 1960. Pp. 220-38.

Reminiscences of GO by his publisher, whose policy of "antifascist publishing which paid no heed to communist susceptibilities" was in effect at the end of 1936. Warburg discusses the contradictory elements in WIGAN PIER and HOMAGE.

Warncke, Wayne. "George Orwell on T.S. Eliot." WHR, 26 (1972), 265-70.

Examines several of GO's essays and reviews that deal with T.S. Eliot's poetry. At various times, GO referred to the aloofness of Eliot's poetry.

───────. "George Orwell's Critical Approach to Literature." SHR, 2 (1968), 484-98.

A substantial essay which discusses many of GO's major critical essays and attempts to see them against the larger perspectives of the history and modes of literary criticism.

Watson, George. "Orwell and the Spectrum of European Politics." JES, 1 (1971), 191-97.

High praise for THE COLLECTED ESSAYS, JOURNALISM, AND LETTERS OF GEORGE ORWELL, above. Watson matches GO's commentaries with the various political events of the 1930's and 1940's and concludes that they provide "the best literary chronicle of England."

Williams, Raymond. GEORGE ORWELL. New York: Viking, 1971.

A provocative, tightly argued study of GO's life and works. Williams argues that GO made "a whole series of attempts to find a new social identity," and that the strength of his work is due to a combination of "the energy of his renunciation" and his openness to each new experience. However, Williams regrets a "characteristic coldness" and narrowness in GO's vision.

George Orwell

———. "George Orwell." In his CULTURE AND SOCIETY, 1780-1950. New York: Harper and Row, 1958. Pp. 276-84.

> A brief but useful chapter which argues that a key concept toward understanding GO is "the paradox of the exile." Williams places GO in a whole tradition of twentieth-century writers who reject compromise but also feel a social impotence.

Wollheim, Richard. "Orwell Reconsidered." PR, 27 (1960), 82-97.

> Harsh criticism of WIGAN PIER. Wollheim calls the book "out-of date journalism" and points out the limitations of GO as a theorist who poses the question: "What is it, really, to be a Socialist?"

Woodcock, George. THE CRYSTAL SPIRIT: A STUDY OF GEORGE ORWELL. Boston: Little, Brown, 1966.

> An important and competent study blending recollections and criticism. Woodcock argues that GO's writings cannot be isolated from his "endlessly controversial" personality. In part 4 of the book, Woodcock provides an especially valuable discussion of GO as critic and prose stylist. Politically, Woodcock identifies himself and GO as "dissident members of the literary left of the 1930's and 1940's."

WORLD REVIEW, No. 16 (1950), 3-60.

> A scarce collection of essays with contributions by Bertrand Russell, Stephen Spender, Aldous Huxley, Herbert Read, Malcolm Muggeridge, and T.R. Fyvel. Several of the essays deal with GO's life as well as WIGAN PIER and HOMAGE.

Young, Dudley. "Still Life Inside the Whale." PNR, 18 (1980), 39-49.

> Praises GO's essay "Inside the Whale" (INSIDE THE WHALE) and speculates on its extended implications. Young argues that GO slights the subject of piety and sex in the essay.

Zwerdling, Alex. ORWELL AND THE LEFT. New Haven, Conn.: Yale Univ. Press, 1974.

> An impressive and objective study of GO's politics with references to GO's COLLECTED ESSAYS; perceptive analysis of DOWN AND OUT, HOMAGE, and WIGAN PIER is also provided. Zwerdling demonstrates that GO became the kind of Socialist he was for a number of reasons, some of them contradictory. In the 1930's and 1940's, GO searched for literary forms that would be appropriate for advancing the cause.

HERBERT READ (1893-1968)

NONFICTIONAL PROSE

ANARCHY AND ORDER: ESSAYS IN POLITICS. London: Faber, 1954.

A compilation of HR's political writings which collects several of his short, previous publications. It is a learned defense of anarchism; HR calls for a rejection of powerful, centralized governments of all political stripes in favor of small communities fostering individual liberty.

ANNALS OF INNOCENCE AND EXPERIENCE. London: Faber, 1940. As THE INNOCENT EYE. New York: Holt, 1947.

An autobiography recounting HR's pastoral childhood on a Yorkshire farm and his subsequent fall into experience at a spartan boarding school, in the city of Leeds, and in WWI. HR traces the development of his interest in poetry, in socialism, and the like. The volume is in part a compilation of previously published short pieces.

ART AND ALIENATION: THE ROLE OF THE ARTIST IN SOCIETY. London: Thames and Hudson; New York: Horizon Press, 1967.

The last of HR's studies of the place of art in society. Part 1 contains general essays on the alienation of the artist in technological civilization; part 2 contains essays on individual artists who have confronted the problem.

ART AND EDUCATION. Melbourne: Cheshire, 1964.

Five lectures on the visual arts delivered during a tour of Australia and New Zealand in 1963.

ART AND INDUSTRY: THE PRINCIPLES OF INDUSTRIAL DESIGN. London: Faber, 1934. New York: Horizon Press, 1954.

Herbert Read

> This argues that the aesthetic sense must be introduced in the machine age and its products; abstract art lends itself best to industrial design, according to HR. Several revised versions appeared beginning in 1944.

ART AND SOCIETY. London: Heinemann; New York: Macmillan, 1937.

> Originally lectures at the University of Liverpool, 1935-36. Rejecting Marx's artistic theory in maintaining the individualist nature of artistic creation, HR nonetheless maintains that the artist expresses the subconscious feelings of his community. The book was revised several times, beginning in 1945.

ART AND THE EVOLUTION OF MAN: LECTURE DELIVERED AT CONWAY HALL, LONDON, ON APRIL 10TH, 1951. London: Freedom Press, 1951.

> Not seen.

ART NOW: AN INTRODUCTION TO THE THEORY OF MODERN PAINTING AND SCULPTURE. London: Faber, 1933. New York: Harcourt Brace, 1937.

> A history of the origins and schools of modernist art, with sections on expressionism, cubism, and the like. The book was revised several times beginning in 1936.

THE ART OF JEAN ARP. New York: Abrams, 1968. As ARP. London: Thames and Hudson, 1968. New York: Praeger, 1969.

> A survey of the career of the artist and poet.

THE ART OF SCULPTURE. London: Faber; New York: Pantheon Books, 1956.

> Originally the A.W. Mellon Lectures in the Fine Arts, delivered in 1954. The book traces the historical development of sculpture and stresses the significance of free-standing form.

A COAT OF MANY COLOURS: OCCASIONAL ESSAYS. London: Routledge and Kegan Paul, 1945. New York: Horizon Press, 1956.

> A collection of seventy-one brief essays on artists and authors.

COLLECTED ESSAYS IN LITERARY CRITICISM. London: Faber, 1938. As THE NATURE OF LITERATURE. New York: Horizon Press, 1956.

> Essentially, the first part of this is taken from FORM IN MODERN POETRY and the second from SENSE OF GLORY, although REASON AND ROMANTICISM and IN DEFENSE OF SHELLEY also contribute essays.

A CONCISE HISTORY OF MODERN PAINTING. London: Thames and Hudson; New York: Praeger, 1959.

A survey of important groups and figures in modernist painting, such as Picasso, Kandinsky, and Klee, who have sought "not to reflect the visible, but to make visible."

A CONCISE HISTORY OF MODERN SCULPTURE. London: Thames and Hudson; New York: Praeger, 1964.

> The companion volume to CONCISE HISTORY OF MODERN PAINTING.

CONTEMPORARY BRITISH ART. Harmondsworth: Penguin Books, 1951.

> An amply illustrated survey. Several revised editions appeared beginning in 1954.

THE CONTRARY EXPERIENCE: AUTOBIOGRAPHIES. London: Faber; New York: Horizon Press, 1963.

> This reprints the contents of ANNALS OF INNOCENCE AND EXPERIENCE and adds "A War Diary" (constructed from HR's letters during the war) and "A Dearth of Wild Flowers" on the appearance and local history of Yorkshire.

THE CULT OF SINCERITY. London: Faber, 1968. New York: Horizon Press, 1969.

> HR's last major work. A credo of sorts, the first part of it contains his views on ethics, poetry, and politics. The second part consists of essays on men who have influenced his ideas: Eliot, Jung, Russell, Aldington, Lawrence, and Muir.

EDUCATION FOR PEACE. New York: Scribner's, 1949. London: Routledge and Kegan Paul, 1950.

> A collection of lectures and essays; all but the title essay were reprinted in REDEMPTION OF THE ROBOT.

EDUCATION THROUGH ART. London: Faber, 1943. New York: Pantheon Books, 1945.

> HR's major statement of the thesis "that art should be the basis of education." He examines such topics as the "aesthetic basis of discipline and morality."

ENGLISH POTTERY: ITS DEVELOPMENT FROM EARLY TIMES TO THE END OF THE EIGHTEENTH CENTURY. With Bernard Rackham. London: Benn, 1924.

> HR's first book. Rackham was a colleague at the Victoria and Albert Museum.

Herbert Read

ENGLISH PROSE STYLE. London: Bell; New York: Holt, 1928.

> A guide to prose style, with examples drawn from great stylists, of whom Swift is the most consistently fine according to HR. The first section discusses such topics as onomatopoeia and metaphor; the second includes a survey of various kinds of prose. Revised editions were issued by HR beginning in 1942.

ENGLISH STAINED GLASS. London and New York: Putnam's, 1926.

> An illustrated history.

FORM IN MODERN POETRY. London: Sheed and Ward, 1932.

> The work in fact focuses on nineteenth-century poets. It praises "organic" form in poetry, and, bringing in Freud, argues that the poet should write from the "personality" (ego) rather than from "character" (the superego, more or less).

THE FORMS OF THINGS UNKNOWN: ESSAYS TOWARDS AN AESTHETIC PHILOSOPHY. London: Faber; New York: Horizon Press, 1960.

> The companion volume to ICON AND IDEA. It is a learned, heavily Jungian study of the workings of the creative imagination.

THE GRASS ROOTS OF ART. London: Drummond; New York: Wittenborn, 1947.

> A compilation of various lectures of art. It enunciates such typical Readian themes as the necessity of reconciling art and machine, the inappropriateness of didactic art, and the conducive influence of small communities to artistic production.

HENRY MOORE: A STUDY OF HIS LIFE AND WORK. London: Thames and Hudson, 1965. New York: Praeger, 1966.

> A study of Moore, the great modernist sculptor and HR's friend, that is organized chronologically by period. HR judges Moore to be a great artist because of his prolific output, his mastery of form, and his penetration of life.

ICON AND IDEA: THE FUNCTION OF ART IN THE DEVELOPMENT OF HUMAN CONSCIOUSNESS. London: Faber; Cambridge, Mass.: Harvard Univ. Press, 1955.

> Originally the Norton Lectures of 1953-54. It argues that "the image always precedes the idea in the development of human consciousness"; therefore art is crucial to human evolution.

IN DEFENCE OF SHELLEY AND OTHER ESSAYS. London: Heinemann, 1936.

> A collection of nine previously published essays on literary and artistic topics. The odd title essay begins the defense of Shelley against T. S. Eliot's charge of puerility by positing homosexual tendencies in the Romantic poet.

A LETTER TO A YOUNG PAINTER. London: Thames and Hudson; New York: Horizon Press, 1962.

> Part 1, the letter, emphasizes the sacrifice demanded of the artist; part 2 consists of numerous brief essays on modern artists; part 3 contains longer essays on abstract art. One of these, "The Social Significance of Abstract Art," argues abstraction is an attempt to get at the vital essence of life, hidden by mechanization.

THE MEANING OF ART. London: Faber, 1931. As THE ANATOMY OF ART: AN INTRODUCTION TO THE PROBLEMS OF ART AND AESTHETICS. New York: Dodd, Mead, 1932.

> A collection of fragments from essays first published in the BBC's LISTENER. The first section deals with aesthetic issues and the elements of the art work; the second surveys the history of art. The book has been revised several times by HR beginning in 1936.

THE ORIGINS OF FORM IN ART. London: Thames and Hudson; New York: Horizon Press, 1965.

> A collection of nine essays on the subject. These include pieces on "The Origin of Form in the Plastic Arts," on "The Disintegration of Form in Modern Art," and on the aesthetics of Ortega y Gasset.

PHASES OF ENGLISH POETRY. London: Hogarth, 1928. New York: Harcourt, Brace, 1929.

> A survey of English poets from medieval balladists to contemporaries that seeks to link periods with subjects (the Romantic period treats nature) and that sees the modernists as affording "the narrowest possible appeal--the poet appealing to himself alone."

THE PHILOSOPHY OF MODERN ART: COLLECTED ESSAYS. London: Faber, 1952. New York: Horizon Press, 1953.

> A collection of fourteen essays. Several are on individual painters such as Klee, Moore, and Picasso. The most interesting of the general essays, "Surrealism and the Romantic Principle," identifies classicism with "the forces of oppression" destroyed by surrealism.

Herbert Read

POETRY AND EXPERIENCE. London: Vision, 1967.

> A collection of nine essays on literature, three reprinted from REASON AND ROMANTICISM. The title piece argues that poetry written from immediate experience will not be as good as poetry written when the subconscious is given time to work over experience.

THE POLITICS OF THE UNPOLITICAL. London: Routledge and Kegan Paul, 1943.

> This expresses HR's important antipathy to centralized governments, whether fascist or democratic, and in the first chapter lays out a social plan stressing the family unit and self-governing guilds. Most of the book, however, deals with the plight of the contemporary artist; his work is treated as a "commodity" in democratic society, for example.

REASON AND ROMANTICISM: ESSAYS IN LITERARY CRITICISM. London: Faber and Gwyer, 1926.

> HR's first book on literature, a collection of eleven essays. Their emphasis on the emotive and psychological components of literature foretells major emphases in HR's criticism.

THE REDEMPTION OF THE ROBOT: MY ENCOUNTER WITH EDUCATION THROUGH ART. New York: Trident Press, 1966. London: Faber, 1970.

> This reprints most of EDUCATION FOR PEACE and some later essays. One of these, "The Redemption of the Robot," discusses the need for aesthetic education for the industrial worker.

THE SENSE OF GLORY: ESSAYS IN CRITICISM. Cambridge: The Univ. Press, 1929.

> A collection of nine pieces from the TIMES LITERARY SUPPLEMENT treating English and French authors who reflect the "glory" of western civilization from the age of chivalry (Froissart) to the twentieth century (Henry James). James, for example, is praised for combining a European sensibility with his native, puritanical morality.

THE TENTH MUSE: ESSAYS IN CRITICISM. London: Routledge and Kegan Paul, 1957. New York: Horizon Press, 1958.

> A collection of forty essays on literature and art. Two of the most interesting are "Ezra Pound" (treating the development of his free verse), and "The Image in Modern English Poetry," which argues that, failing to discover a unifying mythology, modernist poetry does succeed in being imagistically vivid.

TO HELL WITH CULTURE AND OTHER ESSAYS ON ART AND SOCIETY.
London: Routledge and Kegan Paul; New York: Schocken Books, 1963.

> A collection of fifteen essays, several drawn from POLITICS
> OF THE UNPOLITICAL. One of the more interesting, "The
> Problem of Pornography," proposes sublimation through art as
> a cure for the vice.

THE TRUE VOICE OF FEELING: STUDIES IN ENGLISH ROMANTIC POETRY.
London: Faber; New York: Pantheon Books, 1953.

> An expansion of such books as FORM IN MODERN POETRY.
> It traces the evolution of "organic form" from Wordsworth and
> Coleridge down to Hulme, Pound, and Eliot.

TRUTH IS MORE SACRED. New York: Horizon Press; London: Routledge and
Kegan Paul, 1961.

> This odd volume consists of correspondence between HR and
> Edward Dahlberg, who finds modern literature introverted and
> effete. The figures discussed are Joyce, Lawrence, James,
> Graves, Eliot, and Pound.

WORDSWORTH. London: Cape, 1930. New York: Cape and Smith, 1931.

> Originally the Clark lectures at Cambridge in 1930, this critical
> biography argues that both Wordsworth's great creative period
> and subsequent decline result from his emotional responses to the
> affair with Annette Vallon.

WORKS EDITED BY OTHERS

HERBERT READ: SELECTED WRITINGS: POETRY AND CRITICISM. Ed. Allen
Tate. New York: Horizon Press, 1964.

> Includes five essays on "literary criticism," four on "art criticism,"
> three on "social criticism," and three on "education."

BIBLIOGRAPHY

Gerwing, Howard, comp. "A Checklist of the Herbert Read Archive in the
McPherson Library of the University of Victoria." MHREV, 9 (1969), 192-258.

> Especially useful for its sections on HR's editing of books and
> contributions to books.

Richardson, Jillian, comp. SIR HERBERT READ. Guides to the Published Works
of Art Historians. Bournemouth, Engl.: Bournemouth and Poole College of
Art, 1970.

Herbert Read

A chronological listing of HR's articles and books on art.

Woodcock, George, comp. "Bibliography." In his HERBERT READ: THE STREAM AND THE SOURCE. London: Faber, 1972. Pp. 293-97.

The NCBEL aside, this is the fullest listing of HR's books available.

BIOGRAPHY

HERBERT READ: A MEMORIAL SYMPOSIUM. Ed. Robin Skelton. London: Methuen, 1970.

As well as critical articles (listed separately) this handy reprint of the January 1961 number of THE MALAHAT REVIEW contains several brief elegiac memoirs on HR by Denise Levertov, Michael Hamburger, Henry Moore, Ben Nicholson, and Roland Penrose.

Woodcock, George. HERBERT READ: THE STREAM AND THE SOURCE. London: Faber, 1972.

This contains a brief biographical sketch.

CRITICISM

Berry, Francis. HERBERT READ. Writers and Their Work. London: Longmans Green, 1953.

Much of this brief study discusses HR's poetry; the treatment of the criticism, however, is informative and balanced. Coleridge's distinction between fancy and imagination, and Keats's distinction between personality and character are seen as central to HR's ideas and are traced briefly in his writings.

Black, Sam. "Herbert Read: His Contribution to Art Education and to Education through Art." MHREV, 9 (1969), 57-65.

A review of HR's educational theories that frequently cites GRASS ROOTS OF ART.

Davie, Donald. "Herbert Read's Romanticism." TWENTIETH CENTURY, 153 (1953), 295-301.

A scathing review of TRUE VOICE OF FEELING, especially antagonistic to HR's ideal of free verse.

Fishman, Solomon. "Herbert Read." In his THE INTERPRETATION OF ART: ESSAYS ON THE ART CRITICISM OF JOHN RUSKIN, WALTER PATER, CLIVE BELL, ROGER FRY, AND HERBERT READ. Berkeley and Los Angeles: Univ. of California Press, 1963. Pp. 143-86.

A lengthy, learned review of HR's theories on visual art that demonstrates his affinities and disagreements with the extreme positions represented by Ruskin and Fry.

──────. "Sir Herbert Read: Poetics vs. Criticism." JAAC, 13 (1954), 156-62.

> Drawing on works such as COAT OF MANY COLOURS, Fishman argues that HR's antiintellectual poetic theory has negatively affected his critical theory.

Fraser, G. S. "The Last English Imagist: On Sir Herbert Read." ENCOUNTER 28, No. 1 (1967), 86-90.

> Notes the inadequacies of HR's Imagist stance--the disbelief in paraphrasable poetic meaning, the dislike of meter--expressed in his prose note in his COLLECTED POEMS.

Glicksberg, Charles I. "Herbert Read: Reason and Romanticism." UTQ, 16 (1946), 60-67.

> A handy review of HR's main ideas.

Grattan, C. Hartley. "Gentlemen, I Give You Herbert Read." HARPER'S, 194 (1947), 535-42.

> A general review of HR's thought which identifies his critical virtues as "his eclecticism and his libertarianism."

Gropius, Walter. "On Herbert Read." MHREV, 9 (1969), 27-30.

> A summary of HR's ideas in EDUCATION THROUGH ART.

Harder, Worth Travis. A CERTAIN ORDER: THE DEVELOPMENT OF HERBERT READ'S THEORY OF POETRY. The Hague: Mouton, 1971.

> A detailed examination of the development of HR's romantic aesthetic, focusing on the years 1918-1938. Harder identifies HR's belief in the intuitive rather than cognitive nature of the poetic act as the unifying element of this development.

Häusermann, H. W. "The Development of Herbert Read." In HERBERT READ: AN INTRODUCTION TO HIS WORK BY VARIOUS HANDS. Ed. Henry Treece. London: Faber, 1944. Pp. 52-80.

> An excellent tracing of the ways HR's ideas on art changed from the 1920's to the 1940's.

Hendry, J. F. "The Philosophy of Herbert Read." In HERBERT READ: AN INTRODUCTION TO HIS WORK BY VARIOUS HANDS. Ed. Henry Treece. London: Faber, 1944. Pp. 108-15.

> A superficial review of HR's ideas on politics and art.

Hodin, J. P. "Herbert Read's Philosophy of Art." NORSEMAN, 9 (1951), 278-84.

>Places HR in the tradition of artistic and social criticism of Ruskin, Morris, and Fry.

Murry, John Middleton. "The Anarchism of Mr. Herbert Read (I)." ADELPHI, 17 (1941), 369-75; "The Anarchism of Mr. Herbert Read (II)." ADELPHI, 17 (1941), 401-05.

>Murry notes the vagueness of HR's term "natural law" in PHILOSOPHY OF ANARCHISM (ANARCHY AND ORDER).

Raine, Kathleen. "Herbert Read as a Literary Critic." SR, 77 (1969), 405-25.

>An informative and balanced discussion of HR's attitudes toward various poetic movements and poets of his time. HR was too often attracted by the avant-garde, according to Raine.

Ramsay, A. A. W. "Psychology and Literary Criticism." CRITERION, 15 (1936), 627-43.

>An examination of HR's ideas concerning the neurotic sources of poetry and the antithesis of "character" formation and the poetic impulse, as expressed in such works as REASON AND ROMANTICISM and FORM IN MODERN POETRY. Both theories need qualification, according to Ramsay.

Ramsden, E. H. "Herbert Read's Philosophy of Art." In HERBERT READ: AN INTRODUCTION TO HIS WORK BY VARIOUS HANDS. Ed. Henry Treece. London: Faber, 1944. Pp. 42-51.

>Emphasizes the intuitive quality in HR's art criticism.

Ray, Paul C. "Sir Herbert Read and English Surrealism." JAAC, 24 (1966), 401-13.

>A good examination of how HR's increased emphasis in the early thirties on the role of the unconscious in poetic creation led him to embrace surrealism.

Tate, Allen. "Foreword." In his HERBERT READ: SELECTED WRITINGS: POETRY AND CRITICISM. New York: Horizon Press, 1964. Pp. 7-14.

>A brief discussion of the Coleridgean nature of HR's ideas on topics such as psychology and education.

_____. "The Philosopher of Freedom." MHREV, 9 (1969), 68-87.

>A good discussion of the development and principal tenets of HR's anarchistic social philosophy which quotes heavily from such works as POETRY AND ANARCHISM (ANARCHY AND ORDER).

Woodcock, George. HERBERT READ: THE STREAM AND THE SOURCE. London: Faber, 1972.

>   The fullest survey of HR's writings and ideas. Seeing HR as pulled between the antinomies of meditation and action, rationality and romanticism, Woodcock surveys his literary criticism in chapter 4, his art criticism in chapter 5, the extension of his critical ideas to social thought in chapter 6, and his social writings in chapters 7 and 8.

I.A. RICHARDS (1893-1979)

There are a number of handbooks and textbooks that IAR developed with linguistic collaborators which are not listed here.

NONFICTIONAL PROSE

BASIC ENGLISH AND ITS USES. London: Kegan Paul; New York: Norton, 1943.

    Argues the need for an international "second" language. Outlines the history, aims, and rules of Basic English.

BASIC IN TEACHING: EAST AND WEST. London: Kegan Paul, 1935.

    IAR shows teachers how translating from ordinary to Basic English offers valuable exercise in linguistic skills. Mentions how Chinese students approach a verbal message and interpret novels to fit their own preformed categories.

BASIC RULES OF REASON. London: Kegan Paul, 1933.

    Written in Basic English, this slight book discusses theories of knowledge, connections, and instruments in simple language. IAR surveys the opinions of other thinkers and offers his own views on the nature of thought and logic.

BEYOND. London and New York: Harcourt, 1974.

    Analyzes and compares the dramatic perceptions, ideas, and language used in the ILIAD, REPUBLIC, THE DIVINE COMEDY, Job and other parts of the Bible. Eternal questions of freedom, fate, and justice are addressed.

COLERIDGE ON IMAGINATION. London: Kegan Paul, 1934. New York: Harcourt, 1935.

> Important study of Coleridge's critical theory about the power and meaning of words. Offers extended philosophical and psychological treatment of the relationships between subject and object, imagination and fancy, man and nature, thought and feeling in the works of Coleridge and other Romantic writers.

DESIGN FOR ESCAPE: WORLD EDUCATION THROUGH MODERN MEDIA. New York: Harcourt, 1968.

> In essays written over several years, IAR explores the meanings of the words in the book's title "in their interconnections." With an urgent voice, he warns against the "population-productivity threat" and militaristic schemes. The earth is in danger from both planlessness and calculated strategies of "power fiends." The use of innovative instructional methods, such as visual arts, is recommended for responsible education.

THE FOUNDATIONS OF AESTHETICS. London: Allen and Unwin, 1922. New York: Harcourt, 1925.

> With C.K. Ogden and James Wood. Surveys the various theories of aesthetics and concludes that beauty rests in the experience of the perceiver. The critic's job is to analyze precisely what impulses a work of art conveys to its audience.

HOW TO READ A PAGE: A COURSE IN EFFECTIVE READING, WITH AN INTRODUCTION TO A HUNDRED GREAT WORDS. New York: Norton, 1942. London: Kegan Paul, 1943.

> A philosophical-psychological guide to improved and close reading through a purposeful commitment. The reasons for misreading are discussed and the meanings of 103 keywords are clarified in detail. Some of the Basic words include: art, change, feeling, order, purpose, science, and work.

INTERPRETATION IN TEACHING. London: Kegan Paul; New York: Harcourt, 1938.

> IAR outlines practical applications of rhetoric, grammar, and logic for classroom teachers. He argues for increased attention to linguistic study. In a useful blend of general principles and specific examples, IAR treats such topics as metaphor, interpretation, translation, Basic English, usage, and definition.

LEARNING BASIC ENGLISH: A PRACTICAL HANDBOOK FOR ENGLISH-SPEAKING PEOPLE. With Christine Gibb. New York: Norton, 1945.

> A simplified and limited introduction to the vocabulary, rules, and grammar of the English language. The authors hope that the spread of an international language could foster "a more peaceful world."

I.A. Richards

THE MEANING OF MEANING: A STUDY OF THE INFLUENCE OF LANGUAGE UPON THOUGHT AND OF THE SCIENCE OF SYMBOLISM. With C. K. Ogden. London: Kegan Paul, 1923. New York: Harcourt, 1925.

> A pioneering study of semantics. Among other terms and concepts, the important distinction between the "symbolic" meaning of science and the "emotive" meaning of poetry is explained. Includes supplementary essays by B. Malinowski on meaning in primitive languages and by F. G. Crookshank on the theory of signs.

MENCIUS ON THE MIND: EXPERIMENTS IN MULTIPLE DEFINITION. London: Kegan Paul; New York: Harcourt, 1932.

> Includes passages in Chinese and English from Mencius, an important Oriental moralist and philosopher who lived 372-289 B.C. IAR discusses the problems of translation and interpretation that arise from studying Chinese "modes of meaning." He finds Mencius' view of psychology to be relevant to "the vexed question of science and value."

NATIONS AND PEACE. New York: Simon and Schuster, 1947.

> In "straight Basic English" and with a sense of urgency, IAR's brief sentences combine with illustrations by Ramon Gordon to announce better ideas for defining universal human needs and establishing peaceful governments. A new form of world government "to keep us safe from one another" is recommended.

THE PHILOSOPHY OF RHETORIC. London: Routledge; New York: Oxford Univ. Press, 1936.

> A series of six lectures on such rhetorical topics as: "The Aims of Discourse and Types of Context," "Some Criteria of Words," and "Metaphor." IAR urges that rhetoric "should be a study of misunderstanding and its remedies."

PRACTICAL CRITICISM: A STUDY OF LITERARY JUDGMENT. London: Kegan Paul, 1929. New York: Harcourt, 1930.

> Probably IAR's most famous and influential book. He applies theories outlined in PRINCIPLES OF LITERARY CRITICISM to a selection of unidentified poems that were analyzed and often misinterpreted by his students at Cambridge. His goal was to improve the understanding and grounds for judgment of literary works through the application of careful semantic analysis. Some of the ten difficulties readers have with poetry include: stock responses, sentimentality, doctrinal adhesions, and inhibition.

PRINCIPLES OF LITERARY CRITICISM. London: Kegan Paul, 1924. New York: Harcourt, 1925.

I.A. Richards

> One of the most important critical works of the century. IAR employs a psychological foundation to foster the comprehension of poetic meaning. Some key considerations are feeling, tone, and intention. Also covers poetry in relation to value and belief. Historical and biographical background are deemphasized.

SCIENCE AND POETRY. London: Kegan Paul; New York: Norton, 1926.

> Brief but provocative speculations on how new developments in psychology and other sciences will change our beliefs and outlooks. Discusses the nature and future of poetry in general as well as specific poetry by Hardy, De la Mare, Yeats, and Lawrence.

SO MUCH NEARER: ESSAYS TOWARD A WORLD ENGLISH. New York: Harcourt, 1968.

> Ten important essays on the common theme of "what man collectively could be doing for himself" with such new technological advances as computers, mass media, and press. IAR outlines several political and linguistic misunderstandings; he argues for a "World English." Other essays on education, language, and poetry.

SPECULATIVE INSTRUMENTS. London: Routledge and Kegan Paul; Chicago: Univ. of Chicago Press, 1955.

> A series of informal essays to foster clear comprehension of language and better interpretations of literature. Several selections reveal IAR's increasing attention to pedagogic concerns: "The Future of the Humanities," "Education and Culture," "The Idea of a University," and others. In a diagram he lists seven instruments of comprehending: indicating, characterizing, realizing, valuing, influencing, controlling, and purposing.

TECHNIQUES IN LANGUAGE CONTROL. With Christine Gibson. Rowley, Mass.: Newbury House, 1974.

> Advocates a revitalization of the American language through the precise study of "Every Man's English." Exercises in restatement help even the native speaker to grasp the meanings of words and passages and to communicate more effectively.

THE WRITTEN WORD. With Sheridan Baker and Jacques Barzun. Rowley, Mass.: Newbury House, 1971.

> IAR's two essays discuss the future of reading and instructional engineering. In the first essay he surveys the purposes of some of his earlier writings.

I.A. Richards

WORKS EDITED BY OTHERS

COMPLEMENTARITIES: UNCOLLECTED ESSAYS, I.A. RICHARDS. Ed. John Paul Russo. Cambridge, Mass.: Harvard Univ. Press, 1976.

> Collects twenty-seven essays: thirteen deal with critical theory ("Art and Science," "Emotion and Art," "Emotive Language Skill"); eleven deal with practical criticism ("Gerard Hopkins," "A Passage to Forster," "Lawrence as a Poet"); three present autobiographical information on IAR's tastes in sports and art. The essays were written between 1919 and 1975.

POETRIES; THEIR MEDIA AND ENDS: A COLLECTION OF ESSAYS BY I.A. RICHARDS PUBLISHED TO CELEBRATE HIS 80TH BIRTHDAY. Ed. Trevor Eaton. The Hague: Mouton, 1974.

> Collects seventeen essays, a few published for the first time. The essays cover topics in linguistics, philosophy, practical criticism, and semantics; all are related to the improvement of the educational process through the use of literature, especially poetry. The editor hopes the volume will provide "an up-to-date and unified account" of IAR's poetics.

BIBLIOGRAPHY

Karnani, Chetan, comp. CRITICISM, AESTHETICS AND PSYCHOLOGY: A STUDY OF THE WRITINGS OF I.A. RICHARDS. New Delhi: Arnold-Heinemann, 1977. Pp. 157-59.

> Includes a listing of sixteen books and ten articles by IAR. Also selectively lists writings on IAR (thirteen books and eight articles).

Russo, John P., ed. "A Bibliography of the Books, Articles, and Reviews of I.A. Richards." In I.A. RICHARDS: ESSAYS IN HIS HONOR. Ed. Reuben Brower, Helen Vendler, and John Hollander. New York: Oxford Univ. Press, 1973. Pp. 321-65.

> The most complete primary bibliography of IAR's works. Especially useful for its listing of IAR's many articles and reviews. IAR assisted in the preparation. The items are arranged in chronological order (1919-73). The annotations are superb: they often reproduce key quotations and list contents of the works.

Schiller, Jerome P., comp. I.A. RICHARDS' THEORY OF LITERATURE. New Haven, Conn.: Yale Univ. Press, 1969. Pp. 177-84.

> Includes a selective bibliography of works--both books and articles--by and about IAR.

CRITICISM

Abrams, M.H. "Belief and the Suspension of Disbelief." In LITERATURE AND BELIEF, ENGLISH INSTITUTE ESSAYS, 1957. Ed. M.H. Abrams. New York: Columbia Univ. Press, 1958. Pp. 1-30.

> Glancing reference to IAR's theories in SCIENCE AND POETRY and PRACTICAL CRITICISM as Abrams surveys the historical clash between "what poets say and what their readers believe to be true."

Belgion, Montgomery. "What is Criticism?" CRITERION, 10 (1930), 118-39.

> Charges IAR with several misunderstandings of the "nature of aesthetic emotion" and misinterpretations of the effect of poetry on readers. Although PRACTICAL CRITICISM is an instructive book, it betrays IAR's "blindness" to the significance of his student's comments.

Bennett, Joan. "'How It Strikes a Contemporary': The Impact of I.A. Richard's Literary Criticism in Cambridge, England." In I.A. RICHARDS: ESSAYS IN HIS HONOR. Ed. Reuben Brower, Helen Vendler, and John Hollander. New York: Oxford Univ. Press, 1973. Pp. 45-60.

> Interesting assessment of the intellectual climate at Cambridge at the start of IAR's teaching career. A new emphasis was placed on theory of criticism and close analysis of major literary works: thus, opportunity abounded "for new directions in teachings."

Bentley, Eric Russell. "The Early I.A. Richards: An Autopsy." ROCKY MOUNTAIN REVIEW, 8 (1944), 29-36.

> Harsh but lively attack on IAR's theory of value: it is "inconsistent," "inapplicable to criticism," and tied to "unsubstantiated psychology."

Bethell, S.L. "Suggestions Towards a Theory of Value." CRITERION, 14 (1935), 239-50.

> Regrets that IAR is not a philosopher as well as a psychologist and a critic. Although PRINCIPLES makes an important contribution to the psychology of communication, it fails in its theory of value because of IAR's "specialist outlook."

Bhabha, Homi I. "Apologies for Poetry: A Study in the Method of Mill and Richards." JSL, 3 (1975), 71-88.

> Examines the two writers' claims for poetry; finds Mill to be "nostalgic" and IAR "progressive." Bhabha offers worthwhile commentary on IAR's SCIENCES AND POETRIES and PRINCIPLES.

Bilsky, Manuel. "I.A. Richards on Belief." PPR, 12 (1951), 105-15.

I.A. Richards

>Attempts to clarify IAR's position on the relation between beliefs and aesthetic experience in his early writings. Bilsky sees a weakness and contradiction in IAR's definition of an intellectual belief.

_____. "I.A. Richards' Theory of Metaphor." MP, 50 (1952), 130-37.

>Points out discrepancies and weaknesses in IAR's theory of metaphor as outlined in PHILOSOPHY OF RHETORIC and INTERPRETATION IN TEACHING.

_____. "I.A. Richards' Theory of Value." PPR, 14 (1954), 536-45.

>Finds some flaws in IAR's ethical theory: his empiricism leads him toward a naturalistic definition of "good" in PRINCIPLES and SCIENCE AND POETRY.

Black, Max. "Some Objections to Ogden and Richards' Theory of Interpretation." JP, 39 (1942), 281-90.

>Harsh analysis of the "pretentious" doctrines in MEANING OF MEANING. Black finds the crucial terms of the theory to be vague and undefined; he charges that assertions are "unsupported by relevant evidence."

_____. "Some Questions about Emotive Meaning." PHR, 57 (1948), 111-26.

>Grants that IAR's later writings move toward idealism and overcome the "doctrinaire rigidity" of his earlier behaviorism. Recommends Charles L. Stevenson's theories of meaning as a remedy to the weaknesses of IAR's doctrines.

Blackmur, R.P. "San Giovanni in Venere: Allen Tate as a Man of Letters." SR, 67 (1959), 614-31.

>Impressionistic but insightful comparisons are made concerning form and content of the literary criticism produced by IAR, Allen Tate, and John Crowe Ransom.

Blissett, William. "I.A. Richards." UTQ, 14 (1944), 58-66.

>A balanced assessment of IAR's "pioneer" contributions in four main areas. Blissett sees defects in his theories of psychology and value, but praises his distinction between the scientific and the poetic uses of language.

Brooks, Cleanth. "I.A. Richards and the Concept of Tension." In I.A. RICHARDS: ESSAYS IN HIS HONOR. Ed. Reuben Brower, Helen Vendler, and John Hollander. New York: Oxford Univ. Press, 1973. Pp. 135-56.

>A valuable examination of IAR's role in drawing twentieth-century attention to three important aesthetic problems: "disparity in poetry," "kinds of unification possible," and "the positive values of a poetry that makes use of tension in its structural principle."

Brower, Reuben, Helen Vendler, and John Hollander, eds. I.A. RICHARDS, ESSAYS IN HIS HONOR. New York: Oxford Univ. Press, 1973.

> Includes nineteen essays on IAR's ideas and interests by distinguished critics, philosophers, teachers, and linguists. Includes an IAR interview and bibliography. Some of the more important essays (annotated separately) are by Bennett, Brooks, Coburn, Empson, Fletcher, Hartman, Russo, Skinner, Stevenson, Vendler, Willey, and Wimsatt.

Butler, Christopher. "I.A. Richards and the Fortunes of Critical Theory." EIC, 30 (1980), 191-204.

> Valuable survey of IAR's works which explains why, in spite of subsequent developments, his reputation will rest on his two early masterpieces, PRINCIPLES OF LITERARY CRITICISM and PRACTICAL CRITICISM.

Chisholm, Roderick. "Intentionality and the Theory of Signs." PHS, 3 (1952), 56-63.

> Makes brief references to the theory of signs in MEANING OF MEANING.

Coburn, Kathleen. "I.A.R. and S.T.C." In I.A. RICHARDS: ESSAYS IN HIS HONOR. Ed. Reuben Brower, Helen Vendler, and John Hollander. New York: Oxford Univ. Press, 1973. Pp. 237-44.

> A creative and valuable assessment of IAR's contribution to Coleridge studies. Shows how IAR was original in viewing Coleridge as a critic "supremely useful" to "understanding how meanings, words, and imagination work."

Cohn, Jan. "The Theory of Poetic Value in I.A. Richards' PRINCIPLES OF LITERARY CRITICISM and Shelley's A DEFENSE OF POETRY." KSJ, 21-22 (1972-73), 95-111.

> Intelligent and well-documented article which finds the moral defenses of poetry by Shelley and IAR to be similar in their focus on the audience rather than on the art object. Also both support poetry against the attacks of science and utility.

Cox, R. Gordon. "I.A. Richards and Criticism Today." SR, 82 (1974), 705-12.

> Stresses that IAR's influence and critical legacy transcends "the real or alleged excesses of an outmoded New Criticism."

Crane, R.S. "I.A. Richards on the Art of Interpretation." ETHICS, 59, No. 1 (1949), 112-26.

> Although IAR has written many studies on how to interpret philosophical and literary texts, his ideas are often simplistic once the reader moves beyond "the sophisticated diction and

tortuous movement of the prose." Crane rejects IAR's "alluring" scientific modernity and resists his "dogmatic rigor."

Cruttwell, Patrick. "Second Thoughts, IV: I.A. Richards' PRACTICAL CRITICISM." EIC, 8 (1958), 1-15.

> A pedestrian survey which summarizes and questions some of IAR's objectives in PRACTICAL CRITICISM. As a classic of criticism, however, the work stands up to revaluation.

Daiches, David. "Principles of Literary Criticism." NEW REPUBLIC, 98 (1939), 95-98.

> Examines the contemporary reception of IAR's PRINCIPLES, defends his psychological theory of value and its application to literature, and estimates the resonant influence of his ideas. A succinct and worthwhile discussion.

Dickie, George. "I.A. Richards's Phantom Double." BJA, 8 (1968), 54-59.

> Finds IAR's theories in PRINCIPLES about the effects of tragedy on an audience to be inadequate.

Eastman, Max. "A Note on I.A. Richards' Psychology of Poetry." In THE LITERARY MIND: ITS PLACE IN AN AGE OF SCIENCE. New York: Scribner's, 1931. Pp. 295-317.

> A classic in negative brow-beating. Eastman outlines IAR's "troubles" and "all the weaknesses of his books." Eastman charges IAR with the fundamental error of trying to shift practical activity from science to poetry. Further, "his psychology is wrongly based," and "he cannot explain metaphor."

Eliot, T.S. "Introduction" and "The Modern Mind." In his THE USE OF POETRY AND THE USE OF CRITICISM: STUDIES IN THE RELATION OF CRITICISM TO POETRY IN ENGLAND. London: Faber, 1933. Pp. 13-36; 121-42.

> While granting respect for IAR's discriminating taste in poetry, Eliot takes issue with his theory of education in PRACTICAL CRITICISM and with his theory of value that "arises out of his psychology." Shows how IAR is, in his own way, "a serious moralist."

———. "Literature, Science, and Dogma." DIAL, 82 (1927), 239-43.

> Significant discussion of the relation of belief to truth and poetry in IAR's SCIENCE AND POETRY. Eliot objects that the book poses but doesn't answer many important questions.

Empson, William. "The Hammer's Ring." In I.A. RICHARDS: ESSAYS IN HIS HONOR. Ed. Reuben Brower, Helen Vendler, and John Hollander.

New York: Oxford Univ. Press, 1973. Pp. 73-84.

> A balanced discussion of IAR's accomplishments in literary criticism and linguistics. Although his views are respected and influential, Empson speculates on why some critics (such as F.R. Leavis in SCRUTINY) have rejected IAR's theories.

――――. THE STRUCTURE OF COMPLEX WORDS. London: Chatto and Windus, 1952.

> The book is dedicated to IAR; former pupil Empson draws on ideas from many of IAR's books throughout the semantic study.

Fekete, John. "I.A. Richards." In THE CRITICAL TWILIGHT: EXPLORATIONS IN THE IDEOLOGY OF ANGLO-AMERICAN LITERARY THEORY FROM ELIOT TO McLUHAN. London: Routledge and Kegan Paul, 1977. Pp. 25-36.

> Assesses IAR's "powerful" contributions to the modern critical tradition. IAR's critical stance is praised for its "practical and technical relation to reality."

Fisher, Philip. "Questions of English." CE, 40 (1979), 727-39.

> A provocative essay on the careers of IAR and F.R. Leavis. Fisher argues that as IAR worked out the relationship between literature and social questions, he became a Quixotic crusader for lost causes: he "diluted the notion of language and culture in the hope of a future, universal, common reality."

Fletcher, Angus. "I.A. Richards and the Art of Critical Balance." In I.A. RICHARDS: ESSAYS IN HIS HONOR. Ed. Reuben Brower, Helen Vendler, and John Hollander. New York: Oxford Univ. Press, 1973. Pp. 85-100.

> A stimulating discussion. In his criticism IAR tries to analyze the conflicting forces at work in reading and understanding. Like Coleridge, he turns from criticism to poetry as the larger energies of "the analytic and the visionary intelligence" interact during his career.

Fogarty, Daniel. "I.A. Richards' Theory." In his ROOTS FOR A NEW RHETORIC. New York: Columbia Univ. Press, 1959. Pp. 28-55.

> Clear, basic explanation of IAR's theories of abstraction, metaphor, definition, and comprehending. IAR provided "full and positive answers" to Fogarty's questions about his philosophy of rhetoric and its origins.

Foster, Richard. "I.A. Richards: From Laboratory to Imagination." In THE NEW ROMANTICS: A REAPPRAISAL OF THE NEW CRITICISM. Bloomington: Indiana Univ. Press, 1962. Pp. 47-63.

> Views IAR's development as a "shift away from 'positivism'" and "toward a condition of mind that is pretty accurately described

by the word 'romanticism.'" Uses IAR's own words to elaborate changes from earlier intentions and principles.

Fry, Roger. TRANSFORMATIONS: CRITICAL AND SPECULATIVE ESSAYS ON ART. London: Chatto and Windus, 1927.

> Uses some of IAR's theories in PRINCIPLES OF CRITICISM as a point of departure for "further investigations into the nature and ends of pictorial design."

Gentry, George. "Reference and Relation." JP, 40 (1943), 253-61.

> Argues with Ogden's and IAR's fundamental aim in MEANING OF MEANING--sign-situation in naturalistic categories--but views as a weakness their conclusion that reference is a relation. Stimulating reading for the philosophically inclined.

Gilbert, Katherine. "The Intent and Tone of Mr. I.A. Richards." JAAC, 3 (1944), 29-48.

> Interesting analysis of the variety of tones in IAR's writings. Gilbert identifies the tone of the prophet, the reformer, the school-master, and the practical critic. In some cases his intent and tone lead him "into exaggeration."

Glicksberg, Charles I. "I.A. Richards and the Science of Criticism." SR, 46 (1938), 520-33.

> Admires IAR's efforts to lift literary criticism to "a plane of scientific accuracy," but then discusses why he only partially succeeds.

Graff, Gerald E. "The Later Richards and the New Criticism." CRITICISM, 9 (1967), 229-42.

> Contends that, despite the interpretations of several modern critics, IAR's theory both early and late in his career "might be characterized as at once romantic and positivistic." Primarily attacks the views of Richard Foster in THE NEW ROMANTICS (1962).

Gudas, Fabian. "I.A. Richards and the Principle of Complementarity." ESSAYS IN HONOR OF ESMOND LINWORTH MARILLA. Ed. Thomas A. Kirby and William J. Olive. Baton Rouge: Louisiana State Univ. Press, 1970. Pp. 355-66.

> A jargon-ridden essay which shows how IAR's works after 1930 use the Danish physicist Niels Bohr's principle of complementarity. The basic idea that IAR's works move from a dogmatic to a provisional and experimental tone is a commonplace.

Hamilton, G. Rostrevor. POETRY AND CONTEMPLATION: A NEW PREFACE TO POETICS. Cambridge: The Univ. Press, 1937.

> Agrees with IAR's emphasis in PRINCIPLES on the organization and

complex harmony of the poetic experience. However, Hamilton argues that IAR has had a "harmful effect" on criticism and poetry because he is wrong about art and morals as well as the relation of poetry to life. Presents a Bergsonian theory of poetry.

Hamlin, Cyrus. "I.A. Richards (1893-1979): Grand Master of Interpretations." UTQ, 49 (1980), 189-204.

A former student offers praise of IAR's genius and diversity. Many of his keenest interpretive readings of poems never found their way to print; his work in communications theory is being appreciated only now.

Harding, D.W. "I.A. Richards." SCRUTINY, 1 (1933), 327-38.

Analyzes the tone and attitude in IAR's writings and labels it "amateur." Further, he doubts the "practical usefulness" of IAR's attempt to convince the common man of poetry's value or to help settle critical disagreements.

Hartman, Geoffrey H. "The Dream of Communication." In I.A. RICHARDS: ESSAYS IN HIS HONOR. Ed. Reuben Brower, Helen Vendler, and John Hollander. New York: Oxford Univ. Press, 1973. Pp. 157-78.

Examines IAR's theories concerning the influence of art on experience in PRINCIPLES and other works. If, as IAR warns, art can corrupt, then criticism must be "more alive and discriminating then ever." Also relates IAR's ideas to new developments in psychoanalysis.

Hochmuth, Marie. "I.A. Richards and the 'New Rhetoric.'" QJS, 44 (1958), 1-16.

Surveys IAR's works and focuses on PHILOSOPHY OF RHETORIC. Hochmuth examines IAR's concept of language, his theory of communication, his attempt to reorient rhetoric, and his critical principles. Concludes with an estimation of his place "in the great tradition of rhetoric."

Hoopes, James. "Modernist Criticism and Transcendental Literature." NEQ, 52 (1979), 451-66.

Thorough examination of the influence of IAR's critical theories on James Agee's works.

Hotopf, W.H.N. LANGUAGE, THOUGHT, AND COMPREHENSION: A CASE STUDY OF THE WRITINGS OF I.A. RICHARDS. Bloomington: Indiana Univ. Press; London: Routledge, 1965.

A scholarly, comprehensive examination from the psychological viewpoint of IAR's purposes and views of language, thought, meaning, learning, and society. Argues that IAR's greatest influence has been in two areas: education in proper thinking and the appreciation of poetry. His two most important works are, therefore, MEANING OF MEANING and PRACTICAL CRITICISM. Defends IAR against certain criticisms by the New Critics. Also discusses how other critics have received, misunderstood, and been influenced by IAR's theories.

James, David Gwilym. SCEPTICISM AND POETRY: AN ESSAY ON THE POETIC IMAGINATION. London: Allen and Unwin, 1937.

Criticizes IAR's literary aesthetic because his interests in psychology have led him astray "from the theory of the imagination to a theory of the emotional and volitional response to poetry." James explains why IAR has done "a signal disservice to the advance of the theory of poetry." Shows how IAR has misused Coleridge's ideas. A thoughtful attack which makes some subtle discriminations.

Karnani, Chetan. CRITICISM, AESTHETICS AND PSYCHOLOGY: A STUDY OF THE WRITINGS OF I.A. RICHARDS. New Delhi: Arnold-Heinemann, 1977.

Relates IAR's criticism to various schools of psychology--Freudian, gestalt, behaviorism. Traces the sources of his essential critical ideas and argues that many of these "seminal conclusions" are derived from earlier psychologists. Karnani offers some valuable insights concerning the nature of criticism through his technical and interdisciplinary approach. Includes a selected primary and secondary bibliography.

Knight, E. Helen. "Some Aesthetic Theories of Mr. Richards." MIND, N.S. 36 (1927), 69-76.

Argues that IAR does not make a sharp enough distinction between communication and judgment.

Krieger, Murray. "The Critical Legacy of Matthew Arnold: Or, the Strange Brotherhood of T.S. Eliot, I.A. Richards and Northrop Frye." SORA, N.S. 5 (1969), 457-74.

An interesting but flawed juggling act which reaches for various "unexpected" balls of similarity to prove a "theoretical brotherhood." Includes brief discussion of IAR's SCIENCE AND POETRY.

Leavis, F.R. "Dr. Richards, Bentham and Coleridge." SCRUTINY, 3 (1935), 382-402.

A long and negative review of COLERIDGE ON IMAGINATION. Leavis finds the book to be full of scientific "pretensions"; further, he objects that there is "for demonstration, not even a beginning in the serious critical analysis of poetry" and that IAR Benthamizes Coleridge.

Levin, Harry. "I.A. Richards (1893-1979)." NYRB, 6 (6 December 1979), 40-42.

> An appreciative general survey of IAR's life and works. Levin stresses IAR's "panoramic" vision and the influence of Coleridge. Concludes that no other critic in the past fifty years has made a greater impact on the interpretation of poetry than IAR.

McLuhan, H. M. "Poetic vs. Rhetorical Exegesis, the Case for Leavis against Richards and Empson." SR, 52 (1944), 266-76.

> A valuable and balanced discussion of the three critics' methods of evaluating poems. McLuhan argues that Leavis' method has "superior relevance" to that of Empson and IAR because he believes a poem should refine "moral perception" and extend "dramatic awareness."

Patankar, R. B. "Richard's Theory of Value." In his AESTHETICS AND LITERARY CRITICISM. Bombay: Nachiketa Publications, 1969. Pp. 188-203.

> Summarizes and offers some objections to IAR's theories. Attempts to classify his ideas as either moral or aesthetic theory; enumerates certain methodological problems of IAR's theory of value.

Perlis, Alan D. "Science, Mysticism, and Contemporary Poetry." WHR, 29 (1975), 209-18.

> Enthusiastic summary of IAR's prophecies in SCIENCE AND POETRY. Perlis concludes, however, that IAR's view of the relationship between science and poetry is "ahistorical" and has not been realized.

Pollock, Thomas Clark. "A Critique of I. A. Richards' Theory of Language and Literature." In A THEORY OF MEANING ANALYZED. General Semantics Monographs. Ed. M. Kendig and S. I. Hayakawa. Lakeville, Conn.: Institute of General Semantics, 1942. Pp. 1-25.

> With copious documentation, Pollock attempts to argue that in several ways IAR's "central theory of the uses of language is inadequate as a theoretical basis for the study of literature." He finds the overall framework in MEANING OF MEANING and PRINCIPLES to be incomplete; later works confuse or contradict the earlier theories.

Rackin, Phyllis. "Hulme, Richards, and the Development of Contextualist Poetic Theory." JAAC, 25 (1967), 413-25.

> A copiously documented article which shows how IAR eventually succeeds in avoiding the subjectivism of his earlier theory by enlarging the concepts of metaphor and irony. Elaborates IAR's objections to Hulme's more limited views.

I.A. Richards

Ransom, John Crowe. "I.A. Richards: The Psychological Critic. And William Empson, His Pupil." In his THE NEW CRITICISM. Norfolk, Conn.: New Directions, 1941. Pp. 3-101.

> Calls IAR the father of the New Criticism. Close, extended scrutiny of IAR's critical theories. Ransom points out where and how the New Criticism is damaged by "using the psychological affective vocabulary" and by instances of "plain moralism."

_____. "A Psychologist Looks at Poetry." VQR, 11 (1935), 575-92.

> Finds IAR's account of poetry to be too limiting in its rejection of "the Cognitive element." Regrets that IAR has not worked free from his psychological bias.

Rao, B.D. "Expanding Circles: I.A. Richards and the Problems of Verbal Communication." LCRIT, 10, No. 3 (1972), 24-34.

> An ambitious but generalized attempt to link IAR's various volumes--from MEANING OF MEANING through SPECULATIVE INSTRUMENTS--with the "one preoccupation which persists": verbal communication. IAR's later works present some unresolved difficulties.

Righter, William. LOGIC AND CRITICISM. London: Routledge, 1963.

> Contains a brief discussion of IAR's theoretical criterion for making value judgments. Righter also admires IAR's practical criticism, but claims that he sometimes errs in using scientific discipline as a critical tool.

Rudolph, Gerald Allen. "The Aesthetic Field of I.A. Richards." JAAC, 14 (1956), 348-58.

> Ambitious exercise in synthesis. Rudolph argues that many previous critics have misjudged IAR because they have overlooked some dimensions of his theory; he strives to unite IAR's critical remarks "into a perspective of the whole theory."

Russell, Bertrand. "The Meaning of Meaning." DIAL, 81 (1926), 114-21.

> Praises IAR's book of the same title for its scientific methods and theories. Russell embarks on a philosophical discussion of his own in testing the book's theories of meaning.

Russo, John P. "Introduction." In COMPLEMENTARITIES: UNCOLLECTED ESSAYS BY I.A. RICHARDS. Ed. John Paul Russo. Cambridge, Mass.: Harvard Univ. Press, 1976. Pp. vii-xxiv.

> A valuable assessment of IAR's contributions to modern literary criticism, especially to the art and science debate. Russo praises IAR's expansion of the perimeter of criticism, his interest in other disciplines, and his concern with values. IAR is ranked as an "heir of Matthew Arnold's humanistic criticism."

---------. "Meaning and Language Training: The Richards Theory and Method." In USES OF LITERATURE. Harvard English Studies. Ed. Monroe Engel. Cambridge, Mass.: Harvard Univ. Press, 1973. Pp. 275-90.

    Discusses IAR's objections to contemporary reading and language programs based on learning the code. Russo presents IAR's theory of meaning that underlies his own methods for instruction. Some practical exercises are given.

---------. "The Recent Career of I.A. Richards." PLL, 8 (1972), 102-09.

    A competent review essay which relates several books published by IAR in the 1960's to some of his earlier works. IAR's "utilitarian approach to language" challenges the "new formalism" of structural linguistics.

---------. "Richards and the Classical Tradition." In I.A. RICHARDS: ESSAYS IN HIS HONOR. Ed. Reuben Brower, Helen Vendler, and John Hollander. New York: Oxford Univ. Press, 1973. Pp. 245-58.

    A worthwhile account of IAR's "general attitude toward and specific works on classical Greece."

---------. "Richards and the Search for Critical Instruments." In TWENTIETH-CENTURY LITERATURE IN RETROSPECTIVE. Harvard English Studies. Ed. Reuben A. Brower. Cambridge, Mass.: Harvard Univ. Press, 1971. Pp. 133-54.

    Discusses how IAR in PRINCIPLES adapts the model for mental processes proposed in the neurophysiological studies of Sir Charles Scott Sherrington. The model helps to explain the complex processes involved in responding to a poem and the idea of competing but balanced structures.

---------. "A Study in Influence: The Moore-Richards Paradigm." CRITI, 5 (1979), 683-712.

    A thorough and thoughtful essay on the many influences of G.E. Moore on the young IAR at Cambridge University. Moore's impact was "potent and stimulating" in these areas: philosophical problems, critical argument, psychology, and style.

Schiller, Jerome P. "An Alternative to 'Aesthetic Disinterestedness.'" JAAC, 22 (1964), 295-302.

    In arguing for "a very personal, but controlled" approach to significant experiences of art works, Schiller refers to IAR's definitions of "impulses," "interests," and "synaesthesis" in PRINCIPLES.

---------. I.A. RICHARDS' THEORY OF LITERATURE. New Haven, Conn. and London: Yale Univ. Press, 1969.

    Perhaps the finest critical study of IAR's ideas and style to date. Schiller skillfully analyzes misunderstandings of IAR as well as his changes in perspectives, interests, views, and the tone of the writings. Balanced explanation of why IAR's early, brash prose style seems now to be a "barrier" for the reader, whereas the style of "questioning indecisiveness" of later works never was effective. Despite these stylistic weaknesses, Schiller concludes that content-wise, IAR offers "an extremely valuable and contemporary approach to literature." Chapter 6 appraises IAR's theory of literature--with poetry being his deepest concern-- as "coherent," "sound," and "provocative."

Sesonske, Alexander. "Truth in Art." JP, 53 (1956), 345-53.

> Elaborates some implications of IAR's position in SCIENCE AND POETRY that art should be independent of all beliefs.

Skinner, B.F. "Reflections on Meaning and Structure." In I.A. RICHARDS: ESSAYS IN HIS HONOR. Ed. Reuben Brower, Helen Vendler, and John Hollander. New York: Oxford Univ. Press, 1973. Pp. 199-210.

> An eminent psychologist speculates on why certain words are written in a poetic context. He uses Shakespeare's Sonnet 129 to speculate on how a poet sharpens verbal material to improve the effect on the reader.

Spaulding, Gordon. "Elementalism: The Effect of an Implicit Postulate of Identity on I.A. Richards' Theory of Poetic Value." In A THEORY OF MEANING ANALYZED. General Semantics Monographs. Ed. M. Kendig and S.I. Hayakawa. Lakeville, Conn.: Institute of General Semantics, 1942. Pp. 26-35.

> A technical scrutiny of the origin and use of the terms that IAR uses to formulate theories of poetic value and meaning in PRINCIPLES and MEANING OF MEANING. Spaulding finds contradictions and unconscious assumptions at work.

―――. "Richards on the Theory of Value." In I.A. RICHARDS: ESSAYS IN HIS HONOR. Ed. Reuben Brower, Helen Vendler, and John Hollander. New York: Oxford Univ. Press, 1973. Pp. 119-34.

> A philosophical discussion in which Stevenson shows how IAR's two "quite distinct" theories of value--in MEANING and PRINCIPLES--can be combined, with modifications, into a single, unified theory.

Stolnitz, Jerome. AESTHETICS AND PHILOSOPHY OF ART CRITICISM: A CRITICAL INTRODUCTION. Boston: Houghton Mifflin, 1960.

> Includes brief but interesting discussion of IAR's ideas on artistic "truth."

Tate, Allen. "Literature as Knowledge: Comment and Comparison." In REASON IN MADNESS: CRITICAL ESSAYS. New York: Putnam's, 1941. Pp. 20-61.

> Examines the positivist side of IAR's early thought. Concludes that IAR "offers no final solution of the problem of the unified imagination" and his books represent the modern mind's failure "to understand poetry on the assumptions underlying the demi-religion of positivism."

Tomlin, E.W.F. "I.A. Richards and Belief." TWENTIETH CENTURY VERSE, 10 (1938), 46-51.

> A hair-splitting and confusing discussion of emotive and scientific language as well as the problem of belief in SCIENCE AND POETRY.

Vendler, Helen. "Jakobson, Richards, and Shakespeare's Sonnet CXXIX." In I.A. RICHARDS: ESSAYS IN HIS HONOR. Ed. Reuben Brower, Helen Vendler, and John Hollander. New York: Oxford Univ. Press, 1973. Pp. 179-98.

> Praises IAR for elevating paraphrase of poetic meanings to "the high art it rightly is" and also sees value in Jakobson's method of formal linguistic description of the sonnet.

Vivas, Eliseo. "Four Notes on I.A. Richards' Aesthetic Theory." PHR, 44 (1935), 354-67.

> A thorough philosophical discussion of the relation between value-theory and psychological description in IAR's works.

Wellek, Rene. "On Rereading I.A. Richards." SORA, N.S. 3 (1967), 533-54.

> A valuable reassessment of most of IAR's critical writings. Wellek spells out in specific detail why he disagrees with IAR's idea of poetry and his concepts of the reader's relation to it. Wellek concludes that IAR's "greatest and most beneficial influence was due to PRACTICAL CRITICISM."

Willey, Basil. "I.A. Richards and Coleridge." In I.A. RICHARDS: ESSAYS IN HIS HONOR. Ed. Reuben Brower, Helen Vendler, and John Hollander. New York: Oxford Univ. Press, 1973. Pp. 227-36.

> Lists ways in which IAR is like and unlike Samuel Taylor Coleridge. Reviews COLERIDGE ON IMAGINATION in some detail and defines the uniqueness of IAR's "prophetic character" in his writings.

Williams, Raymond. "Two Literary Critics." In his CULTURE AND SOCIETY, 1780-1950. New York: Harper and Row, 1958. Pp. 244-52.

Places IAR's theory of value in the tradition of Arnold's "prescription of culture against anarchy." Also examines and questions some of IAR's basic views concerning the psychology of the artist and the social function of art.

Wimsatt, William K., Jr. "I.A.R.: What to Say about a Poem." In I.A. RICHARDS: ESSAYS IN HIS HONOR. Ed. Reuben Brower, Helen Vendler, and John Hollander. New York: Oxford Univ. Press, 1973. Pp. 101-18.

An appreciative survey of IAR's past and more recent statements about how to analyze and teach poetry.

GEORGE SAINTSBURY (1845-1933)

THE WORKS OF GEORGE SAINTSBURY (New York: Arno Press, 1979) reprints COLLECTED ESSAYS AND PAPERS; CORRECTED IMPRESSIONS; ELIZABETHAN AND JACOBEAN PAMPHLETS; ESSAYS IN ENGLISH LITERATURE: 1780-1860; ESSAYS IN ENGLISH LITERATURE: 1780-1860, SECOND SERIES; MISCELLANEOUS ESSAYS; and PREFACES AND ESSAYS.

NONFICTIONAL PROSE

THE COLLECTED ESSAYS AND PAPERS OF GEORGE SAINTSBURY. 4 vols. London: Dent; New York: Dutton, 1923, 1924.

> Reprints the previous essay collections, with only the third volume containing a substantial amount of hitherto uncollected material, including essays on cooking grouse and partridge.

A CONSIDERATION OF THACKERAY. London: Milford, 1931.

> A collection of the seventeen introductions to GS's Oxford edition of his favorite novelist. GS likes BARRY LYNDON least, ESMOND most, and argues that Thackeray presents too gloomy a picture of human nature in VANITY FAIR.

CORRECTED IMPRESSIONS: ESSAYS ON VICTORIAN WRITERS. London: Heinemann; New York: Dodd, Mead, 1895.

> Twenty-two essays describing GS's initial responses to several major Victorians and his current opinions of them.

DRYDEN. London: Macmillan; New York: Harper, 1881.

> A critical biography, stressing Dryden's representativeness of his age, his great poetic range, and his improvement of literary English.

THE EARLIER RENAISSANCE. Periods of European Literature. London: Blackwood; New York: Scribner's, 1901.

George Saintsbury

> The fifth volume in the series edited by GS. GS finds the period's central trait to be not reason but "the reviving sense of style, of the propriety and power of language."

THE EARL OF DERBY. London: Sampson Low, Marston; New York: Harper, 1892.

> A history of the career of the Tory Prime Minister, with a section on his Latin verse and translation of Homer. GS admires his personal qualities, while admitting he lacked a coherent political theory.

THE ENGLISH NOVEL. London: Dent; New York: Dutton, 1913.

> A survey covering Romance writers to the novelists of the later nineteenth century. It spends a disproportionate amount of space on late eighteenth-century novelists; of nineteenth-century ones, George Eliot is especially undervalued.

ESSAYS IN ENGLISH LITERATURE, 1780-1860. London: Percival, 1890. New York: Scribner's, 1891.

> GS' first essay collection: fourteen pieces from his days as a London journalist. They are on early nineteenth-century authors GS considers undervalued, such as Hogg, Jeffrey, Hazlitt, Hunt, and DeQuincey. The introductory essay argues that the literary critic must shun general formulas on the one hand and pure impressionism on the other.

ESSAYS IN ENGLISH LITERATURE: 1780-1860, SECOND SERIES. London: Dent, 1895.

> Thirteen essays and two-appendixes. They include essays on Southey, Cobbett, Landor, and Hood, three pieces on the development of the historical novel, and a lengthy essay on British war songs.

ESSAYS ON FRENCH NOVELISTS. London: Percival; New York: Scribner's, 1891.

> A collection of twelve essays. GS rips into contemporaries such as Zola ("the dirt-compeller"); earlier novelists are more admired. Despite his revulsion at MADAM BOVARY, GS manages a balanced view of Flaubert.

A FIRST BOOK OF ENGLISH LITERATURE. London: Macmillan, 1914.

> Not seen.

THE FLOURISHING OF ROMANCE AND THE RISE OF ALLEGORY. Periods of European Literature. London: Blackwood; New York: Scribner's, 1897.

The second volume in the series edited by GS. He examines
twelfth- and thirteenth-century literature in chapters on the
Arthur story, on the rise of allegory in France, on the chansons
de geste, on the sagas, and the like. He confesses to using
translations for Welsh and Irish; he does read Icelandic and
Provencal, however, and devotes a chapter to their works.

HISTORICAL MANUAL OF ENGLISH PROSODY. London: Macmillan, 1910.

A condensed version of HISTORY OF ENGLISH PROSODY
intended for use in schools.

A HISTORY OF CRITICISM AND LITERARY TASTE IN EUROPE FROM THE
EARLIEST TEXTS TO THE PRESENT DAY. 3 vols. London: Blackwood;
New York: Dodd, Mead, 1900, 1902, 1904.

One of GS's greatest works, a huge, chronological survey of
critics and critical movements from the Greeks up. It treats
the development of criticism in several European nations other
than England.

A HISTORY OF ELIZABETHAN LITERATURE. London and New York: Macmillan,
1887.

Part of the same series as HISTORY OF NINETEENTH CENTURY
LITERATURE, this covers 1560-1660. GS prefers Spenser to
Milton, while terming Shakespeare the greatest author of all time.

A HISTORY OF ENGLISH CRITICISM. London: Blackwood; New York: Dodd,
Mead, 1911.

The revised British section of HISTORY OF CRITICISM.

A HISTORY OF ENGLISH PROSE RHYTHM. London: Macmillan, 1912.

A survey from the Old English period to the later nineteenth
century that applies GS's foot system to prose and stresses the
importance of variety in prose rhythm.

A HISTORY OF ENGLISH PROSODY FROM THE TWELFTH CENTURY TO THE
PRESENT DAY. 3 vols. London and New York: Macmillan, 1906, 1908,
1910.

One of GS's most important works. It does examine the history
of prosodic theory but mainly concentrates on British poetic
practice in a very inclusive survey. GS perceives the foot to
be the "integer" of British prosody rather than accent or quantity.

A HISTORY OF NINETEENTH CENTURY LITERATURE (1780-1895). London
and New York: Macmillan, 1896.

George Saintsbury

> Written for the same series as HISTORY OF ELIZABETHAN LITERATURE. GS treats no living author save Ruskin. He does devote a great deal of space to the era's nonfiction.

A HISTORY OF THE FRENCH NOVEL (TO THE CLOSE OF THE 19TH CENTURY). 2 vols. London: Macmillan, 1917, 1919.

> GS's last major history, the product of his extraordinarily broad readings in French fiction. He starts all the way back with the chansons de geste--Madame de Stael is not reached until the second volume--and perceives the novel to be a continuation of the romance. His dislike of nineteenth-century Naturalists such as Zola and the Goncourts is evident.

A LAST SCRAP BOOK. London: Macmillan, 1924.

> A last "farrago of literature, politics, gastronomy, religion, anti-Pussyfootism, moral philosophy," and so on. The piece on Byron accuses him of failing to write "pure" poetry, of being too subject-dominated.

THE LATER NINETEENTH CENTURY. Periods of European Literature. London: Blackwood; New York: Scribner's, 1907.

> The twelfth and concluding volume of the series edited by GS. He begins with Tennyson and Hugo; about half the book deals with English and French poetry, fiction, nonfiction, and drama. Chapters on German and southern European literature follow. In the last major chapter, "The New Candidates," GS reveals his aversion to Ibsen, Dostoevsky, and Tolstoy.

A LETTER BOOK: SELECTED WITH AN INTRODUCTION ON THE HISTORY AND ART OF LETTER-WRITING. London: Bell; New York: Harcourt, Brace, 1922.

> For this collection of mostly eighteenth- and nineteenth-century British letters GS writes a one-hundred-page introduction that terms the eighteenth the "very palmiest day of the art."

MANCHESTER. London: Longmans, Green, 1887.

> A thorough, informed history of the city's economic, political, and military activities. Rejecting Dickens' portrait of Manchester in HARD TIMES, GS takes a consistently conservative interpretation of the Peterloo Massacre, the Anti- Com-Law League, and so forth.

MARLBOROUGH. New York, 1883. London: Longmans, Green, 1885.

> A history of the victor of Blenheim that emphasizes his life-long political maneuverings, generally with approval.

MATTHEW ARNOLD. Edinburgh: Blackwood; New York: Dodd, Mead, 1899.

> A critical biography, heavily dependent on Arnold's letters. GS judges Arnold's nonfiction inferior to his poetry, which is likened to Thomas Gray's.

MISCELLANEOUS ESSAYS. London: Percival; New York: Scribner's, 1892.

> A collection of twelve essays mostly on literary topics. "English Prose Style" states it is absolutely distinct from English verse style. "The Present State of the English Novel, 1892" deplores the Jamesian ideal of artistic structuring in the novel.

NOTES ON A CELLAR-BOOK. London: Macmillan, 1920. New York: Macmillan, 1933.

> The first in the SCRAP BOOK line (below), an amusing history of GS's encounters with various types of wine and liquor. GS at his jolliest.

THE PEACE OF THE AUGUSTANS: A SURVEY OF EIGHTEENTH CENTURY LITERATURE AS A PLACE OF REST AND REFRESHMENT. London: Bell, 1916. New York: Oxford Univ. Press, 1946.

> A humorous and idiosyncratic survey of a century GS loves, although he admits it lacks a sense of Shelleyian idealism. Of authors GS prefers Swift, Fielding, and especially Johnson, whose politics are found congenial.

PHILIP AYRES. New York: 1903.

> An examination of the (very) minor seventeenth-century British lyric poet.

PRIMER OF FRENCH LITERATURE. Oxford: Clarendon Press, 1880. New York: Harper, 1881.

> A student's handbook and the first of GS's several books on French literature. He covers its history in 138 pages, stressing in conclusion the uniqueness of its unbroken vitality over eight centuries.

A SCRAP BOOK. London: Macmillan, 1922.

> GS's opinions on many matters, with numerous and amusing footnotes. There are several brief essays on "Education," on "Criticism," on "Politics" (expressing GS's extreme Toryism), and on his deceased friends Andrew Lang, H.D. Traill, W.E. Henley, and Austin Dobson.

A SECOND SCRAP BOOK. London: Macmillan, 1923.

George Saintsbury

> The most significant part of this is a one-hundred page memoir of Merton College and Oxford in the 1860's in which GS explains how he missed a fellowship and failed to graduate with first-class honors in classical studies.

A SHORT HISTORY OF ENGLISH LITERATURE. London and New York: Macmillan, 1898.

> A long, one-volume history, with "interchapters" drawing generalizations about preceding material and often discussing the stylistic development of English poetry.

A SHORT HISTORY OF FRENCH LITERATURE. Oxford: Clarendon Press, 1882.

> A much-expanded version of PRIMER OF FRENCH LITERATURE.

A SHORT HISTORY OF THE LIFE AND WRITINGS OF ALAIN RENE LE SAGE. London: Privately printed, 1881.

> Not seen.

SIR WALTER SCOTT. London: Oliphant, Anderson and Ferrier; New York: Scribner, 1897.

> A critical biography, seeing as Scott's strongest trait his ability to blend realism and romance.

WORKS EDITED BY OTHERS

FRENCH LITERATURE AND ITS MASTERS. Ed. Huntington Cairns. New York: Knopf, 1946.

> This reprints GS's articles on French literature in the eleventh edition of the ENCYCLOPEDIA BRITANNICA.

HISTORICAL MANUAL OF ENGLISH PROSODY. Ed. Harvey Gross. New York: Schocken Books, 1966.

A LAST VINTAGE: ESSAYS AND PAPERS. Ed. John W. Oliver, Arthur Melville Clark, and Augustus Muir. London: Methuen, 1950.

> A sequel to A SAINTSBURY MISCELLANY (p. 393) which contains fifty-one pieces by him, three memorial essays (that by Waddell listed separately), and Parker's bibliography (listed separately).

NOTES ON A CELLAR-BOOK. Ed. Andrew Graham. London: Macmillan, 1963.

PREFACES AND ESSAYS. Ed. Oliver Elton. London: Macmillan, 1933.

> A collection of several prefaces each on Fielding, Smollett, Sterne, and Peacock, with single essays on Donne, Poe, Pater, and others.

A SAINTSBURY MISCELLANY: SELECTIONS FROM HIS ESSAYS AND SCRAP BOOKS, WITH PERSONAL PORTRAITS BY SIR HERBERT GRIERSON AND OTHERS AND A BIOGRAPHICAL MEMOIR BY A. BLYTH WEBSTER. Ed. John W. Oliver and Augustus Muir. New York: Oxford Univ. Press, 1947.

> This contains several memorial essays on GS (that by Webster listed separately) and twenty-four pieces by him, including his inaugural speech upon taking his chair at the University of Edinburgh.

SHAKESPEARE. Ed. Helen Waddell. New York: Macmillan, 1934.

> This reprints GS's essay from the CAMBRIDGE HISTORY OF ENGLISH LITERATURE (1910).

BIBLIOGRAPHY

Leuba, Walter, ed. "George Saintsbury: A Check List." BOOK-COLLECTOR'S QUARTERLY, 12 (1933), 43-51.

> Unannotated, alphabetically arranged listing of GS's books, editions, prefaces, and other contributions to books.

_____. "Selected Bibliography." In his GEORGE SAINTSBURY. Twayne's English Author Series. New York: Twayne, 1967.

> Lists chronologically fifty-one primary titles (unannotated) and alphabetically forty-eight secondary titles (annotated).

Parker, W.M., comp. "A Saintsbury Bibliography." In A LAST VINTAGE: ESSAYS AND PAPERS. Ed. John Oliver, Arthur Clark, Augustus Muir. London: Methuen, 1950. Pp. 244-55.

> The most complete listing, with sections on the books, the translations, and one on "Introductions, Prefaces, and Edited Matter." Chronologically arranged.

BIOGRAPHY

Chrystal, Sir George. "George Saintsbury: 1845-1933." LONDON MERCURY, 28 (1933), 434-41.

> A memorial tribute containing vignettes of GS at the University of Edinburgh.

Waddell, Helen. "The Man of Books." In A LAST VINTAGE. Ed. John W. Oliver et al. London: Methuen, 1950. Pp. 23-28.

> A graceful tribute which notes the paradox that GS, a man of extreme personal prejudices, was nonetheless "the most catholic critic of his time."

Webster, A. Blyth. "A Biographical Memoir." In A SAINTSBURY MISCELLANY. Ed. John W. Oliver and Augustus Muir. New York: Oxford Univ. Press, 1947. Pp. 27-73.

> An informed, miniature critical biography (with almost nothing on the childhood). Webster likens GS's personal manner to Scott's and classes him among critics with Sainte-Beuve.

CRITICISM

Clark, Albert C. PROSE RHYTHM IN ENGLISH. Oxford: Clarendon Press, 1913.

> In HISTORY OF ENGLISH PROSE RHYTHM, GS places too great an emphasis on variety at the expense of regularity.

Collins, John Churton. "Our Literary Guides: I." In his EPHEMERA CRITICA: OR PLAIN TRUTHS ABOUT CURRENT LITERATURE. London: Constable, 1901. Pp. 93-109.

> Assaults SHORT HISTORY OF ENGLISH LITERATURE for reckless generalizations and factual inaccuracies.

Dobson, Austin. "The Oxford Thackeray." In OLD KENSINGTON PALACE. London: Chatto and Windus, 1910. Pp. 271-89.

> High praise for GS's introductions to his edition of Thackeray.

Elton, Oliver. GEORGE EDWARD BATEMAN SAINTSBURY: 1845-1933. London: Milford, 1933.

> A longer survey of the career than below. It chooses Longinus and Pater as GS's critical masters.

---. "George Saintsbury." In ESSAYS AND ADDRESSES. London: Arnold, 1939. Pp. 239-49.

> A very brief, balanced view of the career. Elton notes that at times GS relies on repetition rather than one-shot precision in expressing his critical views.

Gosse, Edmund. "Mr. Saintsbury." In his SILHOUETTES. London: Heinemann, 1925. Pp. 213-18.

George Saintsbury

    Gosse appraises GS as a greater judge of literary quality than a close analyst of literature.

Gross, Harvey. "Introduction." In his HISTORICAL MANUAL OF ENGLISH PROSODY. New York: Schocken Books, 1966. Pp. xv-xxv.

    Gross admires GS's ear, but accuses him of numerous faults as prosodist, including a "naive teleology" in stressing the historical development of the foot system.

Hildick, Wallace. "Rhythm and Blues." KR, 28 (1966), 540-48.

    Although written in "English Don-Jocular" and limited by GS's refusal to consider the uses of rhythm to support or suggest meaning, HISTORY OF ENGLISH PROSE RHYTHM is judged a magnificent anthology and is highly suggestive of future avenues for scholarship.

Leuba, Walter. GEORGE SAINTSBURY. Twayne English Author Series. New York: Twayne, 1967.

    This contains little biographical information but does review the major works and treats GS in his various roles as critic, editor, stylist, and the like. The book is especially informative on GS's contemporary critical reception.

Lynd, Robert. "Mr. Saintsbury." In his THE ART OF LETTERS. New York: Scribner's, 1921. Pp. 172-78.

    Finds GS's enthusiasm in PEACE OF THE AUGUSTANS infectious but his qualitative judgments indiscriminatory.

MacColl, Dugald Sutherland. "Rhythm in English Verse, Prose and Speech." In ESSAYS AND STUDIES BY MEMBERS OF THE ENGLISH ASSOCIATION. Ed. Oliver Elton. London: Oxford Univ. Press, 1914. v, 7-50.

    A thorough and technical lambasting of GS's metrics, which, like Shapiro (p. 396), contrasts them with Sidney Lanier's.

Potter, Stephen. "King Saintsbury." In his THE MUSE IN CHAINS: A STUDY IN EDUCATION. London: Cape, 1937. Pp. 126-39.

    Asserts the interesting thesis that one of GS's problems as professor and critic was that while he could reflect the styles and personalities of his reading, he lacked a definite point-of-view of his own.

Priestley, J. B. "Mr. George Saintsbury." In his FIGURES IN MODERN LITERATURE. London: Lane, 1928. Pp. 170-95.

> A balanced, generally favorable view of GS. Priestley's most interesting point concerns the dualism evident in GS's style: it reflects a literary enthusiast at war with a cautious professor.

Ralli, Augustus. "Saintsbury." In his A HISTORY OF SHAKESPEARIAN CRITICISM. Vol. 2 of two volumes. London: Oxford Univ. Press, 1932. Pp. 287-92.

> Paraphrases GS's views on Shakespeare's works.

Read, Herbert. "George Saintsbury." In his A COAT OF MANY COLOURS. London: Routledge and Kegan Paul, 1956. Pp. 199-202.

> GS avoided those authors who deeply probe life because he was afraid of it.

Richardson, Dorothy. "Saintsbury and Art for Art's Sake in England." PMLA, 59 (1944), 243-60.

> Discusses numerous essays in placing GS in the aesthetic camp of Swinburne and Baudelaire. His aestheticism accounts for his extreme emphasis on form as separable from content and the appreciative rather than analytic quality of his criticism.

Robinson, James K. "A Neglected Phase of the Aesthetic Movement: English Parnassianism." PMLA, 68 (1953), 733-54.

> Notes that GS was in the movement, as witness his early reviews of French authors in FORTNIGHTLY REVIEW.

Shapiro, Karl. ENGLISH PROSODY AND MODERN POETRY. Baltimore: Johns Hopkins Press, 1947.

> An excellent summation (pp. 3-6) of GS's theory of metrics, set against Sidney Lanier's. GS's is flawed because he fails to define his terms, especially "long" and "short."

Sutherland, James R. THE ENGLISH CRITICS. London: Lewis, 1952.

> Picks GS as the fourth great and typical English critic in the line of Dryden, Johnson, and Hazlitt.

Waugh, Arthur. "Living Critics, VIII." BOOKMAN, 10 (1896), 134-36.

> Tempers his praise of GS by complaining that he classifies authors and books too rigidly.

Wellek, René. "George Saintsbury." EM, 12 (1961), 79-96.

> An excellent, balanced introductory essay on GS as a critic

of poetry and fiction. Wellek concludes that GS enormously influenced the subsequent generation of critics for good (e.g., his insistence on comparing works) and for bad (e.g., his avoidance of theory).

Wilson, Edmund. "George Saintsbury's Centenary," and "George Saintsbury: Gourmet and Glutton." In his CLASSICS AND COMMERCIALS. New York: Farrar, Straus, 1950. Pp. 306-10; 366-71.

Wilson terms GS the only first-rate British critic of GS's time. The first piece praises GS's conversational prose style and compares it to Ford's; the second piece discerns a persona in the books used to dramatic effect.

SIEGFRIED SASSOON (1886-1967)

NONFICTIONAL PROSE

THE COMPLETE MEMOIRS OF GEORGE SHERSTON. London: Faber, 1937. As THE MEMOIRS OF GEORGE SHERSTON; MEMOIRS OF A FOX-HUNTING MAN; MEMOIRS OF AN INFANTRY OFFICER; SHERSTON'S PROGRESS. Garden City, N.Y.: Doubleday, 1937.

> Collects works named in the American edition's title; often referred to as the Sherston trilogy.

THE FLOWER SHOW MATCH AND OTHER PIECES. London: Faber, 1941.

> Reprints selections from FOX-HUNTING, INFANTRY, SHERSTON'S PROGRESS, and OLD CENTURY. Depictions of the rustic idyll of Edwardian life in the shires and of some wartime experiences.

MEMOIRS OF A FOX-HUNTING MAN. London: Faber and Gwyer, 1928. New York: Coward-McCann, 1929.

> SS's first and most famous prose work; autobiography that is partly fictional. SS nostalgically describes typical country people and sporting experiences in a remote setting that flourished before World War I (1896-1915). The hero, George Sherston, outgrows the idyllic world as SS's own youthful experiences are delineated.

MEMOIRS OF AN INFANTRY OFFICER, BY THE AUTHOR OF MEMOIRS OF A FOX-HUNTING MAN. London: Faber; New York: Coward-McCann, 1930.

> A semiautobiographical exploration of the disrupting effects of universal conflict on Sherston's character as the hero experiences and records the desolation of World War I. The stark realism of events (1916-17) is often presented in a restrained, matter-of-fact tone, though irony and bitterness are sometimes apparent. Through his wartime experiences as a commander, Sherston grows in compassion and humanity and gains an increased awareness of life's raw realities. Robert Graves and Bertrand Russell are portrayed in the book.

MEREDITH. London: Constable; New York: Viking, 1948.

> Sympathetic and admiring biography of George Meredith. Perhaps the study is most successful in its sensitive treatment of Meredith's relationships with his friends, his first wife, and his son. SS's critical comments on Meredith's poems tend to discuss their ideas and attitudes rather than their technical effects.

THE OLD CENTURY AND SEVEN MORE YEARS. London: Faber, 1938. New York: Viking, 1939.

> SS's autobiography up to 1907; the nostalgic story of the pleasant, carefree days of childhood in the countryside. The narrative style is often childlike to convey the direct impressions of people and places in SS's early years. The account of adolescent years up to age twenty-one is low-keyed, but reflective.

SHERSTON'S PROGRESS. London: Faber; Garden City, N.Y.: Doubleday, 1936.

> Semiautobiographical. Dispassionate analysis of the mental anguish suffered by the hero in this phase of his World War I experiences (1917-18).

SIEGFRIED'S JOURNEY, 1916-1920. London: Faber, 1945. New York: Viking, 1946.

> Autobiography which treats the hero's wartime experience after he has sustained a headwound (1916-18) as well as his adjustments and reactions to the war's end (1918-20). Personal encounters with such literary figures as Thomas Hardy and Wilfred Owen are described; SS's thoughts on socialism are recorded. The book lacks the coherence found in SS's other works.

THE WEALD OF YOUTH. London: Faber; New York: Viking, 1942.

> Autobiography covering the years 1909-14, when the hero enlisted in the army at age twenty-eight. The book records SS's yearnings and ambitions to be a poet, often in a lighthearted tone. Literary figures in pre-World War I London are sketched.

WORKS EDITED BY OTHERS

SIEGFRIED SASSOON: POET'S PILGRIMAGE. Ed. D. Felicitas Corrigan. London: Gollancz, 1973.

Siegfried Sassoon

Reprints selections from SS's diary, letters, prose, and poetry. Interspersed commentary links the material in chronological order.

BIBLIOGRAPHY

Farmer, David, comp. "Addenda to Keynes's Bibliography of Sassoon." PBSA, 63 (1969), 310-17.

> Lists a total of forty-two additions and corrections based on the collections at the University of Texas at Austin.

———, ed. SIEGFRIED SASSOON: A MEMORIAL EXHIBITION. Austin: Univ. of Texas, 1969.

> A catalog of 159 items drawn from the Humanities Research Center collections at the University of Texas in Austin. Careful annotations are provided for books and manuscripts from all phases of SS's life.

Keynes, Geoffrey, ed. A BIBLIOGRAPHY OF SIEGFRIED SASSOON. London: Rupert Hart-Davis, 1962.

> The definitive primary bibliography which is the most comprehensive list of SS's poetry and prose as well as his contributions to books and periodicals.

BIOGRAPHY

Graves, Robert. GOODBYE TO ALL THAT: AN AUTOBIOGRAPHY. London: Cape, 1929.

> Contains a brief reminiscence of Sassoon during the First World War when the two men were close friends.

Jackson, Stanley. THE SASSOONS. New York: Dutton, 1968.

> In this impressive study of the Sassoon family (1832-1961), some biographical details concerning SS are provided. Especially helpful commentary on SS's love of countryside and Rachel Beer, as well as his awkwardness, education, war career, and political ideas. Superficial discussion of his prose autobiographies.

Roth, Cecil. THE SASSOON DYNASTY. London: Hale, 1941.

> Brief discussion of SS's experiences in World War I and of the six autobiographical works.

Thorpe, Michael. SIEGFRIED SASSOON: A CRITICAL STUDY. London: Oxford Univ. Press, 1966.

>The most complete critical biography. Insightful analysis of SS's varied prose styles--poetic, elevated, Paterian, but also plain and ironic; in short, it is flexible enough to describe the light and "savage aspects of existence." Such technical characteristics of style as Latinisms, coinages, and alliteration are treated. Larger structural features of SS's prose accounts are also examined. Thorpe argues that "it is in his prose, not in his poetry, that the memorable achievement of Sassoon's middle years lies." Includes a brief but useful secondary bibliography.

CRITICISM

Braybrooke, Neville. "Rebel of Another Generation." COMMONWEAL, 67 (1958), 429-31.

>Argues that one of the chief forms of SS's rebellion was against the "establishment." Also, the prose is more effective in evoking landscapes than in depicting "scenes of action."

Corrigan, D. Felicitas. "Introduction." In her SIEGFRIED SASSOON: POET'S PILGRIMAGE. London: Gollancz, 1973. Pp. 15-42.

>Maintains that SS's six autobiographical books are "marked by a deep and subtle sense of humour, a profound feeling for the innocence of youth, and a nostalgia for an English way of life destroyed by war and scientific advances." For aesthetic and sociopolitical reasons, SS had a "pre-machine mentality."

Darton, Frederick Joseph Harvey. FROM SURTEES TO SASSOON: SOME ENGLISH CONTRASTS (1838-1928). London: Morley and Kennerley, 1931. Pp. 81-121, 217-22.

>Relates incidents in FOX-HUNTING MAN and INFANTRY OFFICER to events in SS's life. Concludes that the two memoirs exhibit the "mingled detachment and closeness of the essentially English writers." A valuable appendix charts the topography of FOX-HUNTING MAN.

Fussell, Paul. "'My Dear Siegfried': Gosse to Sassoon." JRUL, 38 (1976), 85-97.

>Examines and quotes from a dozen Gosse letters not published in Charteris' biography. Fussell concludes that Gosse helped to refine SS's prose style and provided him with the idea for MEMOIRS OF GEORGE SHERSTON.

Lohf, Kenneth A. "Friends among the Soldier Poets." CLC, 30, No. 1 (1980), 3-18.

>   Discusses SS's meeting with and influence upon Wilfred Owen (as recounted in SIEGFRIED'S JOURNEY).

MacCarthy, Desmond. MEMORIES. London: MacGibbon and Kee, 1953. Pp. 141-44.

>   High praise for SS's writings about World War I. MacCarthy concludes that from a literary point of view, SHERSTON'S PROGRESS is "even more remarkable" than SIEGFRIED'S JOURNEY.

Pinto, V. de Sola. "Siegfried Sassoon." ENGLISH, 2 (1939), 215-24.

>   High praise for SS's prose works, which convey "the wisdom of a fine, sensitive personality, at once imaginative and humorous." Relates the prose to SS's war poetry.

Powell, Dilys. DESCENT FROM PARNASSUS. New York: Macmillan, 1935. Pp. 137-64.

>   Relates SS's war poetry to FOX-HUNTING MAN and INFANTRY OFFICER.

Reid, Hilary. "'The Secret Memoirs of the Human Heart': Siegfried Sassoon's Poetry and Prose." EIGOS [THE RISING GENERATION] (Tokyo), 121 (1975), 201-04.

>   Argues that SS's two prose trilogies are "a more original contribution than the war poems" to twentieth-century literature. Reid admires SS's "direct, unaffected style."

Sassaman, Stephen. "Sassoon and Blunden's Annotation of GOODBYE TO ALL THAT." FRG, 5 (1976), 87.

>   Brief discussion of the many comments and "corrections" made by SS and Blunden in a copy of GOOD-BYE. SS remarks on Graves's style.

Thorpe, Michael. "Introduction." In his THE OLD CENTURY AND SEVEN MORE YEARS. London: Faber, 1968. Pp. 11-22.

>   Interesting analysis of the contemporary reception of THE OLD CENTURY just before World War II. Concludes that the "consolation" it offered was an anachronism. Also discusses the inward and pictorial quality of the narrative, which was partly inherited from Walter Pater's style.

GEORGE BERNARD SHAW (1856-1950)

THE BODLEY HEAD BERNARD SHAW: COLLECTED PLAYS WITH THEIR PREFACES, edited by Dan H. Laurence, London: Max Reinhardt, 1970-74, in seven volumes, contains all the prefaces and some of GBS's essays and letters on his own plays. The STANDARD EDITION OF THE WORKS OF BERNARD SHAW, London: Constable, 1930-1952, ultimately in thirty-six volumes, contains most of the important nonfictional work.

NONFICTIONAL PROSE

THE COMMON SENSE OF MUNICIPAL TRADING. London: Constable, 1904. New York: Lane, 1911.

> Drawing on GBS's experience as borough councilman, this argues for an extension of community control over services, to be supported by taxation.

DOCTOR'S DELUSIONS; CRUDE CRIMINOLOGY; SHAM EDUCATION. London: Constable, 1931. New York: Wise, 1932.

> Volume 22 of the Constable edition, this is a collection of letters and articles on the three topics (IMPRISONMENT is also reprinted). In it GBS shoots at such targets as vaccination and corporal punishment.

DRAMATIC OPINIONS AND ESSAYS WITH AN APOLOGY BY BERNARD SHAW. 2 vols. New York: Brentano's, 1906. London: Constable, 1907.

> A collection of over one hundred reviews written by GBS for the SATURDAY REVIEW from 1895 to 1898. There are numerous reviews of performances of Ibsen, GBS's favorite dramatist, numerous pieces on the deficiencies of Shakespeare, and several on leading actors of the day, such as Irving.

ESSAYS IN FABIAN SOCIALISM. London: Constable; New York: Wise, 1932.

George Bernard Shaw

Collects nine previously published essays and pamphlets including "The Impossibilities of Anarchism" and "Socialism for Millionaires."

EVERYBODY'S POLITICAL WHAT'S WHAT? London: Constable; New York: Dodd, Mead, 1944.

GBS's last major work of Socialist explication, this equates state-subsidized capitalism with fascism. He calls for a reformation of the educational system; in the meantime expert panels rather than "Mr. Everyman" must choose political leaders.

FABIAN ESSAYS IN SOCIALISM. Ed. George Bernard Shaw. London: Scott, 1889.

An important document in the history of British socialism. Edited by GBS, it contains eight introductory essays of which two are by him. "Economic" justifies Socialist economics by reference to an agricultural example rather than an industrial; "Transition" calls for a "gradual transition to Social Democracy...."

FABIANISM AND THE EMPIRE: A MANIFESTO BY THE FABIAN SOCIETY. London: Richards, 1900.

A long pamphlet occasioned by the Boer War. The first part argues that the Empire can survive only by accepting socialism and by tailoring policy to fit specific colonial possessions. The second part examines the plight of "home affairs."

THE FUTURE OF POLITICAL SCIENCE IN AMERICA. New York: Dodd, Mead, 1933. Rev. ed. as THE POLITICAL MADHOUSE IN AMERICA AND NEARER HOME. London: Constable, 1933.

In this New York speech of April 1933, GBS notes contemporary evidence of capitalism's decline. He argues America must reject the individualistic "anarchism" of the Constitution and embrace communism--he adduces the example of Russia.

IMPRISONMENT. New York: Brentano's, 1925. Chislehurst, Kent, Engl.: Prison Medical Reform Council, 1944.

Describing imprisonment as "a worse crime than any of those committed by its victims," GBS discusses the motives for it as a confused mix of retribution, deterrence, and reformation. He argues the state has the right to kill the dangerously incorrigible; those capable of reform should retain most human liberties and opportunities, such as marriage.

THE INTELLIGENT WOMAN'S GUIDE TO SOCIALISM AND CAPITALISM. London: Constable; Garden City, N.Y.: Garden City Publishing, 1928.

A sweeping 500-page survey of social institutions as they exist under capitalism and would exist under socialism. Blaming the former for everything from prostitution to WWI, GBS also rejects various other means of income distribution, such as "to each what she produces," in favor of absolute equality of income.

THE LEGAL EIGHT HOURS QUESTION: A PUBLIC DEBATE BETWEEN MR. GEO. BERNARD SHAW AND MR. G.W. FOOTE AT THE HALL OF SCIENCE, LONDON, JAN. 14 & 15, 1891. London: Forder, 1891.

>   Not seen.

LONDON MUSIC IN 1888-89: AS HEARD BY CORNO DI BASSETTO (LATER KNOWN AS BERNARD SHAW): WITH SOME FURTHER AUTOBIOGRAPHICAL PARTICULARS. London: Constable; New York: Dodd, Mead, 1937.

>   A sequel to MUSIC IN LONDON, consisting of pieces written for THE STAR. It contains a sizable preface on GBS's early exposure to music.

MUSIC IN LONDON, 1890-94: CRITICISMS CONTRIBUTED WEEK BY WEEK TO THE WORLD. 3 vols. London: Constable, 1931. New York: Wise, 1932.

>   A large collection voicing, in part, GBS's preference for Mozart and Wagner and his dislike of Brahms, Italian Opera, and music critics.

OUR THEATRES IN THE NINETIES: CRITICISMS CONTRIBUTED WEEK BY WEEK TO THE SATURDAY REVIEW FROM JANUARY 1895 TO MAY 1898. 3 vols. London: Constable; New York: Wise, 1931.

>   A somewhat expanded version of DRAMATIC OPINIONS AND ESSAYS.

PEACE CONFERENCE HINTS. London: Constable, 1919.

>   A realist's description of the power politics behind WWI and the 1919 Peace Conference. Accurately predicting that the next war would destroy civilian populations, GBS sees the only hope to be the League, with Germany admitted.

PEN PORTRAITS AND REVIEWS. London: Constable, 1931. New York: Wise, 1932.

>   A collection of thirty-six articles, most on contemporary literary men or actors. "The Chesterbelloc" sees Chesterton and Belloc in an unnatural partnership dominated by the latter; "H. G. Wells on the Rest of Us" gives GBS's version of Wells's activities as Fabian. "Shaming the Devil about Shelley" glories in Shelley's radicalism.

George Bernard Shaw

THE PERFECT WAGNERITE: A COMMENTARY ON THE RING OF THE NIBLUNGS. London: Richards, 1898. New York: Stone, 1899.

> Noting Wagner's revolutionary sympathies in the 1848 rebellion, GBS reads the Ring dramas as social allegory with Alberich as capitalist and Siegfried as anarchist.

PREFACES BY BERNARD SHAW. London: Constable, 1934.

> A collection of thirty-seven under the headings "Sociological," "Political," "Religious," "Autobiographical and Professional," and "Miscellaneous."

THE QUINTESSENCE OF IBSENISM. London: Scott; Boston: Tucker, 1891. Rev. ed. London: Constable; New York: Brentano's, 1913.

> An analysis of "Ibsenism" emphasizing social theme solely. GBS sees Ibsen as a social progressive attacking the idealized duties and roles that support the status quo, such as marriage and the self-sacrificing "womanly woman." In the enlarged edition sixteen plays are summarized in accordance with this thesis.

THE SANITY OF ART: AN EXPOSURE OF THE CURRENT NONSENSE ABOUT ARTISTS BEING DEGENERATE. London: New Age Press; New York: Tucker, 1908.

> A reply to Max Nordau's DEGENERATION, which had portrayed modern artists as morbid. GBS, seeing artists as fostering the evolution of the race, first defends Whistler, Wagner, and Ibsen against Nordau and then refutes specific points in Nordau's book.

SHAW GIVES HIMSELF AWAY: AN AUTOBIOGRAPHICAL MISCELLANY. Newton, Montgomeryshire, Engl.: Gregynog Press, 1939.

> Except for two novel prefaces and the miscellaneous "Bits and Scraps," this was reprinted in SIXTEEN SELF SKETCHES.

SIXTEEN SELF SKETCHES. London: Constable; New York: Dodd, Mead, 1949.

> An autobiographical jumble, in which the principal text is accompanied by interviews and letters correcting GBS's biographers. The work centers on his shabby-genteel boyhood in Ireland and early London career as reviewer and Socialist. The chapter "Biographers' Blunders Corrected" presents psychologically ambivalent portraits of the Shaw family circle.

SOCIALISM AND SUPERIOR BRAINS: A REPLY TO MR. MALLOCK. London: The Fabian Society, 1909. New York: Lane, 1910.

> GBS assaults Mallock's position that the able man rather than the laborer produces wealth; he argues that the able must not be confused with capitalists, merely "the holders of land and capital."

STATEMENT OF THE EVIDENCE IN CHIEF OF GEORGE BERNARD SHAW BEFORE THE JOINT-COMMITTEE ON STAGE PLAYS (CENSORSHIP AND THEATRE LICENSING). London: Privately Printed, 1909.

>Not seen.

WHAT I REALLY WROTE ABOUT THE WAR. London: Constable, 1931. New York: Brentano's, 1932.

>A lengthy collection of newspaper articles and retrospective commentary. Although not pacifistic, GBS consistently exposes the hypocrisy and jingoism of both sides.

WILLIAM MORRIS AS I KNEW HIM. New York: Dodd, Mead, 1936.

>A brief, admiring memoir of the man GBS met in Socialist circles in the 1880's. Part of the book portrays Morris as a leader in the factionalized Socialist movement; part depicts life at Kelmscott House. A romance with Morris' daughter is mentioned.

WORKS EDITED BY OTHERS

BERNARD SHAW: A PROSE ANTHOLOGY. Ed. H. M. Burton. London: Longmans, Green, 1959.

>Collects a great many dramatic and nonfictional prose pieces organized under topic headings.

BERNARD SHAW AND KARL MARX: A SYMPOSIUM, 1884-1889. Ed. Richard W. Ellis. New York: Random House, 1930.

>Reprints three GBS reviews of DAS KAPITAL and a debate in writing between GBS and Philip Wicksteed over Jevons.

BERNARD SHAW'S NONDRAMATIC LITERARY CRITICISM. Ed. Stanley Weintraub. Lincoln: Univ. of Nebraska Press, 1972.

>Contains selections on "Novelists," "Poets," and "Memoirists," as well as selections on "Sociology and Sex" (in literature) and "Greatness in Literature."

BERNARD SHAW'S READY-RECKONER: A GUIDE TO CIVILIZATION. Ed. N. H. Leigh-Taylor. New York: Random House, 1965.

>Numerous brief passages from the plays and nonfiction grouped under the headings "Poverty," "Christianity," "Crime and Punishment," "Democracy," "Capitalism," "Socialism," "Human Relations," and "Education."

George Bernard Shaw

COLLECTED MUSIC CRITICISM. New York: Vienna House, 1973.

THE COMPLETE PREFACES OF BERNARD SHAW. London: Hamlyn, 1965.

GEORGE BERNARD SHAW ON LANGUAGE. Ed. Abraham Tauber. New York: Philosophical Library, 1963.

> A collection of letters and prefaces on such GBS enthusiasms as reforming spelling and the alphabet.

THE GREAT COMPOSERS: REVIEWS AND BOMBARDMENTS BY BERNARD SHAW. Ed. Louis Crompton. Berkeley and Los Angeles: Univ. of California Press, 1978.

> The best anthology. Essays on thirty-six composers follow a selection of pieces on general musical topics.

HOW TO BECOME A MUSICAL CRITIC. Ed. Dan H. Laurence. New York: Hill and Wang, 1961.

> A generous selection of GBS's reviews of the 1880's, the 1890's, and the twentieth century (the last issued in 1950).

THE MATTER WITH IRELAND. Ed. Dan H. Laurence and David H. Greene. New York: Hill and Wang, 1962.

> A collection of fifty-two pieces on Irish political questions written throughout GBS's life.

MY DEAR DOROTHEA: A PRACTICAL SYSTEM OF MORAL EDUCATION FOR FEMALES EMBODIED IN A LETTER TO A YOUNG PERSON OF THAT SEX. Ed. Stephen Winsten. New York: Vanguard Press, 1956.

> A lengthy, amusingly iconoclastic "letter" emphasizing the virtues of perceptiveness and self-reliance written in 1878.

PLATFORM AND PULPIT: BERNARD SHAW. Ed. Dan H. Laurence. London: Rupert Hart-Davis, 1962.

> A printing of thirty-seven of GBS's lectures delivered from 1885 to 1946.

PLAYS AND PLAYERS: ESSAYS ON THE THEATRE. Ed. A.C. Ward. London: Oxford Univ. Press, 1952.

> Forty-one are reprinted; the Shakespeare criticism is heavily represented.

George Bernard Shaw

THE PORTABLE BERNARD SHAW. Ed. Stanley Weintraub. New York: Viking-Penguin, 1977.

> This contains no complete play but a great many letters and articles.

PRACTICAL POLITICS: TWENTIETH-CENTURY VIEWS ON POLITICS AND ECONOMICS. Ed. Lloyd J. Hubenka. Lincoln: Univ. of Nebraska Press, 1976.

> A collection of twenty Socialist essays and lectures, mostly written from 1900 to 1930.

THE RATIONALIZATION OF RUSSIA. Ed. Harry M. Geduld. Bloomington: Indiana Univ. Press, 1964.

> An incomplete manuscript from the British Museum collection justifying the excesses of the Soviet regime. It is based on GBS's 1931 visit.

THE ROAD TO EQUALITY: TEN UNPUBLISHED LECTURES AND ESSAYS, 1884-1918. Ed. Louis Crompton. Boston: Beacon Press, 1971.

> A collection of four essays and six lectures from the British Museum collection on Socialist themes.

SELECTED NON-DRAMATIC WRITINGS OF BERNARD SHAW. Riverside Editions. Ed. Dan H. Laurence. Boston: Houghton-Mifflin, 1965.

> Collects the novel AN UNSOCIAL SOCIALIST, QUINTESSENCE OF IBSENISM, and thirteen essays on miscellaneous topics.

SELECTED PASSAGES FROM THE WORKS OF BERNARD SHAW. Ed. Charlotte F. Shaw. London: Constable, 1912.

> A great many included.

SELECTED PROSE. Ed. Diarmuid Russell. New York: Dodd, Mead, 1952.

> A collection of twenty-six pieces under the headings "Biography," "Fiction," "Music," "Theatre," "Socialism," and "Miscellaneous."

SHAW: AN AUTOBIOGRAPHY. 2 vols. Ed. Stanley Weintraub. New York: Weybright and Talley, 1969, 1970.

> A pastiche of nonfictive, autobiographical essays and fragments arranged to form an "autobiography."

SHAW AND IBSEN: BERNARD SHAW'S THE QUINTESSENCE OF IBSENISM AND RELATED WRITINGS. Ed. J.L. Wisenthal. Toronto: Univ. of Toronto Press, 1979.

> Along with QUINTESSENCE OF IBSENISM, this collects and annotates eight other miscellaneous pieces by GBS on Ibsen.

SHAW AND SOCIETY: AN ANTHOLOGY AND A SYMPOSIUM. Ed. C.E.M. Joad. London: Odhams Press, 1953.

> Along with memorial pieces on GBS as Socialist, this extracts passages from some Fabian tracts, prefaces, and articles on Socialist topics.

SHAW ON MUSIC: A SELECTION FROM THE MUSIC CRITICISM OF BERNARD SHAW. Ed. Eric Bentley. Garden City, N.Y.: Doubleday, 1955.

> A generous selection of the reviews, arranged by composers and topics.

SHAW ON RELIGION. Ed. Warren Sylvester Smith. New York: Dodd, Mead, 1967.

> A selection from the plays and nonfiction, including three previously unpublished essays.

SHAW ON THEATRE. Ed. E.J. West. New York: Hill and Wang, 1958.

> A chronologically ordered selection of GBS's precepts on censorship, acting, directing, and other aspects of the theater.

SHAW ON VIVISECTION. Ed. G.H. Bowker. London: Allen, 1949.

> A collection of six brief pieces against vivisection, plus one on vaccination and two on germs.

SHAW'S DRAMATIC CRITICISM (1895-98). Ed. John F. Matthews. New York: Hill and Wang, 1959.

> Fifty-four essays are reprinted.

THE SOCIALISM OF SHAW. Ed. James Fuchs. New York: Vanguard Press, 1926.

> Collects five Socialist pieces, including IMPOSSIBILITIES OF ANARCHISM, and ends with a collection of pithy Socialist remarks by GBS.

BIBLIOGRAPHY

Bevan, E. Dean, ed. A CONCORDANCE TO THE PLAYS AND PREFACES OF BERNARD SHAW. 10 vols. Detroit: Gale Research Co., 1971.

Broad, C. Lewis, and Violet M. Broad, eds. DICTIONARY TO THE PLAYS AND NOVELS OF BERNARD SHAW, WITH BIBLIOGRAPHY OF HIS WORKS AND OF THE LITERATURE CONCERNING HIM WITH A RECORD OF THE PRINCIPAL SHAVIAN PLAY PRODUCTIONS. London: Black, 1929.

> This hodgepodge does contain annotated, chronological listings
> of works by and on GBS.

Carpenter, Charles A., comp. "Modern Drama Studies: An Annual Bibliography."
MD, 17 (1974), 87-89, and continuing.

> Unannotated listing of books and articles alphabetized by author.

─────, ed. "Shaw and Religion/Philosophy: A Working Bibliography." In
SHAW AND RELIGION. Ed. Charles A. Berst. University Park: Pennsylvania
State Univ. Press, 1981. Pp. 225-46.

> An important, extensive primary and secondary bibliography on
> the subject.

Farley, Earl, and Marvin Carlson, comps. "George Bernard Shaw: A Selected
Bibliography (1945-1955) Part One: Books"; "George Bernard Shaw: A
Selected Bibliography 1945-55 Part II: Periodicals." MD, 2 (1959), 188-202,
295-325.

> Unannotated listings, arranged chronologically by author.

Gomme, Geoffrey J.L., et al., eds. "A Continuing Checklist of Published
Shaviana." SHAW BULLETIN [later SHAWR], 1, No. 2 (1951), 13-14.
Continued in subsequent volumes.

> Appearing in almost every number, this contains a well-annotated
> listing of secondary books and articles, as well as a primary
> listing of posthumous editions, collections, and the like.

Henderson, Lucile Kelling, comp. "Shaw and Woman: A Bibliographical
Checklist." SHAWR, 17 (1974), 60-66.

> A listing of GBS statements on women and of works by others
> on his relationship with women.

Hill, Eldon C., ed. "Selected Bibliography." In his GEORGE BERNARD
SHAW. Twayne's English Author Series. Boston: Twayne, 1978. Pp. 165-78.

> Divides the primary works into kinds and lists alphabetically
> by title; the sections on secondary works are annotated.

Keough, Lawrence C., comp. "George Bernard Shaw, 1946-1955: A Selected
Bibliography." BB, 22 (1959), 224-26; 23 (1960), 20-24, 36-41.

> A listing of works by and about GBS issued in this ten-year period.

Rodenbeck, John, comp. "A Shaw/Shakespeare Checklist." SHAWR, 14
(1971), 95-99.

> A listing of GBS's letters and articles about Shakespeare and
> a listing of works by others about him and Shakespeare.

Rosenberg, Edgar, ed. "The Shaw/Dickens File: 1885 to 1950: Two Checklists." SHAWR, 20 (1977), 148-70; 21 (1978), 2-19.

> An annotated listing of GBS's references and allusions to Dickens, completed only up to December 1915.

Shedd, Robert G., comp. "Modern Drama: A Selective Bibliography of Works Published in English." MD, 3 (1960), 154-56. Continued to 1969.

> Unannotated listing of books and articles alphabetized by author.

Townsend, Francis G., et al., comps. "Victorian Bibliography." VS, 1 (1958), 417-19. Continued in subsequent volumes.

> An annual listing of books and articles on GBS; reviews of critical books are also listed.

Ward, A.C., ed. "Bernard Shaw: A Select Bibliography." In his BERNARD SHAW. 1950. Rev. ed. London: Longmans, Green, 1966. Pp. 45-55.

> Useful primarily for its seven-page listing of GBS's book publications in chronological order with some bibliographic annotation.

Weintraub, Stanley. "Bernard Shaw." In ANGLO-IRISH LITERATURE: A REVIEW OF RESEARCH. Ed. Richard J. Finneran. New York: MLA, 1976. Pp. 167-215.

> An excellent review essay on primary and secondary Shavian material, including a section on treatments of the "Early Musical, Dramatic, and Literary Journalism."

Wells, Geoffrey H., ed. A BIBLIOGRAPHY OF THE BOOKS AND PAMPHLETS OF GEORGE BERNARD SHAW. London: Bookman's Journal, 1925.

> Still the best primary bibliography to 1924. It is chronologically arranged with full bibliographic annotation; part 1 treating books and pamphlets by GBS and part 2 contributions by him to others' works.

BIOGRAPHY

Ervine, St. John. BERNARD SHAW: HIS LIFE, WORK, AND FRIENDS. London: Constable, 1956.

> This attempt at major biography contains some mention of the nonfiction but is warped by Ervine's prejudices. There is no table of contents.

Henderson, Archibald. GEORGE BERNARD SHAW: MAN OF THE CENTURY. 1911, 1932. Rev. ed. 2 vols. New York: Appleton-Century-Crofts, 1956.

Still the best biography, this last revision of the massive, authorized original of 1911 contains informative, sizable reviews of the nonfiction.

Irvine, William. THE UNIVERSE OF G. B. S. New York: McGraw-Hill, 1949.

A critical biography emphasizing GBS's roots in late nineteenth-century radical thought.

Weintraub, Stanley. JOURNEY TO HEARTBREAK: THE CRUCIBLE YEARS OF BERNARD SHAW, 1914-1918. New York: Weybright and Talley, 1971.

This detailed history of GBS in the war years includes considerable discussion of his controversial pamphlet COMMON SENSE ABOUT THE WAR and his later writings more favorable to the war effort.

CRITICISM

Abbott, Anthony S. SHAW AND CHRISTIANITY. New York: Seabury Press, 1965.

Reviews GBS's criticisms of Christianity in his plays and non-fiction.

Adams, Elsie B. BERNARD SHAW AND THE AESTHETES. Columbus: Ohio State Univ. Press, 1971.

Cites the nonfiction in showing GBS's affinities with the "moral aesthetes" Ruskin and Morris and argues GBS is closer to the "art for art's sake" movement than he seems.

Barber, George S. "Shaw's Contributions to Music Criticism." PMLA, 72 (1957), 1005-17.

A good, general review of the tendencies in GBS's musical criticism, stressing his emphasis on the economics of concerts and his insistence on jargon-free, opinionated criticism.

Barr, Alan P. "Diabolonian Pundit: G. B. S. as Critic." SR, 11 (1968), 11-23.

GBS misreads Bunyan, Shakespeare, Ibsen, Wagner, and Nietzsche in order to render them relevant contemporary exemplars.

_____. VICTORIAN STAGE PULPITEER: BERNARD SHAW'S CRUSADE. Athens: Univ. of Georgia Press, 1973.

Cites the nonfiction in presenting GBS's Creative Evolution as a Victorian religious impulse.

Bentley, Eric. BERNARD SHAW. 1947. Rev. ed. New York: New Directions, 1957.

> The first two chapters are a strongly favorable review of GBS's Socialist thought.

Bernal, J.D. "Shaw the Scientist." In G.B.S. 90: ASPECTS OF BERNARD SHAW'S LIFE AND WORK. Ed. S. Winsten. New York: Dodd, Mead, 1946. Pp. 120-38.

> Cites several prefaces in laying out GBS's attitudes on Darwinism, vivisection, and vaccination. Bernal deplores GBS's liking of "scientific lost causes."

Berst, Charles A. "In the Beginning: The Poetic Genesis of Shaw's God." In SHAW AND RELIGION. University Park: Pennsylvania State Univ. Press, 1981. Pp. 5-41.

> An important study of GBS's evolving religious ideas. Berst discusses the nonfiction--especially the closely related QUINTES-SENCE OF IBSENISM, SANITY OF ART, and PERFECT WAGNERITE, a "Trinitarian gospel"--in noting the aesthetic nature of GBS's religious impulse.

Bissell, Claude. "The Butlerian Inheritance of G.B. Shaw." DR, 41 (1961), 159-73.

> Cites nonfiction in demonstrating that GBS and Butler are both realists, both Lamarckians, and have similar attitudes toward poverty.

Blissett, William. "Bernard Shaw: Imperfect Wagnerite." UTQ, 27 (1958), 185-99.

> GBS was only a latecomer in Wagner criticism; his treatment of the works is inaccurate; Wagner did not greatly influence GBS's drama.

Boxhill, Roger. SHAW AND THE DOCTORS. New York: Basic Books, 1969.

> While admitting GBS engages in deliberate overstatement, Boxhill defends his writings on medical matters as conforming to "the best humanist tradition of medical writing."

Brome, Vincent. "Shaw versus Wells"; "G.K. Chesterton versus Bernard Shaw." In his SIX STUDIES IN QUARRELLING. London: Cresset Press, 1958. Pp. 1-39; 137-69.

> Two essays citing some nonfiction in retailing GBS's long fights with Wells and Chesterton.

George Bernard Shaw

Brown, Ivor. SHAW IN HIS TIME. London: Nelson, 1965.

> This cites the nonfiction throughout in presenting GBS's attitudes toward social issues of his day.

Chappelow, Allan. SHAW--"THE CHUCKER-OUT": A BIOGRAPHICAL EXPOSITION AND CRITIQUE. London: Allen and Unwin, 1969.

> This encyclopedic hodgepodge quotes a vast array of letters, speeches, and articles in laying out GBS's thoughts on various subjects, of which the economic is predominate.

Cherry, D.R. "The Fabianism of Shaw." QQ, 69 (1962), 83-93.

> Examines the Fabian tracts to indicate GBS's early belief in "the inevitability of gradualness": he "guided English socialism into very English paths."

Chesterton, G.K. GEORGE BERNARD SHAW. New York: Lane, 1910.

> This early, provocative assault on GBS contains a chapter on his criticism which writes down his love of music and his dislike of Shakespeare to his Puritanism.

Costello, Donald P. "G.B.S. the Movie Critic." QUARTERLY OF FILM RADIO AND TELEVISION, 11 (1956), 256-75.

> Pulls together GBS's various statements in articles on the cinema as art form and as mode of mass communication.

Crompton, Louis. "Editor's Introduction." In his THE GREAT COMPOSERS. Berkeley and Los Angeles: Univ. of California Press, 1978. Pp. xi-xxiv.

> An informal essay that sees GBS's "The Religion of the Pianoforte" as the key statement of his musical views and that places him in the nineteenth-century tradition of program music rather than the twentieth-century tradition of absolute music.

──────. "Introduction." In his THE ROAD TO EQUALITY: TEN UNPUBLISHED LECTURES AND ESSAYS, 1884-1918. Boston: Beacon Press, 1971. Pp. ix-xxxvi.

> Along with a lengthy summary of the ten pieces, Crompton adds a brief, handy summation of GBS's Socialist ideas.

Davies, A. Emil. "G.B.S. and Local Government." In G.B.S. 90: ASPECTS OF BERNARD SHAW'S LIFE AND WORK. Ed. S. Winsten. New York: Dodd, Mead, 1946. Pp. 200-208.

> Cites COMMONSENSE OF MUNICIPAL TRADING in noting GBS's rejection of the profit motive in municipal operations.

George Bernard Shaw

Dent, Edward J. "Como Di Bassetto." In G.B.S. 90: ASPECTS OF BERNARD SHAW'S LIFE AND WORK. Ed. S. Winsten. New York: Dodd, Mead, 1946. Pp. 156-69.

> Reviews GBS's music criticisms, stressing his championship of Wagnerian opera.

Dobb, Maurice. "Bernard Shaw and Economics." In G.B.S. 90: ASPECTS OF BERNARD SHAW'S LIFE AND WORK. Ed. S. Winsten. New York: Dodd, Mead, 1946. Pp. 170-82.

> Cites various tracts in arguing that in many of his socialistic ideas GBS was closer to Marx than to Jevons.

Duerksen, Roland A. "Shelley and Shaw." In his SHELLEYAN IDEAS IN VICTORIAN LITERATURE. The Hague: Mouton, 1966. Pp. 166-97.

> A lengthy review of Shelley's influence that cites nonfiction such as "Shaming the Devil about Shelley" (PEN PORTRAITS).

Dukore, Bernard F. BERNARD SHAW, DIRECTOR. Seattle: Univ. of Washington Press, 1971.

_____. BERNARD SHAW, PLAYWRIGHT: ASPECTS OF SHAVIAN DRAMA. Columbia: Univ. of Missouri Press, 1973.

> Both pull together extensive, scattered commentary on these subjects from the nonfiction.

Fromm, Harold. BERNARD SHAW AND THE THEATER IN THE NINETIES: A STUDY OF SHAW'S DRAMATIC CRITICISM. Lawrence: Univ. of Kansas Press, 1967.

> A full-scale treatment of GBS's drama criticism in his SATURDAY REVIEW years, with chapters on his aesthetics, his reactions to nineteenth-century drama, his attitudes toward Shakespeare, Ibsen, censorship, and the like.

Gassner, John. "Bernard Shaw and the Making of the Modern Mind." CE, 23 (1962), 517-25.

> A brief, mediocre review of the drama and music criticism.

_____. "Shaw on Ibsen and the Drama of Ideas." In his IDEAS IN THE DRAMA: SELECTED PAPERS FROM THE ENGLISH INSTITUTE. New York: Columbia Univ. Press, 1964. Pp. 71-100.

> An excellent discussion of the degree to which Ibsen fits GBS's view of him as an iconoclastic dramatist of ideas.

Gerould, Daniel Charles. "George Bernard Shaw's Criticism of Ibsen." CL, 15 (1963), 130-45.

> Defends GBS's criticism of Ibsen by examining the various contexts in which it was written.

Glicksberg, Charles I. "The Criticism of Bernard Shaw." SAQ, 50 (1951), 96-108.

> An impressionistic appreciation of GBS as critic, stressing his intolerant perfectionism.

_____. "Shaw Versus Science." DR, 28 (1948), 271-83.

> A general review of the subject that adduces GBS's religious impulse to account for his antiscientism.

Goldberg, Michael. "The Dickens Debate: G.B.S. vs. G.K.C." SHAWR, 20 (1977), 135-47.

> Cites nonfiction such as GBS's prefaces to GREAT EXPECTATIONS and HARD TIMES (BERNARD SHAW'S NONDRAMATIC LITERARY CRITICISM) in outlining the differences between GBS's Dickens (the social critic) and Chesterton's (the comic).

_____. "Shaw's Dickensian Quintessence." SHAWR, 14 (1971), 14-28.

> Cites various nonfictional works, including prefaces GBS wrote for two of Dickens' novels, in demonstrating that GBS views the social criticism and symbolic bent of the later Dickens as Ibsenesque.

Greiner, Norbert. "Mill, Marx and Bebel: Early Influences on Shaw's Characterization of Women." In FABIAN FEMINIST: BERNARD SHAW AND WOMAN. Ed. Rodelle Weintraub. University Park: Pennsylvania State Univ. Press, 1977. Pp. 90-98.

> On the influence of the three on QUINTESSENCE OF IBSENISM and other nonfictional works presenting the plight of women as economic.

_____. "Shaw's Aesthetics and Socialist Realism." SHAWR, 22 (1979), 33-45.

> A complex discussion of GBS's "combination of socialist and Platonic-Hegelian" aesthetic ideas that cites the nonfiction.

Hadsel, Martha. "The Uncommon-Common Metaphor in Shaw's Dramatic Criticism." SHAWR, 23 (1980), 119-29.

> On GBS's tendency as drama critic to draw his metaphors from the commonplace for the sake of his audience.

Henson, Janice. "Bernard Shaw's Contribution to the Wagner Controversy in England." SHAWR, 4, No. 1 (1961), 21-26.

> GBS was not, in fact, one of the first champions of Wagner, and he was blind to some tendencies of Wagner's art.

Hill, Eldon C. GEORGE BERNARD SHAW. Twayne's English Author Series. Boston: Twayne, 1978.

> This contains virtually nothing on the nonfiction.

Holroyd, Michael. "Women and the Body Politic." In THE GENIUS OF SHAW: A SYMPOSIUM. New York: Holt, 1979. Pp. 166-83.

> Cites the nonfiction in discussing GBS's complex ideas on the subject.

Hubenka, Lloyd J. "Introduction." In his PRACTICAL POLITICS: TWENTIETH-CENTURY VIEWS ON POLITICS AND ECONOMICS. Lincoln: Univ. of Nebraska Press, 1976. Pp. vii-xxv.

> Traces the glimmerings of GBS's late, antidemocratic ideas through the pieces collected.

Hugo, Leon. BERNARD SHAW: PLAYWRIGHT AND PREACHER. London: Methuen, 1971.

> The first three chapters afford a brief, unidolatrous summation of GBS's politics, religion of evolution, and aesthetics.

Hulse, James W. "Shaw: Socialist Maverick." In REVOLUTIONISTS IN LONDON: A STUDY OF FIVE UNORTHODOX SOCIALISTS. Oxford: Clarendon Press, 1970. Pp. 111-37.

> A balanced and learned survey of GBS's socialism in the nineteenth century that cites many of his articles in tracing his uneasy alliance with Marxism and Fabianism.

Hummert, Paul A. BERNARD SHAW'S MARXIAN ROMANCE. Lincoln: Univ. of Nebraska Press, 1973.

> A thorough treatment of the impact of Marx on GBS that devotes considerable space to nonfiction ranging from ESSAYS IN FABIAN SOCIALISM to EVERYBODY'S POLITICAL WHAT'S WHAT.

Irvine, William. "G.B. Shaw's Musical Criticism." MUSICAL QUARTERLY, 32 (1946), 319-32.

> A witty, general discussion of GBS as music critic.

———. "Shaw's QUINTESSENCE OF IBSENISM." SAQ, 46 (1947), 252-62.

> A negative but informed analysis that finds GBS's terms "realist" and "idealist" inadequate as applied to Ibsen.

Kaye, Julian B. BERNARD SHAW AND THE NINETEENTH-CENTURY TRADITION. Norman: Univ. of Oklahoma Press, 1958.

> Cites the nonfiction throughout a penetrating examination of the nineteenth-century sources of GBS's social thought, which, Kaye argues, disabled him from perceiving post-1914 events rightly.

King, Carlyle. "G.B.S. on Literature: The Author as Critic." QQ, 66 (1959), 135-45.

> Notes that GBS's literary criticism is milder than his musical and that he stresses theme over form.

Laurence, Dan H. "Introduction." In HOW TO BECOME A MUSICAL CRITIC. New York: Hill and Wang, 1961. Pp. xi-xxii.

> Notable for its details on the history of GBS's employment as music critic.

Leary, Daniel J. "The Evolutionary Dialectic of Shaw and Teilhard: A Perennial Philosophy." SHAWR, 9 (1966), 15-34.

> Cites the prefaces in noting common Manichean and Pelagian tendencies in the dramatist and the priest.

Le Mesurier, Lillian. THE SOCIALIST WOMAN'S GUIDE TO INTELLIGENCE: A REPLY TO MR. SHAW. London: Benn, 1929.

> Despite the title, a political moderate assaults such radical GBS ideas as equality of income.

Levin, Gerald. "Shaw, Butler and Kant." PQ, 52 (1973), 142-56.

> Cites many of the prefaces in a thickly written discussion of how GBS misinterprets Kant.

Lutz, Jerry. PITCHMAN'S MELODY, SHAW ABOUT "SHAKESPEARE." Lewisburg, Pa.: Bucknell Univ. Press, 1974.

> Cites nonfiction throughout this thorough treatment of GBS's relationship with the Bard. Lutz deals with such subjects as Shakespeare's influence on GBS's plays, GBS's criticism of Shakespeare as empty-headed, and GBS's assaults on the contemporary staging of Shakespeare's plays.

McDowell, Frederick P.W. "Victorian Shaw." VN, 11 (1957), 16-19.

George Bernard Shaw

    A brief presentation of GBS as embodying Victorian tensions, such as tendencies toward rationalism and transcendentalism, that cites QUINTESSENCE OF IBSENISM.

MacKenzie, Norman, and Jeanne MacKenzie. THE FABIANS. New York: Simon and Schuster, 1977.

    This contains a full history of GBS as Fabian with frequent reference to his Fabian tracts.

MacKerness, E.D. "Como Inglese: Notes on the Texture of George Bernard Shaw's Musical Criticism." In RENAISSANCE AND MODERN ESSAYS. Ed. G.R. Hibbard. London: Routledge and Kegan Paul, 1966. Pp. 147-57.

    An informal discussion of GBS's prejudices as music critic, such as his "partiality for dramatic music and his respect for 'organic form. . . .'"

Meisel, Martin. "Shaw and Revolution: The Politics of the Plays." In SHAW: SEVEN CRITICAL ESSAYS. Ed. Norman Rosenblood. Toronto: Univ. of Toronto Press, 1971. Pp. 106-34.

    Cites the Fabian tracts in exploring the discrepancy between the gradualist approach to social change taken by the Fabians and the element of "catastrophism" in many of GBS's plays.

Merritt, James D. "Shaw and the Pre-Raphaelites." In SHAW: SEVEN CRITICAL ESSAYS. Ed. Norman Rosenblood. Toronto: Univ. of Toronto Press, 1971. Pp. 70-83.

    Cites the nonfiction in noting GBS's attitudes toward such figures as Morris and Ford Madox Brown.

Mills, John A. "Acting is Being: Bernard Shaw on the Art of the Actor." SHAWR, 13 (1970), 65-78.

    Cites nonfiction in arguing that GBS supported the psychological "method" approach to acting.

Neill, A.S "Shaw and Education." In G.B.S. 90: ASPECTS OF BERNARD SHAW'S LIFE AND WORK. Ed. S. Winsten. New York: Dodd, Mead, 1946. Pp. 183-99.

    Cites the nonfiction in maintaining GBS overemphasizes intellectual development in education.

Nethercot, Arthur H. "Bernard Shaw, Philosopher." PMLA, 69 (1954), 57-75.

    Cites the nonfiction throughout in noting GBS's references to classical and European philosophers.

_____. MEN AND SUPERMEN: THE SHAVIAN PORTRAIT GALLERY. Cambridge, Mass.: Harvard Univ. Press, 1954.

> Cites nonfictional works, especially QUINTESSENCE OF IBSENISM, as glosses to an anatomy of character types in GBS's plays.

O'Donnell, Norbert F. "Shaw, Bunyan, and Puritanism." PMLA, 72 (1957), 520-33.

> A fuller treatment than Stokes (see p. 423). Citing such sources as the prefaces to MAN AND SUPERMAN and ANDROCLES AND THE LION, O'Donnell argues that GBS's "Bunyan" is much altered from the original and indicates no true puritanism on GBS's part.

Ohmann, Richard M. SHAW: THE STYLE AND THE MAN. Middletown, Conn.: Wesleyan Univ. Press, 1962.

> An excellent analysis of the stylistic features of GBS's non-dramatic prose and of the ways they reflect his habits of thought. Ohmann terms GBS "the most impressive writer of expository English prose in our century."

Osborne, Charles. "The Music Critic." In THE GENIUS OF SHAW: A SYMPOSIUM. Ed. Michael Holroyd. New York: Holt, 1979. Pp. 64-77.

> A review of GBS's music criticism for THE STAR and THE WORLD from 1888 to 1894 that praises his humor, his common sense, and his resistance to the fashions of the hour.

Pallette, Drew B. "An Early Shaw Article on Actors." SHAWR, 4, No. 1 (1961), 27-29.

> Notes an early, parodic article on the art of acting.

Park, Bruce R. "A Mote in the Critic's Eye: Bernard Shaw and Comedy." In G.B. SHAW: A COLLECTION OF CRITICAL ESSAYS. Ed. R.J. Kaufmann. Englewood Cliffs, N.J.: Prentice-Hall, 1965. Pp. 42-56.

> An excellent discussion of GBS's critical undervaluation due to New Critical dislike of didacticism and the modern preference of tragedy over comedy; it cites QUINTESSENCE OF IBSENISM and other works.

Peart, Barbara. "Shelley and Shaw's Prose." SHAWR, 15 (1972), 39-45.

> On GBS's borrowings of ideas and structures for his prose from Shelley's.

Quinn, Martin. "Dickens as Shavian Metaphor." SHAWR, 18 (1975), 44-56.

> Cites nonfiction in noting GBS's frequent use of Dickens as an authority.

George Bernard Shaw

Shenfield, M. "Shaw as a Music Critic." MUSIC AND LETTERS, 39 (1958), 378-84.

> Beginning by comparing GBS with Voltaire, this article stresses the sanity and rationality of GBS's approach to music.

Silver, Arnold. BERNARD SHAW: THE DARKER SIDE. Stanford, Calif.: Stanford Univ. Press, 1982.

> Cites nonfiction in a psychological study of GBS's violent and masochistic tendencies in his plays.

Silverman, Albert H. "Bernard Shaw's Shakespeare Criticism." PMLA, 72 (1957), 722-36.

> GBS's criticism of Shakespeare shows numerous parallels with Jonson's: GBS rejects Shakespeare's "glorification of love and his glorification of pessimism."

Simon, Louis. SHAW ON EDUCATION. New York: Columbia Univ. Press, 1958.

> A thorough survey of GBS's ideas on education (crucial in his system as a guide to evolution) drawn from such works as EVERYBODY'S POLITICAL WHAT'S WHAT and INTELLIGENT WOMAN'S GUIDE.

Small, Barbara J. "Shaw on Standard Stage Speech." SHAWR, 22 (1979), 106-13.

> In his drama criticism GBS calls for correct pronunciation.

Smith, J. Percy. "G.B.S. on the Theatre." TAMR, 15 (1960), 73-86.

> GBS's basic conception of the theater as a church wherein to celebrate the Life Force informs his drama criticism.

_____. "Superman versus Man: Bernard Shaw on Shakespeare." YR, 42 (1952), 67-82.

> An informative review of GBS's Shakespeare criticism. GBS assaults not so much Shakespeare, the Elizabethan playwright, as nineteenth-century bardolatry and the adequacy of Shakespeare as contemporary dramatic model.

_____. THE UNREPENTANT PILGRIM: A STUDY OF THE DEVELOPMENT OF BERNARD SHAW. Boston: Houghton Mifflin, 1965.

> This contains lengthy chapters on GBS as art and music critic (chapter 4), as drama critic (chapter 8), and as Shakespearian critic (chapter 9) that quote him liberally.

Spurling, Hilary. "The Critic's Critic." In THE GENIUS OF SHAW: A SYMPOSIUM. Ed. Michael Holroyd. New York: Holt, 1979. Pp. 129-41.

Reviews GBS's opinions and battles as drama critic for the SATURDAY REVIEW and concludes he attacked as critic sins he later committed as playwright.

Stigler, George J. "Bernard Shaw, Sidney Webb, and the Theory of Fabian Socialism." PAPS, 103 (1959), 469-75.

Cites various GBS tracts in assaulting the Fabian theory of the rent of land.

Stokes, E. E., Jr. "Bernard Shaw and Economics." SOUTHWESTERN SOCIAL SCIENCE QUARTERLY, 39 (1958), 242-48.

A brief review of FABIAN ESSAYS, THE INTELLIGENT WOMAN'S GUIDE, and EVERYBODY'S POLITICAL WHAT'S WHAT that stresses GBS's differences with Marx.

―――. "Bernard Shaw's Debt to John Bunyan." SHAWR, 8 (1965), 42-51.

Cites the nonfiction in discussing the influence of Bunyan, whom GBS admires as a moralistic "artist-philosopher."

―――. "Shaw and William Morris." SHAW BULLETIN, 1, No. 4 (1953), 16-19.

A brief treatment of Morris' impact on GBS's Socialist and artistic ideas.

Stone-Blackburn, Susan. "Shaw on Cutting Shakespeare." SHAWR, 22 (1979), 46-49.

One of GBS's letters is the source of his 1919 article against cutting Shakespeare.

Timko, Michael. "Entente Cordiale: The Dramatic Criticism of Shaw and Wells." MD, 8 (1965), 39-46.

On the similarity of Wells's and GBS's attitudes toward the theater, demonstrated by their reviews of the same eight plays in 1895.

Turco, Alfred. "Ibsen, Wagner, and Shaw's Changing View of 'Idealism.'" SHAWR, 17 (1974), 78-85.

Unlike in QUINTESSENCE OF IBSENISM, in PERFECT WAGNERITE GBS finds some idealism noble.

―――. SHAW'S MORAL VISION: THE SELF AND SALVATION. Ithaca, N.Y.: Cornell Univ. Press, 1976.

A major examination of GBS's philosophy that discusses the evolution of his emphasis on pragmatic realism in QUINTESSENCE OF IBSENISM and PERFECT WAGNERITE.

George Bernard Shaw

Watson, Barbara Bellow. A SHAVIAN GUIDE TO THE INTELLIGENT WOMAN. London: Chatto and Windus, 1964.

> A thorough discussion of GBS's feminism citing such works as QUINTESSENCE OF IBSENISM and MY DEAR DOROTHEA.

Weintraub, Stanley. "In the Picture Galleries." In THE GENIUS OF SHAW: A SYMPOSIUM. Ed. Michael Holroyd. New York: Holt, 1979. Pp. 42-63.

> Reviews GBS's opinions of Rossetti, Whistler, Monet, and others, expressed as art critic for THE WORLD from 1886 to 1890, and links his knowledge of art to his later stage settings.

──────. "Introduction." In BERNARD SHAW'S NONDRAMATIC LITERARY CRITICISM. Lincoln: Univ. of Nebraska Press, 1972. Pp. ix-xxvii.

> A useful survey of GBS's views on novelists and poets, and of his emphasis on didactic literature.

Whitman, Robert F. SHAW AND THE PLAY OF IDEAS. Ithaca, N.Y.: Cornell Univ. Press, 1977.

> Cites the nonfiction throughout the first seven chapters outlining GBS's social and religious thought: Hegel underlies its paradoxical quality.

Wisenthal, J.L. "Shaw and Ibsen." In his SHAW AND IBSEN: BERNARD SHAW'S THE QUINTESSENCE OF IBSENISM AND RELATED WRITINGS. Toronto: Univ. of Toronto Press, 1979. Pp. 3-73.

> An extremely thorough history of GBS's evolving attitudes toward Ibsen as reflected in the nonfiction and of Ibsen's influence on GBS's plays.

OSBERT SITWELL (1892-1969)

NONFICTIONAL PROSE

BRIGHTON. With Margaret Barton. London: Faber; Boston: Houghton Mifflin, 1935.

    OS defends George IV and his patronage of the arts against his many detractors: "George, as Regent and as King, ruled at the most splendid period in English history." The construction history and interior treasures of the Royal Pavilion are described in detail.

DICKENS. London: Chatto and Windus, 1932.

    In a brief and appreciative essay, OS tries to reconcile the "warm and generous tones" of Dickens' novels with the legends of his personality. OS ranks social reform novels set in London as most valuable.

DISCURSIONS ON TRAVEL, ART AND LIFE. London: Richards; New York: Doran, 1925.

    Selected periodical contributions, with revisions. Essays included are: "Lecce," "Puglia," "La Certosa di Padula," "Catania," "A German Eighteenth Century Town," and "Fiume."

ESCAPE WITH ME!: AN ORIENTAL SKETCH-BOOK. London: Macmillan, 1939. New York: Harrison-Hilton, 1940.

    Travel description of Indochina and China. Invaluable pre-World War II descriptions of Saigon, Pnom Penh, Peking, as well as ancient temples and ruins.

THE FOUR CONTINENTS: BEING MORE DISCURSIONS ON TRAVEL, ART AND LIFE. London: Macmillan; New York: Harper, 1954.

    Armchair reflections on the people, animals, and landscapes of various lands visited by OS in his travels. By introducing thoughtful and historical perspective into personal narrative, OS surpasses the limited guidebook approach.

GREAT MORNING! Boston: Little, Brown, 1947. As GREAT MORNING: BEING THE THIRD VOLUME OF LEFT HAND, RIGHT HAND! London: Macmillan, 1948.

> Volume 3 of the autobiography covers the "enchanted" days leading up to the outbreak of WWI. OS provides the first descriptions of Montegufoni (family castle retreat in Italy), outlines his discussions with father concerning the choice of a career, and reports his enjoyment of modern art, opera, theatre, and friends in London.

LAUGHTER IN THE NEXT ROOM. Boston: Little, Brown, 1948. As LAUGHTER IN THE NEXT ROOM: BEING THE FOURTH VOLUME OF LEFT HAND, RIGHT HAND! London: Macmillan, 1949.

> Volume 4 of the autobiography is the most significant and comprehensive. OS describes the disillusionment and suffering while fighting in the trenches in WWI. OS treats various people and events of the twenties, including the Bloomsbury Group and the General Strike of 1926, and of the thirties, including the deaths of his father and mother and other relatives.

LEFT HAND, RIGHT HAND! Boston: Little, Brown, 1944. As LEFT HAND, RIGHT HAND. Vol. 1: THE CRUEL MONTH. London: Macmillan, 1945.

> In volume 1 of his autobiography, OS provides a narrative of his childhood that is full of details and written in prose style that is often poetic and elaborate. Volume 1 covers OS's ancestors, his infancy and childhood. OS includes some interesting descriptions of his first experiences with education, the stage, music, art, and writing. In volume 1 as well as the other volumes, the eccentric escapades of OS's imposing father, Sir George, are a constant source of humor and sometimes pathos.

A LETTER TO MY SON. London: Home and Van Thal, 1944.

> In a brief essay, OS heaps scorn upon politicians for causing "the prevailing disaster" of World War II and reflects on what it means to be an author.

NOBLE ESSENCES OF COURTEOUS REVELATIONS: BEING A BOOK OF CHARACTERS AND THE FIFTH AND LAST VOLUME OF LEFT HAND, RIGHT HAND! London: Macmillan, 1950. As NOBLE ESSENCES: A BOOK OF CHARACTERS. Boston: Little, Brown, 1950.

> In volume 5 of the autobiography, OS mixes character sketches

with reminiscences of creative artists he knew, including Sir Edmund Gosse, Ronald Firbank, Wilfred Owen, Gabriele D'Annunzio, Ada Leverson, and Arnold Bennett. An important premise of the book is OS's conviction that "only by the magic of art, or of individuality, can men save themselves."

THE NOVELS OF GEORGE MEREDITH AND SOME NOTES ON THE ENGLISH NOVEL. London: Oxford Univ. Press, 1947.

In the English Association Presidential Address, 1947, OS judges Meredith to be a great English novelist because he is "a great stylist." Style and humor enliven Meredith's characters and situations.

PENNY FOOLISH: A BOOK OF TIRADES & PANEGYRICS. London: Macmillan, 1935.

Valuable compendium of sixty-nine essays which record OS's early opinions and tastes. Some topics discussed include: private and public schools, reading, friends, manners, Victorianism, snobs, prigs, solitude, and travel.

THE PEOPLE'S ALBUM OF LONDON STATUES. London: Duckworth, 1928.

OS provides historical and aesthetic descriptions of London's squares and statues. Thirty-two line drawings by Nina Hammett are included. With a few reservations, OS believes the monuments "have a charm of romance."

POUND WISE. London: Hutchinson; Boston: Little, Brown, 1963.

Reprints forty-six selected essays or selections from the following previously printed works: SING HIGH!, PENNY FOOLISH, LONDON STATUES, and LETTER TO MY SON.

THE SCARLET TREE. Boston: Little, Brown, 1946. As THE SCARLET TREE: BEING THE SECOND VOLUME OF LEFT HAND, RIGHT HAND! London: Macmillan, 1946.

In volume 2 of the autobiography, OS offers wistful recollections of school days at Bloodsworth and Eton in the Edwardian age. OS is candid about his unpopularity amongst schoolfellows and concludes that "Eton had little effect on my character." OS's fondness for London and Italy as well as his first love are also treated.

SING HIGH! SING LOW! London: Macmillan, 1944.

Reprints fifteen essays (some revised), including "Old Worlds for New," "Save the Old School Tie!," "Picnics and Pavilions," "London" (a fifty-year personal survey from late 1890s to 1943), and "What it Feels Like to be an Author."

Osbert Sitwell

TALES MY FATHER TAUGHT ME: AN EVOCATION OF EXTRAVAGANT EPISODES. London: Hutchinson; Boston: Little, Brown, 1962.

>Record of shared travel experiences with OS's "exceptional" father, Sir George Reresby Sitwell, and Henry Moat, the family butler. Some essays included are: "Going for a Drive," "Catching the Bus," "By Rail and Boat," "Unusual Holidays," "Unforgotten Feasts," "Music," and "Magic."

TRIO: DISSERTATIONS ON SOME ASPECT OF NATIONAL GENIUS. London: Macmillan, 1938.

>With Edith and Sacheverell Sitwell; delivered as the Northcliffe Lectures at the University of London in 1937. Contents by Osbert Sitwell: "Dickens and the Modern Novel" (includes passages from DICKENS), pp. 1-45 and "The Modern Novel: Its Cause and Cure" (includes passages from PENNY FOOLISH), pp. 49-93. In the second essay, Dickens is praised for establishing a modern tradition: he was the first to comprehend and dramatize "the haphazard and ramshackle romance of the nineteenth-century great cities."

WHO KILLED COCK-ROBIN? REMARKS ON POETRY, ON ITS CRITICISM, AND, AS A SAD WARNING, THE STORY OF EUNUCH ARDEN. London: Daniel, 1921.

>An interesting collection of a series of epigrammatic reflections on poetry, and the readers and reviewers who respond to it.

WINTERS OF CONTENT: MORE DISCURSIONS ON TRAVEL, ART, AND LIFE. London: Duckworth; Philadelphia: Lippincott, 1932.

>Includes four revised travel pieces: "The Castel del Monte," "New Year in Bari," "The Secrecy of Venice," and "Winter in Italy."

WINTERS OF CONTENT AND OTHER DISCURSIONS ON MEDITERRANEAN ART AND TRAVEL. London: Duckworth, 1950.

>Travel sketches of Mediterranean lands and culture. Includes WINTERS (1932) "almost in its entirety" and adds several chapters from DISCURSIONS on the South of Italy and Sicily. In a "Preface" OS claims that travel nourishes the cultivated man's mind, defines his personal coinage "discursions," and provides important comments on his own prose style.

WORKS EDITED BY OTHERS

QUEEN MARY AND OTHERS. Ed. Frank Magro. London: Joseph, 1974.

Reprints six essays from POUND WISE and adds six more essays, some of biographical significance--"Portrait of a Very Young Man," "New York in the Twenties," and "Moving House."

BIBLIOGRAPHY

Fifoot, Richard, ed. A BIBLIOGRAPHY OF EDITH, OSBERT AND SACHEVERELL SITWELL. London: Rupert Hart-Davis, 1971. Pp. 143-269.

> The standard primary bibliography which includes a comprehensive listing of OS's original works, contributions to books and periodicals, unpublished books, translations, musical settings, and recordings.

BIOGRAPHY

Lehmann, John. A NEST OF TIGERS; THE SITWELLS IN THEIR TIMES. Boston: Little, Brown, 1968.

> Informative and sympathetic treatment of the lives of OS, Sacheverell, and Dame Edith Sitwell. OS offered factual corrections on the draft. The study tries to access "the impact of the three Sitwells on their times." Some straight-forward commentary on OS's works of travel and autobiography is provided.

Mégroz, Rodolphe Louis. THE THREE SITWELLS: A BIOGRAPHICAL AND CRITICAL STUDY. London: Richards Press, 1927.

> An early and eccentric study of the lives of Edith, Osbert and Sacheverell Sitwell. Mégroz refutes the charge that the Sitwells had "nihilist designs upon form and tradition." Some commentary on OS's COCK ROBIN and DISCURSIONS.

Pearson, John. FAÇADES: EDITH, OSBERT, AND SACHEVERELL SITWELL. London: Macmillan, 1978.

> The definitive biography of the three Sitwells, written in the obsessive and candid spirit of finding out "what really lay behind the various façades Sir Osbert and Dame Edith had assiduously erected in their lifetime." Contains brief commentary on all of OS's works, but especially useful on OS's individual essays and opinions on various topics.

CRITICISM

Bennett, Arnold. "Sitwells." ADELPHI, 1 (1923), 236-38.

Brief remarks on the three Sitwells as writers and personalities.
Bennett calls OS "a born impresario" who "presents" the family
with great originality.

Bower, Anthony. "A View of Sir Osbert Sitwell." PR, 15 (1948), 1364-68.

Interesting summary of an interview with OS. During a visit
to America, OS gives his thoughts on the modern writer's
identity, American writers of the past, and on his own prose
style and composing process.

Burdett, Osbert. "The Sitwells." LONDON MERCURY, 15 (March 1927),
515-25.

Though mainly a discussion of the trio's poetry, Burdett gives
a brief but harsh description of OS's prose style in DISCURSIONS.
He concludes that OS has "less imagination" in his travel books
than his brother Sacheverell because OS does not "lose himself
in a mood of the past" but always "carries modern London with
him." OS is too much "the spectator" of scenes in foreign
lands, and is therefore "less persuasive" as a prose writer.
Burdett's final estimation is that the Sitwells have brought
"nothing new" into the prose tradition.

Fulford, Roger. OSBERT SITWELL. British Council Series. London: Longmans, 1951.

A brief but penetrating study which presents the many sides of
OS and his work. Fulford stresses the theme of the barrier
"between the creative class and the absorbing class" in OS's
writing. OS's humanity and sense of style in the autobiographical volumes are singled out for high praise. Fulford includes
a selected bibliography and a useful index to OS's essays.

Harrison, Elizabeth. "More Geese Than Swans." QQ, 56 (1949), 375-86.

Admires OS's ability in the first four volumes of his autobiography
"to discuss with such detachment his reactions to his age as the
reactions of an artist thoroughly aware of himself." Harrison's
article is marred by her baroque, impressionistic style.

Hartley, L.P. "Sir Osbert Sitwell." TLS, No. 2740 (6 August 1954), xx-xxi.

High praise for the five volumes of OS's autobiography. Hartley
compares the books to a "tapestry" with the qualities of a "dreamlike atmosphere" and an "air of arrested motion," stresses the
importance of the contrasted figure of OS's father, and concludes
that the paradox of OS's "buoyant" temperament and "pessimistic"
convictions must always be remembered.

Jones, Richard. "The Art of Being a Sitwell." VQR, 56 (1980), 470-85.

    Concludes that OS's reputation will survive based on his LEFT HAND RIGHT HAND volumes and on the travel book, ESCAPE WITH ME!

Scott, Winfield Townley. "A Three-Headed Basilisk." SATR, 36 (19 December 1953), 11-14.

    Chatty and anecdotal essay that is somewhat valuable as a chronicle of the Sitwell's rise to literary fame. Includes brief commentary on OS's autobiographical volumes, which Scott calls "the great source of published information on the Sitwells . . . a masterwork, a classic."

Sutton, Eric. "Sitwellismus." OUTLOOK (London), 61 (25 February 1928), 235.

    A general article on the three Sitwells, who are classified as accomplished but minor writers.

Wykes-Joyce, Max. TRIAD OF GENIUS. PART 1. London: Owen, 1953.

    An appreciative survey of the works of Edith and Osbert Sitwell, who both commented on the drafts. Wykes-Joyce praises OS's talent for "vivid portraiture" and demonstrates that his travel books are really "notes and essays on art, literature, places and people."

LYTTON STRACHEY (1880-1932)

THE COLLECTED WORKS (London: Chatto and Windus, 1948) contains six volumes: (1) QUEEN VICTORIA, (2) EMINENT VICTORIANS, (3) ELIZABETH AND ESSEX, (4) BIOGRAPHICAL ESSAYS, (5) LITERARY ESSAYS, (6) LANDMARKS IN FRENCH LITERATURE.

NONFICTIONAL PROSE

BOOKS AND CHARACTERS, FRENCH & ENGLISH. London: Chatto and Windus; New York: Harcourt, 1922.

> A collection of fifteen critical essays, including individual papers on Racine and William Blake as well as several studies on Voltaire and selected Elizabethan figures.

ELIZABETH AND ESSEX: A TRAGIC HISTORY. London: Chatto and Windus; New York: Harcourt, 1928.

> A full-length historical biography of the Virgin Queen. LS analyzes her passionate and intelligent qualities and dramatizes the conflicts and sorrows of the establishment of her sovereign power.

EMINENT VICTORIANS: CARDINAL MANNING, FLORENCE NIGHTINGALE, DR. ARNOLD, GENERAL GORDON. London: Chatto and Windus, 1918. As EMINENT VICTORIANS. WITH FOUR PORTRAITS. Garden City, N.Y.: Garden City Publishing Co., 1918.

> Four biographical sketches of Victorian figures--Cardinal Manning, Florence Nightingale, Dr. Thomas Arnold, and General Charles Gordon--which are clever, concise, and candid. LS's brief preface records the author's method and has been taken as the manifesto of the "new biography."

LANDMARKS IN FRENCH LITERATURE. London: Williams and Norgate; New York: Holt, 1912.

A concise literary history of French literature from the Middle Ages to the nineteenth century. LS concludes that while there has been an "extraordinary wealth" of French writers who have followed the principle of individual deliberation, France has never produced a figure of the stature and power of Shakespeare.

POPE. Cambridge: The Univ. Press, 1925. New York: Harcourt, 1926.

The Leslie Stephen Lecture for 1925, later reprinted in CHARACTERS.

PORTRAITS IN MINIATURE, AND OTHER ESSAYS. London: Chatto and Windus; New York: Harcourt, 1931.

A collection of eighteen concise essays on major and minor figures. The six essays on English historians--Hume, Gibbon, Macaulay, Carlyle, Froude, and Creighton--are especially noteworthy.

QUEEN VICTORIA. London: Chatto and Windus; New York: Harcourt, 1921.

A masterful and generally sympathetic full-length study of the monarch of the nineteenth century. The impressionistic closing reverie is especially famous.

WORKS EDITED BY OTHERS

BIOGRAPHICAL ESSAYS. Ed. James Strachey. London: Chatto and Windus, 1948.

Collects six essays from BOOKS, sixteen from PORTRAITS, twelve from CHARACTERS, and an essay on Charles Greville. The essays are arranged "in the chronological order, not of their composition, but, roughly of the subjects with which they deal."

CHARACTERS AND COMMENTARIES. Ed. James Strachey. London: Chatto and Windus, 1933.

Reprints over thirty of LS's published contributions to various periodicals. Interesting chronological arrangement for studying the development of LS's style over a thirty-year period. Also includes LS's Leslie Stephen Lecture on Pope and an unfinished essay on OTHELLO.

LITERARY ESSAYS. Ed. James Strachey. London: Chatto and Windus, 1948.

Collects eight essays from BOOKS, two from PORTRAITS, and fifteen from CHARACTERS.

LYTTON STRACHEY: THE REALLY INTERESTING QUESTION, AND OTHER PAPERS. Ed. Paul Levy. London: Weidenfeld and Nicolson, 1972.

> Collects some of LS's unpublished papers on such topics as war, politics, men, women, sex, and art. The essays "Art and Indecency" and "The Really Interesting Question" are of some significance.

THE SHORTER STRACHEY. Ed. Michael Holroyd and Paul Levy. New York: Oxford Univ. Press, 1980.

> Collects thirty of LS's essays, originally published between 1904 and 1913. Includes a childhood memoir, a portrait of the Bloomsbury group, and commentaries on such figures as Pope, Dostoevsky, and Sarah Bernhardt.

SPECTATORIAL ESSAYS. Ed. James Strachey. London: Chatto and Windus, 1964.

> Collects thirty-five of the over eighty reviews LS wrote for the SPECTATOR between 1904 and 1914. The essays deal with historical and literary figures of the sixteenth, seventeenth, eighteenth, and nineteenth centuries.

BIBLIOGRAPHY

Edmonds, Michael, ed. LYTTON STRACHEY: A BIBLIOGRAPHY. New York: Garland, 1981.

> A comprehensive descriptive primary bibliography. Edmonds lists and comments upon all English and American editions of LS's books and pamphlets as well as periodical contributions and collected editions. He also lists fourteen secondary sources.

Kallich, Martin, ed. "Lytton Strachey: An Annotated Bibliography of Writings about Him." ELT, 5, No. 3 (1962), 1-77. Continued in subsequent issues.

> The most comprehensive secondary bibliography on LS. The original article includes 467 entries with annotations being provided for nearly all items. Some of the entries are unreliable and the commentaries could be more concise.

Muir, Percy, comp. POINTS: SECOND SERIES, 1866-1934. London: Constable, 1934.

> Contains a handy checklist of LS's books.

Sanders, C.R., comp. LYTTON STRACHEY: HIS MIND AND ART. New Haven, Conn.: Yale Univ. Press, 1957. Pp. 355-66.

> Includes a useful chronological checklist of LS's books, published essays, and some unpublished writings.

BIOGRAPHY

Gadd, David. THE LOVING FRIENDS: A PORTRAIT OF BLOOMSBURY. New York: Harcourt, 1974.

> Detached and relatively unbiased study of LS and the Bloomsbury group. Gadd stresses LS's affairs and homosexuality. Includes brief discussions of VICTORIANS, LANDMARKS, VICTORIA, and ELIZABETH.

Holroyd, Michael. LYTTON STRACHEY: A CRITICAL BIOGRAPHY. Vol. 1: THE UNKNOWN YEARS 1880-1910. London: Heinemann, 1967.

> In volume 1 of the definitive biography, Holroyd discusses LS's early Victorian-Edwardian background. Special praise is reserved for the early critical essays--"so compact and self-contained, yet always elegant and beautifully shaped." Holroyd's biography is controversial in its explanation of LS's psychology; it is useful in treating his various literary accomplishments.

_____. LYTTON STRACHEY: A CRITICAL BIOGRAPHY. Vol. 2: THE YEARS OF ACHIEVEMENT 1910-1932. London: Heinemann, 1968.

> Volume 2 includes valuable discussions of VICTORIANS, VICTORIA, ELIZABETH, and PORTRAITS as well as frank treatment of LS's personal and professional relationships.

_____. LYTTON STRACHEY AND THE BLOOMSBURY GROUP: HIS WORK, THEIR INFLUENCE. Harmondsworth, Engl.: Penguin, 1971.

> Revised edition of critical material previously published in LYTTON STRACHEY: A CRITICAL BIOGRAPHY (1967-68).

Sanders, Charles Richard. LYTTON STRACHEY: HIS MIND AND ART. New Haven, Conn.: Yale Univ. Press, 1957.

> Lavish and unstinted praise for LS; a comprehensive and conscientious survey of his works. While the record of the life could be more balanced and less conservative, there are excellent remarks on LS's ideas and prose style.

_____. THE STRACHEY FAMILY, 1588-1932: THEIR WRITINGS AND LITERARY ASSOCIATIONS. Durham, N.C.: Duke Univ. Press, 1953.

> Valuable background study of the cultural traditions of LS's family. Chapter 15, "Giles Lytton Strachey and His Heritage," sketches LS's life and outlines some of his works. The generation and significance of VICTORIANS, VICTORIA, and SPECTATOR reviews are given special attention.

CRITICISM

Abbott, Wilbur C. ADVENTURES IN REPUTATION. Cambridge, Mass.: Harvard Univ. Press, 1935.

 Contains a harsh condemnation of LS's slanted portraits, "vaudeville" tactics, and condescending attitude.

Adams, James Truslow. "New Modes in Biography." CURRENT HISTORY, 31 (1929), 257-64.

 Good background discussion of the relationship between biographical and scientific truth. Praises LS's works for their personalized character interpretations but denies that they possess "scientific validity." Adams deplores LS's imitators and calls for "genuine taste and standards" in biography.

Annan, Noel. "Introduction." In EMINENT VICTORIANS. London: Collins, 1959. Pp. 9-17.

 Praises LS's humor and "power of writing narrative" but regrets his treatment of the four subjects as "specimens."

──────. LESLIE STEPHEN: HIS THOUGHT AND CHARACTER IN RELATION TO HIS TIME. Cambridge, Mass.: Harvard Univ. Press, 1952.

 Rather than evaluating or moralizing, LS in his literary criticism strove to convey the flavor of the works that he discussed.

Bacon, Leonard. "An Eminent Post-Victorian." YR, 30 (1940), 310-24.

 A rambling, anecdotal tribute to LS. Bacon feels that LS's love of drama and irony prevented him from practicing the art of the historian.

Beerbohm, Max. LYTTON STRACHEY. London: Macmillan, 1943.

 Personal reminiscences of LS. Beerbohm strongly objects to the application of the term "a debunker" to LS's efforts and he includes a brief discussion of VICTORIANS and ELIZABETH.

Bell, Clive. OLD FRIENDS: PERSONAL RECOLLECTIONS. New York: Harcourt, 1956.

 Personal reminiscences of LS and his friends. Bell provides brief commentary on LS's prose style and some background information concerning LS's attitude to the Victorians: "Like all moralists he had his standards" but was "never self-righteous."

Boas, Guy. LYTTON STRACHEY. London: The English Association, 1935.

Includes some valuable commentary on the various features of LS's prose style.

_____. "Lytton Strachey--Reviewer." SPECTATOR, 184 (1950), 456.

Brief but interesting discussion of LS's SPECTATOR reviews of books dealing with history and biography between 1904 and 1914.

Bower-Shore, Clifford. LYTTON STRACHEY: AN ESSAY. London: Fenland Press, 1933.

Early, conventional survey of LS's works. Bower-Shore makes an attempt to analyze LS's prose style.

Bryant, Arthur. "The Art of Biography." LONDON MERCURY, 30 (1934), 236-43.

A dogmatic article which makes superficial comparisons between Victorian and Georgian approaches to writing biography.

Burdett, Osbert. "Experiment in Biography." In TRADITION AND EXPERIMENT IN PRESENT-DAY LITERATURE. London: Oxford Univ. Press, 1929. Pp. 161-78.

Hails LS's milestone achievements in ironic biography but concludes that he is "more in love with analysis than with portraiture, with his method than with man."

Carver, George. ALMS FOR OBLIVION: BOOKS, MEN AND BIOGRAPHY. Milwaukee: Bruce Publishing, 1964.

Brief chapter on LS in a historical survey of biographers. Praises LS's effortless style and simple vocabulary.

Cecil, David. AN ANTHOLOGY OF MODERN BIOGRAPHY. London: Nelson, 1936. Pp. ix-xvi.

Sees a satirist's side to LS: "he looked at his subjects in an ironical mood, keen to notice their comic implications."

Clemens, Cyril. LYTTON STRACHEY. Webster Groves, Mo.: International Mark Twain Society, 1942.

Superficial sketch which contains some anecdotes about the reception of VICTORIANS and VICTORIA.

Clive, John. "More or Less Eminent Victorians: Some Trends in Recent Victorian Biography." VS, 2 (1958), 5-28.

The most intelligent and successful attempt to unravel the disparities between LS's intentions as biographer and later imitators' misguided malpracticings of the art.

Lytton Strachey

Connolly, Cyril. ENEMIES OF PROMISE. London: Routledge, 1938.

> Calls VICTORIANS "a revolutionary book" because of its attack on institutions. Connolly argues that LS's later biographies are not as successful, but as a critic LS is "admirable."

DeVoto, Bernard. "The Skeptical Biographer." HARPER'S, 166 (1933), 181-92.

> Harsh attack on LS and "creative biography." LS's portraits are entertaining but are also studies in "deliberate deception." DeVoto calls for honest biographies written by historians.

Drew, Elizabeth A. "Biography." In THE ENJOYMENT OF LITERATURE. New York: Norton, 1935. Pp. 78-108.

> Drew admires LS's intellectual adroitness but stresses that he is "a moralist at heart." Includes some comparisons with other biographers.

Dyson, A. E. "The Technique of Debunking." TWENTIETH CENTURY, 157 (1955), 244-56.

> Dyson sees LS not as an historian but as a creative artist who wrote memorable but "highly fictitious" caricature. Stylistic devices of irony and ridicule in VICTORIANS are discussed.

Forster, E. M. "English Prose between 1918 and 1939." In his TWO CHEERS FOR DEMOCRACY. London: Arnold, 1951. Pp. 272-84.

> In an important essay about the period's prose, Forster praises LS as the first biographer "to get inside his subject."

Fuess, Claude. "Debunkery and Biography." ATLANTIC, 151 (1933), 347-57.

> Assesses historical importance of LS, who "appeared at a moment when his influence was salutary and stimulating."

_____. "Lytton Strachey." SATURDAY REVIEW OF LITERATURE (NY), 8 (1932), 501-02.

> Assigns LS's popularity to timing ("he catered to an irreverent generation") and style (his works "resembled novels"). Fuess stresses, however, LS's scrupulous scholarship and meticulous revisions for brevity's sake.

Garber, Lawrence. "Techniques of Characterization in Strachey's ELIZABETH AND ESSEX." DR, 56 (1976), 405-28.

Original and intelligent analysis of ELIZABETH. LS intermingled the three methods of the novel, drama, and psychoanalytical study to enliven characters. In the work LS's "inventive powers" were vibrant: "this final experiment in biography extended the imaginative perimeters established in his earlier works."

Gersh, Gabriel. "Lytton Strachey: Pathfinder in Biography." MODA, 11 (1967), 394-99.

A balanced evaluation of LS's works. Gersh admires LS's style and skepticism but berates his lack of "philosophical backing" and "standards of judgement." He concludes that LS remains "a miniaturist."

Gosse, Edmund. "The Agony of the Victorian Age." In his SOME DIVERSIONS OF A MAN OF LETTERS. London: Heinemann, 1919. Pp. 318-32.

Discusses the four figures in VICTORIANS and argues that LS treats them "like puppets." Although LS's method of biography has some merit, it errs in discretion. "It is in sympathy, in imaginative insight, that Mr. Strachey fails."

_____. MORE BOOKS ON THE TABLE. New York: Scribner's, 1923. Pp. 3-10.

Gosse was one of the first critics to point out what is now a commonplace concerning VICTORIA--"that what he started to make a satire has turned in his fingers to an appreciation."

Halperin, John. "EMINENT VICTORIANS and History." VQR, 56 (1980), 433-54.

Provocative and thoughtful revaluation. Finds LS to be a good entertainer in EMINENT VICTORIANS, but lacking in several respects as a historian--he ignores the facts of political history or writes history as polemics.

Heilbrun, Carolyn G. TOWARD A RECOGNITION OF ANDROGYNY. New York: Knopf, 1973.

Examines VICTORIANS, VICTORIA, and ELIZABETH (pages 135-51) in the light of the psychology of masculine and feminine attributes. Heilbrun claims that LS's works are "revolutionary" in their vision of the danger of "sexual polarization" and denial of "full sexual life."

Husain, S. Wigar. "Lytton Strachey: Major Biographies." ALIGARH JOURNAL OF ENGLISH STUDIES, 5 (1980), 211-28.

A critical analysis of LS's EMINENT VICTORIANS, QUEEN VICTORIA, and ELIZABETH AND ESSEX. Husain admires most the "vigorous intellectual quality" and unified theme of the four studies in VICTORIANS. Discusses the special blend of pleasure and instruction in LS's biographies.

Iyengar, K. R. Srinivasa. LYTTON STRACHEY: A CRITICAL STUDY. London: Chatto and Windus, 1938.

> Appreciative survey of LS's major works. The chapters on LS's biographical techniques, irony, and style are the most valuable. Iyengar concludes that LS was "a moralist as well as an ironist."

Johnston, George A. "The New Biography: Ludwig, Maurois, and Strachey." ATLANTIC, 143 (1929), 333-42.

> Useful explanation of the similarities that characterize the three "new biographers." LS's practice differs from his theory: there is a "conscious design" and "strong dramatic sense" throughout his work.

Johnstone, John Keith. THE BLOOMSBURY GROUP. New York: Noonday, 1954.

> Contains a good basic discussion of LS's style and major works. Johnstone stresses the important influence of "the discipline of essay-writing" on LS's later biographies.

Kallich, Martin. THE PSYCHOLOGICAL MILIEU OF LYTTON STRACHEY. New York: Bookman Associates, 1961.

> Kallich argues that an awareness of LS's "direct or indirect indebtedness to Freud contributes to an understanding of Strachey's special psychological insights into human nature . . . and permits an evaluation of his achievement in biography." Some chapters include: "Dual Personalities" in VICTORIANS; "Oedipus Complex" in VICTORIA; and "Hysteria" in ELIZABETH.

King, R. W. "Biography and Curiosity." LIFE AND LETTERS, 10 (1934), 546-53.

> Argues that LS was neither impartial nor scientific in VICTORIANS and VICTORIA. LS's bias, however, was "an essential element in his success."

Kronenberger, Louis. "Lytton Strachey." BOOKMAN (NY), 71 (1930), 375-80.

> Praises LS's erudition, irony, and style. However, style and content are sometimes not united, as in ELIZABETH.

Krutch, Joseph Wood. "Lytton Strachey." NATION (NY), 134 (1932), 199-200.

> High praise for LS's "clear-sighted confidence" and flashing wit. Although he did much for modern biography, LS was "primarily an essayist" rather than a universal historian.

Lehman, B. H. "The Art of Lytton Strachey." In ESSAYS IN CRITICISM. Berkeley: Univ. of California Press, 1929. Pp. 229-45.

> Speculates on writers who may have influenced LS's style. Lehman regrets that LS's irony sometimes leads to disunity and sarcasm.

Levy, Paul. "Introduction." In his LYTTON STRACHEY: THE REALLY INTERESTING QUESTION, AND OTHER PAPERS. London: Weidenfeld and Nicolson, 1972. Pp. ix-xiv.

> Levy explains why LS's previously unpublished "private or esoteric works show a rather different aspect of his mind" which is an aid in understanding his character and his "personal radicalism."

MacCarthy, Desmond. "Lytton Strachey as a Biographer." LIFE AND LETTERS, 7 (1932), 90-102.

> A close friend in discussing the major works points out that as "an artist in biography" LS insisted on freedom in dealing with the subjects of his biographical studies. Insight into LS's intentions and artistic standards.

Maurois, André. ASPECTS OF BIOGRAPHY. Trans. S. C. Roberts. Cambridge: The Univ. Press, 1929.

> Compares LS's methods with those of some of his disciples. Maurois praises LS's human sympathy, psychological perception, humor and poetic style.

_____. "The Modern Biographer." YR, 17 (1928), 227-45.

> LS is both an "idol-breaker" and a "deep psychologist." The common denominator of modern biographers is a refusal to paint masks, a desire "to get to the real man."

_____. PROPHETS AND POETS. Trans. Hamish Miles. New York: Harper, 1935. Pp. 215-42.

> Discusses the tension between art and history and defines LS's "point of view" on the controversy. Maurois concludes that although LS was "French in his style and Voltairean in some of his prejudices, he remains at bottom extremely English."

Pearson, Hesketh. VENTILATIONS: BEING BIOGRAPHICAL ASIDES. Philadelphia: Lippincott, 1930.

> Unrestrained praise for LS as a biographer with imagination and a gift for practicing the art of fusion. The outstanding quality of LS's work "lies in the richness and completeness of its characterization."

Raymond, John. "Strachey's Eminent Victorians." NEW STATESMAN AND NATION, 49 (1955), 545-46.

> Raymond admires the wit and writing in VICTORIANS but harshly condemns LS's "trivial and uncompassionate view of human beings and of the human predicament."

Reilly, Joseph J. "The Passing of Lytton Strachey." CATHW, 135 (1932), 58-68.

> Superficial survey of LS's works, methods, and "psychological insight."

Ritchie, Charles. "Strachey and Guedalla: An Essay in Comparison." DR (Halifax), 12 (1933), 497-502.

> Concludes that in style and subject matter, LS is far superior to Guedalla.

Russell, John. "Lytton Strachey." HORIZON, 15 (1947), 91-116.

> Discusses the French influence on LS's style and method. Russell also provides insightful analysis of LS's attitudes toward the Victorian age.

Saltmarshe, Christopher. "Lytton Strachey." In SCRUTINIES BY VARIOUS WRITERS. Ed. Edgell Rickword. Vol. 2. London: Wishart, 1931. Pp. 184-201.

> Partially admires LS's early achievements but maintains that with ELIZABETH, LS has "exploited his tricks" and his style has "deteriorated beyond belief." Saltmarshe presents a carping catalog of LS's "irritating habits" of style and sentiments.

Sanders, Charles Richard. "Lytton Strachey Improves His Style, 1904-1922." CE, 7 (1948), 215-19.

> A study of LS's revisions in BOOKS AND CHARACTERS reveals important developments in his mature "method, taste, and style." Concludes that LS is a "talented and careful literary craftsman."

_____. "Lytton Strachey's Revisions in BOOKS AND CHARACTERS." MLN, 60 (1945), 226-34.

> Detailed listing of LS's numerous stylistic revisions of his original articles and reviews. Sanders concludes that the changes were "extensive and complex."

Scott-James, Rolfe Arnold. LYTTON STRACHEY. Writers and Their Work. London: Longmans, 1955.

> Brief but useful study of LS's works, with a listing of his essays. Scott-James calls LANDMARKS LS's "greatest triumph in literary criticism" and emphasizes the importance of LS's "point of view."

Smyth, Charles. "A Note on Historical Biography and Mr. Strachey." CRITERION, 8 (1929), 647-60.

> Indicts LS's "sniggering" tendency to ridicule religion and procreation.

Stillman, Clara G. "The Art of Lytton Strachey." NATION, 137 (1933), 686-87.

> Interesting and appreciative review of LS's accomplishments. Stillman compares LS to T.S. Eliot, who was likewise absorbed into a tradition that he initiated.

Strachey, James. "Preface." In his SPECTATORIAL ESSAYS. London: Chatto and Windus, 1964.

> Explains how his brother LS was given the opportunity to write some review essays for THE SPECTATOR. Strachey cautions that the essays underwent some minor editorial revisions--both in style and content.

Stratford, Jenny. "Eminent Victorians." BRITISH MUSEUM QUARTERLY, 32, Nos. 3-4 (1968), 93-96.

> Brief but illuminating discussion of drafts and manuscript of VICTORIANS in the museum.

Wain, John. "The Education of Lytton Strachey." NEW REPUBLIC, 152 (17 April 1965), 20-22.

> Brief discussion of the persona in SPECTATORIAL ESSAYS: "tasteful, well-read, international in outlook." Wain sees the influence of Macaulay's prose style in the essays.

Williams, Orlo. CONTEMPORARY CRITICISM OF LITERATURE. London: Parsons, 1924.

> Praises LS's essay on Racine and admires the one on Stendhal. Williams hopes LS will write more literary criticism of high quality.

Lytton Strachey

Wilson, Edmund. "Lytton Strachey." NEW REPUBLIC, 72 (1932), 146-48.

> Brief survey of strengths and weaknesses of LS's books. Wilson concludes that LS's style was both harmed and aided by his imitation of French models.

Woolf, Virginia. "The Art of Biography." ATLANTIC, 163 (1939), 506-10.

> Discusses biography as art and as craft and argues that VICTORIA is superior to ELIZABETH.

H.M. TOMLINSON (1873-1958)

NONFICTIONAL PROSE

BELOW LONDON BRIDGE. London: Cassell, 1934; New York: Harper, 1935.

> A sequel to LONDON RIVER, with photographs of the London docks by H. Charles Tomlinson. The volume portrays sections such as Limehouse and places such as Lloyd's; HMT repeatedly invokes the clipper CUTTY SARK and Conrad's TORRENS in bemoaning the spread of industrial ugliness.

BETWEEN THE LINES. Cambridge, Mass.: Harvard Univ. Press, 1930.

> A lecture delivered at Harvard in 1927. HMT argues that literature should be the sincere expression of the author's beliefs and that the author's character determines style. He derides the emptiness of Joyce and Eliot, reflecting the emptiness of commercial civilization.

THE FACE OF THE EARTH: WITH SOME HINTS FOR THOSE ABOUT TO TRAVEL. London: Duckworth, 1950. Indianapolis: Bobbs-Merrill, 1951.

> Reprints the travel sketches "A North Devon Estuary," "Some Hints for Those about to Travel," "On the Chesil Bank," "A Spanish Journey," and "The Little Things."

GIFTS OF FORTUNE WITH SOME HINTS FOR THOSE ABOUT TO TRAVEL. London: Heinemann; New York: Harper, 1926.

> A collection of eleven travel and nature sketches. "Some Hints for Those about to Travel" is a lengthy essay advising travelers not to plan and not to remain on "charted paths." "On the Chesil Bank" contains a tribute to Conrad.

LONDON RIVER. London: Cassell; New York: Knopf, 1921.

> Eleven sketches of the geography and atmosphere of the London

H.M. Tomlinson

docks featuring HMT's memories of old shops and personalities in the days of sail. See BELOW LONDON BRIDGE.

MALAY WATERS: THE STORY OF LITTLE SHIPS COASTING OUT OF SINGAPORE AND PENANG IN PEACE AND WAR. London: Hodder and Stoughton, 1950.

> Part travel book set in the Far East, part history of the Straits Steamship Company and its service there during the Japanese invasion and the fall of Singapore.

MARS HIS IDIOT. London: Heinemann; New York: Harper, 1935.

> A lengthy and impassioned volume of antiwar propaganda, based on HMT's memories of the Great War (in which he was a war correspondent), and his observations of the ominous drift of contemporary affairs. He adduces numerous pacifist arguments from the absence of chivalry in mechanized fighting to the imaginary nature of the foreign threat.

A MINGLED YARN: AUTOBIOGRAPHICAL SKETCHES. Indianapolis: Bobbs-Merrill, 1953.

> A collection of eighteen essays and sketches, most reprinted from previous volumes. The title piece reviews HMT's boyhood in the East End of London.

NORMAN DOUGLAS. London: Chatto and Windus; New York: Harper, 1931.

> An appreciation of Douglas' personality and works that compares him to Doughty and finds his travel writing superior to D.H. Lawrence's. Douglas is an aristocratic epicurean whose absence of moral cant and the diversity of whose writings account for his unpopularity.

OLD JUNK. London: Melrose, 1918. New York: Knopf, 1920.

> Twenty-one periodical essays and sketches on nautical and other topics. Two of the more interesting are "The African Coast" (experiences in a native village) and "The Pit Mouth" (on a mining disaster). Four others treat WWI.

OUT OF SOUNDINGS. London: Heinemann; New York: Harper, 1931.

> A collection of sixteen familiar essays and sketches, many deploring the inventions of the machine age. "Beauty and the Beast" is about the "talkies"; "Exploration" is on the modern motives for travel. There are also essays on Trotsky and Hardy.

H.M. Tomlinson

THE SEA AND THE JUNGLE. London: Duckworth, 1912. New York: Dutton, 1913.

> HMT's first and best-known book. It recounts his voyage as purser in a tramp steamer from London to the upper Amazon and is noteworthy both for its evocative sea- and landscapes (reminiscent of Conrad's) and its character portraits of seamen and settlers.

SOUTH TO CADIZ. London: Heinemann; New York: Harper, 1934.

> On the sights and history of Spain, encountered on a trip with friends. HMT repeatedly uses pastoral Spain as a vantage point from which to criticize Europe in crisis. Two unrelated essays are appended: one on ships, one on Thoreau.

TIDE MARKS: SOME RECORDS OF A JOURNEY TO THE BEACHES OF THE MOLUCCAS AND THE FOREST OF MALAYA, IN 1923. London: Cassell; New York: Harper, 1924.

> A vivid account of HMT's six-month journey by ship and foot through the Malay archipelago, with numerous references to the previous travel literature of the region. After encountering leeches, volcanoes, and big game hunters, HMT finds the news from home jejune and vulgar.

THE TURN OF THE TIDE. London: Hodder and Stoughton, 1945. New York: Macmillan, 1947.

> Ten essays in support of the effort to win WWII. The longest, "Log of a Voyage, 1935," works in HMT's message by describing ominous sights during a voyage in the Mediterranean.

UNDER THE RED ENSIGN. London: Williams and Norgate. As THE FORESHORE OF ENGLAND; OR, UNDER THE RED ENSIGN. New York: Harper, 1926.

> A Socialist view of working conditions in the British merchant marine and ports. HMT adduces copious facts and figures about the overloading of ships and underpaying of men. He goes so far as to take an economic approach to Conrad's NIGGER OF THE NARCISSUS.

WAITING FOR DAYLIGHT. London: Cassell; New York: Knopf, 1922.

> Thirty-three essays and sketches. Many are on WWI: "A Raid Night" is a vivid account of a Zeppelin attack. "Literary Critics" states that critical discrimination is instinctive.

THE WIND IS RISING. London: Hodder and Stoughton, 1941. Boston: Little, Brown, 1942.

War propaganda, covering the events of August 1939 to August 1941. HMT explains this divergence from MARS HIS IDIOT by saying the Nazis are worse than war.

WORKS EDITED BY OTHERS

H.M. TOMLINSON: A SELECTION FROM HIS WRITINGS. Ed. Kenneth Hopkins. London: Hutchinson, 1953.

A generous selection of essays and sections of books. Included are pieces on Cunninghame Graham and Robert Lynd.

BIBLIOGRAPHY

Crawford, Fred D., ed. "Selected Bibliography." In his H.M. TOMLINSON. Twayne's English Author Series. Boston: Twayne, 1981. Pp. 245-54.

The best primary and secondary listings: the primary section lists books, articles, and contributions to books.

Hopkins, Kenneth, comp. "A Check List of Books by H.M. Tomlinson." In his H.M. TOMLINSON: A SELECTION FROM HIS WRITINGS. London: Hutchinson, 1953. Pp. 287-88.

A lightly annotated, chronological listing.

CRITICISM

Adcock, St. John. "H.M. Tomlinson." In his THE GLORY THAT WAS GRUB STREET: IMPRESSIONS OF CONTEMPORARY AUTHORS. London: Sampson Low, Marston, n.d. Pp. 311-20.

A brief survey of the career praising HMT's natural style.

Altick, Helen, and Richard Altick. "Square-Rigger on a Modern Mission." CE, 5 (1943), 75-80.

HMT's antiwar writings, springing from his hatred of industrialism, can offer only a vague pastoralism as alternate vision.

Crawford, Fred D. H.M. TOMLINSON. Twayne's English Author Series. Boston: Twayne, 1981.

By far the most useful study of HMT, this larger-than-usual Twayne volume contains chapters on him as essayist, critic, traveler, propagandist, novelist, and the like.

Gay, Alva A. "H.M. Tomlinson, Essayist and Traveller." In STUDIES IN HONOR OF JOHN WILCOX. Ed. A. Dayle Wallace and Woodburn O. Ross. Detroit: Wayne State Univ. Press, 1958. Pp. 209-17.

    Rehashes some of the sea writings and compares HMT to Thoreau.

Hodgson, Stuart. "Mr. H.M. Tomlinson." In his PORTRAITS AND REFLECTIONS. London: Nisbet, 1929. Pp. 185-92.

    HMT's presentation of life is idiosyncratic; his zeal for social reform is excessive.

Hopkins, Kenneth. "Introduction." In his H.M. TOMLINSON: A SELECTION FROM HIS WRITINGS. London: Hutchinson, 1953. Pp. 11-19.

    Hopkins stresses the autobiographical nature of all HMT's writings and the uniqueness of his prose style.

Lynd, Robert. "Mr. H.M. Tomlinson." In BOOKS AND AUTHORS. London: Cobden-Sanderson, 1922. Pp. 226-32.

    A general appreciation, praising HMT's descriptive powers.

Mayer, Frederick P. "H.M. Tomlinson: The Eternal Youth." VQR, 4 (1928), 72-82.

    HMT's enthusiasm is detrimental to his writings: it causes wordiness and prevents objective description.

Severn, Derek. "A Minor Master: A Rereading of H.M. Tomlinson." LONDON MAGAZINE, 18, No. 11 (1979), 47-58.

    A survey of the career that finds the novels least successful, compares HMT's style to Hudson's, and praises HMT's integrity and individuality.

Tomlinson, H.M. "Foreword." In his THE SEA AND THE JUNGLE. Illus. Clare Leighton. London: Duckworth, 1930. Pp. 9-19.

    A brief reminiscence of how HMT came to make his voyage and of the critical reception of the book. HMT stated his writing was influenced by Thoreau.

H.G. WELLS (1866-1946)

THE ATLANTIC EDITION OF THE WORKS OF H.G. WELLS (London: Unwin; New York: Scribner's, 1924-27) collects many of the nonfictional works to that date, although some are abridged: see Hammond's bibliography (p. 458) for details. THE NON-FICTIONAL WORKS OF H.G. WELLS (Totowa, N.J.: Oxford Microfilms, 1980) reproduces seventy-one works on microfiche.

NONFICTIONAL PROSE

AFTER DEMOCRACY: ADDRESSES AND PAPERS ON THE PRESENT WORLD SITUATION. London: Watts, 1932.

> Sixteen essays, including one on "present day morals" and one on divorce.

THE ANATOMY OF FRUSTRATION: A MODERN SYNTHESIS. London: Cresset; New York: Macmillan, 1936.

> Supposedly a synopsis of an eleven-volume work on the forces preventing the creation of a "sane world." These range from the subconscious to the educational system.

ANTICIPATIONS OF THE REACTION OF MECHANICAL AND SCIENTIFIC PROGRESS UPON HUMAN LIFE AND THOUGHT. London: Chapman and Hall, 1901. New York: Harper, 1902.

> HGW's first major work of predictive nonfiction. Beginning with anticipations of new modes of transportation, he works toward the prediction of World War I (and such innovations as the tank). This war will cause the collapse of capitalism, nationalism, and democracy and cause the rise of the New Republicans, a governing class of technocrats.

BOON, THE MIND OF THE RACE, THE WILD ASSES OF THE DEVIL, AND THE LAST TRUMP: BEING A FIRST SELECTION FROM THE LITERARY REMAINS OF GEORGE BOON, APPROPRIATE TO THE TIMES: PREPARED FOR PUBLICA-

TION BY REGINALD BLISS, WITH AN AMBIGUOUS INTRODUCTION BY H. G. WELLS. London: Fisher-Unwin; New York: Doran, 1915.

> All by HGW, supposedly fragments by a novelist who believes in the social utility of art. Chapter 4 is the notorious assault on James as empty aesthete, a "hippopotamus resolved at any cost . . . upon picking up a pea which has got into a corner of its den."

CERTAIN PERSONAL MATTERS: A COLLECTION OF MATERIAL, MAINLY AUTOBIOGRAPHICAL. London: Lawrence and Bullen, 1897.

> A collection of thirty-nine exceedingly occasional newspaper pieces with titles such as "On the Art of Staying at the Seaside." "The Literary Regimen" attributes the styles of Kipling, Stevenson, and others to what they eat.

THE COMMON SENSE OF WAR AND PEACE: WORLD REVOLUTION OR WAR UNENDING. Harmondsworth, Engl.: Penguin, 1940.

> NEW WORLD ORDER redux.

THE CONQUEST OF TIME. The Thinker's Library. London: Watts, 1942.

> A reworking of FIRST AND LAST THINGS.

CRUX ANSATA: AN INDICTMENT OF THE ROMAN CATHOLIC CHURCH. Harmondsworth, Engl.: Penguin, 1943. New York: Agora, 1944.

> Heading his first chapter "Why Do We Not Bomb Rome?" HGW writes an intemperate attack on the history and politics of the Church.

AN ENGLISHMAN LOOKS AT THE WORLD: BEING A SERIES OF UN-RESTRAINED REMARKS UPON CONTEMPORARY MATTERS. London: Cassell, 1914. As SOCIAL FORCES IN ENGLAND AND AMERICA. New York: Harper, 1914.

> A collection of twenty-six essays on a wide variety of topics. "The Contemporary Novel" argues that the novel need not evince the tight structure of the short story, and that it is well suited to the discussion of social issues.

EXPERIMENT IN AUTOBIOGRAPHY: DISCOVERIES AND CONCLUSIONS OF A VERY ORDINARY BRAIN (SINCE 1866). 2 vols. London: Gollancz, 1934. In 1 vol. New York: Macmillan, 1934.

> HGW's long autobiography, a history of how his social theories evolved. Most of it deals with his life in the nineteenth century and affords frank, vivid portraits of his lowly origins, his apprenticeships, his scientific studies, and the like. HGW sees his mental development both in terms of social pressures and as the result of chance accidents.

H.G. Wells

THE FATE OF HOMO SAPIENS: AN UNEMOTIONAL STATEMENT OF THE THINGS THAT ARE HAPPENING TO HIM NOW AND OF THE IMMEDIATE POSSIBILITIES CONFRONTING HIM. London: Secker and Warburg, 1939. As THE FATE OF MAN. New York: Alliance, 1939. Rev. ed. as THE OUTLOOK FOR HOMO SAPIENS. London: Secker and Warburg, 1942.

> A harbinger of MIND AT THE END OF ITS TETHER. HGW asserts that unless the world state is established quickly mankind will regress to barbarism. "There is no reason whatever to believe that the order of nature has any greater bias in favor of man than it had in favor of the icthyosaur. . . ."

FIRST AND LAST THINGS: A CONFESSION OF FAITH AND RULE OF LIFE. London: Constable; New York: Putnam, 1908.

> An ambitious credo. HGW begins by discussing man's limited capacity for accurate perception but next expresses faith in the evolution of a collective racial mind. The rest of the book details practical applications of this belief, such as socialism.

FLOOR GAMES. London: Palmer, 1911.

> Outlines various children's games with toy figures and houses such as "the game of the wonderful Islands." See LITTLE WARS.

'42 TO '44: A CONTEMPORARY MEMOIR UPON HUMAN BEHAVIOUR DURING THE CRISIS OF THE WORLD REVOLUTION. London: Secker and Warburg, 1944.

> A strange amalgam of commentary on contemporary matters such as the U-boat campaign and military intelligence with a historical look at the human propensity for cruelty. It also contains HGW's doctoral thesis written for London University.

THE FUTURE IN AMERICA: A SEARCH AFTER REALITIES. London: Chapman and Hall; New York: Harper, 1906.

> HGW admires the immense material progress of the nation but fears that economic competition will lead to class strife.

GOD THE INVISIBLE KING. London: Cassell; New York: Macmillan, 1917.

> Probably the most rebutted work of an oft-rebutted author. HGW rejects the Trinity (demoting the Father to the inscrutable "Veiled Being") in favor of the God of Love, who is personalized but not quite a person. The second part discusses the new Kingdom of God manifesting many of HGW's social ideas.

H.G. Wells

GUIDE TO THE NEW WORLD: A HANDBOOK OF CONSTRUCTIVE WORLD REVOLUTION. London: Gollancz, 1941.

> A collection of forty-two newspaper pieces on various contemporary political and military topics.

HONOURS PHYSIOGRAPHY. London: Hughes, 1893.

> A cram book written with R.A. Gregory.

IN THE FOURTH YEAR: ANTICIPATIONS OF A WORLD PEACE. London: Chatto and Windus; New York: Macmillan, 1918.

> Originally newspaper articles, the volume calls for the establishment of the League of Nations.

LITTLE WARS: A GAME FOR BOYS FROM TWELVE YEARS OF AGE TO ONE HUNDRED AND FIFTY AND FOR THAT MORE INTELLIGENT SORT OF GIRLS WHO LIKE BOYS' GAMES AND BOOKS WITH AN APPENDIX ON KRIEGSPIEL. London: Palmer, 1913.

> A sequel to FLOOR GAMES. It outlines a complex war game for toy soldiers.

MANKIND IN THE MAKING. London: Chapman and Hall, 1903. New York: Scribner's, 1904.

> The immediate sequel to ANTICIPATIONS, mainly concerned with the education of children in the New Republic. After a discussion of eugenic selection, HGW describes the proper education of youth through college.

MIND AT THE END OF ITS TETHER. London: Heinemann, 1945. Published with THE HAPPY TURNING. New York: Didier, 1946.

> An exceedingly bitter final statement in which HGW repudiates much of his previous work and claims that man is at an evolutionary dead end.

MR. BELLOC OBJECTS TO THE OUTLINE OF HISTORY. London: Watts; New York: Doran, 1926.

> A refutation of Belloc's COMPANION TO MR. WELLS'S OUTLINE OF HISTORY. Opening with the statement, "I am the least controversial of men," HGW closes by accusing Belloc of impudence, ignorance, and dishonesty.

A MODERN UTOPIA. London: Chapman and Hall; New York: Scribner's, 1905.

> A semifictional presentation of a Socialist utopia of the near

future. It will be ruled by the Samurai, reminiscent of Plato's guardians.

THE NEW AMERICA, THE NEW WORLD. London: Cresset; New York: Macmillan, 1935.

Thoughts on FDR and the New Deal in America, where "the intimations of a future world state are to be found."

THE NEW WORLD ORDER: WHETHER IT IS ATTAINABLE, HOW IT CAN BE ATTAINED, AND WHAT SORT OF WORLD A WORLD AT PEACE WILL HAVE TO BE. London: Secker and Warburg; New York: Knopf, 1940. Rev. ed. as THE OUTLOOK FOR HOMO SAPIENS. London: Secker and Warburg, 1942.

A statement of HGW's familiar desire for a Socialist world state.

NEW WORLDS FOR OLD. London: Constable; New York: Macmillan, 1908.

A full-length explanation of socialism. Aimed at a broad readership, much of the book attempts to defuse common fears such as the threat of socialism to the home and its inducement to "vast public corruption."

THE OPEN CONSPIRACY: BLUE PRINTS FOR A WORLD REVOLUTION. London: Gollancz; Garden City, N.Y.: Doubleday, Doran, 1928. Rev. ed. as the OPEN CONSPIRACY: BLUE PRINTS FOR A WORLD REVOLUTION: A SECOND VERSION OF THIS FAITH OF A MODERN MAN MADE MORE EXPLICIT AND PLAIN. London: Hogarth, 1930. Rev. ed. as WHAT ARE WE TO DO WITH OUR LIVES? London: Heinemann, 1931.

HGW predicts his world state will be produced by a quasi-religious political movement of people concerned for the salvation of the race. The loosely federated conspirators will disseminate propaganda and infiltrate industry and government.

THE OUTLINE OF HISTORY: BEING A PLAIN HISTORY OF LIFE AND MANKIND. 2 vols. London: Newnes; New York: Macmillan, 1920.

HGW's monumental and controversial history of the world, which does not bring in man until chapter 7. HGW perceives a pattern of creative elites able to cope with change giving way to rigid bureaucracies unable to do so: thus civilizations wax and wane. The book was an attempt to endow humanity with "common historical ideas" necessary for "common peace and prosperity." See SCIENCE OF LIFE and WORK, WEALTH AND HAPPINESS.

PHOENIX: A SUMMARY OF THE INESCAPABLE CONDITIONS OF WORLD REORGANISATION. London: Secker and Warburg; Girard, Kans.: Haldeman-Julius, 1942.

The first part deals with the "necessary form of world reorganization," noting that the possibility of the blitz dictates world control of transportation, that industrial waste demands a comprehensive plan of conservation, and the like. The second section treats "particular aspects of a world revolution," for example, the place of women and sexual conventions.

THE RIGHTS OF MAN: OR WHAT ARE WE FIGHTING FOR? Harmondsworth, Engl.: Penguin, 1940.

A pamphlet in support of the Sankey Declaration (which HGW was instrumental in drafting).

RUSSIA IN THE SHADOWS. London: Hodder and Stoughton, 1920. New York: Doran, 1921.

Originally articles based on HGW's 1920 visit, during which he met Lenin. HGW stresses the collapse of Russian society, typified by the ruin of Petersburg. He attempts a balanced view of the new government as honest but cruel and inexperienced.

THE SALVAGING OF CIVILISATION. London: Cassell; New York: Macmillan, 1921.

A rehash of HGW's familiar themes of education and world government. The proselytizing impulse that created OUTLINE OF HISTORY now leads him to propose a grander "Book of Necessary Knowledge and Wisdom."

THE SCIENCE OF LIFE: A SUMMARY OF CONTEMPORARY KNOWLEDGE ABOUT LIFE AND ITS POSSIBILITIES. With Julian Huxley and George P. Wells. 3 vols. London: Amalgamated Press, 1930. In 4 vols. Garden City, N.Y.: Doubleday, Doran, 1931.

The second of HGW's efforts at condensing a vast subject for the common man: biology and evolution. See OUTLINE OF HISTORY and WORK, WEALTH AND HAPPINESS.

SELECT CONVERSATIONS WITH AN UNCLE (NOW EXTINCT) AND TWO OTHER REMINISCENCES. London: Lane; New York: Merriam, 1895.

The humorous observations of an uncle from South Africa on the social pretensions of London.

A SHORT HISTORY OF THE WORLD. London: Cassell; New York: Macmillan, 1922.

A briefer version of OUTLINE OF HISTORY.

THE STORY OF A GREAT SCHOOLMASTER: BEING A PLAIN ACCOUNT OF

H.G. Wells

THE LIFE AND IDEAS OF SANDERSON OF OUNDLE. London: Chatto and Windus; New York: Macmillan, 1924.

> A tribute to F. W. Sanderson, whose educational reforms, such as his encouragement of collective rather than competitive activity, HGW admired.

TEXT-BOOK OF BIOLOGY. 2 vols. London: Clive, 1893.

TRAVELS OF A REPUBLICAN RADICAL IN SEARCH OF HOT WATER. Harmondsworth, Engl.: Penguin, 1939.

> HGW collects a series of cantankerous articles and also comments on the difficulties he has experienced getting them published. The hot water includes comments on colonization, the Royal Family, Chamberlain, and Zionism.

WAR AND THE FUTURE: ITALY, FRANCE AND BRITAIN AT WAR. London: Cassell, 1917. As ITALY, FRANCE AND BRITAIN AT WAR. New York: Macmillan, 1917.

> HGW's impressions of the Italian and French fronts from his tour of 1916.

THE WAR THAT WILL END WAR. London: Palmer; New York: Duffield, 1914.

> Eleven newspaper pieces mostly expressing the notion that the allies fight not to destroy the German nation but to end "Prussianism."

WASHINGTON AND THE HOPE OF PEACE. London: Collins, 1922. As WASHINGTON AND THE RIDDLE OF PEACE. New York: Macmillan, 1922.

> A collection of twenty-nine newspaper pieces about the Washington Disarmament Conference. HGW places his hope in a conglomeration of such meetings to engender world peace; he now despairs of the League of Nations.

THE WAY THE WORLD IS GOING: GUESSES AND FORECASTS OF THE YEARS AHEAD. London: Benn, 1928. Garden City, N.Y.: Doubleday, 1929.

> A collection of twenty-seven of HGW's newspaper pieces, mostly on political and international issues.

WHAT IS COMING?: A FORECAST OF THINGS AFTER THE WAR. London: Cassell, 1916. As WHAT IS COMING?: A EUROPEAN FORECAST. New York: Macmillan, 1916.

> HGW predicts a world federation, spurred by the cataclysm

of WWI. The conception of women's roles will alter because of their war work.

THE WORK, WEALTH AND HAPPINESS OF MANKIND. 2 vols. Garden City, N.Y.: Doubleday, 1931. In 1 vol. London: Heinemann, 1932.

> HGW's third attempt at a text for educating the common man about a huge subject, in this case economics and social science. See OUTLINE OF HISTORY and SCIENCE OF LIFE.

WORLD BRAIN. London: Methuen; Garden City, N.Y.: Doubleday, Doran, 1938.

> A collection of four addresses, one article, and appendixes on educational matters. HGW again calls for the creation of a world encyclopedia.

A YEAR OF PROPHESYING. London: Fisher-Unwin, 1924. New York: Macmillan, 1925.

> A collection of fifty-five articles, mostly on politics and international affairs.

WORKS EDITED BY OTHERS

H.G. WELLS: EARLY WRITINGS IN SCIENCE AND SCIENCE FICTION. Ed. Robert M. Philmus and David Y. Hughes. Berkeley and Los Angeles: Univ. of California Press, 1975.

> Collects twenty-eight hitherto unreprinted essays and stories from the 1880's and 1890's.

H.G. WELLS: JOURNALISM AND PROPHECY, 1893-1946: AN ANTHOLOGY. Ed. W. Warren Wagar. Boston: Houghton Mifflin, 1964.

> A generous collection of articles, chapters, and fragments with adequate notation of the sources. The first section contains pieces commenting on political and international issues, the second contains HGW's portraits of famous contemporaries, and the third, major statements of his desire for a world state.

H.G. WELLS'S LITERARY CRITICISM. Ed. Patrick Parrinder and Robert M. Philmus. Sussex: Harvester Press, 1980.

> A well-annotated selection of his drama reviews, his essays for the SATURDAY REVIEW, and the like.

HENRY JAMES AND H.G. WELLS: A RECORD OF THEIR FRIENDSHIP, THEIR DEBATE ON THE ART OF FICTION, AND THEIR QUARREL. Ed. Leon Edel and Gordon N. Ray. Urbana: Univ. of Illinois Press, 1958.

A collection of reviews, essays, and letters by James and HGW on and to each other.

THE LAST BOOKS OF H.G. WELLS: THE HAPPY TURNING AND MIND AT THE END OF ITS TETHER. Ed. G.P. Wells. Tiptree, Essex, Engl.: H.G. Wells Society, 1968.

An odd collection including part of the 1945 revised version of SHORT HISTORY and part of MIND AT THE END OF ITS TETHER for the purpose of demonstrating that HGW was not such a pessimist at the end of his life as supposed.

Stuart, Campbell. SECRETS OF CREWE HOUSE: THE STORY OF A FAMOUS CAMPAIGN. London: Hodder and Stoughton, 1920.

Prints HGW's report (pp. 61-81) on propaganda strategy against Germany in WWI.

WELLS' SOCIAL ANTICIPATIONS. Ed. Harry W. Laidler. New York: Vanguard Press, 1927.

Collects three of HGW's election addresses as a parliamentary candidate in 1922 and six other pieces of Socialist writing. They include "This Misery of Boots," which employs the inequality of footwear as a metaphor for social inequality.

BIBLIOGRAPHY

H.G. Wells Society, comp. H.G. WELLS: A COMPREHENSIVE BIBLIOGRAPHY. 1966. 3rd ed. Middlesex, Engl.: 1972.

A listing of HGW's works which does include a chronological listing of secondary books on him.

Hammond, J.R., ed. HERBERT GEORGE WELLS: AN ANNOTATED BIBLIOGRAPHY OF HIS WORKS. New York: Garland, 1977.

The standard primary bibliography. Along with books and pamphlets, it lists letters, HGW's contributions to books by others, and the contents of the ATLANTIC EDITION. It also contains a three-page listing of secondary material.

Hughes, David Y., and Robert M. Philmus, eds. "The Early Science Journalism of H.G. Wells: A Chronological Survey." SFS, 1 (1973), 98-114.

Abstracts ninety essays, chronologically arranged.

Mullen, R.D., ed. "The Books and Principal Pamphlets of H.G. Wells, A Chronological Survey." SFS, 1 (1973), 114-35.

A chronological listing that usefully annotates the contents of HGW's works.

Parrinder, Patrick, ed. H.G. WELLS: THE CRITICAL HERITAGE. London: Routledge and Kegan Paul, 1972.

Contains contemporary reviews of ANTICIPATIONS, MANKIND IN THE MAKING, MODERN UTOPIA, OUTLINE OF HISTORY, and WORK, WEALTH AND HAPPINESS OF MANKIND.

Philmus, Robert M., ed. "Wells's Literary Reviews in the SATURDAY REVIEW (1895-97)." SFS, 4 (1977), 175-93.

Philmus abstracts ninety-two reviews.

Raknem, Ingvald, comp. H.G. WELLS AND HIS CRITICS. Oslo: Universitetsforlaget, 1962.

This study of HGW's critical reception lists book reviews on the nonfiction and has a chronologically arranged list of articles on HGW.

Ray, Gordon N., comp. "H.G. Wells's Contributions to the SATURDAY REVIEW." LIBRARY, 16 (1961), 29-36.

An unannotated, chronological list of these contributions from 1894 to 1898.

Timko, Michael, comp. "H.G. Wells's Dramatic Criticism for THE PALL MALL GAZETTE." LIBRARY, 17 (1962), 138-45.

A lightly annotated, chronological listing of these reviews of 1895.

Watkins, A.H., ed. CATALOGUE OF THE H.G. WELLS COLLECTION IN THE BROMLEY PUBLIC LIBRARIES. Bromley: London Borough of Bromley Public Libraries, 1974.

A listing of the extensive holdings, both primary and secondary, including introductions by HGW and reviews of his books.

Weeks, Robert P., et al., eds. "H.G. Wells." EFT [now ELT], 1, No. 1 (1957), 37-42. Continued in subsequent volumes.

An alphabetically arranged listing of criticism. The last list appeared 16 (1973), 168-70.

BIOGRAPHY

Brome, Vincent. SIX STUDIES IN QUARRELLING. London: Cresset, 1958.

> Cites numerous nonfictional pieces in detailing HGW's battles with Shaw, Henry Arthur Jones, James, and Belloc.

Dickson, Lovat. H.G. WELLS: HIS TURBULENT LIFE AND TIMES. New York: Atheneum, 1969.

> An antagonistic and unscholarly work, but one that does focus on HGW's decades as social critic and therefore does say a good deal about the nonfiction, especially BOON.

Mackenzie, Norman, and Jeanne Mackenzie. H.G. WELLS: A BIOGRAPHY. New York: Simon and Schuster, 1973.

> The best biography, with information on the writing history, publishing history, and contents of the nonfiction.

Wood, James Playsted. I TOLD YOU SO!: A LIFE OF H.G. WELLS. New York: Pantheon Books, 1969.

> A brief, elementary biography that does contain useful summaries of the major nonfictional works. There is no index, however.

CRITICISM

Archer, William. GOD AND MR. WELLS: A CRITICAL EXAMINATION OF GOD THE INVISIBLE KING. London: Watts, 1917.

> A reasoned criticism of HGW's lack of clarity in GOD, such as his failure to demarcate God's interference in human affairs and his seeming presentation of the Deity as both an entity and a metaphor.

Armytage, W.H G. "Superman and the System, Part I." RQ, 2 (1967), 232-42.

> A very brief discussion of the Nietzschean ubermensch idea in such HGW writings as ANTICIPATIONS and MODERN UTOPIA.

Baylen, Joseph O. "W.T. Stead and the Early Career of H.G. Wells, 1895-1911." HLQ, 38 (1974), 53-79.

> On the literary relationship of HGW and the editor W.T. Stead. Stead's reviews of ANTICIPATIONS and MANKIND IN THE MAKING are described.

Becker, Carl. "Mr. Wells and the New History." AMERICAN HISTORICAL REVIEW, 26 (1921), 641-56.

> A witty but fairly positive review of OUTLINE OF HISTORY that praises HGW's ambition, while noting he becomes less objective when he nears the present.

Belgion, Montgomery. H.G. WELLS. Writers and Their Work. 1953. Rev. ed. London: Longmans, 1964.

>Notes the nonfiction in passing while positing such inane personae as "Baby Wells" and "Giant Wells."

Belloc, Hilaire. A COMPANION TO MR. WELLS'S OUTLINE OF HISTORY. London: Sheed and Ward, 1926.

>A trenchant, thorough refutation of HGW's treatment of Christianity by a Catholic. Belloc accuses HGW of "satisfied ignorance" and a rabid hatred of tradition. The book engendered HGW's MR. BELLOC OBJECTS.

──────. MR. BELLOC STILL OBJECTS TO MR. WELLS'S OUTLINE OF HISTORY. London: Sheed and Ward, 1926.

>Belloc's pamphlet refuting HGW's MR. BELLOC OBJECTS, which in turn refutes Belloc's A COMPANION TO MR. WELLS'S OUTLINE OF HISTORY, which in turn refutes OUTLINE.

Beresford, J.D. H.G. WELLS. London: Nisbet, 1915.

>The last chapter is a weak treatment of HGW's sociological writings.

Bergonzi, Bernard. "Another Early Wells Item." NCF, 13 (1958), 72-73.

>On "The Extinction of Man" (CERTAIN PERSONAL MATTERS) as a source of HGW's early fiction.

──────. "Wells, Fiction and Politics." In his THE TURN OF A CENTURY: ESSAYS ON VICTORIAN AND MODERN ENGLISH LITERATURE. London: Macmillan, 1973. Pp. 99-113.

>A brief review of HGW's utopian writings that discusses MODERN UTOPIA.

Binns, Leonard Elliott. MR. WELLS' INVISIBLE KING: A CRITICISM. London: Society for Promoting Christian Knowledge, 1919.

>HGW's religious views are prejudiced and ignorant; his interpretation of God is mistaken; he is however sincere and does subscribe to some Christian tenets.

Braybrooke, Patrick. SOME ASPECTS OF H.G. WELLS. London: Daniel, 1928.

A jeeringly antagonistic survey of HGW's theological ideas in FIRST AND LAST THINGS and GOD THE INVISIBLE KING; a more even one of his social ideas in FUTURE IN AMERICA, RUSSIA IN THE SHADOWS, and STORY OF A GREAT SCHOOLMASTER.

Brome, Vincent. "H.G. Wells as a Controversialist." UWR, 2, No. 2 (1967), 31-45.

An enumeration of HGW's quarrels. Two of them were with James over BOON and with Belloc over OUTLINE OF HISTORY.

Brooks, Van Wyck. THE WORLD OF H.G. WELLS. London: Unwin, 1915.

An early, well-written study of HGW's socialism that cites the nonfiction throughout, especially FIRST AND LAST THINGS.

Brown, E.K. "Two Formulas for Fiction: Henry James and H.G. Wells." CE, 8 (1946), 7-17.

A ringing defense of James that employs PORTRAIT OF A LADY to indicate HGW's charge of empty characters and overunified structure (voiced in BOON and elsewhere) false.

Brown, Ivor. H.G. WELLS. London: Nisbet, 1923.

An early appreciation that mentions the nonfiction throughout, especially in the chapters "The Social Scene" and "The Hope that Is in History."

Collins, Christopher. "Zamyatin, Wells and the Utopian Literary Tradition." SEER, 44 (1966), 351-60.

The controlled society that HGW embraces in such writings as ANTICIPATIONS is anathema to Zamyatin, whose MY is in part a parody of HGW's utopias.

Costa, Richard Haver. H.G. WELLS. Twayne's English Author Series. New York: Twayne, 1967.

Costa sees HGW the novelist ruined by HGW the social critic, and the nonfiction receives little attention.

Craufurd, Alexander H. "The Religion of H.G. Wells." In his THE RELIGION OF H.G. WELLS AND OTHER ESSAYS. London: Unwin, 1909. Pp. 11-115.

A liberal clergyman largely agrees with HGW's religious and social ideas expressed in FIRST AND LAST THINGS but disagrees with specific points.

Dark, Sidney. THE OUTLINE OF H.G. WELLS: THE SUPERMAN IN THE STREET. London: Parsons, 1922.

> An overly excited defense of HGW against reactionaries like Belloc and aesthetes like Conrad. HGW's nonfiction is surveyed in chapters 3, 6, and 8 to 10.

De La Bedoyere, Michael. WAS IT WORTH IT, WELLS? London: Paternoster Publications, 1943.

> The editor of the CATHOLIC HERALD refutes CRUX ANSATA through reprinting his correspondence with HGW on the book.

Doughty, F.H. H.G. WELLS: EDUCATIONIST. London: Cape, 1926.

> A specialized and informed study of HGW's ideas on education that relies heavily on nonfictional works such as MANKIND IN THE MAKING and SALVAGING OF CIVILIZATION. A handy list is appended noting the chapters in his books (up to 1926) treating the subject.

Downey, Richard. SOME ERRORS OF H.G. WELLS: A CATHOLIC'S CRITICISM OF THE OUTLINE OF HISTORY. 1921. 2nd ed. London: Burns, Oates, and Washbourne, 1933.

> The Archbishop of Liverpool objects to HGW's belief in human evolution and his treatment of the Catholic Church.

Earle, Edward Mead. "H.G. Wells, British Patriot in Search of a World State." In his NATIONALISM AND INTERNATIONALISM: ESSAYS INSCRIBED TO CARLTON J.H. HAYES. New York: Columbia Univ. Press, 1950. Pp. 78-121.

> Cites the nonfiction throughout in discussing HGW's conflicting attitudes toward nationalism.

Edel, Leon, and Gordon N. Ray. "Introduction." In their HENRY JAMES AND H.G. WELLS: A RECORD OF THEIR FRIENDSHIP, THEIR DEBATE ON THE ART OF FICTION, AND THEIR QUARREL. Urbana: Univ. of Illinois Press, 1958. Pp. 15-41.

> Reviews the history of the relationship between the writers.

Ellis, Havelock. "H.G. Wells." In his FROM MARLOWE TO SHAW: THE STUDIES, 1876-1936, IN ENGLISH LITERATURE. London: Williams and Norgate, 1950. Pp. 297-302.

> Although generally admiring, Ellis complains about HGW's ideas on eugenics and evolution.

Farrell, John K.A. "H.G. Wells as an Historian." UWR, 2, No. 2 (1967), 45-57.

> A historian notes the strengths and weaknesses of OUTLINE OF
> HISTORY and the uncannily accurate SHAPE OF THINGS TO
> COME.

Freeman, John. "H.G. Wells." In THE MODERNS: ESSAYS IN LITERARY CRITICISM. London: Scott, 1916. Pp. 53-101.

> This contains a sizeable review of HGW's nonfictional utopian
> writings to 1916.

Gentry, Irene, comp. "Bibliography of H.G. Wells' OUTLINE OF HISTORY." BB, 11 (1922), 160-61, 183-84; 12 (1923), 6-7.

> A listing of works referred to in OUTLINE OF HISTORY.

Glover, Willis B. "Religious Orientations of H.G. Wells: A Case Study in Scientific Humanism." HTR, 65 (1972), 117-35.

> Sees a deep but distorted theological impulse in HGW's works,
> especially GOD THE INVISIBLE KING.

Gomme, Arnold W. MR. WELLS AS HISTORIAN. Glasgow: Maclehose, Jackson, 1921.

> HGW's presentation of Greece and Rome in OUTLINE is unin-
> formed and mistaken: "I rub my eyes, and read this again. . . ."

Haight, Gordon S. "H.G. Wells's 'The Man of the Year Million.'" NCF, 12 (1958), 323-26.

> On an 1893 article that harbingers the TIME MACHINE.

Haynes, Roslynn D. H.G. WELLS: DISCOVERER OF THE FUTURE: THE INFLUENCE OF SCIENCE ON HIS THOUGHT. London: Macmillan, 1980.

> Haynes cites the nonfiction throughout this detailed study of
> how HGW's scientific background influenced his social thought
> and even his literary techniques.

Hopkins, Robert Thurston. H.G. WELLS: PERSONALITY, CHARACTER, TOPOGRAPHY. London: Palmer, 1922.

> An explication of HGW's career addressed to the "man in the
> street." RUSSIA IN THE SHADOWS receives a chapter.

Hughes, David Y. "The Mood of A MODERN UTOPIA." EXTRAPOLATION, 19 (1977), 59-67.

> On the uses of the subjunctive mood in the work.

Huxley, Julian. "THE SCIENCE OF LIFE." In his MEMORIES. New York: Harper, 1970. Pp. 155-78.

> On the writing history of HGW's biology book by his collaborator.

Hyde, William J. "The Socialism of H. G. Wells in the Early Twentieth Century." JHI, 17 (1956), 217-34.

> A thorough review of HGW's Socialist thought, drawing on such books as NEW WORLDS.

Hynes, Samuel. "The Fabians: Mrs. Webb and Mr. Wells." In his THE EDWARDIAN TURN OF MIND. Princeton, N.J.: Princeton Univ. Press, 1968. Pp. 87-131.

> An account of HGW's disruptive effect on the Fabians, with references to his nonfiction of the time such as ANTICIPATIONS and MODERN UTOPIA. "Appendix C" reprints his lecture "Faults of the Fabian."

Ingle, Stephen J. "The Political Writing of H. G. Wells." QQ, 81 (1974), 396-411.

> A slight summation of HGW's socialism; he was better suited to the emotive expression of it in his fiction than the discursive expression of it in his nonfiction.

Johnston, Dillon. "The Recreation of Self in Wells's EXPERIMENT IN AUTOBIOGRAPHY." CRITICISM, 14 (1972), 345-60.

> An excellent discussion of the tension in the volume between the Socialist desire to present the self as merely typical and the desire to present the self as unique.

Jones, Henry Arthur. MY DEAR WELLS. New York: Dutton, 1921.

> A sarcastic assault on Socialist HGW, one of the "haters of England," written as a series of letters to him.

Kagarlitski, J. THE LIFE AND THOUGHT OF H. G. WELLS. 1963. Trans. Moura Budberg. London: Sidgwick and Jackson, 1966.

> A Marxist treatment that notes HGW's frequent political errors. ANTICIPATIONS, MODERN UTOPIA, NEW WORLDS FOR OLD, and RUSSIA IN THE SHADOWS are discussed.

Karl, Frederick R. "Conrad, Wells, and the Two Voices." PMLA, 88 (1973), 1049-65.

> While discussing the conflicting "voices" of these authors (the voices of art and logic), Karl observes that HGW did not always hold the negative opinion of Conrad's art expressed in EXPERIMENT IN AUTOBIOGRAPHY.

Kauffmann, Stanley. "Wells and the New Generation: The Decline of a Leader of Youth." CE, 1 (1940), 573-82.

    States that HGW's popular decline (beginning about 1925) is because his amateurishness in his educational and scientific writings, and his hatred of Marx in his political writings, were resented.

Kazin, Alfred. "H.G. Wells, America and 'The Future.'" ASCH, 37 (1967-68), 137-44.

    Reviews the contents of FUTURE IN AMERICA and compares HGW with other observers of America, such as James.

Leavis, Frank R. "Babbitt Buys the World." SCRUTINY, 1 (1932), 80-83.

    A review of WORK, WEALTH AND HAPPINESS that finds HGW's utopian ideals "trivial."

Lodge, David. "Assessing H.G. Wells." In THE NOVELIST AT THE CROSSROADS AND OTHER ESSAYS ON FICTION AND CRITICISM. Ithaca, N.Y.: Cornell Univ. Press, 1971. Pp. 205-20.

    On the shape of the career and the critical reception of it. A useful overview.

Mirsky, D.S. "H.G. Wells and History." CRITERION, 12 (1932), 1-16.

    A doctrinaire Marxist assault on OUTLINE, arguing that in it HGW reveals "a profound philistinism, a self-satisfied ignorance, and a hatred of democracy."

Mullen, Richard D. "'I Told You So': Wells's Last Decade, 1936-1945." In H.G. WELLS AND MODERN SCIENCE FICTION. Ed. Darko Suvin and Robert M. Philmus. Lewisburg, Pa.: Bucknell Univ. Press, 1977. Pp. 116-25.

    A slight review of the work of the last decade.

National Civic Federation. SYMPOSIUM OF OPINIONS UPON THE OUTLINE OF HISTORY BY H.G. WELLS: VIEWS OF HISTORIANS. New York: 1922.

    A collection of mostly negative replies from historians asked if OUTLINE is suitable as a college text.

Nickerson, C.C. "A Note on Some Neglected Opinions of H.G. Wells." EFT [now ELT], 5, No. 5 (1962), 27-30.

Cites nonfiction (e.g., SELECT CONVERSATIONS) in arguing
that HGW in fact wished a compromise between aestheticism
and didacticism in art.

Nulle, Stebelton H. "The General Education of H. G. Wells." UCQ, 8,
No. 3 (1963), 22-26.

Cites nonfiction in a very general review of HGW's approach
to education.

Orwell, George. "Wells, Hitler and the World State." In THE COLLECTED
ESSAYS, JOURNALISM, AND LETTERS OF GEORGE ORWELL: MY COUNTRY
RIGHT OR LEFT, 1940-1943. Ed. Sonia Orwell and Ian Angus. New York:
Harcourt, 1968. Pp. 139-45.

Reviewing GUIDE TO THE NEW WORLD, Orwell argues that
HGW cannot grasp the danger of Hitler because HGW's view
of life is too rational.

Parrinder, Patrick, and Robert M. Philmus. "Introduction." In their H. G.
WELLS'S LITERARY CRITICISM. Sussex, Engl.: Harvester Press, 1980. Pp.
1-18.

An informed survey of HGW's critical values and connections.

Philmus, Robert M. "H. G. Wells as Literary Critic for the SATURDAY REVIEW."
SFS, 4 (1977), 166-75.

A close analysis of HGW's fiction reviews during 1895-97 that
notes his insistence on the individual quality in good fiction
and his dislike of romance.

―――. "Revisions of His Past: H. G. Wells's ANATOMY OF FRUSTRATION."
TSLL, 20 (1978), 249-66.

Traces the social views in ANATOMY back to HGW's writings
of the 1890's.

Philmus, Robert M., and David Y. Hughes. "Introduction: Outlines." In
H. G. WELLS: EARLY WRITINGS IN SCIENCE AND SCIENCE FICTION.
Berkeley and Los Angeles: Univ. of California Press, 1975. Pp. 1-12.

A good discussion of HGW's ideas on evolution as expressed
in early nonfiction.

Salter, Arthur. "H. G. Wells: Apostle of a World Society." In his PERSONALITY
IN POLITICS: STUDIES OF CONTEMPORARY STATESMEN. London: Faber,
1947. Pp. 120-37.

Cites several of the nonfiction works in noting HGW's obvious
desire for "an ordered world society."

Scheick, William J. "Reality and the Word: The Last Books of H. G. Wells."
ELT, 12 (1969), 151-54.
> On the pessimism of these works, partly expressed in likening
> life to dreams and the cinema.

Sherman, Stuart P. "The Utopian Naturalism of H. G. Wells." In his ON
CONTEMPORARY LITERATURE. New York: Holt, 1917. Pp. 50-84.
> Sarcastic comments on GOD THE INVISIBLE KING and WHAT
> IS COMING?

Steinberg, M. W. "H. G. Wells as a Social Critic." UWR, 2, No. 2 (1967),
9-20.
> A pedestrian review of the subject, seeing ANTICIPATIONS as
> the key expression.

Tilby, A. Wyatt. "The Works of Mr. H. G. Wells." EDINBURGH REVIEW,
237 (1923), 113-32.
> An early review of the career that notes HGW's drive for
> ontological belief in OUTLINE OF HISTORY and GOD.

Timko, Michael. "Entente Cordiale: The Dramatic Criticism of Shaw and
Wells." MD, 8 (1965), 39-46.
> On the similarity of Shaw's and HGW's attitudes toward the
> theater, demonstrated by their reviews of the same eight plays
> in 1895.

UNIVERSITY OF WINDSOR REVIEW, 2, No. 2 (1967), 1-76.
> An HGW number collecting seven articles on him.

Wagar, W. Warren. H. G. WELLS AND THE WORLD STATE. Yale Historical
Publications. New Haven, Conn.: Yale Univ. Press, 1961.
> An excellent treatment of HGW's social thought that discusses
> numerous works of nonfiction. The first chapter, an overview
> of his "prophetic career," is especially useful.

_____. "Introduction." In his H. G. WELLS: JOURNALISM AND PROPHECY,
1893-1946: AN ANTHOLOGY. Boston: Houghton Mifflin, 1964. Pp. xv-
xxvi.
> Contains a brief review of HGW's career as nonfiction writer.

Watkin, E. I. "H. G. Wells: The Frustration of Humanism." In his MEN
AND TENDENCIES. London: Sheed, 1937. Pp. 1-17.

A Christian argues ANATOMY OF FRUSTRATION expresses the frustration of life without Christ.

West, Anthony. "H.G. Wells." ENCOUNTER, 8, No. 2 (1957), 52-59.

HGW's son asserts the important thesis that the utopian social tracts, beginning with ANTICIPATIONS, are mistaken attempts to belie the accuracy of HGW's pessimistic outlook in his first and final periods.

Whittemore, Reed. "The Fascination of the Abomination--Wells, Shaw, Ford, Conrad." In his THE FASCINATION OF ABOMINATION: POEMS, STORIES, AND ESSAYS. New York: Macmillan, 1963. Pp. 129-66.

Notes that despite HGW's distaste for high artistry in fiction, as voiced in EXPERIMENT, his novels are not without art.

Woodcock, George. "The Darkness Violated by Light: A Revisionist View of H.G. Wells." MHREV, 26 (1973), 144-60.

Touches on MIND AT THE END OF ITS TETHER, EXTINCTION OF MAN, MODERN UTOPIA, and FATE OF HOMO SAPIENS in arguing that the pessimism of HGW's last years is also evident in his early career.

Young, Kenneth. H.G. WELLS. Writers and Their Work. London: Longmans, 1974.

The second effort in this series. The fifth section is a balanced view of HGW's Fabianism as reflected in the nonfiction.

VIRGINIA WOOLF (1882-1941)

NONFICTIONAL PROSE

THE COMMON READER. London: Hogarth; New York: Harcourt, 1925.

VW's first essay collection, with twenty-five selections. They include brilliant attempts to capture the essence of Greek and Russian literature; "Modern Fiction," which likens life to a "luminous halo" better depicted by "spiritualists" like Joyce than "materialists" like Bennett; "How It Strikes a Contemporary," noting the literary "age of fragments."

THE COMMON READER: SECOND SERIES. London: Hogarth, 1932. As THE SECOND COMMON READER. New York: Harcourt, 1932.

VW's second essay collection, with twenty-six selections. They include essays on Mary Wollstonecraft, Dorothy Wordsworth, and Christina Rossetti. The essay on Sterne, noting his psychological emphasis, presents him as a forerunner of the moderns. Hardy is judged the major tragic novelist of British literature.

FLUSH: A BIOGRAPHY. London: Hogarth; New York: Harcourt, 1933.

A whimsical biography of Elizabeth Barrett's spaniel. From his perspective, VW depicts the development of Elizabeth and the social stratification in London of the 1840's. The rendering of a dog's sense impressions is vivid.

MR BENNETT AND MRS BROWN. London: Hogarth, 1924.

This final version was originally a paper read to the Heretics Club, Cambridge, May 18, 1924. The essay is VW's famous denunciation of the Edwardians Wells, Bennett, and Galsworthy for their inability to depict human nature, pictured as a Mrs. Brown in a railway carriage. It goes on to discuss the efforts of Georgians such as Eliot and Joyce to do so through new literary techniques. An earlier and inferior version appeared in NATION AND ATHENAEUM, 34 (1923), 342-43.

ROGER FRY: A BIOGRAPHY. London: Hogarth; New York: Harcourt, 1940.

> On the artist and champion of Post-Impressionism, with liberal quotation from his letters and other private writings. The biography focuses less on his art than on his personal life, which was burdened with parental disapproval and a mad wife. The record of his sexual career is largely avoided, however.

A ROOM OF ONE'S OWN. London: Hogarth; New York: Fountain Press, 1929.

> VW's first feminist book, on the difficulties of women writers. Surveying the history of British literature, she concludes that the lack of educational opportunities and financial independence have thwarted these writers. "Judith Shakespeare," who wishes to write and ends a suicide, epitomizes their plight. There is an interesting section on the ideal of the androgynous mind.

THREE GUINEAS. London: Hogarth; New York: Harcourt, 1938.

> VW's second feminist book, much less smiling in tone than ROOM and on extraliterary topics. Asked for a contribution to an antiwar society, she responds with a heavily footnoted survey of the educational and professional plight of women and concludes that the cause of peace is linked to women's rights.

WORKS EDITED BY OTHERS

"'Anon' and 'The Reader': Virginia Woolf's Last Essays." Ed. Brenda R. Silver. TCL, 25 (1979), 356-441.

> Printed for the first time, two sections of a proposed book on British literary history.

BOOKS AND PORTRAITS: SOME FURTHER SELECTIONS FROM THE LITERARY AND BIOGRAPHICAL WRITINGS OF VIRGINIA WOOLF. Ed. Mary Lyon. London: Hogarth, 1977.

> A collection of forty-eight hitherto uncollected reviews.

THE CAPTAIN'S DEATH BED AND OTHER ESSAYS. Ed. Leonard Woolf. London: Hogarth, 1950.

> The fifth essay collection, with twenty-five selections. They include pieces on Marryat, Turgenev, and VW's father. "Memories of a Working Women's Guild" describes her feeling of division from lower-class activists in 1913. MR BENNETT AND MRS BROWN (above) is reprinted.

Virginia Woolf

COLLECTED ESSAYS. Ed. Leonard Woolf. 4 vols. London: Hogarth, 1966-67.

>Reprints the essays from COMMON READER, COMMON READER: SECOND SERIES, MOMENT, DEATH OF THE MOTH, CAPTAIN'S DEATH BED, and GRANITE organized so that volumes 1 and 2 deal with "literary and critical topics" and volumes 3 and 4 deal with "biographical."

CONTEMPORARY WRITERS. Comp. Jean Guiguet. London: Hogarth, 1965.

>Forty hitherto uncollected reviews on modern fiction from the TLS.

THE DEATH OF THE MOTH AND OTHER ESSAYS. Ed. Leonard Woolf. London: Hogarth, 1942.

>The third essay collection, with twenty-eight selections. They include three admiring reviews of James's later works and letters, an essay on Forster that notes his failure to integrate realism and the lyric impulse, and "A Letter to a Young Poet," which deplores the subjectivity of modernist poetry.

THE DIARY OF VIRGINIA WOOLF. Vol. 1: 1915-1919. Ed. Anne Olivier Bell. London: Hogarth, 1977. Vol. 2: 1920-1924. Vol. 3: 1925-1930. Ed. Anne Olivier Bell and Andrew McNeillie. London: Hogarth, 1978, 1980.

>An annotated printing of the thirty-book collection in the Berg Collection, to be issued in five volumes.

GRANITE AND RAINBOW: ESSAYS. Ed. Leonard Woolf. London: Hogarth, 1958.

>The sixth essay collection, with twenty-eight essays under the headings "The Art of Fiction" and "The Art of Biography." Among the more interesting are two pieces on James's supernatural fiction, a balanced essay on the early Hemingway, and "Phases of Fiction," a lengthy division of major British novelists into such groups as "The Truth Tellers" and "The Psychologists."

THE LONDON SCENE: FIVE ESSAYS. New York: Hallman, 1975.

>Reprints "The Docks of London," "Oxford Street Tide," "Great Men's Houses," "Abbeys and Cathedrals," and "'This Is the House of Commons.'"

THE MOMENT AND OTHER ESSAYS. Ed. Leonard Woolf. London: Hogarth, 1947.

>The fourth essay collection, with thirty selections. They include an essay on Lawrence, presenting him as disastrously unconnected

with the fictional tradition, and a review of Forster's ASPECTS
OF THE NOVEL attacking his "unesthetic attitude" toward
fiction.

MOMENTS OF BEING: UNPUBLISHED AUTOBIOGRAPHICAL WRITINGS. Ed.
Jeanne Schulkind. Sussex, Engl.: Sussex Univ. Press, 1976.

> Three papers delivered to the Memoir Club and two other
> reminiscences. Three deal with VW's family life in her
> pre-Bloomsbury days; one deals with her early Bloomsbury
> days; one addresses the question "Am I a Snob?"

THE PARGITERS: THE NOVEL-ESSAY PORTION OF THE YEARS. Ed. Mitchell
A. Leaska. New York: New York Public Library, 1977.

> Prints an early version of YEARS that was written in 1932 and
> takes the form of fiction chapters alternating with essays glossing
> them. The essays discuss the educational, the economic, and,
> especially, the sexual deprivations of women as depicted in the
> fiction.

VIRGINIA WOOLF: SELECTIONS FROM HER ESSAYS. Ed. Walter James.
London: Chatto and Windus, 1966.

> "Political Writings" contains extracts from ROOM and THREE
> GUINEAS and two essays; "Biography" contains two biographical
> essays. There is an ampler selection of critical essays, including
> "Modern Fiction" and "Middlebrow."

VIRGINIA WOOLF: WOMEN AND WRITING. Ed. Michele Barrett. New
York: Harcourt, 1979.

> Part 1 is a collection of seven articles, reviews, and published
> letters on general feminist topics; part 2 collects eighteen pieces
> on women writers.

"Virginia Woolf's 'Byron and Mr. Briggs.'" Ed. Edward A. Hungerford. YR,
68 (1979), 325-49.

> An unfinished essay describing the "common reader's" tendency
> to attempt summarizing conceptions of a writer's career.

"Virginia Woolf's 'Friendships Gallery.'" Ed. Ellen Hawkes. TCL, 25 (1979),
270-302.

> First publication of VW's humorous mock biography of her friend
> Violet Dickinson, written in 1907.

A WRITER'S DIARY: BEING EXTRACTS FROM THE DIARY OF VIRGINIA
WOOLF. Ed. Leonard Woolf. London: Hogarth, 1953.

A selection from VW's diaries covering the years 1918 to 1941 and focusing on her reading, her opinions of other authors, and the writing of her own works. As Leonard Woolf notes, the volume "gives an unusual psychological picture of artistic production from within."

BIBLIOGRAPHY

Beebe, Maurice, comp. "Criticism of Virginia Woolf: A Selected Checklist with an Index to Studies of Separate Works." MFS, 2 (1956), 36-45.

> The "separate works" are all fiction; there is an unannotated, alphabetically arranged section of general criticism.

Kirkpatrick, Brownlee Jean, ed. A BIBLIOGRAPHY OF VIRGINIA WOOLF. Soho Bibliographies. 1957. Rev. ed. Oxford, Engl.: Clarendon Press, 1980.

> The standard, primary bibliography, with sections on books, articles, translations of VW's works, letters, and manuscripts.

Laing, D.A. "An Addendum to the Virginia Woolf Bibliography." N&Q, 19 (1972), 338.

> Notes a one-page foreword (missing in Kirkpatrick) to the catalog of Vanessa Bell's 1934 exhibition.

Majumdar, Robin, ed. VIRGINIA WOOLF: AN ANNOTATED BIBLIOGRAPHY OF CRITICISM, 1915-1974. New York: Garland, 1976.

> Included are sections on critical books, articles, and book reviews. The omission from the index of VW's nonfictional volumes is unhelpful.

Weiser, Barbara, comp. "Criticism of Virginia Woolf from 1956 to the Present: A Selected Checklist with an Index to Studies of Separate Works." MFS, 18 (1972), 477-86.

> The only nonfictional "separate work" is FLUSH; there is an unannotated, alphabetically arranged section of general criticism.

Woolmer, J. Howard, comp. A CHECKLIST OF THE HOGARTH PRESS, 1917-1938. Andes, N.Y.: Woolmer and Brotherson, 1976.

> A descriptive, chronologically organized listing of publications that includes VW's nonfiction.

BIOGRAPHY

Bell, Quentin. VIRGINIA WOOLF: A BIOGRAPHY. London: Hogarth, 1972.

The standard biography, with information on the writing history of the nonfiction.

CRITICISM

Auden, W. H. "A Consciousness of Reality." In FOREWORDS AND AFTERWORDS. Ed. Edward Mendelson. New York: Random House, 1973. Pp. 411-18.

> An admiring review of WRITER'S DIARY, praising the dedication to craft and grasp of commonplace reality shown there.

Barrett, Michele. "Introduction." In her VIRGINIA WOOLF: WOMEN AND WRITING. New York: Harcourt, 1980. Pp. 1-36.

> A good summary of VW's ideas on the subject as expressed in essays and the feminist books. Barrett notes a contradiction between VW's emphasis in ROOM on the material conditions of artistic production and her emphasis elsewhere on the transcendent nature of art.

Batchelor, J. B. "Feminism in Virginia Woolf." ENGLISH, 17 (1968), 1-7.

> Notes VW rejects the stance of militant feminism in THREE GUINEAS and ROOM.

Bazin, Nancy Topping. VIRGINIA WOOLF AND THE ANDROGYNOUS VISION. New Brunswick, N. J.: Rutgers Univ. Press, 1973.

> Chapter 2 cites the nonfiction heavily in outlining VW's aesthetic theories.

Bell, Barbara Currier, and Carol Ohmann. "Virginia Woolf's Criticism: A Polemical Preface." In FEMINIST LITERARY CRITICISM: EXPLORATIONS IN THEORY. Ed. Josephine Donovan. Lexington: Univ. Press of Kentucky, 1975. Pp. 48-60.

> Argues that features of VW's criticism--her biographical approach, her treatment of the reader as equal--constitute a revolt against academic criticism in order to make literature more accessible.

Bell, Millicent. "Virginia Woolf Now." MR, 14 (1973), 655-87.

> Reviews the contents of ROOM and THREE GUINEAS, arguing VW employs a fictive persona in both.

Bell, Quentin. "Introduction." In THE DIARY OF VIRGINIA WOOLF. Vol. 1: 1915-1919. Ed. Anne Olivier Bell. London: Hogarth, 1977. Pp. xiii-xxviii.

> Attempts a brief defense of the veracity of VW's record of others.

Virginia Woolf

Bennett, Arnold. THE AUTHOR'S CRAFT AND OTHER CRITICAL WRITINGS. Ed. Samuel Hynes. Lincoln: Univ. of Nebraska Press, 1968.

    Contains Bennett's antagonistic review of ROOM.

Bennett, Joan. VIRGINIA WOOLF: HER ART AS A NOVELIST. 1945. 2nd ed. Cambridge: The Univ. Press, 1964.

    The second edition adds a chapter on WRITER'S DIARY, which focuses on the entries concerning WAVES, and a chapter on the criticism, which primarily reviews VW's opinions of other novelists.

Bishop, Morchard. "Towards a Biography of FLUSH." TLS, 15 December 1966, p. 1180.

    On inaccuracies about the dog in FLUSH.

Blackstone, Bernard. VIRGINIA WOOLF: A COMMENTARY. New York: Harcourt, 1949.

    This contains a chapter on ROOM, which simply repeats its contents, and a chapter on "Criticism and Biography," which is negligible.

Bogan, Louise. "The Ladies and Gentlemen" and "The Skirting of Passion." In SELECTED CRITICISM: PROSE, POETRY. New York: Noonday, 1955. Pp. 36-39, 365-69.

    The first is a review of THREE GUINEAS; the second wishes that VW's criticism evinced a greater intuitive grasp of passion and evil.

Brewster, Dorothy. VIRGINIA WOOLF. New York: New York Univ. Press, 1962.

    Chapter 2 is a lengthy, casually organized review of the contents of many of VW's essays.

_____. VIRGINIA WOOLF'S LONDON. London: Allen and Unwin, 1959.

    Notes the presentation of London in ROOM, FLUSH, and WRITER'S DIARY. Slight.

Brower, Reuben A. "The Novel as Poem: Virginia Woolf Exploring a Critical Metaphor." In THE INTERPRETATION OF NARRATIVE: THEORY AND PRACTICE. Ed. Morton W. Bloomfield. Cambridge, Mass.: Harvard Univ. Press, 1970. Pp. 229-47.

    Quotes COLLECTED ESSAYS and WRITER'S DIARY in discussing VW's ideal of the poetic novel.

Carroll, Berenice A. "'To Crush Him in Our Own Country': The Political Thought of Virginia Woolf." FEMINIST STUDIES, 4, No. 1 (1978), 99-131.

Draws on both fiction and nonfiction in describing VW's Socialist politics of "confrontation" and "struggle."

Cornwell, Ethel F. "Virginia Woolf's Moment of Reality." In her THE STILL POINT. New Brunswick, N.J.: Rutgers Univ. Press, 1962. Pp. 159-207.

> Cites the nonfiction throughout in discussing VW's use of epiphany in her fiction.

Daiches, David. VIRGINIA WOOLF. New York: New Directions, 1963.

> Chapter 6 discusses VW's critical manner, finding her best at summing up "the atmosphere of a character or a period."

Delord, J. "Virginia Woolf's Critical Essays." RLV, 29 (1963), 126-31.

> On the manner in which VW's reviews attempt to duplicate for the reader her experience of reading the book in question.

DiBattista, Maria. VIRGINIA WOOLF'S MAJOR NOVELS: THE FABLES OF ANON. New Haven, Conn.: Yale Univ. Press, 1980.

> The introduction cites the nonfiction heavily in discussing VW's impersonal narration.

Dil, Anwar S. "Virginia Woolf and Human Rights." VWQ, 3 (1978), 211-16.

> A slight appreciation of ROOM.

Farwell, Marilyn R. "Virginia Woolf and Androgyny." CONL, 16 (1975), 433-51.

> In ROOM, VW vacillates between a conception of androgyny as a balance of male and female qualities and a conception of the fusion of them, denying status to the female.

Fishman, Solomon. "Virginia Woolf on the Novel." SR, 51 (1943), 321-40.

> An informative attempt to deduce the aesthetic theory underlying VW's impressionistic criticism: the Coleridgean imagination is central to it.

Forster, E.M. VIRGINIA WOOLF. Cambridge: The Univ. Press, 1942.

> The Rede Lecture for 1941. Forster judges VW's feminism as expressed in THREE GUINEAS to be old-fashioned and extreme.

Freedman, Ralph. THE LYRICAL NOVEL: STUDIES IN HERMAN HESSE, ANDRE GIDE, AND VIRGINIA WOOLF. Princeton, N.J.: Princeton Univ. Press, 1963. Pp. 185-270.

Cites VW's criticism heavily at the beginning in discussing her creation of the lyrical novel.

Furman, Nelly. "A ROOM OF ONE'S OWN: Reading Absence." In WOMEN'S LANGUAGE AND STYLE. Ed. Douglas Butturff and Edmund L. Epstein. Akron, Ohio: L and S Books, 1978. Pp. 99-105.

A motif of missing items and people, running through the book, suggests the unfulfilled potential of women.

Gish, Robert. "Mr. Forster and Mrs. Woolf: Aspects of the Novelist as Critic." VWQ, 2 (1976), 255-69.

A review of the long critical exchange between Forster and VW that began with Forster's 1915 review of VOYAGE OUT and included MR BENNETT. The fundamental disagreement between them concerned the rendering of character.

Givner, Joan. "Two Leaning Towers: Viewpoints by Katherine Anne Porter and Virginia Woolf in 1940." VWQ, 3 (1977), 85-90.

On similar reactions to WWII expressed in VW's "The Leaning Tower" (COLLECTED ESSAYS, vol. 2) and Porter's story of the same title.

Goetsch, Paul. "A Source of Virginia Woolf's 'Mr Bennett and Mrs Brown.'" ELT, 7 (1964), 188-89.

VW's selection of 1910 as the date "human character changed" was suggested by one of Bennett's own essays.

Goldman, Mark. THE READER'S ART: VIRGINIA WOOLF AS LITERARY CRITIC. The Hague: Mouton, 1976.

A major attempt to place VW's criticism; rather than rampantly impressionistic, it strikes a balance between analysis and emotional response, according to Goldman. He examines in turn her sense of literary periods, her ideas on the novel, and her views on criticism itself.

──────. "Virginia Woolf and E.M. Forster: A Critical Dialogue." TSLL, 7 (1966), 387-400.

Reviews the published exchange between the two and notes that VW cares more for artistic form and criticism itself than Forster.

Gorsky, Susan Rubinow. VIRGINIA WOOLF. Twayne's English Author Series. Boston: Twayne, 1978.

Chapter 2 is a useful attempt to construct VW's general aesthetics from her nonfiction; chapter 7 reviews her feminist writings. An informed study.

Gregory, Horace. "Virginia Woolf: The Spirit of Time and Place." In his SPIRIT OF TIME AND PLACE: COLLECTED ESSAYS OF HORACE GREGORY. New York: Norton, 1973. Pp. 175-79.

> Claims VW revived the familiar essay between the World Wars.

Guiguet, Jean. "A Novelist's Essay: 'The Moment: Summer's Night' by Virginia Woolf." In DER ENGLISCHE ESSAY: ANALYSEN. Ed. Horst Weber. Darmstadt, Ger.: Wissenschaftliche Buchgesellschaft, 1975. Pp. 291-303.

> A close analysis of the imagery and style of "The Moment: Summer's Night" (MOMENT).

──────. VIRGINIA WOOLF AND HER WORKS. 1962. Trans. Jean Stewart. London: Hogarth, 1965.

> The critical nonfiction receives extensive treatment. Guiguet is especially good in outlining VW's ideas about literary criticism and in comparing them to those of her contemporaries.

Gunsteren-Viersen, Julia van. "The Marriage of 'He' and 'She': Virginia Woolf's Androgynous Theory." DQR, 6 (1976), 233-46.

> On how VW's androgynous ideal is reflected in her writing style in the feminist books.

Hamilton, James F. "Woolf's A ROOM OF ONE'S OWN." EXPL, 39, No. 1 (1980), 4-6.

> The tailless condition of the Manx cat described in ROOM suggests the plight of women.

Henig, Suzanne. "D.H. Lawrence and Virginia Woolf." DHLR, 2 (1969), 265-71.

> Reviews VW's various published remarks on Lawrence, and argues she was put off by the sexual frankness of his works.

Hill, Katherine C. "Virginia Woolf and Leslie Stephen: History and Literary Revolution." PMLA, 96 (1981), 351-62.

> A good study of how Stephen's emphasis upon history both in his tutoring of his daughter and in his criticism influenced her criticism. Both see new genres as the products of class shift.

Hoag, Gerald. HENRY JAMES AND THE CRITICISM OF VIRGINIA WOOLF. University Studies, No. 92. Wichita, Kans.: Wichita State Univ. Press, 1972.

Notes broad similarities between James and VW in their theories on the novel. Both mistrust didacticism in fiction and stress form (although she feels it is less the product of conscious deliberation than does he).

Holtby, Winifred. VIRGINIA WOOLF: A CRITICAL MEMOIR. London: Wishart, 1932.

Chapter 2 is an early appreciation of VW's nonfiction that stresses her optimism about the future of literary and social concerns.

Hulcoop, John F. "Virginia Woolf's Diaries: Some Reflections after Reading Them and a Censure of Mr. Holroyd." BNYPL, 75 (1971), 301-10.

The diaries have interesting but not earth-shaking revelations and do not support the view of VW of Strachey's biographer.

Hummel, Madeline M. "From the Common Reader to the Uncommon Critic: THREE GUINEAS and the Epistolary Form." BNYPL, 80 (1977), 151-57.

The form raises reader interest and is well suited to argumentation.

Hungerford, E. A. "Mrs. Woolf, Freud, and J. D. Beresford." L&P, 5 (1955), 49-51.

VW's review of Beresford's AN IMPERFECT MOTHER indicates her attitude toward Freudian literature.

Hunting, Robert. "Laurence Sterne and Virginia Woolf." EA, 32 (1979), 283-93.

Reviews the substance of VW's three main pieces on Sterne and then defends Sterne against her charge of sentimentality.

Johnson, Manly. VIRGINIA WOOLF. New York: Ungar, 1973.

Chapter 1 is a slight review of the nonfiction.

Kenney, Edwin J. "The Moment, 1910: Virginia Woolf, Arnold Bennett, and Turn of the Century Consciousness." CLQ, 13 (1977), 42-66.

Argues VW's choice in MR BENNETT of 1910 as the date of major change owes as much to both the political unrest and her personal problems of that year as to Fry's postimpressionist exhibition.

Kreutz, Irving. "Mr. Bennett and Mrs. Woolf." MFS, 8 (1962), 103-15.

A pro-Bennett piece arguing that he was more interested in the penetration of character than VW admits in MR BENNETT and that she quotes passages from HILDA LESSWAYS out of context.

Kronenberger, Louis. "Virginia Woolf as Critic." In his THE REPUBLIC OF LETTERS: ESSAYS ON VARIOUS WRITERS. New York: Knopf, 1955. Pp. 244-49.

> VW was less interested in literary analysis than in portrait painting. After the first COMMON READER her style is overly rhetorical and clever.

Lakshmi, Vijay. "The Solid and the Intangible: Virginia Woolf's Theory of the Androgynous Mind." LCRIT, 10, No. 1 (1971), 28-34.

> Cites the nonfiction in arguing VW's dualistic approach to life determines her theory that the novel should be a mix of prose and poetry.

─────. "Virginia Woolf and E.M. Forster: A Study of Their Critical Relations." LHY, 12, No. 2 (1971), 39-49.

> A slight review of the critical debate between the two.

Leaska, Mitchell A. "Introduction." In his THE PARGITERS: THE NOVEL-ESSAY PORTION OF THE YEARS. New York: New York Public Library, 1977. Pp. vii-xxii.

> Discusses the writing history of the "novel-essay" and the reasons for the abandonment of the nonfiction component.

Leavis, Q.D. "Caterpillars of the Commonwealth Unite!" SCRUTINY, 7 (1938), 203-14.

> A savaging of THREE GUINEAS that finds it self-indulgent and illogical: "The result affects me like Nazi dialectic without Nazi conviction."

Lewis, Wyndham. "Virginia Woolf." In his MEN WITHOUT ART. London: Cassell, 1934. Pp. 158-71.

> Asserts that VW's dim view of her contemporaries in MR BENNETT is inaccurate.

Leyburn, Ellen Douglass. "Virginia Woolf's Judgment of Henry James." MFS, 5 (1959), 166-69.

> Reviews VW's published statements on James and picks her statement in "Henry James's Ghost Stories" (GRANITE AND RAINBOW) that James was dramatic instead of lyric as explaining why he did not influence her.

Lorberg, Aileen D. "Virginia Woolf: Benevolent Satirist." PERSONALIST, 33 (1952), 148-58.

> An appreciation of the humor in ROOM, MR BENNETT, and FLUSH.

McIntyre, Clara F. "Is Virginia Woolf a Feminist?" PERSONALIST, 41 (1960), 176-84.

> No, because in THREE GUINEAS she derides the organizational impulse.

McLaurin, Allen. VIRGINIA WOOLF: THE ECHOES ENSLAVED. Cambridge: The Univ. Press, 1973.

> Chapter 4 discusses how Roger Fry's ideas about repetition in art influence FLUSH.

Majumdar, Robin. "Virginia Woolf and Thoreau." TSB, 109 (1969), 4-5.

> Draws on VW's 1917 TLS piece about Thoreau in noting both writers value meditation and moments of intense vision.

Majumdar, Robin, and Allen McLaurin, eds. VIRGINIA WOOLF: THE CRITICAL HERITAGE. London: Routledge, 1975.

> Collects contemporary reviews of the several versions of MR BENNETT, COMMON READER, ROOM, FLUSH, THREE GUINEAS, and ROGER FRY.

Manuel, M. "Virginia Woolf as the Common Reader." LCRIT, 7, No. 2 (1966), 28-32.

> In COMMON READER: SECOND SERIES, VW abandons the mask of "common reader" and is revealed as a "creative writer straying into and amusing herself with criticism."

Marcus, Jane. "Art and Anger." FEMINIST STUDIES, 4, No. 1 (1978), 69-98.

> Compares VW's feminist works with the actress Elizabeth Robins' bitter work ANCILLA'S SHARE.

Marder, Herbert. FEMINISM AND ART: A STUDY OF VIRGINIA WOOLF. Chicago: Univ. of Chicago Press, 1968.

> Cites the nonfiction throughout in laying out VW's feminist ideas.

Meisel, Perry. THE ABSENT FATHER: VIRGINIA WOOLF AND WALTER PATER. New Haven, Conn.: Yale Univ. Press, 1980.

Extremely heavy citation of the nonfiction as even ROOM is seen as influenced by Pater. The influence was psychological and stylistic; VW struggled to overcome it.

Novak, Jane. THE RAZOR EDGE OF BALANCE: A STUDY OF VIRGINIA WOOLF. Coral Gables, Fla.: Univ. of Miami Press, 1974.

The first four chapters of this study of VW's dualism draw heavily on the nonfiction. The second chapter contains an interesting summary of VW's attitudes toward James. The third chapter sees the criticism as a mixture of classical and romantic tendencies.

Pacey, Desmond. "Virginia Woolf as a Literary Critic." UTQ, 17 (1948), 234-44.

Argues VW's critical emphases are on "singleness of effect" in art, on impersonality, and on ethics.

Paterson, John. "Virginia Woolf: Fire in the Mist." In his THE NOVEL AS FAITH: THE GOSPEL ACCORDING TO JAMES, HARDY, CONRAD, JOYCE, LAWRENCE AND VIRGINIA WOOLF. Boston: Gambit, 1973. Pp. 184-229.

An excellent discussion of VW's theories on the novel that cites the nonfiction throughout.

Pomeroy, Elizabeth W. "Garden and Wilderness: Virginia Woolf Reads the Elizabethans." MFS, 24 (1978-79), 497-508.

An interesting review of VW's observations on the Elizabethans expressed in seven essays and elsewhere. She admired the "wilderness" of their rich prose style.

Quennell, Peter. A LETTER TO MRS. VIRGINIA WOOLF. London: Hogarth, 1932.

A reply to "Letter to a Young Poet" (DEATH OF THE MOTH) excusing the poet's quirks because of the vitiating social forces he confronts and the dearth of traditional forms still valid.

Rahv, Philip. "Mrs. Woolf and Mrs. Brown." In his IMAGE AND IDEA. Norfolk, Conn.: New Directions, 1949. Pp. 139-43.

VW's spiritual approach to Mrs. Brown (MR BENNETT) is no more adequate than Bennett's materialistic presentation.

Rantavaara, Irma. VIRGINIA WOOLF AND BLOOMSBURY. Helsinki: Annales Academiae Fennicae, 1953.

>   Chapter 11 treats the feminist works and chapter 5 compares
>   VW and her father as critics.

Robb, Kenneth A. "Virginia Woolf's 'Miss Omerod.'" AN&Q, 7 (1968), 71.

>   Notes a misprint in the third part of "Lives of the Obscure"
>   (COMMON READER).

Roberts, John Hawley. "'Vision and Design' in Virginia Woolf." PMLA, 61 (1946), 835-47.

>   Cites ROGER FRY in discussing Fry's influence on VW's aesthetics.

Rogot, Ellen Hawkes. "A Form of One's Own." MOSAIC, 8, No. 1 (1974), 77-90.

>   Cites ROOM and assorted essays in discussing VW's revolt
>   against the "masculine sentence."

Rosenbaum, Stanford P. "The Philosophical Realism of Virginia Woolf." In his ENGLISH LITERATURE AND BRITISH PHILOSOPHY. Chicago: Univ. of Chicago Press, 1971. Pp. 316-56.

>   Notes the influence of G. E. Moore in VW's "Modern Fiction"
>   (COMMON READER).

Rosenthal, Michael. VIRGINIA WOOLF. New York: Columbia Univ. Press, 1979.

>   Chapters 13, 14, and 15 provide usefully close reviews of the
>   contents of the biographies, of the feminist books, and of the
>   most important criticism, respectively.

Rubenstein, Roberta. "Virginia Woolf and the Russian Point of View." CLS, 9 (1972), 196-206.

>   A summation of VW's critical admiration of the Russian novel.

Samuelson, Ralph. "More Than One Room of Her Own: Virginia Woolf's Critical Dilemmas." WHR, 19 (1965), 249-56.

>   VW's "problem of reconciling equality and difference" of the
>   sexes becomes involved with her class ambivalences and skews
>   her critical view of such authors as Joyce and Lawrence.

Schaefer, Josephine O'Brien. "Moments of Vision in Virginia Woolf's Biographies." VWQ, 2 (1976), 294-303.

>   A quick review of VW's biographical essays and books, noting
>   her talent for grasping the essence of the subjects. Schaefer

provides a good analysis of how the dog's viewpoint in FLUSH facilitates this; ROGER FRY fails, however, because VW lacks adequate information about his early, personal life.

Schlack, Beverly Ann. "Virginia Woolf's Strategy of Scorn in THE YEARS and THREE GUINEAS." BNYPL, 80 (1977), 146-50.

> On various rhetorical devices that contribute to the scornful tone of these books.

Schorer, Mark. "Virginia Woolf." YR, 32 (1942), 377-81.

> Accuses VW of lacking objective values in her criticism.

Schulkind, Jeanne. "Introduction." In her MOMENTS OF BEING: UNPUBLISHED AUTOBIOGRAPHICAL WRITINGS. Sussex, Engl.: Sussex Univ. Press, 1976. Pp. 11-24.

> Notes the connections, both of biographical sources and ideas, between these works of nonfiction and the fiction.

Sears, Sallie. "Notes on Sexuality: THE YEARS and THREE GUINEAS." BNYPL, 80 (1977), 211-20.

> Argues the essay, as well as the novel, evinces a basic pessimism about the possibility of social improvement.

Sharma, Vijay L. VIRGINIA WOOLF AS LITERARY CRITIC: A REVALUATION. New Delhi, India: Arnold-Heinemann, 1977.

> Primarily useful for its opening discussion of the cultural influences on VW's criticism.

Showalter, Elaine. "Virginia Woolf and the Flight into Androgyny." In her A LITERATURE OF THEIR OWN: BRITISH WOMEN NOVELISTS FROM BRONTE TO LESSING. Princeton, N.J.: Princeton Univ. Press, 1977. Pp. 263-97.

> Sees the androgyny recommended in ROOM as a retreat from feminine problems and anger.

Sloman, Judith. "Virginia Woolf's Literary History: Integrating the Obscure." VWQ, 3 (1978), 230-40.

> Discusses the reasons (which include her feminism) for VW's tendency to emphasize secondary figures, as in COMMON READER: SECOND SERIES.

Spilka, Mark. VIRGINIA WOOLF'S QUARREL WITH GRIEVING. Lincoln: Univ. of Nebraska Press, 1980.

> Extremely heavy citation, especially in chapters 2 and 3, of
> "A Sketch of the Past" (MOMENTS OF BEING) in the course
> of accounting for VW's difficulties with expressing grief and
> love in psychobiographical terms. Feminist works such as
> PARGITERS receive this approach in the final chapter.

Stubbs, Patricia. "Mr. Lawrence and Mrs. Woolf." In her WOMEN AND FICTION: FEMINISM AND THE NOVEL, 1880-1920. New York: Barnes and Noble, 1979. Pp. 225-35.

> Claims that the examination of women's everyday lives VW
> calls for in ROOM is not present in her novels.

Sugiyama, Yoko. RAINBOW AND GRANITE: A STUDY OF VIRGINIA WOOLF. Tokyo: Hokuseido Press, 1973.

> Chapter 9 explains that some of VW's more hostile and arrogant
> feminist utterances are actually metaphoric; chapter 10 treats
> the biographies and concludes she has no talent for the factual
> variety (ROGER FRY).

Szladits, Lola L. "'The Life, Character, and Opinions of Flush the Spaniel.'" BNYPL, 74 (1970), 211-18.

> Notes parallels between Elizabeth Barrett and VW in connection
> with FLUSH.

Thakur, N. C. THE SYMBOLISM OF VIRGINIA WOOLF. London: Oxford Univ. Press, 1965.

> Chapter 1 compiles VW's various remarks on literary symbolism.

Wellek, René. "Virginia Woolf as Critic." SORA, 13 (1977), 419-37.

> A good review of VW's essays on novelists that demonstrates
> she was more judgmental in her criticism than often assumed.

West, Rebecca. "Autumn and Virginia Woolf." In her ENDING IN EARNEST: A LITERARY LOG. Garden City, N.Y.: Doubleday, Doran, 1931. Pp. 209-13.

> Praises VW's courage in publishing ROOM in the face of prevalent
> antifeminist sentiment.

Wilson, Edmund. "Virginia Woolf and the American Language." In his THE SHORES OF LIGHT: A LITERARY CHRONICLE OF THE TWENTIES AND THIRTIES. New York: Farrar, Straus and Young, 1952. Pp. 421-28.

> Chronicles the flap caused by VW's statement in "On Not
> Knowing French" that American and English are separate tongues.

Woodring, Carl. VIRGINIA WOOLF. Columbia Essays on Modern Writers. New York: Columbia Univ. Press, 1966.

    Contains brief mention of the nonfiction.

W.B. YEATS (1865-1939)

NONFICTIONAL PROSE

AUTOBIOGRAPHIES: REVERIES OVER CHILDHOOD AND YOUTH AND THE TREMBLING OF THE VEIL. London: Macmillan, 1926. New York: Macmillan, 1927.

> Considered by many critics to be WBY's greatest prose work. Important autobiographical record which reveals both the content and style of WBY's personal and artistic life. The disappointments suffered by his friend Synge, the strain and frustration of his relationship with Maud Gonne, his literary tastes, and associates are some of the many topics discussed.

THE AUTOBIOGRAPHY OF YEATS, CONSISTING OF REVERIES OVER CHILDHOOD AND YOUTH, THE TREMBLING OF THE VEIL AND DRAMATIS PERSONAE. New York: Macmillan, 1938.

> Also includes ESTRANGEMENT, DEATH OF SYNGE, and BOUNTY OF SWEDEN.

THE BOUNTY OF SWEDEN: A MEDITATION AND A LECTURE DELIVERED BEFORE THE ROYAL SWEDISH ACADEMY. Dublin: Cuala Press, 1925.

> Includes two essays "The Bounty of Sweden" and "The Irish Dramatic Movement." WBY gratefully reflects that his muse is still young.

THE CELTIC TWILIGHT: MEN AND WOMEN, DHOULS AND FAERIES. London: Lawrence and Bullen, 1893. New York: Macmillan, 1894.

> A collection of twenty-three stories and essays, including "A Teller of Tales," "Belief and Unbelief," "A Visionary," "The Golden Age," "A Remonstrance with Scotsmen," and "The Four Winds of Desire." WBY attempts to discover in the traditions of folk literature and culture an order of experience unspoiled by the materialistic philosophy of modern civilization.

W.B. Yeats

THE CUTTING OF AN AGATE. New York: Macmillan, 1912. London: Macmillan, 1919.

> Reprints "Discoveries," "Poetry and Tradition," "J.M. Synge and the Ireland of His Time," and "Edmund Spenser." The enlarged English edition adds "Certain Noble Plays of Japan." Miscellaneous observations on poetry and drama.

DISCOVERIES: A VOLUME OF ESSAYS. Dundrum, Ireland: Dun Emer Press, 1907.

> A collection of twenty-one essays, including "Prophet, Priest and King," "The Tree of Life," "The Two Kinds of Asceticism," "The Thinking of the Body" and "Religious Belief Necessary to Symbolic Art." In some essays WBY addresses his readers in a prophetic voice.

DRAMATIS PERSONAE. Dublin: Cuala Press, 1935.

> WBY provides descriptions of his collaboration and friendship with Lady Gregory and his part in the establishment of Abbey Theatre.

DRAMATIS PERSONAE 1896-1902, ESTRANGEMENT, THE DEATH OF SYNGE, THE BOUNTY OF SWEDEN. London and New York: Macmillan, 1936.

> A collection of previously published works.

ESSAYS. London and New York: Macmillan, 1924.

> Reprints the essays from GOOD AND EVIL, AGATE, and LUNAE, with a few minor additions.

ESSAYS, 1931 TO 1936. Dublin: Cuala Press, 1937.

> A collection of ten essays, including "Parnell," "Modern Poetry," "Bishop Berkeley" (WBY's interest in philosophy), and "Prometheus Unbound." Several others deal with Oriental religion.

IDEAS OF GOOD AND EVIL. London: Bullen; New York: Macmillan, 1903.

> A collection of nineteen essays, including "What is 'Popular Poetry?,'" "Magic," "The Symbolism of Poetry" ("poetry moves us because of its symbolism"), "The Autumn of the Body," "Emotion of Multitude," and studies of Shelley and Blake. In viewing experience WBY rejects materialism and endorses spiritualism and symbolism.

IF I WERE FOUR-AND-TWENTY. Dublin: Cuala Press, 1940.

W.B. Yeats

In the title essay WBY makes a plea for a unified Irish sensibility. Also includes "Swedenborg, Mediums and the Desolate Places."

MODERN POETRY. London: British Broadcasting Commission, 1936.

One of the National Lectures Series, this lecture-essay was given as a BBC broadcast on 11 October 1936.

ON THE BOILER. Dublin: Cuala Press, 1939.

In an almost informal manner, WBY's "smiling public man" voice considers such topics as eugenics and modern specialization, as well as school testing and training. Interesting record of WBY's late antidemocratic reflections, but not considered one of his major works.

A PACKET FOR EZRA POUND. Dublin: Cuala Press, 1929.

Contains the four essays "Rapallo," "Meditations upon Death," "Introduction to 'The Great Wheel,'" and "To Ezra Pound."

PER AMICA SILENTIA LUNAE. London and New York: Macmillan, 1918.

The title translates to "In the Moon's Friendly Silence." Important statement of the philosophy of the self and anti-self: WBY records his thoughts on man's soul (anima hominis) and the world's soul (anima mundi). Demons, ghosts, and magic are also discussed.

PLAYS AND CONTROVERSIES. London: Macmillan, 1923. New York: Macmillan, 1924.

Essays on the Irish dramatic movement and play production. WBY says he has given up the idea of writing "lovely prose."

POETRY AND IRELAND. With Lionel Johnson. Dundrum, Ireland: Cuala Press, 1908.

REVERIES OVER CHILDHOOD AND YOUTH. Dundrum, Ireland: Cuala Press, 1915. New York: Macmillan, 1916.

Interesting anecdotes and notes concerning WBY's early life. WBY sketches the influence of his father, a portrait-painter, and such early friends as Edward Dowden.

SYNGE AND THE IRELAND OF HIS TIME. Dundrum, Ireland: Cuala Press, 1911.

An essay on Synge's life and works. WBY discusses the harsh public response to Synge's plays and treats some of the quarrels in which he became embroiled.

W.B. Yeats

A VISION. London: T. Werner Laurie, 1925.

> WBY's complex and challenging treatise on human nature and destiny. The twenty-eight phases of the system's linked opposites cover all types of human personality and transformations of the soul after death. A complete system of historic theory outlines the cyclic nature of civilization. Some key concepts include: "mask," "will," "gyres," "body of fate," "the anti-self," and "the phases of the moon." WBY published a revised edition in 1937.

WORKS EDITED BY OTHERS

AUTOBIOGRAPHY. Ed. Mrs. W.B. Yeats. New York: Macmillan, 1953.

> Contains REVERIES, TREMBLING, DRAMATIS, ESTRANGEMENT, SYNGE and BOUNTY OF SWEDEN.

A CRITICAL EDITION OF YEATS'S A VISION (1925). Ed. George Mills Harper and Walter Kelly Hood. London: Macmillan, 1978.

> This edition includes important scholarly apparatus--an introduction which traces the development of the book, an index, endnotes that identify historical personages and places, and a bibliography of works cited.

ESSAYS AND INTRODUCTIONS. Ed. Mrs. W.B. Yeats. London: Macmillan, 1961.

> Contains GOOD AND EVIL, AGATE, later critical essays and introductions, four of which deal with Oriental religion. Also includes the important and revealing "General Introduction for My Work" on the content and style of his poetry. The most important collection of WBY's critical essays.

EXPLORATIONS. Ed. Mrs. W.B. Yeats. London: Macmillan, 1962.

> Essays, introductions, and articles are selected by Mrs. Yeats. Some important paragraphs are omitted without explanation in this edition. Topics covered include: spiritualism, Irish mythology, Irish cultural sensibility, and Irish theatre. An important collection of WBY's critical essays.

LETTERS TO THE NEW ISLAND. Ed. Horace Reynolds. Cambridge, Mass.: Harvard Univ. Press, 1934.

> Reprints essays and a few reviews that were contributed by WBY to THE BOSTON PILOT and THE PROVIDENCE JOURNAL between 1889 and 1891. Essays included are: "Browning," "Ireland's Heroic Age," "The Rhymers' Club," and "The Irish National Literary Society."

W.B. Yeats

MEMOIRS OF W. B. YEATS. Ed. Denis Donoghue. London: Macmillan, 1972.
> Contains first drafts of the journals of 1908-14.

MYTHOLOGIES. Ed. Mrs. W. B. Yeats. London: Macmillan, 1959.
> Contains TWILIGHT and PER AMICA. WBY considers Irish country folklore to be important for revealing the anima mundi (world soul).

SELECTED CRITICISM. Ed. A. Norman Jeffares. London: Macmillan, 1964.
> A useful selection of WBY's literary criticism over several decades.

SELECTED PROSE. Ed. A. Norman Jeffares. London: Macmillan, 1964.
> Includes selections from WBY's autobiographical writings, essays, and introductions.

THE SENATE SPEECHES OF W. B. YEATS. Ed. Donald R. Pearce. Bloomington: Indiana Univ. Press, 1960.
> The selection of speeches reveals the witty and practical bent of WBY as statesman during the years 1922-28. Some selected topics include "League of Nations," "Damage to Property," "Censorship of Films," "Inspection of Prisons," "Debate on Divorce," "Condition of Schools," and "Copyright Protection."

UNCOLLECTED PROSE OF W. B. YEATS, I. Ed. John P. Frayne. London: Macmillan, 1970.
> A collection of WBY's early reviews and critical articles. WBY comments upon such figures as A. E. Symons, Tennyson, and Allingham; he discusses myths and legends as well as his dealings with editors.

UNCOLLECTED PROSE OF W. B. YEATS, II. Ed. John P. Frayne and Colton Johnson. London: Macmillan, 1975.
> Volume 2 provides a useful general index.

BIBLIOGRAPHY

Adams, Hazard. "Yeats Scholarship and Criticism: A Review of Research." TSLL, 3 (1962), 439-51.
> A useful survey essay covering primary and secondary sources.

Cross, K. G. W. "The Fascination of What's Difficult: A Survey of Yeats Criticism and Research." In IN EXCITED REVERIE: A CENTENARY TRIBUTE

TO WILLIAM BUTLER YEATS, 1865-1939. Ed. A. Norman Jeffares and K. G. W. Cross. New York: Macmillan, 1965. Pp. 315-37.

>A useful essay presenting the history of Yeats scholarship.

Cross, K. G. W., and R. T. Dunlop, eds. A BIBLIOGRAPHY OF YEATS CRITICISM, 1887-1965. New York: Macmillan, 1971.

>Good secondary bibliography. Although not as recent or comprehensive as Jochum's (below), the editors list bibliographies, reviews, books, pamphlets, articles, dissertations, and theses that are wholly or partly about WBY's works. Helpful index.

Dougan, R. O., comp. W. B. YEATS MANUSCRIPTS AND PRINTED BOOKS EXHIBITED IN THE LIBRARY OF TRINITY COLLEGE, DUBLIN, 1956. Dublin: Lochlainn, 1956.

>Important specialized listing.

Jochum, K. P. S., ed. W. B. YEATS: A CLASSIFIED BIBLIOGRAPHY OF CRITICISM: INCLUDING ADDITIONS TO ALLAN WADE'S BIBLIOGRAPHY OF THE WRITINGS OF W. B. YEATS AND A SECTION OF THE IRISH LITERARY AND DRAMATIC REVIVAL. Urbana: Univ. of Illinois Press, 1978.

>The best and most comprehensive secondary bibliography on writings about WBY. Many items are annotated and the indexing is lucid and useful.

Stoll, John Edward, comp. A BIBLIOGRAPHY OF THE WRITINGS OF W. B. YEATS. 1958. Rev. ed. Ed. Russell K. Alspach. London: Rupert Hart-Davis, 1968.

>Based on Wade's original 1958 compilation. Several lists (some annotated) are added, including Alspach's "additions to Allan Wade's Bibliography of W. B. Yeats," "The Cuala Press," "Some Books about Yeats and His Work," and "Yeats and Broadcasting." A comprehensive primary bibliography.

──────. THE GREAT DELUGE: A YEATS BIBLIOGRAPHY. Troy, N. Y.: Whitston, 1971.

>Contains over one thousand titles of works by and about Yeats. The definitive primary bibliography.

BIOGRAPHY

Ellmann, Richard. YEATS: THE MAN AND THE MASKS. New York: Macmillan, 1948.

>An important study of the development of WBY's ideas and works with special attention to the influence of John Butler Yeats.

Hone, Joseph. W. B. YEATS, 1865-1939. London: Macmillan, 1965.

> Authorized by Mrs. Yeats as the "official" biography, Hone's anecdotal study records some important details but lacks critical perspective in dealing with the complexities of WBY's thought. Significant storehouse of information.

Jeffares, A. Norman. W. B. YEATS: MAN AND POET. New York: Barnes and Noble, 1966.

> Jeffares' ten chapters are arranged in strict chronological order. Many quotations from WBY's published and unpublished works are given. Jeffares was assisted by Mrs. Yeats and granted access to unpublished diaries and documents. The study shows the "rewarding" and "revealing" conjunction between WBY's prose and verse.

CRITICISM

Adams, Hazard. "Symbolism and Yeats's A VISION." JAAC, 22 (1964), 425-36.

> Adams argues that A VISION does not fit neatly into any previous critical categories, but that it can be called "a grammar of poetic symbolism." Critics have overlooked the book's ironic strategies.

_____. "Yeats, Dialectic and Criticism." CRITICISM, 10 (1968), 185-99.

> A noted scholar discusses the influences of William Blake on WBY's concept of dialectical opposition in AUTOBIOGRAPHY and A VISION. Adams carefully discriminates between artistic and scientific truth.

_____. "Yeatsian Art and Mathematic Form." CENTR, 4 (1960), 70-88.

> Original and interesting discussion of WBY's use of mathematics in A VISION.

Auden, W. H. "The Private Life of a Public Man." MID-CENTURY, No. 4 (1959), 8-15.

> Ostensibly a review of WBY'S MYTHOLOGIES. Auden makes some revealing comments about what he does and does not understand about WBY's work in general. Especially critical of WBY's 1890's period.

Barrow, Craig Wallace. "Comprehensive Index to William Butler Yeats's A VISION." BNYPL, 77 (1973-74), 51-62.

A useful reference tool which indexes by subject and name the contents of the revised (1938) Macmillan edition of A VISION.

Berryman, Charles Beecher. W. B. YEATS: DESIGN OF OPPOSITES. A CRITICAL STUDY. New York: Exposition Press, 1967.

    Includes a rather narrow and pedestrian discussion of A VISION.

Blake, Barton. "Yeats and Youth." YR, 6 (1917), 410-12.

    Blake maintains that REVERIES is "quite unmistakably" in the Romantic tradition and displays much less exhibitionism than George Moore's contemporary work.

Bloom, Harold. YEATS. New York: Oxford Univ. Press, 1970.

    Bloom argues that WBY was among the last writers of the Romantic tradition. Reexamining his works in this light, Bloom concludes that his reputation is often exaggerated. Valuable treatment of PER AMICA; extensive discussion of A VISION.

Boynton, H.W. "Air and Earth." ATLANTIC MONTHLY, 92 (1903), 565-69.

    Boynton believes that the two main theories in GOOD AND EVIL are "that the middle classes have been the death of good literature, and that symbolism is to be its new birth." He praises the power of WBY's "vigorous imaginative prose."

Bradford, Curtis. YEATS AT WORK. Carbondale: Southern Illinois Univ. Press, 1965.

    Commentary on early drafts of some prose pieces, including sections from DISCOVERIES, AUTOBIOGRAPHIES, and ON THE BOILER. Bradford demonstrates that "Yeats made many changes in the texts of his prose works."

Brooks, Cleanth. "William Butler Yeats as a Literary Critic." In THE DISCIPLINES OF CRITICISM: ESSAYS IN LITERARY THEORY, INTERPRETATION, AND HISTORY. Ed. Peter Demetz, Thomas Greene, and Lowry Nelson. New Haven, Conn.: Yale Univ. Press, 1968. Pp. 17-41.

    A balanced and comprehensive discussion of WBY's prose and literary criticism, including A VISION, AUTOBIOGRAPHY, MYTHOLOGIES, ESSAYS AND INTRODUCTIONS, and EXPLORATIONS. Brooks admires WBY's "provocative comments" and "revealing insights" but warns that he could also be arbitrary and unfair.

_____. "Yeats: The Poet as Myth-Maker." In his MODERN POETRY

AND THE TRADITION. Chapel Hill: Univ. of North Carolina Press, 1939. Pp. 173-202.

> Illuminating discussion which relates several poems to A VISION, "the most ambitious attempt made by any poet of our time to set up a 'myth.'"

Buckley, Vincent. "Yeats: The Great Comedian." MHREV, 5 (1968), 77-89.

> An interesting discussion of WBY's sense of humor in AUTO-BIOGRAPHIES--"a human rooted in an immense variousness of energy and perception . . . so alive and purposeful."

Burke, Kenneth. "On Motivation in Yeats." SOR, 7 (1941-42), 547-61.

> Discusses A VISION and several related poems in an effort to consider "some basic correlation of theme, or motif."

Bushrui, S. B. "Yeats's Arabic Interests." In EXCITED REVERIE: A CENTENARY TRIBUTE TO WILLIAM BUTLER YEATS, 1865-1939. Ed. A. Norman Jeffares and K.G.W. Cross. London: Macmillan, 1965. Pp. 280-314.

> Original discussion of a unique aspect of A VISION.

Cary, Meredith Ray. "Yeats and Moore--An Autobiographical Conflict." EIRE, 4, No. 3, (1969), 94-109.

> Cary maintains that Moore is far more successful in describing WBY in HAIL AND FAREWELL than is WBY in describing Moore in DRAMATIS PERSONAE.

Cooke, Michael G. "Modern Black Autobiography in the Tradition." In ROMANTICISM: VISTAS, INSTANCES, CONTINUITIES. Ed. David Thorburn and Geoffrey Hartman. Ithaca, N.Y.: Cornell Univ. Press, 1973. Pp. 267-70.

> Brief analysis of some organizational strategies in AUTOBIOGRAPHY. Cooke concludes that WBY's achievement in the form was "considerable" because he "invented" a sort of mosaic or pointillist form which both represents and controls incertitude of mind, and futility of action."

Coxhead, Elizabeth. "'Collaboration'--Yeats." In her LADY GREGORY: A LITERARY PORTRAIT. 2nd ed. London: Secker and Warburg, 1976. Pp. 98-107.

> Attacks WBY's "disloyalty" to Lady Gregory: "he belittled her personality and made no mention of her plays" in DRAMATIS PERSONAE. Coxhead explores the problems of their collaborative effort.

W.B. Yeats

Daiches, David. "The Practical Visionary." ENCOUNTER, 19, No. 3 (1962), 71-74.

> High praise for WBY's ESSAYS AND INTRODUCTIONS which allows readers to turn away from the esoteric explicators of his poetry to "the poet's own prose discussions of his intentions and his ideas about the nature of poetry."

Donoghue, Denis. "Introduction." In his MEMOIRS: AUTOBIOGRAPHY--FIRST DRAFT; JOURNAL. London: Macmillan, 1972. Pp. 9-15.

> Brief comparison of style and content of first draft of WBY's AUTOBIOGRAPHY and JOURNAL. The style in the AUTOBIOGRAPHY is "often rough, his first draft imperfect, but for most of the way it moves with the freedom of reverie and meditation."

_____. WILLIAM BUTLER YEATS. New York: Viking, 1971.

> Donoghue examines some of WBY's key concepts in order to compile a composite picture of his "sensibility." The "sense of consciousness as conflict" is important throughout his works, including several essays and A VISION.

Eglinton, John. "Mr. Yeats's Autobiographies." DIAL, 83 (1927), 94-97.

> WBY's life story is honest and has "much psychologic interest"; his prose style is exact and has the precise tone of a public speaker.

Ellmann, Richard. THE IDENTITY OF YEATS. New York: Oxford Univ. Press, 1954.

> A basic study of the development of WBY's work with particular attention to the poetry. Some prose works discussed include: AUTOBIOGRAPHIES, CELTIC TWILIGHT, DISCOVERIES, ESSAYS, and most extensively, A VISION.

Engleberg, Edward. THE VAST DESIGN: PATTERNS IN W.B. YEATS'S AESTHETIC. Toronto: Univ. of Toronto Press, 1964.

> A study of WBY's criticism and aesthetic. Especially valuable in its treatment of many of WBY's individual critical essays.

Finneran, Richard J. "Yeats's Revisions in THE CELTIC TWILIGHT, 1912-1925." TSE, 20 (1972), 97-105.

> Points out the many revisions that have been "overlooked by almost all Yeats scholars." Finneran's findings are based on a collation of six printings of CELTIC TWILIGHT and include the interesting element of increasing doubt or skepticism of the narrator.

Fishwick, Marshall. "Yeats and Cyclical History." SHENANDOAH, 1, No. 2 (1950), 52-56.

> A basic but useful discussion of A VISION. Fishwick concludes that WBY's cyclical theory allowed him to transcend "the confusion and mediocrity that ensnared so many artists in his time."

Fletcher, Ian. "History and Vision in the Work of W. B. Yeats." SORA, 4 (1968), 105-26.

> A useful survey which reveals how A VISION has been received and interpreted by scholars and critics over the years.

──────. "Rhythm and Pattern in AUTOBIOGRAPHIES." In AN HONOURED GUEST: NEW ESSAYS ON W. B. YEATS. Ed. Denis Donoghue and James Ronald Mulryne. London: Arnold, 1965. Pp. 165-89.

> A rather rambling commentary which treats the form and content of REVERIES, TREMBLING, and DRAMATIS PERSONAE.

──────. "Yeats's Quest for Self-Transparency." TLS, 72, No. 3698 (1973), 53-55.

> A valuable discussion of the relationship between the draft and published phases of WBY's AUTOBIOGRAPHIES.

Frayne, John P. "Introduction." In his UNCOLLECTED PROSE. Vol. 1. New York: Columbia Univ. Press, 1970. Pp. 19-77.

> Frayne provides useful information concerning WBY's life, the figures who influenced him, and the principles of literary criticism worked out in his early critical articles and reviews.

Freyer, Grattan. W. B. YEATS AND THE ANTI-DEMOCRATIC TRADITION. Totowa, N. J.: Barnes and Noble, 1981.

> Brief, but illuminating study which links WBY's political ideas to his prose and poetry. Freyer offers a balanced discussion, though he stresses the importance of Irish nationalism.

Frye, Northrop. "The Rising of the Moon: A Study of A VISION." In AN HONOURED GUEST: NEW ESSAYS ON W. B. YEATS. Ed. Denis Donoghue and James Ronald Mulryne. London: Arnold, 1965. Pp. 8-33.

> Compares WBY's pattern of symbolism to Dante's and Blake's. A useful discussion which details why A VISION "increased Yeats's awareness of and power to control his own creative process."

Gilomen, Walther. "George Moore and His Friendship with W. B. Yeats." ES, 19 (1937), 116-20.

Discusses the portraits that each author draws of the other in their
autobiographies and concludes that both are "biased in their mutual
description and observation, . . . very often merciless and harsh."

Greene, David H. "Yeats's Prose Style: Some Observations." In MODERN
IRISH LITERATURE: ESSAYS IN HONOR OF WILLIAM YORK TINDALL. Ed.
Raymond J. Porter and James D. Brophy. New York: Twayne, 1972. Pp.
301-14.

> Helpful article which explains how to approach WBY's prose.
> Discusses his different prose styles and shows how they were
> used for polemic and reverie as well as for conveying his
> thoughts on art and life.

Grubb, H.T. Hunt. "A Poet's Dream." POETRYR, 29 (1938), 123-41.

> Argues that the whole conception of A VISION is "dreamlike,"
> and elaborates why some people say that it presents "a nightmare
> procession of beings" from a former existence.

_____. "A Poet's Friends." POETRYR, 27, (1936), 317-22.

> Discusses the various friends presented in DRAMATIS PERSONAE,
> a work which enhances WBY's reputation "as a prose writer of
> elegance and refinement."

Häusermann, H.W. "W.B. Yeats's Criticism of Ezra Pound." ES, 29, (1948),
97-109.

> WBY's most extensive and penetrating discussion of Pound occurs
> in A VISION where "Yeats's criticism of Pound is tempered by
> his affection for the man and by his psychological more than
> literary interest in the poet."

Henn, Thomas Rice. THE LONELY TOWER: STUDIES IN THE POETRY OF
W.B. YEATS. London: Methuen, 1950.

> A diffuse study which contains a chapter on A VISION. Mrs.
> Yeats read and commented upon Henn's manuscript.

Hoffman, Daniel G. "Folklore and Literature." JAF, 76 (1963), 83-86.

> Stresses as background to MYTHOLOGIES WBY'S seeking through-
> out the 1890's "both spiritual experience and political unity" in
> Irish folk tradition and legends. The extent of WBY's knowledge
> of Irish folklore is impressive but the folklorist will be most
> interested in CELTIC TWILIGHT.

Jeffares, A. Norman. "Gyres in Yeats's Poetry." In his THE CIRCUS
ANIMALS: ESSAYS ON W.B. YEATS. London: Macmillan, 1970. Pp. 103-14.

Some references are made to the most complex ideas contained in A VISION, with focused attention on gyres and tinctures.

——————. "Introduction." In his SELECTED CRITICISM. London: Macmillan, 1964. Pp. 7-16.

Traces the main currents of development in the scope and style of WBY's critical writings. A useful survey of how he assimilated and altered his Anglo-Irish heritage in prose.

——————. W.B. YEATS: THE CRITICAL HERITAGE. London: Routledge and Kegan Paul, 1977.

Valuable for ascertaining the critical reception given to some of WBY's works by his contemporaries. Interesting reviews (signed and unsigned) of GOOD AND EVIL, AGATE, A VISION, and AUTOBIOGRAPHIES are included.

——————. "Yeats, Critic." In his THE CIRCUS ANIMALS: ESSAYS ON W.B. YEATS. London: Macmillan, 1970. Pp. 47-77.

A valuable analysis of WBY's prose and prose style, covering its early forms, influences upon it, and its increasing allusiveness. Also provides a good summary of WBY's critical views on modern poetry.

Kenner, Hugh. "Yeats's 'Essays.'" JUBILEE, 9, No. 10 (1962), 39-43.

Lucid survey of the form and subject matter of WBY's essays. Kenner stresses the writer's struggle and intellectual developments reflected in ESSAYS AND INTRODUCTIONS.

Kermode, John Frank. ROMANTIC IMAGE. London: Routledge and Kegan Paul, 1957.

Discusses the artist's role in society and examines several images in such prose works as A VISION and GOOD AND EVIL.

King, B.A. "Yeats's Irishry Prose." In W.B. YEATS, 1865-1965: CENTENARY ESSAYS ON THE ART OF W.B. YEATS. Ed. D.E.S. Maxwell and S.B. Bushrui. Ibadan, Nigeria: Ibadan Univ. Press, 1965. Pp. 127-35.

Drawing upon specific examples from ESSAYS and EXPLORATIONS, King shows how WBY's prose style violates many of the rules of good English prose; nonetheless, it has a definable charm because it is modeled upon the patterns of Irish speech. Demonstrates how WBY's prose is designed for the ear rather than for the printed page.

Krans, H.S. In his WILLIAM BUTLER YEATS AND THE IRISH LITERARY REVIVAL. Garden City, N.Y.: Doubleday, 1904. Pp. 147-91.

A superficial discussion of some of WBY's essays which concludes that GOOD AND EVIL is "a strikingly fresh, vital, and subtle piece of criticism." Basic introduction to Irish background of WBY's works.

Langbaum, Robert. "Growth of a Great Critic." ASCH, 41 (1972), 460, 462, 464, 466.

Langbaum stresses that it was through writing book reviews early in his career that WBY developed "the prose style and critical concepts" that distinguished his later serious criticism.

Lenoski, Daniel S. "W. B. Yeats: God and Imagination." ESC, 6 (1980), 84-93.

Provides fresh philosophical analysis of WBY's aesthetic theories in his essays and letters. Defines his concept of "imagination" by relating it to his attitude toward "God."

Lentricchia, Frank. In THE GAIETY OF LANGUAGE: AN ESSAY ON THE RADICAL POETICS OF W. B. YEATS AND WALLACE STEVENS. Berkeley and Los Angeles: Univ. of California Press, 1968. Pp. 39-87.

Extended discussion of GOOD AND EVIL, which is motivated by WBY's "need to escape naturalist conceptions of reality and art." Also includes a basic introduction to PER AMICA and A VISION.

Levin, Gerald. "The Yeats of the Autobiographies: A Man of Phase 17." TSLL, 6 (1964), 398-405.

Levin points out relationships between AUTOBIOGRAPHIES and A VISION. The autobiographical writings are the dramatized tensions of a man who is living in a wrong age and exploring "the possibilities of Unity of Being without coming to a final answer."

Lucas, F[rank] L. "Sense and Sensibility." In his AUTHORS DEAD AND LIVING. New York: Macmillan, 1926. Pp. 241-44.

Lucas expresses his admiration for the form and content of PLAYS AND CONTROVERSIES. WBY's "patience and good sense" work well against the enemies of a national theatre.

Lucas, John. "From Naturalism to Symbolism." In DECADENCE AND THE 1890'S. Ed. Ian Fletcher. London: Edward Arnold, 1979. Pp. 130-48.

Refers to WBY's AUTOBIOGRAPHIES, IDEA OF GOOD AND EVIL, and A VISION as he champions symbolism over naturalism: "for Yeats the true function of art is to be visionary."

W.B. Yeats

Lynd, Robert. "Poets as Patriots." BRITISH REVIEW, 6, No. 2 (1914), 264-80.

    Elaborates on WBY's definition (in GOOD AND EVIL) of patriotism as "an impure desire in an artist."

Maccallum, H.R. "W.B. Yeats: The Shape Changer and His Critics." UTQ, 32 (1963), 307-13.

    Brief but highly informed survey of WBY's prose. Maccallum argues that in the early essays "there is the charming ambiguity of the Pateresque prose" whereas in the later essays there is "a more extravagant and wilful evasiveness."

MacNeice, Louis. THE POETRY OF W.B. YEATS. New York: Oxford Univ. Press, 1941.

    A reasonable and well-written study which touches on WBY's prose style in AUTOBIOGRAPHIES and A VISION. Calls ON THE BOILER "impudently occasional."

Melchiori, Giorgio. THE WHOLE MYSTERY OF ART: PATTERN INTO POETRY IN THE WORK OF W.B. YEATS. London: Routledge and Kegan Paul, 1960.

    An ambitious study of WBY's images, symbols, and emblems which includes a discussion of A VISION and many of the critical essays. Melchiori stresses that "true symbolism" has "magical overtones."

Moore, Virginia. THE UNICORN: WILLIAM BUTLER YEATS' SEARCH FOR REALITY. New York: Macmillan, 1954.

    An unorganized and anecdotal study which offers, among other things, "a re-evaluation of that esoteric 'net,' A VISION [and] a reassessment of Yeats' relation to Christianity."

Muller, Herbert J. "The New Criticism in Poetry." SOR, 6 (1941), 811-39.

    Muller offers his interpretation of A VISION and is especially critical of Cleanth Brooks's narrow view of the uses of imagination.

Noon, William. "Yeats and the Human Body." THOUGHT, 30, No. 117 (1955), 188-98.

    Noon refers to A VISION in his discussion of WBY's ideas concerning the opposition between body and soul.

Ohmann, Richard M. "Appendix I." In his SHAW: THE STYLE AND THE MAN. Middletown, Conn.: Wesleyan Univ. Press, 1962. Pp. 169-85.

An interesting study which uses statistical methods to compare WBY's prose style in PER AMICA to six other writers, including Shaw and Chesterton. Ohmann concludes that stylistically WBY differs "a great deal from Shaw."

Pascal, Roy. DESIGN AND TRUTH IN AUTOBIOGRAPHY. Cambridge, Mass.: Harvard Univ. Press, 1960.

Brief but provocative discussion of several key tensions in AUTOBIOGRAPHIES. Because WBY records "that intangible, disturbing relationship between poetry and life," the work has "a dream-like flow, yet is concrete and precise."

Pearce, Donald [R.]. "Philosophy and Phantasy: Notes on the Growth of Yeats's 'System.'" UKCR, 18, No. 3 (1952), 169-80.

Discusses A VISION as a handy dictionary of WBY's symbols.

_____. "Introduction." In his THE SENATE SPEECHES. Bloomington: Indiana Univ. Press, 1960. Pp. 11-26.

Brief sketch of WBY's involvement in politics and a survey of the concerns in the speeches. Pearce believes that the speeches shed light on WBY's developing "eloquence and power" as a poet with "that syntax of 'public speech.'"

Peterson, Richard F. WILLIAM BUTLER YEATS. Twayne English Author Series. Boston: Twayne, 1982.

A lucid and well-researched introductory study of WBY's life and works.

Rai, Rama Nand. "A Study of W.B. Yeats's A VISION." JSL, 6, Nos. 1-2 (1978-79), 34-41.

A careful, but unoriginal explanation of WBY's symbolic system in A VISION. Rai focuses on the book's categories of humanity and "its method of dealing with history."

Rajan, Balachandra. W.B. YEATS: A CRITICAL INTRODUCTION. London: Hutchinson, 1965.

A good basic introductory study of Yeats: "Some of Yeats' critical ideas have been briefly discussed and the System has been given such attention as it deserves."

Reynolds, Horace. "Introduction." In his LETTERS TO THE NEW ISLAND. Cambridge, Mass.: Harvard Univ. Press, 1934. Pp. 3-66.

Discusses WBY's participation in the Irish dramatic and literary revival and the influence of several figures on his career.

Ronsley, Joseph. YEATS'S AUTOBIOGRAPHY: LIFE AS SYMBOLIC PATTERN. Cambridge, Mass.: Harvard Univ. Press, 1968.

> While primarily a study of "the design underlying Yeats's presentation of events, people, and ideas" in the AUTOBIOGRAPHY, considerable attention is also given to A VISION.

Seiden, Morton Irving. WILLIAM BUTLER YEATS: THE POET AS MYTHMAKER, 1865-1939. East Lansing: Michigan State Univ. Press, 1962.

> Provides an original and informative approach to WBY's A VISION. Seiden sees the central work in the context of WBY's prose works written before it and his later reflections upon its influence.

Skene, Reg. THE CUCHULAIN PLAYS OF W.B. YEATS: A STUDY. London: Macmillan, 1974.

> An original approach whereby Skene argues that each of the five plays in the Cuchulain cycle gains considerable power in its correspondence to "an important phase of the great wheel of symbolic moon phases which is at the heart of the system of A VISION."

Spender, Stephen. "Honey-Bubblings of the Boilers." THE NEW STATESMAN AND NATION, 18 (1939), 686-87.

> Spender admires the observations and obsessions in ON THE BOILER: "The finest thing in the later Yeats is this single-minded gesture of the ranting, raging old man, a character from late Shakespearean tragedy."

Stanford, W.B. "Yeats in the Irish Senate." REL, 4, No. 3 (1963), 71-80.

> Brief discussion of WBY's political speeches in the Irish Senate. Stanford concludes that WBY "never mastered the subtle art of effective parliamentary humour," was sometimes "callous," but always took seriously his senatorial work.

Stauffer, Donald A. THE GOLDEN NIGHTINGALE: ESSAYS ON SOME PRINCIPLES OF POETRY IN THE LYRICS OF WILLIAM BUTLER YEATS. New York: Macmillan, 1949.

> Treats WBY's theory of the symbol and discusses A VISION with some insight. Stauffer also relates a few of the essays to the principles of poetry exemplified in WBY's lyrics.

_____. "The Modern Myth of the Modern Myth." EIE, 6 (1947), 36-49.

> Appreciative discussion of A VISION, which Stauffer calls "an enthralling study in its delicate balances between fantasy and revelation."

Stock, A.G. W.B. YEATS: HIS POETRY AND THOUGHT. Cambridge: The Univ. Press, 1961.

>Although Stock discusses mainly WBY's poetry and intellectual background, there are two chapters on A VISION. Useful introduction for the general reader.

Torchiana, Donald T. W.B. YEATS AND GEORGIAN IRELAND. Evanston, Ill.: Northwestern Univ. Press, 1966.

>Torchiana argues that WBY's political and religious ideas were influenced by such eighteenth-century figures as Berkeley, Burke, Goldsmith, and Swift. The study discusses some of WBY's uncollected essays and reviews, his speeches and lectures, and ON THE BOILER.

Tschumi, Raymond. "Yeats's Philosophical Poetry." In his THOUGHT IN TWENTIETH-CENTURY ENGLISH POETRY. London: Routledge and Kegan Paul, 1950. Pp. 29-73.

>Analysis of WBY's ideas in A VISION and several related poems. The explanation of the philosophy contained in A VISION is particularly concise and helpful.

Ure, Peter. YEATS. Edinburgh: Oliver and Boyd, 1963.

>Contains a superficial introduction to WBY's prose.

Vendler, Helen. YEATS'S VISION AND THE LATER PLAYS. Cambridge, Mass.: Harvard Univ. Press, 1963.

>Detailed analysis of A VISION and the late plays related to it. Vendler views A VISION "as a symbolic statement, somewhat cluttered up with psychic paraphernalia, which yields itself quite well to reasonable interpretation."

Watson, George. "The Essays of Yeats." OXFORD MAGAZINE, N.S. 1, No. 18 (1961), 324.

>Argues that WBY's essays reveal his "uncritical and syncretic" intelligence.

Webster, Brenda S. YEATS: A PSYCHOANALYTICAL STUDY. Stanford, Calif.: Stanford Univ. Press, 1973.

>Categorizes the several traumatic experiences in WBY's early years and relates them to his various works, including A VISION. Standard psychological fare.

Wells, Warre Bradley. IRISH INDISCRETIONS. London: Allen and Unwin, 1923. Pp. 188-222.

> An interesting personal account of WBY's composition of IF I WERE FOUR-AND-TWENTY and his negative opinions of other Irish prose writers.

Whitaker, Thomas R. SWAN AND SHADOW: YEATS'S DIALOGUE WITH HISTORY. Chapel Hill: Univ. of North Carolina Press, 1964.

> Though primarily a study of WBY's poetry, some attention is given to A VISION and other prose works as they illuminate the poetry.

Wilson, Edmund. AXEL'S CASTLE: A STUDY IN THE IMAGINATIVE LITERATURE OF 1870-1930. New York: Scribner's, 1931.

> A classic treatment of WBY as symbolist (pages 26-63) with particular attention to A VISION. Demonstrates how WBY abandoned florid reverie to recreate a "solid, homely and exact" style.

Wright, David G. "Behind the Lines: Strategies of Self-Portraiture in Yeats and Joyce." CLQ, 16 (1980), 148-57.

> Excellent comparison between the autobiographical strategies--in theory and practice--of the two writers.

Zabel, Morton D. "The Thinking of the Body: Yeats in the Autobiographies." SOR, 7 (1941-42) 562-90.

> A highly skillful article which relates WBY's growth as a poet to his AUTOBIOGRAPHIES.

INDEXES

AUTHOR INDEX

This index includes all authors, editors, compilers, translators, and other contributors to works cited in the text. It is alphabetized letter by letter and numbers refer to page numbers.

A

Abbott, Anthony S. 413
Abbott, Wilbur C. 436
Abrahams, William 345
Abrams, M.H. 373
Acton, Harold B. 41, 123
Adams, E.W. 306
Adams, Elsie B. 413
Adams, Hazard 16, 214, 492, 494
Adams, James Truslow 436
Adams, Robert Martin 154
Adamson, Donald 123
Adcock, Arthur St. John 186
Adcock, St. John 448
Ades, John I. 267
Aiken, Conrad 123-24
Aithal, S. Krishnamoorthy 283
Aldington, Richard 114, 124, 253, 274
Allan, Mowbray 124
Alldritt, Keith 345
Allendorf, Otmar 257
Allum, M.P. 283
Alpers, Paul 154
Alspach, Russell K. 493
Altick, Helen 448
Altick, Richard D. 6, 10, 448
Amelinckx, Frans C. 23
Anderson, Norman A. 197

Anderson, Perry 284
Andrews, Carolyn S. 243
Angus, Ian 467
Annan, Noel 436
Antrim, Harry T. 124
Applejoy, Petronius 222
Arana, R. Victoria 186
Archer, William 460
Armstrong, Terence Ian Fytton 273
Armytage, W.H.G. 460
Arnold, Armin 255, 257
Arthur, Anthony 186
Asquith, Michael 85
Atkins, John Alfred 244, 345
Attwater, Donald 92
Auden, W.H. 41, 82, 85, 475, 494
Austin, Allen 124
Aycock, Wendell M. 133

B

Bacon, Leonard 436
Bahlke, George W. 31
Bailey, Richard W. 3
Baines, Jocelyn 104
Baker, James R. 173
Baker, Joseph E. 191
Baker, Richard 85
Baker, Sheridan 371

Author Index

Baker, William 282
Bal, Sant Singh 345
Bantock, Geoffrey H. 125, 257
Barber, George S. 413
Barfield, Owen 306
Barfoot, Gabriella 125
Barker, Dudley 84
Barr, Alan P. 413
Barrett, Michele 473, 475
Barrett, William 125
Barrington-Ward, Simon 306
Barrow, Craig Wallace 494
Barton, Margaret 425
Barzun, Jacques 371
Batchelor, J.B. 475
Bates, E. Stuart 10
Bates, Ralph 320
Bateson, F.W. 125, 284
Batho, E.C. 6
Baugh, Albert C. 6
Baum, Paull 13
Baxter, Frank C. 273
Baylen, Joseph O. 187, 460
Bazin, Nancy Topping 475
Beach, Joseph Warren 29
Beadle, Gordon B. 346
Beal, Anthony 254
Beard, Paul 70
Beards, Richard D. 255, 257
Becker, Carl 460
Beckett, Samuel 320
Bedford, Sybille 244
Bedford, William 284
Beebe, Maurice 103, 165, 172, 255, 474
Beer, J.B. 338
Beer, John 174, 177, 178
Beerbohm, Max 187, 436
Behrman, S.N. 40
Beker, Miroslav 257
Belgion, Montgomery 125, 132, 233, 373, 461
Bell, Anne Olivier 472, 475
Bell, Barbara Currier 475
Bell, Clive 436
Bell, Millicent 475
Bell, Quentin 474, 475
Belloc, Hilaire 85, 461
Bennett, Arnold 429, 476
Bennett, J.A.W. 312

Bennett, James R. 339
Bennett, Joan 306, 373, 476
Bentley, Eric Russell 373, 410, 414
Bentley, Joseph 244
Beresford, J.D. 461
Bergonzi, Bernard 6, 85, 122, 243, 284, 461
Bernal, J.D. 414
Berry, Francis 364
Berryman, Charles Beecher 495
Berst, Charles A. 411, 414
Berthoud, Jacques 105
Bethell, Samuel Leslie 284, 373
Bevan, E. Dean 410
Bhabha, Homi I. 373
Bilan, R.P. 282, 284-85
Bilsky, Manuel 373-74
Binns, Leonard Elliott 461
Binyon, Laurence 187
Birnbaum, Milton 245
Bishop, Morchard 476
Bissell, Claude 414
Bissell, E.E. 187
Black, Max 374
Black, Michael 285
Black, Sam 364
Blackmur, R.P. 125-26, 275, 374
Blackstone, Bernard 476
Blair, John G. 31
Blake, Barton 495
Blissett, William 126, 374, 414
Block, Haskell M. 187
Bloom, Harold 495
Bloomfield, B.C. 29
Bloomfield, Morton W. 476
Bloomfield, Paul 16, 203, 205
Boas, Guy 41, 436-37
Bogaerts, Anthony M.A. 86
Bogan, Louise 31, 476
Bolgan, Anne C. 126
Bollier, Ernest Philip 126-27
Bond, Raymond T. 83
Bone, Christopher 31
Booth, Wayne C. 173
Boothby, Lord 289
Bornhauser, Fred 166
Borowitz, Helen Osterman 166
Borrello, Alfred 172
Boulton, James T. 257

Author Index

Bourne, John 285
Bower, Anthony 430
Bower-Shore, Clifford 437
Bowker, G.H. 410
Boxhill, Roger 414
Boyd, John D. 127
Boyers, Robert 285
Boyle, Ted E. 214
Boynton, H.W. 495
Bradbrook, B.R. 86
Bradbrook, M.C. 127, 155
Bradbury, Malcolm 286
Bradford, Curtis 495
Bradshaw, Graham 286
Brandabur, Edward 233
Brander, Laurence 173, 245, 346
Brandt, William J. 307
Braybrooke, Neville 127, 128, 401
Braybrooke, Patrick 41, 62, 81, 86, 187, 461
Bredin, Hugh 127
Bredsdorff, Elias 185, 187
Brett, Dorothy 256
Brewster, Dorothy 476
Bridson, D.G. 320
Britten, Benjamin 173
Broad, C. Lewis 410
Broad, Violet M. 410
Brogunier, Joseph 172
Brombert, Victor H. 127
Brome, Vincent 414, 459, 462
Brooke, N.S. 307
Brooks, Cleanth 21, 31, 127, 374, 495
Brooks, Van Wyck 132, 462
Brophy, James D. 499
Bross, Addison C. 41
Brower, Reuben A. 372, 373, 374, 375, 376, 377, 379, 383, 384, 385, 476
Brown, Christopher 228
Brown, E.K. 462
Brown, Father (Monsignor John O'Connor) 86
Brown, Huntington 13
Brown, Ivor 415, 462
Brown, Wallace Cable 128
Browne, Wynyard 286
Bruss, Elizabeth W. 10
Bryant, Arthur 437

Bryer, Jackson R. 121
Buck, Philo M., Jr. 128
Buckley, Jerome Hamilton 188
Buckley, Vincent 128, 286, 496
Budberg, Moura 465
Buddicom, Jacintha 344
Buell, Frederick 31
Burdett, Osbert 63, 430, 437
Burgess, Anthony 254
Burgum, Edwin Berry 32
Burke, Kenneth 128, 320, 496
Burkhart, Charles 188
Burns, Aidan 258
Burton, Dolores M. 3
Burton, H.M. 407
Burton, S.H. 13
Bush, Douglas 128
Bushrui, S.B. 496, 500
Butler, Christopher 375
Butler, Colin 286
Butler, Lance St. John 264
Butor, Michel 22
Butt, John 340
Butturff, Douglas 478
Bynner, Witter 256
Byrne, Peter 287

C

Cahill, Patrick 61
Cahoon, Herbert 229
Cairns, Huntington 392
Calder, Jenni 346
Callan, Edward 29, 32
Calverton, V.F. 128
Cameron, J.M. 128
Cammerts, Emile 86
Canary, Robert H. 121
Canovan, Margaret 86-87
Carlock, Mary Sue 3
Carlson, Marvin 411
Carnell, Corbin Scott 307
Carne-Ross, D.S. 129
Carpenter, Charles A. 411
Carpenter, Humphrey 30, 305
Carroll, Berenice A. 476
Carswell, John 338
Carter, Huntly 321
Carter, Thomas H. 321
Carver, George 437

511

Author Index

Cary, Meredith Ray 496
Cary, Richard 245
Casey, John 16
Cassell, Richard A. 166
Cattani, Georges 129
Cavitch, David 258
Cecil, David 39, 41, 42, 437
Chace, William M. 129, 321
Chambers, Leland H. 87
Chanda, S.M. 346
Chapman, Robert 321
Chappelow, Allan 415
Chapple, J.A.V. 6
Charles, R.H. 229
Charteris, Evan 185, 186
Chaundy, Leslie 204
Cherry, D.R. 415
Chesterton, Cecil 57, 87
Chesterton, G.K. 321, 415
Chew, Samuel E. 6
Child, Ruth C. 129
Chisholm, Roderick 375
Chisholm, Sir Joseph 87
Christensen, Michael J. 304
Christopher, Joe R. 305
Chrystal, Sir George 393
Churchill, R.C. 8, 87, 346
Clancy, Joseph 29
Clareson, Thomas D. 243
Clark, Albert C. 394
Clark, Arthur 393
Clark, Jon 299
Clark, L.D. 258
Clark, Ronald W. 244
Clarke, Margaret 87
Clay, N.L. 39, 42
Clemens, Cyril 437
Clements, Frank 273
Clifford, James L. 10
Clipper, Lawrence J. 87
Clive, John 437
Clutton-Brock, Arthur 188
Coburn, Kathleen 375
Coffey, Thomas P. 63
Coffey, Warren 321
Coffman, Stanley K., Jr. 233
Cohen, John Michael 214
Cohn, Alan M. 121
Cohn, Jan 375
Colbert, Robert Edward 287

Cole, Chris 353
Collin, W.E. 129
Collins, Christopher 462
Collins, Dorothy 81, 82, 83
Collins, John Churton 188, 394
Colmer, John 174
Como, James T. 305, 307, 309
Condon, James P. 129
Conlon, D.J. 88
Conn, Harvie M. 307
Conner, Frederick W. 245
Connolly, Cyril 438
Connolly, John J. 85
Conquest, Robert 307
Conrad, Jessie 167
Cooke, Michael G. 496
Cookson, William 322
Corke, Helen 258
Cormican, L.A. 129
Cornelius, David Krause 287
Cornwell, Ethel F. 258, 477
Corrigan, D. Felicitas 399, 401
Corrin, Jay P. 63, 88
Costa, Richard Haver 462
Costello, Donald P. 415
Coulson, Peter 287
Cowan, James C. 259
Cowley, V.J.E. 129
Cox, C.B. 18
Cox, James Trammell 167
Cox, R. Gordon 32, 155, 375
Coxhead, Elizabeth 496
Crane, R.S. 16, 158, 375
Craufurd, Alexander H. 462
Crawford, Fred D. 448
Crewe, J.V. 130
Crick, Bernard 344
Crompton, Louis 408, 409, 415
Cronin, Anthony 287
Cross, K.G.W. 492, 493, 496
Cross, Wilbur J. 42
Cruttwell, Patrick 376
Cunard, Nancy 113
Cunliffe, J.W. 6
Cunningham, Lawrence S. 88
Cunningham, Richard B. 307
Curle, Richard 103
Currie, Robert 71
Czamanske, Palmer 130

Author Index

D

Dahlberg, Edward 259
Daiches, David 7, 16, 32, 233, 376, 477, 497
Daniel, John 287
Daniells, J.R. 130, 233
Daniels, Mary F. 318
Dark, Sidney 463
Darton, Frederick Joseph Harvey 401
Das, G.K. 174, 177, 178
Davenport, John 114
Davie, Donald 130, 233, 287-88, 364
Davies, A. Emil 415
Davies, Horton 308
Davies, Hugh Sykes 108
Davies, Laurence 204-5, 206
Davis, Dennis D. 243
Davis, Eugene 4
Davis, Harold E. 167
Davis, Herbert 189
Davis, Robert Gorham 130
Davison, Trevor 33
Dawson, Christopher 130
Dawson, E.W. 259
Day, Douglas 214
Day, Martin S. 22
Deakin, William 259
DeBell, Diane 214
De Blácam, Aodh 88
DeChantigny, J.A. 61, 63, 64
de Fonseka, J.P. 81, 82
De La Bedoyere, Michael 463
De la Mare, Walter 13, 229
Delany, Paul 256
DeLaura, David J. 130
Delord J. 477
Demetz, Peter 17, 495
Denhardt, Robert Moorman 203
Dent, Edward J. 416
Derus, David L. 88
DeVoto, Bernard 438
DiBattista, Maria 477
Dickie, George 376
Dickson, Lovat 460
Dil, Anwar S. 477
Dobb, Maurice 416
Dobie, J. Frank 203, 227
Dobrée, Bonamy 6, 13, 31
Dobson, Austin 394

Dodd, Philip 188
Dodsworth, Martin 155
Dohmen, William F. 322
Donaghy, Henry J. 89
Donaldson, E. Talbot 308
Donoghue, Denis 131, 492, 497, 498
Donovan, Josephine 475
Dooley, David J. 89, 346
Dougan, R.O. 493
Doughty, F.H. 463
Downey, Richard 463
Doyle, Brian 71
Draper, Michael 71
Draper, R.P. 259
Drew, Elizabeth A. 438
Drinkwater, John 186
Duchene, Francois 33
Duerksen, Roland A. 416
Duffy, John J. 131
Dukore, Bernard F. 416
Duncan, Joseph Ellis 131, 188
Dunlop, R.T. 493
Dupee, F.W. 322
Duval, Elizabeth 273
Duval, Hanson R. 244
Dyson, A.E. 18, 438

E

Eaker, J. Gordon 89
Eames, Elizabeth R. 121
Earle, Edward Mead 463
Eastman, Max 376
Edel, Leon 11, 457, 463
Edmonds, Michael 434
Edwards, A.S.G. 213
Edwards, Dorothy 89
Eglinton, John 497
Ehrsam, Theodore G. 104
Eleanore, Sister Mary 14
Eliot, T.S. 17, 189, 259, 322, 339, 376
Ellis, A.E. 99
Ellis, David 260
Ellis, Havelock 463
Ellis, P.G. 131
Ellis, Richard W. 407
Ellmann, Richard 11, 493, 497
Elsbree, Langdon 260
Elton, Oliver 393, 394, 395

Author Index

Elwin, Malcolm 189
Empson, William 376-77
Engel, Elliot D. 89
Engel, Monroe 382
Engleberg, Edward 497
Enright, D.J. 215
Epstein, Edmund L. 478
Epstein, Jacob 232
Ervine, St. John 412
Eschelbach, Claire J. 244
Espey, David B. 346
Estrich, Helen Watts 246
Evans, B. Ifor 7
Evans, David 89
Evans, Maurice 89
Everett, Barbara 33
Every, Brother George 131
Ewart, Gavin 101

F

Fahey, William A. 260
Fairchild, Hoxie Neale 233
Falck, Colin 131
Farley, Earl 411
Farmer, David 400
Farrell, John K.A. 463
Farrer, Austin 308
Farwell, Marilyn R. 477
Faulkner, Peter 33
Fay, Eliot 256
Fedden, Robin 22
Feeney, Leonard 89
Fekete, John 132, 377
Felstiner, John 42
Ferguson, Francis 132
Fernandez, Ramon 132
Fichte, Joerg O. 308
Fifoot, Richard 429
Finneran, Richard J. 412, 497
Fisher, Philip 288, 377
Fishman, Solomon 364-65, 477
Fishwick, Marshall 498
Fitzgerald, John J. 346
FitzGibbon, Constantine 113, 114
Fjelde, Rolf 322
Fleishman, Avrom 105
Fletcher, Angus 377
Fletcher, Ian 498, 501
Fletcher, James V. 229

Fletcher, John Gould 33
Flint, F.S. 233
Flint, R.W. 114
Flory, Evelyn A. 114
Fogarty, Daniel 377
Fogle, Richard Harter 339
Folkenflik, Robert 189
Folkenflik, Vivian 189
Ford, Boris 7
Ford, Ford Madox 229
Forster, Anthony 61, 65
Forster, E.M. 33, 275, 438, 477
Foster, Joseph 256
Foster, Richard 260, 377-78
Fowler, Alastair 305
Fowler, Roger 347
Fox, C.J. 317, 318, 322, 326, 329
Frank, Armin Paul 121, 132
Frank, Frederick S. 215
Frank, Mechthild 121
Frankel, Hyman 71
Fraser, G.S. 7, 33, 100, 155, 289, 323, 365
Fraser, John 288-89
Fraser, Keath 114
Frayne, John P. 492, 498
Frederick, John T. 229
Freed, Lewis 132-33
Freedman, Ralph 477
Freeman, Donald 14
Freeman, John 189, 464
Freeman, Mary 260
French, Philip 289
Freyer, Grattan 498
Fricke, Donna G. 43
Fricke, Douglas C. 43
Fromm, Harold 416
Fry, Roger 378
Fry, Varian 121
Frye, Northrop 17, 323, 498
Fuchs, James 410
Fuess, Claude 438
Fulford, Roger 430
Fuller, John 155
Fuller, Roy 155
Furbank, P.N. 173, 174
Furlong, William B. 90
Furman, Nelly 478
Fussell, Paul 22, 189, 401
Fyvel, T.R. 347

Author Index

G

Gabbay, Lydia Rivlin 167
Gabrieli, Vittorio 310
Gadd, David 435
Gallatin, A.E. 40
Gallup, Donald 121
Garber, Lawrence 438
Gardiner, Linda 227
Gardner, Averil 156
Gardner, Helen Louise 133, 189
Gardner, Philip 156, 174
Garnett, David 254, 272
Garnett, Edward 103, 204, 227, 229-30
Garnett, Richard 74, 189
Garraty, John 11
Gassner, John 416
Gauss, Christian 63
Gawsworth, John [Terence Ian Fytton Armstrong] 323
Gay, Alva A. 449
Gedder, Gary 105
Geduld, Harry M. 409
Gentry, George 378
Gentry, Irene 464
George, Arapura G. 133
Gerber, Helmut E. 104, 165, 172
Gerhardi, William 289
German-Reed, T. 273
Gerould, Daniel Charles 417
Gersh, Gabriel 260, 289, 439
Gerwing, Howard 363
Getti, Hilary 260
Gibb, Christine 369
Gibb, Jocelyn 305, 306
Gibson, Christine 371
Gilbert, Allan H. 308
Gilbert, Douglas 306
Gilbert, Katherine 378
Gill, Roma 154, 155, 156, 157, 158, 159, 160
Gillie, Christopher 7
Gillis, Everett A. 133
Gillon, Adam 106
Gilomen, Walther 498
Gingerich, Martin E. 30
Gish, Robert 478
Givner, Joan 478
Glasheen, Adeline 323

Glicksberg, Charles I. 133, 156 260, 339, 347, 365, 378, 417
Glicksberry, Charles I. 323
Glover, Willis B. 464
Godshalk, William Leigh 174
Goetsch, Paul 478
Goldberg, Michael 417
Goldberg, S.L. 289, 308
Goldknopf, David 105
Goldman, Mark 174, 478
Goldring, Douglas 323
Gomme, Andor 289
Gomme, Arnold W. 464
Gomme, Geoffrey J.L. 411
Goodheart, Eugene 261
Gordon, David J. 261
Gordon, George S. 190
Gordon, Lyndall 122
Gordon, Ramon 370
Gorman, Herbert S. 42
Gorsky, Susan Rubinow 478
Gosse, Edmund 394, 439
Gracie, William J., Jr. 190
Graff, Gerald E. 378
Graham, Andrew 392
Graham, C. 323
Graham, Stephen 206
Grant, Patrick 215
Grattan, C. Hartley 128, 365
Graves, Robert 14, 274, 400
Gray, Hugh 105
Gray, Piers 133
Gregory, Horace 479
Green, Martin 261, 290
Green, Robert 167
Green, Roger Lancelyn 306
Green, V.H.H. 90
Greenberg, Clement 134
Greenberg, Martin 290
Greenberg, Robert A. 190
Greenburg, Herbert 34
Greenburg, Martin 34
Greene, David H. 408, 499
Greene, Thomas 495
Greenlees, Ian 115
Greenwood, Edward Baker 283, 290
Gregor, Ian 264
Gregory, Horace 323
Gregory, R.A. 453
Greiner, Norbert 417

Author Index

Gribble, James 290
Griffin, C.W. 347
Griffin, Ernest G. 339
Griffin, William 304
Griffith, Philip Mahone 339
Grigson, Geoffrey 290, 323
Gropius, Walter 365
Gross, Harvey 392, 395
Gross, John 17
Gross, Miriam 345
Grosskurth, Phyllis 190
Grover, Philip 319
Grubb, H.T. Hunt 499
Grushow, Ira 42
Gudas, Fabian 378
Guest, John 82
Guiguet, Jean 472, 479
Gullick, Norman 185
Gunn, Drewey, W. 246
Gunsteren-Viersen, Julian van 479
Gunter, Bradley 121
Gupta, N. Das 134
Gurling, Freda E. 261
Gutierrez, Donald 261
Guttman, Allen 134

H

Hadsel, Martha 417
Haight, Gordon S. 464
Haldane, J.B.S. 308
Halliburton, David G. 185
Halperin, John 439
Hamalian, Leo 256
Hamilton, Alastair 324
Hamilton, Carol J. 308
Hamilton, George Rostrevor 309, 378-79
Hamilton, James F. 479
Hamilton, Robert 63, 90, 230
Hamlin, Cyrus 379
Hammond, J.R. 458
Hand, Harry E. 290
Handsacre, Alan. See White, Albert C.
Handy, William J. 17
Hannay, Margaret Patterson 309
Hanquart, Evelyn 174
Hansen, Miriam 233
Harap, Louis 71
Harder, Worth Travis 365
Harding, D.W. 134, 379

Harper, Howard M., Jr. 262
Harris, Harold J. 347
Harrison, Elizabeth 430
Harrison, John R. 134, 262, 324
Hart, Jeffrey 90
Hart-Davis, Rupert 39, 40
Hartley, L.P. 430
Hartman, Geoffrey H. 379, 496
Hartshorne, Charles 309
Harvey, David Dow 165
Harvey, J. 290-91
Hassall, Christopher 262
Häusermann, Hans Walter 246, 365, 499
Hawkes, Ellen 473
Hawley, Andrew R. 71
Hay, Eloise Knupp 105-6
Hayakawa, S. Ichiye 134, 381, 384
Haymaker, Richard E. 206, 230
Hayman, Ronald 283
Haynes, Renée 62, 63
Haynes, Roslynn D. 464
Hayward, John 120, 134
Headings, Philip R. 134
Heath, William W. 339
Heilbrun, Carolyn G. 439
Heinemann, Margot 299
Helsinger, Howard 190
Henderson, Alexander 246
Henderson, Archibald 412
Henderson, Lucile Kelling 411
Hendry, J.F. 234, 365
Henig, Suzanne 479
Henighan, T.J. 275
Henn, Thomas·Rice 499
Henson, Janice 418
Hepburn, James 185, 190
Heppenstall, Rayner 338, 340
Herendon, Richard 167
Hertz, Karl 130
Hervouet, Yves 106
Herz, Judith Sherer 174
Hetzler, Leo A. 90
Heyl, Bernard 291
H.G. Wells Society 458
Hibbard, G.R. 264, 266, 420
Higdon, David Leon 106
Higgins, Bertram 135
Higginson, Fred Hall 213

Author Index

Highet, Gilbert 347
Hijmans, Ben L. 215
Hildick, Wallace 395
Hill, Eldon C. 411, 418
Hill, Katherine C. 479
Hillebrand, Harold N. 43
Hind, C. Lewis 190
Hinz, Evelyn J. 262
Hirsch, David 291
Hirsch, E.D., Jr. 17
Hoag, Gerald 479
Hobsbaum, Philip 17, 156
Hobson, Harold 191
Hochman, Baruch 262
Hochmuth, Marie 379
Hodge, Alan 210, 212
Hodge, Bob 347
Hodges, Robert R. 106
Hodgson, Stuart 449
Hodin, J.P. 366
Hoffman, Daniel G. 215, 499
Hoffman, Frederick J. 18, 262-63, 266, 324
Hogarth, Paul 210
Hoggart, Richard 34, 347-48
Holbrook, David 291
Holder, Alan 135
Hollander, John 372, 373, 374, 375, 376, 377, 379, 383, 384, 385
Hollis, Christopher 64, 90, 348
Holloway, John 291, 324
Holloway, Mark 114
Holmer, Paul L. 309
Holmes, Charles M. 246
Holroyd, Michael 418, 421, 422, 424, 434, 435
Holtby, Winifred 480
Hone, Joseph 494
Hooper, Walter 304, 305, 306, 309
Hoopes, James 379
Hopkins, Kenneth 448, 449
Hopkins, Robert Thurston 464
Hopkinson, Tom 348
Hoskins, Katherine Bail 34
Hotopf, W.H.N. 379
Hough, Graham 14, 18, 135, 156, 263
House, Humphrey 135
Howarth, Herbert 122, 135, 324
Howe, Irving 275
Hubenka, Lloyd J. 409, 418

Hughes, David Y. 457, 458, 464, 467
Hughes, Glenn 234
Hugo, Leon 418
Hulcoop, John F. 480
Hull, Keith N. 275-76
Hulse, James W. 418
Hummel, Madeline M. 480
Hummert, Paul A. 418
Hungerford, Edward A. 473, 480
Hunt, Bishop C., Jr. 22
Hunt, Peter 91
Hunter, Lynette 91
Hunting, Robert 480
Huntley, Frank L. 191
Huntley, H. Robert 167
Husain, S. Wigar 439
Huss, Roy 43
Hutchins, Robert Maynard 135
Huttar, Charles 310
Huxley, Julian 250, 455, 465
Hyde, H. Montgomery 274
Hyde, William J. 465
Hyman, Stanley Edgar 18, 135
Hynes, Samuel 7, 70, 72, 136, 167, 231, 232, 234, 465

I

Ingle, Stephen J. 348, 465
Inglis, Fred 291
Irvine, William 185, 191, 413, 418-19
Irwin, W.R. 174, 263
Isherwood, Christopher 27
Iyengar, K.R. Srinivasa 440

J

Jackson, R.L.P. 291
Jackson, Stanley 400
Jago, David 64
Jamal, Zahir 348
James, Clive 292
James, David Gwilym 380
James, Stanley B. 64
James, Walter 473
Jameson, Frederic 324
Janik, Del Ivan 263
Jarrell, Randall 216

517

Author Index

Jarrett-Kerr, Martin 263, 292
Jebb, Eleanor 62
Jebb, Reginald 62, 64
Jeffares, A. Norman 492, 493, 494, 496, 499-500
Jensen, James 156-57
Jerrold, Douglas 64
Joad, C.E.M. 246
Jochum, K.P.S. 121, 493
John, V.V. 91
Johnson, Colton 492
Johnson, Edgar 11
Johnson, Lesley 136, 292
Johnson, Lionel 490
Johnson, Manly 480
Johnson, Maurice 136
Johnson, Michael L. 154
Johnson, Richard A. 34
Johnson, Robert G. 165
Johnston, Dillon 465
Johnston, George A. 440
Johnstone, John Keith 175, 440
Jones, Alun R. 18, 231, 232, 234, 292, 299
Jones, Henry Arthur 465
Jones, John 340
Jones, Richard 431
Jones, W.S. Handley 91
Joseph, David I. 175
Joy, Neill R. 106

K

Kagarlitski, J. 465
Kalechofsky, Roberta 348
Kallich, Martin 434, 440
Kalnins, Mara 253, 263
Kamerbeek, J., Jr. 234
Kantra, Robert A. 64
Kaplan, Morton 18
Karl, Frederick R. 104, 106, 115, 167, 465
Karnani, Chetan 372, 380
Katz, Wendy R. 349
Kauffmann, Stanley 466
Kaufmann, R.J. 299, 340, 421
Kaye, Julian B. 419
Kazin, Alfred 466
Keating, Karl 64
Keefe, Carolyn 306

Keith, W.J. 22, 263
Kelly, Hugh 91
Kelvin, Norman 175
Kendall, Paul 11
Kendig, M. 381, 384
Kenedy, R.C. 324
Kenner, Hugh 91, 136, 157, 292, 318, 319, 325, 500
Kenney, Edwin J. 480
Kenny, Herbert A. 64
Keough, Lawrence C. 411
Kermode, John Frank 500
Kermode, Frank 120, 136-37, 234, 263-64, 284
Kertzer, J.M. 106
Keskinen, Kenneth 349
Kessler, Jascha 264
Keynes, Geoffrey 400
Kilby, Clyde S. 304, 306, 309
Killham, John 292
Killigrew, Michael 165
Kimbrough, Robert 108
King, B.A. 500
King, Carlyle 247, 349, 419
King, R.W. 440
Kings, J.A. 239
Kingsmill, Hugh 137
Kinkead-Weekes, Mark 264
Kirby, Thomas A. 378
Kirk, Russell 137, 325, 349
Kirkham, Michael 216
Kirkpatrick, Brownlee Jean 172, 474
Kirkwood, M.M. 247
Klaus, Carl H. 15
Klein, Holger 214
Klein, Theodore M. 133
Klingopulos, G.D. 175, 264
Kloss, Robert 18
Knickerbocker, William S. 137
Knight, E. Helen 380
Knight, G. Wilson 340
Knightly, Philip 191
Knox, E.V. 83
Knox, Ronald 65
Kojecký, Roger 137
Kramer, Jurgen 137
Krans, H.S. 500
Kreeft, Peter 309
Kress, Gunther 347

Author Index

Kreutz, Irving 480
Krieger, Murray 18, 137, 234, 380
Kronenberger, Louis 43, 440, 481
Krutch, Joseph Wood 441
Krzyzanowski, Ludwik 106
Kubal, David L. 349
Kuehn, Robert E. 247
Kuhn, Daniel K. 310
Kumar, Jitendra 138
Kuna, F.M. 138

L

La Bossiere, Camille Rene 106
Lafourcade, Bernard 319
Laidler, Harry W. 458
Laing, D.A. 474
Lakshmi, Vijay 175, 481
Lambert, J.W. 100
Land, Berel 349
Landow, George P. 190
Langbaum, Robert 43, 501
Las Vergnas, Raymond 65, 92
Laurence, Dan H. 403, 408, 409, 419
Lauterbach, Edward S. 4
Lawlor, John 310
Lawrence, A.W. 272, 274
Lea, F.A. 92, 338, 340
Leary, Daniel J. 419
Leary, Lewis 115
Leaska, Mitchell A. 473, 481
Leavis, Frank R. 138, 325, 380, 466
Leavis, Q.D. 280, 281, 481
LeBrun, Philip 138
Ledger, Marshall 43
Lee, Brian 139, 264
Lee, Ernest George 310
Lee, Robert A. 350
Leer, Norman 168
Lehman, B.H. 441
Lehmann, John 7, 100, 429
Leigh, David J. 92
Leigh-Taylor, N.H. 407
Leighton, Clare 449
Le Mesurier, Lillian 419
Lemon, Lee T. 19
Lenoski, Daniel S. 501
Lentricchia, Frank 501

Lester, John A., Jr. 8
Leuba, Walter 393, 395
Levin, Gerald 419, 501
Levin, Harry 381
Levy, Hyman 69, 72
Levy, Paul 434, 441
Levy, William Turner 139
Lewis, D.B. Wyndham 82, 92
Lewis, Wyndham 235, 481
Lewisohn, Ludwig 191
Leyburn, Ellen Douglass 481
Liddell, Robert 292
Lief, Ruth Ann 350
Leinhardt, R.G. 101
Lilley, George 338
Lindeman, Ralph D. 115
Lindsay, Jack 325
Littell, Philip 43
Litzenberg, Karl 191
Lock, D.R. 223
Lodge, David 19, 292, 466
Lohf, Kenneth A. 104, 402
Longaker, Mark 11
Longville, Timothy 264
Looker, Samuel J. 228
Lorberg, Aileen D. 482
Lothian, John M. 247
Low, D.M. 113, 115
Lowbridge, Peter 154
Lowndes, Marie Belloc 62
Lowther, F.H. 92
Lu, Fei-Pai 139
Lucas, E.V. 60, 82, 83
Lucas, F.L. 14, 216, 501
Lucas, John 35, 501
Lucy, Seán 139
Ludwig, Richard M. 121
Luhan, Mabel Dodge 256
Lunn, Arnold 92
Lutz, Jerry 419
Lynch, J.G. Bohun 44
Lynd, Robert 44, 65, 115, 395, 449, 502
Lyon, Mary 471

M

McAlister, F.L. 293
Macaulay, Rose 175
Maccallum, H.R. 502
MacCarthy, Desmond 65, 402, 441

Author Index

McCarthy, John P. 65, 93
MacColl, Dugald Sutherland 191, 395
McCormack, Arthur 247
MacCurtain, Austin 66
McDiarmid, Hugh 205
McDonald, Edward D. 113, 115, 254, 255-56, 265
Macdonald, Gregory 93
McDowell, Frederick P.W. 19, 172, 175-76, 419
McDowell, M. Jennifer 344
McElderry, Bruce R., Jr. 44
McIntyre, Clara F. 482
Mack, John E. 274
Mack, Maynard 264
McKenzie, D.F. 283
Mackenzie, Jeanne 420, 460
Mackenzie, Norman 420, 460
MacKerness, E.D. 420
McLaurin, Allen 482
McLuhan, H.M. 93, 157, 293, 381
McMahon, Francis E. 66
MacNeice, Louis 28, 502
McNeillie, Andrew 472
McNeir, Waldo F. 144
McNelly, Cleo 350
Macphail, Andrew 276
MacShane, Frank 165, 166, 168, 206, 325
Madden, William A. 19
Madeleva, Sister M. 66
Magnusson, Sigurdur A. 34
Magro, Frank 428
Mairet, Philip 340
Mais, S.P.B. 191
Majumdar, Robin 474, 482
Malraux, Andre 276
Mandel, Barrett J. 192
Mandell, C.C. 66
Mann, Charles W. 265
Manuel, M. 482
March, Richard 131
Marcus, Jane 482
Marcus, Philip L. 139
Marder, Herbert 482
Margolies, David N. 72, 299
Margolis, John D. 139
Marie Virginia, Sister 93
Marks, Emerson R. 139

Marovitz, Sanford E. 247
Marriott, Paul J. 274
Marthaler, Joyce Shober 244
Martin, Dexter 265
Martin, Graham 140, 152
Martin, John 93
Martin, Kingsley 247
Martin, Mildred 121
Martin, W. 232
Martin, Wallace 235
Martindale, C.C. 65, 92
Mason, Ellsworth 213
Mason, H.A. 157
Mason, Michael 66, 93
Massingham, H.J. 230
Masterman, C.F.G. 94
Masterman, Margaret 310
Materer, Timothy 325
Mattheisen, Paul F. 192
Matthews, G.M. 72
Matthews, John F. 410
Matthews, T.S. 100
Matthews, William 4
Matthiessen, F.O. 140
Maud, Ralph N. 265
Maurois, André 94, 441
Maxwell, D.E.S. 140, 500
Maycock, A.L. 83
Mayer, Frederick P. 449
Mayne, Richard 326
Meckier, Jerome 247
Megaw, Moira 154
Megay, Joyce N. 23
Mégroz, Rodolphe Louis 429
Mehoke, James S. 216
Meilaender, Gilbert 310
Meisel, Martin 420
Meisel, Perry 482
Meixner, John A. 168
Melchiori, Giorgio 502
Mellichamp, Leslie 350
Mellown, Elgin W. 4
Melville, Cecil F. 326
Melville, Lewis 80
Mendelson, Edward 28, 29, 30, 34, 475
Merivale, Patricia 265
Merritt, James D. 420
Meyers, Jeffrey 206, 273, 276, 318, 320, 321, 322, 326, 327, 330, 344, 350

Author Index

Meyers, Valerie 344
Michel, Walter 318, 326
Miko, Stephen J. 265
Miles, Josephine 14
Milic, Louis 4
Miller, Karl 157
Millgate, Michael 192
Mills, A.R. 293
Mills, George 491
Mills, Gordon 276
Mills, John A. 420
Milner, Andrew 293
Mirsky, D.S. 466
Mitchell, Peter Todd 265
Mix, Katherine L. 44
Mizener, Arthur 166
Moers, Ellen 44
Moloney, Michael F. 140
Monod, Sylvere 94
Montgomery, Marion 123, 140
Moore, George 192
Moore, Harry T. 176, 254, 255, 256-57, 260, 266, 267
Moore, Virginia 502
Morf, Gustav 104
Morris, Tom 265
Morrison, Claudia C. 19
Morrissette, Bruce 192
Morrow, Bradford 319
Morse, J.I. 140
Morton, John Bingham 61, 62, 66
Moser, Thomas C. 168
Mosher, T.B. 60
Most, Glenn W. 293
Mudrick, Marvin 109, 293
Muir, Augustus 393, 394
Muir, Edwin 140, 176
Muir, Percy 434
Mulhern, Francis 294
Mullen, Richard D. 458, 466
Muller, Herbert J. 502
Mulryne, James Ronald 498
Munton, Alan 70, 326
Murray, D.L. 223
Murray, Henry 94
Murry, Byron D. 141
Murry, John Middleton 14, 366
Murry, Mary Middleton 338
Myers, W.A. 310

N

Najder, Zdzislaw 103
National Civic Federation 466
Natwar-Singh, K. 172
Nehls, Edward 266
Neill, A.S. 420
Nelson, Francis W. 235
Nelson, Lowry 495
Nethercot, Arthur H. 420-21
Nettels, Elsa 107
Newton-De Molina, David 125, 131, 135, 136, 141, 142, 144, 147
Nichols, Ann Eljenholm 266
Nichols, William 294
Nickerson, C.C. 466
Nicolson, Harold 11
Nisbet, Robert 67
Noon, William 502
Noonan, James 141
Norris, Christopher 157
Norwood, W.D., Jr. 311
Notopoulos, James A. 277
Nott, Kathleen 235, 311
Novak, Jane 483
Noyes, Alfred 94
Nulle, Stebelton H. 467

O

O'Connor, Monsignor John. See Brown, Father
O'Connor, William Van 19
O'Donnell, Norbert F. 421
O'Donnell, Thomas J. 277
O'Flinn, J.P. 351
Ogden, C.K. 369, 370
Ohmann, Carol 475
Ohmann, Richard M. 35, 421, 502
O'Leary, John Gerard 192
Olive, William J. 378
Oliver, John W. 392, 393, 394
Oliver, L.M. 40
Olney, James 12, 192
Olsen, Elder 158
Orage, Alfred R. 94, 326
Orwell, George 343, 467
Orwell, Sonia 343, 467
Osborne, Charles 30, 421

Author Index

Osterwalder, Hans 141
Ostling, Joan K. 305
Oxley, B.T. 351

P

Pace, Claire 129
Pacey, Desmond 483
Pallette, Drew B. 421
Palmer, Paul R. 266
Panichas, George A. 141, 266, 294
Park, Bruce R. 421
Parker, G.B. 172
Parker, W.M. 206, 393
Parkinson, Thomas 141
Parrinder, Patrick 457, 459, 467
Pascal, Roy 503
Patankar, R.B. 381
Paterson, John 107, 266, 483
Paul, Leslie 141
Paulin, Tom 35
Pawling, Chris 351
Payne, John R. 227
Payne, Robert 274, 277
Peacock, R. 142
Pearce, Donald R. 492, 503
Pearlman, E. 192
Pearson, Hesketh 62, 67, 94, 442
Pearson, John 429
Peart, Barbara 421
Perlis, Alan D. 381
Peschmann, Hermann 216
Peters, Robert L. 185, 193
Peterson, Richard F. 214, 503
Peterson, Sven 142
Petitpas, Harold M. 94
Peyre, Henri 23
Pfleger, Karl 95
Phelps, Gilbert 193
Philipson, Morris 243
Philmus, Robert M. 351, 457, 458, 459, 466, 467
Pierle, Robert C. 266
Pinchin, Jane Lagoudis 176
Pinion, F.B. 266
Pinto, Vivian de Sola 266, 402
Pollock, Thomas Clark 381
Pomeroy, Elizabeth W. 483
Pondrom, Cyrena N. 235
Poole, Roger C. 294

Porter, Peter 35
Porter, Raymond J. 499
Porter, Roger J. 193
Porteus, Hugh Gordon 326
Potter, Stephen 395
Pound, Ezra 142, 193, 230, 235, 327
Pound, Omar S. 319
Powell, Dilys 35, 142, 402
Pownall, David E. 213
Poynter, J.W. 67
Pradhan, S.K. 294
Praz, Mario 142, 327
Priestley, J.B. 294, 395
Primeau, Ronald 235
Pritchard, William H. 319, 327-28
Pritchett, V.S. 95, 193
Pryce-Jones, Alan 67, 100
Pulos, C.E. 19, 168, 235
Purcell, J.M. 67
Purnell, George 95
Putt, S. Gorley 295

Q

Quennell, Peter 100, 142, 248, 483
Quiller-Couch, Arthur T. 143
Quinn, Martin 421

R

R., E. 230
Rackham, Bernard 359
Rackin, Phyllis 236, 381
Rahv, Phillip 295, 483
Rai, Rama Nand 503
Raina, M.L. 143
Raine, Kathleen 366
Rajan, Balachandra 127, 143, 503
Rajnath 143
Raknem, Ingvald 459
Raleigh, John H. 143
Ralli, Augustus 396
Ralston, W.R.S. 193
Ramsay, A.A.W. 366
Ramsden, E.H. 366
Ramsey, Roger 351
Rank, Hugh 351
Ransom, John Crowe 143-44, 158, 382

Author Index

Rantavaara, Irma 483
Rao, B.D. 382
Rascoe, Burton 193
Rawlings, Donn 176
Ray, Gordon N. 457, 459, 463
Ray, Paul C. 72, 366
Raymond, John 95, 442
Read, Herbert 15, 231-32, 236, 259, 396
Reckitt, Maurice B. 95
Reed, Henry 144
Rees, Richard 337, 340, 351
Rees, Thomas Richard 144
Reeves, James 213, 216
Regnery, Henry 328
Reid, Hilary 402
Reilly, Joseph J. 442
Reynolds, Horace 491, 503
Rhys, Ernest 84
Rice, Philip Blair 144
Richards, I.A. 20, 158-59
Richardson, Dorothy 396
Richardson, Jillian 363
Richardson, John Adkins 267
Riches, Phyllis M. 4
Ricks, Beatrice 122
Ricks, Christopher 295
Rickword, Edgell 69, 72, 89, 135, 328, 442
Riding, Laura 236, 328
Rieff, Philip 255, 267, 352
Riewald, Jacobus Gerhardus 40, 45, 46
Righter, William 20, 144, 382
Ringbom, Hakan 352
Ringrose, C.X. 295
Ritchie, Charles 223, 442
Robb, Kenneth A. 484
Roberts, John Hawley 484
Roberts, Mark 267, 311
Roberts, Michael 231, 236
Roberts, Morley 228
Roberts, S.C. 39, 45
Roberts, Warren 254, 256
Robinson, A.D. 236
Robinson, Ian 295
Robinson, James K. 193, 396
Robson, W.W. 8, 144, 159, 295
Rodenbeck, John 411
Rodker, John 230

Rodway, Allan 311
Rogot, Ellen Hawkes 484
Rolo, Charles J. 243
Ronsley, Joseph 504
Rose, Alan M. 107
Rose, William K. 319, 328
Rosenbaum, Stanford P. 126, 484
Rosenberg, Edgar 412
Rosenblood, Norman 420
Rosenthal, Michael 484
Rosenthal, Raymond 318
Ross, Fredric R. 194
Ross, William T. 352
Ross, Woodburn O. 449
Rota, Bertram 277
Roth, Cecil 400
Roughead, W.N. 61, 64
Routh, Harold V. 8
Rovere, Richard H. 343
Rubenstein, Roberta 484
Rucker, Mary E. 15
Rudolph, Gerald Allen 382
Russell, Bertrand 382
Russell, Diarmuid 409
Russell, John 442
Russell, Leonard 191
Russo, John Paul 372, 382-83
Ruthven, R.K. 20

S

Sadock, Geoffrey 296
Said, Edward W. 107
Saintsbury, George 15
St. Vincent, Edwin 287
Sale, Roger 159, 311
Salgado, Gamini 267
Salmon, Christopher V. 144
Salter, Arthur 467
Saltmarshe, Christopher 442
Sampson, George 8
Samuelson, Ralph 484
Sanders, Charles Richard 434, 435, 442
Sandison, Alan 352
San Juan, E., Jr. 194
Sassaman, Stephen 402
Savage, Derek S. 145
Saxena, H.S. 267
Scarfe, Francis 145

Author Index

Schaefer, Josephine O'Brien 484
Scheick, William J. 468
Schiller, Jerome P. 372, 383
Schlack, Beverly Ann 485
Schmerl, Rudolf B. 176, 248
Schmude, Karl G. 95
Schneider, Elizabeth 145
Schneiderman, Leo 267
Scholes, Robert 15
Schorer, Mark 267, 485
Schuchard, Ronald 145, 236
Schulkind, Jeanne 473, 485
Schwartz, Delmore 146
Sclater, P.L. 224
Scott, William T. 95
Scott, Winfield Townley 431
Scott-James, Rolfe Arnold 8, 443
Scruggs, Charles 352
Sears, Sallie 485
Seccombe, Thomas 194
Seaver, George 341
Seiden, Melvin 168
Seiden, Morton Irving 504
Sellers, W.H. 35
Sencourt, Robert 123
Sesonske, Alexander 384
Severn, Derek 449
Sewell, Elizabeth 96
Seymour-Smith, Martin 216, 328, 341
Shahane, Vasant A. 177, 178
Shaheen, M.Y. 177
Shand, John 45
Shanks, E.B. 66
Shanks, Edward 67
Shapiro, Karl 146, 236, 396
Shapiro, Marjorie 352
Shapiro, Stephen 12
Sharma, Arvind 248
Sharma, Vijay L. 485
Sharrock, Roger 146, 311
Shaw, Charlotte F. 409
Shaw, George Bernard 96, 404
Shedd, Robert G. 412
Sheed, F.J. 81
Sheed, Wilfrid 82, 96
Sheehy, Eugene P. 104
Shelston, Alan 12
Shenfield, M. 422
Shepard, Odell 227
Shepherd, Henry F. 194

Sherman, Stuart P. 194, 468
Sherry, Norman 105, 169
Shober, Joyce Lee 244
Shorter, Clement 194
Showalter, Elaine 485
Shrubb, Peter 296
Shrubsall, Dennis 228
Shumaker, Wayne 12
Silver, Arnold 422
Silver, Brenda R. 471
Silverman, Albert H. 422
Simon, Brian 146
Simon, Louis 422
Singh, Frances B. 177
Singh, G.S. 296
Sisson, C.H. 329
Sitesh, Aruna 268
Sitwell, Edith 296
Sitwell, Sir Osbert 194
Sked, Alan 353
Skelton, Robin 213, 364
Skene, Reg 504
Skinner, B.F. 384
Slater, Montagu 329
Sleight, Richard 159
Sloman, Judith 485
Slosson, Edwin E. 96
Small, Barbara J. 422
Small, Christopher 353
Small, Michel 268
Smith, Carol H. 146
Smith, David R. 103, 107
Smith, Grover 169
Smith, J. Percy 422
Smith, James 146, 159
Smith, Logan Pearsall 45
Smith, Malcolm 353
Smith, Page 329
Smith, Warren Sylvester 410
Smyer, Richard I. 353
Smyth, Charles 443
Snee, Carole 299
Snow, C.P. 296
Soldo, John J. 147
Solomon, Eric 107
Sossaman, Stephen 217
Spanos, William V. 329
Spaulding, Gordon 384
Speaight, Robert 62, 67
Spears, Monroe K. 35-36

Author Index

Spencer, Theodore 149, 189
Spender, Stephen 31, 36, 100, 123, 147, 268, 329, 504
Spengemann, William C. 23
Sperber, Murray A. 353
Spilka, Mark 485
Sprug, Joseph W. 96
Spurling, Hilary 422
Squire, J.C. 195
Srinath, C.N. 147
Stade, G. 217
Stallman, Robert W. 206
Stallybrass, Oliver 173, 177
Stanford, Derek 45-46, 341
Stanford, W.B. 504
Stang, Sondra J. 169
Stansky, Peter 345
Stapleton, Laurence 147
Starkman, M.K. 311
Stauffer, Donald A. 504
Stavrou, Constantine N. 268
Stead, C.K. 147
Steadman, John M. 147
Stein, Joseph 46
Stein, Walter 296
Steinberg, M.W. 468
Steiner, George 217, 296
Stephen, Leslie 195
Stevenson, David L. 46, 147
Stevenson, John 353
Stewart, Desmond 274
Stewart, Jean 129, 479
Stewart, John L. 268
Stigler, George J. 423
Stillman, Clara G. 443
Stock, A.G. 159, 505
Stokes, E.E., Jr. 423
Stoll, Elmer Edgar 311
Stoll, John Edward 493
Stolnitz, Jerome 384
Stone, Geoffrey 148, 329
Stone, Wilfred 177
Stone-Blackburn, Susan 423
Stonier, G.W. 329
Stovall, Floyd 143
Strachey, James 433, 434, 443
Strachey, John 70, 73
Strachey, Lytton 195
Stratford, Jenny 443

Strickland, Geoffrey 160, 297
Stuart, Campbell 458
Stubbs, Patricia 486
Sugiyama, Yoko 486
Sullivan, John 84, 96
Sundaram, P.S. 312
Sutherland, James R. 15, 396
Sutton, Denys 100
Sutton, Eric 431
Suvin, Darko 466
Swan, Michael 116, 268
Swigg, Richard 268
Swinnerton, Frank 8
Symons, Arthur 195
Szladits, Lola L. 486

T

Tabachnick, Stephen Ely 277
Takács, Ferenc 148
Takayanagi, Shunichi 148
Tamaizumi, Yasuo 312
Tambimuttu, Thurairajah 131
Tanner, Michael 297
Tanner, Stephen L. 148
Tarnawski, Wit 108
Tate, Allen 122, 123, 142, 236, 363, 366, 385
Tauber, Abraham 408
Teets, Bruce E. 104
Temple, Ruth Z. 4, 195
Thakur, N.C. 486
Thayer, C.G. 341
Thody, Philip 68, 248
Thomas, Edward Morely 108, 353
Thomas, R. Hinton 148
Thomas, William David 213
Thompson, Denys 279
Thompson, E.P. 353
Thompson, Eric 148
Thomson, George H. 69, 70, 73, 171, 177
Thomson, J.A.K. 15
Thorburn, David 108, 496
Thorpe, Michael 401, 402
Thumboo, Edwin 177
Tierney, Frank M. 195
Tilby, A. Wyatt 468
Tillyard, E.M.W. 148

Author Index

Timko, Michael 423, 459, 468
Tindall, William York 9, 254
Titterton, W.R. 84
Todd, Ruthven 30
Tolomeo, Diane 213
Tomalin, Ruth 228
Tomlin, E.W.F. 318, 320, 330, 385
Tomlinson, H. Charles 445
Tomlinson, H.M. 116, 449
Tommasi, Anthony 255
Torchiana, Donald T. 505
Toulmin, Stephen 289
Townsend, Francis G. 412
Tracy, Billy T. 268-69
Traubitz, Nancy Baker 195
Traversi, Derek 297
Treece, Henry 365, 366
Trevelyan, G.M. 178
Trew, Tony 347
Trilling, Diana 255
Trilling, Lionel 148, 178, 217, 297-98, 354
Tripp, Raymond P., Jr. 306, 308, 311, 312
Trivedi, H.K. 178
Truitt, Willis H. 178
Tschiffely, Aime Felix 203, 205
Tschumi, Raymond 505
Tucker, Martin 4
Tuell, Anne K. 46
Turco, Alfred 423
Turnell, G. Martin 149

U

Ullman, Stephen 15
Unger, Leonard 122, 149
Ure, Peter 505
Utley, Francis Lee 312

V

Van Doren, Mark 149
Van Thal, Herbert 60
Vendler, Helen 372, 373, 374, 375, 376, 377, 379, 383, 384, 385, 505
Verma, Rajendra 149
Versfeld, M. 96
Vickery, John B. 217

Vidan, Ivo 169
Villars, Jean Beraud 275
Vinaver, Eugene 312
Vines, Sherard 330
Vitoux, Pierre 248
Vivas, Eliseo 20, 149, 298, 385
Vorhees, Richard J. 354

W

Waddell, Helen 393, 394
Wagar, W. Warren 457, 468
Wagner, Geoffrey 169, 319, 330-31
Wagner, Jeanie 269
Wain, John 100, 160, 312, 354-55, 443
Walker, John 204, 206
Wallace, A. Dayle 449
Walsh, Chad 312-13
Walsh, William 269, 398
Warburg, Frederic J. 355
Ward, Alfred C. 9, 408, 412
Ward, Anne 237
Ward, David 150
Ward, Leo R. 97
Ward, Maisie 81, 84-85
Ward, Wilfrid P. 97
Waring, Hubert 97
Warmsley, Nigel 217
Warncke, Wayne 355
Warren, Austin 150
Warren, Robert Penn 36
Wasson, Richard 150
Watkin, E.I. 95, 248, 468
Watkins, A.H. 459
Watson, Barbara Bellow 424
Watson, C.B. 150
Watson, Garry 298
Watson, George 20, 108, 355, 505
Watson, Sheila 331
Watt, Donald J. 178, 248
Watt, Ian 108
Watts, Cedric T. 204-5, 207
Watts, Frederick 308
Watts, Harold H. 247, 249
Waugh, Alec 195
Waugh, Arthur 196, 396
Waugh, Evelyn 60
Weatherby, H.L. 313
Weathers, Winston 313

526

Author Index

Weber, Horst 263, 268, 479
Webster, A. Blyth 394
Webster, Brenda S. 505
Webster, Grant T. 150
Webster, H.T. 116, 249
Wecter, Dixon 237
Weeks, Robert P. 459
Weinblatt, Alan 150
Weiner, S. Ronald 269
Weintraub, Rodelle 272, 278
Weintraub, Stanley 272, 275, 278, 407, 409, 412, 413, 424
Weisberg, Robert 151
Weiser, Barbara 474
Weisinger, Herbert 217
Weiss, Margene E. 197
Welby, T. Earle 196
Wellek, René 20, 151, 298-99, 385, 396, 486
Wells, Geoffrey H. 412
Wells, George P. 455, 458
Wells, H.G. 55, 68
Wells, Stanley 46
Wells, Warre Bradley 505
Wert, Paul 269
Wertheimer, Douglas 196
West, Alick 20
West, Anthony 469
West, E.J. 410
West, Herbert Faulkner 205, 228
West, Julius 97
West, Rebecca 486
Weston, John Howard 108
Wheatley, Elizabeth D. 116
Whitaker, Thomas R. 269, 506
White, Albert C. 97
White, Richard L. 269
White, William Luther 196, 256, 313, 344
Whitehorn, K.E. 81
Whiteside, George 151
Whitman, Robert F. 424
Whittemore, Reed 469
Wildi, Max 270
Wiley, Paul L. 169
Wilhelmsen, Frederick 68
Will, Frederick 130
Willey, Basil 385
Williams, J.E. Hodder 79
Williams, Joy 254

Williams, Orlo 151, 196, 443
Williams, Raymond 73, 151, 237, 254, 270, 299, 348, 353-54, 355-56, 385
Williams, Stanley T. 196
Williamson, George 151
Willis, John H. 154, 160
Willison, I.R. 5
Wills, Garry 97
Wilson, Angus 299
Wilson, Colin 218, 331
Wilson, Edmund 41, 46, 97, 101, 116, 152, 397, 444, 486, 506
Wilson, George F. 228
Wimsatt, William K. 21, 152, 386
Winslow, Donald J. 5
Winsten, S. 408, 414, 415, 416, 420
Winston, George P. 152
Winters, Yvor 152
Wise, Thomas J. 104
Wiseman, James 152
Wisenthal, J.L. 409, 424
Wolf, Howard R. 197
Wolfe, Peter 108
Wollheim, Richard 152, 356
Wood, James 369
Wood, James Playsted 460
Woodcock, George 36, 249, 320, 356, 364, 367, 469
Woodring, Carl 487
Woodruff, Douglas 64
Woods, Richard D. 249
Woodward, Daniel A. 152
Woolley, C. Leonard 271
Woolf, Cecil 113
Woolf, James D. 185, 186, 197
Woolf, Leonard 178, 197, 223, 471, 472, 473
Woolf, Virginia 47, 178, 197, 444
Woolmer, J. Howard 474
Worsley, J.C. 27
Worth, George J. 108
Worthen, John 270
Wright, David G. 506
Wright, George T. 36
Wright, Iain 299
Wright, Nathalia 152
Wright, Walter F. 103, 109

Author Index

Wyke, Clement H. 198
Wykes-Joyce, Max 431

Y

Yeats, Mrs. W.B. 491, 492
Yoder, Edwin M. 249
Young, Alan 70
Young, Dudley 36, 356
Young, Kenneth 469
Young, Vernon 331

Z

Zabel, Morton Dauwen 109, 152, 506
Zable, Arnold 331
Zaehner, Robert C. 249
Zahner, Lilly 249
Zak, William F. 299
Zeitlin, Jacob Israel 250
Zeke, Zoltan G. 344
Zudeck, Ronald 85
Zwerdling, Alex 356

TITLE INDEX

This index includes titles of books cited in the text. References are to page numbers and alphabetization is letter by letter.

A

Abinger Harvest 170
Abolition of Man, The 300
Abroad: British Literary Traveling between the Wars 22
Absent Father: Virginia Woolf and Walter Pater, The 482
Achievement of T.S. Eliot, The 140
Adam and Eve 332
Adonis and the Alphabet and Other Essays 238
Adventures among Birds 224
Adventures in Reputation 436
Advice 60
Aesthetics and Philosophy of Art Criticism 384
Afoot in England 224
After Democracy 450
Aftermath, or Gleanings from a Busy Life Called upon the Outer Cover for Purposes of Sale "Caliban's Guide to Letters," The 48
After Strange Gods 117, 259
Age of Criticism, 1900-1950, An 19
Alarms and Discursions 74
Albergo Empedocle and Other Early Writings 171
Albert Schweitzer 341
Aldous Huxley (Henderson) 246
Aldous Huxley (Watts) 249
Aldous Huxley: A Bibliography 244

Aldous Huxley: A Bibliography, 1916-1959 244
Aldous Huxley: A Biographical Introduction 248
Aldous Huxley: A Biography 244
Aldous Huxley: A Collection of Critical Essays 247
Aldous Huxley: A Critical Study 245
Aldous Huxley: A Literary Study 244
Aldous Huxley: On Art and Artists 243
Aldous Huxley: The Critical Heritage 248
Aldous Huxley and the Way to Reality 246
Aldous Huxley's Quest for Values 245
Aldous Huxley's Stories, Essays, and Poems 238
Alexandria: A History and a Guide 170
Alexandria Still 176
Alfred Tennyson (Chesterton) 74
Allegory of Love, The 300
All Is Grist 74
All I Survey 74
All Things Considered 75
Almanac, An 110
Alms for Oblivion 437
Alone 110

Title Index

Along the Road   238
America, I Presume   314
America: The Diary of a Visit, Winter 1884-1885   185
America and the Cosmic Man   314
American and British Writers in Mexico, 1556-1973   246
Analytical Bibliography of Universal Collected Biography, An   4
Anarchism Is Not Enough   328
Anarchy and Order   357
Anatomy of Art, The   361
Anatomy of Criticism   17
Anatomy of Frustration, The   450
Ancient Lights and Certain New Reflections   161
And Even Now   37
Anglosaxy: A League That Works   314
Anna Karenina and Other Essays   279
Annals of Innocence and Experience   357
Annotated Check-List of a Collection of Writings by and about T.E. Lawrence, An   273
Annotated Checklist of the Works of W.H. Auden (1924-1957), An   29
Annotations of Some Minor Writings of "T.E. Lawrence"   273
Another Ego   262
Anthology of Modern Biography, An   437
Anticipations of the Reaction of Mechanical and Scientific Progress upon Human Life and Thought   450
Apes, Japes, and Hitlerism   323
Apocalypse   251
Apocalypse and the Writings on Revelation   253
Apostle and the Wild Ducks, and Other Essays, The   81
Appeal of Fascism, 1919-1945, The   324
Appetite of Tyranny, The   75
Appreciations and Criticism of the Works of Charles Dickens   75
Argentine Ornithology   224
Argentine Tango   219
Armed Vision, The   18
Around Theatres   37, 38, 40

Art and Alienation   357
Art and Education   357
Art and Industry   357
Art and Painting: D.H. Lawrence   253
Art and Society   358
Art and the Evolution of Man   358
Arthurian Torso   300
Art Now   358
Art of Being Ruled, The   314
Art of Biography, The   11
Art of Jean Arp, The   358
Art of Reading, The   326
Art of Rearrangement, The   175
Art of Sculpture, The   358
Art of Seeing, The   238
As I Was Saying   75
Aspects and Impressions   179
Aspects of Biography   441
Aspects of Literature   332
Aspects of Modern Poetry   296
Aspects of the Novel   170
Assorted Articles   251
Atlantic Edition of the Works of H.G. Wells, The   450
At the Sign of the Lion, and Other Essays from the Books of Hilaire Belloc   60
Attitudes to Criticism   289
Attitudes toward History   320
Auden   33
Auden: An Introductory Essay   34
Authordoxy   97
Author's Craft and Other Critical Writings, The   476
Autobiographical Acts   10
Autobiographies: REVERIES OVER CHILDHOOD AND YOUTH and THE TREMBLING OF THE VEIL   488
Autobiography (Chesterton)   75
Autobiography (Yeats)   491
Autobiography: Essays Theoretical and Critical   12
Autobiography of G.K. Chesterton, The   75
Autobiography of John Middleton Murry, The   332
Autobiography of Yeats, The   488
Avowals   192
Avowals and Denials   75

Title Index

Avril: Being Essays on Poetry of the French Renaissance 48
Axel's Castle 506

B

Barbarism of Berlin, The 75
Barbarous Knowledge 215
Basic English and Its Uses 368
Basic in Teaching 368
Basic Rules of Reason 368
Battle Ground, The 48
Belloc: A Biographical Anthology 60
Belloc Essays 61
Below London Bridge 445
Bernal Diaz del Castillo 199
Bernard Shaw (Bentley) 414
Bernard Shaw: A Prose Anthology 407
Bernard Shaw, Director 416
Bernard Shaw: His Life, Work, and Friends 412
Bernard Shaw, Playwright 416
Bernard Shaw: Playwright and Preacher 418
Bernard Shaw: The Darker Side 422
Bernard Shaw and Karl Marx 407
Bernard Shaw and the Aesthetics 413
Bernard Shaw and the Nineteenth-Century Tradition 419
Bernard Shaw and the Theater in the Nineties 416
Bernard Shaw's Marxian Romance 418
Bernard Shaw's Nondramatic Literary Criticism 407
Bernard Shaw's Ready-Reckoner 407
Best of W.H. Hudson, The 227
Betrayal of Christ by the Churches, The 332
Between St. Dennis and St. George 161
Between the Lines 445
Between Two Worlds 332
Beyond 368
Beyond Personality 300
Beyond the Mexique Bay 239
Bibliographical Notes on T.E. Lawrence's SEVEN PILLARS OF WISDOM and REVOLT IN THE DESERT 273

Bibliography of D.H. Lawrence, A 256
Bibliography of Edith, Osbert and Sacheverell Sitwell, A 429
Bibliography of E.M. Forster, A 172
Bibliography of John Middleton Murry, A 338
Bibliography of Joseph Conrad, A 104
Bibliography of Norman Douglas, A 113
Bibliography of Siegfried Sassoon, A 400
Bibliography of the Books and Pamphlets of George Bernard Shaw 412
Bibliography of the First Editions of the Works of Robert Bontine Cunninghame Graham, A 204
Bibliography of the Works of Max Beerbohm, A 40
Bibliography of the Works of Robert Graves, A 213
Bibliography of the Writings of D.H. Lawrence, A 255
Bibliography of the Writings of Norman Douglas, A 113
Bibliography of the Writings of W.B. Yeats, The 493
Bibliography of the Writings of W.H. Hudson, A 228
Bibliography of the Writings of Wyndham Lewis, A 319
Bibliography of Virginia Woolf, A 474
Bibliography of Yeats Criticism, 1887-1965, A 493
Biographical Essays 433
Biography (Shelston) 12
Biography as an Art 10
Birds and Beasts of the Greek Anthology 110
Birds and Man 224
Birds in a Village 225
Birds in London 225
Birds in Town and Village 225
Birds of La Plata 224
Blasting and Bombardiering 314
Bloomsbury Group: A Study of E.M. Forster, Lytton Strachey, Virginia Woolf, and Their Cycle, The 175

Title Index

Bodley Head Bernard Shaw, The   403, 440
Bodley Head Ford Madox Ford, The   161
Bodley Head Max Beerbohm, The   39
Bonnet and Shawl   219
Book of a Naturalist, The   225
Book of the Bayeux Tapestry, The   48
Books and Characters, French and English   432
Books and Portraits   471
Books on the Table   179
Boon, the Mind of the Race, the Wild Asses of the Devil, and the Last Trump   450
Bounty of Sweden, The   488
Brave New World Revisited   239
Brazilian Mystic, A   199
Brighton   425
Bright Shadow of Reality   307
British Autobiographies   4
British Birds   225
Broadcast Talks   300
Brought Forward   199
But It Still Goes On   208

C

Caliph's Design, The   315
Cambridge Edition of the Letters and Works of D.H. Lawrence, The   251
Campaign of 1812, and the Retreat from Moscow, The   48
Capri: Materials for a Description of the Island   110
Captain's Death Bed and Other Essays, The   471
Carchemish: A Report on the Excavations of Djerabis on Behalf of the British Museum   271
Cartagena and the Banks of the Sinu   199
Case for Christianity, The   300
Case of the Helmeted Airman, The   33
Catalogue of the H.G. Wells Collection in the Bromley Public Libraries   459
Catholic Church and Conversion, The   75

Catholic Church and History, The   49
Cave and the Mountain, The   177
Celtic Twilight, The   488
Center of Hilarity, The   93
Certain Order, A   365
Certain Personal Matters   451
Certain World, A   27
Challenge of Schweitzer, The   332
Characters and Commentaries   433
Characters of the Reformation   49
Charity   199
Charles Dickens (Chesterton)   76
Charles Dickens: A Critical Study   76
Charles the First, King of England   49
Charted Mirror, The   291
Chaucer   76
Checklist of the Hogarth Press, 1917-1938, A   474
Chesterton, Belloc, Baring   92
Chesterton: Man and Mask   97
Chesterton and the Victorian Age   86
Chesterton Calendar, A   76
Chesterton Catholic Anthology, A   81
Chesterton Continued   84
Chesterton Essays   81
Chesterton on Shakespeare   81
Christendom in Dublin   76
Christian Behaviour   301
Christian Reflections   304
Christian World of C.S. Lewis, The   309
Christmas Garland, A   37
Christocracy   333
Chronicles of Conscience   346
Cinque Ports, The   161
Classical Influences on English Prose   15
Coat of Many Colours, A   358
Coleridge on Imagination   368
Collected Essays (Huxley)   239
Collected Essays (Woolf)   472
Collected Essays, Journalism, and Letters of George Orwell   342
Collected Essays and Papers of George Saintsbury, The   387
Collected Essays in Literary Criticism   358
Collected Essays of Edmund Gosse   179

Title Index

Collected Music Criticism 408
Collected Works, The (Strachey) 432
Collected Works of Aldous Huxley 238
Collected Works of W.H. Hudson, The 224
Coloured Lands, The 81
Come to Think of It . . . a Book of Essays 81
Common Asphodel, The 208
Common Man, The 81
Common Pursuit, The 279, 325
Common Reader, The 470
Common Reader: Second Series, The 470
Common Sense of Municipal Trading, The 403
Common Sense of War and Peace, The 451
Community Farm 333
Companion to Mr. Wells's OUTLINE OF HISTORY, A 49, 461
Complete Memoirs of George Sherston, The 398
Complete Prefaces of Bernard Shaw, The 408
Concept of Freedom, The 69
Concepts of Criticism 20
Concise Cambridge History of English Literature, The 8
Concise History of Modern Painting, A 358
Concise History of Modern Sculpture, A 359
Concordance to the Plays and Prefaces of Bernard Shaw, A 410
Condemned Playground, The 98
Confessions of T.E. Lawrence, The 277
Congo Diary 103
Conquest of Death, The 333
Conquest of New Granada, The 200
Conquest of the River Plate, The 200
Conquest of Time, The 451
Conquistador, American Fantasia 219
Conrad Library, A 104
Conrad's Eastern World 105
Conrad's Manifesto 103
Conrad's Politics 105
Conrad's Prefaces to His Works 103

Conrad's Romanticism 108
Consideration of Thackeray, A 387
Considerations on Edmund Gosse 187
Contemporary Biography 11
Contemporary British Art 359
Contemporary Criticism of Literature 151, 196, 443
Contemporary Techniques of Poetry 208
Contemporary Writers 472
Contrary Experience, The 359
Contrast, The 49
Conversation with a Cat, and Others, A 49
Conversation with an Angel and Other Essays, A 49
Corrected Impressions 387
Countries of the Mind: Essays in Literary Criticism 333
Countries of the Mind: Essays in Literary Criticism: Second Series 333
County of Sussex, The 50
Count Your Dead 315
Coventry Patmore 179
Craft of Letters in England, The 7
Crane Bag, and Other Disputed Subjects, The 208
Cranmer, Archbishop of Canterbury, 1533-1556 50
Creation and Discovery 20
Crimes of England, The 76
Crisis and Criticism and Literary Writings 20
Crisis in Physics, The 69
Crisis of Our Civilization, The 50
Critical and Historical Principles of Literary History 16
Critical Approaches to Literature 16
Critical Assumptions 20
Critical Attitude, The 161
Critical Edition of Yeats's A VISION 491
Critical Essays 342
Critical Kit-Kats 179
Critical Writings of Ford Madox Ford 165
Criticism, Aesthetics and Psychology 372, 380
Criticism of Prose, The 13

Title Index

Criticism of T.S. Eliot, The 127
Cromwell 50
Crowning Privilege, The 208
Cruise of the NONA, The 50
Crusader Castles 272
Crusades, The 50
Crux Ansata 451
Crystal Spirit, The 356
C.S. Lewis (Hannay) 309
C.S. Lewis: A Biography 306
C.S. Lewis: A Critical Essay 309
C.S. Lewis: An Annotated Checklist of Writings about Him and His Works 305
C.S. Lewis: Apostle to the Skeptics 312
C.S. Lewis: Defender of the Faith 307
C.S. Lewis: Images of His World 306
C.S. Lewis: Speaker and Teacher 306
C.S. Lewis: The Shape of His Faith and Thought 309
C.S. Lewis and Some Modern Theologians 310
C.S. Lewis at the Breakfast Table and Other Reminiscences 305
C.S. Lewis on Scripture 304
Cuchulain Plays of W.B. Yeats, The 504
Cult of Sincerity, The 359
Culture and Environment 279
Culture and Society, 1780-1950 73, 299
Cultures in Conflict 287
Cunninghame Graham: A Centenary Study 205
Cunninghame Graham: A Critical Biography 205
Cutting of an Agate, The 489
Cyril Connolly (Spender) 100

D

Dante 117
Danton: A Study 51
Dark Sun, The 263
Dawn and the Darkest Hour 249
Day in Windsor, A 239

Death of the Moth and Other Essays, The 472
Defence of Cosmetics, A 37
Defence of Democracy, The 333
Defendant, The 76
Demon and Saint in the Novels of Aldous Huxley 249
Demon of Progress in the Arts, The 315
Descent from Parnassus 402
Descriptive Catalogue of the Bibliographies of 20th Century British Poets, Novelists, and Dramatists, A 4
Design and Truth in Autobiography 503
Design for Escape 369
Destructive Element, The 329
Development of English Biography, The 11
Devils of Loudon, The 239
D.H. Lawrence (Leavis) 279
D.H. Lawrence: A Basic Study of His Ideas 260
D.H. Lawrence, A Checklist 256
D.H. Lawrence, Novelist 280
D.H. Lawrence: Selected Literary Criticism 254
D.H. Lawrence: Selected Essays 253
D.H. Lawrence: The Critical Heritage 259
D.H. Lawrence: The Croydon Years 258
D.H. Lawrence: The Crusader as Critic 268
D.H. Lawrence and America 257
D.H. Lawrence and Italy 254
D.H. Lawrence and Maurice Magnus 110
D.H. Lawrence and the Idea of the Novel 270
D.H. Lawrence and the New World 258
D.H. Lawrence as a Literary Critic 261
D.H. Lawrence Companion, A 266
D.H. Lawrence in Italy 256
D.H. Lawrence in Taos 256
D.H. Lawrence on Education 254
D.H. Lawrence's American Journey 259

Title Index

D.H. Lawrence's Nightmare 256
Diabolical Principle and the Dithyrambic Spectator, The 315
Diary of Virginia Woolf, The 472
Dickens 425
Dickens, Dali and Others 342
Dickens the Novelist 280
Dictionary to the Plays and Novels of Bernard Shaw, with Bibliography of His Works and the Literature Concerning Him with a Record of the Principal Shavian Play Productions 410
Difficult Questions, Easy Answers 209
Disagreements: A Polemic on Culture in the English Democracy 346
Discarded Image, The 301
Discoveries: A Volume of Essays 489
Discoveries: Essays in Literary Criticism 333
Discursions on Travel, Art and Life 425
Doctor's Delusions 403
Documentary and Imaginative Literature, 1880-1920 6
Don Roberto: Being the Account of the Life and Works of R.B. Cunninghame Graham, 1852-1936 205
Doom of Youth 315
Doors of Perception, The 240
Doughty Deeds 200
Do We Agree? 51
Do What You Will 239
Down and Out in Paris and London, a Novel 342
Dramatic Opinions and Essays with an Apology by Bernard Shaw 403
Dramatic Personae 489
DRAMATIC PERSONAE 1896-1902, ESTRANGEMENT, THE DEATH OF SYNGE, THE BOUNTY OF SWEDEN 489
Dryden 387
Dual Heritage of Joseph Conrad, The 106
Duke, The 219
Dyer's Hand and Other Essays, The 27

E

Earlier Renaissance, The 387
Earl of Derby, The 388

Early Auden 30
Economics for Helen 51
Education and the University 280
Education for Peace 359
Education through Art 359
Education Today--and Tomorrow 27
Edwardian Occasions 7
Elected Circle, The 147
Elements of the Essay 15
Elements of the Great War, The 53
Eliot and His Age 137
Eliot in Perspective 140
Eliot's Early Years 122
Elizabeth: Creature of Circumstance 51
Elizabethan Commentary 51
Elizabeth and Essex 432
Elizabethan Essays 117
E.M. Forster (Kelvin) 175
E.M. Forster (McDowell) 175
E.M. Forster (Moore) 176
E.M. Forster: A Critical Study 173
E.M. Forster: A Life 173
E.M. Forster: An Annotated Bibliography of Secondary Materials 172
E.M. Forster: An Annotated Bibliography of Writings about Him 172
E.M. Forster: A Study 178
E.M. Forster: A Tribute 172
E.M. Forster: Selected Writings 172
E.M. Forster: The Critical Heritage 174
E.M. Forster: The Personal Voice 174
Eminent Victorians 432
Enchafèd Flood, The 27
End of the Armistice, The 81
Ends and Means 240
Enemies of Promise 98, 438
Enemy: A Biography of Wyndham Lewis, The 320
Enemy Salvoes 317
England, Your England, and Other Essays 343
England and the English 162
English Auden, The 28
English Autobiography 12
English Critics, The 396
English Essayists 13

535

Title Index

English First Editions of Hilaire Belloc, The 61
English Literary History and Bibliography 192
English Literature: An Illustrated Record 180
English Literature and Ideas in the Twentieth Century 8
English Literature between the Wars 7
English Literature in Our Time and the University 280
English Literature in the Sixteenth Century excluding Drama 301
English Literature in the Twentieth Century 6
Englishman Looks at the World, An 451
English Novel, The 388
English Novel: From the Earliest Days to the Death of Joseph Conrad, The 162
English Pastoral Poetry 153
English People, The 342
English Pottery 359
English Prose Style 15, 360
English Prosody and Modern Poetry 396
English Stained Glass 360
English Stylistics 3
English Travellers in the Near East 22
Eric and Us 344
Escape with Me! 425
Essay on the Nature of Contemporary England, An 51
Essay on the Restoration of Property, An 51
Essays (Yeats) 489
Essays, Ancient and Modern 117
Essays, 1931 to 1936 489
Essays and Introductions 491
Essays and Poems 82
Essays by G.K. Chesterton 82
Essays in English Literature, 1780-1860 388
Essays in English Literature: 1780-1860, Second Series 388
Essays in Fabian Socialism 403
Essays New and Old 240
Essays of a Catholic Layman in England 52

Essays of To-Day and Yesterday 76
Essays on French Novelists 388
Essays on Literary Criticism and the English Tradition 284
Essential R.B. Cunninghame Graham, The 203
Essential T.E. Lawrence, The 272
Esto Perpetua 52
Etruscan Places 251
Eugenics and Other Evils 76
Europe and the Faith 52
Europe in Travail 333
Evening Colonnade, The 98
Everlasting Man, The 77
Everybody's Political What's What? 404
Evolution of an Intellectual, The 333
Evolution of a Revolt 272
Experiment in Autobiography 451
Experiment in Criticism, An 301
Experiments 111
Explorations 491
Eye-Witness, The 52
Ezra Pound (Fraser) 323
Ezra Pound: His Metric and Poetry 117

F

Fabian Essays in Socialism 404
Fabianism and the Empire 404
Fabians, The 420
Fables of Aggression 324
Façades: Edith, Osbert, and Sacheverell Sitwell 429
Face of the Earth, The 445
Faith 200
Fancies versus Fads 77
Fantasia of the Unconscious 251, 255
Far Away and Long Ago 225
Fate of Homo Sapiens, The 452
Fate of Man, The 452
Father and Son 185
Father and Son: A Study of Two Temperaments 180, 185
Father Archangel of Scotland and Other Essays 202
Fathers of the Revolution 220
Feminism and Art 482

Title Index

Fern-Seed and Elephants and Other Essays on Christianity 304
Fifty Years of English Literature, 1900-1950 8
Filibuster. A Study of the Political Ideas of Wyndham Lewis, The 320
Filibusters in Barbary 315
First and Last 52
First and Last Things 452
First Book of English Literature, A 388
5 Pens in Hand 209
Five Types: A Book of Essays 77
Floor Games 452
Flourishing of Romance and the Rise of Allegory 388
Flower Show Match and Other Pieces, The 398
Flush: A Biography 470
Food for Centaurs 209
Footnote on Capri 111
For a Hudson Biographer 228
Forces in Modern British Literature, 1885-1956 9
For Continuity 280
Ford Madox Brown 162
Ford Madox Ford (Smith) 169
Ford Madox Ford (Stang) 169
Ford Madox Ford: A Study of His Novels 166
Ford Madox Ford, 1873-1939 165
Ford Madox Ford: Prose and Politics 167
Ford Madox Ford: The Critical Heritage 168
Ford Madox Ford's Novels 168
Foreshore of England, The 447
Forewords and Afterwords 28
For Lancelot Andrewes 118
Form in Modern Poetry 360
Forms of Things Unknown, The 360
'42 and '44 452
Foundations of Aesthetics, The 369
Fountains in the Sand 111
Four Absentees 338
Four Continents, The 425
Four Loves, The 301
Four Men, a Farrago, The 52
Free Press, The 52
Free Society, The 334

French Literature and Its Masters 392
French Profiles 179, 180
French Revolution, The 52
Freud and the Critic 19
F.R. Leavis (Greenwood) 290
F.R. Leavis (Walsh) 298
F.R. Leavis: A Check-List 283
F.R. Leavis, Judgment and the Discipline of Thought 285
From Pampas to Hedgerows and Downs 230
From Puzzles to Portraits 10
From Shakespeare to Pope 180
From Surtees to Sassoon 401
Frontiers of Criticism, The 118
Function of Literature, The 72
Further Speculations by T.E. Hulme 231, 232
Further Studies in a Dying Culture 69
Future in America, The 452
Future of Political Science in America, The 404
Fyodor Dostoevsky: A Critical Study 334

G

Gallery, A 219
Gauchos of the Pampas and Their Horses 203, 227
GBS/GKC: Shaw and Chesterton, the Metaphysical Jesters 90
Generally Speaking: A Book of Essays 77
General Sketch of the European War: The First Phase 53
General Sketch of the European War: The Second Phase, A 53
George Bernard Shaw (Chesterton) 77, 415
George Bernard Shaw (Hill) 418
George Bernard Shaw: Man of the Century 412
George Bernard Shaw on Language 408
George Edward Bateman Saintsbury 394
George Herbert 118
George Orwell (Brander) 346

Title Index

George Orwell (Hopkinson) 348
George Orwell (Kalechofsky) 348
George Orwell (Oxley) 351
George Orwell (Williams) 355
George Orwell: A Life 344
George Orwell: A Literary and Biographical Study 345
George Orwell: An Annotated Bibliography of Criticism 344
George Orwell: Fugitive from the Camp of Victory 351
George Orwell: The Critical Heritage 350
George Orwell: The Ethical Imagination 345
George Orwell as Essayist 352
George Saintsbury (Leuba) 395
Georgian Literary Scene, 1910-1935, The 8
Gerard Manley Hopkins 280
G.F. Watts 77
Gifts of Fortune with Some Hints for Those about to Travel 445
Gilbert Keith Chesterton 86
G.K.C. as M.C.: Being a Collection of Thirty-Seven Introductions by G.K.C. 82
G.K. Chesterton (Clipper) 87
G.K. Chesterton (Evans) 89
G.K. Chesterton (Hollis) 90
G.K. Chesterton (Ward) 84
G.K. Chesterton: A Bibliography 84
G.K. Chesterton: A Biography 84
G.K. Chesterton: A Centenary Appraisal 96
G.K. Chesterton: A Critical Study 97
G.K. Chesterton--A Criticism 87
G.K. Chesterton: An Anthology 82
G.K. Chesterton: A Portrait 84
G.K. Chesterton: A Selection from His Non-Fictional Prose 82
G.K. Chesterton: Explorations in Allegory 91
G.K. Chesterton: Radical Populist 87
G.K. Chesterton: The Critical Judgments 88
G.K. Chesterton and Hilaire Belloc 63, 88

G.K. Chesterton and His Biographer 87
G.K. Chesterton's Evangel 93
Glass Walking-Stick, and Other Essays from THE ILLUSTRATED LONDON NEWS, 1905-1936, The 82
Gleaming Cohort, A 82
God: Being an Introduction to the Science of Metabiology 334
God and Mr. Wells 460
God Approached, The 156
God in the Dock 304
God the Invisible King 452
Golden Codgers 11
Golden Nightingale, The 504
Goldsworthy Lowes Dickinson 171
Goodbye to All That 209, 400
Goodbye to Western Culture 111
Gossip in a Library 180
Grand Man 113
Granite and Rainbow 472
Grass Roots of Art, The 360
Gray 180
Great Composers, The 408
Great Deluge, The 493
Great Heresies, The 53
Great Inquiry, The 53
Great Morning! 426
Great Short Works of Aldous Huxley 243
Great Trade Route 162
Great Tradition, The 281
Greek Myths, The 209
Grey Eminence 240
Grief Observed, A 301
Guide to the New World 453

H

Half-Century of Eliot Criticism, A 121
Hampshire Days 225
Handful of Authors, A 82
Hans Holbein the Younger 162
Hatchment, A 200
Heart of the Country, The 162
Heaven--and Earth 334
Heaven and Hell 240
Hebrew Myths, The 209

Title Index

Henry James: A Critical Study 162
Henry James and H.G. Wells 457
Henry James and the Criticism of Virginia Woolf 479
Henry Moore: A Study of His Life and Work 360
Herbert George Wells: An Annotated Bibliography of His Works 458
Herbert Read (Berry) 364
Herbert Read: A Memorial Symposium 364
Herbert Read: Selected Writings 363
Herbert Read: The Stream and the Source 364, 367
Heretics 77
Hernando de Soto: Together with an Account of One of His Captains, Goncalo Silvestre 200
Heroes of Thought 334
Heroes' Twilight 6
Hero or Fool? 309
H.G. Wells (Belgion) 461
H.G. Wells (Beresford) 461
H.G. Wells (Brown) 462
H.G. Wells (Costa) 462
H.G. Wells (Young) 469
H.G. Wells: A Biography 460
H.G. Wells: A Comprehensive Bibliography 458
H.G. Wells: Discoverer of the Future 464
H.G. Wells: Early Writings in Science and Science Fiction 457
H.G. Wells: Educationist 463
H.G. Wells: His Turbulent Life and Times 460
H.G. Wells: Journalism and Prophecy, 1893-1946 457
H.G. Wells: Personality, Character, Topography 464
H.G. Wells: The Critical Heritage 459
H.G. Wells and His Critics 459
H.G. Wells and the World State 468
H.G. Wells's Literary Criticism 457
Hilaire Belloc (Haynes) 63
Hilaire Belloc: A Memoir 62
Hilaire Belloc: An Anthology of His Prose and Verse 61
Hilaire Belloc: An Introduction to His Spirit and Work 63

Hilaire Belloc: Edwardian Radical 65
Hilaire Belloc: No Alienated Man 68
Hilaire Belloc: The Man and His Work 66
Hilaire Belloc Keeps the Bridge 67
Hilaire Belloc's Prefaces 61
Hilaire Belloc's Stories, Essays, and Poems 61
Hill of Devi, The 171
Hills and the Sea 53
Hind in Richmond Park, A 225
His People 201
Historical Manual of English Prosody 389, 392
Historic Thames, The 53
History of Criticism and Literary Taste in Europe from the Earliest Texts to the Present Day, A 389
History of Eighteenth Century Literature, 1660-1780 181
History of Elizabethan Literature, A 389
History of England, A 53
History of English Criticism, A 389
History of English Prose Rhythm, A 15, 389
History of English Prosody 389
History of English Prosody from the Twelfth Century to the Present Day, A 389
History of Nineteenth Century Literature (1780-1895), A 389
History of the French Novel (to the Close of the 19th Century), A 390
Hitler 315
Hitler Cult, The 316
H.M. Tomlinson (Crawford) 448
H.M. Tomlinson: A Selection from His Writings 448
Holy Face and Other Essays 241
Homage to Catalonia 343
Homage to John Dryden 118
Homage to Oceania 350
Honours Physiography 453
Hope 201
Horses of the Conquest, The 201, 203

Title Index

House of Commons and Monarchy, The 54
How About Europe? 111
How the Reformation Happened 54
How to Become a Musical Critic 408
How to Read a Page 369
How to Teach Reading 281
Hudson Anthology, A 227
Hundred Days, The 220
Hundredth Year, The 220
Hundred Years, The 220
Huxleys, The 244

I

I.A. Richards' Theory of Literature 372, 383
Ibsen 181
Icon and Idea 360
Idea of a Christian Society, The 118
Ideas and Places 98
Ideas of Good and Evil 489
Identity of Yeats, The 497
Idle Days in Patagonia 226
Idylls of the Queen 220
If I Were Four-and-Twenty 489
Ignes Fatui, a Book of Parodies 220
Illusion and Reality 69
Image of Man in C.S. Lewis, The 313
Imagism and the Imagists 234
Imprisonment 404
Incomparable Max, The 39
In Defence of Shelley and Other Essays 360
Independence Day, a Sketch Book 220
Index to G.K. Chesterton, An 96
Inklings, The 305
Innocent Eye, The 357
Inside Out 10
Inside the Whale and Other Essays 343
Intelligent Woman's Guide to Socialism and Capitalism, The 404
Inter Arma 181
Interests of Criticism, The 16
Interpretation in Teaching 369
In the Fourth Year 453
Invisible Poet: T.S. Eliot, The 136

Ipane, The 201
Irish Impressions 77
Irish Indiscretions 505
Italy, France and Britain at War 456
I Told You So! 460
It Was the Nightingale 163

J

Jacobean Poets, The 181
James the Second 54
Jeremy Taylor 181
Jesting Pilate 241
Jesus, Man of Genius 335
Jews, The 54
Jews: Are They Human?, The 316
J. Middleton Murry: Selected Criticism: 1916-1957 337
Joan of Arc 54
John Clare and Other Studies 334
John Dryden: The Poet, the Dramatist, the Critic 118
John Middleton Murry (Griffin) 339
John Middleton Murry (Mairet) 340
Jonathan Swift 334
Jose Antonio Paez 201
Joseph Conrad: A Critical Biography 104
Joseph Conrad: An Annotated Bibliography of Writings about Him 104
Joseph Conrad: A Personal Remembrance 163
Joseph Conrad: The Major Phase 105
Joseph Conrad: The Three Lives 104
Joseph Conrad and His Circle 167
Joseph Conrad and the Fiction of Autobiography 107
Joseph Conrad at Midcentury 104
Joseph Conrad on Fiction 103
Journey through Despair, 1880-1914 8
Journey to a War 27
Journey to Heartbreak 413
Journey with Genius 256
Joyful Christian, The 304

K

Katherine Mansfield and Other

Title Index

Literary Portraits 334
Katherine Mansfield and Other Literary Studies 337
Keats 334
Keats and Shakespeare 335
Knowledge and Experience in the Philosophy of F.H. Bradley 118

L

Landmarks in French Literature 432
Land's End, The 226
Language, Thought, and Comprehension 379
Language and Style 15
Language of Criticism, The 16
Language of Fiction 292
Languages of Criticism and the Structure of Poetry, The 16
Lars Porsena: Or the Future of Swearing and Improper Language 210
Last Books of H.G. Wells, The 458
Last Days of the French Monarchy, The 54
Last Essays 103
Last Man in Europe, The 352
Last Rally, The 55
Last Scrap Book, A 390
Last Theatres, 1904-1910 39
Last Vintage, A 392
Late Harvest 111
Later Auden, The 31
Later D.H. Lawrence, The 254
Later Nineteenth Century, The 390
Laughing Prophet, The 86
Laughter in the Next Room 426
Lawrence, Hardy, and American Literature 268
Lawrence and Brett 256
Lawrence and the Arabian Adventure 210, 274
Lawrence and the Arabs 210
Lawrence of Arabia: A Biographical Enquiry 274
Lawrence of Arabia: A Triumph 274
Lawrence of Arabia: The Literary Impulse 278
Learning ASIC English 369
Leaves and Fruit 181
Leavis (Hayman) 283

Leavises, the "Social," and the Left, The 298
Lectures in America 281
Left Hand, Right Hand! 426
Left Wings over Europe 316
Legal Eight Hours Question, The 405
Leo Tolstoy 77
Leslie Stephen: His Thought and Character in Relation to His Time 436
Letter Book, A 390
Letters from Iceland 28
Letters to Malcolm 302
Letters to the New Island 491
Letter to a Young Painter, A 361
Letter to Mrs. Virginia Woolf 483
Letter to My Son, A 426
Liberators, with Portraits by F.K. Kormis, The 220
Library of Literary Criticism, A 4
Lies of Art, The 42
Life and Ideas of Sanderson of Oundle, The 456
Life and Letters of John Donne 181
Life and Letters of Sir Edmund Gosse, The 186
Life and Opinions of T.E. Hulme, The 231, 232
Life and Thought of H.G. Wells, The 465
Life and Works of Ford Madox Ford, The 166
Life in the Fiction of Ford Madox Ford, The 168
Life of Algernon Charles Swinburne, The 182
Life of Hilaire Belloc, The 62
Life of Jesus, The 335
Life of John Middleton Murry, The 338
Life of Philip Henry Gosse, F.R.S., The 182
Life of William Congreve 182
Light on C.S. Lewis 306
Limited Hero in the Novels of Ford Madox Ford, The 168
Linguistics and Literary Style 14
Lion and the Fox, The 316
Lion and the Unicorn, The 343

541

Title Index

Literary Biography (Edel) 11
Literary Biography (Ellmann) 11
Literary Criticism 21
Literary Criticism of F.R. Leavis, The 285
Literary Criticism of T.S. Eliot, The 140
Literary Critics, The 20
Literary Essay in English, The 14
Literary Essays 433
Literary Legacy of C.S. Lewis, The 313
Literature and Science 241
Literature of Politics, The 118
Little Wars 453
Lives and Letters 10
Living Principle, The 281
Logic and Criticism 20, 382
London Music in 1888-89 405
London River 445
London Scene, The 472
London Street Games 111
Lonely Tower, The 499
Long Week-End, The 210
Looking Back 111
Looking before and after 335
Lorenzo in Search of the Sun 256
Lorenzo in Taos 256
Louis XIV 55
Love, Freedom and Society 335
Love among the Haystacks and Other Pieces 254
Loving Friends, The 435
Lunacy and Letters 83
Lyrical Novel, The 477
Lytton Strachey (Beerbohm) 37, 436
Lytton Strachey (Boas) 436
Lytton Strachey (Clemens) 437
Lytton Strachey (Scott-James) 443
Lytton Strachey: A Bibliography 434
Lytton Strachey: A Critical Biography. Vol. 1: The Unknown Years 1880-1910 435
Lytton Strachey: A Critical Biography. Vol. 2: The Years of Achievement 1910-1932 435
Lytton Strachey: A Critical Study 440
Lytton Strachey: An Essay 437
Lytton Strachey: His Mind and Art 434, 435
Lytton Strachey: The Really Interesting Question and Other Papers 434
Lytton Strachey and the Bloomsbury Group 435

M

Mainly on the Air 38
Majorca Observed 210
Making, Knowing, and Judging 28
Making of George Orwell, The 345
Making of the Auden Canon, The 29
Malay Waters 446
Mammon and the Black Goddess 210
Manchester 390
Mankind in the Making 453
Man's Natural Powers 312
Man's Place 34
Man Who Was Chesterton: A Centenary Essay 1874-1974, The 95
Man Who Was Chesterton: The Best Essays, Stories, Poems and Other Writings of G.K. Chesterton, The 83
Man Who Was Orthodox, The 83
March of Literature, The 163
Marianne Thornton: A Domestic Biography 171
Marie Antoinette 55
Marlborough 390
Mars His Idiot 446
Marx, Engels, and the Poets 17
Mass Civilization and Minority Culture 281
Master of Our Time, A 323
Masters and Men 220
Matter with Ireland, The 408
Matthew Arnold 391
Max, a Biography 41
Max and the Americans 44
Max Beerbohm (McElderry) 44
Max Beerbohm: Selected Essays 39
Max Beerbohm in Perspective 44
Meaning of Art, The 361
Meaning of Dreams, The 210
Meaning of Meaning, The 370
Memoirs of a Fox-Hunting Man 398
Memoirs of an Infantry Officer, by the Author of MEMOIRS OF A FOX-HUNTING MAN 398

Title Index

Memoirs of George Sherston 398
Memoirs of W.B. Yeats 492
Memories 402
Memories and Impressions 161
Men and Supermen 421
Mencius on the Mind 370
Men in Print 272
Men of Affairs 221
Men of Letters 221
Men of War 221
Men without Art 316
Mere Christianity 302
Meredith 399
Merrill Checklist of T.S. Eliot, The 121
Metaphors of Self 12
Metri Gratia 221
Metropolitan Critic, The 292
Middle East, 1940-1942, a Study in Air Power 221
Middleton Murry: A Study in Excellent Normality 340
Mightier Than the Sword 163
Milton 55
Milton's God 153
Milton's Grand Style 295
Mind at the End of Its Tether 453
Mind Awake, A 304
Mind of Chesterton, The 90
Minerva Edition of the Works of G.K. Chesterton 74
Mingled Yard, A 446
Miniatures of French History 55
Minoan Distance, The 258
Mint, The 271
Miracles: A Preliminary Study 302
Mirages 201
Mirror of the Sea, The 102
Mirror to France, A 163
Miscellaneous Essays 391
Miscellany of Men, A 78
Missing Muse and Other Essays, The 221
Modern Age, The 7
Modern Conquistador, A 205
Modern English Literature 8
Modern Movement, The 99
Modern Poetry 490
Modern Prose Style 13
Modern Utopia, A 453

Modern Writer and His World, The 7
Mogreb-El-Acksa 201
Moment and Other Essays, The 472
Moment of SCRUTINY, The 294
Moments of Being 473
Monarch: A Study of Louis XIV 55
More 38
More Books on the Table 182, 439
More Theatres 1898-1903 39
Mornings in Mexico 252
Movements in English Literature, 1900-1940 7
Movements in European History 252
Movements in Modern English Poetry and Prose 330
Mr. Belloc Objects to THE OUTLINE OF HISTORY 68, 453
Mr. Belloc Still Objects to Mr. Wells's OUTLINE OF HISTORY 55, 461
Mr. Bennett and Mrs. Brown 470
Mr. Churchill, a Portrait 221
Mr. Wells' INVISIBLE KING 461
Mrs. Fisher: Or the Future of Humour 211
Mrs. Markham's New History of England 55
Mr. Wells as Historian 464
Music at Night and Other Essays 241
Music in London, 1890-94 405
My Dear Dorothea 408
My Dear Wells 465
Mysterious Mr. Bull, The 316
Mystery of Keats, The 335
Mythologies 492

N

Napoleon 56
Napoleon's Campaign of 1812 48
Nations and Peace 370
Naturalist in La Plata, The 226
Nature and Culture in D.H. Lawrence 258
Nature in Downland 226
Nature of Biography, The 11
Nature of Literature 358
Nazarene Gospel Restored, The 211
Necessity of Communism, The 335
Necessity of Pacifism, The 335

Title Index

Nest of Tigers, A 429
New Age under Orage, The 235
New America, the New World, The 454
New Apologists for Poetry, The 18
New Bearings in English Poetry 281
New Cambridge Bibliography of English Literature, The 5
New Jerusalem, The 78
New World Order, The 454
New Worlds for Old 454
New York Essays 163
New York Is Not America 163
Noble Essences of Courteous Revelations 426
No Enemy 163
Non-Fictional Works of H.G. Wells, The 450
Norman Douglas (Greenlees) 115
Norman Douglas (Leary) 115
Norman Douglas (Lindeman) 115
Norman Douglas (Tomlinson) 116, 446
Norman Douglas: A Biography 114
Norman Douglas: A Pictorial Record 114
Norman Douglas: A Selection from His Works 113
Nor Shall My Sword 282
Northern Studies 182
Notes on a Cellar-Book 391, 392
Notes on Life and Letters 102
Notes on Some Figures behind T.S. Eliot 122, 324
Notes on the District of Menteith for Tourists and Others 201
Notes towards the Definition of Culture 119
Novelist of Three Worlds 169
Novels of George Meredith and Some Notes on the English Novel, The 427

O

Occupation: Writer 211
Of Other Worlds 304
Old Calabria 112
Old Century and Seven More Years, The 399
Old Friends 436
Old Gang and the New Gang, The 316
Old Gods Falling 189
Old Junk 446
Old Road (from Canterbury to Winchester), The 56
Olive Tree and Other Essays, The 241
On 56
On Anything 56
One Day 112
One Mighty Torrent 11
On English Poetry 211
One Thing and Another 61
On Everything 56
On Nothing and Kindred Subjects 56
On Poetry: Collected Talks and Essays 211
On Poetry and Poets 119
On Running after One's Hat and Other Whimsies 83
On Sailing the Sea 61
On Something 56
On the Boiler 490
On the Margin 241
On the Place of Gilbert Chesterton in English Letters 56, 85
Open Conspiracy, The 454
Orators, The 28
Oriental Assembly 272
Origins of Form in Art, The 361
Orthodoxy 78
Orwell (Thomas) 353
Orwell and the Left 356
Orwell Reader, The 343
Orwell's Fiction 350
Osbert Sitwell 430
Other Harmony of Prose, The 13
Our Examination Round His Factification for Incamination of Work in Progress 320
Our Theatres in the Nineties 405
Outline of H.G. Wells, The 463
Outline of History, The 454
Outline of Sanity, The 78
Outlook for Homo Sapiens, The 452, 454
Out of Soundings 446
Outside the Whale 349

Title Index

Oxford Addresses on Poetry   211
Oxford's Legendary Son   274

P

Packet for Ezra Pound, A   490
Paleface: The Philosophy of the "Melting-Pot"   316
Palmerston, 1784-1865   222
Pamphlet against Anthologies, A   212
Paneros   112
Paradise Lost in Our Time   128
Paradox in Chesterton   91
Paradox of George Orwell, The   354
Pargiters, The   473
Paris   57
Partial Critics, The   19
Partition of Europe, a Textbook of European History, 1715-1815, The   222
Party System, The   57
Path to Rome, The   57
Patterns of Love and Courtesy   310
Les Pavillons   99
Peace Conference Hints   405
Peace of the Augustans, The   391
Pearl of Days, The   191
Pedro de Valdivia: Conqueror of Chile   202
Peep into the Past and Other Prose Pieces   40
Pencillings: Little Essays on Literature   335
Penny Foolish   427
Pen Portraits and Reviews   96, 405
People's Album of London Statues, The   427
Per Amica Silentia Lunae   490
Perennial Philosophy, The   241
Perfect Wagnerite, The   406
Personal Heresy, The   302
Personal Record, A   102
Pharos and Pharillon   171
Phases of English Poetry   361
Philip Ayres   391
Philosophy of Modern Art, The   361
Philosophy of Rhetoric, The   370
Phoenix: A Summary of the Inescapable Conditions of World Reorganisation   454
Phoenix: The Posthumous Papers of D.H. Lawrence   254

Phoenix II: Uncollected Unpublished, and Other Prose Works by D.H. Lawrence   254
Picked Company   60
Pitchman's Melody, Shaw about "Shakespeare"   419
Places   57
Platform and Pulpit   408
Plays and Controversies   490
Plays and Players   408
Pledge of Peace, The   336
Poet as Critic, The   19
Poetic Art of W.H. Auden, The   31
Poetic Craft and Principle   212
Poetic Unreason and Other Studies   212
Poetry and Contemplation   378-79
Poetry and Drama   119
Poetry and Experience   362
Poetry and Ireland   490
Poetry and Morality   128, 286
Poetry in Prose   13
Poetry of W.B. Yeats, The   502
Poetry of W.H. Auden, The   36
Poets, Critics, Mystics   337
Points: Second Series, 1866-1934   434
Points of View   120
Polish Heritage of Joseph Conrad, The   104
Political Madhouse in America   404
Politics of the Unpolitical, The   362
Pope   433
Pornography and Obscenity   252
Portable Bernard Shaw, The   409
Portable D.H. Lawrence, The   255
Portrait of a Dictator   202
Portrait of Max   40
Portraits and Sketches   182
Portraits from Life   163
Portraits in Miniature, and Other Essays   433
Poste Restante   256
Pound Wise   427
Practical Criticism   370
Practical Politics   409
Prefaces and Essays   393
Prefaces by Bernard Shaw   406
Preface to PARADISE LOST, A   302
Pre-Raphaelite Brotherhood, The   164

Title Index

Present Age in British Literature, The 7
Previous Convictions 99
Price of Leadership, The 336
Priest of Love, The 257
Primer of French Literature 391
Prince-Errant and Evocator of Horizons 206
Prince of Our Disorder, A 274
Principles of Literary Criticism 20, 370
Private Shaw and Public Shaw 275
Problem of Pain, The 302
Problem of Style, The 14, 336
Progress and Other Sketches 202
Proper Studies 242
Prophets and Poets 441
Propos of LADY CHATTERLEY'S LOVER, A 252
Prose Literature since 1939 134
Prose Rhythm in English 394
Prose Styles 13
Provence: From Minstrels to the Machine 164
Psychoanalysis and the Unconscious 252, 255
Psychological Milieu of Lytton Strachey, The 440
Pyrenees, The 57

Q

Queen Mary and Others 428
Queen Victoria 433
Quest for the Necessary 34
Question and the Answer, The 57
Questions at Issue 182
Quintessence of Ibsenism, The 406

R

Rag-Time and Tango 222
Rainbow and Granite 486
Raleigh 183
Rare, Vanishing and Lost British Birds 227
Rationalization of Russia, The 409
Razor Edge of Balance, The 483
Reactionaries, a Study of the Anti-Democratic Intelligentsia, W.B.

Yeats, Wyndham Lewis, Ezra Pound, T.S. Eliot, D.H. Lawrence, The 134, 324
Reader over Your Shoulder, The 14, 212
Readers and Writers (1917-1921) 326
Reader's Art, The 478
Reader's Guide to George Orwell, A 350
Reader's Guide to Joseph Conrad, A 106
Reader's Guide to T.S. Eliot, A 151
Reason and Romanticism 362
Redeemed and Other Sketches 202
Redemption of the Robot, The 362
Reflection on the Psalms 302
Reflections on the Death of a Porcupine 252
Rehabilitations and Other Essays 303
Reminiscences of D.H. Lawrence 336
Reputations. Essays in Criticism 323
Resurrection of Rome, The 78
Return to Chesterton 85
Return to the Baltic 57
Return to Yesterday 164
Revaluation 282
Reveries over Childhood and Youth 490
Revolt in the Desert 271
Richelieu, a Study 57
Rights of Man, The 455
Rise and Fall of the Man of Letters, The 17
River of London 58
Road, The 58
Road to Equality, The 409
Road to Miniluv, The 353
Road to Wigan Pier, The 343
Robert Browning (Chesterton) 78
Robert Browning: Personalia 183
Robert Graves (Cohen) 214
Robert Graves (Seymour-Smith) 216
Robert Graves (Stade) 217
Robert Graves: Peace-Weaver 216
Robert Graves and the White Goddess 217
Robert Louis Stevenson 78
Robespierre: A Study 58
Rodeo: A Collection of Tales and Sketches of R.B. Cunninghame Graham 203

Title Index

Roger Fry: A Biography 471
Romance and Realism 70
Romantic Image 137, 500
Room of One's Own, A 471
Rossetti: A Critical Essay on His Art 164
Rotunda: A Selection from the Works of Aldous Huxley 242
Royalist in Politics, T.S. Eliot and Political Philosophy 149
Rude Assignment 317
Rural Tradition, The 22
Russia in the Shadows 455

S

Sacred Wood, The 119
Saddest Story, The 166
St. Francis of Assisi 78
Saintsbury Miscellany, A 393
St. Thomas Aquinas 78
Salvaging of Civilization, The 455
Sanity of Art, The 406
Sassoon Dynasty, The 400
Sassoons, The 400
Scarlet Tree, The 427
Scepticism and Poetry 380
Science, Liberty and Peace 242
Science and Poetry 371
Science of Life, The 455
Scottish Stories 202
Scrap Book, A 391
Sea and Sardinia 253
Sea and the Jungle, The 447
Season of Youth 188
Secondary Worlds 28
Second Common Reader, The 470
Second Empire, The 222
Second Scrap Book, A 391
Secret Dispatches from Arabia 272
Secrets of Crewe House 458
Seeing through Everything 327
Select Conversations with an Uncle (Now Extinct) and Two Other Reminiscences 455
Selected Criticism (Yeats) 492
Selected Essays (Auden) 28
Selected Essays (Chesterton) 83
Selected Essays (Eliot) 17
Selected Essays, First Series 183

Selected Essays, 1917-1932 119
Selected Essays, Second Series 183
Selected Essays of Hilaire Belloc 61
Selected Literary Essays 304
Selected Non-Dramatic Writings of Bernard Shaw 409
Selected Passages from the Works of Bernard Shaw 409
Selected Poetry and Prose of Robert Graves 213
Selected Prose (Eliot) 120
Selected Prose (Shaw) 409
Selected Prose (Yeats) 492
Selected Prose of T.S. Eliot 120
Selected Writings of Cunninghame Graham 204
Selection from AROUND THEATRES, A 38, 40
Senate Speeches of W.B. Yeats, The 492
Sense of Glory, The 362
Servile State, The 58
Seven Men 38
Seven Men and Two Others 38
Seven Pillars of Wisdom 271
Seventeenth Century Studies 179, 183
Seven Types of Ambiguity 153
Seven Writers of the English Left 70
Sex, Literature and Censorship 255
Shakespeare (Murry) 336
Shakespeare (Saintsbury) 393
Shavian Guide to the Intelligent Woman, A 424
Shaw: An Autobiography 409
Shaw--"The Chucker-Out" 415
Shaw: The Style and the Man 421
Shaw and Christianity 413
Shaw and Ibsen 409
Shaw and Society 410
Shaw and the Doctors 414
Shaw and the Play of Ideas 424
Shaw Gives Himself Away 406
Shaw in His Time 415
Shaw on Education 422
Shaw on Music 410
Shaw on Religion 410
Shaw on Theatre 410
Shaw on Vivisection 410
Shaw's Dramatic Criticism (1895-98) 410

Title Index

Shaw's Moral Vision 423
Shepherd's Life, A 226
Sherston's Progress 399
Shilling for My Thoughts, A 83
Shooting an Elephant and Other Essays 343
Shorter History of England 58
Shorter Strachey, The 434
Short History of England, A 79
Short History of English Literature, A 392
Short History of French Literature, A 392
Short History of Modern English Literature, A 183
Short History of the Life and Writings of Alain Rene Le Sage, A 392
Short History of the World, A 455
Short Talks with the Dead, and Others 58
Sidelights on New London and Newer York, and Other Essays 79
Siegfried Sassoon: A Critical Study 401
Siegfried Sassoon: A Memorial Exhibition 400
Siegfried Sassoon: Poet's Pilgrimage 399
Siegfried's Journey, 1916-1920 399
Silence of the Sea, and Other Essays, The 58
Silhouettes 184
Sing High! Sing Low! 427
Sir Edmund Gosse 197
Siren Land 112
Sir Herbert Read 363
Sir Max Beerbohm: Bibliographical Notes 40
Sir Max Beerbohm, Man and Writer 45
Sir Thomas Browne 184
Sir Thomas Browne: A Biographical and Critical Study 191
Sir Walter Scott 392
Six British Battles 58
Six Studies in Quarrelling 459
Sixteen Self Sketches 406
Social Forces in England and America 451
Socialism and Superior Brains 406

Socialism of Shaw, The 410
Socialist Woman's Guide to Intelligence, The 419
Soldier of Humor and Selected Writings, A 318
Solitary in the Ranks 274
Some Aspects of H.G. Wells 461
Some Diversions of a Man of Letters 184
Some Errors of H.G. Wells 463
Some Reminiscences 102
Some Thoughts on Hilaire Belloc 62
Some Versions of Pastoral 153
So Much Nearer 371
Son of Woman 336
Soul of London, The 164
South American Sketches of R.B. Cunninghame Graham, The 204
South to Cadiz 447
Spectatorial Essays 434
Speculations 232
Speculative Instruments 371
Spenser's Images of Life 305
Spice of Life, and Other Essays, The 83
Spirit of the People, The 164
Standard Edition of the Works of Bernard Shaw, The 403
Stane Street, The 59
Statement of the Evidence in Chief of George Bernard Shaw before the Joint-Committee on Stage Plays (Censorship and Theatre Licensing) 407
Steps: Stories, Talks, Essays, Poems, Studies in History 212
Still Life 222
Stories, Essays, and Poems 84
Story of a Great Schoolmaster, The 455
Strachey Family, 1588-1932, The 435
Structure of Complex Words, The 153, 377
Studies and Further Studies in a Dying Culture 70
Studies in a Dying Culture 70
Studies in Classic American Literature 253
Studies in Keats 336

Title Index

Studies in Keats: New and Old 336
Studies in Medieval and Renaissance Literature 305
Studies in the Literature of Northern Europe 184
Studies in Words 303
Study of George Orwell: The Man and His Works, A 348
Style 14
Style and Proportion 14
Style and Stylistics (Hough) 14
Style and Stylistics (Milic) 4
Success 202
Summer Islands 112
Supers and Supermen 222
Superstition of Divorce, The 79
Surprised by Joy 303
Surprise of Excellence, The 45
Survey of Modernist Poetry, A 212
Survival of English, The 295
Survivals and New Arrivals 59
Sussex 59
Swan and Shadow 506
Swifter Than Reason 214
Swinburne 184
Symbolic Meaning, The 255
Symbolism of Virginia Woolf, The 486
Symposium of Opinions upon THE OUTLINE OF HISTORY by H.G. Wells 466
Symposium on Formalist Criticism, A 17
Synge and the Ireland of His Time 490

T

Tactics and Strategy of the Great Duke of Marlborough, The 59
Talent of T.S. Eliot, The 151
Tales My Father Taught Me 428
Talking to India 343
Taste for the Other, The 310
Techniques in Language Control 371
T.E. Hulme (Roberts) 236
T.E. Lawrence (Stewart) 274
T.E. Lawrence (Tabachnick) 277
T.E. Lawrence: A Bibliography (Duval) 273
T.E. Lawrence: A Bibliography (Meyers) 273
T.E. Lawrence: A Reader's Guide 273
T.E. Lawrence: The Search for the Absolute 275
T.E. Lawrence by His Friends 274
Tenth Muse, The 362
Testimony to Hilaire Belloc 62
Text-Book of Biology 456
Texts and Pretexts 242
Themes and Variations 242
Theory and Personality 139
Theory of Criticism (Hobsbaum) 17
Theory of Criticism (Krieger) 18
Theory of My Time, A 340
They Asked for a Paper 303
Thing, The 79
Things to Come 337
Thirteen Stories 203
Thirty Tales and Sketches 204
This and That, and the Other 59
Thomas Carlyle 79
Thought, Words and Creativity 282
Thoughts after Lambeth 119
Thoughts in the Wilderness 294
Three French Moralists, and the Gallantry of France 184
Three Guineas 471
Three of Them 112
Three Persons 276
Three Sitwells, The 429
Three Voices of Poetry, The 119
Thus to Revisit 164
Tide Marks 447
Time and Western Man 317
To Criticize the Critic and Other Writings 120
Today the Struggle 34
Together 112
To Hell with Culture and Other Essays on Art and Society 363
To Keep Faith 338
Tomorrow and Tomorrow and Tomorrow 238
To the Unknown God 337
Toward a Recognition of Androgyny 439
Toward WOMEN IN LOVE 265
Towns of Destiny 59
Transformations 378
Transitional Age in British Literature, 1880-1920, The 4

Title Index

Transposition and Other Addresses 303
Traveller in Little Things, A 227
Travels of a Republican Radical in Search of Hot Water 456
Tremendous Trifles 79
Triad of Genius 431
Trio: Dissertations on Some Aspect of National Genius 428
True Voice of Feeling, The 363
Truth about the New Party (and Much Else Besides Concerning Sir Oswald Mosley's Political Aims, the "Nazi" Movement of Herr Adolph Hitler, and the Adventure in Political Philosophy of Mr. Wyndham Lewis), The 326
Truth Is More Sacred 363
T.S. Eliot (Bergonzi) 122
T.S. Eliot (Bradbrook) 127
T.S. Eliot (Cattani) 129
T.S. Eliot (Headings) 134
T.S. Eliot (Spender) 123
T.S. Eliot (Unger) 149
T.S. Eliot: A Bibliography 121
T.S. Eliot: A Bibliography of Secondary Works 122
T.S. Eliot: A Collection of Critical Essays 136
T.S. Eliot, Aesthetics and History 133
T.S. Eliot: A Memoir 123
T.S. Eliot: A Selected Critique 122, 149
T.S. Eliot: A Symposium for His Seventieth Birthday 127
T.S. Eliot: His Mind and Art 133
T.S. Eliot: Metaphor and Metonymy, a Study of His Essays and Plays in Terms of Roman Jakobson's Typology 141
T.S. Eliot: Moments and Patterns 149
T.S. Eliot: The Critic as Philosopher 133
T.S. Eliot: The Dialectical Structure of His Theory of Poetry 139
T.S. Eliot: The Literary and Social Criticism 124
T.S. Eliot: The Man and His Work 123

T.S. Eliot: The Metaphysical Perspective 148
T.S. Eliot: The Pattern in the Carpet 145
T.S. Eliot: The Poet and His Critics 121
T.S. Eliot and Education 125
T.S. Eliot and the Idea of Tradition 139
T.S. Eliot Criticism in English, 1916-1965 121
T.S. Eliot's Concept of Language 124
T.S. Eliot's Dramatic Theory and Practice, from Sweeney Agonistes to the Elder Statesman 146
T.S. Eliot's Impersonal Theory of Poetry 124
T.S. Eliot's Intellectual and Poetic Development, 1909-1922 133
T.S. Eliot's Intellectual Development 1922-1939 139
T.S. Eliot's Social Criticism 137
T.S. Eliot's Theory of Poetry 143
Turn of the Tide, The 447
Twelve Types 79
Twenties, The 324
Twentieth Century British Literature 4
Twentieth-Century English Literature, 1901-1960 9
Twilight in Italy 253
Two Cheers for Democracy 171
Two Cultures? 282
Two Maps of Europe, and Some Other Aspects of the Great War, The 59
Two Marshals, The 222
Two Visits to Denmark 184

U

Uncollected Prose of W.B. Yeats, I 492
Uncollected Prose of W.B. Yeats, II 492
Under the Red Ensign 447
Unicorn, The 502
Universe of G.B.S., The 413
Unknown Orwell, The 345

Title Index

Unprofessional Essays 337
Unquiet Grave, The 99
Unrepentant Pilgrim, The 422
Use of Imagination, The 269
Use of Poetry and the Use of Criticism, The 120
Uses of Diversity, The 80
Utopian Vision of D.H. Lawrence, The 261
Utopia of Userers and Other Essays 80

V

Valet to the Absolute 235
Validity in Interpretation 17
Vanished Arcadia, A 203
Varied Types 79
Variety of Things, A 38
Vast Design, The 497
Ventilations: Being Biographical Asides 442
Venus in the Kitchen 113
Victorian Age in Literature, The 80
Victorians and After (1830-1914) 6
Victorian Stage Pulpiteer 413
Virginia Woolf (Brewster) 476
Virginia Woolf (Daiches) 477
Virginia Woolf (Forster) 477
Virginia Woolf (Gorsky) 478
Virginia Woolf (Johnson) 480
Virginia Woolf (Rosenthal) 484
Virginia Woolf (Woodring) 487
Virginia Woolf: A Biography 474
Virginia Woolf: A Commentary 476
Virginia Woolf: A Critical Memoir 480
Virginia Woolf: An Annotated Bibliography 474
Virginia Woolf: Her Art as a Novelist 476
Virginia Woolf: Selections from Her Essays 473
Virginia Woolf: The Critical Heritage 482
Virginia Woolf: The Echoes Enslaved 482
Virginia Woolf: Women and Writing 473
Virginia Woolf and Bloomsbury 483

Virginia Woolf and Her Works 479
Virginia Woolf and the Androgynous Vision 475
Virginia Woolf as Literary Critic 485
Virginia Woolf's London 476
Virginia Woolf's Major Novels 477
Virginia Woolf's Quarrel with Grieving 485
Vision, A 491
Vortex: Pound, Eliot, and Lewis 325
Vulgarity in Literature 243

W

Waiting for Daylight 447
War and the Future 456
Warfare in England 59
War That Will End War, The 456
Washington and the Hope of Peace 456
Washington and the Riddle of Peace 456
Was It Worth It, Wells? 463
Way the World Is Going, The 456
W.B. Yeats: A Classified Bibliography of Criticism 493
W.B. Yeats: A Critical Introduction 503
W.B. Yeats: Design of Opposites 495
W.B. Yeats: 1865-1939 494
W.B. Yeats: His Poetry and Thought 505
W.B. Yeats: Man and Poet 494
W.B. Yeats: The Critical Heritage 500
W.B. Yeats and Georgian Ireland 505
W.B. Yeats and the Anti-Democratic Tradition 498
W.B. Yeats Manuscripts 493
Weald of Youth, The 399
Well and the Shallows, The 80
Wellington 219
Wells' Social Anticipations 458
What Are We to Do with Our Lives? 454
What I Really Wrote about the War 407
What Is a Classic? 120

Title Index

What I Saw in America 80
What Is Coming? 456
What's Wrong with the World 80
W.H. Auden (Wright) 36
W.H. Auden, a Bibliography, 1924-1969 29
W.H. Auden: A Biography 30
W.H. Auden: A Reference Guide 30
W.H. Auden: A Tribute 31
W.H. Auden: The Life of a Poet 30
W.H. Auden as a Social Poet 31
W.H. Hudson (Tomalin) 228
W.H. Hudson: A Bibliography 227
W.H. Hudson: A Portrait 228
W.H. Hudson: The Vision of Earth 230
W.H. Hudson: Writer and Naturalist 228
W.H. Hudson's Reading 228
When Blood Is Their Argument 165
White Goddess, The 212
Who Killed Cock-Robin? 428
Whole Mystery of Art, The 502
Why I Am a Catholic 60
Wild Body, The 317
Wilderness of Zin, The 272
Wild Knight of Battersea, The 92
William Blake (Chesterton) 80
William Blake (Murry) 337
William Butler Yeats (Donoghue) 497
William Butler Yeats (Peterson) 503
William Butler Yeats: The Poet as Mythmaker, 1865-1937 504
William Cobbett 81
William Empson (Willis) 160
William Empson: The Man and His Work 156
William Empson and the Philosophy of Literary Criticism 157
William Henry Hudson (Frederick) 229
William Henry Hudson: A Tribute by Various Writers 228
William Morris as I Knew Him 407
William the Conqueror 60
Wind Is Rising, The 447
Winters of Content 428
Winters of Content and Other Discursions on Mediterranean Art and Travel 428

Wisdom of G.K. Chesterton, The 86
W.M. Thackeray 80
Wolsey 60
Women and Men 165
Wordsworth 363
Work, Wealth and Happiness of Mankind, The 457
Works of George Saintsbury, The 387
Works of Max Beerbohm 38
Works of Max Beerbohm, The 37
Works of Max Beerbohm with a Bibliography by John Lane, The 38
World Brain 457
World of Aldous Huxley, The 243
World of George Orwell, The 345
World of H.G. Wells, The 462
World's Last Night and Other Essays, The 303
Wounded Spirit, The 276
Writer and the Absolute, The 317
Writer's Diary, A 473
Writings of D.H. Lawrence 1925-30, The 256
Writings of E.M. Forster, The 175
Writ in Sand 203
Written Word, The 371
Wyndham Lewis (Kenner) 319
Wyndham Lewis (Pritchard) 327, 328
Wyndham Lewis (Tomlin) 320
Wyndham Lewis: A Descriptive Bibliography 319
Wyndham Lewis: A Descriptive Catalogue of the Manuscript Material in the Department of Rare Books Cornell University Library 318
Wyndham Lewis: A Discursive Exposition 326
Wyndham Lewis: An Anthology of His Prose 318
Wyndham Lewis: A Portrait of the Artist as the Enemy 331
Wyndham Lewis: A Revaluation 326
Wyndham Lewis: Fictions and Satires 321
Windham Lewis at Cornell 319
Wyndham Lewis in Canada 320
Wyndham Lewis on Art 318
Wyndham Lewis the Artist, from BLAST to Burlington House 317

Y

Year of Prophesying, A 457
Yeats (Bloom) 495
Yeats (Ure) 505
Yeats: A Psychoanalytical Study 505
Yeats: The Man and the Masks 493
Years at Work 495
Yeats's Autobiography 504
Yeats's VISION and the Later Plays 505
Yet Again 39
Young Hilaire Belloc, The 62
Your Mirror to My Times 165

Ref Z 2014 .P795 B76 1983
Brown, Christopher C.
English prose and criticism,
 1900-1950

JUL 2 6 1985